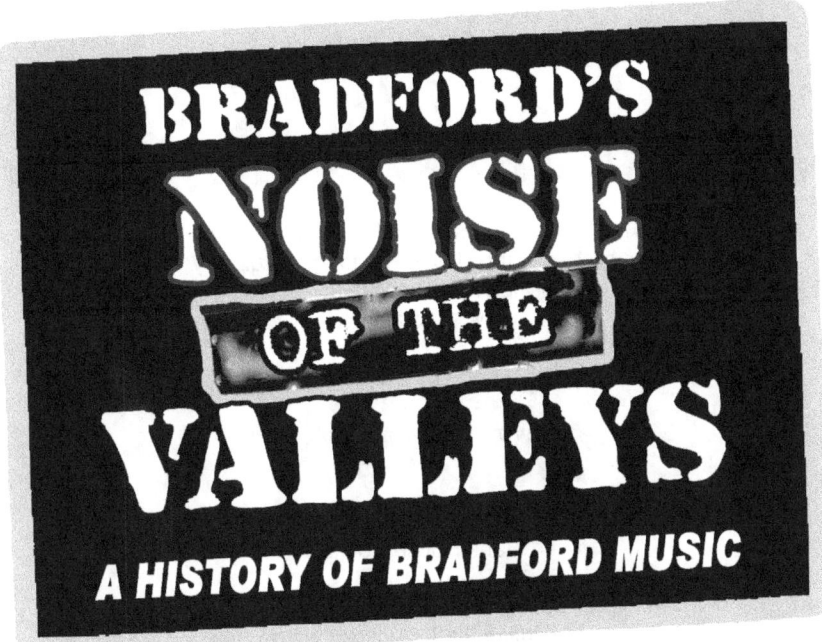

VOLUME 1 • 1967 - 1987
GARY CAVANAGH AND MATT WEBSTER

LS ARTS BOOKS
A Bradford Noise Production

Dedicated to three Virgos and a Sagittarian, by Gary.

Dedicated to a Hippy, by Matt.

Bradford 2025 Edition

This revised, updated and expanded edition
published in the United Kingdom in 2025 by
LS Arts Publishing
West Yorkshire

Leeds Streets Ltd

www.leeds-streets.uk

First published in the United Kingdom in 2009 by
Bank House Books

Second edition published in the United Kingdom in 2013 by
Mutiny 2000 Publications
Bradford
West Yorkshire

bradfordnoise.com
mutiny2000.com

© 2009, 2013, 2025 Gary Cavanagh and Matt Webster, 2009

The Authors hereby assert their moral rights to be identified as the Authors of the Work.

Written and researched by Gary Cavanagh and Matt Webster
Graphic design by Matt Webster
Layout by Matt Webster and Gary Cavanagh
Family trees drawn by Gary Cavanagh

All images in this book are copyright of the original creators.

All rights reserved. No part of this publication may be reproduced, stored in a retrieval system, or transmitted, in any form or by any means, electronic, mechanical, photocopying, recording or otherwise, without the prior permission of the publisher and copyright holders.

British Library Cataloguing in Publication Data
A catalogue record for this book is available from the British Library

ISBN 978-1-7391481-3-3

Printed in the UK by Lightning Source

FOREWORD

Bradford has always been a bit unsung. But not any more, thanks to this work of breathtaking scholarship. Its scope, reach and minute attention to detail mean that just about anybody who ever joined in with a tap room sing-song or whistled along to a pop tune on their way down Great Horton Road is included. The authors Gary Cavanagh and his mate Matt Webster both deserve a medal as big as a dustbin lid or at the least the freedom of the metropolitan borough. The text is lively, well researched and very readable and it had me reaching to find my own Bradford musical memories.

I saw Thin Lizzy at the St George's Hall sometime in the 1970s and after that gig ate my first proper curry, meat and peas, I shovelled it down with half a dozen chapattis for about eighty five pence and the girl I'd gone with told me that I should grow my hair like Scott Gorham. That never happened, but an affair with that grand old venue did start that night, I saw Elvis Costello there and was mesmerised by Mary Coughlan who gargled in between songs with honey and whiskey, to fight off the flu. But my favourite Bradford musical memories are of the festivals of the 1980s when bands played live in front of the city hall. A big band called Loose Tubes came one year and in teeming rain gave a mad brass band concert of salsa tunes full of sunshine while hundreds of wool city rockers danced and splashed in the puddles. It was glorious and I didn't dry out properly until I got back to our house, two trains and a bus ride away.

Books like this do that to you, they send you spiralling back through the landscapes of your memory to find the lovely days when we danced and sang. A lot of work is being done now on intangible heritage, the history that is not in the guidebooks, not in the listed buildings, but in the people, the stories and yes, the songs of our own personal and collective memories.

The authors of this book have tapped into that rich tapestry and woven a bonny book. One that encompasses Charlie Watts and Ray Davies's wedding days, the psychedelic "happening" that was Moonkyte and a potted history of Britain's longest running folk club. How good is that?

Ian Clayton
author of *Bringing It All Back Home*

Little old textile town...

Bradford is in some ways still a small town, surrounded by a number of smaller townships that all merge into the city as we know it today. Situated at its centre is a natural bowl provided by the great valleys of the rivers Aire and Wharfe.

Since 1974 Bradford has been enlarged to a metropolitan district, taking in the townships of Shipley, Bingley, Haworth, Keighley and Ilkley, making it the seventh largest urban / rural conurbation in the UK.

Nationally over the last few decades the City of Bradford has perhaps been perceived in a negative light. Despite this it has continued to provide a positive and diverse multi-cultural heritage. This is reinforced by the city's continually thriving local music scene. The expression of individual musicians from all the migrant cultures has embraced and celebrated a cross-cultural network of musical alliances which has produced a rich, yet often under-appreciated, musical history.

This book's research is an attempt to chronicle the social history of the local music scene during the years 1967 to 1987, the bands who formed and the clubs that opened to cater for the emerging scene. It is a study of the interconnections and links that have strengthened the scene and provided a mix of vibrant, creative and often socially aware talent.

It draws on information from various sources, including the Rock On column and other relevant news stories originally published in the Telegraph & Argus, to present a largely as yet unwritten but vital history of Bradford's music culture which deserves to be recognised in the same way that the music histories of places such as Manchester, Liverpool and London has been.

The research has as its central basis a series of local 'rock family trees' which recognise the individual members of bands that have contributed to the scene during the time period under discussion.

Prices from Record Collector's Rare Record Guide have been used for some of the more collectable records.

Any work of this type will always appear incomplete to some extent as it is nigh on impossible to document everything with total success. While every effort has been made to provide a clear and detailed study, it is no doubt riddled with minor flaws, errors and omissions as well as the odd wrongly spelt name due, in some part, to the notoriously vague memories of some musicians or, more often, to the simple lack of a research source for some bands. The use of nicknames on the 'trees' is in order to keep a continuity where musicians may have been better, or only, known by a nickname rather than their real name.

The authors have set up a website (see below) in order to create a forum for feedback and rectify any mistakes and to deal with queries that can be verified for future revisions.

Lastly this research is especially dedicated to Rob Heaton (RIP 2004), Clive Royston (RIP 2007), and Willi Beckett (RIP 2007) who were all very helpful in my early research and it is a tribute to them and all the other musicians no longer with us whose sweat, energy, skill, talent and dedication produced music that collectively gave pleasure to so many of us.

Bradford,
November 2008

www.bradfordnoise.com

How to read the Rock Family Trees

Just in case anybody has difficulties in understanding the Rock Family Trees, below is a basic key on how to read them. Firstly they are read downwards and in chronological order by year date. Year dates in closed brackets indicate the years a band was active, and the rear end open brackets denotes that no information is available as to when the band ceased to be active.

Symbols and abbreviations

#2 etc – denotes the 2nd incarnation of a band
voc – vocals
gtr – guitar
drm – drums
keyd – keyboards
harm – harmonica
hamm – hammond organ
trump – trumpet and so on
- - - ! denotes an occasional guest or studio member
(RIP 2000) – As a mark of respect for the fallen, this denotes the year known of the individual's passing.

CONTENTS

Preface: 1963-66 From Rock'n'roll To The Beat Boom & The Halifax Connection   1-26

Bradford Clubs • The Gaumont • The Beatles & The Stones • The Club Scene In The Sixties • The Cresters • Two Pop Stars Married In Bradford • Lorraine & The Bah'Tats • Brian T Strollers • Linda Russell • Robin Hood & His Merry Men • Allen Pound's Get Rich • The Bradfords • The Quare Fellows • The Forgers • The Followers • The Yen/Essence • TheThree Good Reasons • The Outer Limits • TheThimbleriggers • John's Fiollowers • Root & Jenny Jackson • Blues Singer Lives Locally

Chapter 1: 1967-70 Psychedelia To Heavy Rock   27-64

Hendrix Hits Ilkley • Music At Bradford University • Lulu Comes To Town • Pearson's Records • Barbara Moore • The Casuals • The Accent • Zany Woodruff Operation • Love Affair • Welfare State • Black Dyke Beatle • Love Affair • Allan Holdsworth • Now Group Of 1969 • Crystallised Anthem • Rodney Bewes • Dave Lee Sound • Junior's Eyes • Hogsnort Rupert's Original Flagon Band • Samantha Promotions • The First Yorkshire Free Festival • The Zanties/Midnight Hearse • Kindness • The Original Bradford (Arts) Festival • Now Group Of 1970 • The Ambition • First Local Free Festival • Trevor Hockey • The Disaster Of The Krumlin Festival

Chapter 2: 1971-76 Prog Rock To Punk Rock   65-102

The Second Bradford Arts Festival • Demons In The Park • Kaboss • Spiral Highway • Rawdon Festival • 1971 Clubs • Bickershaw Festival • Jonathan Swift • Park Avenue Pop Festival • John Verity • Rivington Pike • Catherine Howe • Bradford Gay Liberation Front • Rock Strife • The Collection • Midas • Living Next Door To Smokie • Moonchild • The Battle Of Bradford • The Princeville Rock Club • Kiki Dee Hits Top Spot • Mutton Chops • Azel • Foxy Lady • Malcolm Jackson • First Aid • Punch Up North • Alan Whittaker • Black Dyke Mills Band • Valances • US Soul Star Settles In Shipley

Chapter 3: 1956-87 Local Folk   103-120

Topic Folk Club • Wild Oats • Quiet Farm/Maidenhead Farm • Jan Dukes de Grey • Moonkyte • Roy Bailey • Keighley Folk • Jovial Crew • Swan Arcade • Janet Jones • Folkweave • Mountain Ash Band • Roger Sutcliffe • Tim Moon • Brendan Croker • The Mekons

Chapter 4: 1977-80 Punk Rock/New Wave/NWOBHM   121-168

Jed's Blues Band • Rockabilly Rebs • Omen • Judy Blue • Roy Sundholm • Ocean • Phoenix • NWOBHM • Baby Tuckoo • Shadowfax • Dawnwatcher • Dedriger • Turbo • After Hours • Rhabstallion • New Electric Warriors • Stormer • Challanger • Stormtrooper • Black Onyx • The Punk/New Wave Scene • Royal Standard • Vaults Bar • Hokum • The Invaders • Smash Hits • Vex • Excel • Rock Against Rascism • Fascist Attacks On Local Alternative Bookshop • The Negatives • Look Records • Ulterior Motives • Checkmate Gets Married • Silver Screen Girls • Sid & Maggie • The Donkeys • Local Comics • Local Sound Systems • Bradford's Experimental Electric Noise Scene • Counterdance • Eaten Alive By Insects • The Scene • Cameras In Cars • Violation • Futurama • Radio 5 • Hicks From The Sticks • The Elements • Chainsaw

Chapter 5: 1980-83 Post Punk/Anarcho Punk/Goth   169-238

Futurama 2 • Anarcho Punk Hits Bradford • Fassbender-Russell • Palm Cove • Panache • Manhattan Club/Bibi's • New Model Army • Chronic/Living Dead • Requiem • Claimant's Union • The1981 Riots • The Birth Of The 1 In 12 Club • The Word • Boys From The East • Bad News 1 • Single File • 1919 • Bradford 12 • West Indian Community In Bradford • Trish Cooke • Roots Records • Ramon Martino • Complete Disorder • Screaming Plastic Turtles • Southern Death Cult • The Bradford Poets/Ranters • Joolz • Little Brother • Seething Wells • Wild Willi Beckett • Nick Toczek • Dirk Spig • Ginger John • The Worst Of The 1 In 12 Club Cassettes • The Cathedral Centre • Roger Higgins • George Blake • Wow It's Now • Cannibal Feast • Something Else • The Beginning Of Flexible Response • The 1 In 12 First Anniversary • Fanzines • Gory Details • Bradford Centre Against Unemployment • The Return Of The 1 In 12 Club • Complete Harmony • The Keighley Scene • Teenage & The Wildlife • The Shakes • Skeletal Family • Muggin's Blight • Montage • Bradford International Jazz Festival • The 1 In 12 Club At Tickles • Raw • Isolation • Anti-System • Morbid Humour • The Negativz • The Convulsions • We're From Bradford • Skive Off & Jive Free Festival • Fritz The Cat • Futurama 5 • The 1 In 12 Club At The Market Tavern • People's Squat For Peace • Social Spastix

Chapter 6: 1984-86 Indie/Alternative Rock   239-300

The 1 In 12 Club At The Market Tavern • People's Squat For Life • Stop The City II • Creation Roots • The Rootsman • Third Anniversary Of The 1 In 12 Club • The Miner's Strike 1984/85 • Not The International Garden Festival • Enemies Of The State •

Heavy Metal/Rock 2 • Excalibur • Harlequyn • Siren • NME Reviews • Hindle's Gears Dispute • The Nerve Agents • Swamp Flower • Vegetable Section • Manningham Community Centre • Women's Music Collective • Belle & The Devotions • Griff's Magic Theatre • Checkpoint • Getting The Fear • Tuxedo • Vanishing Point • Another Cinema • El Loco • Passmore Sisters • The Best Way To Walk • Ghost Dance • Anti-Fascist 12 • Catch 22 • Bradford City Fire Disaster • The Crowd • Systembeat • The Milky Way Club • Rebecca Storm • The Liberty Club • Systembeat 2 • Handful Of Dance • The Keighley Scene • The Saturday Club • Red Wedge Tour • Fifth Anniversary Of The 1 In 12 Club • The Moon • Theatre Tavern • Mr Love • Silent Night Strike • Janet Cook • Annie & The Aeroplanes • Psycho Surgeons • Flexible Response Records • Bradford Package Tour • Happiness Ad • The Frog & Toad • Western Dance • Tisma Project • Circus • Damien Wolfe • Eazy Street • Talula Gosh • Pro Patria Mori

Chapter 7: 1987 & The Second Summer Of Love   301-318

From The Underworld • Guido • Jayver • JJ's Bones • Milan Lad • Malcolm Hanson • Battle Of The Bands 1987 • Far North Music • Somebody's Brother • Zodiac Mindwarp & The Love Reaction • Slammer • Spoilt Bratz • John Peel Comes To The 1 In 12 Club • Bradford Festival • Bad News • Joe Johnson • Club Rio Campus/Rio's

References/Bibliography   319-326

Index Of Bands On Trees   327-334

From A1 to Zzebra

Afterwords   335-344

About The Authors • Acknowledgements • The Music 1967-1987 CDs • The Missing Music 1 & 2

From Rock 'N' Roll To The Beat Boom

And the Halifax Connection!

Preface: 1963 to 1966!

British rock'n'roll music quickly developed during the years 1959-66 and, like most towns and cities, Bradford had a vibrant local scene - an epicentre of rock'n'roll youth culture with a host of talented groups and artists - before the onslaught of Beatlemania and the R'n'B / beat boom silenced about ninety per cent of the city's indigenous groups. They faded into the background and, as bingo began to commandeer most of the old dance halls, the few surviving groups plied their trade on the working men's club cabaret circuit.

As Derek Lister points out in his book Bradford Rock'n'Roll, *'The Beatles… reflected and inspired this new mood among the nation's youth, which had its roots in a growing economic independence. By the end of 1964, even The Beatles were moving into new musical waters and challenging others to follow them. British pop was already beginning to change in character and content, as more young R'n'B groups came to the fore. They were less interested in playing our rock'n'roll dance music, than to make what amounted to anti-establishment statements and took their music seriously. Looking back, it felt like the end of an era. The mod style and music would take over for a couple of years, this in turn being taken over by pop art progressing to psychedelically painted trucks, long hair, drugs, flower power and hippies.'* (1)

As a tribute to this early period, some bands from that era are mentioned in this book and documented with Rock Family Trees, showing their growth and willingness to adapt (or not!) to the new direction British music was evolving into.

Trees tend to grow both ways, the roots reaching into the past and the new growth spreading to the future. Where it has been possible, we have continued the lineups of bands to the present day, rather than stay within the confines of dates on the front of the book. These dates can be confusing as they really indicate the period bands formed or came to prominence, and we try to tell as complete a tale as possible, whether they lasted fifty days or fifty years.

It may help to think of the cover dates as a focus point. Maybe it was the time of a band's first record or their first big gig. Some members may have been in an earlier band or found greater success later on. If you read on you might just find out!

This book also covers social and cultural events that influenced or brought attention to our city.

Courtesy of the Telegraph & Argus

Bradford came to public attention on the silver screen in 1963 when the motion picture *Billy Liar* was filmed in and around the city. It was co-written by Leeds lads Keith Waterhouse and Wallis Hall and directed by John Schlesinger. It starred Julie Christie and Tom Courtney and featured local Bingley lad Rodney Bewes who became famous as one of *The Likely Lads*, with James Bolam.

It was filmed in and around the city in 1962. Locations include Bradford landmarks like Broadway, Forster Square, the War Memorial, the Locarno Ballroom on Manningham Lane, Undercliffe Cemetery and streets in Baildon.

Although the BAFTA-nominated film was not a huge box office success when released, *Billy Liar* was named number 76 in the *British Film Institute*'s list of the top 100 British films in 1999.

THE BEATLES AND THE STONES

The Gaumont Theatre (The Odeon) was the major venue at this time. Built in 1930 as the New Victoria Cinema, it was one of the biggest outside London with 3,318 seats, a restaurant and a ballroom. This twin-towered art deco-style brick building was built on the site of one of Bradford's original early breweries, Whitaker & Co, which was founded in 1757, and was famous for the XXXX Stingo Ale.

It was renamed the Gaumont in 1950 and became a popular music venue until it was remodelled as a two-screen cinema and renamed The Odeon in 1969. The closure of the cinema in 2000 led to years of uncertainty. The Save The Odeon campaign lasted for years as Bradford residents battled to save the building from demolition. It finally re-opened as a music venue in 2025, now known as Bradford Live.

Beatles fans queue for tickets

Weeks before, thousands of teenagers had queued in Bradford overnight (some for over seventeen hours) to get tickets for the group's return concert. On the night 6,000 screaming teenagers (seventy percent girls!) drowned out the group's two-set show and tried to swamp the stage, those who got too hysterical had to be treated by the St John's Ambulance Brigade attendants.

After the show, the fans tried to find out where the group were staying, but The Beatles were already on their way back to Liverpool.

In the late 1950s, The Gaumont featured American rock'n'roll stars like Eddie Cochrane and Gene Vincent (30/1/60) and Buddy Holly & The Crickets (9/2/58) before showcasing the sixties 'package tours' with the emerging stars of the pop charts.

On February 2, 1963, teenage pop singer Helen Shapiro was supported by The Beatles on what was the opening night of their first nationwide tour.

This was the first appearance of the Fab Four in Bradford and within weeks of the show the nation was gripped by Beatlemania!

By their next visit, on December 21, they were the headlining stars of The Beatles' Christmas Show which featured The Beatles, Billy J Kramer & The Dakotas, The Fourmost, The Barron Knights, Cilla Black, Rolf Harris and Tommy Quickly.

The Gaumont was chosen to host the first of only two special northern previews (the second being the following night in Liverpool) of The Beatles' Christmas Show, which continued at the Astoria Cinema in London from December 24 to January 11, 1964.

The Beatles made their third and final appearace at the Gaumont on October 9, 1964, which was John Lennon's 24th birthday. Before they took to the stage that night support act, Mary Wells, made history by becoming the first Motown star ever to appear on a British stage.

Another Beat group from Liverpool, The Dennisons, who had a couple of minor hits on Decca Records, have a slight  connection with Bradford; their drummer, the late Clive Hornsby (pictured second from right), became better known as Jack Sugden in Yorkshire TV's long-running soap *Emmerdale*.

PREFACE - FROM ROCK'N'ROLL TO THE BEAT BOOM 1963 - 1966

The Gaumont was the venue for The Rolling Stones' first appearance in Bradford when they supported The Everley Brothers and Little Richard on October 19, 1963. They returned as headliners on Saturday, September 26, 1964.

On December 11, 1963, Bradford music promoter Garth Cawood booked the Stones for a student dance at **Queen's Hall**. Garth was a friend of Brian Jones and booked them for £200 just as their debut single *Come On* was shooting up the charts. The band were pelted by jelly babies by the student crowd, much to their amusement.

On July 12, 1964, Garth brought the Rolling Stones back to the Queen's Hall when they were supported by Lulu and Ray Anton & The Peppermint Men, for the door charge of 10/6d.

THE CLUB SCENE IN THE SIXTIES

Between 1961 and 1968 a group of Halifax youth set up and ran their own jazz and blues club called **The Plebians** (Plebs for short!) with enough success that they even ventured into Bradford to try to imitate the same scene here too. Between June and November, they set up **The Reelement Discotheque** - Bradford's first disco - which was run as a private club with a doorman.

The Greek owners, Messrs Senducaris and Papadopolis, allowed members of the Halifax Plebs Club to hire their Rendezvous Coffee Bar in Piece Hall Yard for a Friday night disco.

The door was fitted with a bell and a sliding peephole to vet customers, flyers were distributed around the Art College and the Allasio Coffee Bar with membership cards being printed and sold before the opening night. Every Friday for about six months the disco attracted around a hundred customers as cool art student types packed the place, dancing to beat groups and French pop, which created a continental mood of mystery. (2)

The Mojo Club (Market Tavern) opened on September 26, 1963; it ran until 1969. Kiki Dee used to sing there and the regular DJ was 'friend to the stars' Carl Gresham, who later worked as the DJ at the Mecca (Locarno) Ballroom on Manningham Lane, as well as writing the *Top Ten* column for the local evening paper the *Telegraph & Argus (T&A)*.

There must have been hundreds of such named clubs all over the country, the most famous being **Peter Stringfellow's** in Sheffield.

Other famous clubs in the North at this time were **The Twisted Wheel** in Manchester and **The Three Coins** in Leeds.

1964 saw the mod (modernist) scene, derived initially from the modern jazz scene, becoming the archetypal youth cult of smart suits, Italian scooters and amphetamines, dancing to the music of R'n'B, soul and Jamaican ska. On the bank holiday weekend of August 3 and 4, riots took place in the South coast towns of Hastings, Clacton and Brighton as the suited mods took on the leather-clad rockers.

Around the same time the first pirate radio stations, like Radio Caroline off the east coast and Radio Veronica operating off the Dutch coast, began playing all the latest pop and independent hits.

After the success of the Reelement Disco certain Pleb members were keen to start a new venture in Bradford. They soon found a property to rent a huge cellar (Millergate) owned by Patchett's of Queensbury. This ran at the back of the new bar development on the site of the old Provincial House, adjacent to what is now Centenary Square. They obtained planning permission and conversion work started, with the room being redecorated and a stage and snack bar built as well as the installation of a sound system.

A Poster designed by Jake Morton for the Cat and printed by Canfield Bros Bradford.

On Saturday August 14, 1964, Bradford's first independently run music club was born. It was named **The Little Fat Black Pussycat Club** after a San Francisco poetry club.

On the opening night, The Pretty Things were a great success and after that, the club opened every Friday and Saturday as a members club, with DJ Dave Wilcock working the all-nighter. Kiki Dee was amongst those who attended the all-nighters and apparently worked in the cloakroom.

Many groups appeared, including London's The Action and Preston's The Mood who, after playing the club, changed their name to The Little Fat Black Pussycats in honour of the Club.

When The Moody Blues played there on October 31, they were paid £55, which was a lot of money in those days, and a sure sign the club was packing the punters in. Unfortunately, the local police were concerned about the size of the crowds and the potential drug problems, so they put pressure on the landlord and the organisers and in the end, the club had to shut down. (3) It had lasted for around nine months.

Sometime during 1964, **The Dungeon** (at 85 Westgate, later the site of the Northern Drum Centre) was opened. It was meant to be a 'cellar club' but it was based on the first floor, up a flight of steps. It was referred to by contemporaries as *'the only upstairs dungeon in the world'* and was also decked out with 'plastic skeletons' chained to the walls with blacked out windows on the outside. It was run by Readmore Productions which was a partnership of Don Read (who was road manager for UK jazz elders Johnny Dankworth and Cleo Laine) and Ray Kennan. Ray played in many bands including Ray Kennan & The Guvners who once had a residency at the legendary Star Club in Hamburg and featured future Deep Purple guitarist Ritchie Blackmore. (2)

The Blue Sounds were the resident band. They were a six-piece R'n'B group containing mostly ex-Leeds University students with eight degrees between them. The group included The Beatles' German friend and future Manfred Mann man Klaus Voorman on bass guitar. They toured around the UK regularly and played at the Marquee Club in London.

On September 12, Long John Baldry & His Hoochie Coochie Band played; a six piece band which included Rod Stewart on vocals and Jeff Bradford on guitar.

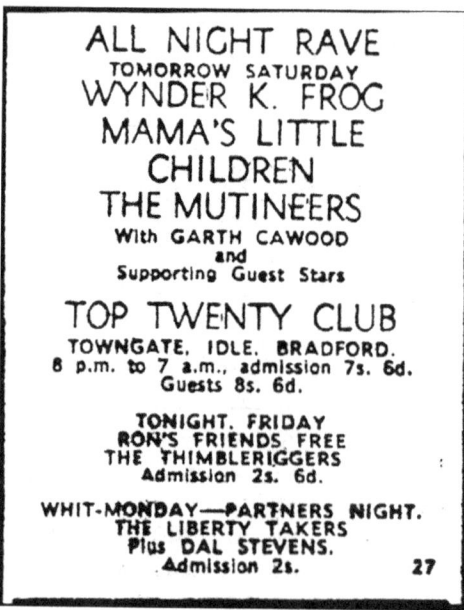

On the outskirts of Bradford from 1964 to 1966 was **The Top 20 Club** in Idle, which is now the Idle/Thackley Conservative Club, owned by Frank Thorpe, manager of Keighley group The Thimbleriggers, who also ran the popular Thorpe's

DAL STEVENS / DAVE ARRAN & THE CRUSADERS

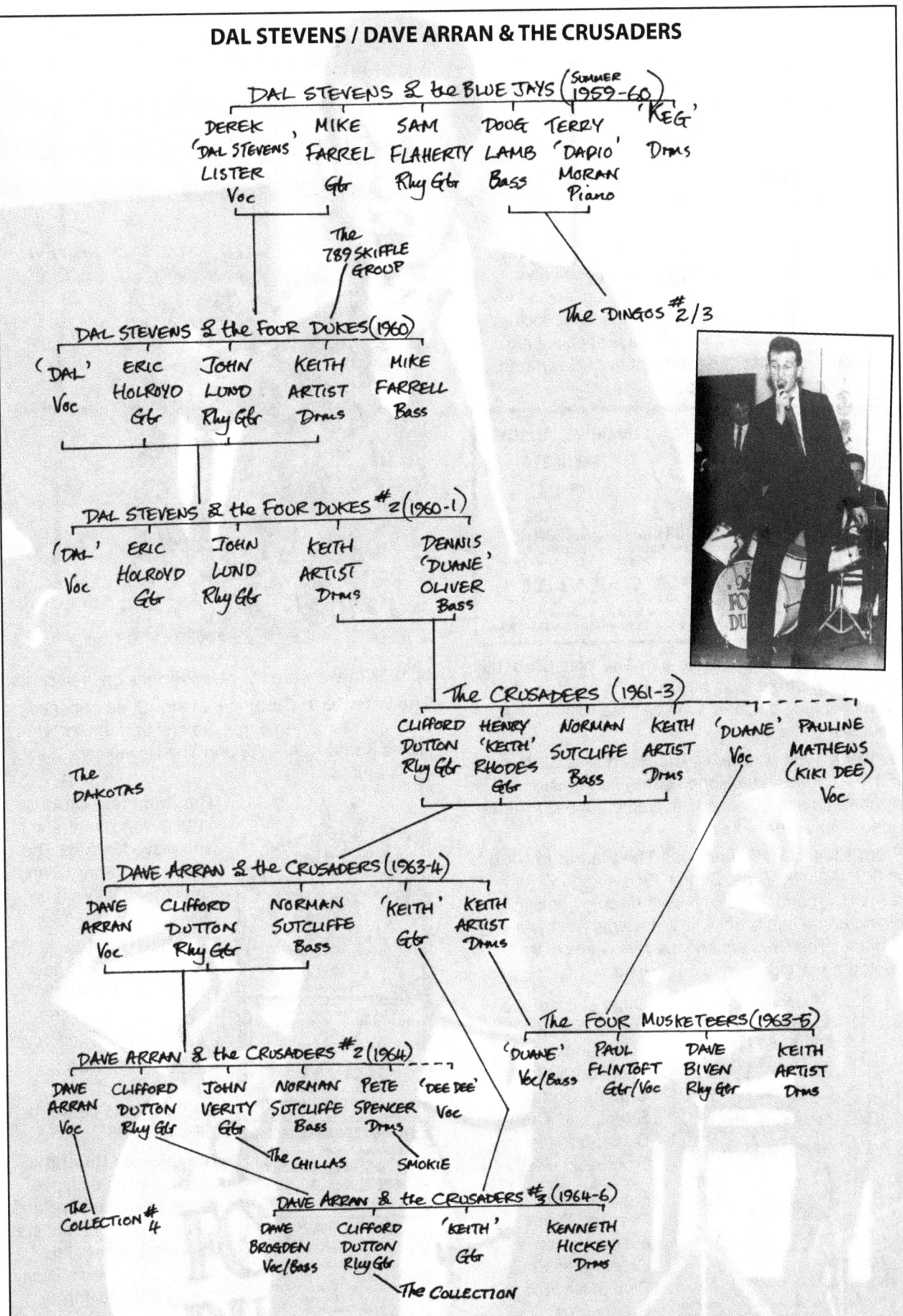

Ice Cream Co. It was managed for him by Garth Cawood as DJ and compere (MC) who, besides giving local group The End regular gigs, also booked the likes of The Pretty Things, The Kinks (30/4/66 for 10/6d), Screaming Jay Hawkins (3/3/65), Screaming Lord Sutch & The Savages (24/3/65) and Tom Jones, amongst a host of others. Billy (Wicherly) Fury often visited as his Uncle Ernest Wicherly was the landlord of the White Bear pub over the road.

The Coffin Club (35 Ivegate) opened for its first night on June 4, 1964, run by Owner Paul Flynn. On July 1, Herman's Hermits / The Vigilantes performed there; other groups who played include The Rockin' Vicars who had a bassist called Ian 'Lemmy' Kilminster, later a member of Hawkwind and founder of Motorhead.

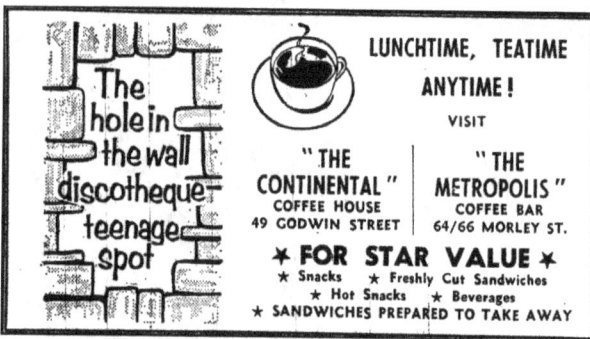

From 1964 to 1969 **The Hole In The Wall Club**, at 49 Godwin Street, was a café during the day which on an evening became a regular 'teenage spot' for discos and live gigs.

Between 1964 and 1970, **The Heartbeat Club** (Silver Blades, Little Horton Lane) had mainly discos with some concerts. In September 1971 it re-opened as **Annabella's**.

From 1964 to 1969 there was **The Flamingo Club** at 8-9, Walmer Villas. During 1964 and 1965 for a few short months this club, with discos, gambling, dining and a late licence till 2 am, was run by Mike Sagar of The Cresters and his wife Glenice. It hosted a few gigs during this period.

Other clubs of the period included, from 1964 to 1966, **The Romantica Club** on Godwin Street, and **The DJ Club** at the Troutbeck, Ilkley.

A club called **The Red Den** put on gigs at Greengates Social Club at Newline, Greengates.

In 1965 these were the newest clubs on the scene:

The Witchbarn Club, at 8 Manor Street, opened on the 12th March. Amongst the first performers were Alexis Korner (24/3/65) and The Downliner's Sect (27/3/65).

The Somerset Club, at 11 Idle Road, where acts who played include The Kingpins on May 15 and The Lykes Of Witch on July 16.

The Blue Dolphin at White Cross, Guiseley, where Van Morrison's Belfast R'n'Bers Them played live on April 2.

The Top Hat Club, 2 Manor Street, held regular discos between 1965 and 1966.

The Lyceum Rainbow Club on Wardley Drive, off the top of Leeds Road, was a casino and cabaret venue that put on the likes of Joe Brown, Dusty Springfield and Tom Jones.

PREFACE - FROM ROCK'N'ROLL TO THE BEAT BOOM 1963 - 1966

THE STROLLERS

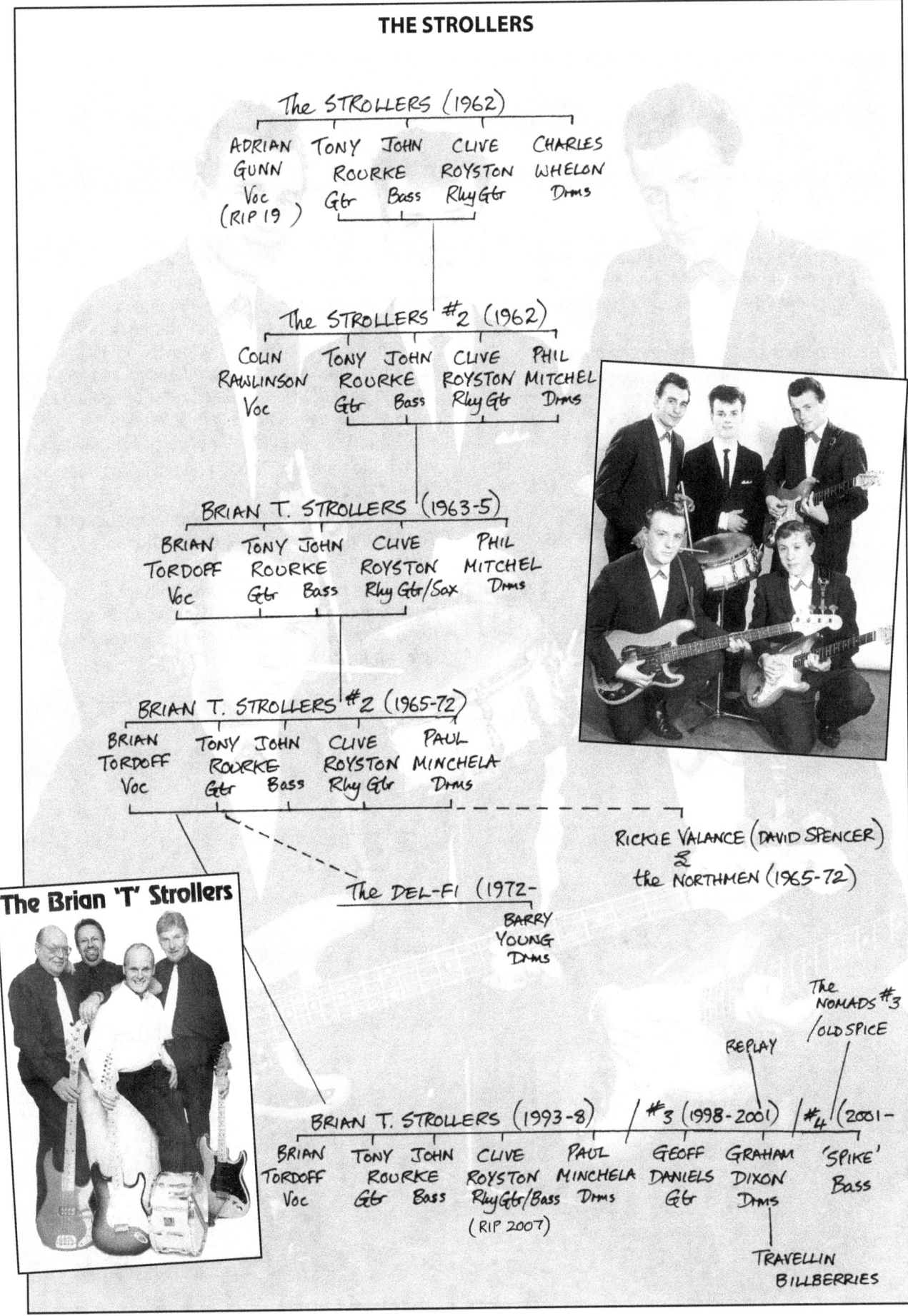

The STROLLERS (1962)
- ADRIAN GUNN - Voc (RIP 19)
- TONY ROURKE - Gtr
- JOHN ROYSTON - Bass
- CLIVE ROYSTON - Rhy Gtr
- CHARLES WHELON - Dms

The STROLLERS #2 (1962)
- COLIN RAWLINSON - Voc
- TONY ROURKE - Gtr
- JOHN ROYSTON - Bass
- CLIVE ROYSTON - Rhy Gtr
- PHIL MITCHEL - Dms

BRIAN T. STROLLERS (1963-5)
- BRIAN TORDOFF - Voc
- TONY ROURKE - Gtr
- JOHN ROYSTON - Bass
- CLIVE ROYSTON - Rhy Gtr/Sax
- PHIL MITCHEL - Dms

BRIAN T. STROLLERS #2 (1965-72)
- BRIAN TORDOFF - Voc
- TONY ROURKE - Gtr
- JOHN ROYSTON - Bass
- CLIVE ROYSTON - Rhy Gtr
- PAUL MINCHELA - Dms

The DEL-FI (1972-)
- BARRY YOUNG - Dms

RICKIE VALANCE (DAVID SPENCER) & the NORTHMEN (1965-72)

The NOMADS #3 / OLD SPICE

REPLAY

BRIAN T. STROLLERS (1993-8) / #3 (1998-2001) / #4 (2001-)
- BRIAN TORDOFF - Voc
- TONY ROURKE - Gtr
- JOHN ROYSTON - Bass
- CLIVE ROYSTON - Rhy Gtr/Bass (RIP 2007)
- PAUL MINCHELA - Dms
- GEOFF DANIELS - Gtr
- GRAHAM DIXON - Dms
- 'SPIKE' - Bass

TRAVELLIN BILLBERRIES

The Brian 'T' Strollers

THE CRESTERS

The Cresters were a Pudsey / Bramley based group who released two singles in 1964 on the HMV record label. They had previously released two singles as Mike Sagar & The Cresters (1960-62) and their guitarist Richard Harding (who played a Gretsch White Falcon guitar) had also released a solo instrumental single in 1961.

They supported The Beatles and, at the time, Richard was universally acknowledged as the best guitarist of his generation, admired by Paul McCartney and Tom Jones.

Richard and John's father Arthur Harding (below left), who had a musical background as a violinist in several West Riding orchestras, ran a recording studio in the attic of 84 Hough Lane, Bramley. As a skilled studio engineer in the homemade eight-track, mainly mono studio Arthur produced hundreds of excellent demo tapes for a wide range of local Yorkshire musicians. With his son's help he was '...dedicated to showing 'em in London, that the North was capable of making top class music... even in his little studio.' (4)

The group's drummer Johnnie Casson from Halifax went on to be a top TV comedian working with the likes of Des O'Connor.

On the August 30, 1964, The Cresters supported The Rolling Stones at **The Oasis Club** in Manchester.

One of the only other local independent recording studios at this time was the Excel at 49 Bradford Road, Shipley. It was run by F Thistlethwaite who also ran his own Excel record label.

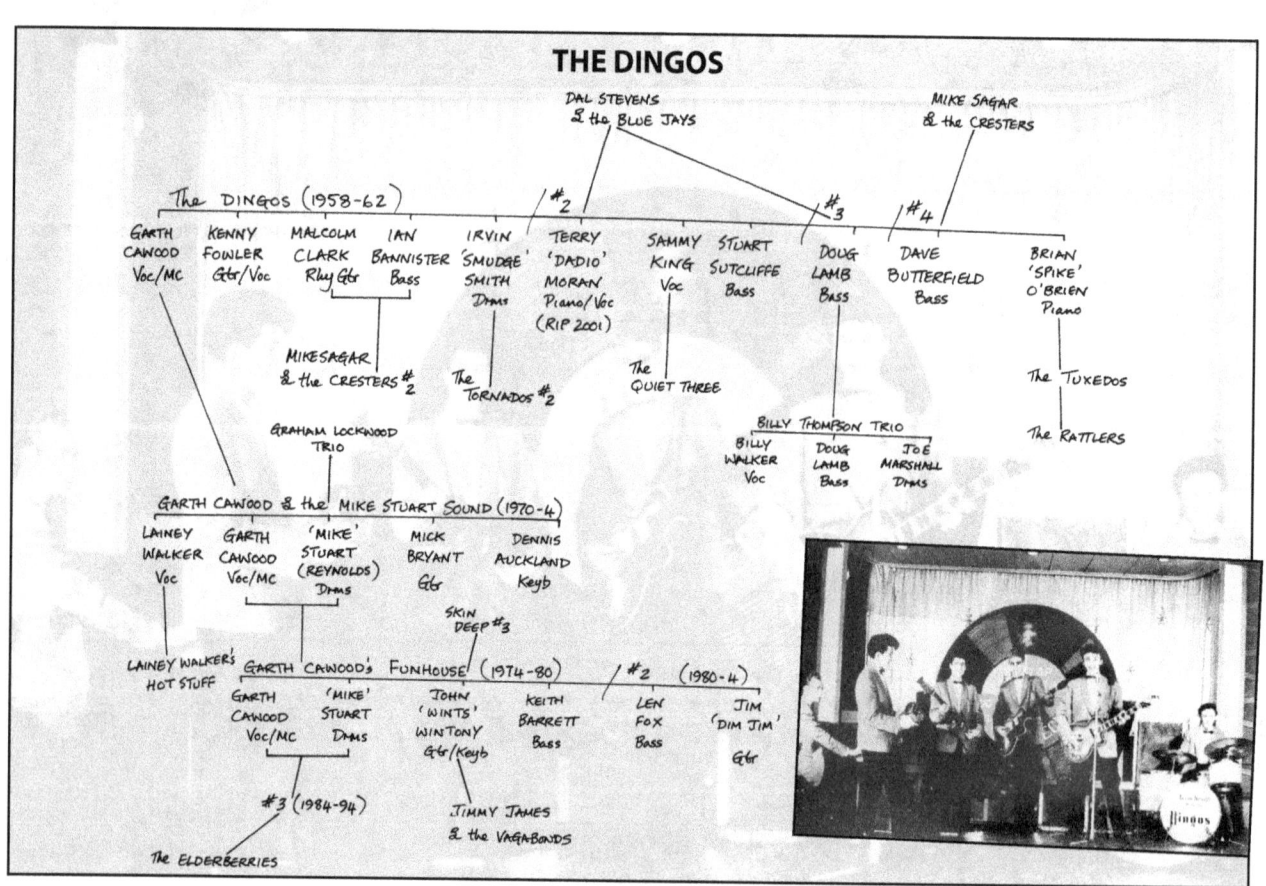

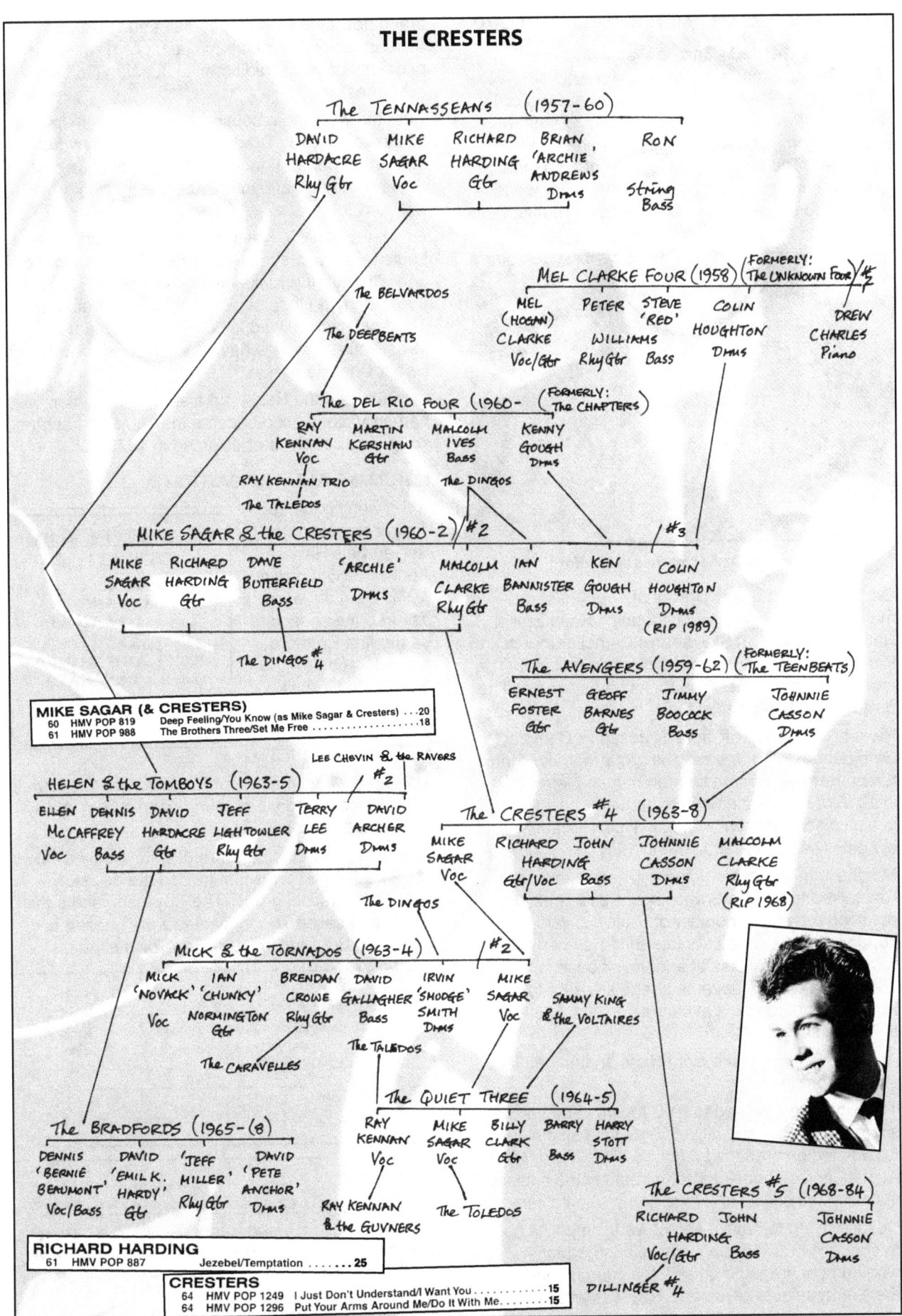

TWO POP STARS GET MARRIED IN BRADFORD

On October 14, 1964 Charlie Watts, drummer of the Rolling Stones, secretly wed twenty-six-year old art student Shirley Sheppard at Bradford Register Office. Their friends Andy and Jeanette Hoogenboom, who were based in Bradford, were witnesses. The two couples later went for a meal at a country pub near Ripon, before the newly weds returned to London. Charlie and Shirley remined together for the rest of their lives.

Kinks' Ray Davies marries in Bradford

On December 12, Ray Davies of The Kinks married eighteen-year-old Lithuanian Rasa Emiija Halina Didzpetris at St Joseph's Catholic Church, Parkington Street, Bradford. They had first met earlier that year, when The Kinks had played at **The Esquire Club** in Sheffield. (5)

Rasa had 'skipped off' from St Joseph's Convent Girls School to go and see the group with her friend Eileen Fernley. Rasa had been born in Germany in 1948 of Lithuanian parents and after being in a displaced persons' camp in Hull, the family eventually settled in Bradford in 1951.

Months later, while recording a TV show in Bristol, Ray talked to Kiki Dee, who knew Rasa, and obtained the phone number of Rasa's sister in London. A few phone calls later and Ray had arranged to meet Rasa at a friend's house in London. Soon Ray became a regular visitor to Bradford and hung out at coffee bars like The Hole In The Wall.

At a club in Halifax one night Rasa announced that she was pregnant.

The Kinks were signed to PYE records and had scored a number one hit with their third single, the fuzz/distortion drenched riff of *You Really Got Me*, in August. In October Rasa contributed some backing vocals at the sessions for the group's first album.

Despite trying to have a secret wedding police had to control a crowd of about three hundred fans who had congregated outside the church during the twenty-minute ceremony. Ray was wearing a brand new blue pin-stripped suit and Rasa had on a cream and white satin and lace gown whilst the bridesmaids wore traditional Lithuanian national costumes.

After the wedding reception at Ray's new in-laws at 31 Howard Street, Bradford, the couple flew from Yeadon Airport to London and then caught a train to Exeter for their honeymoon, before settling down in London.

On May 23, 1965, Rasa gave birth to a girl named Louisa. Ray wrote the lullaby *I Go To Sleep* for her and although the Kinks never recorded it Peggy Lee, Sonny & Cher, sixties groups The Truth and The Applejacks all did, as did The Pretenders in 1981, whilst Ray was having a relationship with singer Chrissie Hynde.

In 1968 Ray and Rasa had a second daughter, named Victoria, who became the subject of another song. The couple later divorced in 1973. (6)

LORRAINE AND THE BAHT'ATS

After winning the *Top Town* competition at St George's Hall, on April 1, 1965, Lorraine & The Baht'ats were assured the chance to be the first Bradford group to appear on Hughie Green's *Opportunity Knocks* TV show. They did so on November 19, 1966.

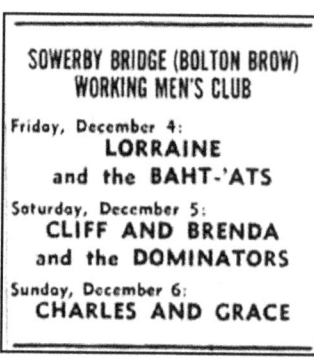

The other winning act from Bradford was the Krylati Folk Dancers who were young people born locally of Ukrainian parents. (7)

Fourteen other acts performed, watched by a crowd of 1,500. The Baht'ats just gained the decision over another local group, The Royalists, and a third local band called The Vigilantes were chosen to represent Bradford in future *Top Town* contests.

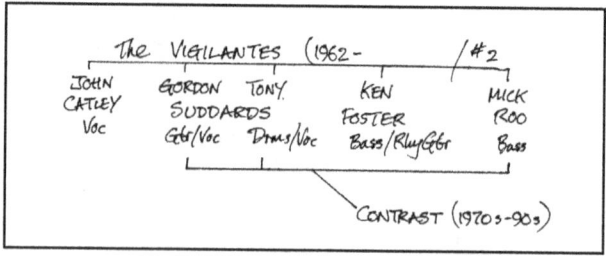

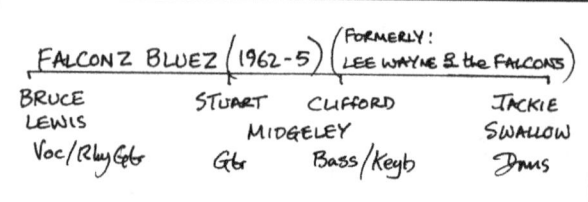

PREFACE - FROM ROCK'N'ROLL TO THE BEAT BOOM 1963 - 1966

LORRAINE AND THE BAHT'ATS / THE CARAVELLES

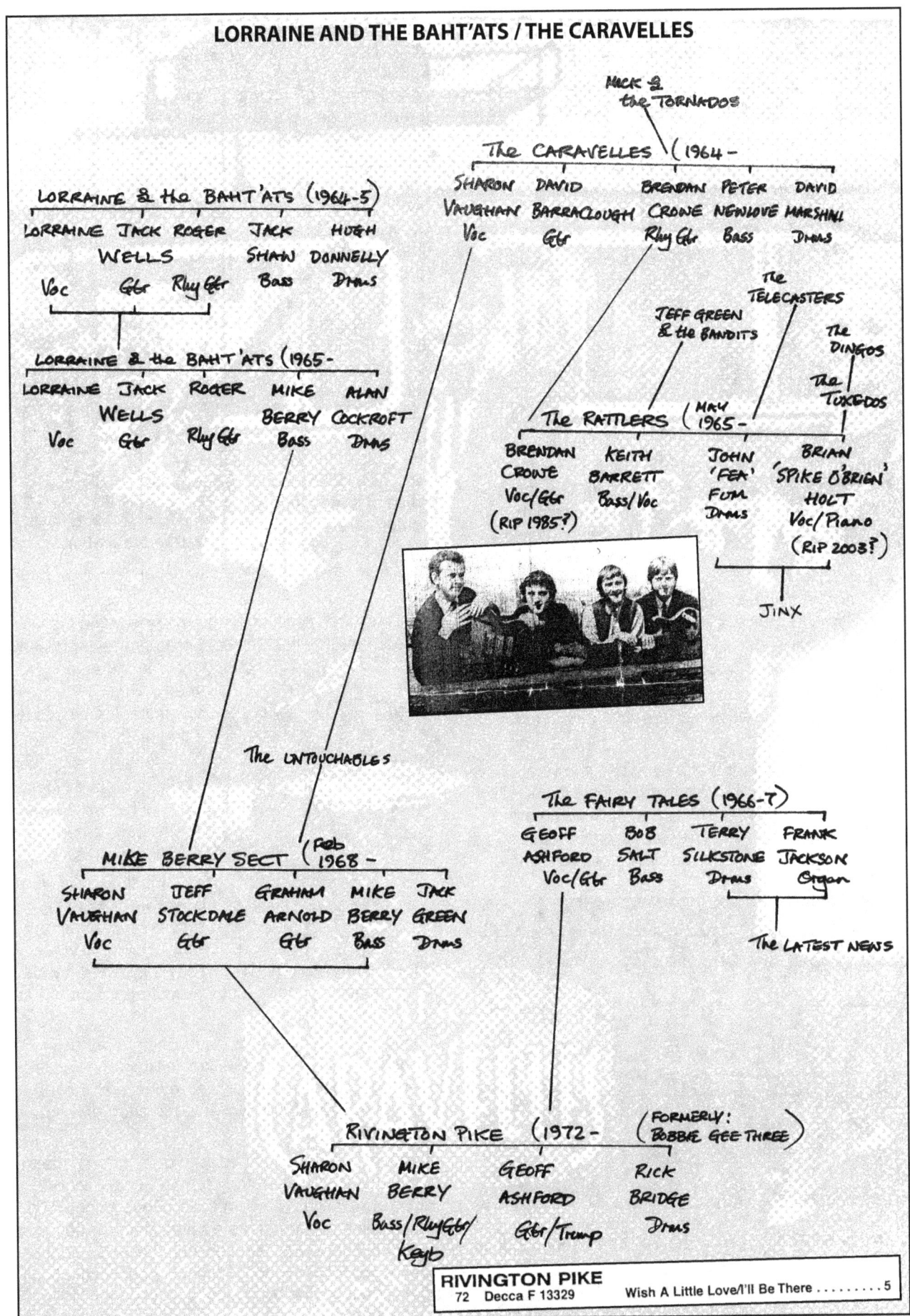

LORRAINE & the BAHT'ATS (1964-5)
- LORRAINE — Voc
- JACK WELLS — Gtr
- ROGER WELLS — Rhy Gtr
- JACK SHAW — Bass
- HUGH DONNELLY — Dms

LORRAINE & the BAHT'ATS (1965-
- LORRAINE — Voc
- JACK WELLS — Gtr
- ROGER WELLS — Rhy Gtr
- MIKE BERRY — Bass
- ALAN COCKROFT — Dms

The CARAVELLES (1964- (← MICK & the TORNADOS)
- SHARON VAUGHAN — Voc
- DAVID BARRACLOUGH — Gtr
- BRENDAN CROWE — Rhy Gtr
- PETER NEWLOVE — Bass
- DAVID MARSHALL — Dms

The RATTLERS (MAY 1965- (← JEFF GREEN & the BANDITS; The TELECASTERS; The DINGOS; The TUXEDOS)
- BRENDAN CROWE — Voc/Gtr (RIP 1985?)
- KEITH BARRETT — Bass/Voc
- JOHN 'FEA' — Dms
- BRIAN 'SPIKE O'BRIEN' HOLT — Voc/Piano (RIP 2003?)
→ JINX

The Untouchables →

MIKE BERRY SECT (Feb 1968-
- SHARON VAUGHAN — Voc
- JEFF STOCKDALE — Gtr
- GRAHAM ARNOLD — Gtr
- MIKE BERRY — Bass
- JACK GREEN — Dms

The FAIRY TALES (1966-7)
- GEOFF ASHFORD — Voc/Gtr
- BOB SALT — Bass
- TERRY SILKSTONE — Dms
- FRANK JACKSON — Organ
→ The LATEST NEWS

RIVINGTON PIKE (1972- (FORMERLY: BOBBIE GEE THREE)
- SHARON VAUGHAN — Voc
- MIKE BERRY — Bass/Rhy Gtr/Keyb
- GEOFF ASHFORD — Gtr/Trump
- RICK BRIDGE — Dms

RIVINGTON PIKE
72 Decca F 13329   Wish A Little Love/I'll Be There 5

On May 19, legendary blues guitarist John Lee Hooker played at the Queen's Hall on Morley Street.

In June 1965, Bradford got a higher education 'red brick' institution when Bradford University was opened by Labour Prime Minister, Harold Wilson.

BRIAN T STROLLERS

Local group The Brian T Strollers (the T stands for singer Brian Tordoff's favourite drink) were described as *'young, exuberant, smart, punctual and polite to promoters. Prepared to sweep up after the job and inexpensive at the moment'*.

Ricky Valance

From 1965 to 1972 they were the backing band (under the name The Northmen) for Ricky (David Spencer) Valance who'd had a number one single in August 1960 with *Tell Laura I Love Her* on Columbia Records.

On August 21, 1965, at **The Silver Slipper Club** on Salt Street (first opened in 1961) owner Jerome Morgan was arrested for possession of cannabis in a police raid for which he received a two-year sentence.

Another package tour that played two shows at The Gaumont was: The Rolling Stones, Unit 4 + 2, Spencer Davis Group, The End, The Checkmates and Charles Dickens & The Habits, on October 4, 1965. Again, the fans had camped out overnight for tickets.

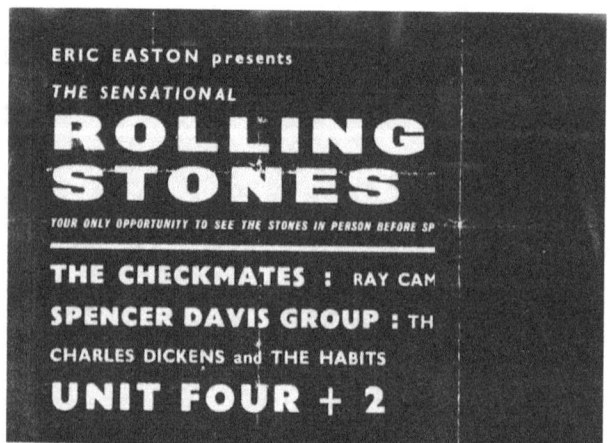
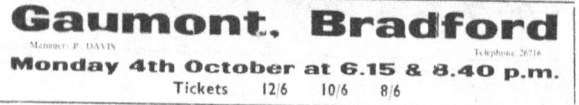

LINDA RUSSELL

Linda Nixon started out in a group called The Presidents (1958-61) with her brother Malcolm (who left to join The Garry Lee Three) and her future husband Bruce Russell. She then became the vocalist of The Beat Squad, who rehearsed at St Marks Youth Club in Uttley, in 1961, later changing their name to The Keymen.

In 1965, Linda went solo and signed a deal with EMI Records to produce a minimum of four singles a year. A single she recorded, written by comedian and songwriter Kenny Lynch, *Under The Smile of Love / If You've Never Been In Love*, was meant for release on the HMV Label but never saw the light of day.

Linda and Bruce Russell

On December 8, 1967, Linda made her first TV appearance, on the Granada programme *Firstimers*, where she sang the Georgie Fame Hit *Sunny* accompanied by Bruce on guitar.

In January 1969, she did release a single - *We've Got A Need For Each Other* on PYE Records.

At this time, she and Bruce were enjoying a successful support act residency of over 78 weeks at the **Batley Variety Club**. They supported a wide range of acts including Louis Armstrong, Eartha Kitt, and Gracie Fields.

In July 1969 Linda represented England at the *Golden Orpheus Song Festival* in Bulgaria, backed by a forty-piece orchestra, where she won the top prize as foreign singer which led to a ten-date tour of Bulgaria.

Linda and Bruce continued as a duo on the cabaret circuit until 1973 when they formed a new act with Joyce and David Killington called Peppercorn. The two couples performed as a quartet until 1980, when Linda and Bruce reverted to being a duo. In 1995 Linda finally retired from live performances after a thirty-seven-year career.

PREFACE - FROM ROCK'N'ROLL TO THE BEAT BOOM — 1963 - 1966

LINDA RUSSELL

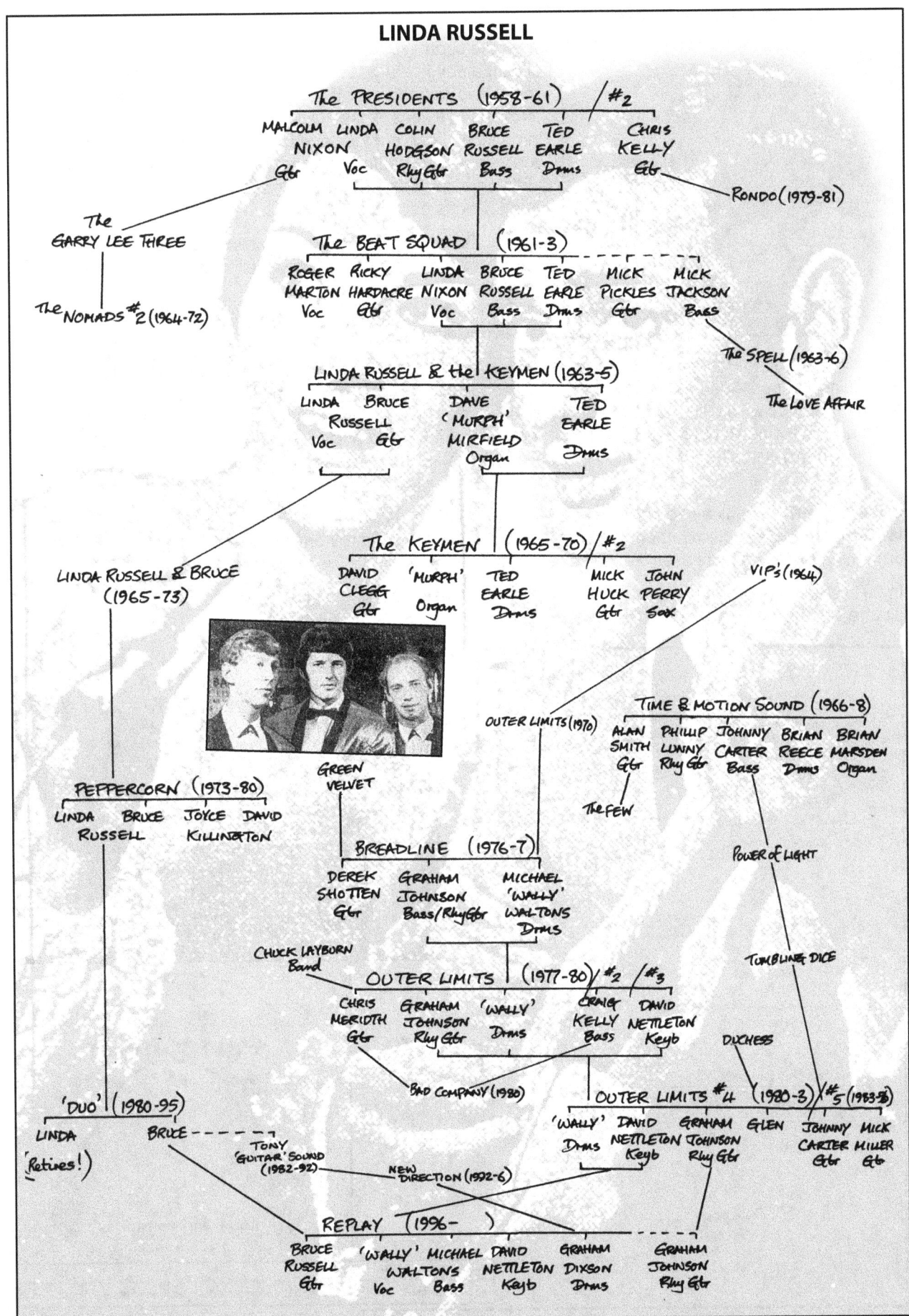

ROBIN HOOD & HIS MERRY MEN / GET RICH / ALLEN POUND'S GET RICH

When the short lived local group, Robin Hood & His Merry Men called it a day in early 1966, singer Allen Marston and drummer Trevor MacPartland set off down South to try and make it in the music business. They quickly settled in Southsea on the Hampshire coast, got jobs and formed a new group called Get Rich with fellow Bradford guitarist Barry Morris and local lad John Curtis on bass The group travelled to their gigs in a van with pound £ signs painted on it.

In June, the lads were featured in a two-page spread in the *Daily Mirror*. Despite this, they split up. Allen and Trevor returned to Bradford and formed Allen Pound's Get Rich with local musicians Allan Davies and Brian Wardley.

The band signed to Parlophone Records in 1966 to record their only 7" single, *Searching In The Wilderness*, a classic freak-beat number. It was produced by Norman 'Hurricane' Smith, the sound engineer on all the early Beatles albums up to and including Rubber Soul. Smith later produced Pink Floyd (including their legendary first album, Piper At The Gates Of Dawn) and The Pretty Things.

In the late 1970s, punk audiences picked up on the *Searchin' In The Wilderness* single at discos. It became revered, probably due to its rhythmic drumming sounding quite a lot like the early Adam & The Ants.

In 2017, *Record Collector Magazine* repressed and released the single in a picture sleeve, which quickly sold out.

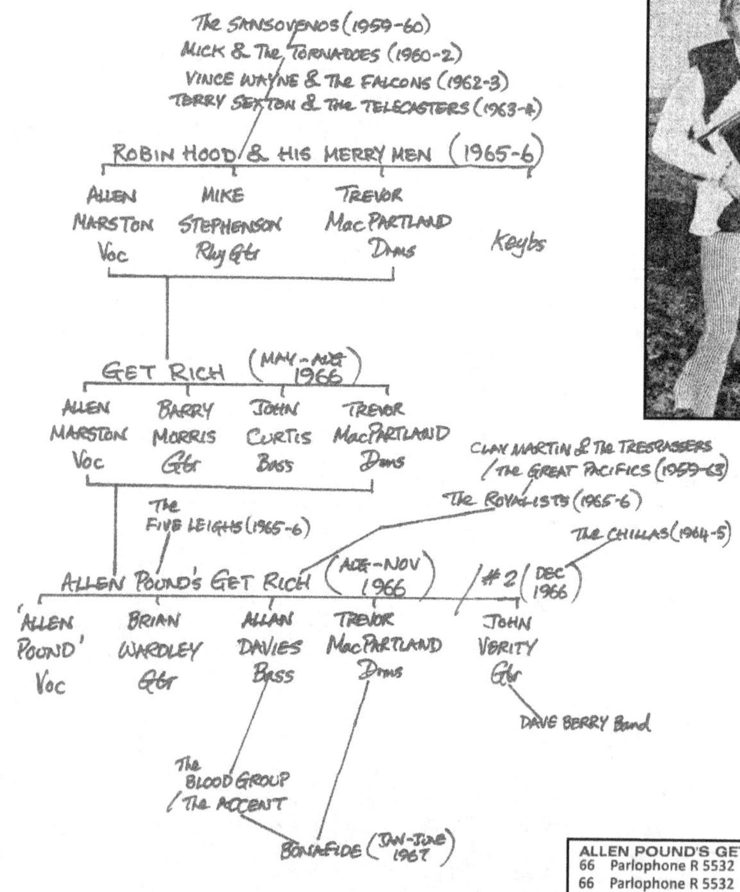

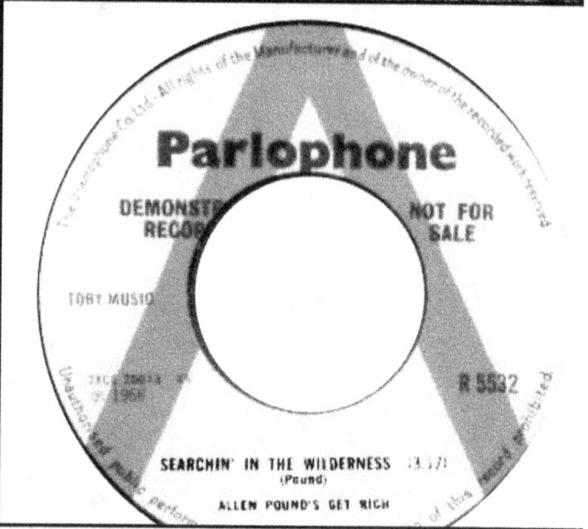

	ALLEN POUND'S GET RICH		
66	Parlophone R 5532	Searchin' In The Wilderness/Hey You (rare stock copy)	1000
66	Parlophone R 5532	Searchin' In The Wilderness/Hey You (more common demo)	600

PREFACE - FROM ROCK'N'ROLL TO THE BEAT BOOM   1963 - 1966

THE CHEERFUL DOUBLE LIFE OF FOUR ORDINARY LADS IN CALF-SKIN JACKETS

With their aim as their name: GET RICH

DAILY MIRROR, Monday, June 6, 1966

FRIDAY evening. The clock ticks round to five o'clock. It strikes—and the lives of four boys move into top gear.

As the weekend begins, their tidy, slicked-back hair comes tumbling down busby-like over their foreheads and ears.

Flung away is their conventional nine-to-five restraint. And put away are their conventional weekday clothes.

by SALLY MOORE
PICTURES:
ALISDAIR MACDONALD

In their place come calf-skin jackets, patterned bell-bottomed trousers, polo-necked sweaters and an uninhibited enthusiasm for the excitement of the Big Beat.

Exit four ordinary working boys.
Enter The Get Rich beat group.

They gather in Waterlooville, near Southsea, Hants, in a suburban semi-detached, rented for eight guineas a week from a sailor now abroad.

Pots

Behind the orthodox net curtains, guitars, bongo drums, amplifiers, microphones, a harmonica, an autoharp and all the other assorted clobber essential to the Beat, litter the green wall-to-wall carpet of the lounge.

ALLEN MARSTON, 20, the blond singer of the group and Trevor MacPartland, 18, the drummer, live there with a large Alsatian called Tiger.

Pocket-sized Barry Morris, the 22-year-old lead guitarist, lives in a Southsea bedsitter only just big enough to do his yoga exercises on the floor.

John Curtis, 20, the bass guitarist, is a local boy and lives at home in Southsea with his father.

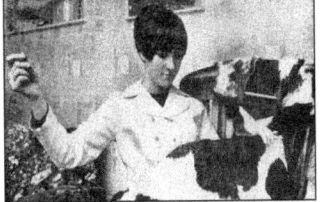

There's a girl, too — urchin-faced Liz Lee, 19, a cheerful get-them-organised sort, who works in a Southsea dress shop.

She spends her spare time sewing up any holes in the group's gear, making endless pots of coffee and carrying around a silver tube of Indi-moved from home two months ago to try to break into the "big time" down South.

On the way, their soft calf-skin jackets got wet in the removal van and went starch-stiff—but the boys don't worry.

"We've got away from the working men's clubs of the North and that's the main thing." says Allen.

Blues

"Audiences there only want to hear Beatles' music and the stuff they can sing along to. We couldn't play what we wanted or how we wanted and they kept telling us to turn the volume down. Here we can play the way we like."

Their own music is a mixture of blues, beat and pop which they call Blues-Beat.

In fact, the Beat is their life. They would all turn professional if they could, but at present they do ordinary jobs because they need the money.

Allen, who started the group in Yorkshire two years ago, is a £16-a-week representative for a loans firm. As he drives round on business in his firm's white Cortina GT, he sings and thinks up new songs.

Trevor, nicknamed "Little Plum" by the group because of his red hair, gets £8 a week as an assistant in a tailor's shop.

His Mum, who is very with it," bought him his first drum kit and his father, he says, "washes water" at Bradford Waterworks.

Barry is the "different" one. rod and line on the end of Southsea's Victoria Pier. He caught an eel the other day but mostly he catches nothing.

He works "in the rag trade, cutting up old rags or dusters and things."

John, an £11-a-week Admiralty rigger at Portsmouth dockyard, has been in several groups in the area and joined The Get Rich when they appeared on the Southsea scene.

He says he think up new songs and works on new arrangements in his mind while he's waiting on the jetty for a ship to come in.

UNDERGROUND in the dim red glow of The Indigo Vat beat club in Hampshire-terrace, Southsea, the boys listen to the throb of the St. Louis Checks, a popular local group.

So far The Get Rich are an "unknown quantity" to most of the other semi-professional groups and beat fans in the area.

Their name is known through mentions in a local paper—but few have heard them play yet.

It's all part of the plan, explains Allen.

"We've not played much here." he says, "because we haven't been here long and we're concentrating on building our image first. We went round to all the club managers and got them interested and now everyone's heard of us from here to Bognor Regis.

ing out new songs. Now people want to hear us, clubs want to book us, and we're ready to move in."

In an upstairs room above the Borough Arms pub in St. Paul's-road, Portsmouth, the Big Beat reverberates as the boys rehearse.

Cold, half-drunk cups of tea and left-over ham sandwiches lie forgotten on a table as they concentrate on putting together a new song, written by Allen, called "Don't Look Through My Window."

Drums

Barry works out the main theme on lead guitar as John works out the bass notes. Trevor on drums is planning the beat.

"Can you try it faster?" says Allen, and demonstrates. "Like this—boom boom, boom boom, boom!"

Their individual working lives are forgotten. They have become one unit, intent only on the Beat.

At night, behind the drawn curtains of the semi-detached in Bernina-close, Allen and Trevor play beat records before they go to bed. "Then we dream of the day we shall turn professional," said Trevor.

I remember the Rockin' Berries having similar dreams some years ago. "If we ever get into the Top Ten we'll buy you a Cadillac," they told me.

Well, I never got my Cadillac. But the Rockin' Berries *did* make the Top Ten and the "big time."

Perhaps The Get Rich will too, one day.

But till then it's back to stage one and work on Mondays . . .

15

THE BRADFORDS

Local singer Ellen McCaffrey (pictured left) of the group Helen & The Tomboys (1963-65) was very popular on the local scene and had sung previously under the stage name of Dee Lawrence.

In 1965 The Tomboys, minus Helen and with new drummer Pete Archer, emigrated to Canada and from there started working under the name of The Bradfords.

Their first album The 1234 Sides Of The Bradfords, was released in Canada as a four-piece with the band using made up names.

They released three singles on Capital Records; *Leaning On A Lamppost / Together We Have Stayed* (1965), *What Are You Doing To My Friend / Babette* (1966) and *I Really Don't Want To Know / The Merry Plowboy* (1968).

By 1968 the group had been in residence at The Rathskeller Club in Minneapolis for the previous two years and had also made a TV appearance.

The group played under their new stage names, which emulated the flower power movement.

While based in Minneapolis the group opened their own club and also diversified into running a local studio and management company. They continued to perform during the 1970s with extra vocalist Linda Kendall.

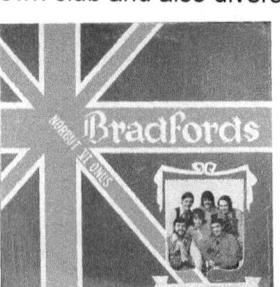

A fourth single, *Laurel And Hardy*, appeared on the Trolley label in 1971. They recorded two LPs for Trolley Records. The first had the unusual title Norbut VI Onus (1972). For their second *Take Off Your Clothes (1973)* they were billed as 'The Bradfords From England.

Original Tomboy's vocalist (also bassist Bernie's sister) Ellen McCaffrey had rejoined the band in time for their second album.

A later album *It Turned Out Better Than We Hoped* appeared with almost the same cover as their first album but completely different track listing. The Bradford's called it a day some time in the early 1980s.

James Bordass outside The Bradford's club in 1971

The band's drummer David 'Pete Anchor' Archer opened a fish & chip shop in Vancouver which also had a bar selling English ale.

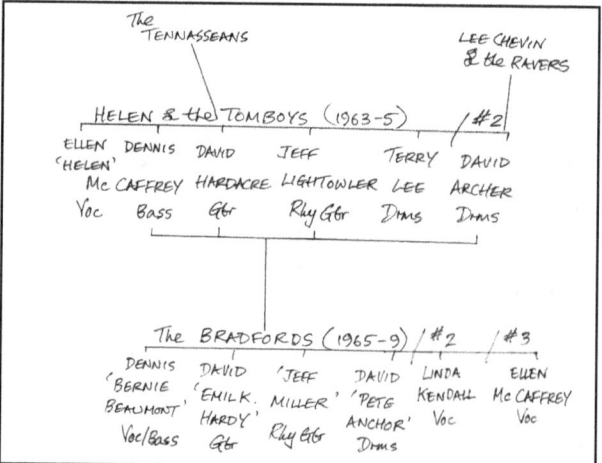

PREFACE - FROM ROCK'N'ROLL TO THE BEAT BOOM 1963 - 1966

THE NOMADS / MARK RUSSELL FOUR

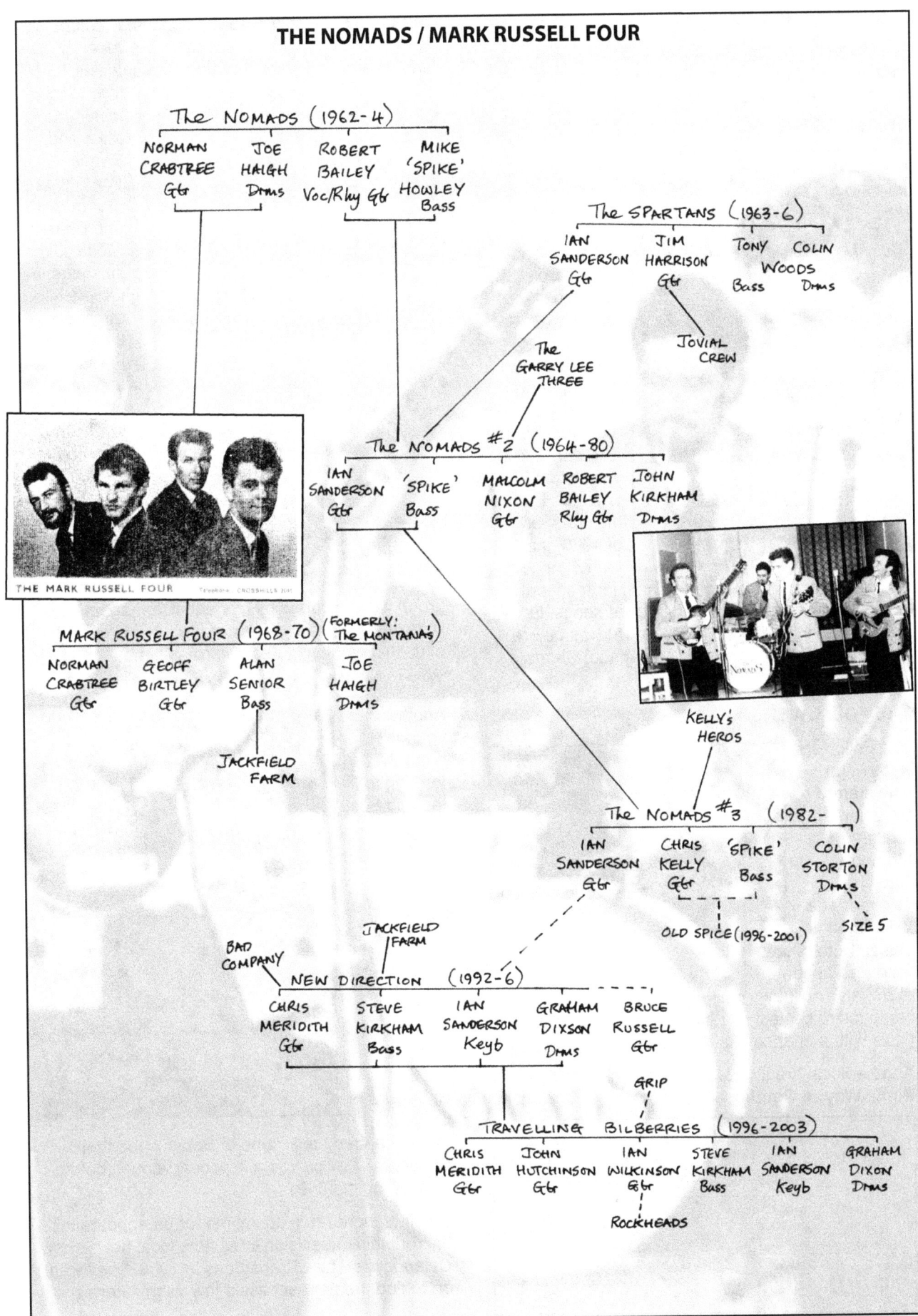

THE QUARE FELLOWS

In Halifax the group The Quare Fellows (1964-65) had bleached blond hair and wore outrageous clothes for their stage show.

THE FORGERS

The Forgers (July 1966 - Melvin Jeffrey Voc, Neil Addison Gtr, Brian Stuart Bass, Andy Jackson Drms)

The Forgers were teenagers, originally at Carlton school, and three of the group worked as office clerks. They all intended to give up their jobs in a bid to become the first Bradford area group to 'hit the top'. During the summer of 1966, they toured the north east of England with twelve newly composed songs. One prestigious gig in Burnley (August 13) was before a crowd of 25,000 at Lucas' (Areospace) *Sports & Gala Day*.

THE FOLLOWERS

The Followers (1966 - John Iredale, Paul, Peter Adams)

The Followers were a trio who started by 'doing a turn' at a local Methodist Church Concert. The lads from the Odsal/Buttershaw area also appeared at a Welsh holiday camp talent contest in 1966, reaching the area finals with a chance of a top prize of £1,000.

Another local group around at this time was **The Vince Wayne Combo.**

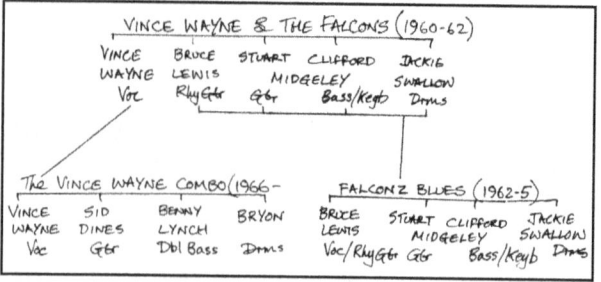

Vince Wayne & The Falcons (1960-62): Vince Wayne Voc, Bruce Lewis Rhy Gtr, Stuart Midgeley Gtr, Clifford Bass/Keys, Jackie Swallow Drms

The Vince Wayne Combo (1966 - Vince Wayne Voc, Sid Dines Gtr, Benny Lynch Dbl Bass, Bryon Drms)

Falconz Blues (1962-5): Bruce Lewis Voc/Rhy Gtr, Stuart Gtr, Clifford Midgeley Bass/Keys, Jackie Swallow Drms

On Sunday, March 13, 1966, at Odsal Stadium there was a charity football match between TV Allstars and Yorkshire Sporting Personalities.

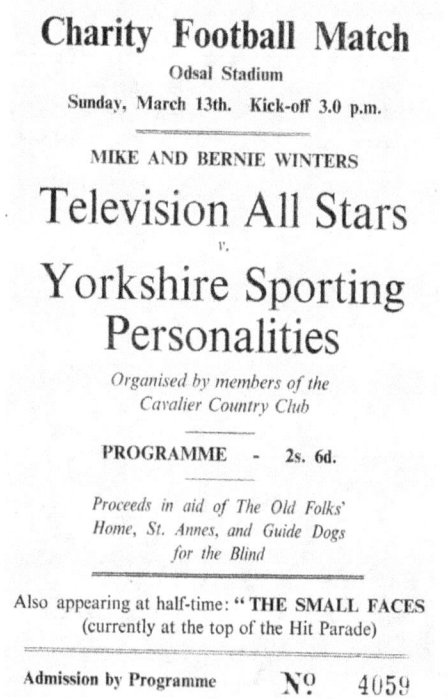

Charity Football Match
Odsal Stadium
Sunday, March 13th. Kick-off 3.0 p.m.

MIKE AND BERNIE WINTERS

Television All Stars
v.
Yorkshire Sporting Personalities

Organised by members of the Cavalier Country Club

PROGRAMME - 2s. 6d.

Proceeds in aid of The Old Folks' Home, St. Annes, and Guide Dogs for the Blind

Also appearing at half-time: "THE SMALL FACES (currently at the top of the Hit Parade)"

Admission by Programme   No. 4059

The teams included Mike and Bernie Winters, Fred Trueman and Brian Close. Over six thousand people attended the match. Fresh from the success of their top three single, *Sha-La-La-La-Lee*, the Small Faces made an appearance. At the end of their set, the group were mobbed by hysterical teenagers while collecting for charity. They made a hasty retreat out of town, twenty minutes before halftime.

THE YEN / ESSENCE / ELIZABETHANS

Another young band was forming in the mid-60s. The lineup of Chris Norman, Alan Silson, Terry Uttley and Ron Kelly played their first show as The Yen in February 1965 at Birkenshaw School.

They changed their name to Sphynx and then Essence. They played a few local venues before splitting up in 1966.

The four were reunited in time for an appearance on Yorkshire Television's tea time local news show *Calander* as The Elizabethans in 1968. They went on to find greater success a few years later as Smokie.

PREFACE - FROM ROCK'N'ROLL TO THE BEAT BOOM — 1963 - 1966

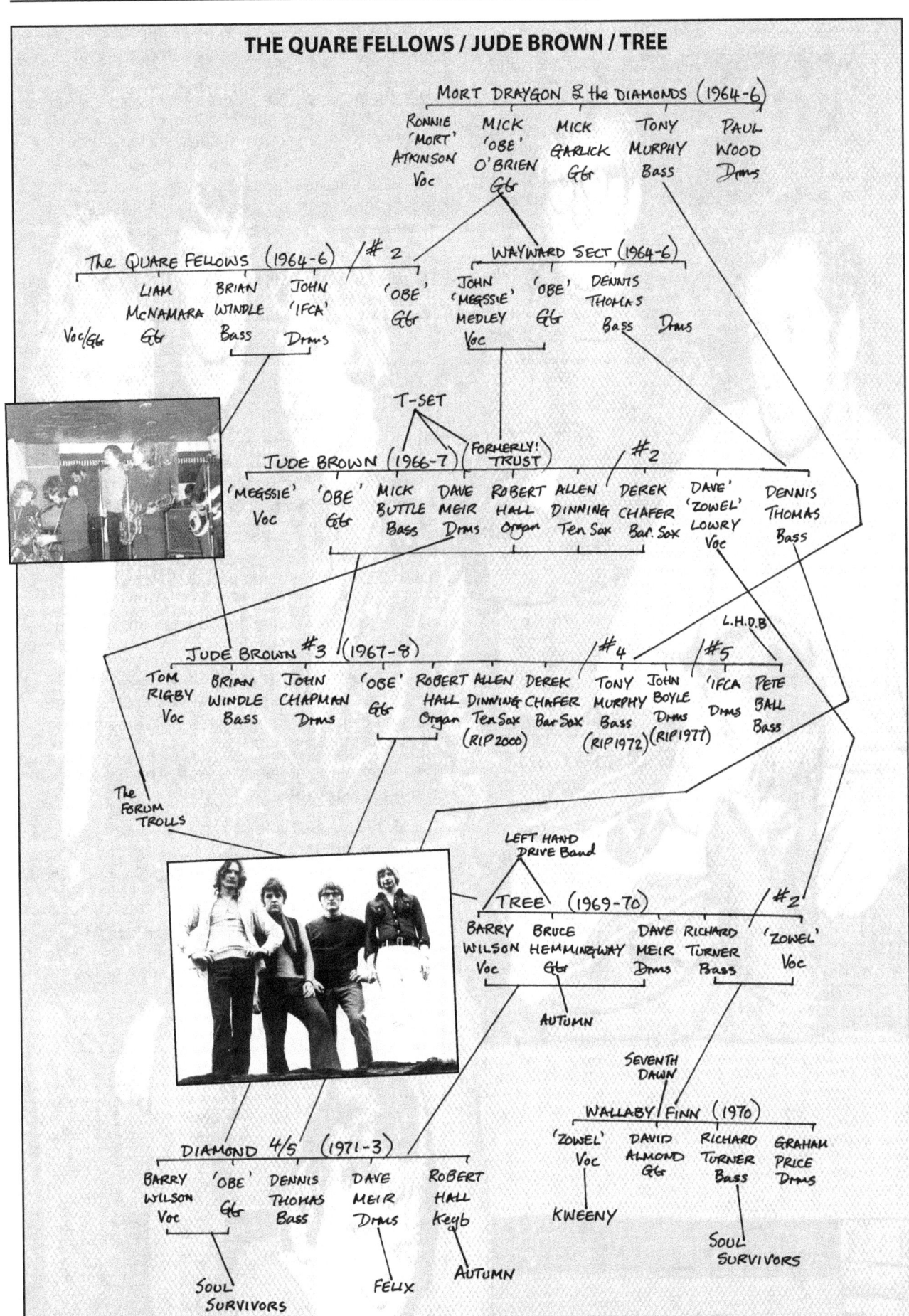

THE THREE GOOD REASONS

Local trio Peter & Ann Clegg and 'Danny' Radivoj released three singles on the Mercury label between 1965-66. Their second single was a cover of The Beatles' *Nowhere Man* which got to No 47 in the UK charts and reached No 1 in the Dutch charts.

Their manager Farrol Kelly was convicted of being 'drunk in charge of the band's van' one night after getting caught driving home from a concert at the Imperial Ballroom in Nelson, Lancashire. His response to the police was, *'Delighted, I am going to the nick!'*

THREE GOOD REASONS			
65	Mercury MF 883	Build Your Love/Don't Leave Me Now	10
65	Mercury MF 899	Nowhere Man/Wire Wheels	18
65	Mercury MF 929	The Moment Of Truth/Funny Kind Of Loving	10

Peter had begun his musical career with local favourites The Phantoms and later formed Hi-Fly (left), who were on the local scene from 1976 to 1981 and included former members of Fogg, Mouldy Warp, Dave Lee Sound and Ritz.

The Texan singer P J Proby caused a storm of controversy during his 1965 tour as he manipulated 'pant splitting' episodes at concerts in Croydon and Luton, leading to his ban from ABC theatres. As his later career spiralled into bankruptcy and alcoholism, he spent time in the mid-1980s as a poverty-stricken stable hand near Haworth!

Also in 1965, Halifax 'harmonica blues' group **Mort Daygen & The Diamonds** released a single entitled *If I Had A Ticket*.

CHAD WAYNE & the CHESSMEN (1964-				
TINA KNIGHT	CHAD WAYNE	ROGER DAVIES	'DUKE' EVEREST	PETER VERNON
Voc	Voc/Gtr	Rhy Gtr	Bass	Dms

Some of the other groups around at this time were: **Chad Wade & The Chessmen, The Cheats, The Amperes, The Hombres** from **Keighley, The Frrends** from Ilkley, and **The Rocking Birds** from Halifax.

In 1966 the newest club around town was **The Penny Farthing Club**, at the Ritz Building on Charles Street, which changed its name to **Scamps** in the 1970s.

In Idle **The O-O (Double O) Club** began at the world-famous **Idle Working Men's Club** as a mod inspired club. The band John's Followers played there on December 16.

Two other clubs at this time were **The Brazilla Club** and **Mareena Club.**

The Big Rave Ball was held at the Queen's Hall, Leeds, on January 22, 1966, featuring The Kinks, The Outer Limits, The Peppers and Garth Cawood. The entrance fee was 7/6d.

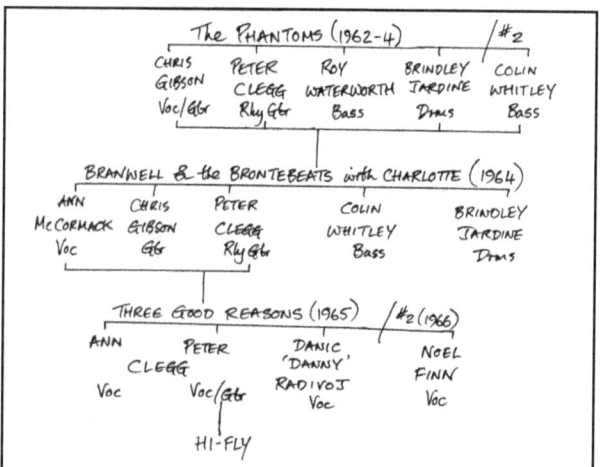

THE CHEATS / THE CALDERBEATS

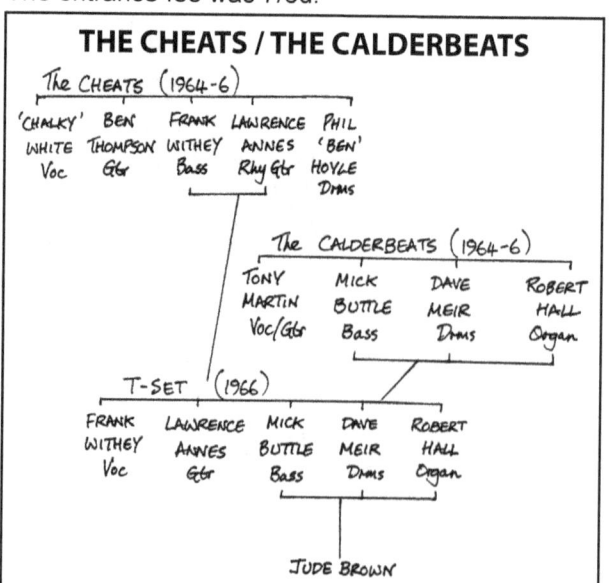

PREFACE - FROM ROCK'N'ROLL TO THE BEAT BOOM 1963 - 1966

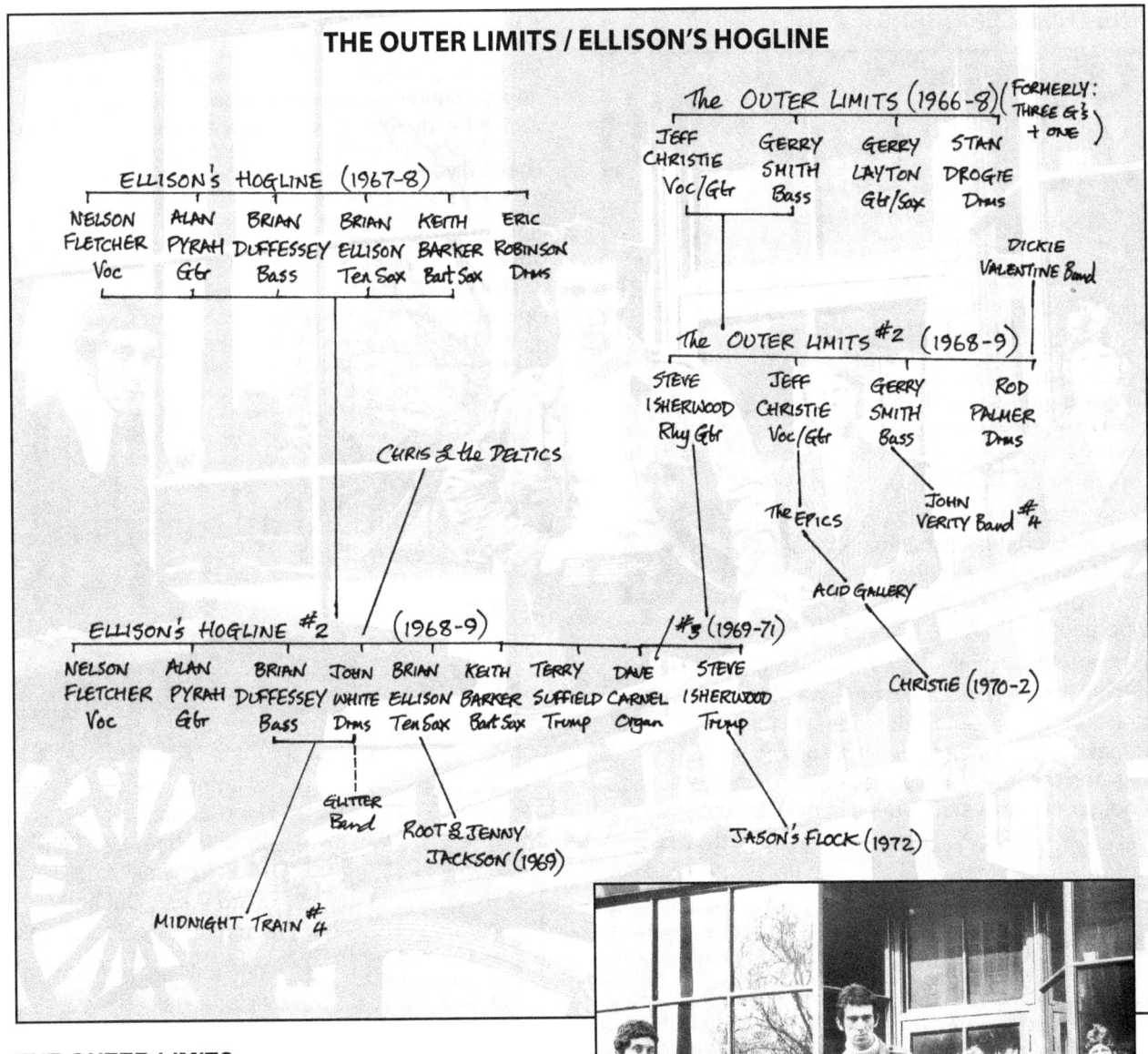

THE OUTER LIMITS

The Outer Limits were a Leeds based group, with Bradford lad Gerry Smith on bass, who had evolved out of skiffle group The Three G's + One.

They had their first release, *When The Work Is Through*, on a Leeds student charity disc before they signed to Deram Records. Their Deram single, *Just One More Chance*, was a hit in Berlin and has since attracted attention from Northern Soul DJs as a dance floor classic.

By 1968 the group had an eight-hundred-strong fan club and had drafted in two more Bradford lads, Steve Isherwood and Rod Palmer.

They moved to Immediate Records to record the single *Great Train Robbery* (inspired by the original 1899 Robbery) which was released on the Immediate off-shoot label Instant Records.

The group's singer Jeff Christie eventually (via bands The Epics and Acid Gallery) formed Christie, who had a 1970 number one with Yellow River.

		OUTER LIMITS	
67	Elephant LUR 100	When The Work Is Thru'/5 MAN CARGO: What A Wonderful Feeling (Leeds Students Charity Rag record)	50
67	Deram DM 125	Just One More Chance/Help Me Please	18
68	Immediate IM 067	Great Train Robbery/Sweet Freedom (demo only)	65
68	Instant IN 001	Great Train Robbery/Sweet Freedom	20
71	Decca F 13176	The Dark Side Of The Moon/Black Boots	8

THE THIMBLERIGGERS

Keighley group The Thimbleriggers (1962-66), whose name means 'one who plays a sleight-of-hand trick', were originally known as The Karavelles but changed their name to avoid confusion with the girl duo The Caravelles who appeared on the scene in August 1963.

In 1964, The Thimbleriggers did some recording at a local Riddleston studio, run by ex-big band leader and songwriter Ken Henderson. He hired the lads to back a female singer he was promoting and, besides recording two songs with her, they also did another of Ken's songs *Beg, Borrow Or Steal*, which

they never played live. In payment for their services, they were allowed to record some of their own

material. What they recorded was mainly jamming, but it was still closer to their live sound. (8)

The band played a range of venues, including a support slot for Wayne Fontana & The Mindbenders at the Imperial Ballroom in Nelson, on its revolving stage, on April 3, 1965. Just before the group split, they met the then Rolling Stones manager Andrew Loog Oldham who tried to sign them.

```
The THIMBLERIGGERS (1962-6) / #2
JOHN      JOHN      DAVID     TONY      KEITH          PHIL
LOVEDAY   'GUS'     TEA       TRETTON                  PICKLES
Voc       SUGDEN    Bass      Gtr       Dms            Rhy Gtr
          Rhy Gtr

     JOHN'S FOLLOWERS (DEC 1966 - (8))
JOHN      JOHN      TREVOR    JOHN      ANDY
LOVEDAY   MARTIN    TILLOTSON SWAIN     PICKLES
Voc       Gtr       Bass      Dms       Keybs
```

JOHN'S FOLLOWERS

After four years playing with The Thimbleriggers singer John Loveday left to form his own group, John's Followers, in December 1966.

They played some of their first gigs at Bradford's Hole In The Wall and Double O clubs during the years 1967-68 as well

as further afield in places like Gainsborough (Lincolnshire) Drill Hall, billed as The Return of the Freak Out and supported by Ultrasonics.

Gigs at Keighley's Victoria Hall, the Technical College and Central Youth Club cemented their thriving local fan base, as did a gig at Thornton's Manor Blues Club.

By May 1968, the group had signed a three-year contract with an Italian agency after a successful tour there. In Italy, they appeared on six half-hour TV programmes, as well as twenty-one live radio performances.

John's Followers went into the studio in Milan to record a 7" single, *Buone Vacanze (Good Holidays) / Crystal Mountals* on the Arlecchino label.

On Saturday, August 3, 2013, the group reformed for a one-off free gig at the Variety Club, Russell Street, Keighley, with John Loveday flying in from New Zealand where he'd emigrated to years before.

THE KINGPINS / THE LADYKILLERS / MOULDY WARP

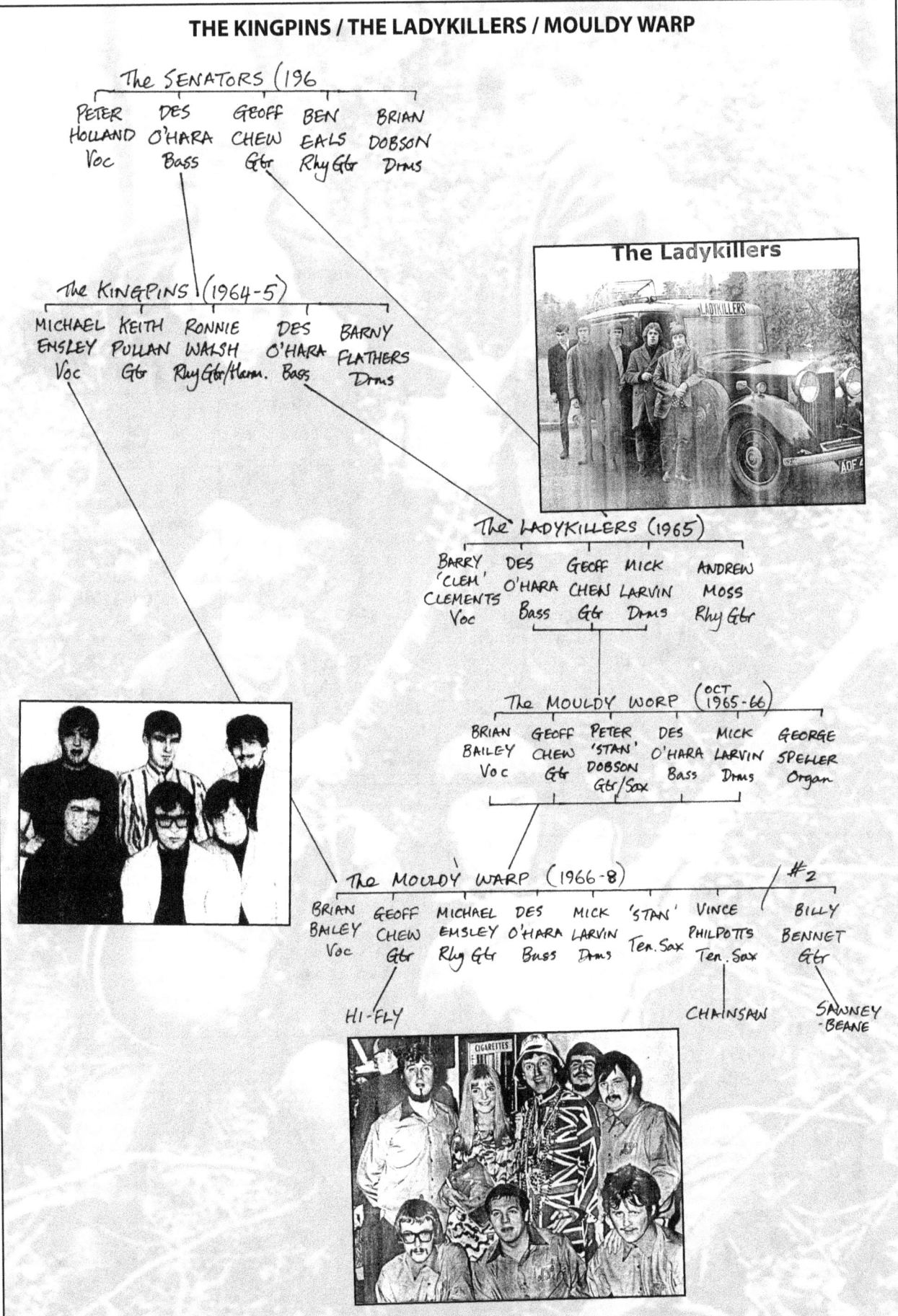

ROOT 'N' JENNY JACKSON

Root and Jenny Jackson were a brother and sister soul act based in Mirfield, near Huddersfield. They played regularly at the Plebs in Halifax from 1966.

From 1967 to 1970 they were backed by The Hightimers. They released two singles on the German Beacon label, *Lean On Me / Please Come Home* (1968) and *Let's Go Somewhere / If I Didn't Love You* (1969).

The Hightimers were also used as the backing band for chart hits by Bob & Marcia - *Young, Gifted & Black* (number five in 1970), and Dave & Ansil Collins - *Double Barrel* (number one in 1971). Three members of the Hightimers later formed the reggae band Jab Jab in the 1970s.

In 1970, Root 'n' Jenny had a new backing group, The Zenith Band. They released the single, *So Far Away*, written by Huddersfield songwriter Abington Ledwidge.

A second single, *Save Me / If I Didn't Love You*, followed later that year.

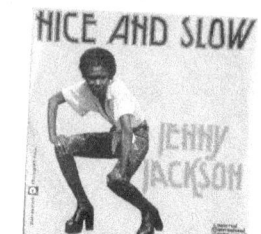

Jenny Jackson later released the solo single *Nice And Slow* on the Universal International Music label.

Their agent was Danny Pollock who ran the S&D Enterprise agency in Leeds with Stuart Frais. He also managed local acts Ellison Hogline and Horsforth psych-folk duo Jan Dukes de Grey.

ROOT & JENNY JACKSON			
69	Beacon BEA 110	Please Come Home/Lean On Me	15
69	Beacon BEA 136	Let's Go Somewhere/If I Didn't Love You	10
ROOTS & JENNY JACKSON			
70	Beacon BEA 164	Save Me/If I Didn't Love You	25

sat, aug 19, 7.45
ROOT'N' JENNY JACKSON
and the
HIGHTIMERS

bring your own tamborine ! ! !

OPENING SUNDAYS
3 shilling's
7.45 - 11.0

Plebeian, Halifax

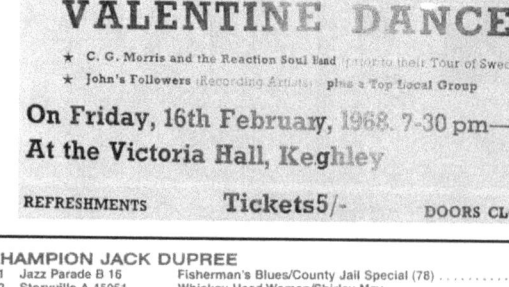

KEIGHLEY COUNCIL OF YOUTH PRESENT
VALENTINE DANCE
★ C. G. Morris and the Reaction Soul Band *prior to their Tour of Sweden*
★ John's Followers *Recording Artists* plus a Top Local Group
On Friday, 16th February, 1968. 7-30 pm—12-30 am
At the Victoria Hall, Keighley
REFRESHMENTS   Tickets 5/-   DOORS CLOSE 10-15 pm

CHAMPION JACK DUPREE			
51	Jazz Parade B 16	Fisherman's Blues/County Jail Special (78)	30
62	Storyville A 45051	Whiskey Head Woman/Shirley May	20
67	Decca F 12611	Barrelhouse Woman/Under Your Hood	22
67	Blue Horizon 45-1007	Get Your Head Happy/Easy Is The Way (with T.S. McPhee)	130
68	Blue Horizon 57-3140	I Haven't Done No-One No Harm/How Am I Doing It (with Stan Webb)	22
69	Blue Horizon 57-3152	Ba'la Fouche/Kansas City	22
69	Blue Horizon 57-3158	I Want To Be A Hippy/Goin' Back To Louisiana	22
61	Storyville SEP 381	BLUES ANTHOLOGY VOL. 1 (EP)	30
64	RCA RCX 7137	RHYTHM AND BLUES VOL. 1 (EP)	30
64	Decca DFE 8586	LONDON SPECIAL (EP, with Keith Smith Climax Band)	60
65	Ember EMB 4564	JACK DUPREE (EP)	25
60s	XX MIN 716	CHAMPION JACK DUPREE (EP)	20
59	London Jazz LTZ-K 15171	BLUES FROM THE GUTTER (LP)	85
61	London Jazz LTZ-K 15217	CHAMPION JACK'S NATURAL AND SOULFUL BLUES (LP, also stereo SAH-K 6151)	80/110
65	Storyville SLP 145	TROUBLE TROUBLE (LP)	35
65	Xtra XTRA 1028	CABBAGE GREENS (LP)	25
65	Storyville SLP 161	PORTRAITS IN BLUES (LP)	35
66	Decca LK/SKL 4747	FROM NEW ORLEANS TO CHICAGO (LP)	90
67	Storyville 670 194	CHAMPION JACK DUPREE (LP)	40
67	Decca SKL 4871	CHAMPION JACK DUPREE AND HIS BIG BLUES BAND (LP)	90
68	Blue Horizon 7-63206	WHEN YOU FEEL THE FEELING YOU WAS FEELING (LP)	80
69	Blue Horizon 7-63214	SCOOBYDOOBYDOO (LP)	80
70	Sonet SNTF 614	THE INCREDIBLE CHAMPION JACK DUPREE (LP)	18
72	Sonet SNTF 626	LEGACY OF THE BLUES (LP)	18
75	Atlantic K 40526	BLUES FROM THE GUTTER (LP)	12

CHAMPION JACK DUPREE

One of the many tales on the local music scene over the years was about a US blues singer living in the area, and yes, it was true. In 1966, American blues singer and 'barrel-house' pianist Champion Jack Dupree settled in Halifax, at 173 Ovenden Way.

'Champion Jack' was born William Thomas Dupree, on July 4, 1910, in New Orleans. He was brought up at the Waifs Home Orphanage after his parents (his father was a black African-American and his mother a Cherokee Indian) had been murdered by the Ku Klux Klan in a fire at their grocery store. At that time, Louis Armstrong was at the same orphanage and played a battered bugle as a signal to go to bed.

At the age of fourteen or fifteen, Jack left the orphanage and hit the 'hobo trail' - riding the trains, sleeping rough and begging for food. He learned to play the piano 'barrelhouse' style on his travels around the bars by watching the pianists ply their trade.

By 1931, at the height of the Great Depression and inspired by watching the boxers at Kid Green's Gym in Chicago, he had taken up boxing. He began his career in the ring as a sparring partner before becoming an amateur fighter, later turning professional as a southpaw (left-handed) fighting for $40 for six rounds or $90 if he lasted ten rounds. He went on to win the California State boxing title in 1938 and became USA Lightweight Champion (hence his moniker) before retiring undefeated after one hundred and seventy fights.

In 1937 Jack's first wife died, leaving him to cope with two young sons.

In the early 1940s in New York, he became friends and worked with Sonny Terry & Brownie McGhee with whom he recorded material for small 'black orientated' labels.

During the Second World War, Jack served as a cook in the US Navy. He was shipwrecked and became a POW where he found that his Japanese captors treated black GIs better than the white prisoners.

In 1958, Champion Jack recorded his first album, *Blues From The Gutter*, on Atlantic Records. The track *Junker's Blues* became the inspiration for Fats Domino's debut recording, *The Fat Man*. (8)

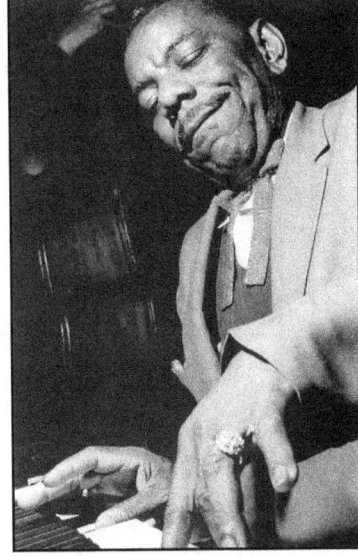

By 1959/1960, tired of the racist abuse, he left the USA for Europe where he hoped to find some semblance of freedom. While visiting a London club, Jack met eighteen-year-old Shirley Harrison from Halifax, whom he later married. The couple first settled in Switzerland, before moving to Halifax.

In 1966, in London, he recorded the LP *From New Orleans To Chicago* for Decca Records. The album was produced by Mike Vernon and featured British blues guitarists Eric Clapton and Tony McPhee.

That same year, his second daughter Georgiana was born; daughter Christine was the eldest and Jackie was born in 1969.

Now firmly settled in his wife's home town of Halifax, Jack played a gig at the local Folk Club **The Grass Roots**, based at the Plummet Line Hotel, on November 27. Then on January 14, 1968, he appeared at the newest club in town, **Clarence's**. In early October 1971, Jack and Shirley were able to buy their council house on Ovenden Way for £1,600 and immediately started refurbishing both the outside and the interior. They gave the house its own name, *Jackie*, after their youngest. During the 1970s Jack played widely in the north of England and the rest of the UK, including the Vaults Bar in Bradford in 1972, as well as being featured in the Yorkshire TV documentary *A Kind of Freedom*.

At some point in the mid-1970s, he played in Ireland at Dublin's Slattery's Bar and was helped out on harmonica by a pre-Boomtown Rats Bob Geldof.

In 1976 Jack and his family left Halifax and moved back to Europe, first to Copenhagen and then to Zurich, before finally settling down in Hanover, Germany. On January 22, 1992, Champion Jack Dupree died, aged 81, after a lifetime of performing mainly his own material, drawn from his everyday life experiences, in a style not matched by many of the old blues legends. (9)

Chapter 1: Psychedelia to Heavy Rock 1967–1970

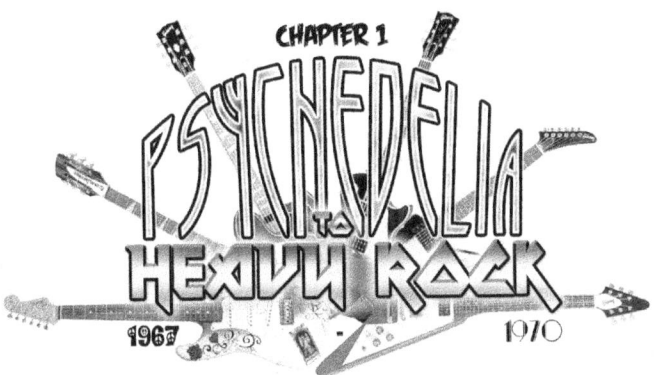

The year 1967 would forever be associated with the hippy cultural phenomenon of the 'Summer of Love' and the emergence of psychedelia which in Bradford, led to the opening of a new club.

The String O' Beads Club, at 47 Cheapside, ran until 1968. Opened as a response to the lack of entertainment for young people, this was the only

club that catered for sixteen to twenty-year-olds. It was run as a members club, with no alcohol, and put on all-night gigs which ran from 10 pm to 8 am for a charge of fifteen shillings (75p), as in July 1967 when Ellison's Hogline performed.

In 1968 an incident at an all-night rave threatened the club's existence when seven young people were rushed to hospital after overdosing on downers. The club's manager Susan Sproat said, *'We try our very best to keep drugs out of the club, and the drug pushers, but with a membership of around 4,000 it is the people who use the club that make it what it is.'* (1)

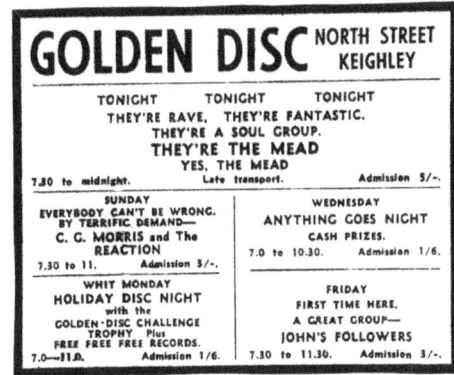

A similarly run club was **The Golden Disc Club**, on North Street in Keighley, which changed its name to **The Silhouette Club** in 1968.

HENDRIX HITS ILKLEY

Sunday, March 12, 1967, was the night that Ilkley had its most famous rock'n'roll incident when the Jimi Hendrix Experience played at **The Gyro Club**, based at the Troutbeck Hotel, as part of their first UK tour.

Their debut single, Hey Joe, had got to number six in December 1966, and the group's next release, Purple Haze, which eventually reached number three, was due out on March 17.

Unfortunately, due to sketchy and conflicting reports in the local press, what happened is a little bit fragmented but the gig was stopped midway through the second number Stone Free, when, as DJ Stuart Frais remembers, *'This plainclothes police sergeant mounted the stage at eight-fifteen and began in a condescending tone; 'Listen, boys and girls…' There was bound to be trouble, after all, everyone was over eighteen; there would have been no trouble if Jimi had been allowed to finish his act.'* (2)

The police were reacting to the 'gross overcrowding' at the venue, as the more than seven hundred people (three times the allowed capacity) who were crammed into the venue were a fire risk. Hendrix responded by backing into his Marshall stack, thus drowning out the policeman's words with feedback.

The group left the stage and the police started to clear the room. It took over two hours as glasses were smashed, pictures knocked off walls in the corridor and a door pulled off its hinges by the crowd in the crush to vacate the premises. Those who waited for a refund were annoyed at only receiving half of the ten shillings (50p) admission price, and at having to wait until 11.15pm.

After the gig Jimi and the group went down the road for a drink or two at a local pub. They stayed the night at the Crescent Hotel and left for London in the morning.

The next day the national press wrote conflicting and sensationalist accounts, such as, *'Pop Fans Run Amok At Hotel'* and *'700 In Uproar At Beat Club As Police Stop Show'*, when in fact the local police recorded a peaceful dispersal with no arrests.

Pink Floyd played an eight hour *'Psycho-Chromatic Fantasy'* at Bradford University on June 22.

MUSIC AT BRADFORD UNIVERSITY (1965-79)

From its inception as a new 'plate glass' university in 1965, under its first  chancellor Labour Prime Minister Harold Wilson (a Huddersfield lad) live music played a an important part of student life on campus.

Folk, jazz, rock, punk and indie musicians graced the stages of the University's Great and Small Halls, in the Richmond Building, and later on the bigger Communal Building stage, some of whom are now of legendary status.

A short list of some of the more famous artists is offered below, compiled from the research of Bradford University Library's Special Collections Assistants, John Booker and Martin Levy. (3)

Their research was mainly from archived copies of the Student Union newspaper, *Javelin* (1966-81), which alongside listings of future concerts and gig reviews contained related articles on student interests and social life, as well as local and national campaigns around issues of social justice, by an increasingly radical student population.

Jazz greats such as Duke Ellington (twice) and Roland Kirk played during the late 1960s, plus British jazz fusion artists Graham Collier and Ian Carr's Nucleus.

Folk artists were evident from the beginning, and the University had its own Union Folk Club from 1971 and a Folk Singing Circle from the same year.

Fairport Convention, The Spinners, The Strawbs, Pentangle, John Martyn, Roy Harper, Ralph McTell and Irish acts Horselips and Planxty were amongst some of the better known acts who appeared, as did local lad Roger Sutcliffe.

In November 1971, in the hope of beating a world record, folk singer Steve Elliot, from Bradford Technical College, played on the Union Bar for 27 hours.

Between 1965-75 a host of famous rock bands appeared, to name just a few: John Mayall's Blues Breakers, Moody Blues, Ten Years After, Pink Floyd, Deep Purple, Black Sabbath, Status Quo (above), Family, Neil Young, Yes and Supertramp, as well as many lesser known artists and local bands.

This was the era when most of the major names in British music regularly played the university/college circuits as part of their major tours. (4)

Many local 'townies' and non students were able

CHAPTER 1 - PSYCHEDELIA TO HEAVY ROCK 1967 - 1970

to see these gigs in the 1970s only after the restrictions on Student Union Card holders being the only ones allowed into concerts was relaxed.

When punk and new wave arrived in the late 1970s bands including Generation X, The Stranglers (whose bassist Jean Jaques Burnel, pictured above, was a Bradford University student in the early 1970s), Tom Robinson Band, Wire, Gang Of Four, The Skids, Squeeze, The Undertones, Penetration, Dr Feelgood and John Cooper Clarke all played, as did local acts The Negatives and The Invaders.

LULU COMES TO TOWN

On July 17, 1967, seventeen-year-old Scottish pop singer Lulu (real name Marie McDonald McLaughlin Lawrie) took time out from playing at Jimmy Corrigan's' Batley Variety Club to visit ten-year-old Paul MacKenzie of Buttershaw Drive, Bradford, who had recently undergone a series of leg operations

Lulu had just had a number six hit single in April with *The Boat That I Row*. News of her visit spread quickly, as she had turned up in a Rolls Royce to take tea and sign Paul's autograph book. The surrounding streets were soon crowded with people as kids were trying to catch a glimpse of the flame-haired singer.

The petite 5ft 2in red-headed Lulu had shot to the top of the UK singles chart with the single *Shout* in 1964, and was the first British girl artist to perform behind the Iron Curtain when she played Poland in March 1966.

PEARSON'S RECORD SHOP

Tommy and Ethel Pearson had started their family business in 1959 as a stall on the old John Street Market, selling 78s and the newer 45s, before opening their first shop on Manchester Road.

By 1967, they had opened *Pearson's Disc-a-Go-Go* in Kirkgate (on the frontage of the old Kirkgate Market - see picture above) to great success and later opened outlets in Brighouse and Leeds.

The shop relocated to Rawson Place (on the same side as the old Rawson Market) in 1972, after hearing news of the prospective demolition of Kirkgate Market. (4)

The smart new premises were on three floors, one whole floor dedicated to 'progressive' music and a fashion section in its 'Fellas Department' and a budget 50p LP section in the basement. The shop lasted until 1980, before it became Bostocks and finally closing prior to the demolition of the market. (5)

BARBARA MOORE

Bradford-born Jazz singer and pianist Barbara (Birkby) Moore became the first wife of 'easy listening' arranger/composer Pete Moore, who is famous for *Asteroid* which is the 1968 signature music to the Pearl & Dean cinema advert.

She also sang the 'DoooOh's' on the title theme for the 1960s Roger Moore TV series *The Saint*.

She became an in-demand session singer, working with her friend Jackie Lee as part of the vocal backing group the Jackie Lee Singers. She also co-wrote songs with Jackie Lee, such as *Well, That's Loving You* which was the B-side to Jackie's 1968 Phillips single, *We're Off And Running*.

Barbara accompanied comedian Peter Cook on the theme tune to the film *Bedazzled* which came out as a single, with music by the Dudley Moore Trio (no relation). She also appeared in episodes of Pete and Dud's *Not Only... But Also* TV series. She was part of The Ladybirds trio of singers who sang live backing vocals for artists appearing on Top Of The Pops, including Jimi Hendrix's live performance of his 1966 *Hey Joe* single.

She also appeared on the *Dusty Springfield Show*.

In the 1970s, she formed her own group, the Barbara Moore Singers. They backed up stars of the day like Glenn Cambell, Bobby Gentry and Mike Yarwood on BBC TV shows.

Barbara was also in demand as an arranger. She led the choir on Elton John's *Border Song*. In 1971, she arranged the vocals on the famous Coco-Cola advert *I'd Like To Teach The World To Sing*.

She also wrote the theme tune to Terry Wogan's BBC radio show.

Barbara became acknowledged as one of the UK's 'wickedest scat jazz vocalists'. She appeared on numerous LPs between 1966 and 1970, including the two volumes of *Birds 'N' Brass* (Rediffusion); Tony Evans' *Golden Brass And Satin Voices* (Columbia); *From Chico...With Love* by Chico Arnez & His Cubana Brass; and the very collectable 1966 first LP by German producer Mark Wirtz, *Latin A Go-Go* (Ember).

Barbara recorded the one-off LP *Something Cool* with the band The Voices In Latin which was a collection of 1960s hits and original songs given a rhythmic Latin feel.

Barbara's first solo LP appeared in 1967 on CBS / Ember Records and was called *A Little Moore Barbara*.

Her 1971 LP, *Vocal Shades And Tones*, on the rare De Wolfe library label, is a desirable classic in jazz circles, renowned for its wide-ranging vocal style The single *Hot Heels*, from the LP, was released on the Jazzman label in 2001.

She also released a compilation album of her work, entitled *Sing Sweet Barbara: 1966-1990*, on Ember Records. The double CD also featured some of the jingles she recorded for brands like Toshiba and Moulinex.

Barbara continued to arrange, compose and perform in her later years until her passing in 2021, aged 89.

BARBARA MOORE			
67	CBS (S) BPG 62839	A LITTLE MOORE BARBARA (LP)	40
81	527 HMC	Headline (Barbara Moore)	12

BARBARA MOORE (SOUND)			
70s	De Wolfe	VOCAL SHADES & TONES (Barbara Moore Sound)	100
01	Jazzman JM 018	Hot Heels/Grey Sigh	5

THE CASUALS / THE COLLECTION

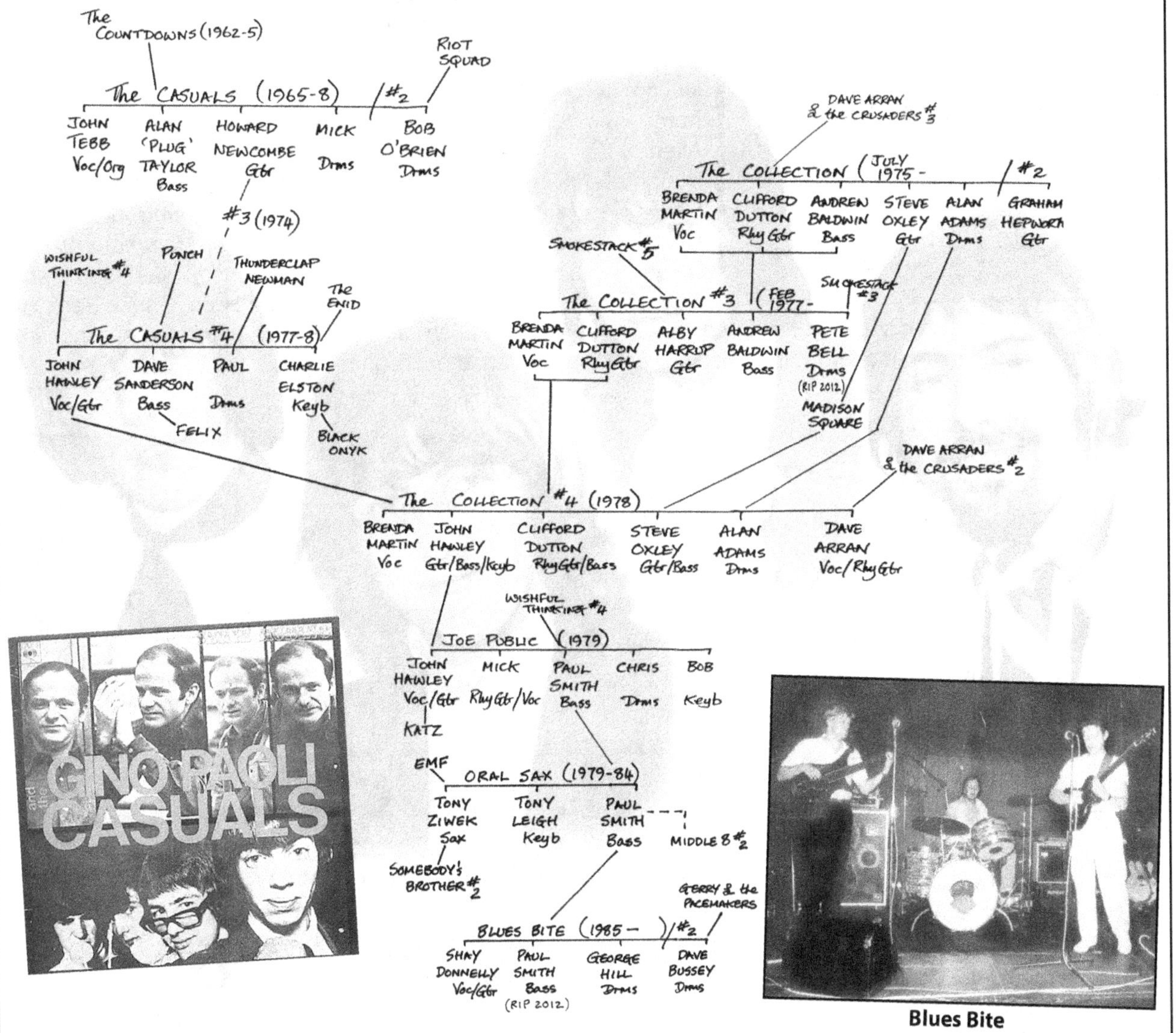

THE CASUALS

Halifax bass guitarist Alan 'Plug' Taylor was an ex-mechanic whose father had taught him how to play the ukulele. Formerly a member of The Easybeats and The Countdowns, Alan joined Lincolnshire-based group The Casuals in 1965. In the mid-1960s, the group were based in Milan, Italy, playing clubs around central Europe. They released a couple of singles and the album *Gino Paoli And The Casuals,* with Italian singer Gino Paoli.

They returned to England in 1967. In September 1968, they released the single *Jezemine* on Decca Records, which got to number two in the hit parade. The song was co-written by rocker Marty Wilde and had previously been recorded by Welsh group The Bystanders (members of whom went on to be in the rock band Man).

The Casuals' next single, *Toy,* also reached the Top 30 at the end of 1968. Their only album, *Hour World,* came out in 1969. The group released their last single *Witch* on Dawn Records in 1974 before splitting up in 1975. A version of the band which included none of the original line-up was performingon the live circuit in 1977.

THE ACCENT

The Accent were a Bradford band who had started life as The Blue Blood Group, with bass player, Alan Davis joining from Allen Pound's Get Rich. They changed their name to The Accent - apparently because 'southern folk' couldn't understand their Yorkshire accents!

> **AIRE VALLEY YOUNG FARMERS' CLUB**
> **BARN BEAT BARBECUE**
> at EAST MANYWELLS FARM, CULLINGWORTH
> Music by THE BLOOD GROUP
> 8 p.m.—12 midnight.
> **WHIT MONDAY, JUNE 7th, 1965**
> Tickets: 4/- before the day; 5/- on the day. Obtainable from club members.
> CAR PARKS FREE.

The group rehearsed in John Hebron's dad's cow shed at Fall Top Farm in Clayton and were managed by guitarist Rick Birkett's dad, Lance Birkett.

Whilst on tour, The Accent were spotted by London talent agent Ricki Molloy who recommended them for a residency at ex-boxer Billy Walker's **Upper Cut Club** in London. After an appearance at another London venue, The Flamingo, record producer Mike Vernon offered them a chance to record a single for Decca Records. The result was the group's only release, *Red Sky At Night / Wind Of Change*, which unfortunately made no impact on the charts in October 1967. It has since been highly acclaimed by collectors of 1960s 'psych rock' as a phenomenal double-sider and is rated as one of the best records of the genre.

The loud 'bone-crunching sledgehammer' style power chords dominate the A-side's general aura of strangeness, while the B-side, Wind Of Change, has an eerie atmosphere of menace.

The group's colourful and distinctive 'psychedelic clobber' (clothes) emulated the US West Coast hippy influence and were designed and made by the group's girlfriends. To promote the single, on Saturday, October 13, the group performed a warm-up gig at Bradford Park Avenue's football ground before the club's home game against Port Vale.

After the 'Summer of Love' The Accent continued to gig. On February 2, 1968, they were playing bottom of the bill at the ten-hour *Mammoth All Nite Festival* at Queen's Hall, Leeds. It was headlined by The Move and featured The Herd, Chuck Berry and Edwin Starr, all for the price of sixteen shillings in advance or £1 on the door.

THE ACCENT

> LATEST RELEASE
> "red sky at night"
> on
> *Decca*
> by
> THE ACCENT

> **MAMMOTH ALL NITE FESTIVAL**
> Ten hours non-stop
> AT THE
> **QUEEN'S HALL**
> LEEDS
> NEXT FRIDAY, FEB. 2nd
> **THE MOVE**
> **HERD**
> **EDWIN STARR**
> **CHUCK BERRY**
> **JIMMY SAVILE**
> **CHRIS FARLOWE**
> BRIAN AUGER TRINITY with JULIE DRISCOLL
> SAMMY SMALL and the UNION BLUES RAVE BAND
> THE ACCENT
> Tickets from VALLANCES in advance 16/-
> Tickets at the door £1
> or s.a.e. to
> **17a BRIGGATE, SHIPLEY**

When the group split, guitarist Rick released a solo LP as *Rick Hayward* on Mike Vernon's Blue Horizon label, before working with Jellybread, Christine Perfect (later of Fleetwood Mac) and the second version of The Zombies. Rick also worked as a session guitarist, appearing on various albums for Blue Horizon Records. As well as performing solo, from 1988 he played guitar with East Anglian band The Big Easy. He is also an astrologer, contributing to *Prediction* magazine under the alias of 'Remus'.

Rick Hayward in 1972

Rick's brother-in-law John Hebron, The Accent's rhythm guitarist, later owned a butcher's shop in Queensbury and continued to perform on the working men's club circuit until his tragic death on holiday in the early 1990s.

Bass player Allan continued to work with various bands over the years.

CHAPTER 1 - PSYCHEDELIA TO HEAVY ROCK 1967 - 1970

THE ACCENT

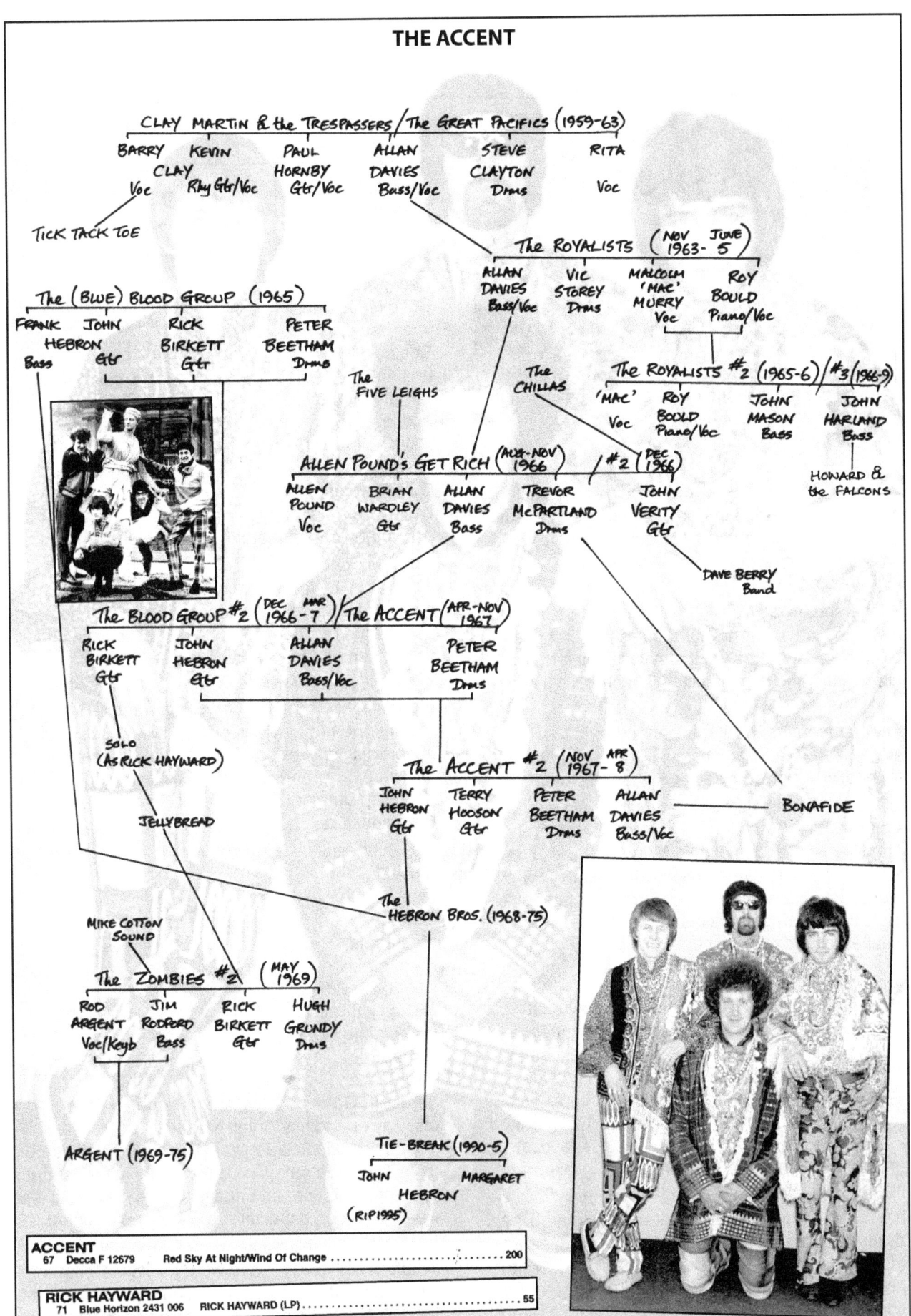

ACCENT			
67	Decca F 12679	Red Sky At Night/Wind Of Change	200

RICK HAYWARD			
71	Blue Horizon 2431 006	RICK HAYWARD (LP)	55

ZANY WOODRUFF OPERATION

ZWO were a Cleckheaton-based soul group, amongst many such groups in West Yorkshire. They won the Bradford area final of the *Search For*

Sound competition and went on to perform at the national competition final in April, only losing out to local London group Mud!

During 1967, like many other local Yorkshire groups, they recorded some original and cover songs at Matt Mathias's small studio at the back of his radio repair shop in Huddersfield. Matt became world famous for manufacturing his 'Matamp' guitar amplifier, which was marketed in the south as the Orange amp.

By the end of 1967 ZWO, like many bands, dissolved into other new groups as the changes brought on by the rise of the psychedelic era made inroads into the domination of Northern Soul in the Yorkshire gig scene.

Another tenuous Bradford connection: in the TV series *Man In A Suitcase*, McGill, the ex-CIA agent for hire, was played by actor Richard Bradford.

Other local groups around at this time in 1967 included: The Squeeze, The Mirage & Margaret, The Raveso Band (featuring Maurice Thomas on vocals), and The Quarry Men from Keighley, who must surely have been unaware of John Lennon's band of the same name that morphed into The Beatles.

In 1968 **The Bluesville '68 / Jook Joint Club** started around February at the Farmer's Inn at Thornbury, with Sunday night showcasing national up-and-coming rock groups such as Free, Jethro Tull and Fleetwood Mac. Gigs attracted crowds upwards of two hundred, and local groups who played on Wednesday nights pulled in around fifty.

It was run by a young manager and promoter Dave Stansfield (later of Moonkyte, see folk chapter) and friends until early 1969, when it was closed by the police for not having the correct music licence. For some reason, the police took exception to 'a bunch of mainly long-haired Hippy freaks' organising their own entertainment. The organisers tried to keep a similar club going under the title **The Workhouse** on Sundays at the Electric Circus, Troutbeck Hotel, Ilkley, but it only lasted a couple of weeks. It seems that they were allowed to continue at the Farmer's Inn, as the Jook Joint continued there until 1971.

Dave Stansfield also managed Pearson's Record Shop (which later became Bostocks) originally in Kirgate Market and later in Rawson Market. He and owner Tom Pearson became the first promoters to start featuring major rock groups like Deep Purple, at **St George's Hall**, in 1969.

The hall is a two-thousand-seat venue, built in 1853 by local architects Lockwood & Mawson to be used as a venue originally for local choral societies and for concerts by Manchester's Halle Orchestra.

A few gigs were organized by Dave Stansfield and blues singer Grahame 'Grom' Kelly at the Central Library Theatre, such as one on Wednesday 19th June which was billed as a *Festival (Concert) Of The Blues* and featured Alexis Korner / Free / Aynsley Dunbar's Retaliation / Grom / The Broomdusters.

In September 1974 Dave became manager of Airedale Records, situated at 20-22 Barry Street (around the corner from The Castle pub) with Grom as assistant manager. It was officially opened by Bryan Moseley (Alf Roberts from *Coronation Street*) who lived in Shipley at the time. The shop ran as a conventional record shop opening until 8pm on Fridays, but its main business was mail order, especially to Eastern Bloc countries.

Later, after finishing a degree in Peace Studies at Bradford University, Dave went to live in Rome for the next eight years as a rock correspondent for the *Record Mirror, Billboard Magazine* and others.

CHAPTER 1 - PSYCHEDELIA TO HEAVY ROCK 1967 - 1970

ZANY WOODRUFF OPERATION / SKIN DEEP

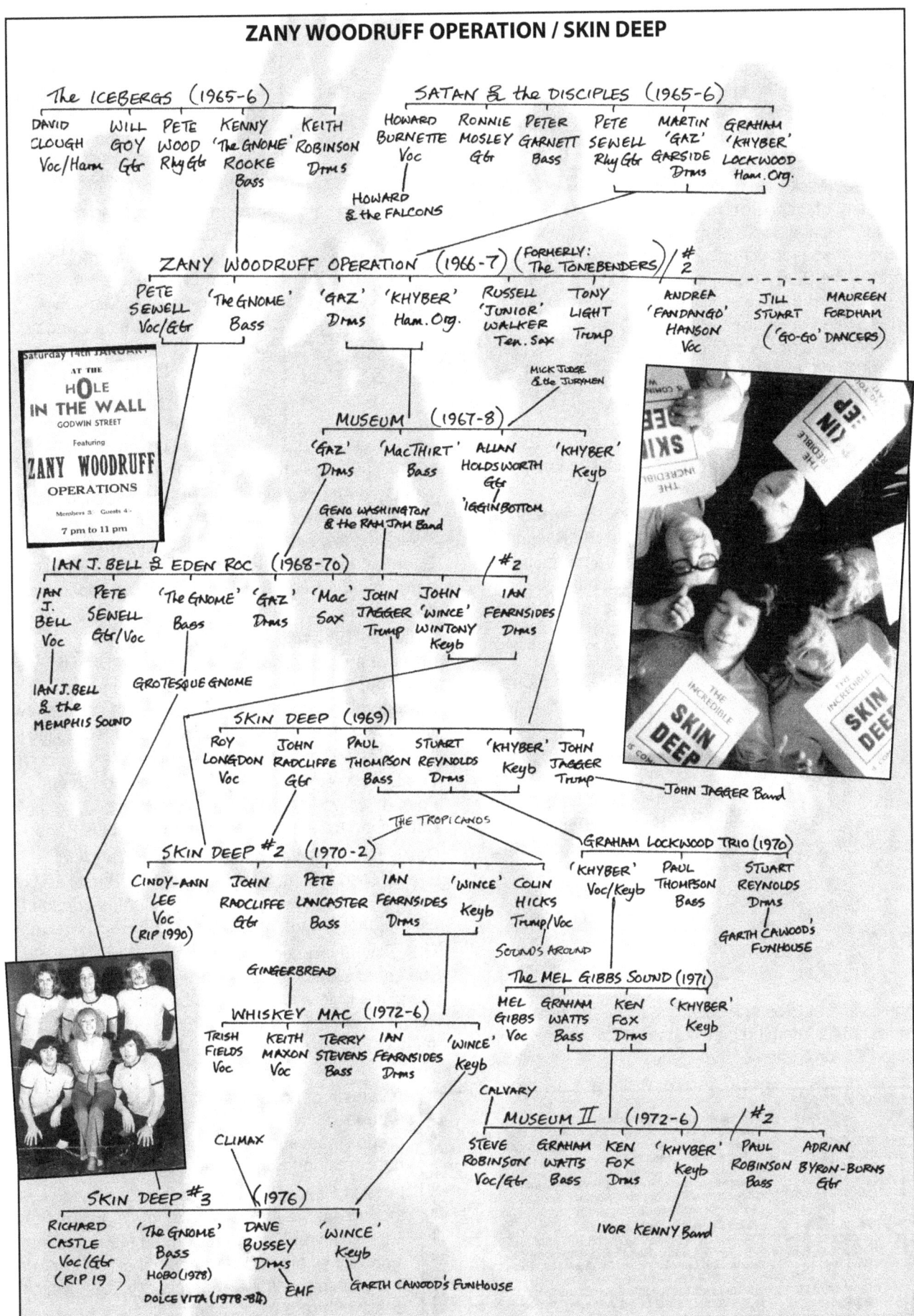

LOVE AFFAIR

Michael Jackson was the first Bradford artist to make it to number one in the charts, with Love Affair's *Everlasting Love* in 1968.

When Hanson School old boy Michael (Mick to his mates), formerly of local group The Spell, finished a £25 per week summer season with his current group The Beat Squad, from Keighley, at Butlin's in Filey, he was invited down to London by members of the soul/beat group Timebox. In late 1966 he answered an advert for a bass guitarist in the music paper Melody Maker. He got the job

L to R: Michael Jackson, Morgan Fisher, Steve Ellis, Rex Brayley & Maurice Bacon - 1969

and his musical career with the band The Love Affair began.

The group had been originally formed in early 1966 by successful handbag manufacturer Sid Bacon, as a vehicle for his fifteen-year-old drummer son Maurice (Mo), whose uncle Max Bacon had been a jazz drummer. The group enjoyed a residency at **The Marquee Club** in Wardour Street, before turning professional in mid 1967.

Their first single was a cover of The Rolling Stones' *She Smiled Sweetly* on Decca Records, which failed to chart.

Love Affair's second single was a cover of the soul singer Robert Knight's *Everlasting Love* in January 1968 on CBS Records which got regular airplay on Radio Caroline.

During a publicity stunt/photo shoot at the statue of Eros in Piccadilly Circus, the group got arrested for climbing on the statue. They were each fined £8 for breach of the peace.

The single climbed the charts to number one, becoming a classic of the day. They were criticised for not actually playing on the single, which wasn't unusual at the time, but they did all play on their LP *The Everlasting Love Affair*.

Fresh from their chart success, Love Affair toured heavily around Europe and the UK, including what were, for eighteen-year-old Mick, two home town shows on Sunday, October 6, at The Gaumont, with Scott Walker, The Casuals and The Paper Dolls. (7)

At the shows, half the girls in the 1,500 crowd were screaming for Mick in true 'teenybop' style.

The Love Affair's next single for CBS was *Rainbow Valley*, which reached number five in the charts. Their next few singles were written by Phillip Goodhand-Tait; *A Day Without Love*, *One Road* and *Bring On Back The Good Times* all became top twenty hits.

Between 1967 and 1969 the group enjoyed massive success and, being one of the UK's biggest pop groups, the boys' photos were on many a teenage girl's bedroom wall, courtesy of magazines like Jackie. In early 1969 Mick was also managing local Bradford group 'Igginbottom.

The Love Affair became the first UK group to tour Poland. When singer Steve Ellis quit to go solo in December 1969 they recruited vocalist Gus Eadon.

Despite a short-lived name shortening to LA for their second album, the group continued until 1971 when Mick left, saying he was *'tired of the constant touring and general music-biz crap.'*

That July he married his longtime girlfriend Patricia Speight of Shipley. They had originally met as young teenagers at the coffee bar/disco/venue The Hole In The Wall in the early 1960s. Later, Mick gained success selling cars and became UK sales director for Alfa Romeo.

A version of Love Affair appeared sometime around 1973, hoping to capitalize on the group's past success by stalking the club circuit but contained none of the original members.

In 1991 Steve Ellis went back on the road, touring as 'Steve Ellis's Love Affair' and in 1999 Mick, Mo and Morgan re-formed the group for a charity single and video on behalf of Bradford Royal Infirmary's Ward 7 Specialist Unit, which deals with rare blood disorders.

LOVE AFFAIR

Year	Label	Title	
67	Decca F 12558	She Smiled Sweetly/Satisfaction Guaranteed	60
67	CBS 3125	Everlasting Love/Gone Are The Songs Of Yesterday	6
68	CBS 3366	Rainbow Valley/Someone Like Us (some in p/s)	20/8
68	CBS 3674	A Day Without Love/I'm Happy	6
69	CBS 3994	One Road/Let Me Know	6
69	CBS 4300	Bringing On Back The Good Times/Another Day	6
69	CBS 4631	Baby I Know/Accept Me For What I Am	7
70	CBS 4780	Lincoln County/Sea Of Tranquility	6
70	Pye 7N 45218	Let Me Dance/Love's Looking Out At You	8
71	Parlophone R 5887	Wake Me I Am Dreaming/That's My Home	12
71	Parlophone R 5918	Help (Get Me Some Help)/Long Way Home	12
73	CBS 1144	Everlasting Love/Bringing On Back The Good Times (p/s, 'Hall Of Fame Hits' series)	5
77	Creole CR 146	Private Lives/Let A Little Love Come In	5
68	CBS 63416	THE EVERLASTING LOVE AFFAIR (LP, mono/stereo)	22

CHAPTER 1 - PSYCHEDELIA TO HEAVY ROCK 1967 - 1970

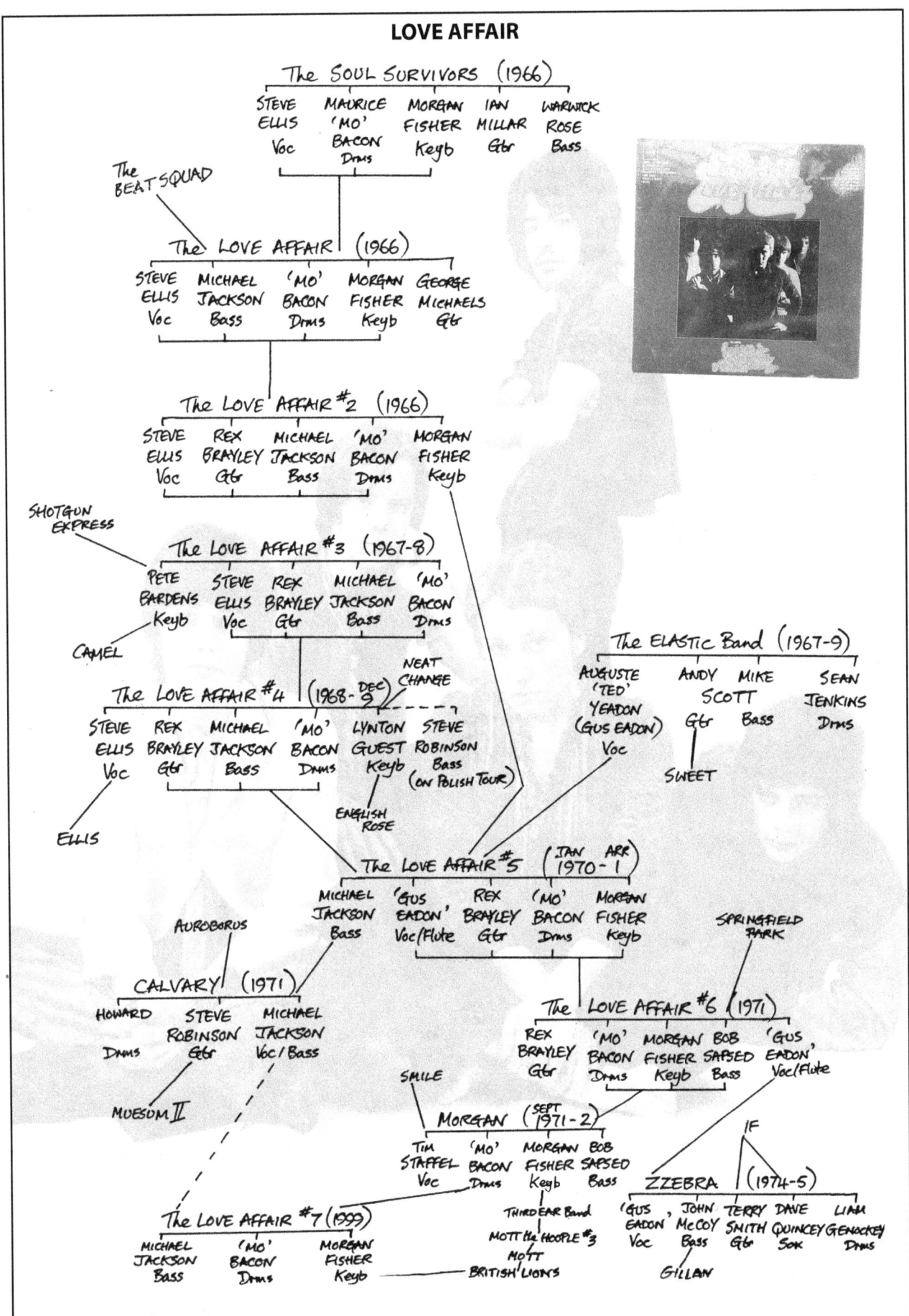

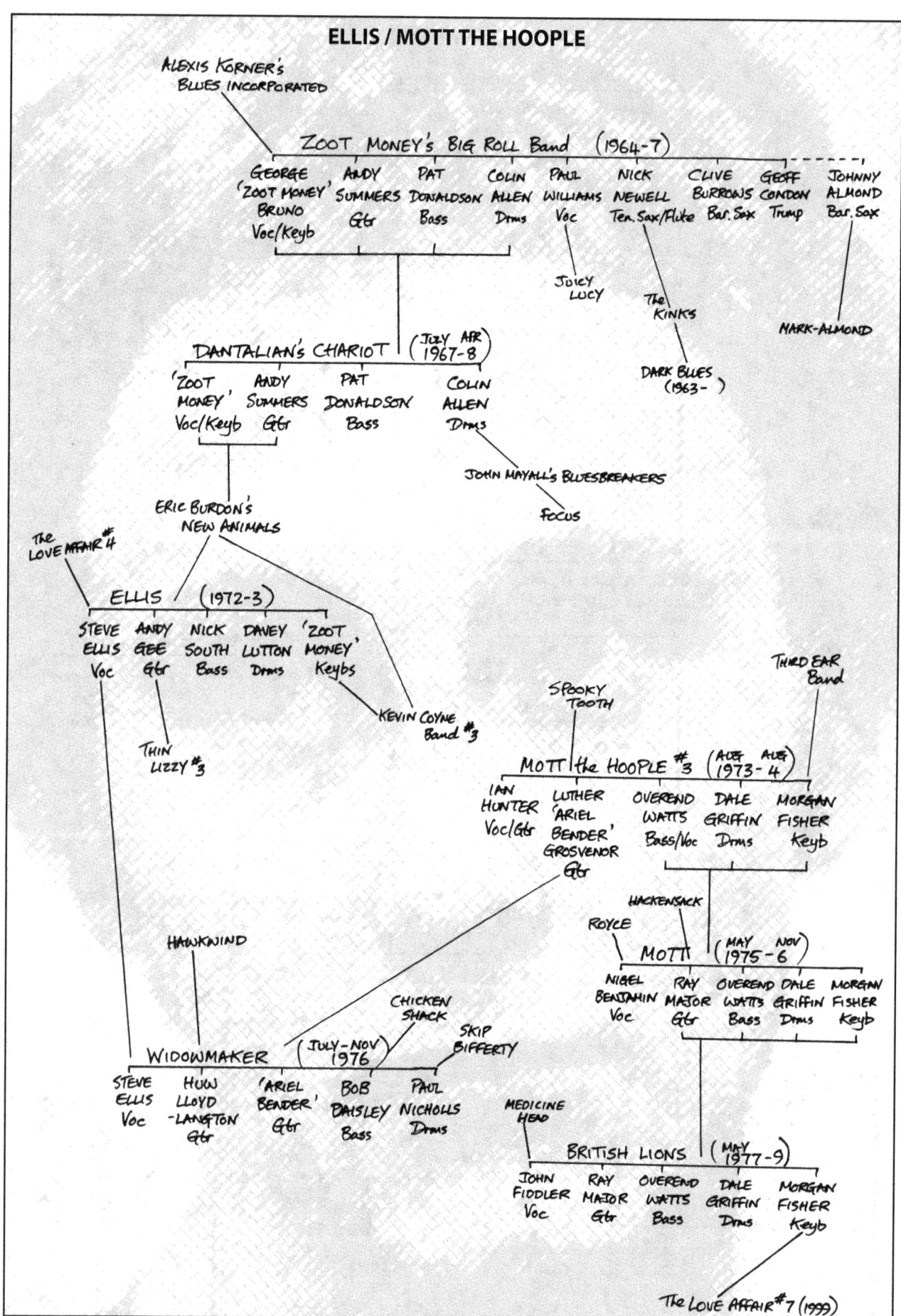

WELFARE STATE

Welfare State was founded on December 6, 1968, by principal members John Fox and Sue Gill, as a loose arrangement of multi-media art students and teachers at Bradford's Art College. The name was a satire of the real welfare state of free health and social care, translated into offering 'art for all'. They were inspired by the work of the then head of the Complementary Studies Department, the Lancastrian poet and playwright Albert Hunt, who had turned his department into the UK's most progressive theatre workshop. (8)

These 'art college freaks' also included a couple of ex-members of Halifax group The Left Hand Drive Band. As Welfare State they produced a track called *Silence Is Requested In The Ultimate Abyss* for John Peel's *Top Gear Radio Show* LP in 1969. The track also featured the electronic effects of The White Noise, under the direction of David Vorhaus. Quoting from John Peel's sleeve notes on the LP: '*...a mixture of alchemists, earth goddess, monsters, poets and freaks...weird but interesting.*'

In 1970, one of Welfare States' experimental performance pieces, *Circus Time*, was commissioned for the first Bradford Arts Festival.

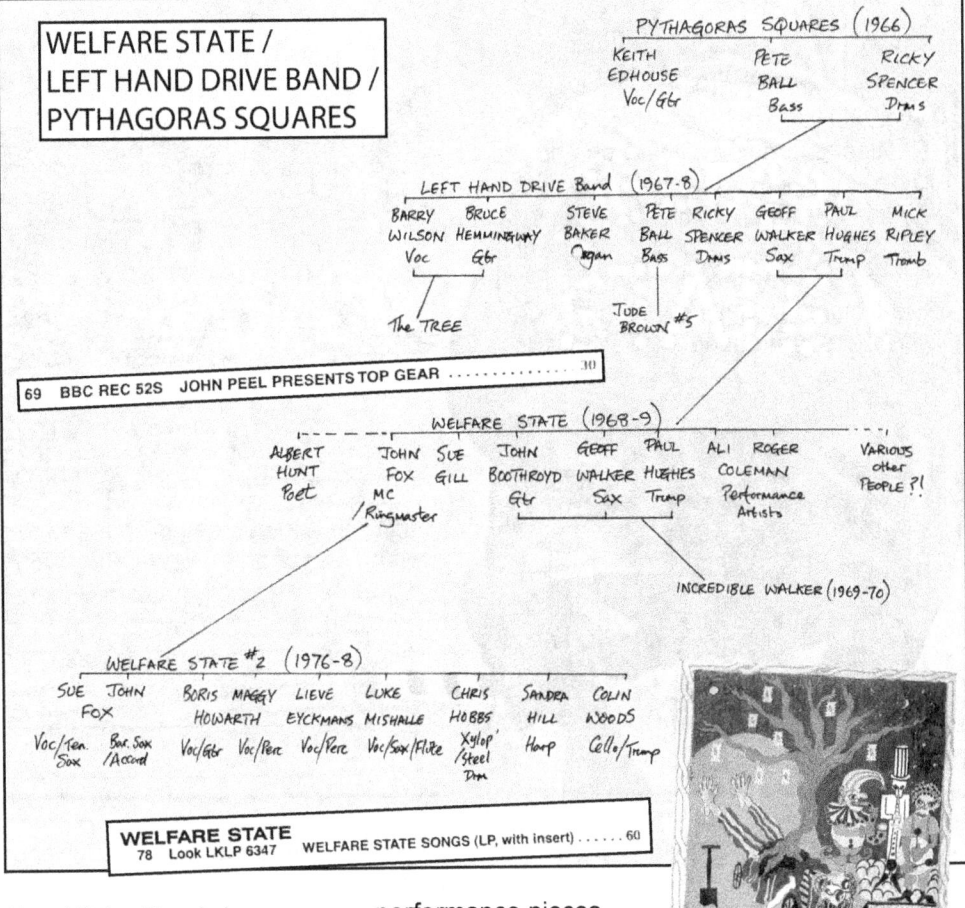

Leaving Bradford in 1971, Welfare State took their wandering troupe to perform the art of the galleries and theatres onto the streets of northern industrial towns. They evolved into a remarkable group of musicians, engineers, performers, sculptors, poets and pyro-technicians who invented and developed large site-specific theatre in the landscape.

In 1978, a new incarnation of Welfare State musicians recorded and released their only LP, *Welfare State Songs*, put out on the local Look Record label, before evolving into their new title of Welfare State International.

As WSI they moved to Cumbria in 1983 and eventually set up the pioneering arts project Lanternhouse in Ulverston. This incorporated *'a role for art that weaved into the fabric of people's lives and allowed collaboration rather than mere passive spectacle. Their long-term aim was to establish partnerships in the local community, supporting any individual potential and developing active opportunities for the dispossessed to thrive in an imaginative and creative environment.'*

This innovative creativity continued until 2006, when WSI was wound down after the retirement of artistic director John Fox. (9)

DAN MARSHALL AND HIS FRIENDS WERE CERTAINLY PART OF THE MODERN BOHEMIA THAT PURSUED LOVE, PACIFISM AND PLEASURE.

1967 - 1970   BRADFORD'S GROOVY SOUNDS OF THE VALLEYS

BLACK DYKE BEATLE

On the 30th June 1968, at Shipley's Victoria Hall, Paul McCartney of The Beatles recorded a single with The Black Dyke Mills Band entitled *Thingumybob* for the TV sitcom of the same name. The world-famous brass band had originally formed as The Queenshead Band at the Old Dolphin pub in 1816. John Foster (1799 -1879), founder of the company that bears his name, played the French horn.

In 1855, the name was changed to the Black Dyke Mills Band and over the years, they won many finals of the UK Brass Band Championships. During his short stay in Bradford, Paul McCartney stayed at the Victoria Hotel with his sheepdog, Martha. He was hounded by Beatles fans, coming from near and far.

BLACK DYKE MILLS BAND
68 Apple APPLE 4   Thingumybob/Yellow Submarine.......50

Local Keighley country and western trio **The Doveston Brothers** were still going in 1971 when they appeared at the London Palladium in a national talent contest after winning the regional series of finals at Butlin's Holiday camps. The first prize for the winners was £2,900.

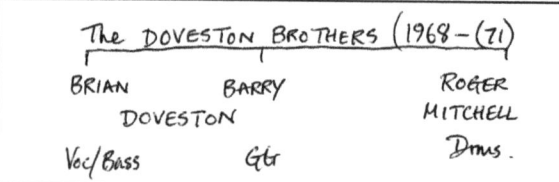

Other groups around at this time in 1968 were; **The Gentry**, and **Pipedream** With Beverly. From Keighley, there was **Ginger Wheelbarrow** and **Plastic Dream Machine**.

The Talismen were a Halifax group who recorded two songs by Halifax songwriter Cedric Thomas, at Hebden Bridge's Calder Recording Co., but there is no information on whether they were ever released.

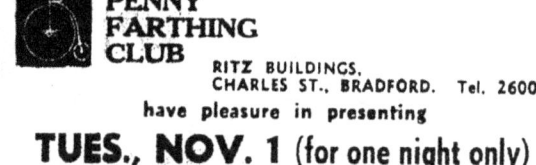

Another local group was **The Elizabethans**, who were on the local scene in the late 1960s. They dressed in frilly shirts and played covers of the hits of the day. After a name change to Kindness, they were signed to RCA Records and released their first single *Light Of Love / Lindy Lou* in 1970.

Later they recorded three singles for Decca before another name change, this time to Smokey.

Also around at this time from Halifax were; **Fact & Fiction** (whose Housey brothers were born in Egypt), **Quo Vadis**, **The Rainbows**, **Desolation Row** and **The Felix Complex** (ex-The Dominoes).

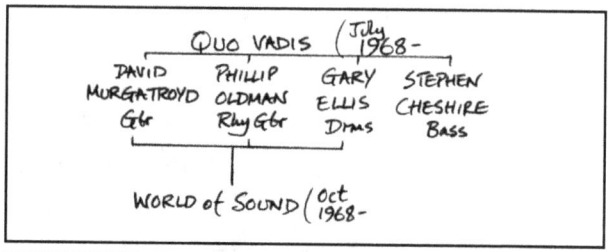

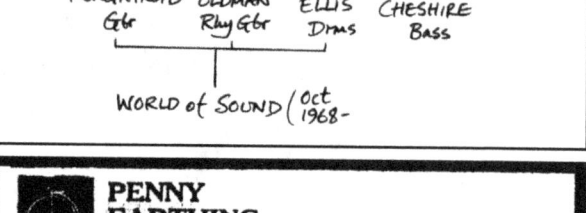

PENNY FARTHING CLUB
RITZ BUILDINGS,
CHARLES ST., BRADFORD. Tel. 26001
have pleasure in presenting

TUES., NOV. 1 (for one night only)
" LIVE " — ON STAGE
THE FANTASTIC RAVE SOUND OF

JOHN NAYALL'S BLUESBREAKERS

LIMITED ADMISSION BY TICKET ONLY
ON SALE AT THE CLUB
MEMBERS AND GUESTS ONLY

CHAPTER 1 - PSYCHEDELIA TO HEAVY ROCK   1967 - 1970

FREE EXPRESSION

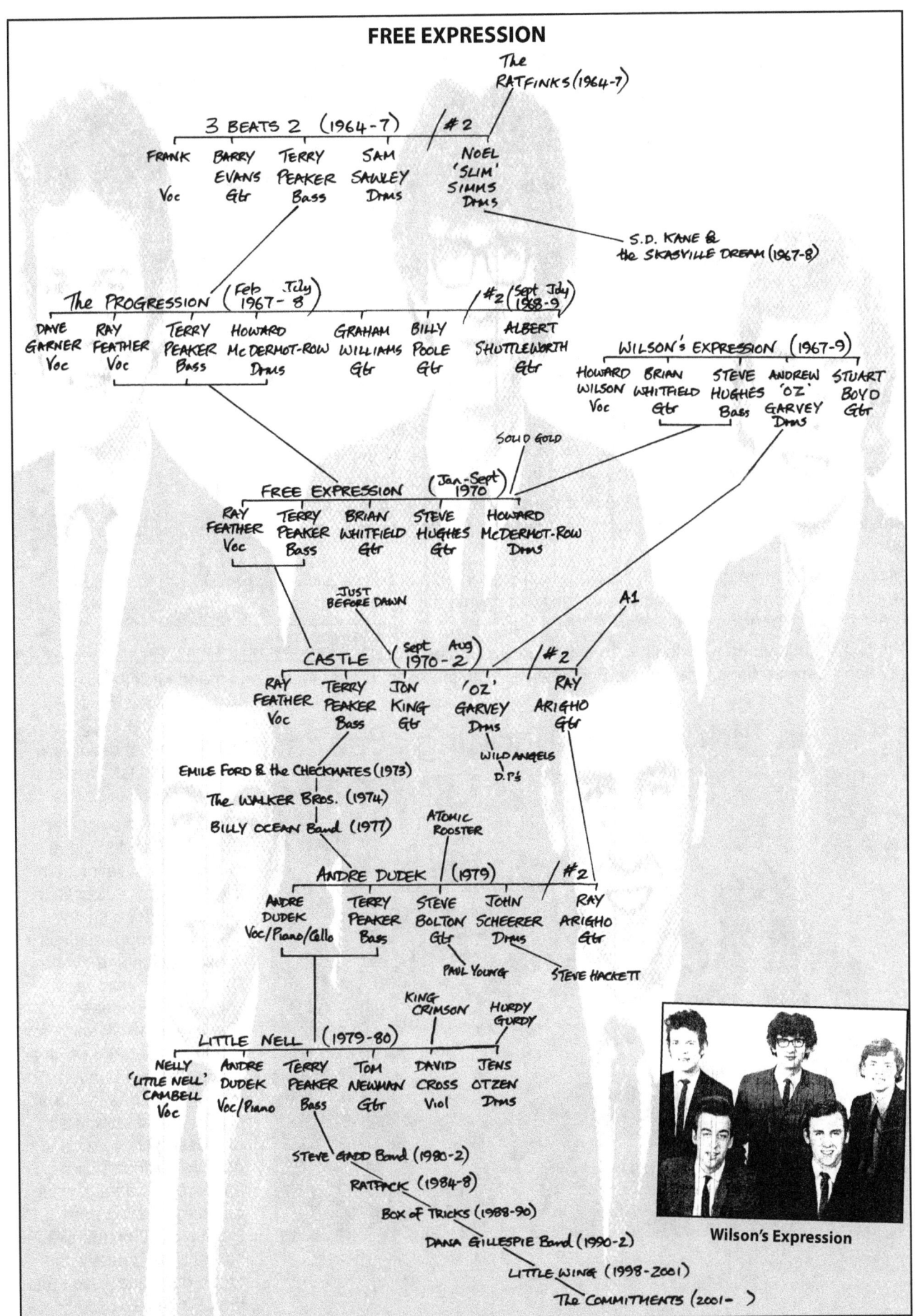

Wilson's Expression

ALLAN HOLDSWORTH

'If a candidate is needed for the most technically skilled guitarist of all, there is no need to look further than Allan Holdsworth. Whether playing jazz or rock or something in between, the speed of his fingers on the fretboard is seldom less than jaw-dropping.'

As the above quote demonstrates, Bradford guitarist Allan Holdsworth was highly regarded as the 'guitarist's guitarist' with accolades from other guitarists like the late Gary Moore, Eddie Van Halen, Journey's Neal Schon and Frank Zappa - who lauded him as *'one of the most interesting guys on guitar on the planet.'*

Steven, Allan, Mick and Dave

'IGGINBOTTOM
69   Deram DML/SML 1051   'IGGINBOTTOM'S WRENCH (LP) 100

Despite being widely regarded by fans and fellow musicians as one of the twentieth century's most prominent and extraordinary innovative guitarists, guitarist Allan Holdsworth was hardly known in his own town.

He had only picked up a guitar at the age of eighteen when his father, an amateur musician, bought him one. Within a year he was playing in local semi-pro bands.

Music became more important to his life, which presented a difficult choice whether to become a professional musician or to devote his life to his other great love, cycle racing. Music won.

His first serious group was 'Igginbottom, started with mates at Allan's parents' flat on the Thorpe Edge estate. With the support of manager and friend Mick Jackson (of Love Affair fame), the group did a regular Monday night residency at The Old Oak Tree pub, near Kirkstall in Leeds.

Before long they played their first London gig at a Guitar Festival night in Ronnie Scott's Jazz Club in Soho. After a shaky start, the group received a massive standing ovation. They soon recorded their only LP release, *'Igginbottom's Wrench*, for the Deram label, at a small studio in West London. The album was done in virtually one take and attempted to cross-fertilize jazz and pop. When the record appeared it had a glowing recommendation from Ronnie Scott on the sleeve notes. Unfortunately, the group disbanded soon after the LP's release.

They're Bradford's budding Beatles

MR. ALLAN HOLDSWORTH (left), aged 18, of Thorold House, Thorpe Edge, Idle, taking a class of would-be guitar players at Thorpe Evening Institute, Idle, last night. Allan is a member of the Bradford group "Mike Judge and the Jurymen." This course in guitar playing, which started last night, is the first in the Bradford Education Department Evening Institutes.

Courtesy of the Telegraph & Argus

CHAPTER 1 - PSYCHEDELIA TO HEAVY ROCK — 1967 - 1970

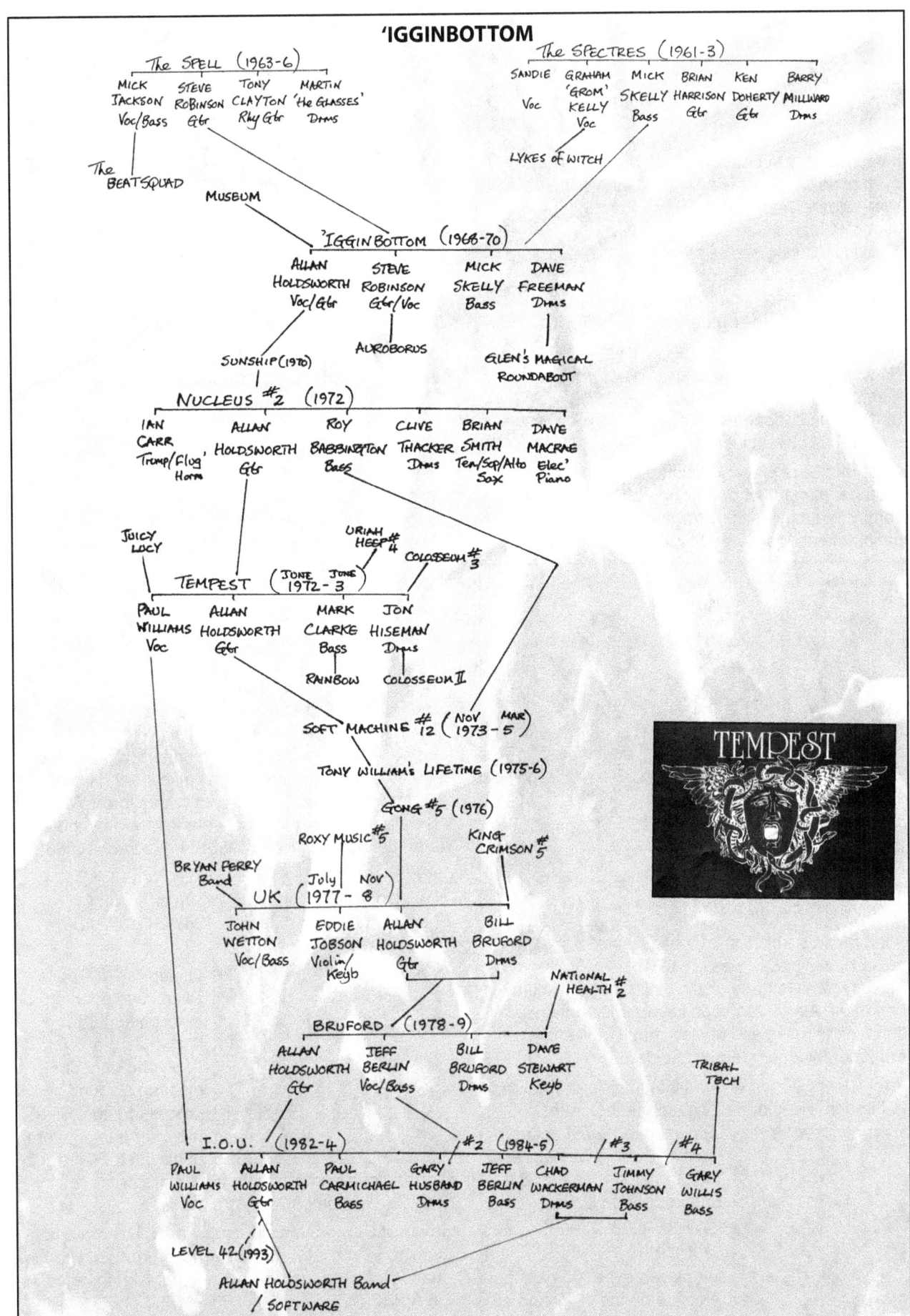

Allan started to get session work, notably appearing with Jimmy Page and playing the guitar parts on Donovan's 1968 single, *Hurdy Gurdy Man*.

Invited to stay in London by jazz saxophonist Ray Warleigh, he had a brief stint with jazz-fusion band Nucleus, playing on their 1972 *Belladonna* album before joining drummer Jon Hiseman's prog-rock group Tempest.

Between November 1973 and March 1975, he was part of Soft Machine, appearing on their 1975 Harvest label LP *Bundles*.

Allan met bass player Alphonse Johnson (ex-Weather Report) who mentioned him to drummer Tony Williams. Tony later invited Allan to join his band, Lifetime (pictured below).

He appeared on their albums *Believe It* (1975) and *Million Dollar Legs* (1976) and, while in New York, was signed to Creed Taylor's CTI Records.

Allan recorded his first solo LP, *Velvet Darkness* in 1976, at Rudy Van Gelder's studio using former Lifetime bandmate Alan Pasqua on keyboards, Alphonse Johnson on bass and Mahavishnu Orchestra's drummer Michael 'Narada' Walden.

After leaving Tony William's Lifetime, Allan returned to London. He joined Gong, appearing on their LP *Gazeuse* (1976) before teaming up with former Yes/King Crimson drummer Bill Bruford to form UK with bassist John Wetton (ex-Family/King Crimson).

UK played over 200 gigs in America during 1977 and 78, where Allan was never entirely comfortable in the stadium rock spotlight. Allan recorded two albums with Bruford, *Feels Good to Me* (1978) and *One Of A Kind* (1979) before finally going out as a solo performer.

In the 1980s he relocated to Southern California in the USA. Based at his home studio The Brewery, he became a successful solo artist. He put out the album *IOU* on his own label in 1982. His 1983 12-inch EP *Road Games* was released on Warner Brothers Records. These were followed by the albums *Metal Fatigue* (1985), *Atavachron* (1986), *Sand* (1987), and *Secrets* (1989).

He also guested on many jazz/rock albums (including Stanley Clarke's 1988 LP *If This Bass Could Only Talk*).

During the 1990s, Allan developed an innovative guitar known as the 'Synth Axe', and various electronic sound processing tools like the 'Harness'. Several of his custom designs for baritone and piccolo guitars were produced by the Carvin Company in America.

Allan still visited his old mates in the UK when he was touring the world with various projects, like his band Software, up until his untimely death, aged 70 in April 2017.

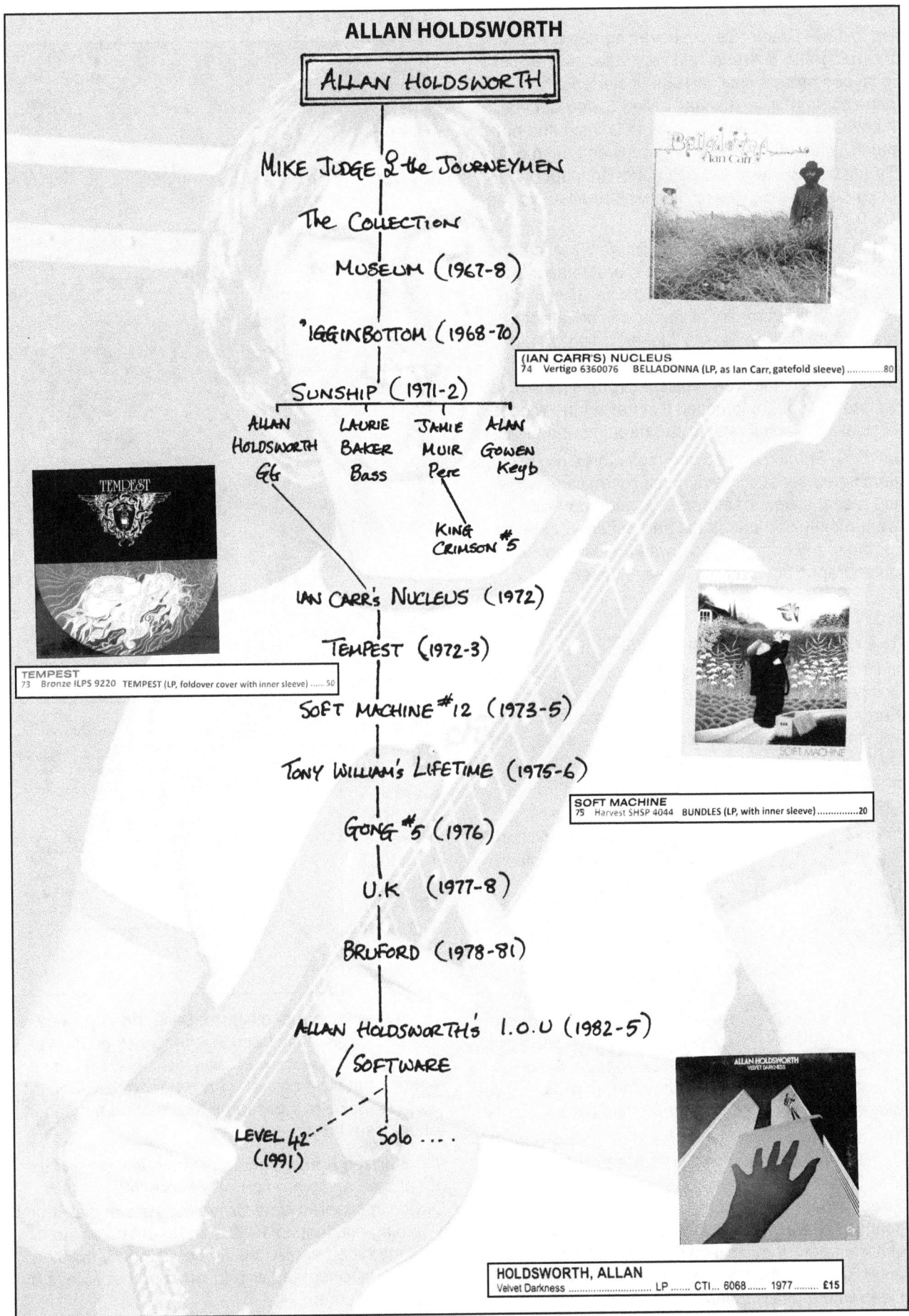

NOW

Up to 1969 Bradford's local evening newspaper, the *Telegraph & Argus*, had very little coverage of local pop groups until, in 1969, it started a half-page column on a Tuesday called *Swing Section*. It covered current youth trends in fashion and pop music, with articles on local groups and a gig guide. The main reporter was Leon Hickman, supported by Anne Webster. The column was re-titled *Now* in 1970.

In the commercial world of the music weeklies, the coverage of popular music was more detailed than the local newspaper's weekly column. The whole national and international scene was covered in magazines like the *Melody Maker*, which was the oldest and had started in 1926 as a music trade paper. Its rival the *New Musical Express (NME)*, started in 1952, outstripped it in having the widest circulation which it maintained throughout the '70s.

In 1970, *Sounds* arrived and these three magazines dominated serious British music journalism, while the rest, the *Record Mirror, Disc* and *Top Pops*, were mainly pop-orientated and generally catered for the teeny bop audience, with profiles, colour photographs and other harmless nonsense.

NOW GROUP OF 1969

The *T&A*, trying to keep abreast of popular trends in society, sponsored the *Now Group Of 1969* competition, which was staged at the nearby Penny Farthing Club. Nineteen groups entered the contest; with the winners receiving the first prize of 33 guineas (£35.70) and a free audition with the 'go ahead' label President Records. (10)

An additional audition was promised by a Polydor Records talent spotter, and Paul Collins, the booking agent for the Penny Farthing Club, offered to put on a gig for the winning band.

The eventual winners were the Brighouse group, Skin Deep (pictured above). They auditioned on May 22 at Regent Sound Studios in Denmark Street, where they recorded two self-penned songs, *The Ballad of Robin Hood* and *Whiskers*. Unfortunately, they split up soon after. Guitarist John Radcliffe soon formed a new version of Skin Deep with a totally different lineup. (11)

CRYSTALLIZED ANTHEM

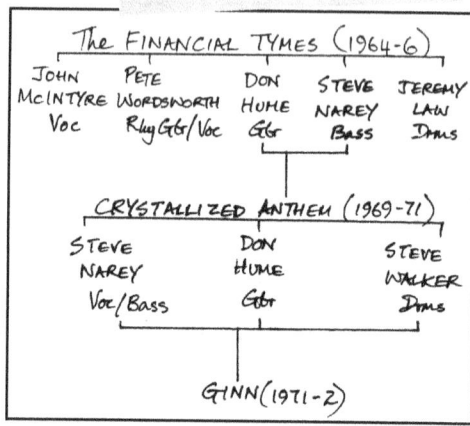

Formed in 1969, from the ashes of the Bradford group The Financial Tymes, the band were a tight blues-rock trio. Bassist Steve Narey was influenced by his dad's jazz collection, especially the bass lines that kept running through his head. His first bass guitar was constructed in woodwork classes in his last year at school. Later he converted a Hofner hollow-bodied bass to look like a Gibson EB3, creating a meatier, chunky sound.

Crystallized Anthem gigged extensively around the local area and were finalists in both *Telegraph & Argus* sponsored *Now Group* contests at the Penny Farthing nitespot, in 1969 and 1970. The group later changed their name to Ginn before finally splitting up. Steve rehearsed with local group Lazy Days but did not join them.

CHAPTER 1 - PSYCHEDELIA TO HEAVY ROCK 1967 - 1970

My Bass Is...
STEVE NAREY'S HOFNEEBEE3!

I suppose it's all my Dad's fault, really, for playing all those Glen Miller and Tommy Dorsey 78s back in the 50s. I'd be walking home from school in the afternoons and it wouldn't be the melody line from *Sunny Side Of The Street* going through my head, it was the bass. And then in 1963 I heard Macca playing that overgrown fiddle, and that was it. I made my first bass in my last year of school woodwork class, a violin bass copy, but of course, I didn't have any money to buy strings, so I had to rescue some from a scrapped piano, which were effectively roundwounds with a lovely twangy tone when you could only otherwise buy thumping flatwounds in the shops.

In 1964, I paid seven quid for a second-hand Höfner hollow-bodied bass with a good neck and fingerboard, which I gigged with for about two years until the body joints fell apart, an old Höfner trick – its instruments used traditional animal-based adhesives which gradually dried out over the years until with, quite literally, a bang, the glued-in neck was no longer a glued-in neck and you had a two-part bass.

The neck was rescued, as were the pick-ups, machine heads and a few other bits, and I then set about carving a body, to a shape which looked a bit like that of a Gibson EB-3, from a solid lump of mahogany bought as a cut-off from a local timber yard.

Tools were at an absolute minimum – I only had an old spokeshave, and a saw to cut out and shape the whole thing. It took me ages! (*spirit of Val Singleton there – that's what we like to hear – Ed*). However, the thing is still going strong some 30 years later, having had only one facelift.

Steve Narey's Frankenstein of a bass is still going strong 30 years on

Custom Circuits

The original single coil Höfner pick-ups have been combined into one unit with the aid of eight magnets and a few bits of mild steel, and wired through a series/parallel switch. This gives either a nice clean single coil sound, or meaty chunky (that's dog food isn't it?) humbucking tones.

The scale length is only 30inches but with the appropriate 45 – 105 gauge strings (*wouldn't be a hint there, Steve, would it? Ed*) it's nice and tight right down to the open E string.

No, I'm not selling it!

Steve Narey

RODNEY BEWES

Bingley actor, Rodney Bewes (RIP 2017) was best known for playing 'Bob' in the 1970s TV series *The Likely Lads* (1964-68). He was cast by writers Dick Clement and Ian Le Frenais after they saw him in the 1963 film *Billy Liar*.

Rodney's dalliance with the pop charts began when former Rolling Stones' manager Andrew Loog-Oldham released the 7" single *Dear Mother, Love Albert* in 1970 on his off-shoot label, Revolution.

Rodney sang the theme song of the same-titled TV sitcom that was broadcast between September 1969 and June 1972. The lyrics were co-written by Rodney and former Manfred Mann drummer Mike Hugg. The TV show ran for 26 episodes, at thirty minutes per episode. The first series was produced by Thames Television, the subsequent series 2-4 by Yorkshire Television.

The plot concerns the Rodney Bewes character (Albert Courtney) leaving the North to live in London, where he finds work in a confectionery factory, moves into a flat with two young ladies and writes home to his mother grossly exaggerating all these events. By the fourth and final series, the show title was shortened to just *Albert* when the character lost his job and was finding it hard to survive in London.

Rodney returned to play Bob Ferris, alongside co-star James Bolam, in *Whatever Happened to the Likely Lads?* (1973–74). The 1976 film of series featured another Bradford actor - future *Doctor Who* assistant Mary Tamm.

In 2010, a three-disc set containing series 2-4 of *Dear Mother... Love Albert* came out on DVD. Series one has sadly been erased, like many early TV shows.

```
FROM NEW ORLEANS
CHAMPION JACK DUPREE
IN CONCERT AT

MISTER
CLECKHEATON TOWN HALL
SATURDAY / SUNDAY - NOVEMBER 28/29
DANCING 9-00 - 12-00    CONCERT 12-00 - 3-00
TICKETS 10/-

MAYOR'S
FEATURING
SOUND CITY DISCO
KINDNESS
(FROM RADIO ONE)

MIDNIGHT
GROTESQUE GNOME      MORNING DAWN
TONY BARRETT         ISENGARD
CRYSTALLIZED ANTHEM

MUSICAL
LICENCED BAR, REFRESHMENTS
TICKETS FROM CLECKHEATON TOWN HALL
OR COUNCILLOR J. M. HEY FLAT 4 THE HOLLIES BRADFORD ROAD
CLECKHEATON

MARATHON
IN AID OF THE MAYOR OF SPENBOROUGH'S APPEAL FOR THE CHILDBIRTH RESEARCH CENTRE
```

There was a special charity event in November 1969, at Cleckheaton Town Hall. Over two nights, *Mister Mayor's Midnight Musical Marathon* featured local groups Kindness, Isengard and Crystalized Anthem, plus Halifax resident blues legend Champion Jack Dupree.

RODNEY BEWES
69	Revolution REV 1003	Remember When/Dear Mother Love Albert	10
70	Revolution Pop REVP1001	Dear Mother Love Albert/Meter Maid	10

HIGHLY LIKELY
74	BBC RESL 10	Whatever Happened To You?/God Bless Everyone	30

47

DAVE LEE SOUND

Dave Lee was a self-taught pianist who virtually single-handedly kept the authentic 1950s rock'n'roll revival scene alive in Bradford. With his band The Dave Lee Sound, he played all over the country and the world. Their first gig was in 1964 at the Red Lion, Bankfoot.

In 1970 his trio came second on Hughie Green's *Opportunity Knocks* TV Show. By 1971, after playing regularly at the Oddfellows Arms in Greengates, the landlord Patrick Killen started the Bradford Rock'n'Roll Club on December 15, with an eventual membership of over 200 drawn from Bradford, Leeds, York and Dewsbury. (12)

The band regularly packed out the Oddfellows Arms in Eccleshill, Brian Rishworth's HQ for Revivalists.

The highlight of Dave's career was undoubtedly meeting his idol 'The Killer', Jerry Lee Lewis, in Manchester in 1971 when he joined him on stage as well as having a drink backstage after the show.

The band also had their own record label in the 1970s, called Throstle's Nest, based in Bingley, which released three LPs and two EPs.

The trio recorded at least three LPs, including *Live At The Stardust,* on Southern Sound Records, which was recorded at a show bar in Brighouse in 1975.

Tragically, Dave died in 2004. He was a brilliant musician, sadly missed by his many fans.

JUNIOR'S EYES

Vocalist/harmonica player Grahame 'Grom' Kelly, an ex-Belle Vue Grammar School pupil, played with many local bands, including Midnight Train. In 1968, Grom moved to London to join progressive rock band Junior's Eyes as lead singer. The band's album, *Battersea Power Station*, was first released in the USA and linked to an American tour before coming out in the UK in June 1969.

With Grom as singer, they released the singles *Woman Love / White Light Part 2* and *Circus Days* as well as the 4-song 7-inch EP *Star Child*, all produced by Bowie producer Tony Visconti.

Junior's Eyes, led by guitarist Mick Wayne but without Grom, backed David Bowie on a BBC radio session and members played on early Bowie tracks including *Space Oddity*.

Their much sought-after *Battersea Power Station* LP changes hands for well over £100 if you can find one. It was re-released on CD in 2000 with completely different cover artwork and tracks from the band's singles, demos and radio sessions.

Halifax group **Tree** recorded some tracks at a session in 1969.

CHAPTER 1 - PSYCHEDELIA TO HEAVY ROCK 1967 - 1970

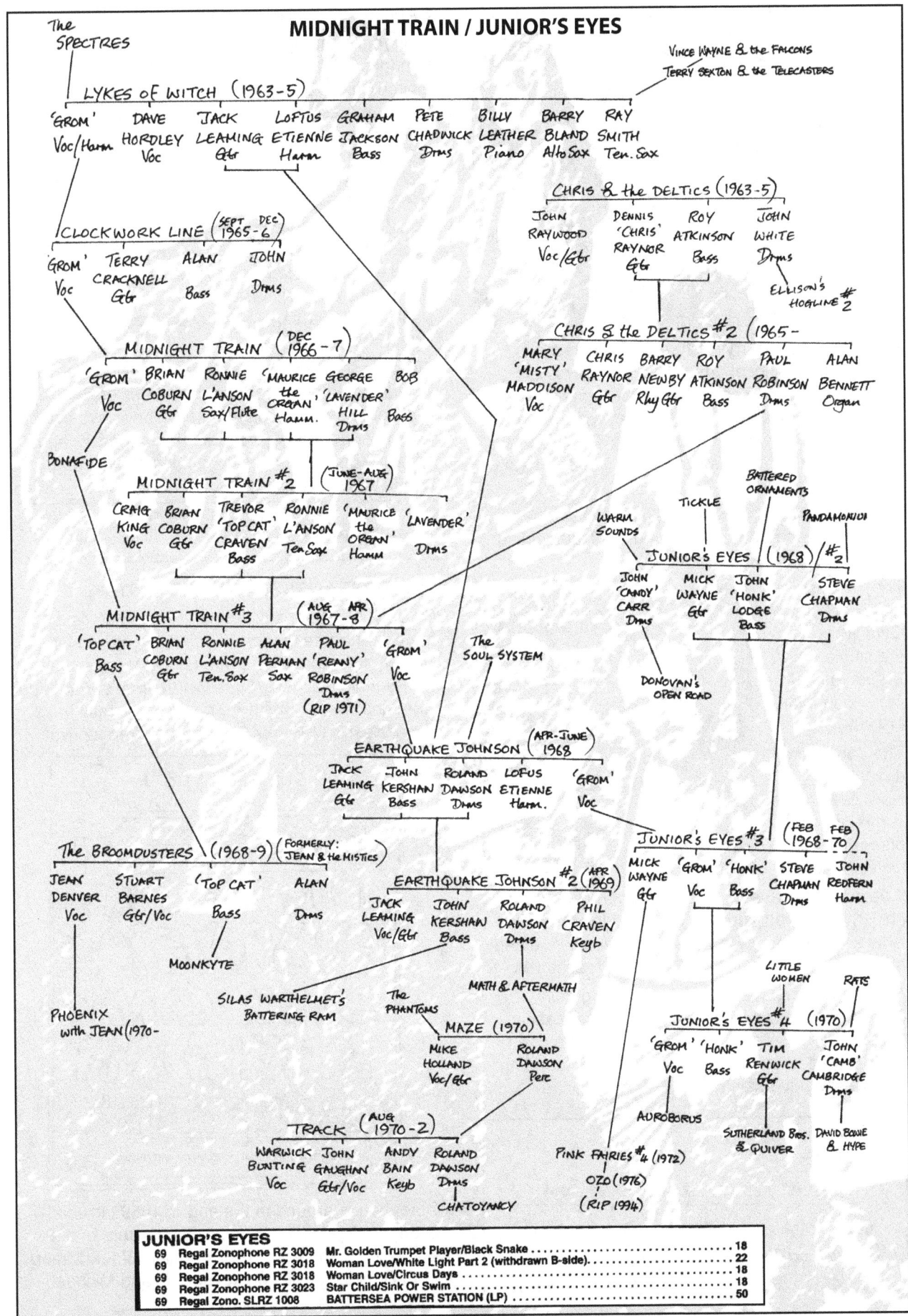

JUNIOR'S EYES
- 69 Regal Zonophone RZ 3009 Mr. Golden Trumpet Player/Black Snake ... 18
- 69 Regal Zonophone RZ 3018 Woman Love/White Light Part 2 (withdrawn B-side) ... 22
- 69 Regal Zonophone RZ 3018 Woman Love/Circus Days ... 18
- 69 Regal Zonophone RZ 3023 Star Child/Sink Or Swim ... 18
- 69 Regal Zono. SLRZ 1008 BATTERSEA POWER STATION (LP) ... 50

HOGSNORT RUPERT'S ORIGINAL FLAGON BAND

Bradford lad Ian Terry (pictured above, second left), formerly of local group The Instruders, had emigrated to New Zealand in 1965. He landed a record contract with HMV for his new group, five English ex-pats who formed to enter TV's *New Faces*. Their name was Hogsnort Rupert's Original Flagon Band!

(A Windsor-based group called Hogsnort Rupert & His Good Good Band had played the Troutbeck in Ilkley on May 2, 1965.)

They released an LP, *All Our Own Work*, and the single *When I Was Young / Maggie Maggie*, in 1969.

The band were described in New Zealand as *'a mix of r'n'b, bluegrass and skiffle.'*

A second LP, *Have A Hogsnort Rupert Summer* (1970), appeared after Ian Terry had left the band. Now a three-piece with Luther and Wisehart joined by John Reilly, their single *Pretty Girl* reached No 1.

After shortening the bands name to Hogsnort Rupert, Luther and Wisehart continued releasing albums with different lineups. They became one of New Zealand's longest running bands, celebrating their 40th anniversary in 2010.

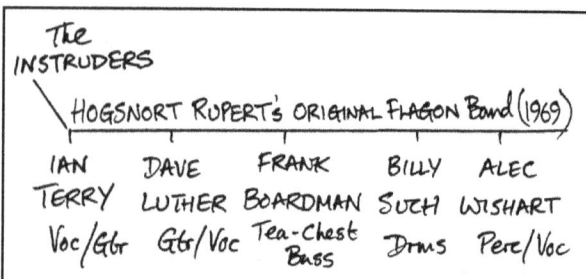

SAMANTHA PROMOTIONS

Two young entrepreneurs, based in Earl's Court, London, G Robin and N Van Grieken at Transworld, placed an advert in *Melody Maker* for young rock bands interested in getting a recording contract. Applicants were duly auditioned and the better ones were selected to submit a song for a potential record release. They soon got enough material to produce and release two compilation LPs. The first, *Samantha Promotions Volume 1* (SPLP101), appeared in 1969, featuring eleven bands. The second, *Samantha Promotions Volume 2* (SPLP102), was released in 1970. It included the track *Nightmares* by Keighley progressive rock band Free Expression.

These promotional LPs were produced in limited amounts and sent to colleges and universities to get live work for the bands featured. They have become the rarest psych/prog-related LPs in the UK, and because only a few copies survive, they change hands for four-figure sums.

70	Transworld SPLP 101	SAMANTHA PROMOTIONS (orange cover, private pressing, a few with poster)	600
70	Transworld SPLP 102	SAMANTHA PROMOTIONS (purple cover, private pressing, a few with poster)	600

THE FIRST YORKSHIRE FREE FESTIVAL

On July 26, 1969, at Clarence Park, Wakefield, there was a free outdoor concert, organised by Bill Nelson. It featured his band, Global Village, along with Buffalo Canvas, (Silas Warthelmet's) Battering Ram and Alistair Smith & Friends. This may have been West Yorkshire's first open-air free festival.

Other bands around at the end of 1969 included **Grail**, the imaginatively titled **The Group**, and a skiffle/soul band from Skipton called **Black Sheep** (with Donald Newiss on keyboards and Michael Jones on drums).

CHAPTER 1 - PSYCHEDELIA TO HEAVY ROCK 1967 - 1970

TOASTED GROWLE / JACKFIELD FARM

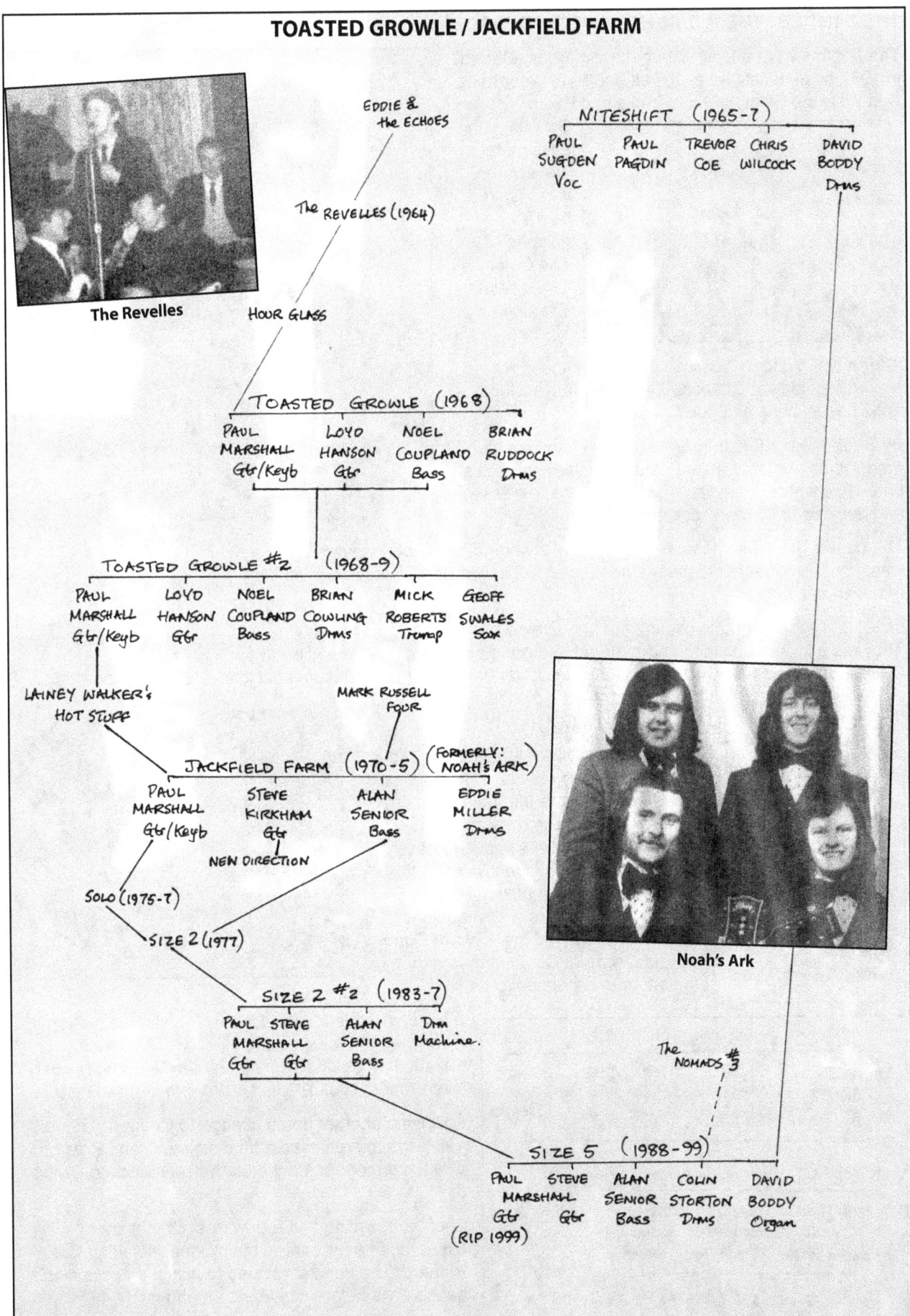

THE ZANTIES / THE MIDNIGHT HEARSE / CHARLES 1

The Zanties were a Queensbury-based group, started in 1967 by guitarists Keith Jowett and Paul Woodhead with Keith's brother John on drums and Peter Schofield on bass guitar. Their name was inspired by a TV episode of *The Outer Limits* called *The Zanti Misfits*.

After a first gig for a local scout group dance, they played regularly at Queensbury Conservative Club and various clubs and pubs.

By September 1968, they were managed by Ronnie Fairbrother who brought in David Appleyard on vocals until 1969 when Ronnie and David became restless and decided to go their separate ways.

The band signed with agent Norman Thewlis who got them work seven nights a week, before Peter left to pursue his studies but suggested Trevor Jones as his replacement.

In 1970, Keith decided to change the band name to The Midnight Hearse. They did a tour of Scotland and returned to organise a dance at Victoria Hall in Queensbury. The band played regularly on US air bases, toured Wales and did lots of club dates. They also began to write their own songs. In 1975, Paul Woodhead left and the band continued as a trio.

The next year they released their debut single, *We're Gonna Have A New World Champion*. It was a tribute to Bradford boxer Richard Dunn (pictured right with the band), who was due to have a crack at the World Heavyweight title in Germany against boxing legend Muhammad Ali. After a spirited fight, Richard lost but had the *Richard Dunn Sports Centre* at Odsal named after him in honour of his endeavours.

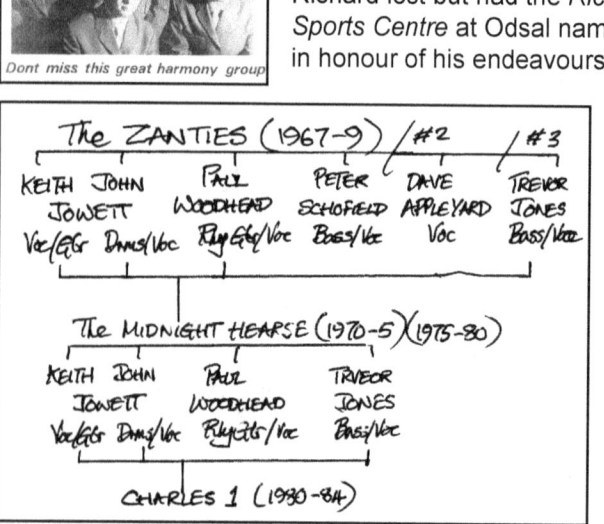

A second single followed in 1977, called *25 Years On*, a song written to celebrate the Silver Jubilee of Queen Elizabeth II, again released on Mat Records, which was broadcast on BBC's *Look North* programme.

Following another name change to Charles 1 in late 1980, the trio released a third single, *Glory! Bradford City* to commemorate the team's promotion to Division 3.

Their songwriting abilities were such that some big names have covered their tunes, including Cliff Richard. The band continued to play pubs, clubs and dance halls before coming to an end in 1984.

KINDNESS

Prior to re-inventing themselves as Smokey/Smokie, and going on to have eleven Top 20 hit singles between 1974-76, these Bradford lads had been known as Kindness between 1970 and 1973 and before that, The Elizabethans.

As The Elizabethans in 1968, managed by Mark Jordan, they became fully professional, appearing on Yorkshire TV's news magazine show *Calendar* and recorded their first five song demo; *Colours Of The Rainbow, Do You Love Me?, For My Country, Jamaica*, and *Rock'n'Roll Is Here To Stay*. (These early tracks turned up on a rare Russian CD called *Mega Rarities Of Smokie Career* years later.)

By January 1970, RCA Records showed an interest, suggested a name change to Kindness and signed the band. They recorded their debut single, the double A-sided *Light Of Love / Lindy Lou*, which unfortunately sold only 300 copies and RCA subsequently ended their contract.

In late 1971, their management was taken over by Dave Eager, the early Radio 1 DJ, who introduced the band to Decca Records. Their first single for Decca, *Oh Julie (Oh Oh July) / I Love You Carolina*, was released in February 1972. A second single, *Let The Good Times Roll / Oh Yea*, followed later in that year and was selected as the opening theme to Radio 1's *Saturday Show* by DJ Emperor Rosco.

In 1973, their third and final single for Decca, *Make It Better / Lonely Long Lady*, flopped and Decca Records terminated their contract. The song *Lonely Long Lady* was the first of their releases to be written by the band themselves, credited to Kindness.

They were recruited as Peter Noone's backing band and did a nationwide tour with him. Drummer Ron Kelly left the band, replaced by Pete Spencer.

The band were re-branded as Smokey in 1974 and signed to Mickey Most's RAK Records. Most teamed them up with the songwriting team of Nicky Chinn and Mike Chapman, who were already writing for Mud, Suzi Quatro and The Sweet. Smokie's 1970s chart success began and the rest is history.

INNER MIND / CROWN JOOLS

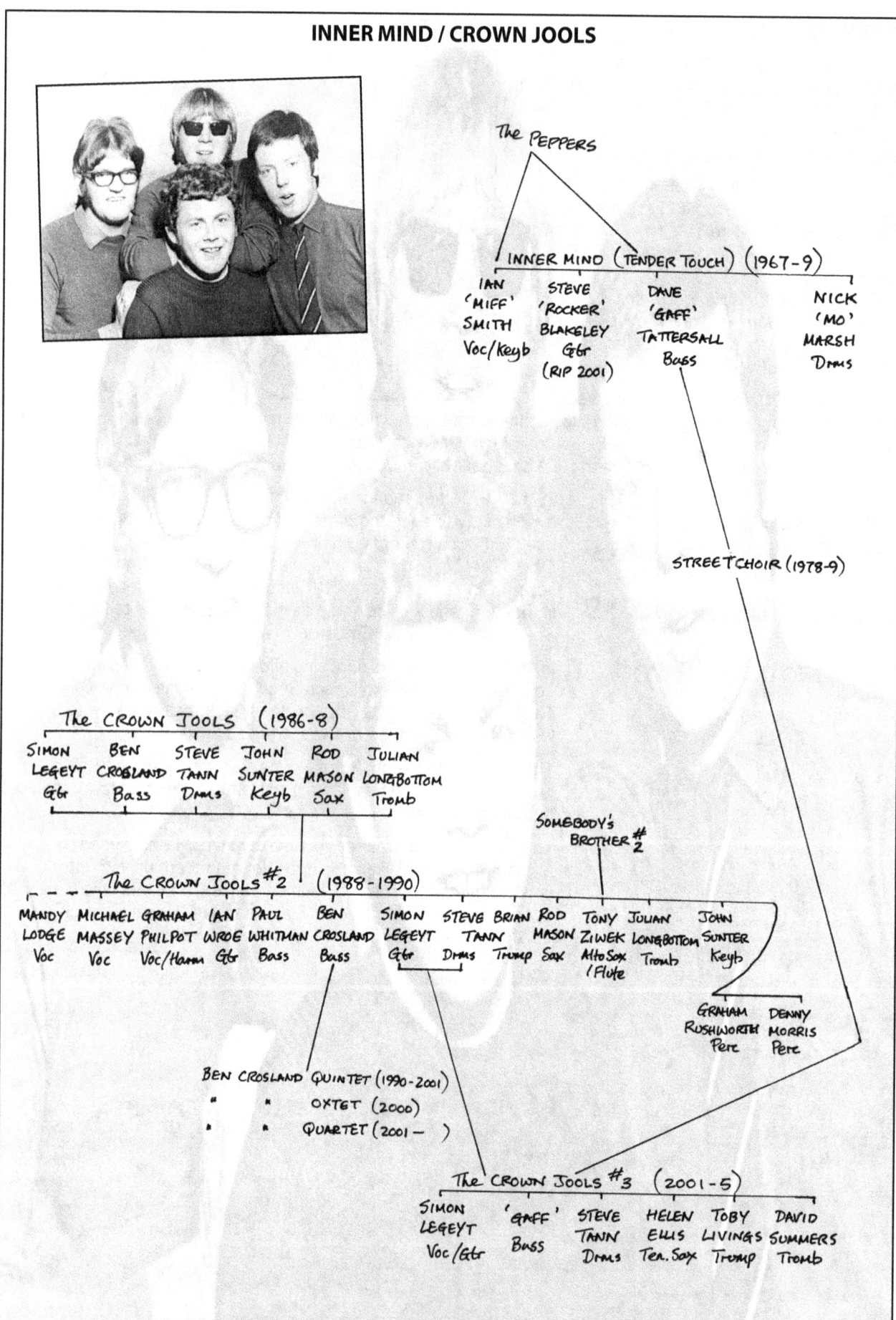

CHAPTER 1 - PSYCHEDELIA TO HEAVY ROCK   1967 - 1970

THE ORIGINAL BRADFORD (ARTS) FESTIVAL.

The first Bradford Arts Festival ran from February 22 to March 1, 1970. It aimed to *'provide a focal point for local arts activities, stimulated by the concentrated inclusion of top-class professional artists and hopes to further such activities in the region by involving as many sections of the community as possible.'* (15)

The eight days of music concerts, drama, poetry, films and exhibitions took place at various venues around the city, from the university to St George's Hall. It was organised by the Bradford Students Association (directors Ian White and Alan Hulse - a local playwright and later TV actor) in conjunction with the University, the City Council, Yorkshire Arts and the Bradford Area Development Association.

Some of the key musical events were;

Monday, February 23, at Queen's Hall - a Jazz Club night with the Mike Westbrook Band and the Joe Markey Septet.

Tuesday, February 14, at St George's Hall - a Folk Club event with Bridget St. John, The Johnsons, Mike Cooper, Ewan McCall and Peggy Seeger.

Wednesday, February 25, at the University Great Hall - another jazz night with Graham Collier Sextet (who had premiered a specially commissioned piece for the festival called *Smoke Blackened Walls And Curlews*), and the classical guitarist John Williams.

Thursday 26, at St George's Hall - folk act Pentangle.

Friday 27, at the University Great Hall - a special *Arts Fest Ball* featuring Manfred Mann, Idle Race (Jeff Lynne's pre-ELO band), Eire Apparent (whose LP was produced by Jimi Hendrix) and local folk act Jan Dukes de Grey.

Saturday, February 28, at St George's Hall - a special afternoon and evening show of Mike Westbrook and John Fox's *Circus Time* - a mixed media event involving seventy musicians (including Welfare State), fire-eaters, wrestlers, clowns, etc!

Also on the same evening at Queen's Hall was an all-night seminar (seven hours) called, *Pop Culture & Deviance*, organised by university sociology lecturer Paul Walton, which, even though The Incredible String Band didn't turn up, still attracted a crowd of around 600. A stripper called Estelle opened the proceedings, followed by drag act Paul Reid and the theatre group The People Show, who were asked to leave the stage after stripping and pretending to be homosexuals. Stewards and audience were involved in violent scuffles during this and also during Leeds Art College lecturer Jeff Nuttal's set of poem readings, due to his use of crude four-letter words and 'flashing his todger'!

Although there were long gaps between the various acts, Bob Dylan's *Don't Look Back* film was shown and the local band Auroborus managed to play before the whole event finally ended at six o'clock in the morning.

At the end of the Festival, the director Ian White commented on the whole affair, *'After so much work over many months by so many people to get this recognised as the city's festival, I'm afraid it's all gone down the drain.'*

NOW GROUP OF 1970

In April, the *T&A* sponsored another local talent contest. The *Now Group Of 1970*, held for the second year at the Penny Farthing, run by manager Bill McGarry (ex-manager of Gerry & The Pacemakers).

There were twenty five entrants, some of whom had entered the previous year, each playing a twenty-minute set. The competition ran in three rounds, with the last eight going through to play at the final on Friday, April 10.

The finalists stood to win £50, a £50 hand-made Orange microphone and a record audition with CBS Records through their A&R talent-spotter Derek Johns, who was one of the judges.

The *Now Group Of 1970* contestants were: Fresh Garbage, Scorched Earth, Auroborus, Crystalized

Scorched Earth

Anthem, Smokestack, Track, Young Generation, Electric City Sound, The Sun, The Ambition, Guest (from Heckmonwike), Smokey Ring Hat Band, Free Expression (both from Keighley), Talismen (from Halifax), Sweet Ice, Pendulum, Capricorn (all from Leeds), Whiskey Poker Orchestra (Huddersfield), Free Speech (Manchester).

The winners were Bradford / Leeds group Fresh Garbage (one of the groups managed by Dave Stansfield), with two other Bradford bands, Scorched Earth and Auroborus, coming second and third respectively. Auroborus vocalist Grom was upset at their sound due to feedback problems, but their material was original and described as a 'gulping blues style'. Penny Farthing manager Bill McGarry handed over the cheque for £50 to winners Fresh Garbage, with the *T&A*'s Mike Priestley looking on.

In July Fresh Garbage recorded four tracks in a four-hour session at a studio in London; Jazz, Life, Free Woman and You Need Love, and then announced, as a few disillusioned acts had before them, that they would leave the 'dead scene' of Bradford for London, giving up their jobs and renting a cottage to concentrate on improving their set.

A Leeds band called Capricorn were spotted by an agent and later appeared on *Opportunity Knocks*.

Mike Holland, guitarist of local band Maze, had done the rounds as a busker and was working on a 'pop opera' called *Professor Of The Streets*.

On Saturday, April 11, 1970, the *Halifax Pop & Blues Festival 70* took place at Thrum Hall Rugby League ground; entrance fee £1 or 25 shillings. It was the area's first-ever outdoor event, taking place from 6 pm until midnight, at the 35,000-capacity venue, but due to icy winter weather, only around 2,500 turned up. This may also have been partly due to a too varied musical line-up but even so, the crowd brought a party mood to the evening.

The first group were Bradford's Midnight Hearse, who only managed to play one number, but as a consolation, a London booking agent got them a gig at the Marquee Club. Also, in the end, headliners Fleetwood Mac turned up too late to play! The local press described the event as, *'a brave attempt - but a flop!'*

CHAPTER 1 - PSYCHEDELIA TO HEAVY ROCK — 1967 - 1970

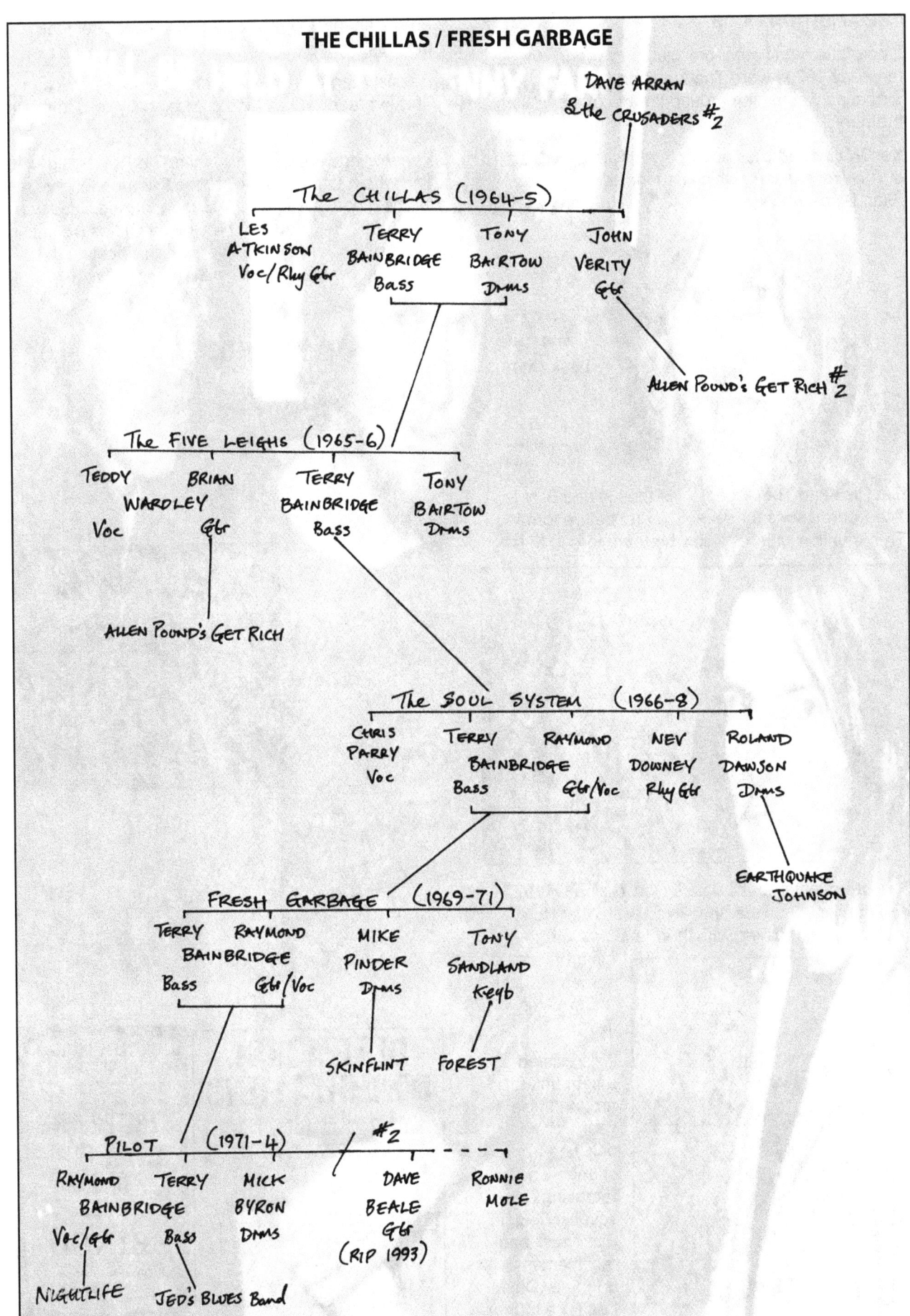

THE AMBITION / AXIS

One of the many semi-pro 'clubland' groups in the early 1970s were The Ambition / Axis whose formation was based around the trio of the Waller brothers.

Ken Waller had previously played with Clay Martin & The Trespassers, which had included bassist Allan Davis who went on to play with Allen Pound's

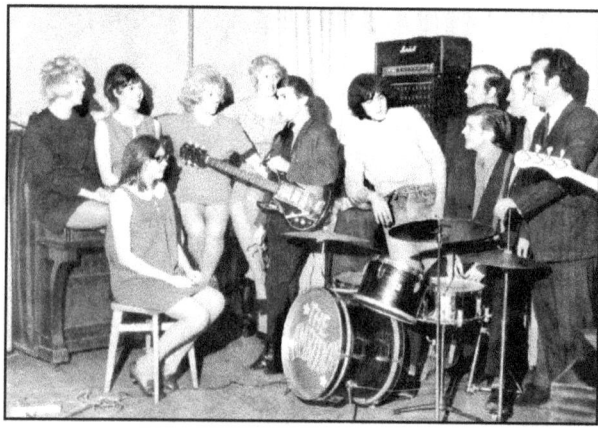

Get Rich and The Accent. Ken then joined Billy & The Fourmasons for several years, before forming The Ambition with his fellow brothers Ian and Alan.

The group entered the *T&A's Now Group Of 1970* competition, but were short lived, with Alan Berry replacing Ken Waller, who then reunited with his brothers sometime later to form Axis in 1971.

Axis existed as a tight unit for around three years, their only line-up change was recruiting extra vocalist Maggie Pickersgill and replacement drummer Dave Lee for a tour of American Air Force bases in Morocco, after which they disbanded,

Bassist Alan Waller would later tour Germany with The Average White Band but tragically died in a car crash in 1976.

Ken Waller went on to play with The Roy Bould Trio who had a residency at the Furnace Inn for the next couple of years. He then formed Sundown (1978-80), followed by The Golden Oldies (reuniting with brother Ian) before eventually relocating to Australia, where he lived with his wife Vivian.

CHAPTER 1 - PSYCHEDELIA TO HEAVY ROCK 1967 - 1970

THE AMBITION / AXIS

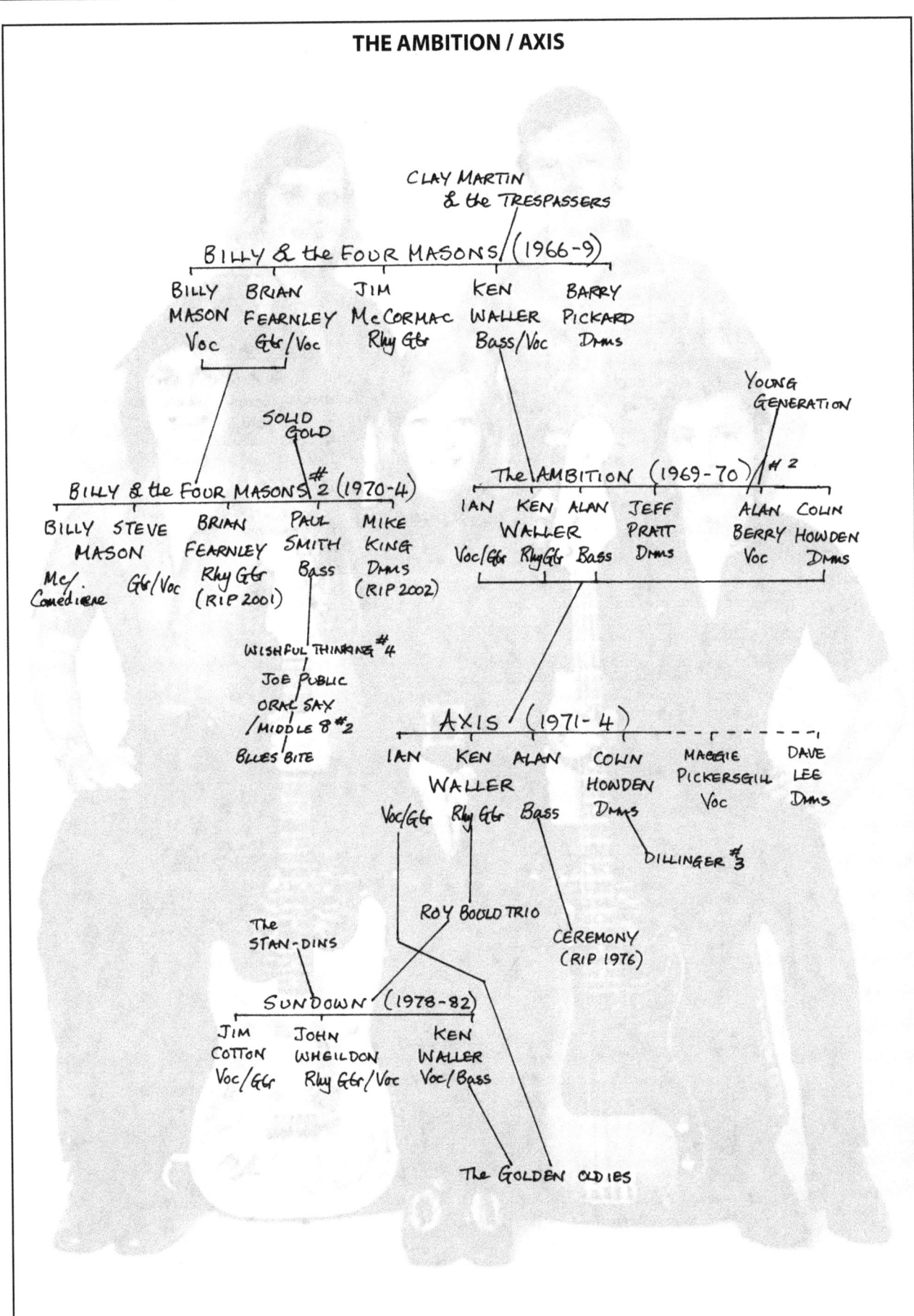

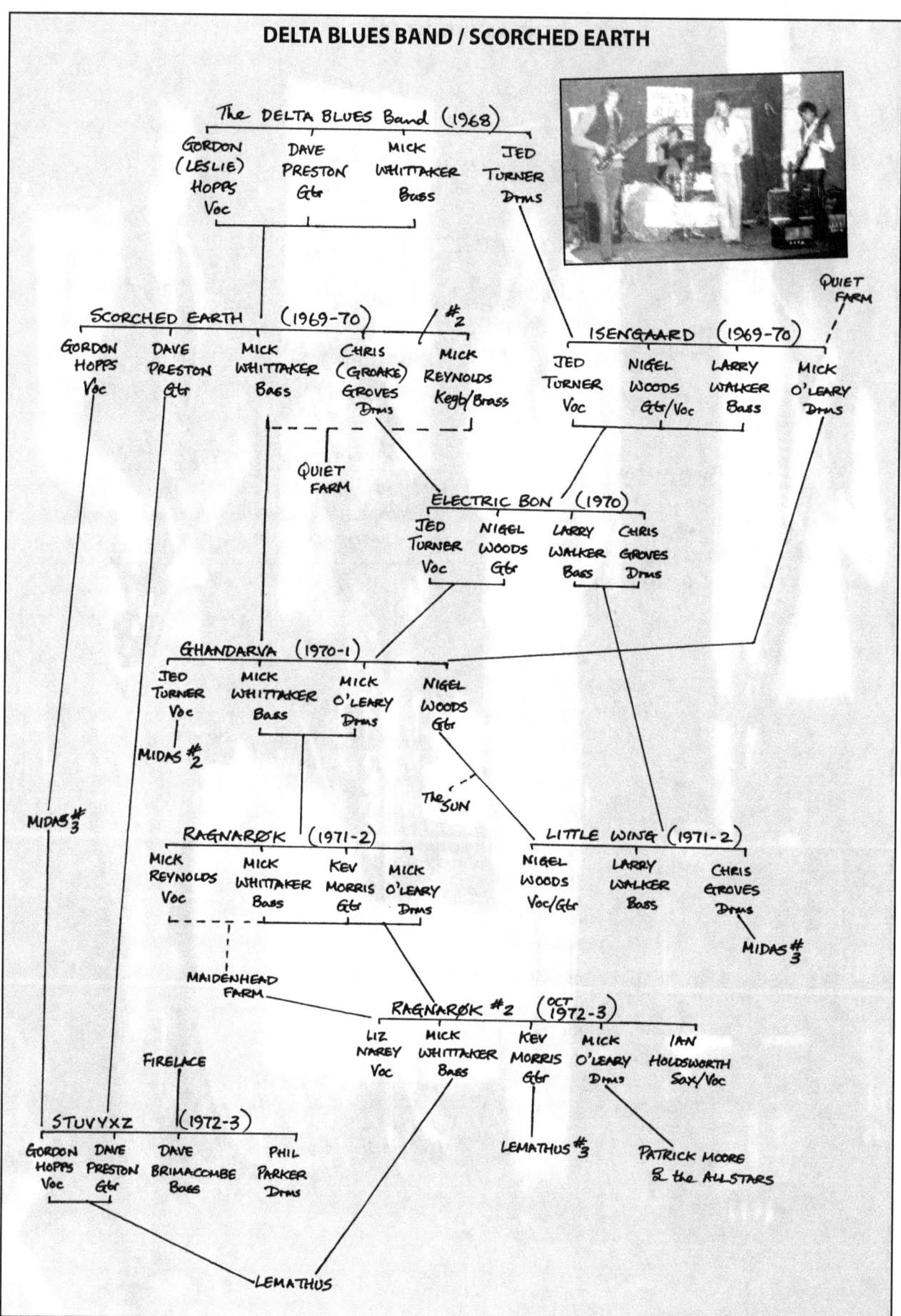

CHAPTER 1 - PSYCHEDELIA TO HEAVY ROCK   1967 - 1970

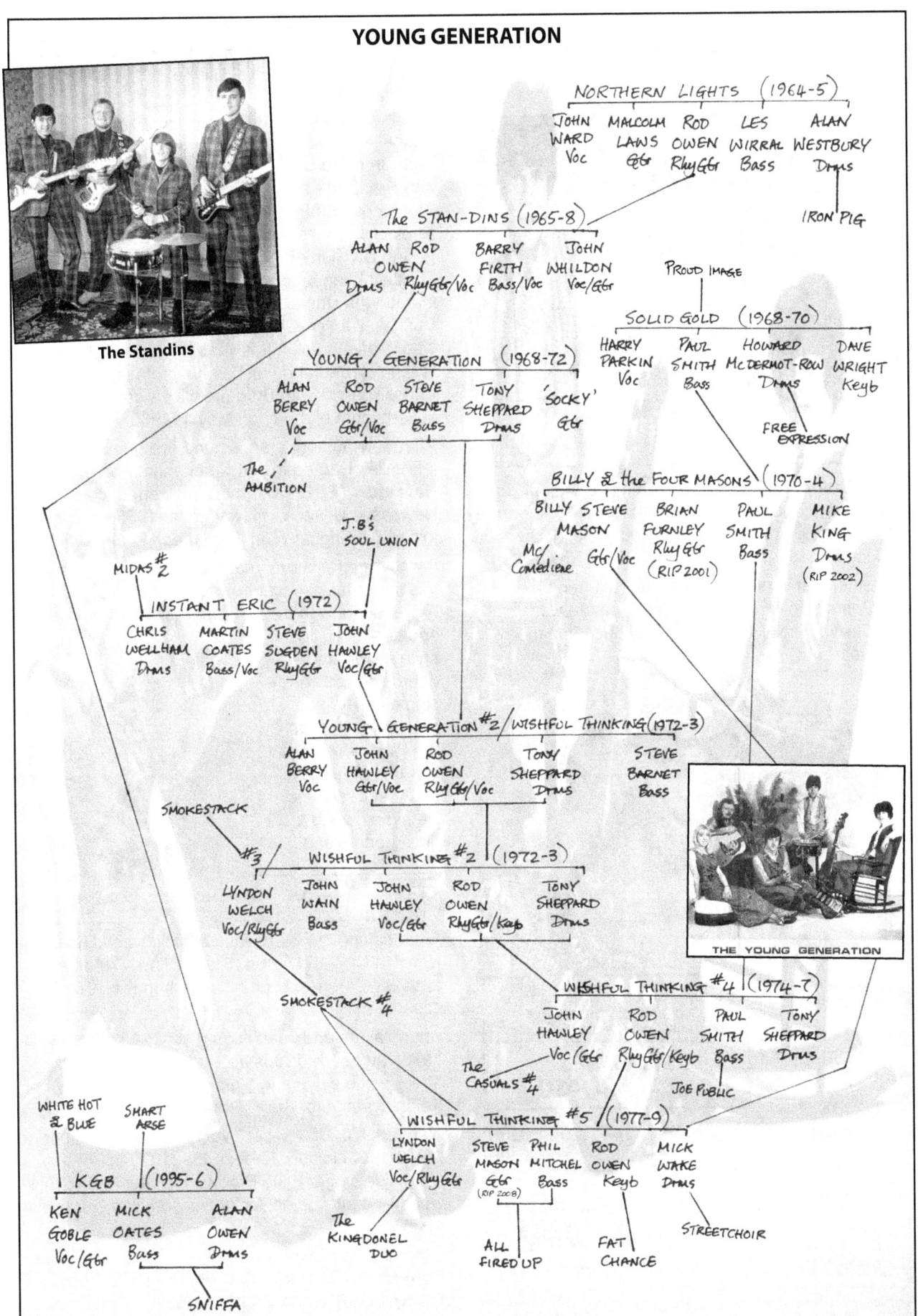

THE FIRST BRADFORD FREE FESTIVAL

The first outdoor festival in Bradford district was on July 23, 1970, when there was a free concert at Cliffe Castle.

Free Expression playing at the Cliffe Castle Park Pop Festival in July 1970. Left to right: Brian Whitfield, Ray Feather, Howard McDermot-Row (partially hidden), Terry Peaker and Steve Hughes.

This was the line-up: Smokey Ring Hat Band, Free Expression (above), Isengard, Mad Green Octopus (Burnley prog rockers), August Tramp (folk), Dave Falkingham (poet), Tony Jackson (from Newcastle).

In September **The Gorgon II Club** opened up at the County Hotel. This short-lived venture was obviously trying to establish a similar club to the 1968 one.

TREVOR HOCKEY (1943-87)

Until 1970, Bradford, like Manchester, was a two-team football city, with both Bradford City and Bradford Park Avenue, until BPA lost re-election to the then Fourth Division of the Football League to Cambridge United.

But it was an ex-City player called Trevor Hockey who is of interest in this year. A local Keighley lad, he started and finished his professional football career with Bradford City, signing on his seventeenth birthday on May 1, 1960.

After only 53 appearances and five goals, he left Valley Parade to join Nottingham Forest in November 1961. From there he went to play for Newcastle United until November 1965 when he joined Birmingham City for a fee of £25,000.

It was during his five years at St Andrews that this tough-tackling central midfielder became a big favourite with the fans, no more so than when sporting a Beatles-style hairdo and beard. He recorded a single for Birmingham, called *Happy 'Cos I'm Blue*, which has become a much sought-after single. He even owned a pink grand piano!

TREVOR HOCKEY
70s Beau Brummie TET 120ST Happy 'Cos I'm Blue/THE BLUES PLAYERS: Keep Right On To The End Of The Road (p/s) 40

After leaving the Blues for Sheffield United, then Norwich City, and Aston Villa, he finally returned to Valley Parade to end his career in the 1974-5 season.

After playing and coaching in the USA in the late 1970s and early 1980s he sadly died of a heart attack while playing five-a-side in his home town of Keighley, aged only forty-three, on April 2, 1987.

Also in 1970, Batley-born vocalist Robert Palmer (1949-2003) joined Vinegar Joe (1970-1974) alongside singer Elkie Brooks. He later had several worldwide hit singles, including *Addicted To Love* in 1986.

Other bands around at the end of 1970 were; **The Four Mates**, **Traction Sound**, **The Lyric Show Group** and **Electric City Sound**.

CHAPTER 1 - PSYCHEDELIA TO HEAVY ROCK 1967 - 1970

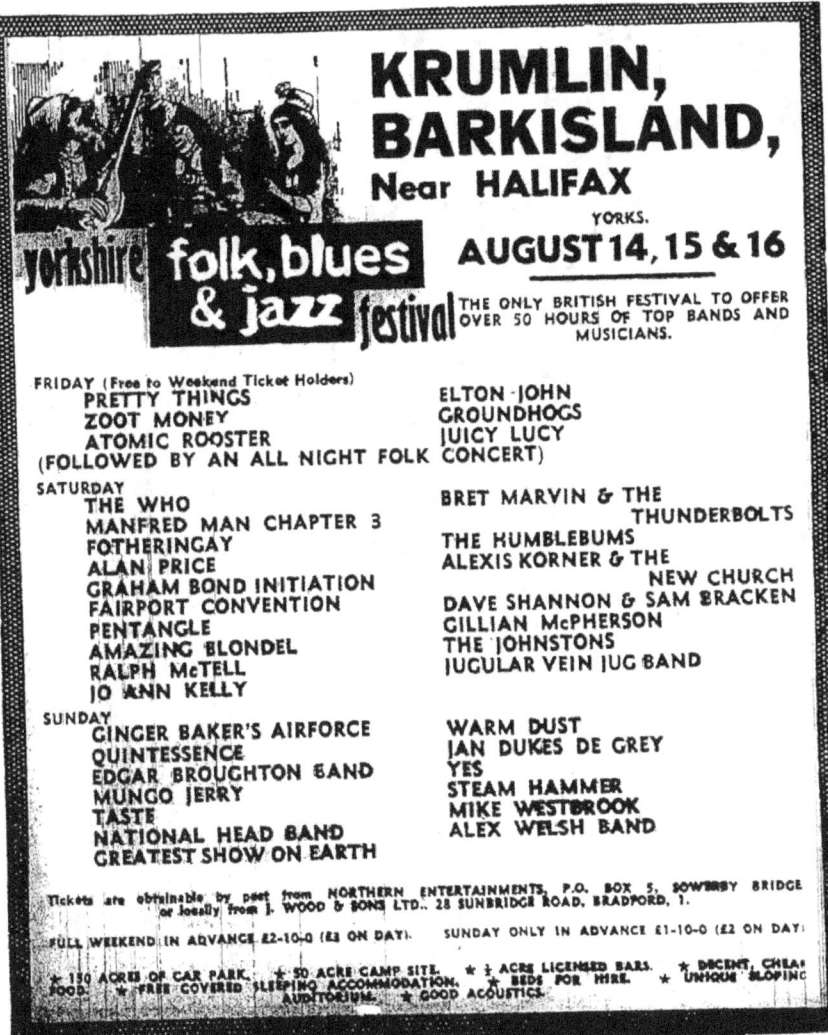

THE DISASTER OF THE KRUMLIN FESTIVAL

The Krumlin Festival was Yorkshire's first big open-air festival. It was organised by two entrepreneurs; Derek McEwen and Brian Highley, from Northern Entertainment. Brian, besides being the landlord of The Anchor pub in Mill Bank, Halifax, had been lead singer of Brian Highley & The Highlights and won Halifax's Gala's Battle Of The Bands in 1963.

Fifty thousand people were expected to turn up to see a star-studded bill at the fifty-acre natural amphitheatre site on Banquet House Farm, Barkisland - a tiny village just outside Halifax.

With over 8,000 tickets, at £3 for the weekend, sold within weeks of going on sale, the promoters were hopeful of making their target and breaking even. They also expected quite a few European visitors en route to the Isle of Wight Festival later that month (here the promoters lost £100,000 despite 600,000 attending, as gatecrashers broke down the fences).

On the Friday, the first group were meant to be on stage at three o'clock, but with last-minute hitches, the folk duo The Humblebums (Gerry Rafferty and Billy Connolly) didn't get on stage until ten to eight. Their Scottish humour and lively folk music were well received, despite the fall of the first rain.

The next artist was Elton John, making his festival debut. He became the star of the Friday night line-up making it hard for Georgie Fame, who was the next act, to follow. Atomic Rooster were next, the first proper group, who worked hard and deserved their encore from the crowd. Then The Pretty Things (slightly drunk!) took over before the last of the day's acts, Juicy Lucy, struggled to keep the tired crowd interested, whilst sparring with the windy elements.

For those still awake, there was an all-night folk concert in the Balloon Tent to end the first day's events.

The next day, Saturday, was advertised as starting at 10 am but the music didn't get underway until midday, with a continuation of the previous night's folk celebration, with Joanne Kelly, Ralph McTell, The Johnstons and Honey Dew all performing their sets during intermittent rain.

Meanwhile, the police praised the crowd for 'their courteous manner' whilst arresting at least eight people for drug offences (cannabis). The plain-clothed drug squad officers were all wearing the same Army & Navy combat jackets and were five stones heavier than anyone else!

The Festival DJ, Jeremy Floyd, was fined £25 for insulting

Krumlin kid catching the vibe

the drug squad over the PA with the following message; *'In your midst are DS officers, one is a tall ginger-haired pig, if any of them get you, go to the Release Tent and they'll help you.'* The police also arrested a man regarding forged tickets, and three London men were remanded, accused of 'demanding money with menaces' from the festival stalls.

Krumlin crowd camping in cold and cramped conditions

On the stage next were Pentangle, whose blend of electric folk received a big ovation from the audience. As the rain came down and the gales began The Groundhogs hit the stage, playing a ferocious heavy blues set which went down well. (Pictures taken of the band on the stage at the festival would later grace the inside and back cover of their next LP, *Split*.)

Krumlin Festival debris

Fairport Convention stole the afternoon show with a rousing set, even getting the rain-soaked crowd up on their feet to applaud. They were followed by Graham Bond and Alexis Korner, then Sandy Denny's Fotheringay and finally Alan Price and Zoot Money were left to finish off the night. Their set eventually had to stop as rain was pouring onto the stage and there was a fear of electrocution.

This was effectively the end of the festival as the gales and rain stopped any further performances.

Release's fourteen staff members (including four doctors) with the St John's Ambulance Service, voluntary organisations and Civil Aid battled to help the festival crowd by handing out 2,000 cups of free soup and by treating over two thousand people for exposure. At least two dozen festivalgoers were taken to Huddersfield Royal Infirmary. A local entrepreneur sold orange plastic bags from a stall, probably saving hundreds from exposure.

On Sunday, which was supposed to be the final day of the festival, the site was devastated by the harsh weather and aid workers checked people to see that they hadn't asphyxiated. No groups performed on that day and rumours of financial problems were facing the promoters spread. In fact, Derek McEwen had cracked under the strain and was last seen walking off over the bleak moors. The police searched for him but he went missing for a week. The promoters' losses were between fifteen and twenty thousand pounds, mainly due to forged tickets, and they had to declare themselves bankrupt.

Postscript: In March 1972, West Yorkshire Police received a cheque for £59.22 from the Official Receiver as settlement for their services at the festival. The rest of the £2,820 bill was written off as unrecoverable. (17)

Chapter 2
Prog Rock to Punk Rock
1971-1976

In 1971, the year Britain went metric with decimalisation and lost its old system of pounds, shillings and pence (£/s/d), one of Bradford's most popular venues was **The Queen's Hall.**

It was built in 1914 at the top end of the Alhambra complex and was one of the city's main dance halls up until 1968. It was then taken over by Bradford College Students' Union, which promoted bands from the national gig circuit and also held regular Friday and Saturday night late discos until 2 am which attracted virtually every 'freak, head and rock fan' in the town.

One of the most spectacular and individual dancers at these events was a guy called Jimmy Iqbal who had very long raven-black hair. He was last seen as an extra in a 1990s TV advert for a major building society. (1)

MR. MAYOR MEETS THE 'POP' FANS

Courtesy of the Spenborough Guardian

On January 15, Cleckheaton Councillor Michael Hey and local musician Graham Lockwood handed over a cheque for £110 to Mayor Jack Dewhirst for his appeal into childbirth research. The money was raised at a jazz-rock concert the previous November at the Town Hall. The show attracted over four hundred people who saw a line-up featuring ex-members of ZWO (who appeared as Grotesque

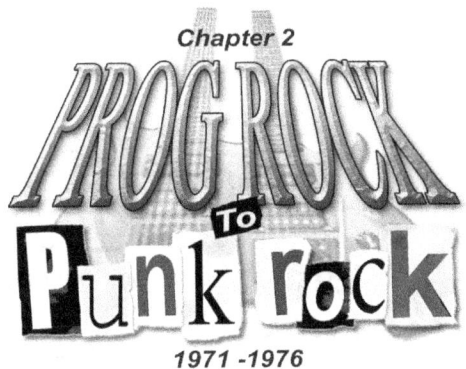

BOB DESANT TRIO (1970)
DES BRADY — Bass
ANTHONY SMITH — Piano
BOB KERSHAW — Drums

Gnome for this particular gig), The Graham Lockwood Trio, Ian Bell & The Memphis Sound, The Bob Desant Trio, and a special appearance by Champion Jack Dupree. (2)

By 1969-1970, the Tavern In The Town on Westgate had become one of Bradford's premier live music venues, featuring jazz, pop and blues on different nights of the week. Between 1971 and 1976 it became **The Tavern In The Town Rock Club.** The new club was set up by Dave Preston, Gordon Hopps, Phil Parker and Mick Whitaker as a place for local bands to play, due to a lack of suitable venues in the city. The opening night was a free gig by local band Stuvxyz on Wednesday, November 17. The door take was split, as on subsequent nights, 75 percent to the band 25 percent to the venue. As a consequence of the frequent early seventies power cuts the club had to cancel Sunday night gigs in March and April.

The Gorgon II Club (a new version of the original club) at Butterfield's Social Club in Shipley had a big following when it first opened, attracting over one hundred gig-goers a week. It later changed to **The Medusa Club** and was run as a rock venue by Chris Ormanroyd in Keighley.

From April 18, 1971, **The Argonaut Club**, at the Victoria Hotel on Park Lane, Bradford, held 'prog rock' nights every two weeks for the princely admission fee of 30p, or thirty 'new pence'.

June 23 saw the opening of **The Pentagon** nightspot at 45, Westgate. Originally, in 1963, this venue had been known as **The Europa** nightclub and was the first in Bradford to gain a late licence. When it re-opened as the Pentagon in 1971, glam rockers Mud were the opening act at the club. Later it was taken over by the West Indian community and became known as Checkpoint.

A venue called **The Gatto Bianco Club** opened at 33 Salem Street, off Manor Row.

In Keighley, **The Apollo Club**, organised by Paul Suckley from Cullingworth, put on weekly Wednesday night gigs from early November 1971. The first was by local Keighley band Kaboss on the 3rd.

The *T&A* stated that it had opened because there was, *'nothing for people who like music which is progressive, heavy, underground... This enterprise could harden into a steady source of music and fun for Keighley's frustrated freaks!'* (3)

Many local bands played at **The Afro Club** at 55 Godwin Street, which also put on some more bizarre forms of entertainment as in 1971 when a show called *Exorcism Of Shit* was performed by avant-garde duo Chris & Cosey. (4)

THE SECOND BRADFORD ARTS FESTIVAL

The second Bradford Arts Festival took place from March 4-14, organised again by the Bradford Students Association and Bradford Council. Ian White was again the festival director, with Alan Hulse as festival administrator.

The festival was another mixture of plays, film and music; the main music events were;

On Thursday 4, at St George's Hall - Quintessence / Edgar Broughton Band, entrance fee: 15s (75p).

On Saturday 6, at Bradford University - a folk concert by The Corries for 10s (50p).

Also on Saturday 6, at St George's Hall - a choral society event with The Hammond Sauce Works Band.

On Monday, March 8, at the Central Library - a 'group electronic' music production.

Wednesday 10 saw rock 'n' roll revival band The Wild Angels play at St George's Hall, with Emperor Rosko's Disco.

A folk club gig took place at Queen's Hall on Thursday 11.

On Friday 12, there was a concert by the Halle Orchestra at St George's Hall.

And, on Saturday 13 at St George's Hall, the Syd Lawrence Orchestra performed.

Pulse Productions was new promotional organization set up by Ian Barton and Phillip Featherman, who felt there was enough room for local promoters to operate in the area. The first organised gig was at St George's Hall on April 19; it featured Mungo Jerry and Demon Fuzz.

Their second was at the same venue on May 23, when the Edgar Broughton Band and Kevin Ayres played. By 1972, Ian Barton was back working as a DJ at Keighley Variety Club, two nights a week.

DEMONS IN THE PARK

On Saturday, June 5, 1971, Keighley's Cliffe Castle played host to its second free outdoor festival, named Demons In The Park. It featured headline band Blonde On Blonde plus local Bradford and Keighley groups Spiral Highway, Kaboss, Castle, Factory, Otherland and acoustic duo Joss & Trev (Joss Grundy & Trevor Carolan).

Over two thousand people attended, despite it being a very windy day. There were complaints about the noise from local residents, as the sound was carried by the very blustery winds on the day. Five people were arrested in the town for minor misdemeanours and a fight broke out.

'At the end of Spiral Highway's performance trouble broke out,' said Chris Gillott, one of the organisers, *when a group of skinheads and rockers started fighting. 'I went up to try and stop them but they started on me, police soon broke them up and everything ran smoothly. We had about 2,000 people there to start with and only about 50 intent on causing trouble. All the rest only wanted to hear the music.'* (5)

CHAPTER 2 - PROG ROCK TO PUNK ROCK   1971 - 1976

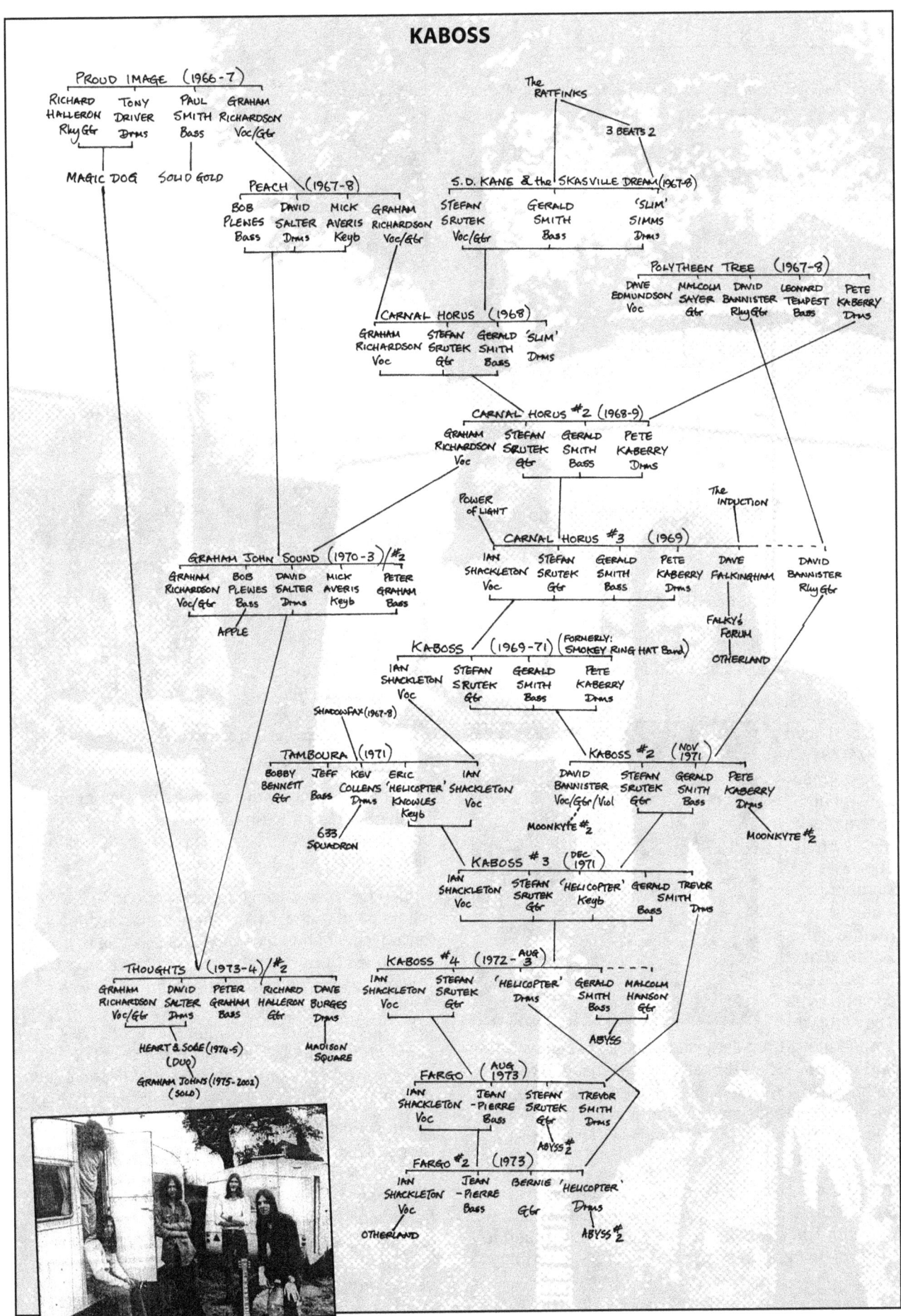

KEIGHLEY NEWS

Free festival brought 2,000 to Keighley park, but..
POP CONCERT A "FLOP"

The festival wasn't a flop, as the local paper stated, but due to the trouble and local pressure, it would be quite a few years before there was another free festival in the Cliffe Castle grounds.

KABOSS

Kaboss were one of the bands that played that day. They moved to London in 1972 where they lived in two caravans, trying to scratch a living and make a name for themselves in the music scene.

SPIRAL HIGHWAY

Spiral Highway (1971-73) were formed by Grahame 'Grom' Kelly after a brief spell with Auroborus when he returned to Bradford after the demise of Junior's Eyes. They toured around the UK regularly and, at a gig in Jarrow as part of Newcastle Art Festival, they encountered the growing 1970s far-right movement, when 'about seventy skinheads tried to start trouble, but the audience turned on them en masse and the police had to rescue them.'

In 1982, after being in a couple more bands in the 1970s, Grom resurrected his old blues band Midnight Train, with a new line-up, and continued to perform on the local music scene for the next thirty years.

RAWDON FESTIVAL

In July there was a free festival at Nunroyd Park, Rawdon, where more than two thousand people went to see eight groups, including Kaboss and Jan Dukes de Grey, who'd driven up overnight from London. It had been organised by students and staff from Aireborough Grammar School and raised £70 for the *Save The Children* charity.

1971 MORE CLUBS

In September men were targeted by staff at the Penny Farthing and Annabella's clubs for wearing the essence of petunia oil, as it was believed to disguise the smell of cannabis!

During October, a lively debate went on in the letters page of the *T&A*, around the subject of 'giving local bands a chance'. As Les Lea of Fagley bemoaned, *'I've seen the rise and fall of many clubs trying to desperately reconstruct the Bluesville / Jook Joint idea of good music. The reason why they fail is apathy on the part of the audience. I ask the Bradford rock fans, please don't put down our local groups, we have some fine ones that deserve your support.'* (6)

Then a week later in support of Les was Dave Stone of Undercliffe's letter; *'Many of the bands I've seen at the Tavern in the Town have been really first class, having good material of their own. A good band doesn't have to play the same sort of riffs all the time, does it? Groups with original material, whether they be local or not, are the ones which will be the groups of tomorrow.'* (7)

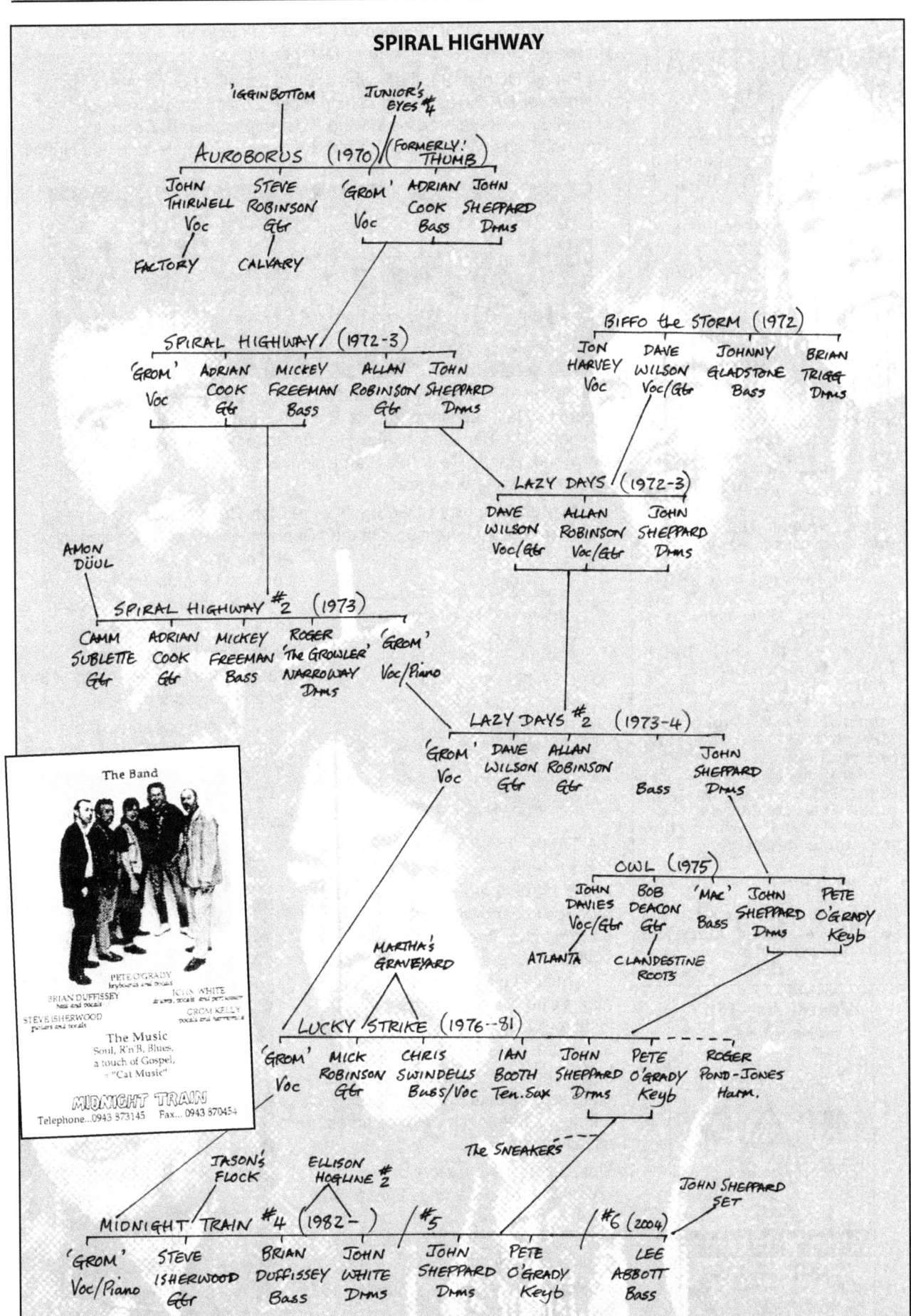

SKYNYRD STEAL THE SHOW

After coming on to the stage to a recorded fanfare of "I Wish I Was In Dixie" blaring through a few thousand watts, American group Lynyrd Skynyrd bounced into some good modern rock 'n roll music at St. George's Hall, Bradford last night.

Under an enormous confederate flag, the seven-piece band with four guitarists, proved to be even better "live" than on record. They have an excellent EMI album out a present called Second Helping and they performed many of the tracks themselves from it.

It is Lynyrd's first British tour but they are already establishing themselves as a very popular act.

Top of the bill Dutch band, Golden Earring — famed for their hit single Radar Love, were too jumbled. Poor amplification distorted a lot of their material.

Many of their songs are too repetitive and the group rely too much on echo chambers and various other electronic devices.

But the 1,100-strong audience didn't seem to care although I saw a few leaving before the end. Maybe the terrific volume of noise had got through to them.

SIMON ORRELL

Pink Floyd played for the second (and last) time in the city, at Bradford University Great Hall on Sunday, October 10.

On Friday, October 23, there was a 'Bust' benefit at St George's Hall where over £100 was raised to help those 'busted' for possession of marijuana. It featured Hawkwind (no surprise there!), Coum Transmissions, Wild Oates, Gentle Revolution, Stumble, and Jeff Nuttall. (8)

During the 1970s, many new and innovative bands performed at St George's Hall, like Deep Purple, Black Sabbath, Hawkwind, Lynyrd Skynard, The Sensational Alex Harvey Band, Wishbone Ash, Dr Feelgood, Randy California, Van Halen, Steve Hillage, Man, Be Bop Deluxe, to name but a few.

Another band to play St George's were Mott The Hoople who have a slight Bradford connection. On their September 1973 number ten hit *All The Way From Memphis*, from the LP *Mott*, the lyrics state, *'Through the Bradford cities in the Orioles.'*

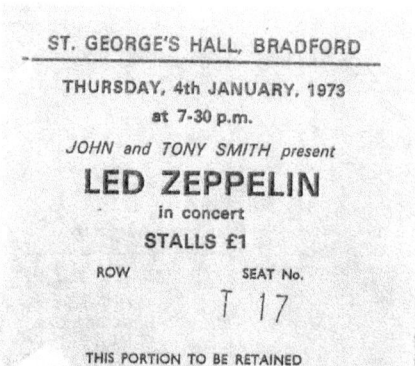

As the ticket shows, even probably the greatest band of that decade played too. (9)

Lez Zeppelin appeared there promoting their 1973 LP *Houses Of The Holy*, for princely the sum of £1 in the stalls.

German electronic pioneers Tangerine Dream also played on their first UK tour.

In the 1970s there was a lively local prog rock scene with many bands playing either their own material, standard covers or a mixture of both. They mainly gigged on the working man's club circuit or at the various local rock clubs that sprung up here and there.

Membership of the local scene was often very incestuous and group members' memories of those times are usually hazy.

Most bands have a story or two to tell, like *'selling a bike and gas fire to buy a PA amp'* or *'playing a full-on gig, complete with lights and a 5000 watt PA in a council flat'*.

Two other local groups around in 1971 were **Orion** and **Pigpen**.

CHAPTER 2 - PROG ROCK TO PUNK ROCK — 1971 - 1976

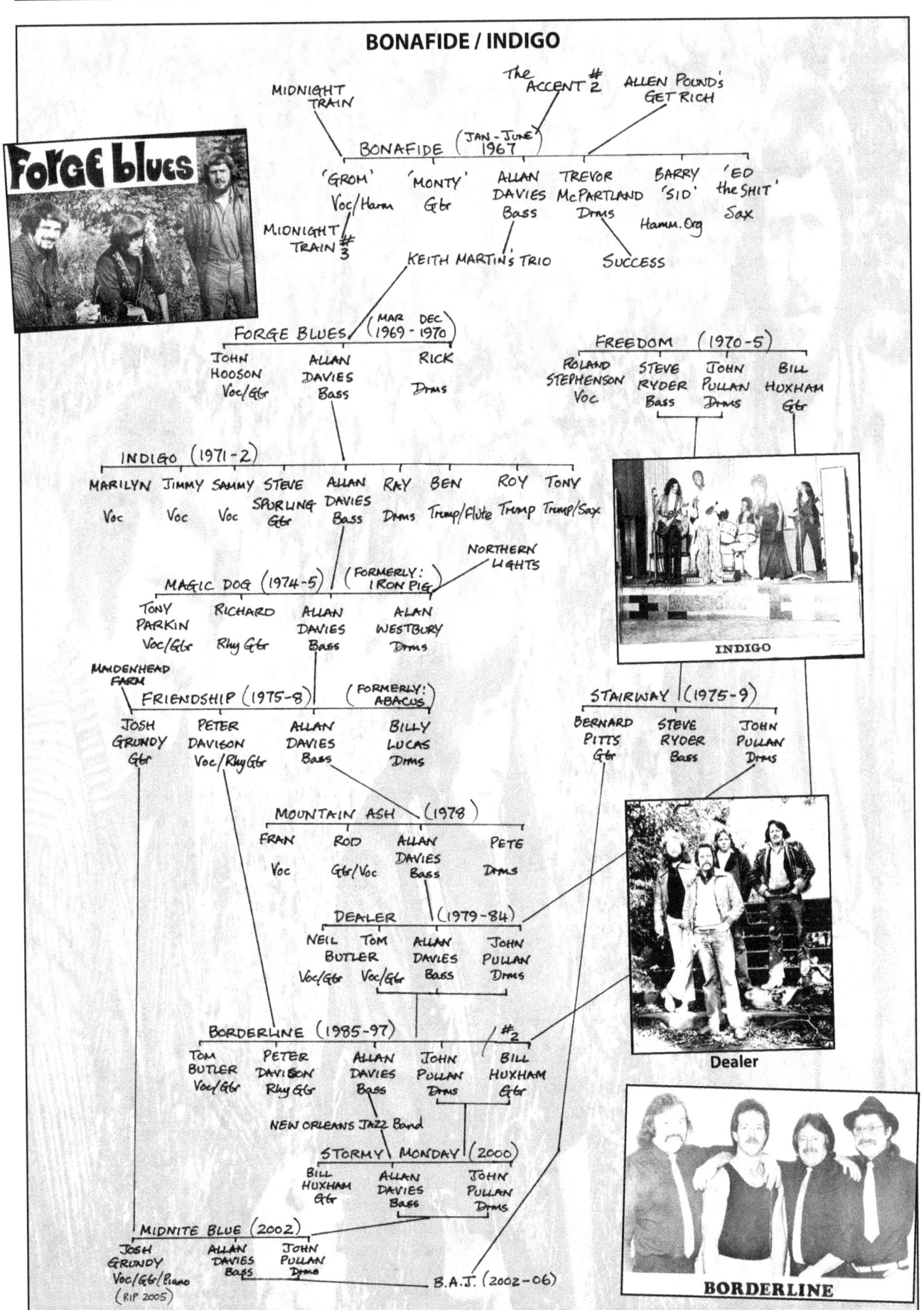

BONAFIDE / INDIGO

BICKERSHAW FESTIVAL 1972

Over the weekend of May 5-7 1972, in the Lancashire mining town of Bickershaw, entrepreneur Jeremy Beadle (the TV prankster, later to host shows including *Game For A Laugh*, *Beadle's About* and the original *You've Been Framed*) organised a pop and rock festival with some impressive bands. From the US came the mighty Grateful Dead, Quicksilver Messenger Service and Country Joe, with Bradford's own art-performance terrorists Welfare State being one of the opening acts.

In Idle, a team of karate experts demolished a stone cottage using only their bare hands, head and feet. Among the team were the brothers Mike and Denny from the Yorkshire rock and harmony group Greengage.

Other bands around in 1972 were: **Hadrian's Wall**, **Bitch, Hot Buttered Leg**, and **Gritt** from Pudsey.

HADRIAN'S WALL (1972)			
MARTIN KITSON	RAY BAXTER	JOHN HOWARD	CHRIS BOTTOMLEY
Voc	Gtr	Bass	Dms

In January, **The Rock Workshop** on Godwin Street closed down. It had been started by members of Spiral Highway, although at this time it was run by Pete Beaumont and Pat and Rod Long.

As Pete put it, *'We didn't aim to make a profit; any money we made went to the bands. It had been a good opportunity for new bands to play.'*

In the same month **The Medusa Club**, which was run from **The Criterion Discotheque** in Shipley, was also forced to close due to poor attendances.

On March 23, 1973, the Talbot Hotel on Darley Street (built in 1879) closed. It had once been the drinking haunt of Branwell, brother of the Bronte sisters, who also apparently purchased his laudanum (opium) from the establishment.

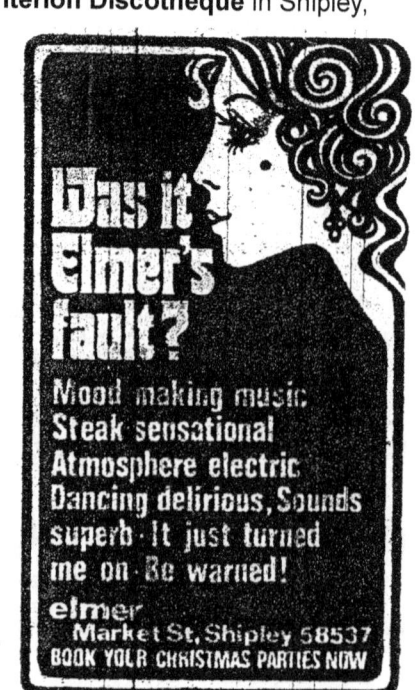

CHAPTER 2 - PROG ROCK TO PUNK ROCK 1971 - 1976

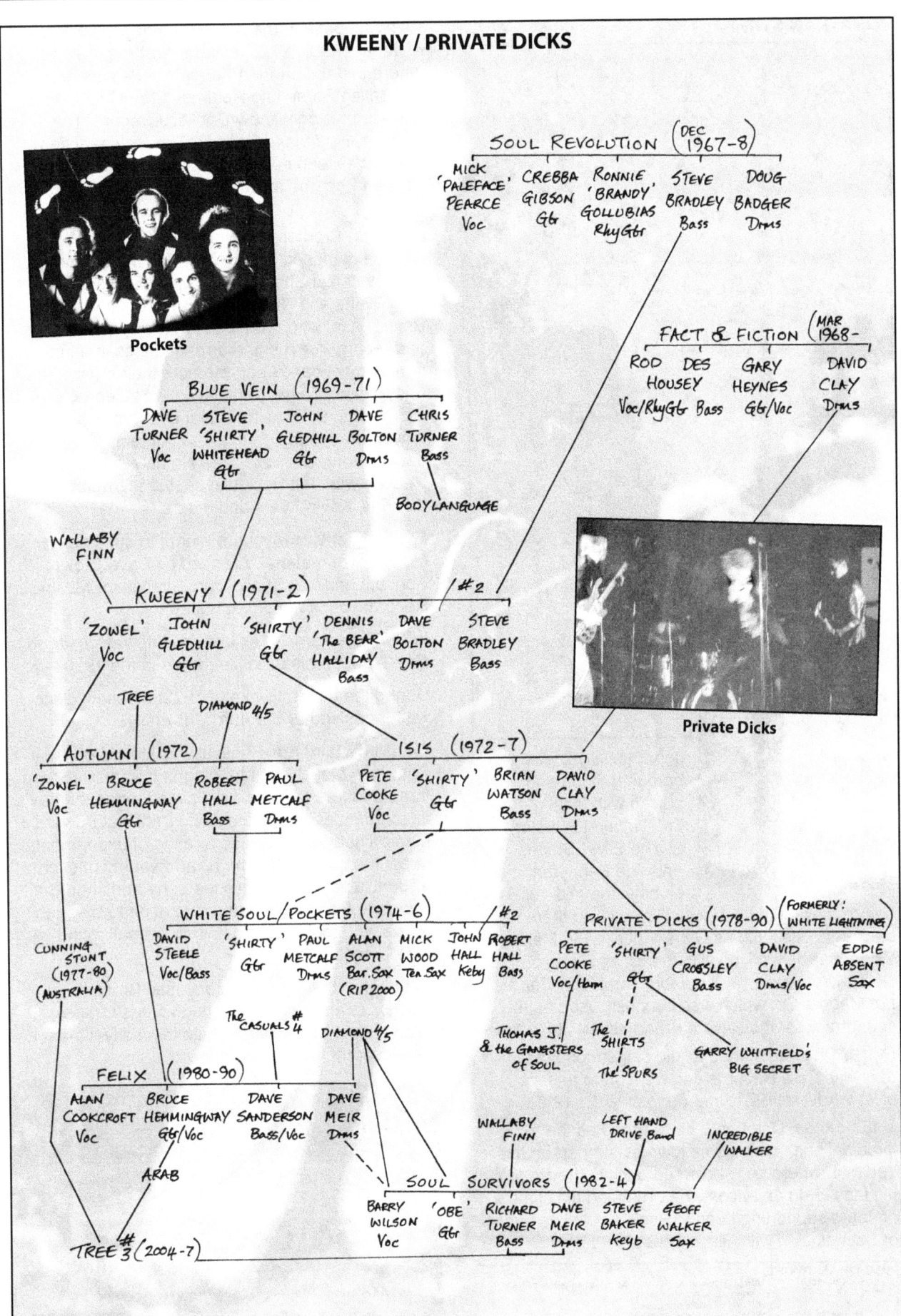

KWEENY / PRIVATE DICKS

JONATHAN SWIFT

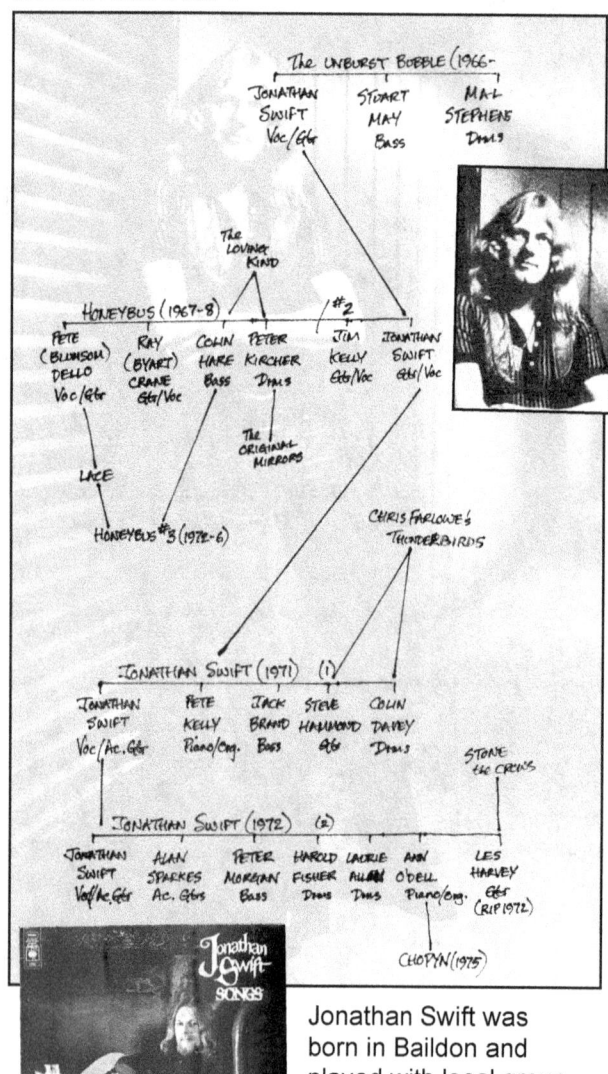

Jonathan Swift was born in Baildon and played with local group The Unburst Bubble at The Silver Blades and The Pennyfarthing clubs in the mid-1960s, before moving to Liverpool. Whilst living there he backed artists such as Gene Vincent and Marty Wilde, before working with the group Honeybus. He co-wrote their 1968 number eight hit, *I Can't Let Maggie Go*, which was famously used as the soundtrack for the Nimble Bread advert at the time.

By 1971 he had signed a solo singer/songwriter deal with CBS Records and went on to release two LPs; *Introvert* (1971) and *Songs* (1972). (9)

On Saturday, October 2, he returned as the 'prodigal son' to his home town as support on the Yes tour, where he was forced back to the stage by his fans to do an encore. He promoted his albums on tours supporting Leon Russell, as well as a tour of Scandinavia with Black Sabbath.

JONATHAN SWIFT			
70	MCA MU 1130	Afraid Of Tomorrow/I Haven't Got Anything Better To Do	5
72	CBS 7931	Corinna/Just This Morning	5
71	CBS 64412	INTROVERT (LP, nude cover)	12
72	CBS 54751	SONGS (LP, with lyric insert)	12

As a response to the Bloody Sunday massacre of January 30, 1972, in Derry, Northern Ireland, where thirteen unarmed people were shot dead by the British Parachute Regiment, Paul McCartney released his only known 'political' record. The single, *Give Ireland Back To The Irish*, reached number sixteen in the charts and then was promptly banned from the airwaves by the BBC on February 26!

In March, Bradford's Community & Information Service launched a self-contained management agency called Shaft. It was run by David Brown, Mick Watts and Nick Nicholson of Mandrake Enterprises, who produced and designed posters and record sleeves and arranged gigs in an attempt to help local bands and promote their music. They had to cancel a gig organised for St George's Hall, featuring Stray and East Of Eden, but then they started to put on gigs at Fountain Hall, at the back of John Street Market. Notably, on March 30, Heaven with Jeff Beck played, then Graham Bond, Kweeny, Kevin Ayers and others.

Local band **Kweeny** were meant to cut a demo of their own material, financed by Dave Brown, in April at London's Chalk Farm Studios for Mushroom Records, but it never happened.

In 1975 the name of **Fountain Hall** was changed to **Gatsby's**, and later to **Benson's** in the 1980s.

During the miners' strike of 1972, a benefit disco was organised at Bradford University.

Bradford's third Arts Festival was staged on Saturday, May 26, at Manningham Park. Between three and four thousand people attended the day's assortment of bands, including Principal Edward's Magic Theatre, as well as a range of experimental street theatre artists. The bizarre variety of events also included a children's tea party and John Bull Puncture Repair Outfit, a group of performance artists who took a public bath in a small round plastic pool.

At the end, the organisers accused Bradford Council of not providing enough funds for the festival, and of wanting to oust the festival team and take over the events themselves.

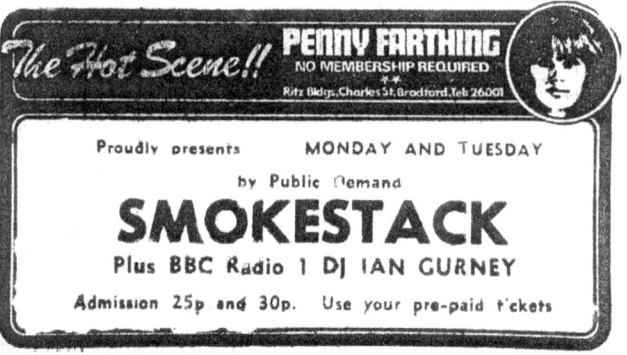

PARK AVENUE POP FESTIVAL

On the bank holiday Monday, May 28, 1972, Bradford's first-ever outdoor 'pop festival' was held at Park Avenue football ground. It ran from 11 am to 8 pm for an entry fee of one pound in advance. The festival was organised by *Five Star Promotions* of Driffield and cost around £10,000 to stage.

The directors of Five Star, Dave Thorley and Dave Barker, expected a crowd of twenty thousand; they said, *'the festival was aimed at the average disco user, the average girl who works in a shop… not for people into folk or the 'heavy' stuff.'* (10)

The main bands were: Gary Glitter, Mungo Jerry, Blackfoot Sue, and The Equals (featuring Eddie Grant who later had hits in the 1980s, including Electric Avenue).

Most of these acts had had top ten hits in the year before the festival, so it should have been a success.

Other bands included first on the bill Midnight Blue, Pagan Chorus from Barnsley, and The Weasels.

On the day of the event, the promoters had tried to prevent ticket fraud, but despite fans sleeping out overnight, and coach parties coming from as far as Plymouth, Wales and London the event ended as a flop as only two thousand people attended and the promoters lost money.

In 1972 Keighley born Simon Frith, a senior lecturer in sociology at Warwick University, completed a 'youth survey' of Keighley's music scene. He interviewed one hundred and five youths between the ages of fourteen and eighteen at schools and colleges in the town about their attitudes and opinions on British music culture.

What he noticed was a distinct separation on the lines of class and age between fans of rock and fans of pop. Rock fans were into progressive/heavy/ folk music, buying LPs, going to gigs and were mainly middle class (although in no way exclusively) who tended to stay on at school to do A levels, whilst fans of commercial pop chart/radio music bought singles, watched *Top Of The Pops* and went to discos. They were mainly working-class kids who had left school at sixteen.

Obviously, not all youth fitted this easy pigeon-holing, as one said, *'I have assorted friends; some 'hairys' (long hairs/hippies), some Crombie Boys and Girls (skinheads gone 'smooth' who wore Crombie overcoats). I can sit and listen to both sorts of music and don't mind either. I'm in between a skinhead and a hippy, I wear mod clothes, but I like both kinds of music.'*

Another interviewee clearly identified with the rock scene, saying, *'Progressive and heavy are fantastic. If they were not there life would not be worth living. They are the backbone behind music as a whole, showing us what it should really be like.'*

Overall, at this time period, what Simon identified was that *'both types of different, but occasionally crossing over music cultures provided a background soundtrack to the youths' everyday life, fitting their individual interests and leisure needs with the radio or records that were always on.'*

JOHN VERITY

Queensbury lad John Verity worked with various local groups in the 1960s, but by 1969, he was living and working in America.

Whilst there, he formed the original lineup of the John Verity Band, who supported many of the big names of the day. On returning to the UK in 1971, he began work with producer Steve Rowland in a new version of his band Family Dogg.

By March 1972, John was back in his hometown village of Queensbury, building his homemade SHY Studio in a cellar, and helping to produce demo tapes for local bands.

He formed the second version of the John Verity Band with other local musicians and recorded and released his first LP, *John Verity Band*, on Probe Records.

The band got a management deal with Argent's manager Mel Collins, and over the next few years, they gathered a large loyal local following from their constant gigging.

That line-up played their last gig at the Tavern In The Town Rock Club on December 22, 1974.

After the departure of original lead guitarist and vocalist Russ Ballard John joined Argent in 1975. Ballard was the band's joint songwriter (with Rod Argent and Chris White) and had written their top twenty 1973 single *God Gave Rock'n'Roll To You*. American rock band Kiss revived the song in 1992 and their cover version was a huge hit, reaching No 4 in the charts.

Lead guitarist John Grimaldi (pictured, far left) joined Argent at the same time as John.

The band left CBS and signed a record deal with RCA. The new lineup released the albums *Counterpoints* in 1975 and *Circus* in 1976.

John Verity stayed with Argent until they split in 1976. He then formed the band Phoenix with the Argent rhythm section of Jim Rodford and Bob Henrit (both of whom later joined The Kinks).

As Phoenix, the trio released a self-titled LP in 1976, produced by John Verity on CBS Records. Their second album, *In Full View*, came out in 1979 on the Carisma label. They later played at the Princeville Rock Club in Bradford.

After Phoenix, John and drummer Bob Henrit joined the band Charlie in 1980.

The next band John fronted was the simply named Verity. He teamed up with fellow Bradfordians Terry Uttley of Smokie on bass and Andy 'Tiddy' Wells, formerly of Baby Tuckoo, on keyboards. They recorded the album *Interrupted Journey*, released on PRT Records in 1981. The album, *Rock Solid*, followed in 1989.

By 1992, he had relocated from his native Yorkshire to rural Bedfordshire, where he continued to gig with a version of the John Verity Band in the UK and abroad. He has released many solo albums, including *Its A Mean Old Scene* (2012), *Tone Hound On The Last Train To Corona* (2014), *My Religion* (2016), *Blue To My Soul* (2017) *Passion* (2020) and *Blue* (2022) on the VaVoom Records label.

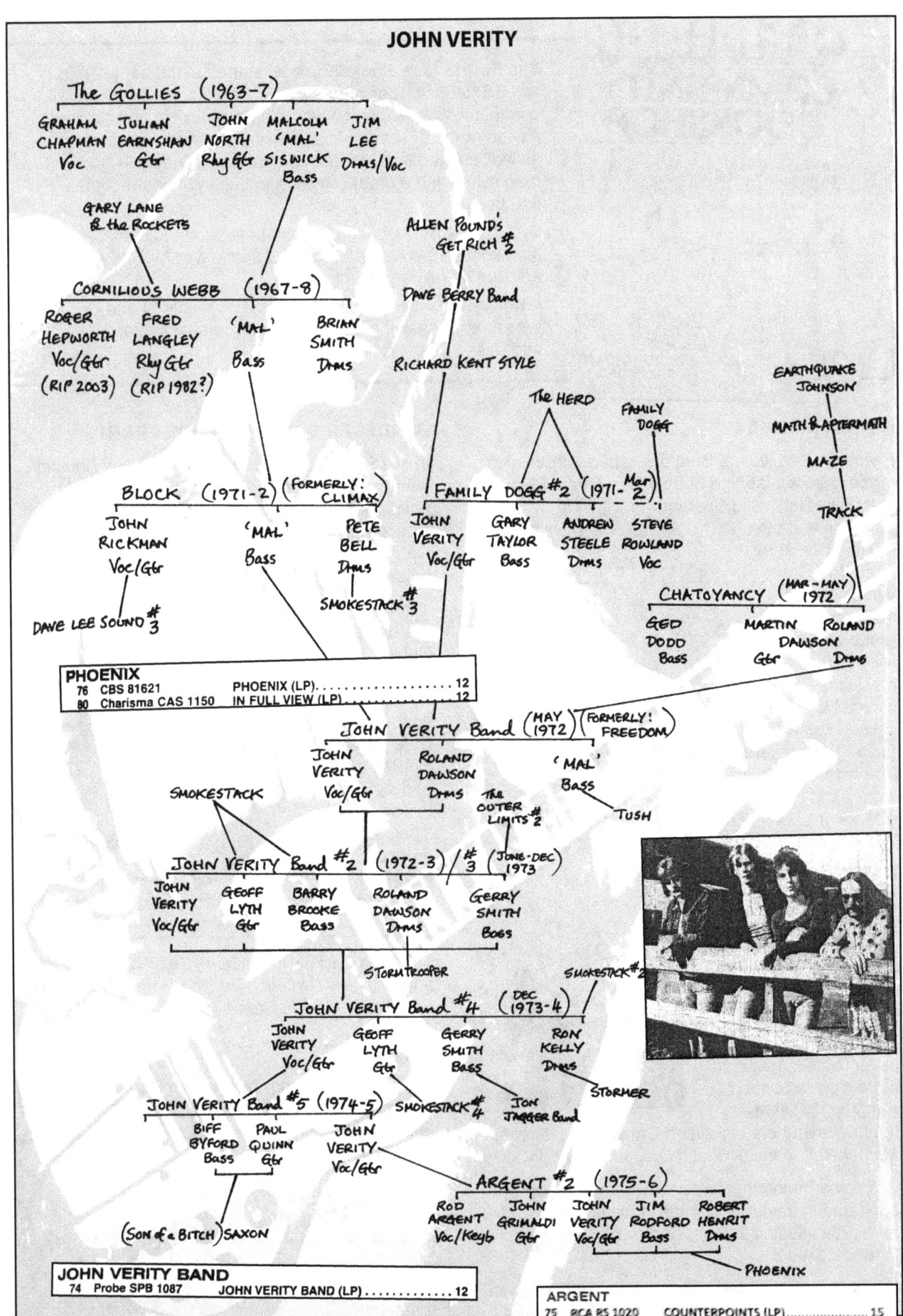

The Fourth Idea Bookshop was started in the early 1970s at 14 Southgate (behind the old Sunwin House) as a radical, community bookshop. It was run as a collective and stocked a wide range of academic books on humanities subjects, as well as the latest independent novels, periodicals and magazines and a great selection of second-hand records and books.

By 1974 it was described as, *'the best alternative/radical bookshop in the North-East, good stock, well laid out and efficient as well as friendly.'* (12)

It was also a meeting place for Bradford's activist and pressure groups who used the premises as a contact address.

RIVINGTON PIKE

Rivington Pike were a Bradford cabaret group formerly known as The Bobbie Gee Three. Before that, Mike Berry and Sharon Vaughan had been in The Mike Berry Sect. They were a versatile, multi-instrumental group who released a single on Decca Records in October 1971, called *Wish A Little Love / I'll Be There*. The record sold well locally and got them plenty of work, including a date at London's **Talk Of The Town** club and fifteen weeks on a world cruise.

CATHERINE HOWE

Catherine Howe, a folk singer/songwriter from Halifax, released her debut LP, *What A Beautiful Place*, on Reflection Records in 1971. During the mid seventies she released three more albums; *Harry* in 1975 (which features members of Fairport Convention), *Silent Mother Nature* in 1976, and *Dragonfly Days* in 1979.

Before her recording career, she was an actor and appeared in many TV dramas in the late '60s and early '70s inluding *Z-Cars*, *Doctor Who* and *Dixon Of Dock Green*.

She returned to recording years later with *Patience Street* in 2005.

BRADFORD GAY LIBERATION FRONT

In 1975, the *Campaign For Homosexual Equality* (which had started in 1964) released a limited edition four track EP entitled *Bradford Gay Liberation Front* on their own Chebel Records. (13) Only around two or three hundred copies were pressed and it is now very collectable.

The main vocalist on the single was Tom Robinson, who had joined the London based acoustic trio Cafe Society in 1973 and had signed to The Kinks' Kong label and produced one LP in 1975.

```
TOM ROBINSON (BAND)
75   Chebel SRT/CUS 015   GOOD TO BE GAY (EP, as Bradford Gay Liberation Front)...15
```

The EP's tracks were side A; *Glad To Be Gay* and *The Gay Switchboard Jingle*, and, side B; *Schizophrenia* and *Stand Together*.

The song *Glad To Be Gay* was a precursor to the 1978 hit *Sing If You're Glad To Be Gay* (although a totally different song) by the Tom Robinson band off their four track EP *Rising Free*. The band had previously had a number 5 hit single with *2-4-6-8 Motorway* in October 1977. Tom's only other big hit was in June 1983 with *War Baby* as a solo artist, which reached number 6.

CHAPTER 2 - PROG ROCK TO PUNK ROCK   1971 - 1976

ROCK STRIFE

During the early 1970s, the *Telegraph & Argus* ran an article in it's music column by Simon Orrell about the decline in the music club scene. Clubs had helped and encouraged the growth of new bands on the local scene since the mid-1960s, with the start of clubs like The Little Fat Black Pussycat, The Hole in the Wall, The Penny Farthing, The Silhouette, Bluesville/Jook Joint, The Appollo, Rock Workshop and The Medusa.

Scorched Earth

Rock strife — and trouble lifts ugly head at Medusa

The boom in rock music has hit Bradford but two clubs, offering good music at low prices, are struggling for funds.

They are the Tavern in the Town Club and the Rock Workshop, Godwin Street. And in Shipley, the Medusa which ran at the Criterion Discotheque, has closed after difficulties.

Both city centre clubs cater for people who like heavy, bluesy groups with plenty of guts. Much of it is local talent, although the Tavern club is now looking further afield for new groups.

The Tavern is run by Gordon Hopps and Dave Preston, two former members of the Bradford band Scorched Earth.

The club, which meets every Sunday night, has been running for over a year and is doing better than ever. It runs, remarkably, on an admission fee of 25p and sometimes less.

"We don't make much profit," said Gordon. "In fact, I have to guarantee a certain amount of money to groups myself, and often have to make the amount up."

The atmosphere is good with everyone there to hear one thing — good rock music.

By SIMON ORRELL

The rock workshop, run by Pete Beaumont, with Pat and Rod Long, has seen bad times recently.

The workshop was originally started by local group, Spiral Highway and then about two months ago Pete, Pat and Rod started booking different groups.

Although the admission fee was only 15p for an evening's entertainment very few people took advantage.

"We do not aim to make profit," said Peter. "Any money we do make goes to the bands. It is a good opportunity for new bands to play at the club."

A wrong type of member has forced the closure, for the second time in two years, of the Medusa Club. Chris Ormondroyd, who ran the club, said: "Last week the rock band Honk were jeered at. We feel we just cannot carry on."

Poor attendances caused concern but recent behaviour has just been too much.

Chris was bitterly upset: "Running the Medusa has been costing us money and although we didn't want to make any profit, we have been losing too much."

Medusa had a big following about two years ago when the Club was held at Butterfields Social Club, Shipley.

"We had well over a hundred people who used to come every week come rain or shine," said Chris. "A lot of these have settled down now, though and don't want to leave their firesides."

With discotheques running at large profits and charging up to £1.50 entrance fee, it amazes me why, especially on week days, people do not flock into the rock clubs.

The few who do support the clubs each week certainly appear to enjoy themselves. The atmosphere is friendly and many local groups go along to watch other bands at work.

THE COLLECTION

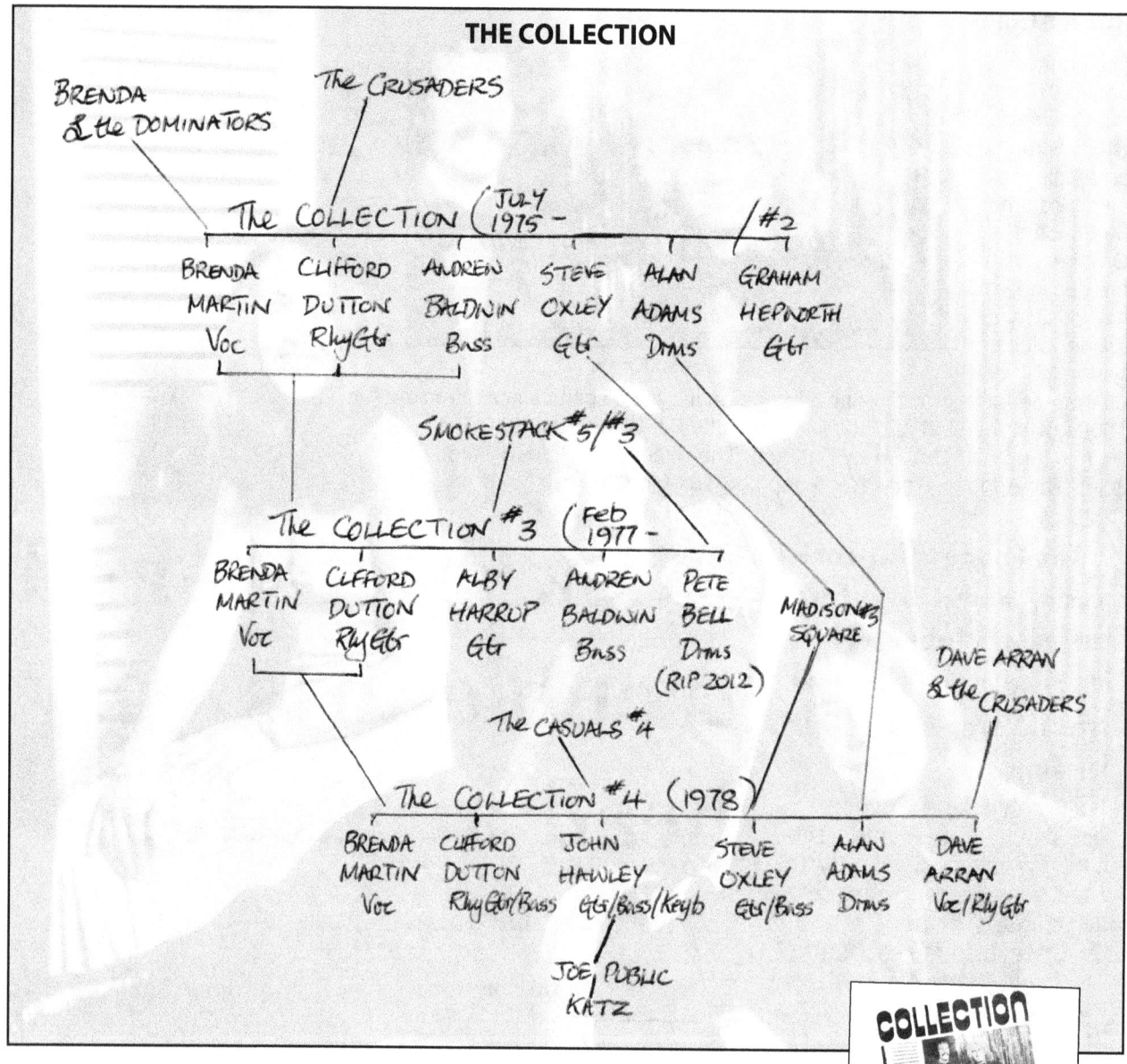

THE COLLECTION

Out of the many semi-professional local bands of the 1960s to '70s who plied their trade playing covers on the working men's club scene, The Collection were one of the most proficient and were highly regarded by fellow local musicians.

The group released their self-titled twelve track LP of cover versions in 1976. The album was recorded at Fair View Studios in Hull.

The back cover sleeve notes are reproduced here (pictured right).

Lead by guitarist Clifford Dutton, the band continued gigging around the local scene into the late 1970s.

Since its birth in 1966 "Collection" like every other band has had it's ups and downs, changes in personnel etc. But the determination of it's founder Cliff has finally paid off. During the ten years to the present line-up many fine musicians have worked with the band; notably Alan Holdsworth voted Britain's No. 1 Jazz Guitarist and drummer Pete Spencer of "Smokie".

It was in 1970 when with the absence of a lead vocalist, the band decided to take a chance and change from the most popular format of a four piece all male line-up, to one of a five-piece, with a female lead vocalist, the right decision? The music on this Album answers that. The band have managed to re-create here on wax the warmth generated by their music during a live stage show from which this is a short selection. This Album represents the years of hard work and the thousands of miles travelled by the band always with the inner belief that "One Day It Will Happen". All the members of the band would like to thank you for buying the Album and sincerely hope you enjoy this new addition to your "Collection".

CHAPTER 2 - PROG ROCK TO PUNK ROCK — 1971 - 1976

VIRGIN DUDES / NEW THREAT / OMEN

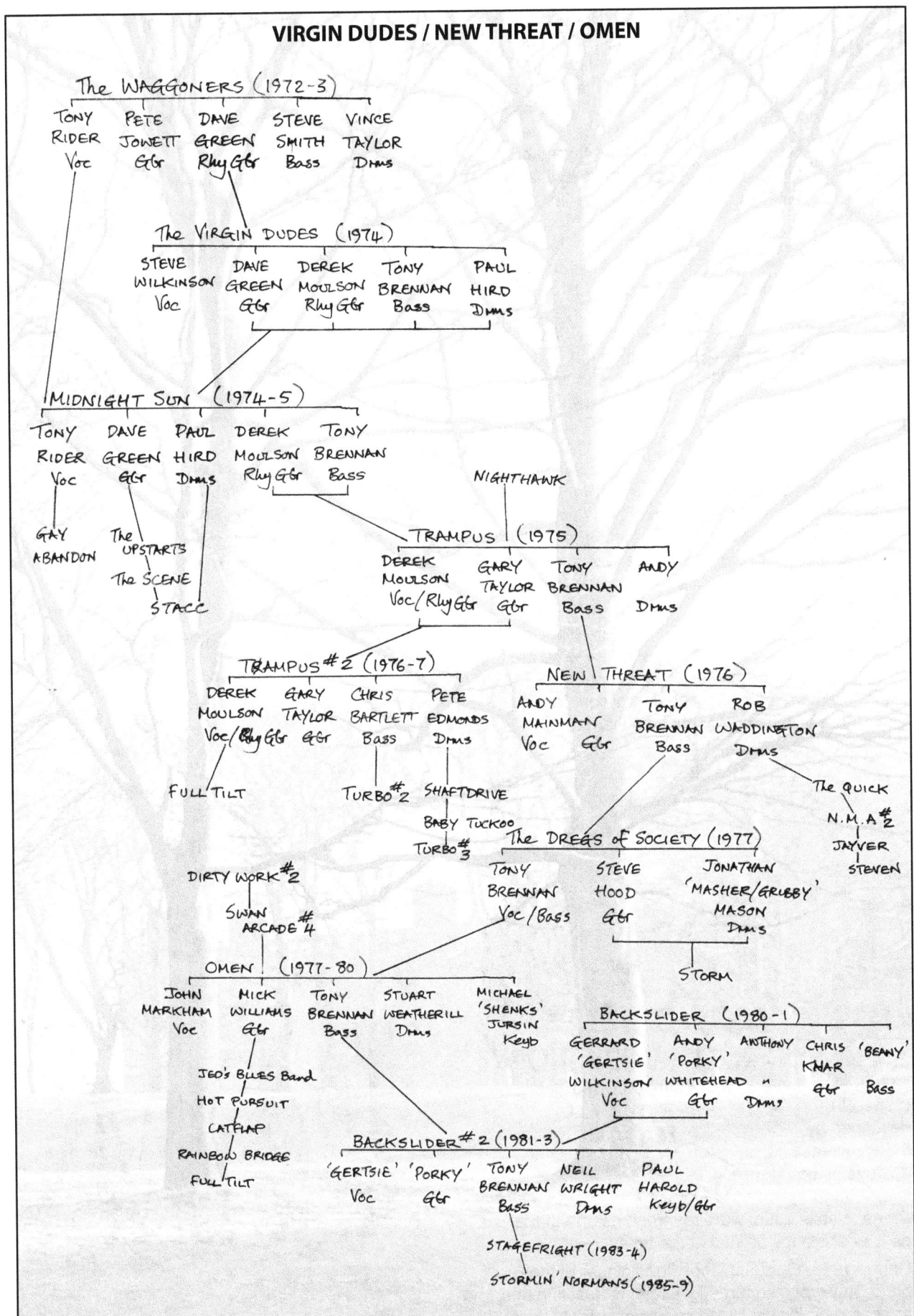

> **Court told of 'payment by cannabis'**
>
> Instead of paying for two LPs with money, a man gave a girl shop assistant a quantity of cannabis in exchange, Mr David Jones, prosecuting, told Bradford magistrates yesterday
>
> Jeffrey Exley, aged 28, unemployed, of 4 Carleton House, Bradford, pleaded guilty to receiving two stolen records, three cases of being in unauthorised possession of cannabis and supplying cannabis without being authorised.
>
> The case was adjourned for three weeks for medical and social inquiry reports to be prepared.

Dope For LPs! T&A 24th May '73

On September 22, 1973, the first ever Northern Soul night was run at the Wigan Casino. Two days later, on the 24th, author Gary Cavanagh had his first taste of live music when he went to see Status Quo and Savoy Brown at St George's Hall, for only 50p. *'The next ten gigs I went to included; Hawkwind, Focus, Mott The Hoople, The Strawbs, Black Sabbath, Alex Harvey Band, Tangerine Dream, Golden Earring and Lynyrd Skynyrd. This was quite an introduction to the live music scene for a young lad in the seventies, in an era when major bands still played in Bradford on a regular basis.'*

Bradford's fondly remembered Kirkgate Market was demolished on November 3, to make way for John Poulson's hideously designed concrete mall. A protest demo tried to stop the demolition, leading to thirty-three arrests on obstruction charges.

MIDAS

Local groups **Larry Ankle** and **Why Not Sneeze** were also around in 1973.

In April 1974, Bradford was enlarged and turned into a Metropolitan District Council, taking in the townships of Keighley, Bingley, Haworth and Ilkley. It became a larger urban-rural conurbation as part of local government reform. This made Bradford the seventh-largest city in the UK.

By 1974 the *T&A's* half-page feature on the local rock and pop scene was renamed the *Rock On* column, under the stewardship of reporter Simon Orrell.

In June Rock On did an article on Bradford's 'dying' concert scene, under the headline, *'Where have all the fans gone?'* in which local concert promoter Jane Beeker stated that she would not book bands for Bradford in the near future, because of *'the poor ticket sales and lack of response at attracting people to gigs.'* (14)

A number of musicians, unable to find enough paying gigs as members of prog rock groups, formed club bands in order to get work with agencies playing cover versions on the club circuit.

On August 30, 1974, the police raided the Windsor Free Festival and caused a major battle as undercover officers arrested hippies for drug related offences.

Bradford band Midas (1969-75), described by the local press as developing into a King Crimson style outfit, were regarded as one of the best local groups around at the time.

During 1973, Gordon Hopps (lead singer of the band Stuvxyz) also turned his talents to acting and appeared on locally filmed soap *Emmerdale Farm*.

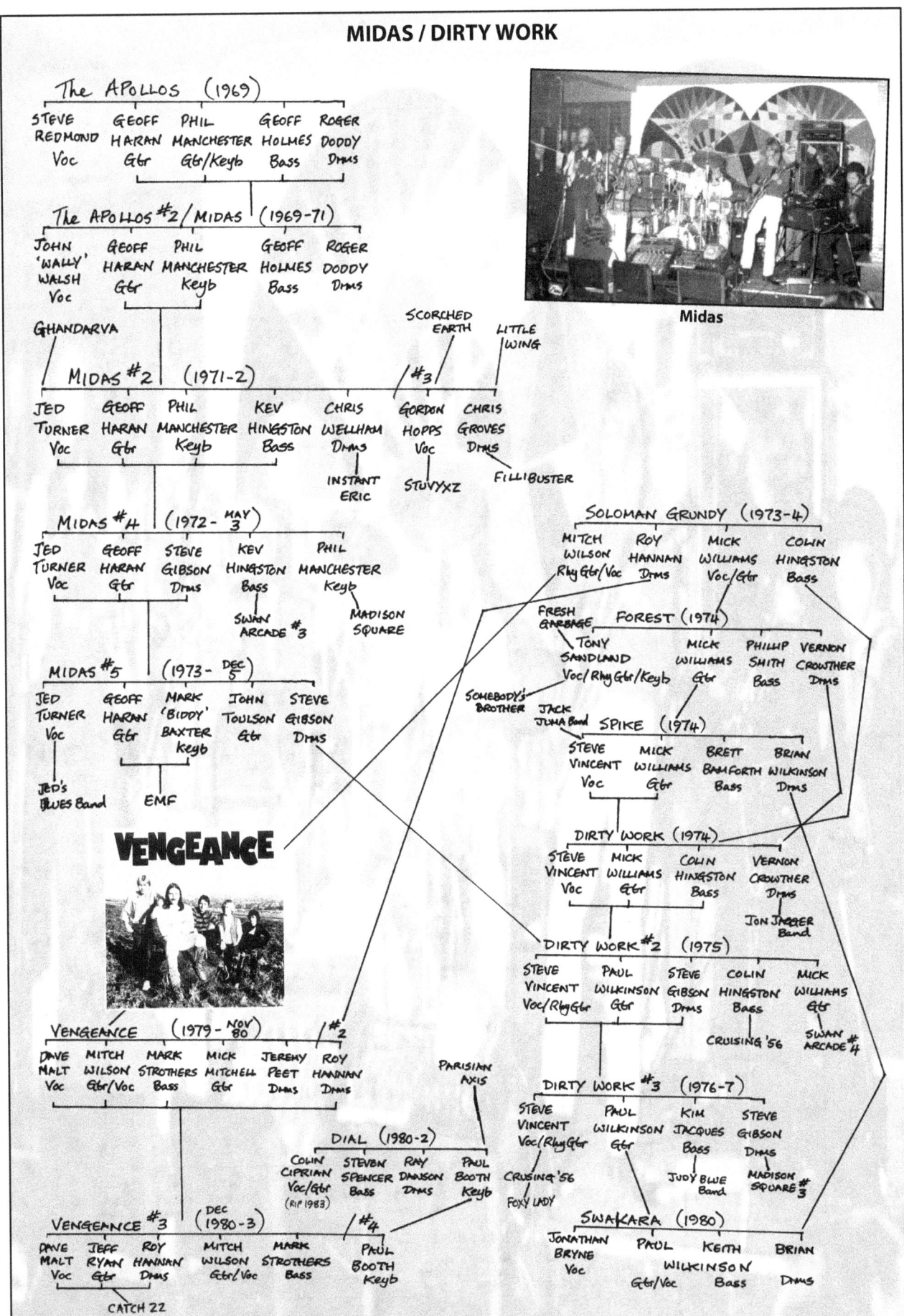

Midas

SMOKESTACK

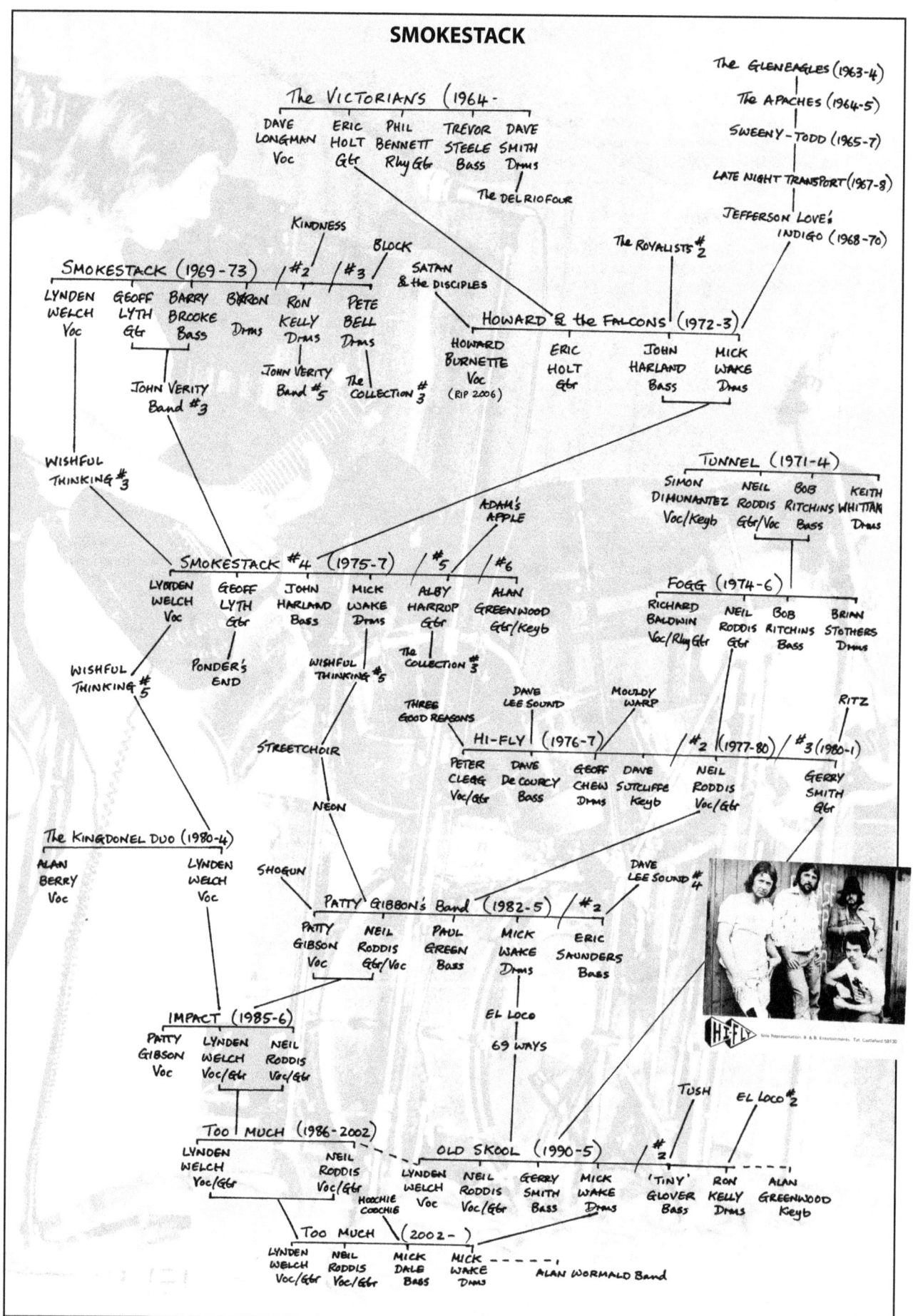

CHAPTER 2 - PROG ROCK TO PUNK ROCK — 1971 - 1976

SPLASH ALLEY

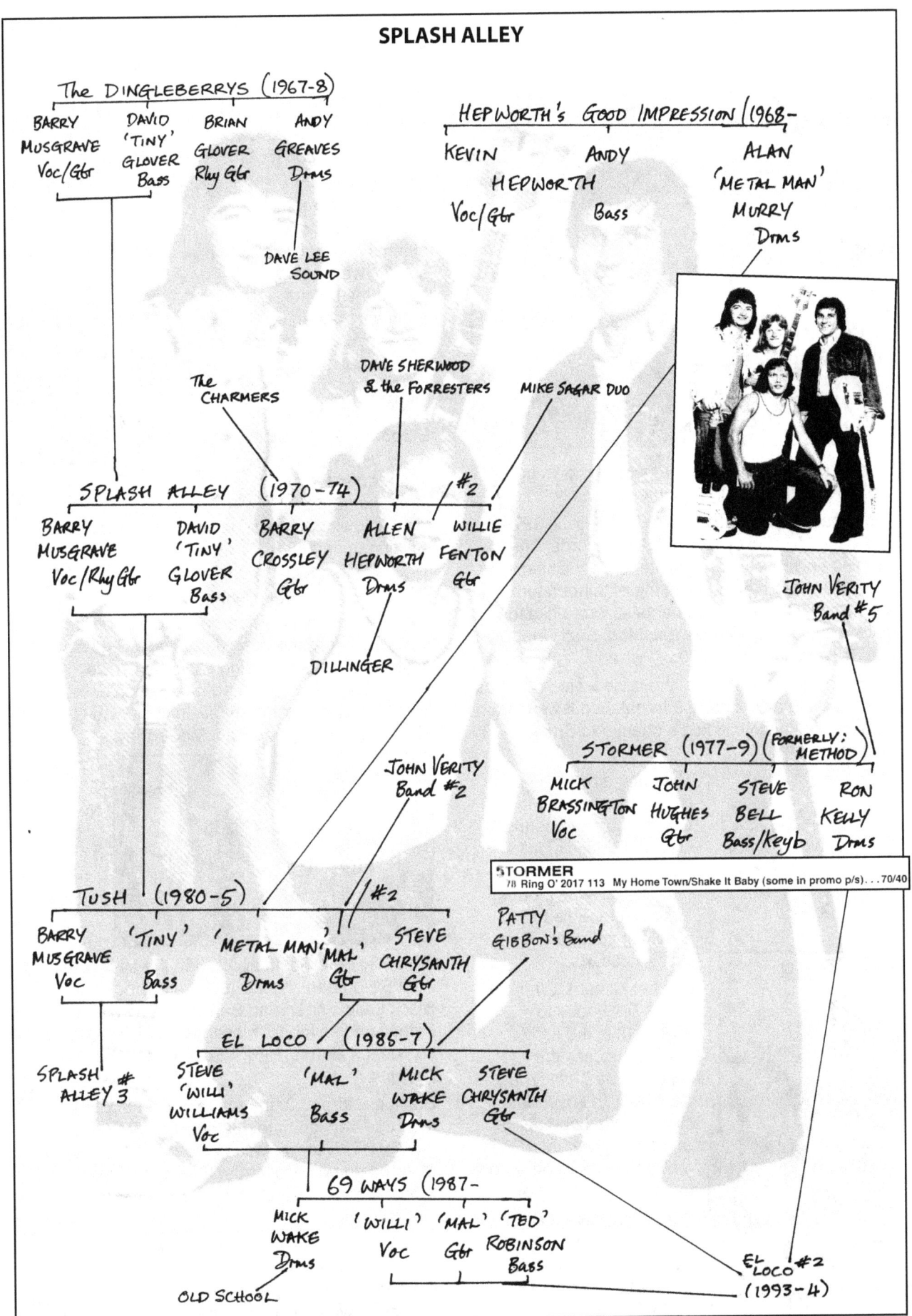

The Dingleberrys (1967-8)
- Barry Musgrave — Voc/Gtr
- David 'Tiny' Glover — Bass
- Brian Glover — Rhy Gtr
- Andy Greaves — Drms

Dave Lee Sound

Hepworth's Good Impression (1968-)
- Kevin Hepworth — Voc/Gtr
- Andy — Bass
- Alan 'Metal Man' Murry — Drms

The Charmers →
Dave Sherwood & the Forresters →
Mike Sagar Duo →

Splash Alley (1970-74) #2
- Barry Musgrave — Voc/Rhy Gtr
- David 'Tiny' Glover — Bass
- Barry Crossley — Gtr
- Allen Hepworth — Drms
- Willie Fenton — Gtr

Dillinger

John Verity Band #5

Stormer (1977-9) (formerly: Method)
- Mick Brassington — Voc
- John Hughes — Gtr
- Steve Bell — Bass/Keyb
- Ron Kelly — Drms

STORMER
78 Ring O' 2017 113 My Home Town/Shake It Baby (some in promo p/s)...70/40

John Verity Band #2

Tush (1980-5) #2
- Barry Musgrave — Voc
- 'Tiny' — Bass
- 'Metal Man' — Drms
- 'Mal' — Gtr
- Steve Chrysanth — Gtr
- Patty — Gibbon's Band

Splash Alley #3

El Loco (1985-7)
- Steve 'Willi' Williams — Voc
- 'Mal' — Bass
- Mick Wake — Drms
- Steve Chrysanth — Gtr

69 Ways (1987-)
- Mick Wake — Drms
- 'Willi' — Voc
- 'Mal' — Gtr
- 'Ted' Robinson — Bass

Old School

El Loco #2 (1993-4)

85

LIVING NEXT DOOR TO SMOKIE

Smokie are probably Bradford's best-known group of the 1970s, nationally and internationally.

They changed their name from Kindness in 1974 and signed to Mickey Most's RAK Records. After teaming up with chart songwriters Nicky Chinn and Mike Chapman they had a string of thirteen top twenty hits. Chinn & Chapman also wrote hits for many groups, including Sweet, Mud, Suzi Quatro and Racey during the 1970s.

For their first three albums, the band were known as Smokey (with a 'y') before a threatened lawsuit from Smokey Robinson initiated a change to Smokie (ending in 'ie').

Their first album, *Pass It Around*, spawned the Chinn\Chapman penned title track which didn't make the BBC Radio playlist as it was thought to be a reference to smoking cannabis. Both failed to charts.

Their next album, *Changing All The Time*, rose to number 18 in the charts after the success the singles *If You Think You Know How To Love Me*, which reached number 3, and *Don't Play Your Rock 'n' Roll To Me*, another top ten, getting to number 8.

Both singles were Chinn/Chapman compositions although band members wrote the majority of album tracks.

After their rise to popularity in 1975 with two albums and two hit singles the next year brought more success. 1976's Midnight Cafe spawned two more chart singles but two non-album singles brought them the biggest success. *I'll Meet You At Midnight* got to number 11 followed by their most famous hit, *Living Next Door To Alice*, which reached number five.

The next two years brought two more albums and a run of six top twenty singles before their chart popularity began to wane in 1979, the era of new wave and the ska revival.

With regular tours in Europe (they became really big in Germany) and around the world the band gathered a loyal following and sold millions of records before splitting up in 1983.

They re-formed in 1985, initially for a one-off benefit concert in aid of the Bradford City Fire Disaster. The man responsible for their reformation was fellow Bradford musician John Verity, who also organised the benefit single by The Crowd. *You'll Never Walk Alone* featured a collection of musicians from Bradford and further afield, including Gerry Marsden, Lemmy and Paul McCartney.

Singer Chris Norman had started a solo career and decided not to continue and drummer Pete Spencer also left the band. Guitarist Alan Silson and bassist Terry Uttley recruited Black Lace singer Alan Barton, drummer Steve Pinnell and keyboard player Martin Bullard for their comeback album, 1989's *Boulevard Of Broken Dreams*.

Smokie returned to the top ten in 1995 with a re-recorded version of teir biggest hit. The retitled *Living Next Door to Alice (Who the F**k Is Alice)* featured guest vocals from blue comedian, Roy 'Chubby' Brown which reached number three in the charts. (15)

Despite personnel changes, Smokie continued to perform to loyal fans around the world. After the death of bassist Terry Uttley in 2021, Smokie continued with no original members in the lineup.

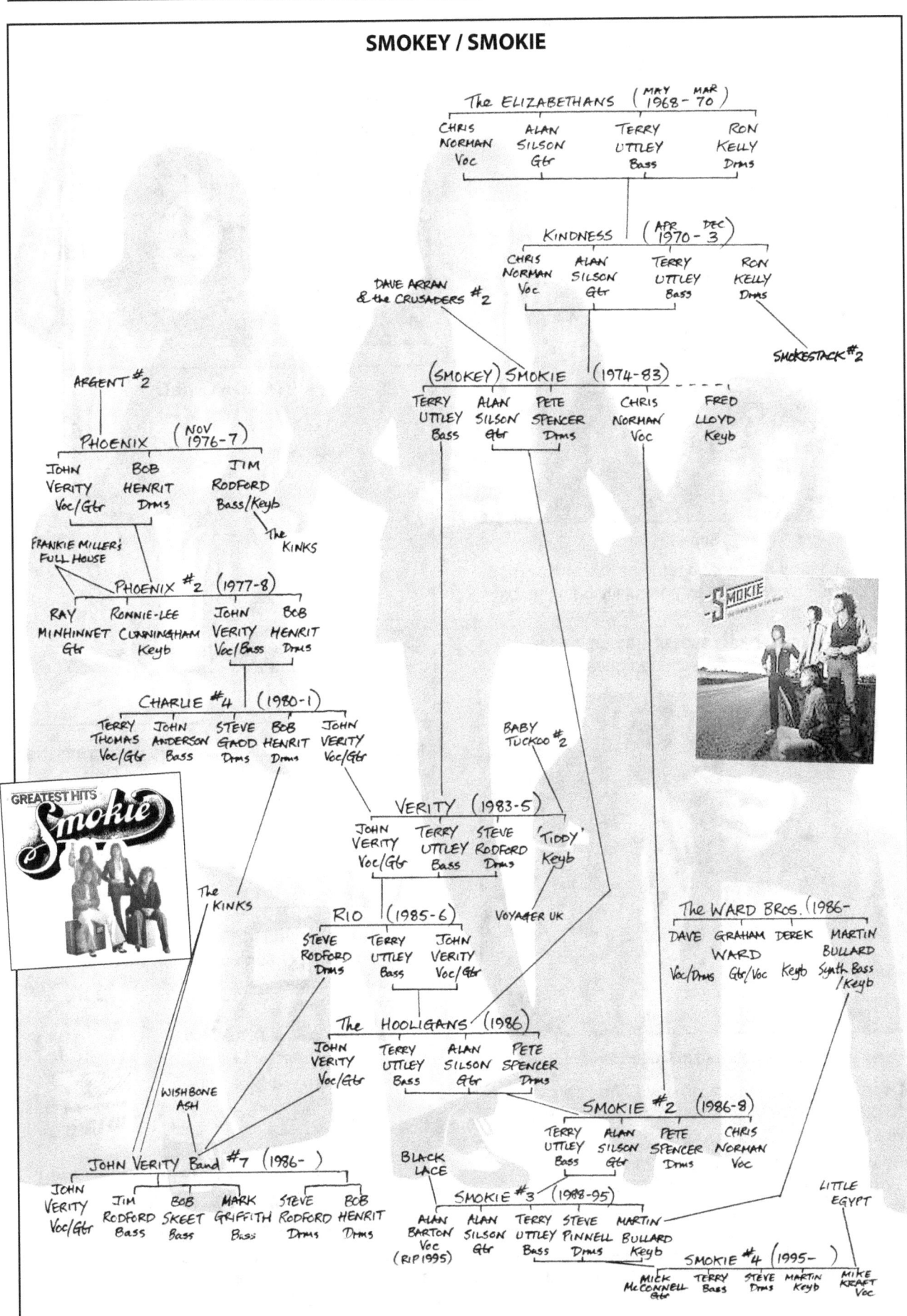

On February 11, 1975, the British Conservative (Tory) Party elected a new leader, Margaret Thatcher, who later would become prime minister. Depending on your view of her reign, she would be responsible for British rejuvenation and economic prosperity or the asset-stripping of traditional industries, mass unemployment, war-mongering and economic deprivation for the least able in society.

In the same month, local Black African-Caribbean band Superfly (who had been around since 1969)

Superfly

were touted by their manager Mike Watson (a BBC technician/cameraman) as potentially being as big as the then chart group Sweet Sensation.

They could have had a shot at stardom as their vocalist, Desmond Jefferson, had once been in

Medicine Head at Queen's Hall

Desmond Dekker's backing band The Aces. In September Superfly supported chart act Medicine Head at Queen's Hall.

Between 1975 and around 1982 in Halifax, **The Good Mood Club** at 15 Crown Street, previously known as **Clarence's** and before that **Big Daddy's**, was putting on regular gigs. Gary Cavanagh went to see Welsh rockers Budgie play there and also saw The 101ers, Joe Strummer's pre-Clash band, on January 31, 1976.

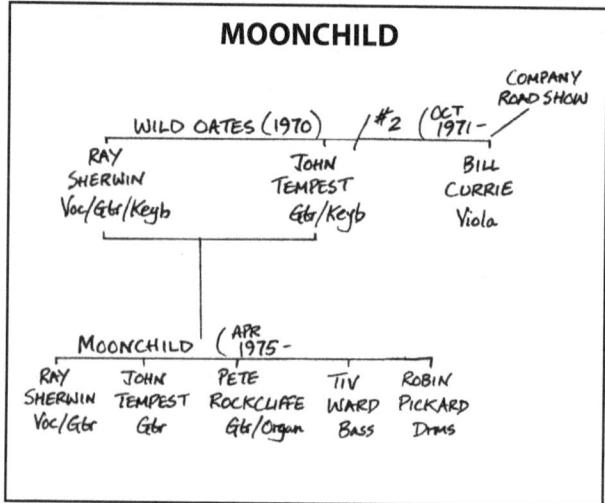

Moonchild, a Bradford band whose line-up included two ex-members of local folk duo Wild Oats, released a single in 1975 before even doing a gig! That first gig was at The Tavern In The Town Rock Club in October 1975.

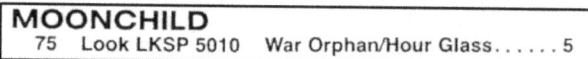

Another band around in 1975 was a bunch of Bradford University students called **Dirty But Nice**.

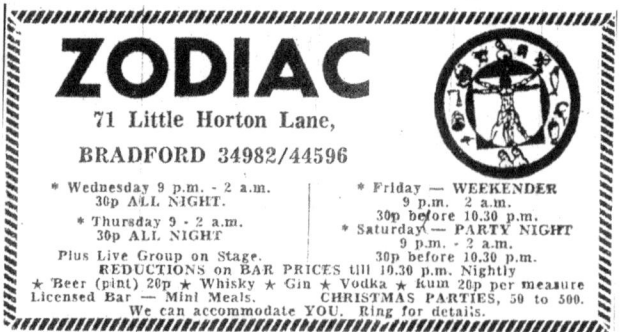

In 1976 **The Zodiac Discotheque**, at the bottom of Little Horton Lane (later the site of 1980s rock venue **The Frog And Toad**), was another venue putting on gigs at the time.

CHAPTER 2 - PROG ROCK TO PUNK ROCK   1971 - 1976

HIGHTIMERS / SUPERFLY

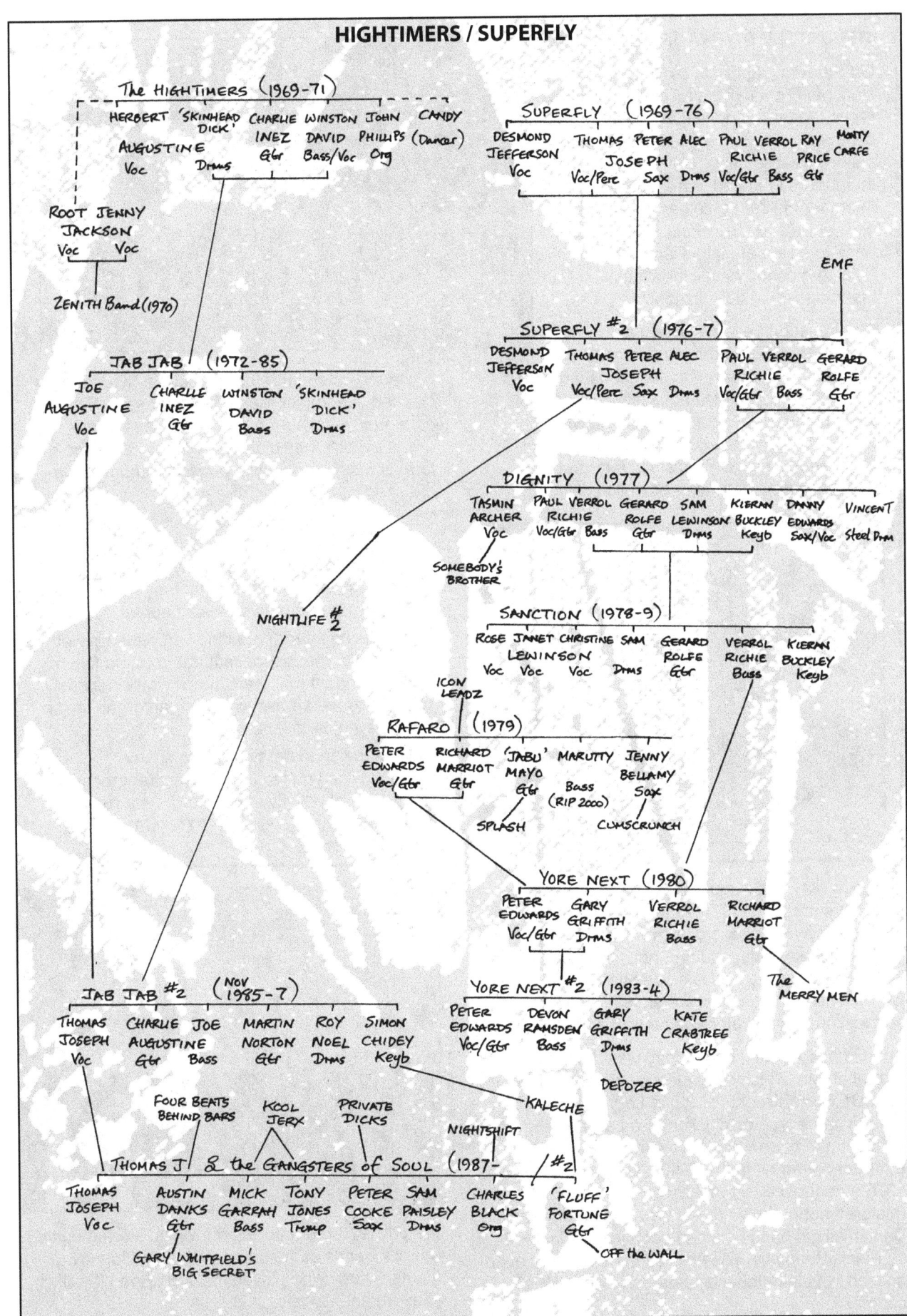

THE BATTLE OF BRADFORD

On Saturday, April 24, 1976, the National Front (NF), a fascist/racist organisation, held a rally to commemorate St Georges Day for the second year running. The 1,500 NF supporters intended to march from Infirmary Fields (Lumb Lane) into the city centre and then along Manningham Lane to a rally at Lister Park before holding a controversial meeting at Manningham Middle School.

What ensued became known as *The Battle Of Bradford*. A counter demonstration of three to five thousand anti-fascists, made up of various left-wing groups, trade union workers, and Asian and white working class was organised by the *Ad-Hoc Committee Against Fascism* to interrupt the march. Around four hundred police officers battled to defend the fascists as the two groups clashed. NF leader Martin Webster said, *'These communists (sic) mobs must understand that organisations they disagree with have a right to express their opinions publicly without being attacked.'* (16)

The police were attacked by the anti-fascist demonstrators with stones, bottles, bricks and eggs. Helmets were sent flying and two police cars were overturned as they made the obligatory arrests of twenty-six people.

Whilst the counter demo didn t stop the rally or the meeting, the response it got from the folk of Bradford meant that the Council would seriously think again before allowing such an organisation to hold a similar event.

It also showed the resistance to such organisations and led to a future strengthening of anti-fascist activity in Bradford. As a result, the Asian Youth Movement (AYM) was formed later that year.

Between May and August Britain suffered the long hot summer of 1976. At the time it was the hottest ever on record, with withering heat, plagues of ladybirds, and drought, with most towns in the South having to use standpipes. People were advised to conserve water, leading to the suggestion, 'Save water - bathe with a friend!'

Then in mid-August, the country was deluged by torrential rain, which continued for ten days. **The Talk Of Yorkshire**, at the top of Leeds Road, was still the same type of 'chicken-in-a-basket' cabaret venue it had been when it was known as **The Lyceum Rainbow** in the 1960s. On August 21, 1976 a controversial band called The Ladybirds (pictured right) played there; they were a topless Danish all girl band who had been formed in 1968 by Pierre Beauvais. They toured the world and even caused riots in Indonesia, a predominantly Muslim country.

In April 1978 promoter Martin Wood started putting on rock bands at the same venue on Monday nights. Those who played included Son Of A Bitch (Saxon) and Gygafo. (17)

CHAPTER 2 - PROG ROCK TO PUNK ROCK 1971 - 1976

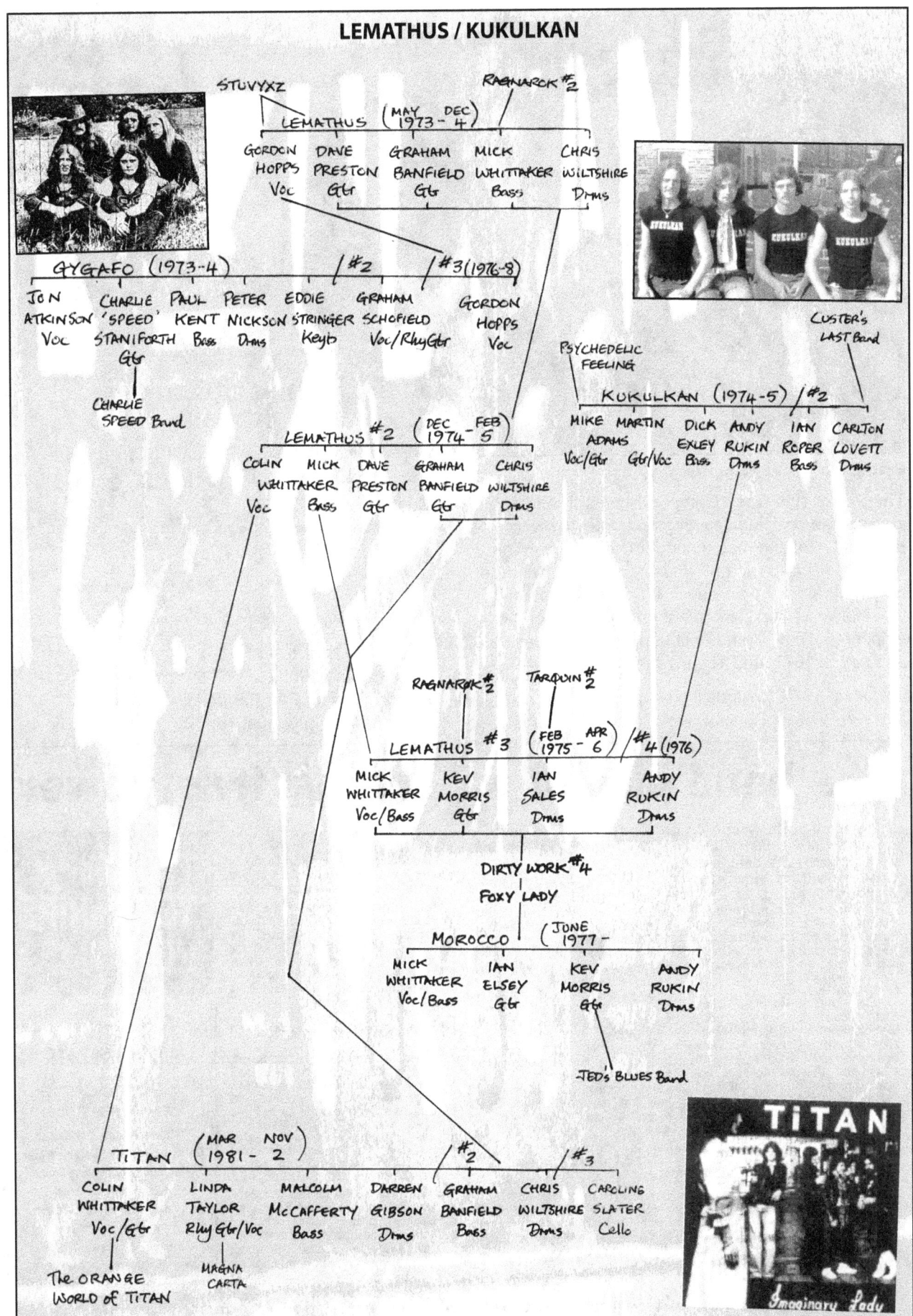

LEMATHUS / KUKULKAN

Bradford heavy rockers Azel

The Princeville Rock Club, on Princeville Street, was started on Thursday, September 2, 1976, by the band Azel and their manager Dave King. In the early days it also ran on Sunday lunchtimes with the added attraction of a stripper! It became a haven for local West Yorkshire talent (the bands - not the strippers!). Dirty Work / Phobia played there on January 3, 1977, and The Invaders on April 24.

From late 1978 onwards it championed the rise of the New Wave of British Heavy Metal (NWOHM) which included bands like Saxon, Samson, Vardis, Limelight, and lots more.

It later moved to Gatsby s, where it ran until June 1982, and then to **The Pile Bar** on Lilycroft Road, Manningham, in August 1982.

The band played on — using free power

Although the supply had been disconnected because of unpaid bills, electricity was free for the band practices at a house in Woodlands Road, Bradford, the city magistrates heard.

It presented no problem to the occupier, 24-year-old Ian Sales, when his friends brought their instruments for rehearsals because he just plugged in to the houses next door, the court was told.

Sales, now of Horton Grange Road, Bradford, pleaded guilty to dishonestly using electricity, attempting to dishonestly use electricity, burglary at an office and two offences of unlawful possession of drugs.

He was jailed for six months.

Mr. John O'Kane, prosecuting, said Sales plugged into the supply at two houses on each side of his own when he was living in Woodlands Road.

From bedroom

The offences were discovered when PC Michael Hopwood, attending a fire in the street, saw an electric lead going from the bedroom of one house to another. Further inquiries revealed that there had also been a lead going from Sales's kitchen to the kitchen of another house.

When Sales was questioned he made a statement in which he said he had had his own supply cut off and had used electricity from one house next door after the occupiers had left.

When the supply to that house had been disconnected he had run a lead to another empty house, but claimed he had not started to use electricity from that house before he was caught.

Meters unread

Mr. O'Kane said it was not possible to calculate how much electricity had been used dishonestly because the meters at the houses had not been read when the previous occupiers left.

Mr. O'Kane said that Sales had also been arrested late at night inside an office in Laisteridge Lane, Bradford. A window had been broken and a calculator had been moved.

On another occasion he was at a house in Oak Villas, Bradford, when it was visited by police officers of the drug squad. He admitted to them that he had recently had an injection of pethidine and had smoked cannabis.

Small amount

Mr. David Taylor, for Sales, said Sales connected to the electricity of the houses next door when he was unemployed and had been unable to pay his bills, but only a small amount was used. He said Sales claimed the electricity was used only for lighting for a brief period.

Mr. Taylor said the burglary was committed when Sales had been drinking excessively. He was not addicted to drugs and the evidence about the drug offences was solely his frank admission.

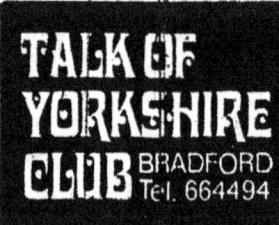

TALK OF YORKSHIRE CLUB BRADFORD Tel. 664494

CABARET
All this Week

LOVE AFFAIR

TUESDAY
is mid-week party nite.

Wining, Dining, Dancing to Garth Cawood and Rainey Walker plus the Mike Stewart Sound.

Open 9 p.m. to 2 a.m.
It's only 25p before 10.30 p.m.
Monday to Friday
50p before 10.30 p.m. Saturday.
NO MEMBERSHIP REQUIRED

Rehearsals were powered for free from the house next door! Telegraph & Argus 1st July 1976

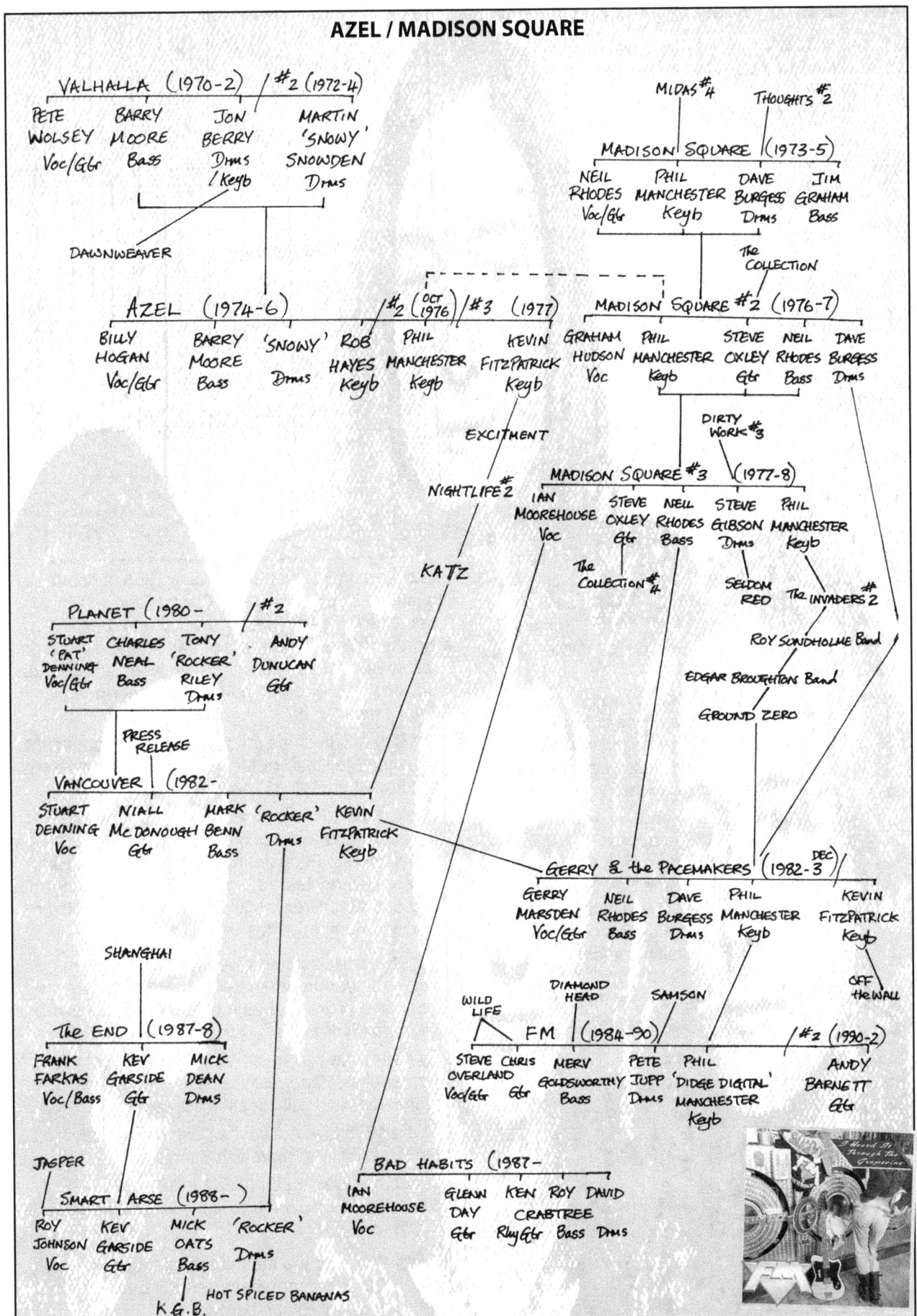

KIKI DEE HITS TOP SPOT

In July 1976 local lass Kiki Dee topped the pop charts with *Don't Go Breaking My Heart* – a duet with Elton John which was at the top for six weeks and stayed in the charts for another eight weeks.

On November 21, she played a hometown gig at St George's Hall for two thousand enthusiastic fans. The highlight of the evening was the encore when Elton arrived on stage wearing a Bradford Northern (Bulls) scarf, which was a total surprise to Kiki, with whom he then performed their number-one hit song. The next year she was voted *Top Female Singer* in the UK in the music press.

Kiki was born Pauline Matthews in March 1947. After leaving school she worked as a counter assistant at Boots the Chemists while singing in local dance bands in the evening.

She was given her stage name by songwriter Mitch Murray and her manager Vic Billing before she released her debut single *Early Night* in March 1963. The next year she turned professional.

In February 1965 she appeared at the International San Remo Song Festival in Italy and in the same year appeared in the British comedy *Dateline Diamonds* - a film about a jewel thief involved with a pirate radio ship.

Her debut LP, *I'm Kiki Dee* was

released on Fontana Records in 1968. It contained a later B-side, *On A Magic Carpet Ride*, which, because of its psychedelic/soul sound, became a Northern Soul classic. In the same year, she helped fellow Bradfordian Mick Jackson when she provided backing vocals for Love Affair's number-one hit, *Everlasting Love*.

In 1969 Kiki became the first female British artist to be signed to Detroit's Motown Records, where she recorded her *Great Expectations* LP.

Back in the UK in the early 1970s, she was in a musical limbo and working the cabaret circuit before she signed to Elton John's Rocket Records. Her career was revitalized, and in 1973 she had her first of six top twenty hits with *Amoureuse*, which reached number thirteen.

In 1981, whilst signed to Ariola Records, she had another number thirteen hit with *Star*, which was used years later as the theme to ITV's *Bob's Opportunity Knocks*.

By 1984, she was in the West End musical *Pumpboys & Dinettes* which included ex-Manfred Mann vocalist Paul Jones in the cast.

At the 1985 Live Aid concert she performed *Don't Go Breaking My Heart* with Elton John.

In another West End musical in 1988, Willy Russell's *Blood Brothers*, she was nominated for an Oliver Award.

She reached the top ten again in 1993 with *True Love*, another duet with Elton John, which got to number two.

CHAPTER 2 - PROG ROCK TO PUNK ROCK 1971 - 1976

The next year she met her future musical partner Carmelo Luggeri with whom she began writing songs and performing as a duo.

An LP called *Almost Naked* was released in 1995, and in 2004, after more than forty years in the music business, Kiki released a new album, *Walk Of Faith*.

KIKI DEE

63	Fontana TF 394	Early Night/Lucky High Heels	15
63	Fontana TF 414	I Was Only Kidding/Don't Put Your Heart In His Hand	10
64	Fontana TF 443	Miracles/That's Right, Walk On By	18
64	Fontana TF 490	(You Don't Know) How Glad I Am/Baby I Don't Care	12
65	Fontana TF 596	Runnin' Out Of Fools/There He Goes	10
66	Fontana TF 669	Why Don't I Run Away From You?/Small Town	15
67	Fontana TF 792	I'm Going Out (The Same Way I Came In)/We've Got Everything Going For Us	10
67	Fontana TF 833	I/Stop And Think	8
67	Fontana TF 870	Excuse Me/Patterns	8
68	Fontana TF 926	Can't Take My Eyes Off You/Hungry Heart	8
68	Fontana TF 983	Now The Flowers Cry/On A Magic Carpet Ride	65
70	Tamla Motown TMG 739	The Day Will Come Between Sunday And Monday/ My Whole World Ended (The Moment You Left Me)	15
73	Rocket PIG 2	Lonnie And Josie/The Last Good Man In My Life	7
65	Fontana TE 17443	KIKI DEE (EP)	35
66	Fontana TE 17470	KIKI DEE IN CLOVER (EP)	30
68	Fontana (S)TL 5455	I'M KIKI DEE (LP)	40
70	Tamla Motown STML 11158	GREAT EXPECTATIONS (LP)	55

MUTTON CHOPS

Local band Mutton Chops (the nick-name of men's long sideburns) were described as '*a poor man's Bonzo Dog Doo Dah Band*'.

They were a cabaret turn cum heavy rock outfit who performed a collection of old vaudeville songs and send-ups of current chart hits. (18)

MUTTONCHOPS / MIDDLE 8

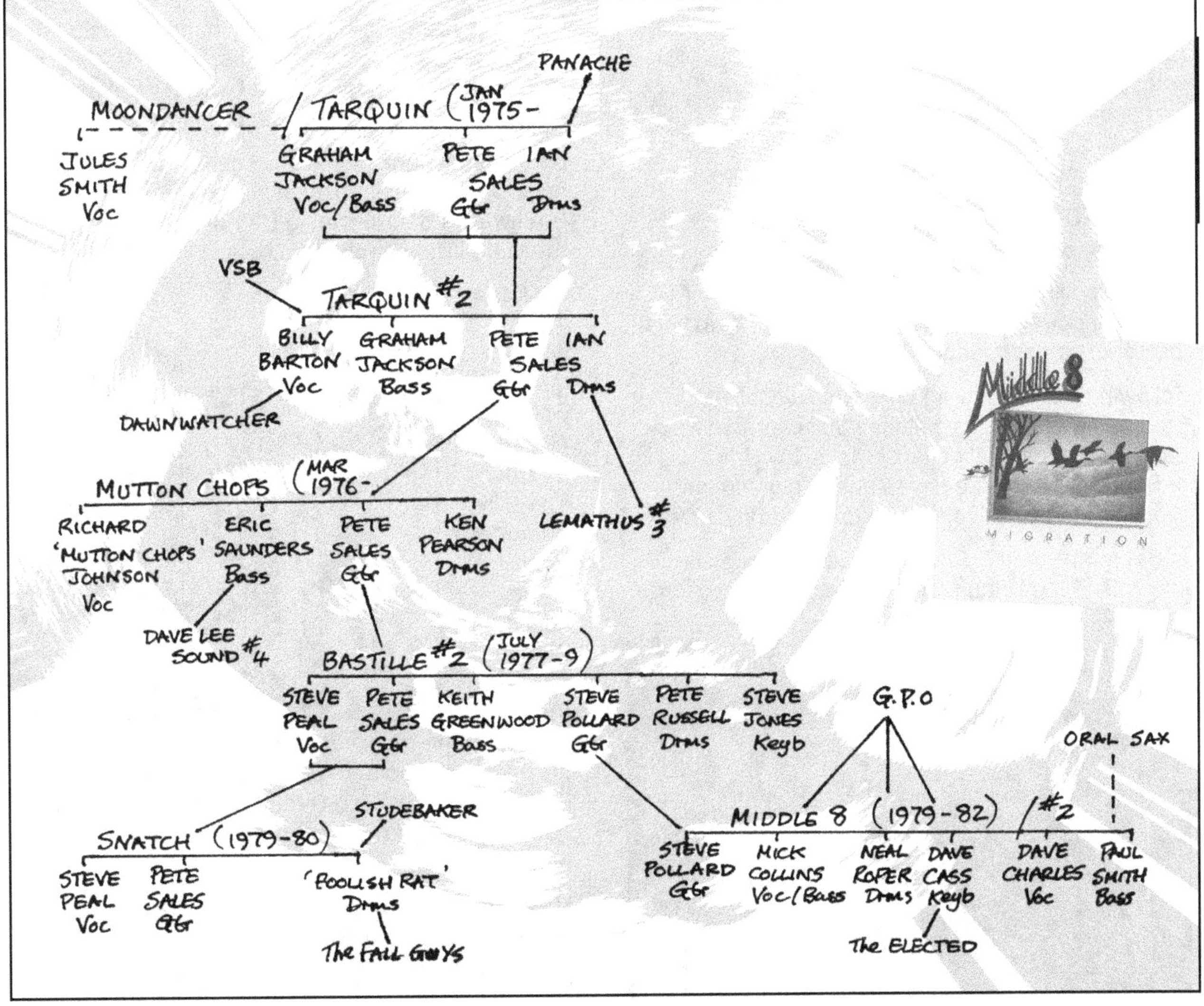

AZEL

Local prog-rock band Azel (1974-77), had built up such a large local following, that former Students' Union Social Secretary Paul Tarran invited them to play a showcase gig at Bradford University on March 15, 1977.

Four major record companies (EMI, Phonogram, A&M and Pye) were invited to see the band, plus Leeds outfit Bastille and Pudsey band Skinny Cat, all hoping to get the recognition they deserved. Paul said, *'They're all first class outfits and they should go far. if they get the right breaks.'* (13). Unfortunately, none of the bands were signed.

After Azel split, bassist Barry Moore started PA company PSS, hiring equipment to bands, then went on to manage local rock group Krakatoa and produced their 1992 CD *Building Bridges*.

FOXY LADY / THE HAWKS

Andy Rukin, former Kukulkan drummer, as well as playing locally with prog-rockers Lemathus, joined the last incarnation of Dirty Work to help them finish their club commitments.

Following this, Andy with Dirty Work vocalist Steve Vincent and his girlfriend Julia, formed Foxy Lady, with additional guitarist Matti-Roy Unnuk of Shadowfax, to take advantage of gigs on the Working Men's Club circuit up to Christmas 1976.

In September 1977, Andy and Matti-Roy were joined by Allan Unnuk (also of Shadowfax) and the Whittaker brothers, Colin and Mick, to form The Hawks (pictured above). They had previously tried calling themselves The Rowdies, but couldn't get any bookings under that name.

MALCOLM JACKSON

Local lad Malcolm Jackson embarked on his musical career in 1961 when he, along with two fellow pupils from Whetley Lane school, sang on the recording of the TV advert for *Soreen Fruit Malt Loaf* at Elite Studios which was at the back of the old Elite Picturehouse on Lilycroft Road.

Malcolm later became an accomplished guitarist and harmonica player who followed the old blues harp tradition of soaking harmonicas in beer to make them sound louder, except he used vodka.

Between 1969 and 1972 Malcolm played solo around the working men's clubs. By 1972-73, Malcolm was a roadie for the biggest local band of the time, The John Verity Band.

As the local punk/new wave scene emerged in the late 1970s Malcolm played with Beezer Bob & The Brainwaves before joining Barnoldswick quartet The Amazing Whipps (pictured below) in 1979.

In October 1986, while guesting with seven piece local jazz band The Billy Thompson Band at the Junction Pub in Scholes (near Thornton), he received three standing ovations for his harmonica solo in one song. The next year he joined local rock band Siren for a three month stint, before building and concentrating on his home recording studio.

Malcolm also played harmonica in over eighty bands as guest musician.

Sadly, Malcolm passed away in 2018.

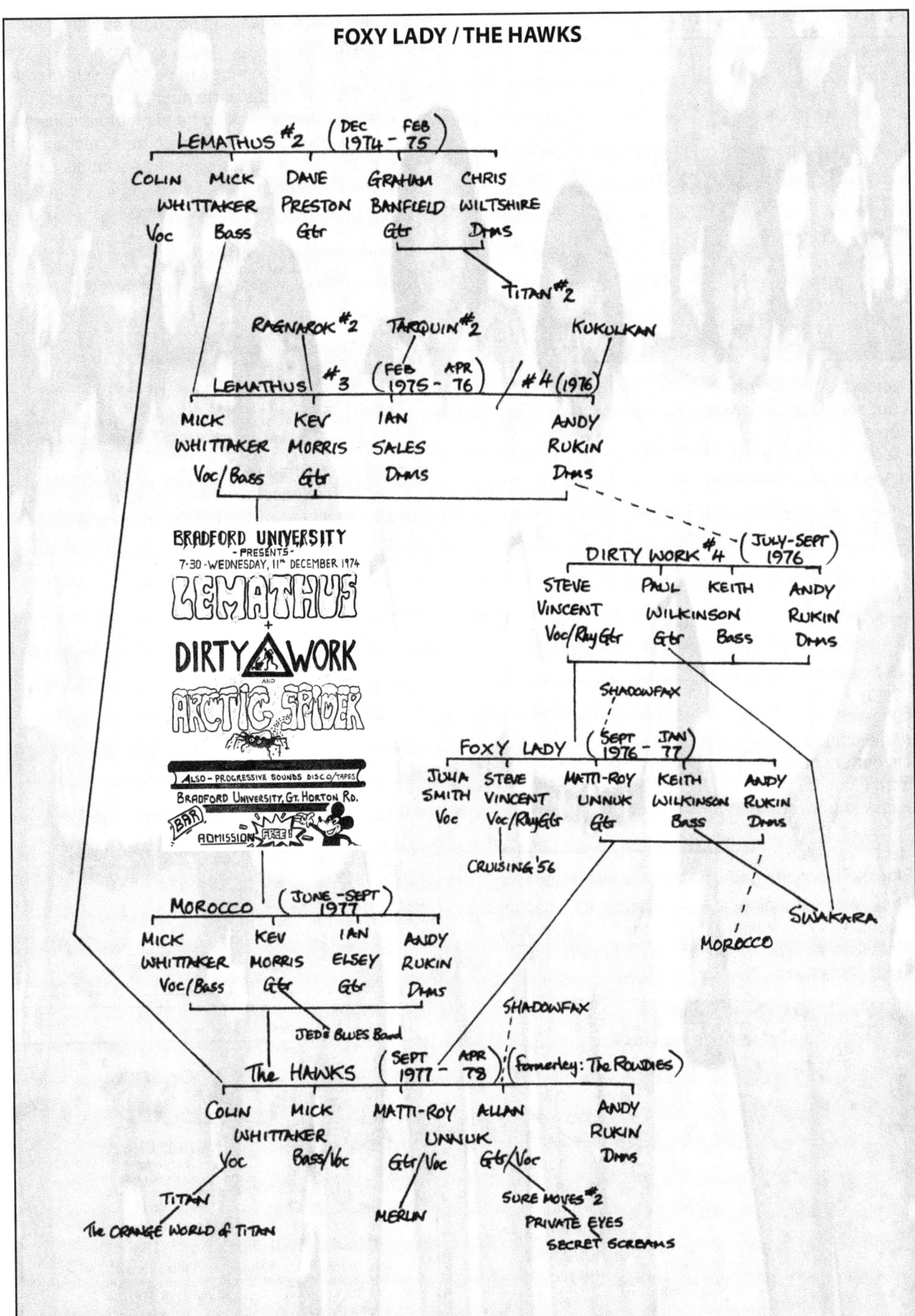

FIRST AID

Although Alan Wormald was born in Holbeck, Leeds (of Bradfordian parents) he was a friend and contemporary of Allan Holdsworth. He worked the Mecca Ballroom scene in the 1960s and 70s with many Bradford sidemen.

He also worked with Glen South and the band Huckleberry. They played at a club called **The Cat's Whiskers** in Meanwood, Leeds, in the early 1970s.

In 1976 his manager Jimmy Parson suggested a name change for his current band, from Flock to First Aid (maybe because of the US band called Flock). They soon got a record deal with Decca.

They released their epic *Nostradamus* as a concept album in 177. It was inspired by the book Alan had recently read, *The Prophecies Of Nostradamus*, by Erika Cheetham.

Author Erika Cheetham visited the band in the studio a couple of times and was hoping to tie the LP in with her book. Unfortunately, her agent tried to demand 50 per cent of the album's royalties and so consequently this never happened.

In the 1980s Alan continued to perform with various local bands, as well as a member of Tommy Hunt and Freddie Starr's backing bands, before joining Shakatak in 1994. He has worked here and abroad with them for many years, as well as with his own four-piece jazz fusion outfit.

Bradford band Shadowfax started in 1973 and in 1979/1980 released two singles as well as supporting rockers UFO at St George's Hall on December 15, 1979.

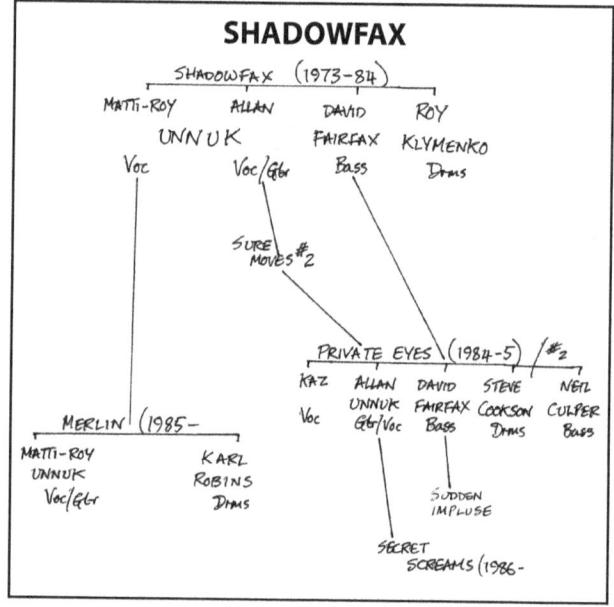

SHADOWFAX			
79	BFD SFX 100	Really Into You (p/s)	50

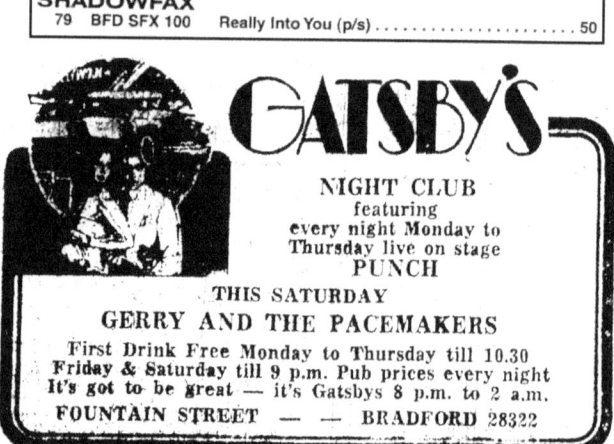

CHAPTER 2 - PROG ROCK TO PUNK ROCK   1971 - 1976

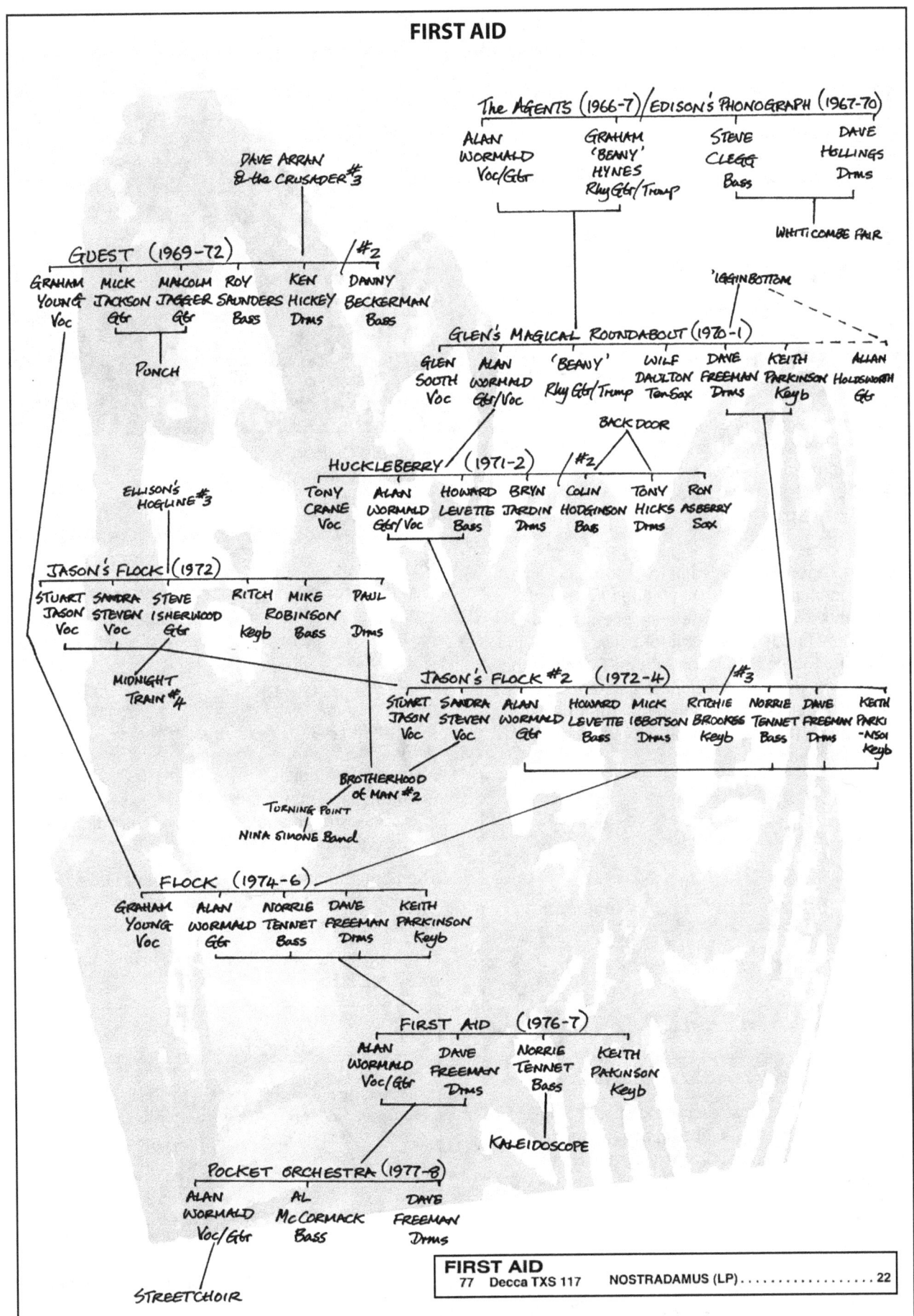

FIRST AID
77 Decca TXS 117   NOSTRADAMUS (LP).................22

PUNCH UP NORTH

Local four-piece pop-rock band Punch were immortalised in a thirty-minute BBC documentary called *Punch On The Road* in 1976. It was one of the BBC regional local affairs *Close Up North* programmes and aired on BBC 2 after the national and local news.

The film followed the band as they travelled the highways on their way to and from gigs at Northern working men's clubs. The documentary shows them travelling to places like Sunderland and Hull in their trusty Transit van.

The band members had all given up their jobs and found an agent in an attempt to become full-time professional musicians. They generally played two or three forty-minute sets of covers of mid-seventies chart hits per night for between £30 and £40 a gig. Punch auditioned for the ITV talent show *Opportunity Knocks* and went to appear on the Hughey Green hosted programme. After passing the audition, they hoped to land a record deal with one of their self-penned songs.

and Pete Callander. Murray had written massive hits for the likes of Gerry & The Pacemakers *(I Like It)*, Freddie & The Dreamers *(You Were Made For Me)* and Paper Lace *(Billy Dont' Be A Hero)*. Unfortunately, the hit-making magic failed to work for Punch and their single didn't didn't hit the heights they had dreamed of.

Then band folded after a year. Bassist Dave Sanderson went on to join The Casuals in 1977 and then spent ten years in Felix.

Singer Mick Kershaw (born Mick Novak) passed away in 2018.

The documentary is a fascinating snapshot of the life on the road of a jobbing covers band in the 1970s. While no mini polystyrene Stone Henge on show, it could sit alongside later spoof rockumentaries like *Spinal Tap* and *Bad News*. *Punch On The Road* can be found on YouTube.

Punch's only single, *The Ballad Of Good Luck Charm / On The Gan*g, came out on Bus Stop Records in 1976. Both songs were by Mitch Murray

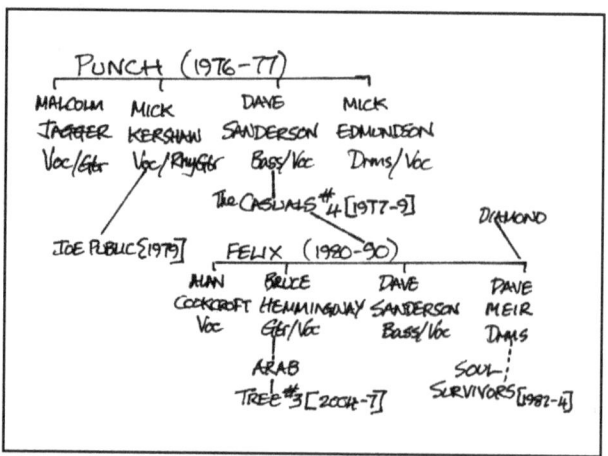

ALAN WHITTAKER

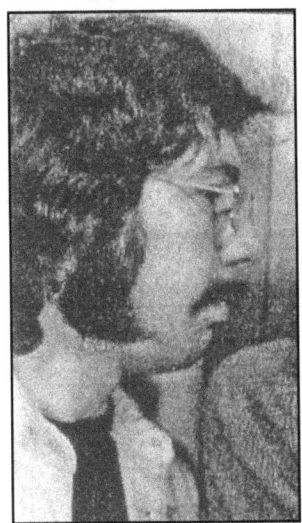

On the roll-call of *T&A* reporters who had overseen the paper's various music columns is Alan Whittaker.

Alan, a Thornton lad, was friends with many members of local 1970s bands such as Midas, Swan Arcade, Rhabstallion and The Donkeys and tried to sympathetically do justice to the local music scene while writing for the *Rock On* column.

Between 1975-79, he and a few mates worked on the band project Rodent. They were a prog-folk group who, it is said, refused to play live. It is no surprise that the group were completely unknown at the time. Their musical endeavours only came to light in 2002 when a CD of their warts and all home recordings called In Passing was released.

BLACK DYKE MILLS BRASS BAND

The world-famous brass band Black Dyke Mills Band was originally formed in 1855 at Queensbury, Bradford. In July 1860 at the Crystal Palace, London, they became British National Brass Band Champions for the first time. In subsequent years (1902-2005) the band won the National Championship 19 times, and second and third place 17 and 11 times. They also won the British Open Championship (1862-2005), held at Manchester's Belle Vue Gardens, twenty seven times and were European Champions (1978-2005) eleven times as well as World Brass Band Champions in 1970.

The year 2025 marked the 170th anniversary of their existence, in which time they have toured the world, made over five hundred radio broadcasts and recorded over two hundred 10"/LPs/CDs of their music.

VALLANCES

All through the 1970s, retail chain store Vallances was on Bank Street in the area once occupied by Bradford's Victorian Swan Arcade. Besides selling fridges, cookers, washers and other 'white goods' on the second foor there was a musical department which sold a small collection of popular/comptemory, jazz and classical music singles and LPs, where, if you dug deep, you could sometimes find a bargain.

Although in competion with the HMV Shop, Bostocks, Woods and other shops, Vallances could occaisionaly be the source of rare releases or cheaper versions of sought after vinyl.

After the store left Bradford, Vallances began selling Sir Clive Sinclair's C5 mini-trike electric car at under £400 in the early 1980s.

In mid-December 1976, local DJ Colin Peters did a charity marathon 100-hour record-playing session at the Victoria Hotel, Park Lane, Manningham. He managed to raise £100 to buy Christmas presents for pensioners.

'His stint wasn't so bad when the pub was open, as he managed to walk around and talk to customers. But in those days pubs closed in the middle of the day, and Sundays had a long, dry stretch between 2 pm and 7 pm. Towards the end, he actually started to suffer the occasional hallucination from sleep deprivation, while his girlfriend had to keep an eye on him to stop him drifting into limbo when the record wanted changing. But he went the distance in the end, all four days and a bit, at the time when randomly played CDs were undreamed of and vinyl 45 rpm discs had to be changed by hand.' (19)

US SOUL STAR SETTLES IN SHIPLEY!

Around 1976, American soul singer Tommy Hunt settled in Shipley with his second wife Susan. Born in 1933 in Pittsburgh, his first group were the Five Echoes. He went on to join The Flamingoes and have a big hit with *I Only Have Eyes For You* in 1958.

After the decline of the Northern Soul scene in the mid-eighties, Tommy moved to live in Holland and performed on the cabaret circuit, travelling the world.

He moved back to England in 1997 during the Northern Soul scene revival.

TOMMY HUNT
62	Top Rank JAR 605	The Door Is Open/I'm Wondering	18
68	Direction 58-3216	I Need A Woman Of My Own/Searchin' For My Baby Looking Everywhere	10
72	Polydor 2058 236	Mind, Body & Soul/One More Mountain To Climb	6
74	Pye 7N 45325	Sleep Tight Honey/Time Alone Will Tell	6
75	Spark SRL 1132	Crackin' Up/Get Out	6
85	Kent TOWN 103	The Work Song/IVORYS: Please Stay	8

After he arrived in the UK in the 1970s, he soon became a big favourite on the Northern Soul scene, singing at the second anniversary of the Wigan Casino.

In August 1976 his single, *Loving On The Losing Side*, taken from his *A Sign Of The Times* LP on Spark Records, reached number 28 in the charts.

In 2001, The Flamingos were inducted into the *Rock & Roll Hall Of Fame* in recognition of their thirty-year outstanding contribution to music.

He settled in Yorkshire and continued to perform selected solo shows, like the one he did at The Tyke pub, on Thornton Road in 2003.

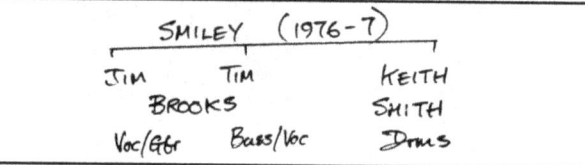

SMILEY (1976-7)
JIM — TIM — KEITH
BROOKS — SMITH
Voc/Gtr — Bass/Voc — Drms

In December, local bands who knew each other mainly from the Vaults Bar / Queen's Hall scene organised their own gig at Bingley Arts Centre.

The bands that played were; Dust Blue, Vedas, Phobia and QED. Phobia's set was recorded that night through the PA by Mick Gibson of the Halifax-based Full Circle Mobile Recording Service.

It proved to be a very popular event and so many of the bands' friends, fans and family turned up that the small theatre bar ran out of beer before the end of the night's performances!

Some other bands around and about in 1976 were **Spitz** and **Ill Wing**.

Chapter 3
Local folk!
1956-1987

Folk music in the United Kingdom was essentially the music created by and for the common people. For hundreds of years, people made songs or ballads which were transmitted orally from one generation to the next by word of mouth, within a population that generally didn't write them down.

The songs/ballads were associated with the everyday social life of the working class, usually dramatic narratives set around a central theme.

Love, relationships, murders, disasters, strikes; local and national political issues and current events were amongst the wide range of subjects these songs covered.

After the first printing presses were set up in England, the collective 'folk' memory was preserved in ballads, also known as 'broadsides'.

Reuben Holder

In a culture before there were newspapers, bibles and prayer books were almost all working class folk had to read, if in fact they could read, and therefore they had to rely on street literature to find out what was going on. The most popular form of these were known as broadsides; single sheet newsletters which were the tabloids of their day. Sometimes pinned up on walls in houses and ale houses, broadsides carried news, public notices, speeches and songs that could be read or sung aloud.

They were printed and then sold by vendors on the streets of London, and later in the new urban provincial towns for a penny; 1d or ½d a sheet. The musical broadsides contained three to six columns of verse and a refrain (chorus) and were printed on a handbill (flyer) size sheet and may have circulated in more than one version, often sung to the popular tunes of the day.

These popular traditional songs were based on a 'system of six diatonic modes', unlike the modern common

THE WEAVER'S LAMENT.
A POEM IN THE YORKSHIRE DIALECT.

BY BENJAMIN PRESTON, BRADFORD.

Aw'm a weyver ya knaw, an awf deead,
  So aw du all at ivir aw can
To put away aat o' my heead
  The thowts an the aims of a man!
Ten shillin a wick's whot aw arn
  When aw've varry gooid wark an full time,
An aw think it a sorry consarn
  Fur a hearty young chap in his prime!

But ar maister says things is as well
  As they hae been, ur ivir can be;
And aw happen sud think soa mysel,
  If he'd nobud swop places wi me;
But he's welcome ta all he can get,
  Aw begrudge him o' noan o' his brass,
And aw'm nowt bud a madlin ta fret,
  Ur ta dream o' yond bewtiful lass!

Aw nivir sal call hur my wife,
  My love aw sal nivir mak knawn,
Yit the sorra that darkens hur life
  Thraws a shadda across o' my awn;
An aw'm suar when hur heart is at ecas,
  Thear is sunshine an singin i' mine,
An misfortunes may come as they pleeas,
  Bud they nivir can mak ma repine.

When aw laid i' my bed day an neet,
  And wur geen up by t' doctur fur deead—
God bless hur—shoo'd come wi' a leet
  An a basin o' grewil an breead;
An aw once thowt aw'd aht wi' it all,
  But sa kindly shoo chattud an smiled,
Aw wur fain tu turn ovvur ta t'wall,
  An ta bluther an sob like a child!

An aw said as aw thowt of hur een,
  Each breeter fur't tear at wur in't;
Its a sin ta be niver furgeen
  Ta yoke hur ta famine an stint;
So aw'l e'en travel torrud thru li'e,
  Like a man thru a desert unknawn,
Aw mun ne'er hev a hoam an a wife.
  Bud my sorras will all be my awn!

practice of the harmonic chromatic scale in the stable major and minor notes of classical - art music. (1)

A local 19th century Bradford example of the type of street vendor who sold broadsides was the local character, Reuben Holder.

He had been born in Hunslet, Leeds, in 1797 as Samuel Holdsworth and was a child collier. At five years old he was driving the 'gin horse' at the pit head and at eight was sent down the pit to mine. As a joke he was baptized 'Reuben' at Rothwell Church when he was twenty years old. In his later years, he spent time as a fish hawker and ballad seller. His own verses were printed and he sold them at Bradford Market on Saturday nights. As a teetotaller, he was a pioneer of the early Temperance Movement. His work was mainly about the conditions of the working people and support for the Chartist movement, with titles like; 'Lines on the Distressed State of Trade', 'The New Starvation Law.', 'The Flight of Peter Bussey' and 'Lines on the Teetotal Barrel'. His poetic fame brought him little gain during his lifetime and he always had the appearance of a down-at-heel, poor man. (2)

Another local 'workman' poet was Ben Preston; a dialect poet of the poor.

In the 1850s, a very popular northern artist was Ned Corvan (1830-65) from Newcastle, who composed his own songs about topical issues of the day set to current tunes.

At the end of the 19th century, many folk traditions were beginning to be lost as rural folk moved increasingly into the urban cities. Around 1899, in an attempt to preserve the folk heritage, Cecil Sharp helped to found the English Folk Song and Dance Society, touring the country to collect old folk songs and recording them on wax cylinders. But, with the massive death toll of the First World War, interest in this first folk revival was dissipated.

The second, post World War II, folk revival began in the early 1950s and expressed the concerns of the working class on a political level. Old folk traditions were rediscovered by political progressives and the growing 'Ban the Bomb' peace movement.

The prime mover of the new folk revival was the Lancastrian Ewan McColl (real name James Miller, and father of Kirsty McColl). McColl was a Marxist who started the first UK folk club, 'The Ballad & Blues', in London in 1951 with his American wife Peggy Seeger. Unfortunately, he gave the nascent folk movement a rather unflattering image of a 'traditional reactionary folkie'- finger in ear, bearded, and wearing an Arran sweater - that continues to this day. He also wrote two of the most timeless songs, 'Dirty Old Town' and 'The First Time Ever I Saw Your Face', among many others as well as writing radio ballads, radio plays that bordered on ballad operas.

In 1956 Lonnie Donegan, a member of Chris Barber's Jazz Band, recorded an old Leadbelly song called 'Rock Island Line' which got to number eight in the charts

Cartoon (and above) by Leeds jazz guitarist Diz Disley

and kick-started a national craze for washboard and string bass 'skiffle'. All over the country, young people were rediscovering folk music through the American-orientated urban blues of skiffle, and in Bradford, a resurgence began.

THE TOPIC FOLK CLUB

On the 11th of November 1956 Alex Eaton, a guitar-playing French teacher at Carlton (Bolling) Grammar School, started meeting on Friday evenings with his wife Louise and other folk music enthusiasts. They met in the upstairs room of what used to be the old 19th Century radical meeting house Laycock's Temperance Hotel (Albion Court) which at the time was Bradford's first Chinese restaurant, Mr Yung's Golden Dragon (now Giuseppe's Pizza Place!) (3).

The members met to sing, talk and start informal 'floor singing' sessions, which became a proving ground for many local singers of authentic local material, like Dave Kiddie's 'The Methody Parson' and Alan Emmott's 'The Dyer's Prentice'. This was the beginning of what would

become the oldest and longest-running folk club in the world - the Topic Folk Club.

The club took the name from the only folk record label in the UK at that time and, because a friend worked there, they were loaned a record player and some early releases.

The Topic grew quickly and moved to a bigger space in Unity Hall (Rawson Square) in 1957-58 with a membership of three hundred and four. They soon supplemented the Friday evening sessions with occasional Saturday night concerts, some of the first of which featured US artists Ramblin' Jack Elliot and Shirley Collins.

At the floor singing sessions in the early days of the Topic, a couple of urban myths were produced. Legend has it that during the 1960s both Bob Dylan and Paul Simon turned up to perform while in the country. Unfortunately, nobody can verify that either event took place.

During the first three or four years Alex Eaton helped to impress his particular form on the club's existence, but later he only visited the club occasionally, although he continued to put up visiting singers.

After moving to another five venues during the 1960s - The Fox & Goose on Canal Road (1959-64), The Sun Inn on Sunbridge Road (1964-8), The Market Tavern (1968-69), then the Rawson Hotel, the Ukrainian Club, and The Market Tavern again - the club was finally established at The Star, on Westgate, in 1969. (4)

The folk revival of the 1960s inspired a new generation of singer-songwriters like Donovan, Roy Harper and Nick Drake, and encouraged a revival in Celtic traditional music by groups such as Planxty, The Chieftains, The Wolfe Tones and the Breton harpist Alan Stivell to name only a few. It also sparked a new sub-genre of folk-rock led by groups like Pentangle, Incredible String Band, Fairport Convention and others.

During the Topic's years at the Star (1969-91), it played host to an impressive list of UK artists who performed on Friday evenings, such as Dick Gaugan, Rab Noakes, Andy Irvine and Christy Moore (both ex-Planxty), Bolton's Bernard Wrigley, Ewan McColl & Peggy Seeger, The Watersons, Magna Carta and the First Lady of British Folk, June Tabor, as well as many of the local groups/artists.

WILD OATS

Local folk duo Wild Oats - Ray Sherwin and John Tempest -, who had supported Hawkwind at St. George's Hall in 1970, became a trio after meeting classically trained viola player Bill Currie, a Huddersfield lad, in East Grinstead, Sussex. The original duo then formed the prog-rock band Moonchild in 1975 and played their first gig at the Tavern In the Town Rock Club..

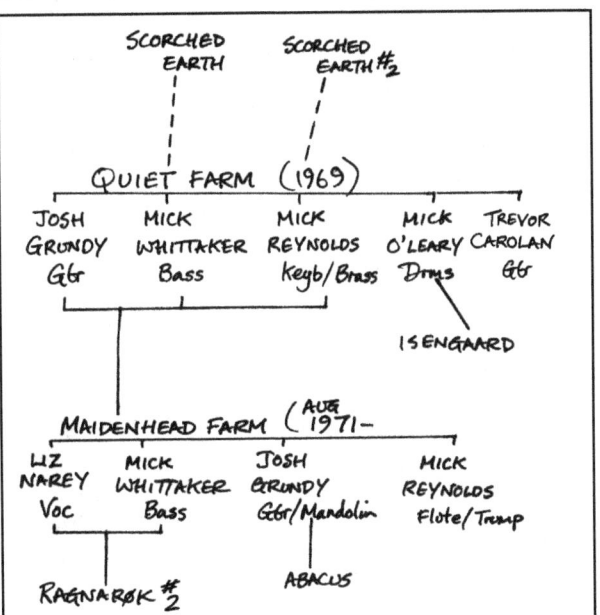

QUIET FARM / MAIDENHEAD FARM

Quiet Farm and Maidenhead Farm were two groups formed as offshoots from local rock bands and moonlighted as folk incarnations. Maidenhead Farm was Mick Whittaker of Ragnarok's offshoot, which included Josh Grundy who was well known in his own right on the local folk scene. The group, despite only being in existence for six weeks, entered a competition at the Syon Park Folk Festival with fifty other groups. Even when they had to borrow equipment to perform, they still came second, with their own material described as 'jazz/folk fusion in a Pentangle-ish style.'

On the 18th of October 1971, they supported Hull heavy prog-rockers Red Dirt at Bradford University. They continued until the following October when Mick Whittaker and Liz Narey re-formed Ragnarok. (5)

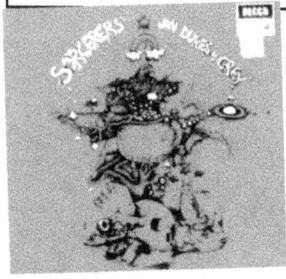

JAN DUKES de GREY

Jan Dukes de Grey were a Horsforth 'psychedelic-acid folk' duo of Mick Bairstow and Derek Noy who had formed in 1968 and were managed by Danny Pollock. Their first LP, 'Sorcerers', was released on the Deram offshoot label Nova in 1970. By the time their second album, 'Mice and Rats in the Loft', was released, they were signed to Transatlantic Records and had become a trio with the addition of percussionist Denis Conlan.

JAN DUKES DE GREY			
70	Decca Nova (S)DN 8	SORCERERS (LP)	50
71	Transatlantic TRA 234	MICE AND RATS IN THE LOFT (LP)	80

In the 1960s a few rival folk clubs formed, some as breakaways from the Topic, such as The Bradford Folk Club, at the Commercial Hotel on James Street, which opened on Sunday nights in 1968. The club was set up by Paul Tattersal as a reaction against the pop/folk/skiffle sound, and members were all staunch and stern traditionalists.

As they couldn't afford to book established artists they relied on their own members and local amateurs to play at the club. One was a young, smooth and charming Irishman called James 'Irish Jim' Hayden (RIP 2001) who roundly abused the crowd during his performance, especially when they only half-heartedly joined the choruses of the passionately sung Irish rebel songs. 'I don't come to the club every Sunday, I sing when I feel like it. That's the only way to sing folk songs.'(6)

Bradford's popular Market Tavern hosted yet another club at this time, called DB's Folk Club, on Sunday nights.

Also performing on the local folk scene in 1969/1970 were The Black Line Elders from Cowling, Tony Black from Bingley, Linda Roper, and the duo Baz & Steve.

MOONKYTE

Whilst visiting London's Regent Studios in 1970 as manager of Fresh Garbage, Dave Stansfield slipped a rough tape of his own tunes recorded with sidekick Dave Foster to the producer. Two weeks later, the producer rang to ask if he wanted to record an LP. Enlisting bass player Trevor Craven and drummer Mick Humphreys, they promptly set off to London and recorded an album in eleven hours called 'Count Me Out' as Moonkyte. The resulting album was a strange mix of Delta blues and folk-rock with lyrics about their experimentation with LSD and hashish.

Released in October 1971, on DJ Emperor Rosko's Mother label, it was endorsed with sleeve notes by John Peel. It has now become a very collectable 'psyche-folk' album for aficionados of that genre.

In a T&A interview Trevor said, 'We don't want to go down to London and let the showbiz sausage machine get us. We want to build up a 'rep' from a base in Bradford then let London see us on our own terms.' (7)

Although the band didn't do many live gigs (they were often too 'out of it') they did return to the studio in London to record a second album, 'Cuckoo', with new drummer Pete Kaberry, late of Kaboss. Unfortunately, the LP was never released and the band drifted apart although they never formally disbanded. Who knows, maybe they'll resurface soon and do some gigs.

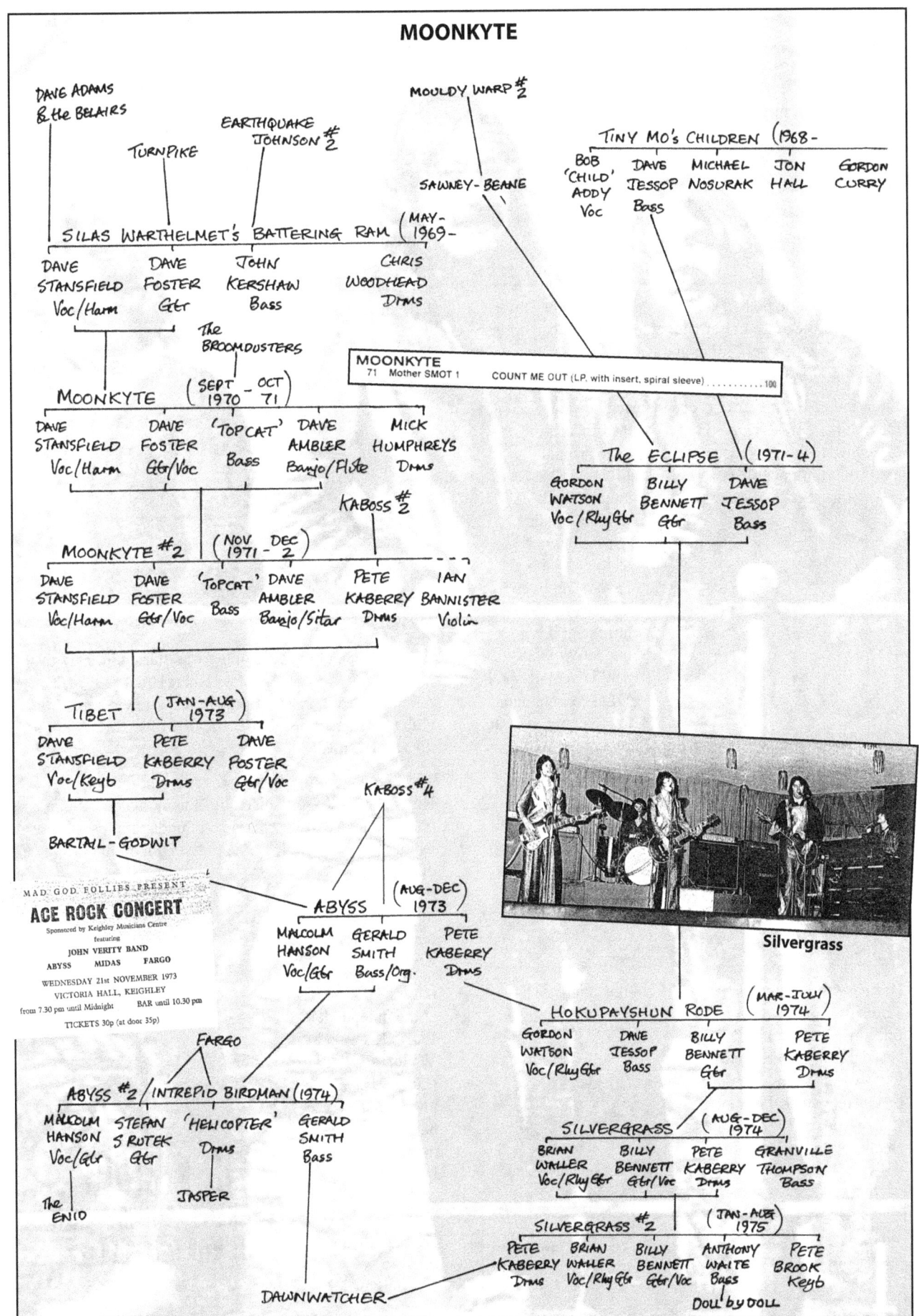

ROY BAILEY

In 1971 folk singer Roy Bailey was living in Shipley with his wife Val and two children. He had been a sociology lecturer at Bradford University before transferring to Sheffield University as head of the applied social studies department.

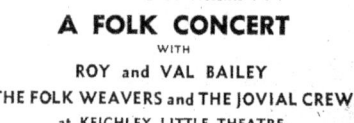

Roy had started as a vocalist in a skiffle group in 1958, before singing with his wife Val, and he had sung with a pre-Strawbs Dave Cousins while at Leicester University. He released three LPs on the folk label Trailer and was a popular regular at the Topic Folk Club.

Interviewed by the T&A's Ann Webster, he said, 'In the old days, folk singers used to be the modern-day equivalent of journalists. They used to go around the country telling people of events. That function has, of course, died. The modern media of television, radio and newspapers have taken over. Yet modern folk singing has the ability to put across what people actually feel. Whatever changes are to come, we can be sure of one thing: folk music will reflect the world, but sadly it will never change it.' (8)

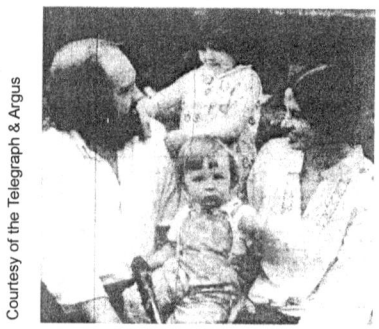

After retiring from academic life Roy received an MBE for services to folk music in 2000. In 2003 he embarked on a successful tour with MP Tony Benn called 'Writing on the Wall' with Tony reading various quotations from history and Roy singing protest songs.

ROY BAILEY (U.K.)			
71	Trailer LER 3021	ROY BAILEY (LP)	15
76	Fuse AC 262	NEW BELL AWAKE (LP)	12
82	Fuse CF 382	HARD TIMES (LP, with insert)	12

Hebric, whose name is derived from the Gaelic 'Tha e breagh' - meaning 'it is fine', were a Cleckheaton based group who released at least two privately pressed LPs, 'Hebric', in 1976 and 'Later Ron' in 1978, on the Heckmondwike Box Studios label.

HEBRIC (1972-(78)				#2
JOHN BROMLEY	DAVE CALVERT	PHILLIP 'JIMMY' BOND	MALCOLM STOCKS	RON DARNBROUGH
Voc/Bodhram	Gtr/Banjo/Mandolin/Voc	Gtr/Mand/Voc	Piano/Voc	Voc/Gtr

In the 1970s more of folk clubs were set up around the Bradford district, such as The Talisman Folk Club at the New Inn, Idle, in 1971, where groups like **Idle Well** and **Hawg's Folly** played, and one at the Moonrakers pub on Halifax Road, run by the landlord Tom Bresline, which started on Tuesday nights from September 1971.

Bradford Art College also ran a folk club around this period at the Ambassador Club.

In 1972 students from Bradford College's Margaret McMillan building ran a Sunday night folk club at the Queen's Hall from the 23rd of October, featuring artists such as Jovial Crew, Martin Carter, Roger Sutcliffe and Roy Bailey.

More folk concerts were put on at the Prospect pub, on Bolton Road, by the Pennie Folk Club on Saturday nights in May 1972.

KEIGHLEY FOLK

The first folk club in Keighley was started in 1967 by Ben Ellison and others at the Albert Hotel (1967-72). After a meeting in The Lord Rodney, they renamed the club the 'Bacca Pipes' after the title of a 'Morris jig' of the same name.

The club later moved to a large room in the Wellington Hotel (1972-80), organised by Jim Whitehead, and put on many successful concerts on Sunday nights. It moved again in the 1980s, this time to the Globe Inn (1980-2000), where regular Friday night concerts continued for the next twenty years.

After a short stay at the independent Worth Brewery Visitors Centre (2000-01), which unfortunately had to close, the Bacca Pipes moved to the Welcome Inn (a working men's club) and from there to the Ukrainian Club. (9)

The New Starvation Law examined,

And some Description of the Food, Dress, Labour, and Regulations, imposed upon the poor and unfortunate Sufferers in the New British Bastiles.

Come you men and women unto me attend,
And listen and see what for you I have penn'd;
And if you do buy it, and carefully read,
T'will make your hearts within you to bleed.

The lions at London, with their cruel paw,
You know they have pass'd a Starvation Law;
These tigers and wolves should be chained in a den,
Without power to worry poor women and men.

Like the fox in the farm-yard they shly do creep;
These hard-hearted wretches, O, how dare they sleep,
To think they should pass such a law in our day,
To bate and to stop the poor widow's pay.

And if they don't like their pay to be stopp'd,
'Gainst their own will, into th' Bastile they're popp'd;
Their homes must break up, and never return,
But leave their relations and children to mourn.

The three pension'd paupers in grandeur do live,
Pon riches that they from the taxes receive;
Which poor people pay from their scanty week's wage,
Though pinch'd, and confin'd like a bird in a cage.

But if they'd to work before they were fed,
They'd not go a tolling the poor children's bread,
Which fathers do earn very hard every day,
While they in carriages are dashing away.

There's many poor children go ragged and torn,
While they and their horses are pamper'd with corn;
Now is not this world quite unequally dealt?
The Starvation Law by some few is felt.

When a man and his wife for sixty long years
Have toiled together through troubles and fears,
And brought up a family with prudence and care,
To be sent to the Bastile it's very unfair.

And in the Bastile each woman and man
Is parted asunder,—is this a good plan?
A word of sweet comfort they cannot express,
For unto each other they ne'er have access.

Of their uniform, too, you something shall hear,—
In strong Fearnaught jackets the men do appear;
In coarse Grogram gowns the women do shine,
And a ninepenny cap,—now won't they be fine?

On fifteenpence halfpenny they keep them a week;
Had Commissioners this we should have them to seek,
They'd not come to Yorkshire to visit us here,
And of such vile vermin we soon should be clear.

To give them hard labour, it is understood,
In handmills the grain they must grind for their food,
Like men in a prison they work them in gangs,
With turning and twizing it fills them with pangs.

I'll give you an insight of their regulations,
Which they put in force in these situations,
They've school, chapel, and prison all under a roof,
And the governor's house stands a little aloof.

The master instructs them the law to obey,
The governor minds it's all work and no play,
And as for religion the parson doth teach
That he knows the gospel,—no other must preach.

Ye hard-working men, wherever you be,
I'd have you watch closely these men, d'ye see;
I think they're contriving, the country all o'er,
To see what's the worst they can do to the poor.

But if that their incomes you wish for to touch,
They'll vapour, and grumble, and talk very much,
The Corn Laws uphold, the poor will oppress,
And send them to th' Bastile in th' day of distress.

Courtesy of West Yorkshire Archive Service

1d Broadsheet by Reuben Holder 1838

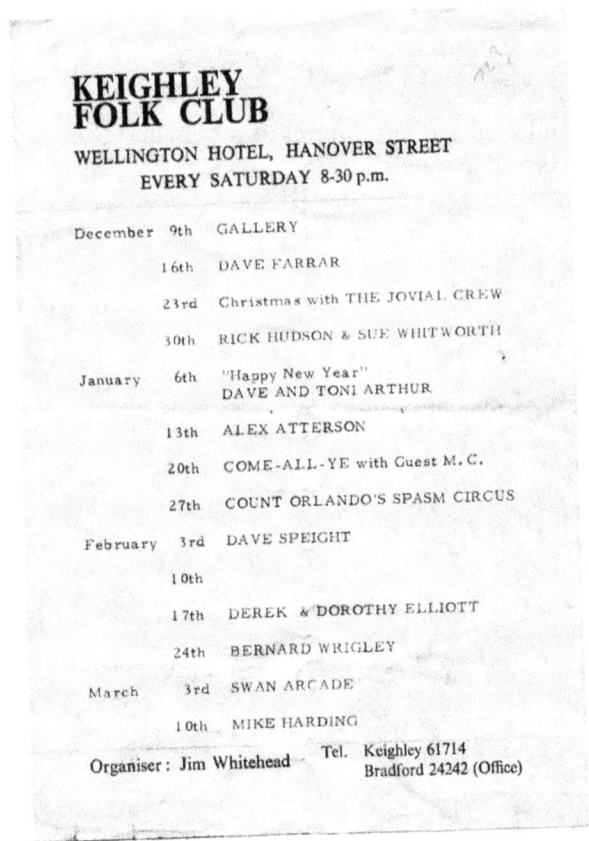

There was another folk club at the Devonshire Hotel started in 1972 by Jim O'Brien of the local group Talisman. Jovial Crew and Roger Sutcliffe played on the opening night on the 25th of March.

JOVIAL CREW

Jovial Crew were formed in December 1966 at the Granby Pub, Keighley, where they practised in the tap room once a week. Their name was derived from the line, 'Come over the hill together to join the Jovial Crew,' from the song 'Four Jolly Brothers'.

They played around the Dales and West Yorkshire folk scene and won the 1970 Dales National Folk Contest at Skipton town hall.

In 1971, after recording a few private live gigs, they released their only LP, 'The Jovial Crew' (FHR 0205), on the Folk Heritage label. It consisted of eleven songs and only 100 copies of the album were pressed.

In January 1972, they recorded the song 'Santiano' for Yorkshire TV, which was broadcast on the teatime news show, Calendar.

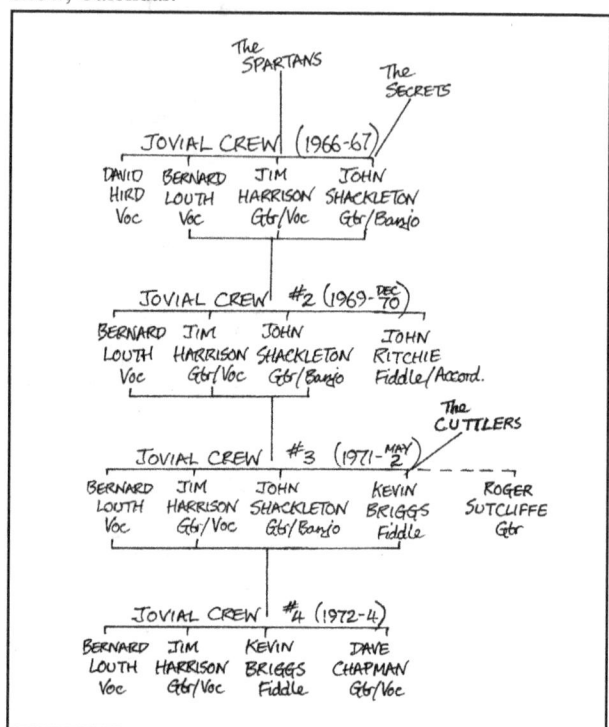

Jovial Crew were big favourites on the local scene, supporting various artists like Christy Moore, Tim Hardin, Dave Burland and the Yetties. They played their last performance in Grassington in 1974.

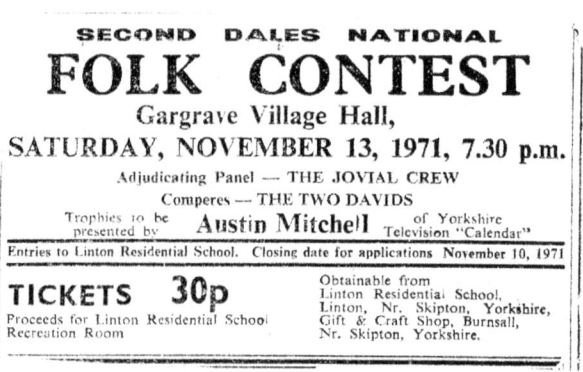

SWAN ARCADE

Haworth-based folk group Swan Arcade took their name from the old 1880 Bradford four-storey Victorian arcade built by Angus Holden MP on the site of the White Swan Inn. The landmark arcade was demolished in March 1962 as part of Bradford's 1960s city centre modernisation during a spree of City Council-backed vandalism that saw the destruction of many of Bradford's landmark buildings.

The group was started in 1970, by Bradford lad Dave (Bradley) Brady (1944-2006) and his wife Heather Johnston, whom he had met at a Leeds folk club, and

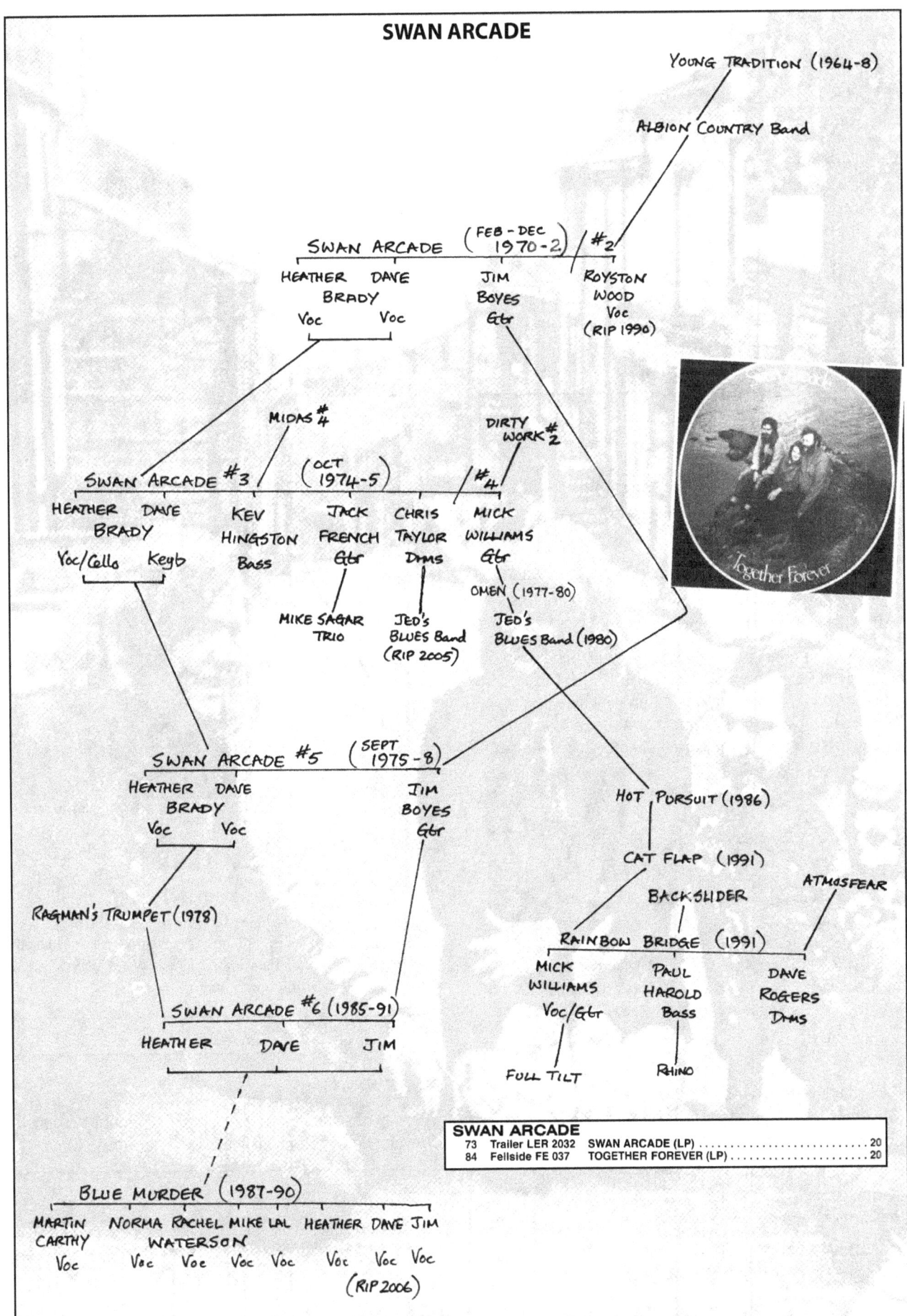

augmented into a trio when Jim Boyes joined. Jim was replaced for a while by former 'Young Tradition' member Royston Wood before returning to the line-up in 1975.

Their first LP 'Swan Arcade' was recorded in a dusty attic in Haworth in 1972. It consisted of twelve tracks featuring mainly three-part vocal harmonies and was released on Bill Leader's Trailer folk label. (Bill had also lived in Shipley.)

The group went electric for a while in the 1970s, adding extra members on bass, drums and guitar.

They were regulars at the Topic Folk Club, playing at least seven times between 1972 and 1987, as well as successfully touring the UK and Europe where they appeared on Dutch TV with Kate & Anna McGarrigle. During their career they released another five albums; the

Swan Arcade turn electric!

second, 'Matchless' (1976), stayed in the Belgian folk charts for three years.

Their other four LPs included two on Fellside Records; 'Together Forever' (1983) and 'Diving For Pearls' (1986), and two on their own Sygnet label.

After finally disbanding in 1987, Dave and Heather combined with members of the Waterson family to form the harmony group Blue Murder.

Later Dave worked as a road manager for the Scottish Chamber Orchestra before retiring in 2005. Sadly, he died the following year.

JANET JONES

When remedial teacher Janet Jones bought a cheap Chinese made guitar for £5 in 1970 she started singing and strumming behind closed doors with no thought of appearing in front of an audience. By 1971, and after her first real gig at the Fleece, Addingham, she took the folk scene by storm, going on to win the female section of the Dales National Folk Contest. In November 1972 she appeared on TV's 'Opportunity Knocks', singing the Lancashire folk song, 'Old Pendle'. She also tried to broaden her appeal by doing the occasional

cabaret spot, even working on some pop material composed by local Keighley songwriter Ken Henderson.

She released her only, and now very collectable, LP, 'Sing to Me Lady', on the Midas record label in 1974, the title track of which had been written by Ilkley folk singer Martin Carter. In 1976, she appears to have also released a privately pressed EP called 'A Fresh Wind Waves' on Folk Heritage, which contained an insert.

JANET JONES		
74 Midas MR 005	SING TO ME LADY (LP)	80

FOLKWEAVE

A group of schoolteachers from the Horsforth, Yeadon, Rawdon area formed the band Folkweave in 1972.

FOLKWEAVE (1972 –			
MARILYN OOULTER	'BRAD' BRADSHAW	JOHN VIPOND	GILL WILKINSON
Voc	Acs. Gt/Bass /Voc	Mand./Banjo /Voc	Drms/Voc

CHAPTER 3 - LOCAL FOLK — 1956 - 1987

MONTAIN ASH / THREEFOLD

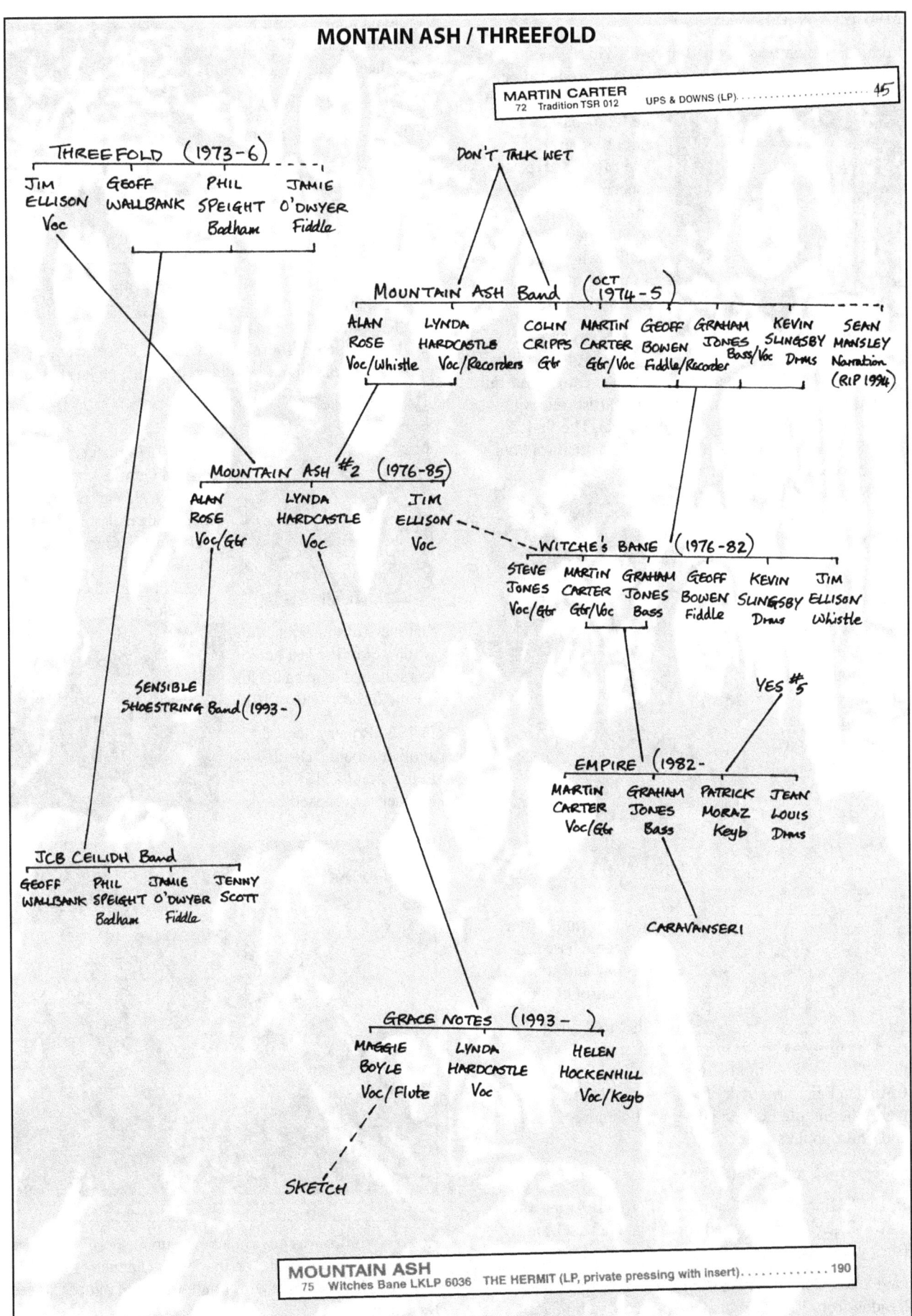

MOUNTAIN ASH BAND

Formed by members of the Burley-in-Wharfedale Folk Club in 1975, this mix of local musicians produced one

album 'The Hermit' on the Ilkley based folk label Witches Bane. The LP was a type of concept album, based on the life of the 19th century hermit Job Senior who lived in a mud and stone kennel on Rumbold's Moor.

After a string of concerts during 1976-77 to publicise the LP, the various members went their separate ways. One member, Martin Carter, had been a renowned local folk artist, releasing at least two albums on the Tradition label. The first was 'Someone New' (TSR008) in 1971, which sold out in two weeks.

The following year's LP, 'Ups & Downs', was a mix of traditional tunes, interspersed with five of Martin's original songs. He was helped out on that album by Phil Langham of the Ripley Wayfarers, on fiddle and mandolin, and Sue

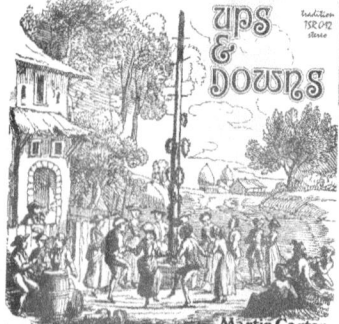

Lloyd on flute. Later he became based in Glasgow and continues to be a 'troubadour'.

Other folk groups/artists around in the 1970s were: - Thimblestone, The Two Daves and Christine Fairbairn, both of Ilkley. From Halifax there were The Simple Folk and the duos Labrador, Creatikon and The Cobblers.

Other venues at this time were:-

In 1972, Bingley Folk Club at the Ferrands Arms, a folk club at The Star, Ilkley, and another at the Red Lion, Burley-in-Wharfedale.

On Easter Monday 1972, there was a folk festival at Yeadon from 12 – 11 pm, at the princely sum of 75p.

While on the Bradford folk scene during the 1970s and '80s, there was...

ROGER SUTCLIFFE

A Bradford-born folk/blues guitarist Roger Sutcliffe has been a feature of the local folk scene since the late 1960s and was also a keen supporter of the Topic Folk Club.

He is a qualified music teacher, who had taught me at Clayton Junior High when I was a lad. Proficient at performing traditional US blues originals, he has become

something of a living legend.

Since 1974 he has regularly visited Germany and has gained a strong reputation there, releasing his first German LP 'Games Being Run' in 1976 on the Bonn-based Froggy Records. 'He belongs to

that class of musician with whom, after the last note has sounded, you can drink a wine or beer with.' (10)

In 1976 Roger released another album, 'Death Letter', on local Huddersfield-based Look Records.

SINGERS NIGHT — with added nostalgia — at the Topic with, left to right in the foreground, Roger Sutcliffe, Paul Tattersall, Louise Eaton, Alwyn Daley and Alex Eaton.

Roger Sutcliffe was always a keen supporter of the Topic Folk Club. For example, on the 29th of January 1980, he hosted a singers' night with Frank Cahill in aid of Cancer Research.

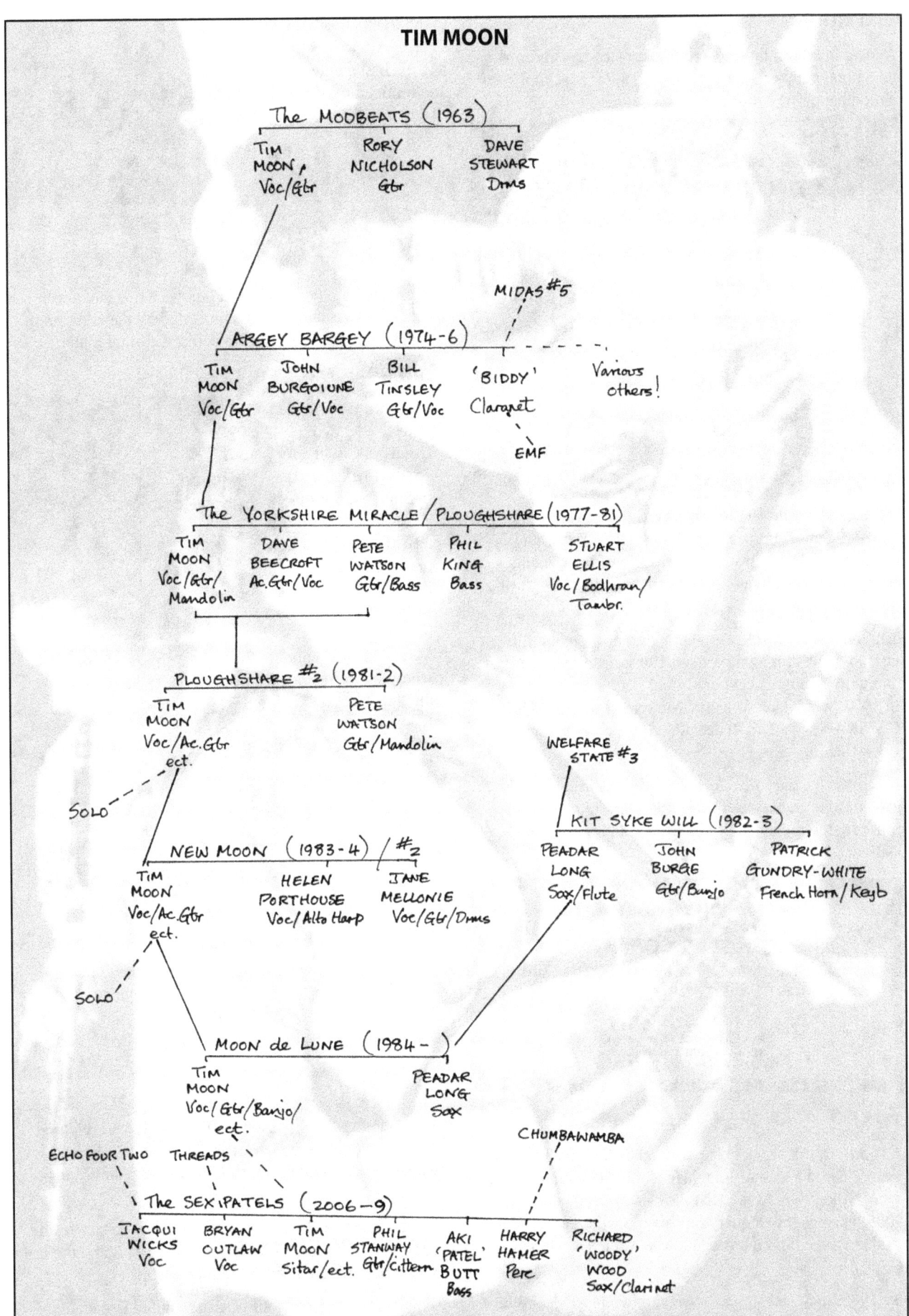

TIM MOON

A local lad, born in Shelf (Halifax postcode, Bradford telephone number!) started playing guitar at school with a mod band The Modbeats.

Influenced by the 1960s new electric folk groups like Fairport Convention and The Incredible String Band, he started to learn how to play a range of instruments, eventually joining various folk-orientated groups during the 1970/80s as well as going solo.

Tim gained a growing reputation as a proficient multi-instrumentalist, playing around 100 instruments - guitars, mandolins, violins, keyboards and saxophones, etc. In 1977, with 'The Yorkshire Miracle', a single, 'The CAMRA Song / The Redeemin' Grace,' was recorded on Look Records.

He continued his solo career and worked with other group projects, besides DJing a regular Monday night folk programme on BCB, the local community radio station.

```
GRAND OPENING NIGHT
of Bradford's Newest Folk Club
SINGERS CORNER
Metropole Hotel, Sunbridge Road, Bradford
Wednesday 13th April at 8 p.m. prompt.
This Week the fabulous
GRAHAM SHAW
Plus many surprise guests.
All floor singers welcome.
Tetley's Hand Pumped Beer
```

TITAN

A Bradford folk /rock group formed by Colin Whittaker, who released a single 'Imaginary Lady / Guaranteed You Won't Like It' on Misty River Music in 1982.(In July 2005, in answer to a query in Record Collector's 'Value Added Fax' column, this single was valued as worth £200!)

By 1983, they had signed a two single/one LP deal with the CBS subsidiary label After Hours, and their first single was a remixed version of the previous years,

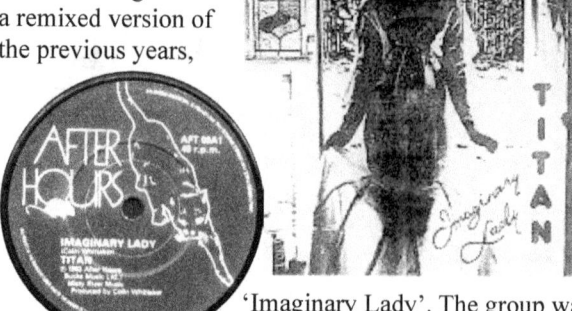

'Imaginary Lady'. The group was also augmented by the addition of Leeds Symphony Orchestra cellist Caroline Slater.

BRENDAN CROKER

Bradford lad Brendan Croker attended Bradford College for a year, then studied in Sheffield for three years, before becoming a British Rail guard, a refuse collector and a theatre set designer at Leeds Playhouse. There he met guitarist Steve Phillips with whom he formed the duo Nev & Norris.

He formed The 5 O'Clock Shadows in 1984 and recorded his debut LP 'A Close Shave' on Dave Foster's (late of Moonkyte) Leeds indie label Unamerican Activities.

During 1986, now based in Leeds, he teamed up with local folk/punks The Mekons as an auxiliary member and featured on their LPs until 1989.

He still kept a version of The 5 O'Clock Shadows going and released a second album, 'Boat Trips In The Bay', in 1987.

He signed to the Silvertone label in 1989 and released a third album, 'Brendan Croker and the 5 O'Clock Shadows', which featured Tanita Tikaram and Mark Knopfler.

Both the above albums featured in the Indie charts; the first reached number nineteen in June 1987, and the last got to number eight in September 1989.

This alliance with Knopfler also reunited Brendan

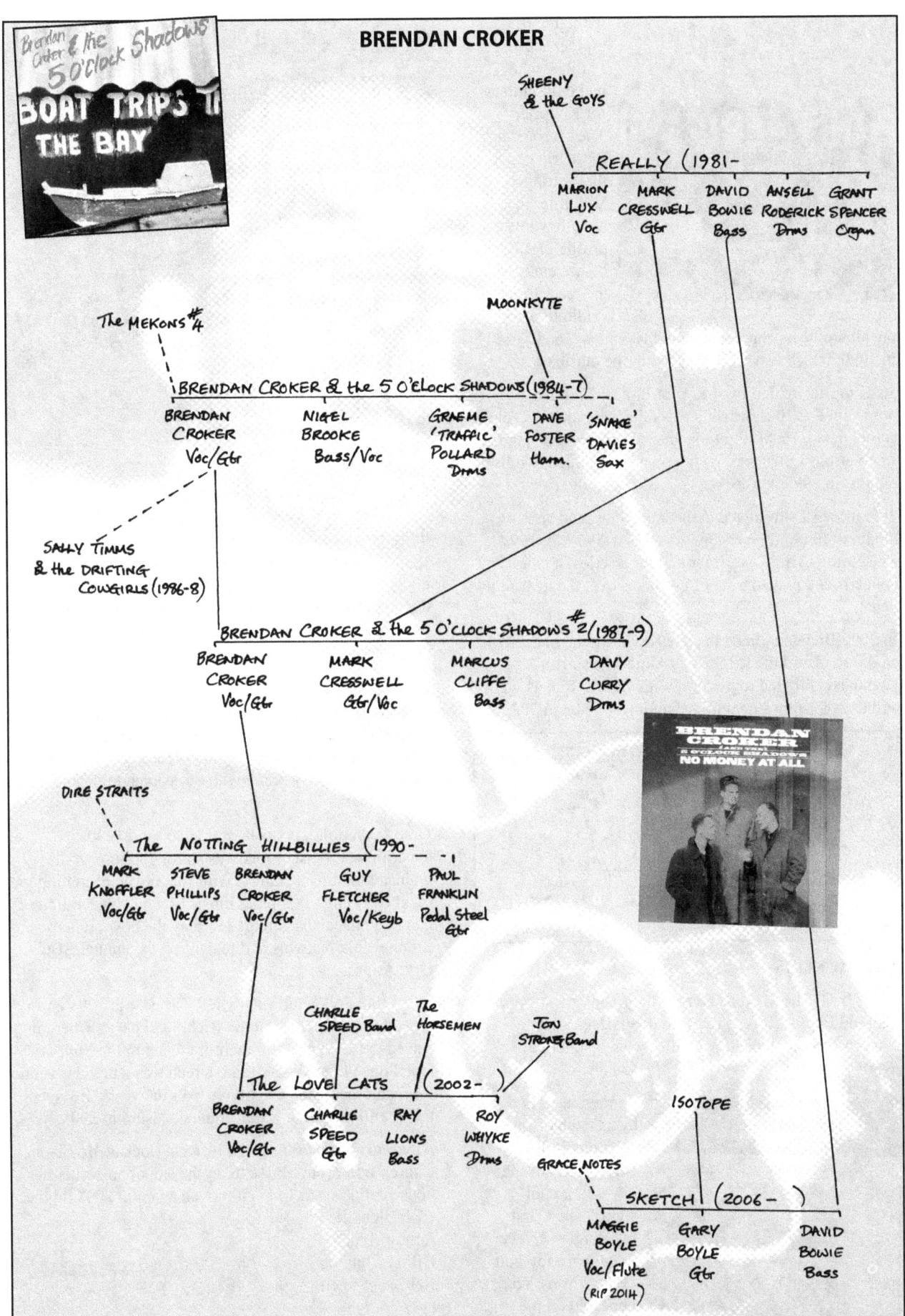

with guitar builder Steve Phillips, who had built guitars for Knopfler. They formed a loose trio called the Notting Hillbillies, and did a few low profile gigs before entering the recording studio to record the album, 'Missing… Presumed Having a Good Time' in 1990, which was well received in the music press.

As Knopfler drifted back to Dire Straits, Brendan, by now hailed as 'the British Ry Cooder', pursued his solo career again. He also got together a new backing band, The Serious Offenders, with whom he recorded two live albums in 1993 and 1994.

Two more LPs followed in the late 1990s, and an album of his Andy Kershaw sessions in 1995. In 1997 The Notting Hillbillies reformed for a series of charity concerts and played a set of UK dates over the next few years.

In 2002 Brendan joined the late Kevin Coyne in the studio to record the LP 'Life Is Almost Beautiful'. Brendan continued to perform with various folk as well and do solo shows up until his untimely death in 2023.

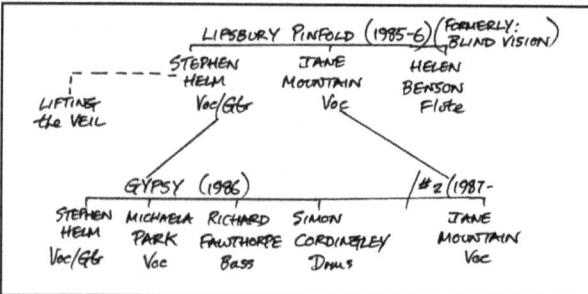

THE MEKONS

Leeds band The Mekons merged their punk rock roots with old English folk to reinvent themselves as an alt-country-folk-punk band, with their own distinctive sound.

Formed in 1977 by a bunch of fine art students, they became one of the city's first punk bands. Their first two singles, 'Never Been in a Riot' and 'Where Were You', appeared on the Fast Products label, before the band signed to Virgin Records in 1980 and produced a double LP called 'The Quality of Mercy is Not Strnen.'

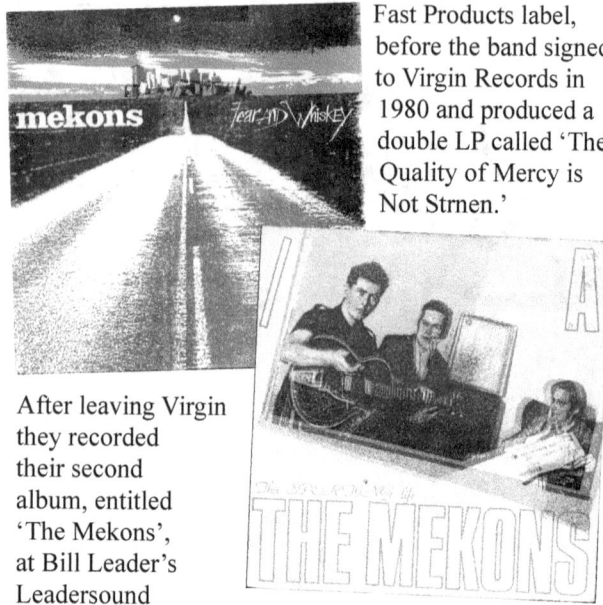

After leaving Virgin they recorded their second album, entitled 'The Mekons', at Bill Leader's Leadersound studios, just outside Halifax, with engineer John Gill. The album would eventually surface on the York label Red Rhino in 1981 reaching number seventeen in the Indie charts.

Joining Leeds-based CNT Records in 1983 they released the twelve-inch single 'English Dancing Master' which would establish their new evolution and future sound, drenched in Americana country & western and urban electric folk.

Between 1985 and 1990 they had three top twenty LPs in the Indie charts, including the acclaimed 'Fear and Whiskey', before certain members relocated to Chicago, USA. Up to the present they continue to charm the US alternative country scene with occasional tours and gigs and albums.

Despite the folk purists by the 1980s and 1990s, experimental/twisted folk was starting to impact the mainstream music culture, with folk music becoming the 'next big thing' in popular music as a new generation of talented musicians emerged to play the now numerous summer folk festivals and feature on the annual BBC Folk Awards.

The Topic Folk Club finally left The Star in 1991 and moved to the Peel Hotel, on Richmond Road, where it stayed until 1994. From there it moved to the Melborn Hotel on White Abbey Road, which was a popular venue for many local music ventures over the years. It stayed there until the venue's unfortunate closure in 2005.

After moving in 2006 to the historic Cock & Bottle on Church Bank (built in 1820 on the site of an earlier ale house dating from 1747) it moved again in 2008, to the Irish Club, the former John Dillon Club, on Rebecca Street. (11)

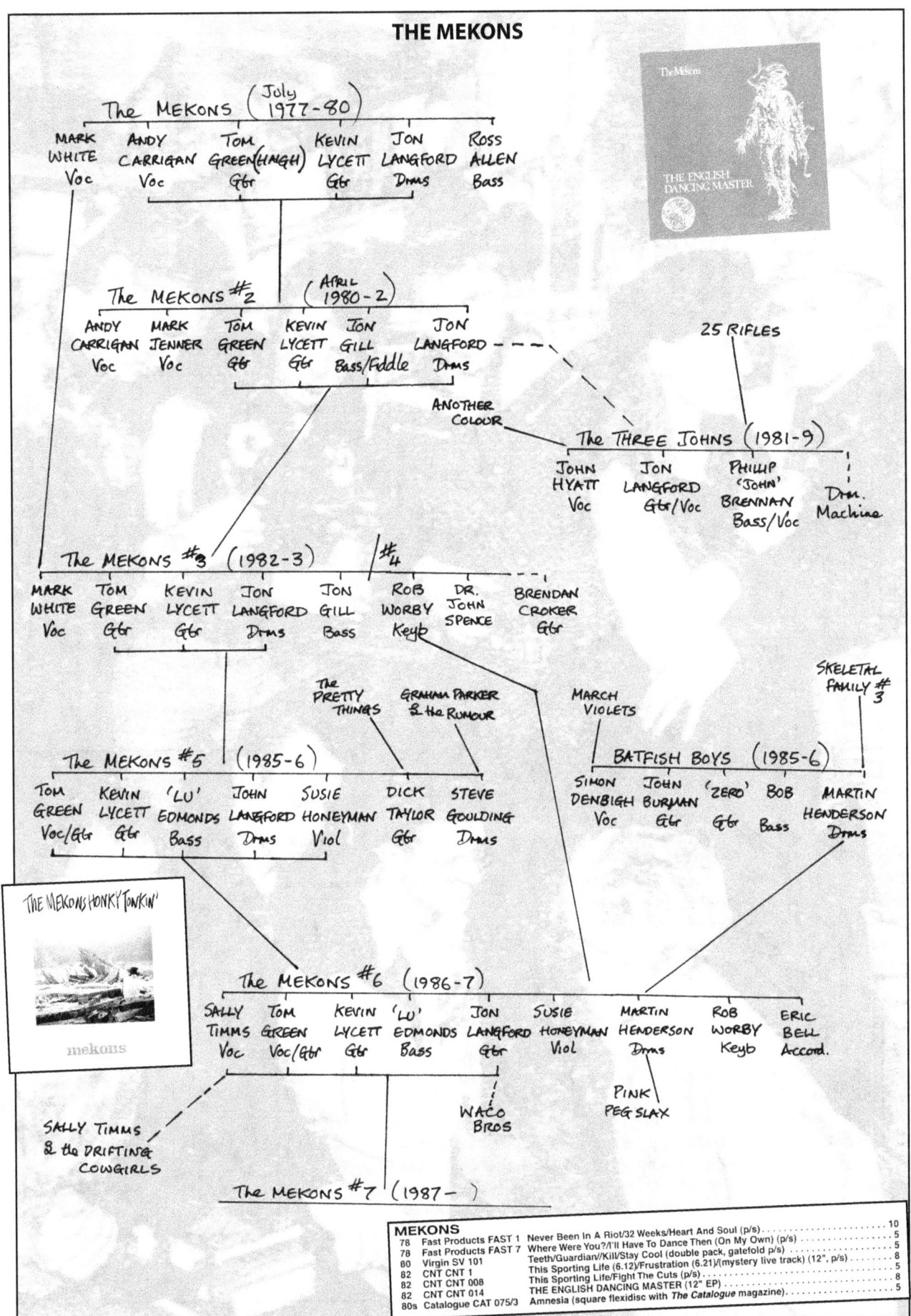

1956 - 1987 BRADFORD'S NOISE OF THE VALLEYS

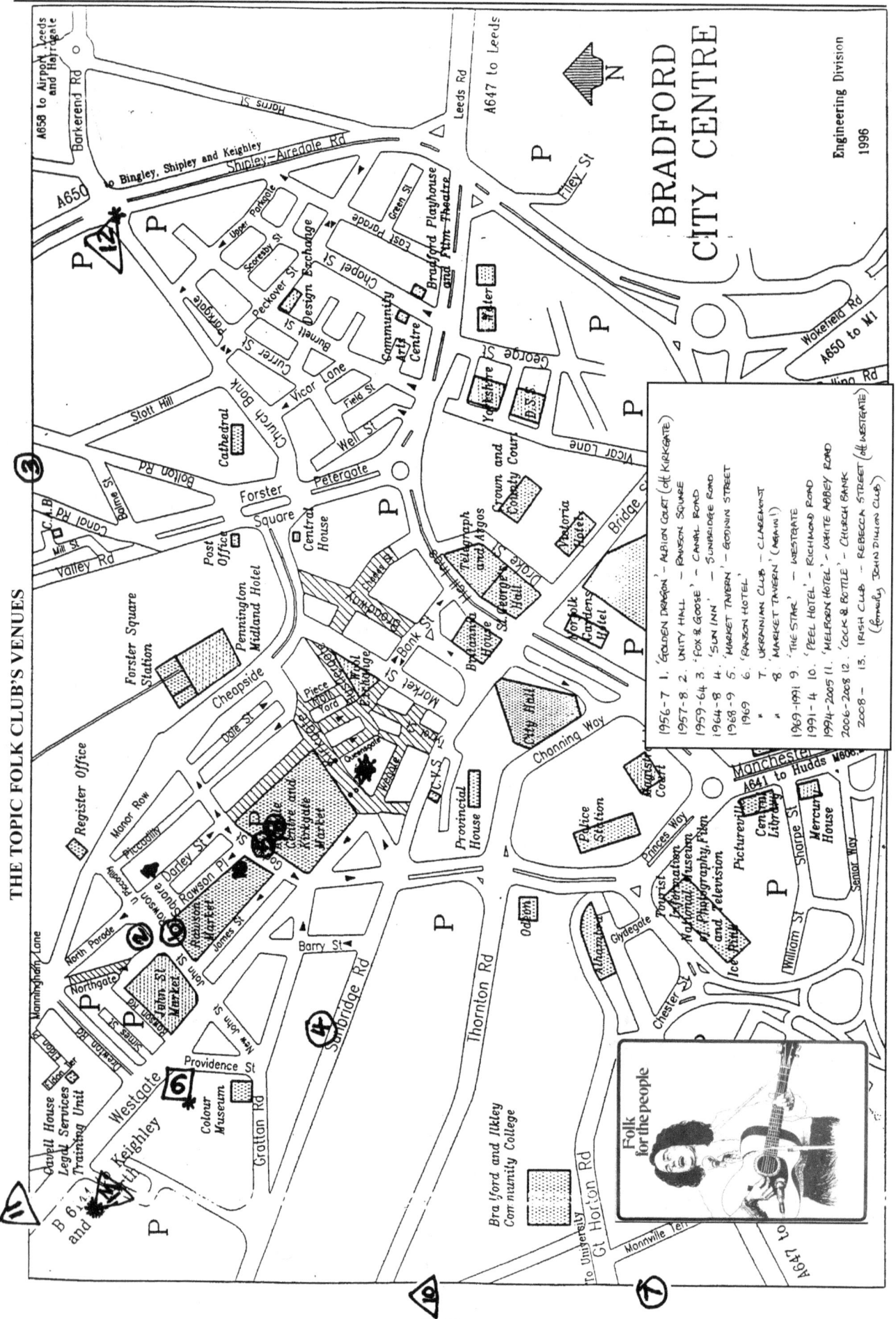

Chapter 4
PUNK NEW WAVE Heavy Metal
1977 - 1980

The British rock music culture of the late 1970s was becoming a staid, safe, self-congratulatory affair. With most major bands having already sold out, living as tax exiles or flaunting excessive lifestyles to an audience in the throes of severe economic recession with unemployment at around two million in 1977, music was starting to become dangerously bland, pompous and boring. A breath of fresh air was needed.

In 1976 it arrived - with punk, initially influenced by late 1960s - early '70s American groups like Velvet Underground, MC5, Iggy & The Stooges and the New York Dolls.

The movement was kick-started by 'garage' style groups like The Ramones, The Dictators, Television, Blondie, Patti Smith, Richard Hell & The Voidoids and Talking Heads between 1975 and 1976 at a low-life bar in New York's Bowery district called CBGB's.

In the UK in 1976 bands like the Sex Pistols, The Clash, The Damned and The Stranglers were the forerunners

The Ramones outside CBGB's

of what became known as 'punk rock' and seemed to epitomise a very different British version of this new music revolution. The fledgling punk rockers were initially based in London and its surrounding suburbs, and were closely followed by the likes of Chelsea, 999, Siouxsie & The Banshees and, in Manchester, The Buzzcocks.

What was a revelation to many was the general punk rock ethic; it was anti-establishment, political and helped to create a new do-it-yourself youth culture with people designing their own home-made fashions, hair styles, 'Fanzines' (Mark Perry's 'Sniffin' Glue' was a blueprint for thousands to come!) and of course there was the music - raw, basic and experimental.

In the past bands had to go cap in hand, touting demos to record companies with the hope of a record deal, competing with thousands of others. With the DIY culture, bands no longer had to do this; they could record and produce their own single on their own label, thus shaking up the music industry by demystifying the production process. (1)

Because punk took a little longer to hit the north, it didn't start to have a real impact until around 1978, so the old rock scene continued to dominate the local music culture.

Bradford's main venues were still St George's Hall, Queen's Hall and the university Great Hall and Communal Building where touring rock groups were still drawing crowds.

JED'S BLUES BAND

After leaving rock band Midas, vocalist Jed Turner formed the first incarnation of his long-running self-named blues band who, after playing for over more than thirty years, became something of a Bradford institution. After

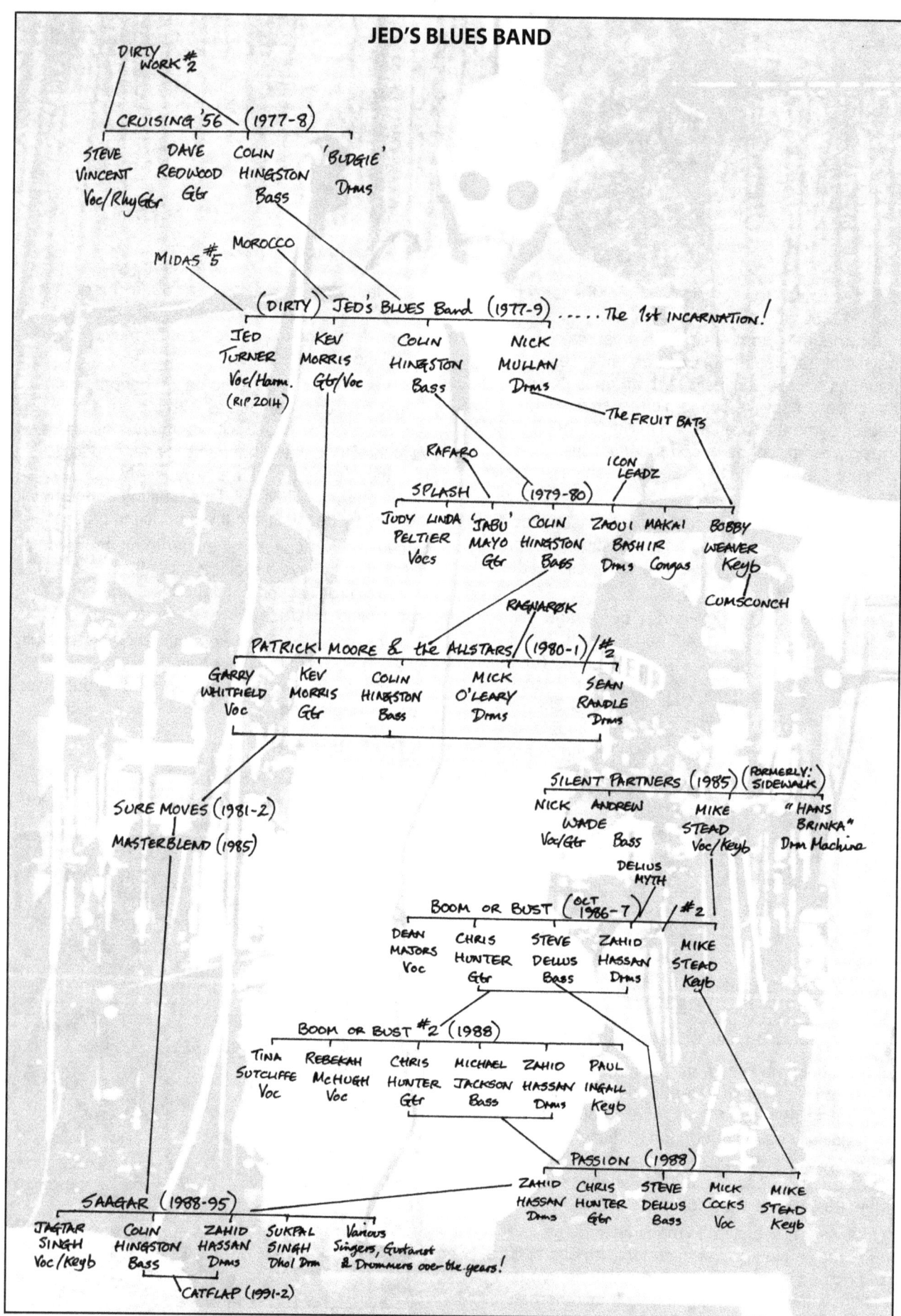

the original band split in 1979, it became a loose jamming outfit with various line-up changes over the years which included many famous local guest appearances.

In the early 1980s they played a regular residency on Sunday nights at the Palm Cove Club with Jed as the central figure, singing and playing harmonica. Sadly, Jed passed away in 2014.

A wide range of other semi-pro rock and pop bands, such as **Katzz**, were still plying their musical wares on the lucrative working men's club circuit as well as performing on the increasing pub rock scene.

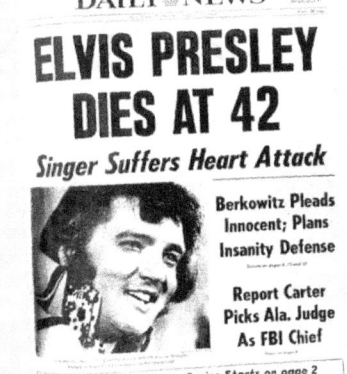

The world of music was shaken by the death of Elvis Presley, the king of rock'n'roll, on August 16, 1977. Elvis died on the toilet from a barbiturate overdose aged only forty-two. At his funeral over 75,000 people gathered outside his Graceland residence in Memphis, Tennessee.

THE ROCKABILLY REBS

Formed in 1977, as an Edwardian (Ted) rockabilly band from Bradford/Leeds The Rockabilly Rebs gigged extensively on the local pub and working men's club circuit. In 1979, they released a self-financed 7" EP single *Boothill Boogie / Ain't Nothin' Shakin'/ One Way Train / Alabama Shake* on SRT Records.

Original members Gary Strain and Paul 'Poppa" Harrison were joined by bassist Graham Kearns and guitarist Nigel Hope in time to play at an EMI/Tetley's sponsored *Band Of The North* competition. They were signed to EMI for a one-album deal, releasing their debut LP *Rockabilly Rebs* in 1981.

Hope was replaced by guitarist Dean Strain for their second album. *Rebels Till The End*, was released on the London-based JSP label in 1982.

This was followed by another 7" single, *Boppin' Bullfrog / Rag-Bones* on their own Bullfrog Records based at Coal Hill Lane, Rodley in Leeds.

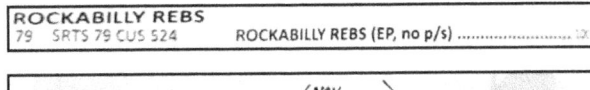

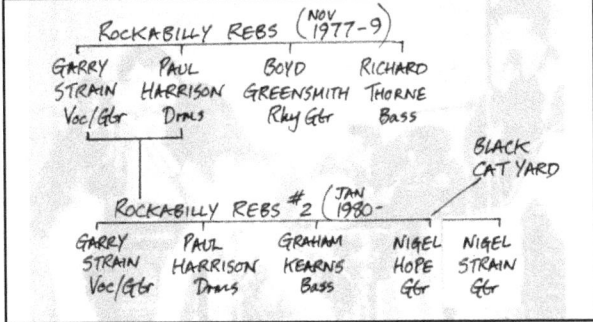

STREET CHOIR / KATZZ

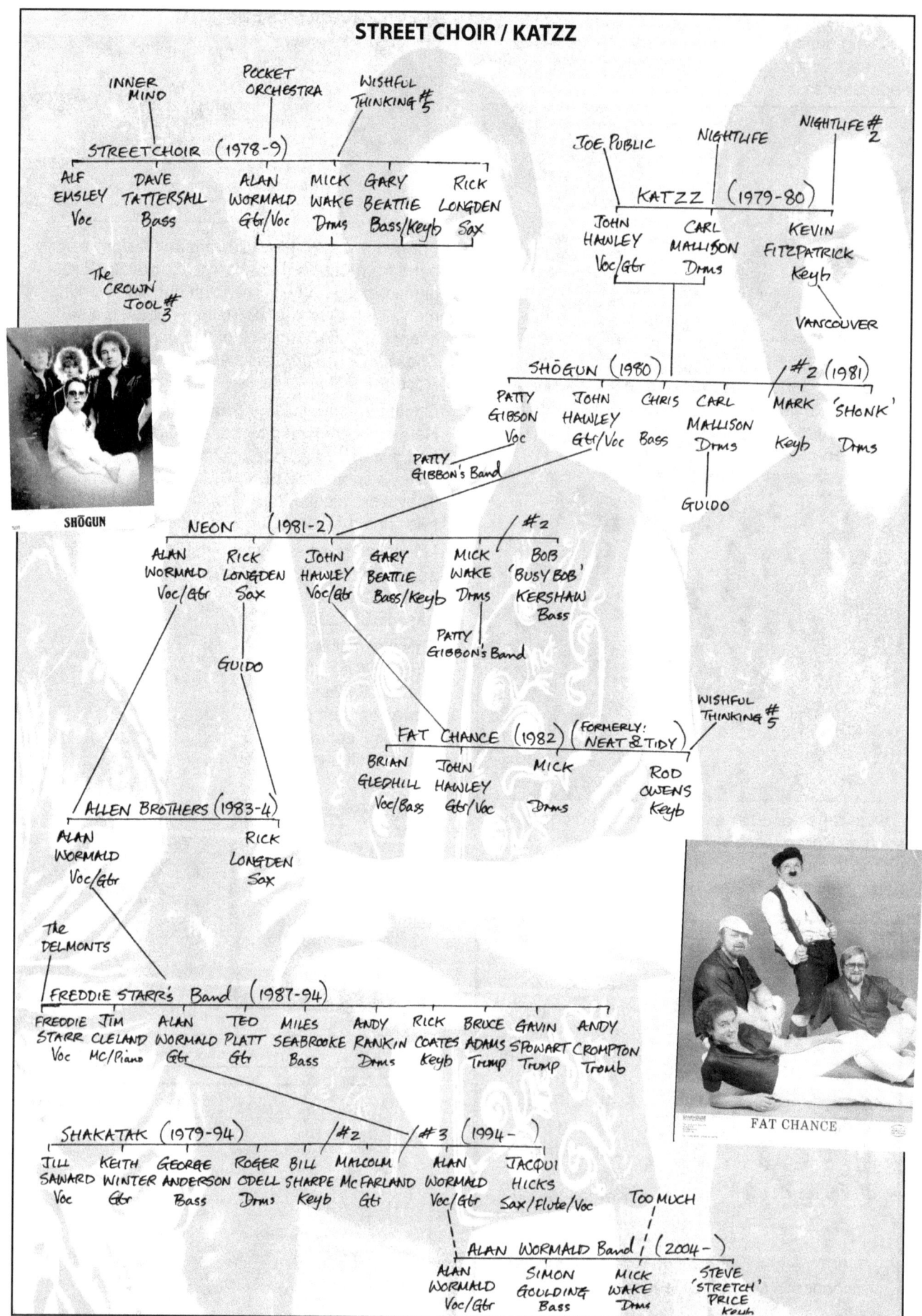

SHŌGUN

FAT CHANCE

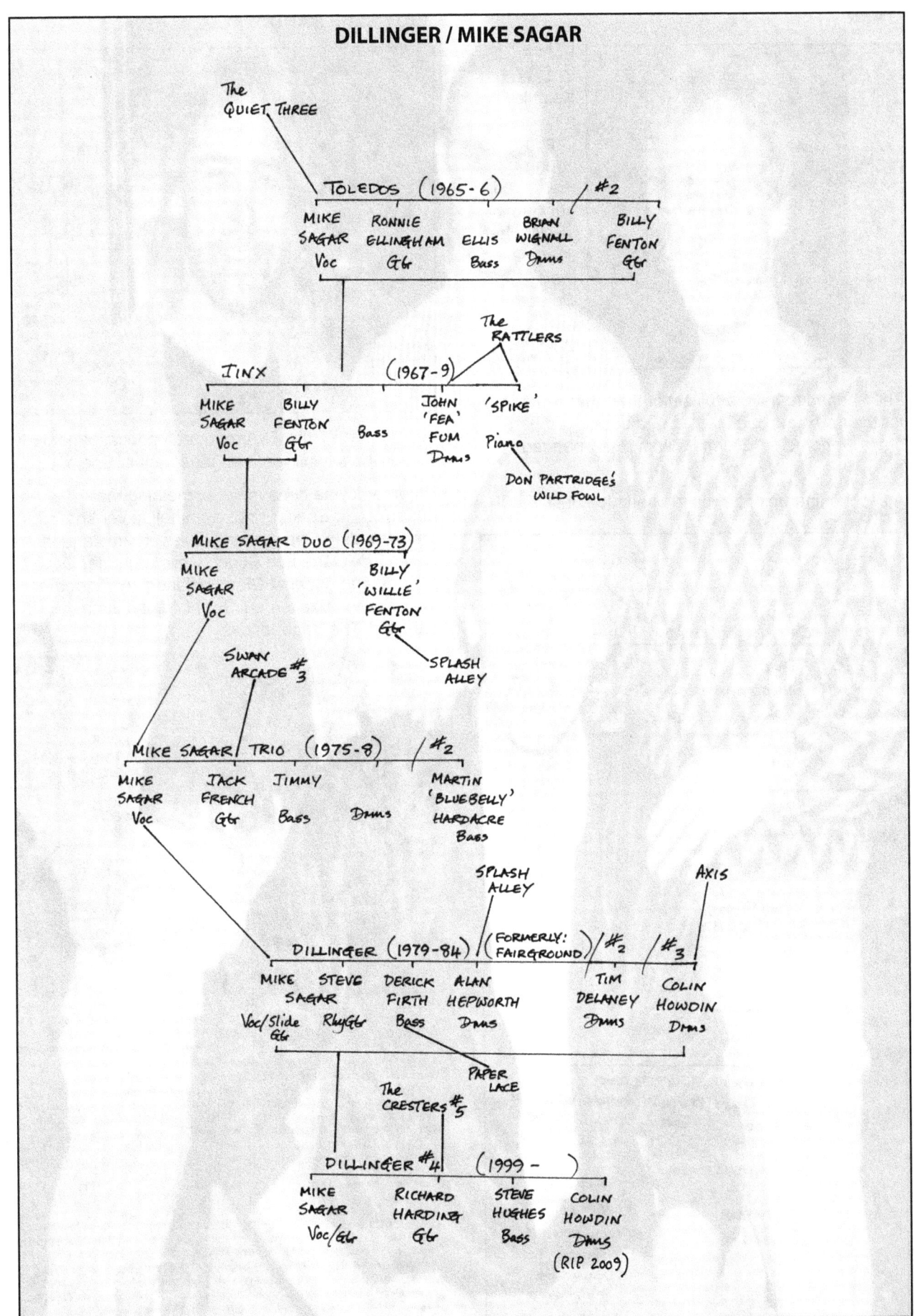

OMEN

Formed in 1977, Keighley rock band Omen were young men aged between 18-21 when they played their debut gig at the town's Downtown Club.

They hoped to have a full set of their own material for their next gig, but in a set of a dozen numbers only *Overlords Of Evermore* was a self-penned tune.

A second line-up of the band continued until 1980.

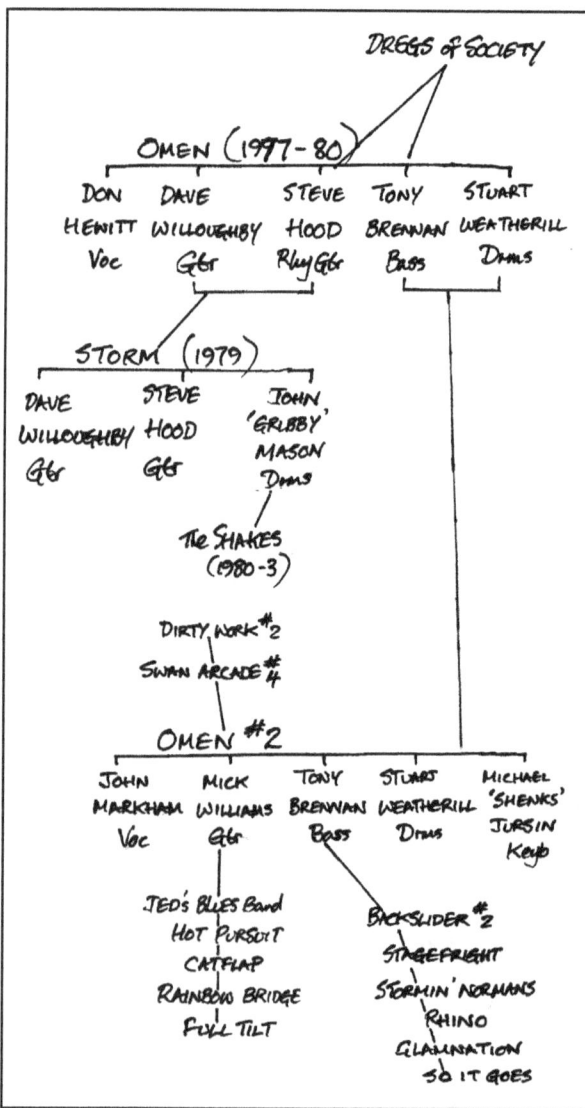

JUDY BLUE BAND

In March 1977 the T&A reported on local band Judy Blue Band's two month engagement in Spain.

Whether it was because of something that happened in Spain or not, we shall never know, but the band didn't last for long. Bassist Kim Jaques joined The Dave Lee Sound while drummer Dave Bussey and guitarist Glen Harland played together in the bands Excitement, Nightlife and Jimmy James & The Vagabonds.

Spain-bound band

A new Bradford group, formed only three months ago, leave tomorrow for a two-month engagement in Spain.

The Judy Blue Band—four men and a girl—have been appearing on the local club circuit and rehearsing for their overseas engagement.

The five—vocalist Julia Smith, David Bussey (drums), Glen Harland (lead guitar), Michael Walker (keyboard) and Kim Jaques (bass guitar)—are all from Bradford. They play a variety of music in their cabaret and disco act.

David Bussey, who was mainly responsible for getting the group together, said they would spend a month at a United States Air Force base at Zaragosa and the second month at a United States Marine camp at Rota, near Gibraltar.

"Last year I returned to Bradford after appearing with another band in summer season and found out that the other members of the group were out of work. We decided to get together and after playing the clubs we auditioned for the tour in Spain and were successful.

"We are delighted and hopefully the summer will bring us a season at one of the major holiday camps," said David.

Picture shows (from the left): David Bussey, Glen Harland, Julia Smith, Kim Jaques and Michael Walker.

CHAPTER 4 - PUNK / NEW WAVE / HEAVY METAL   1977 - 1980

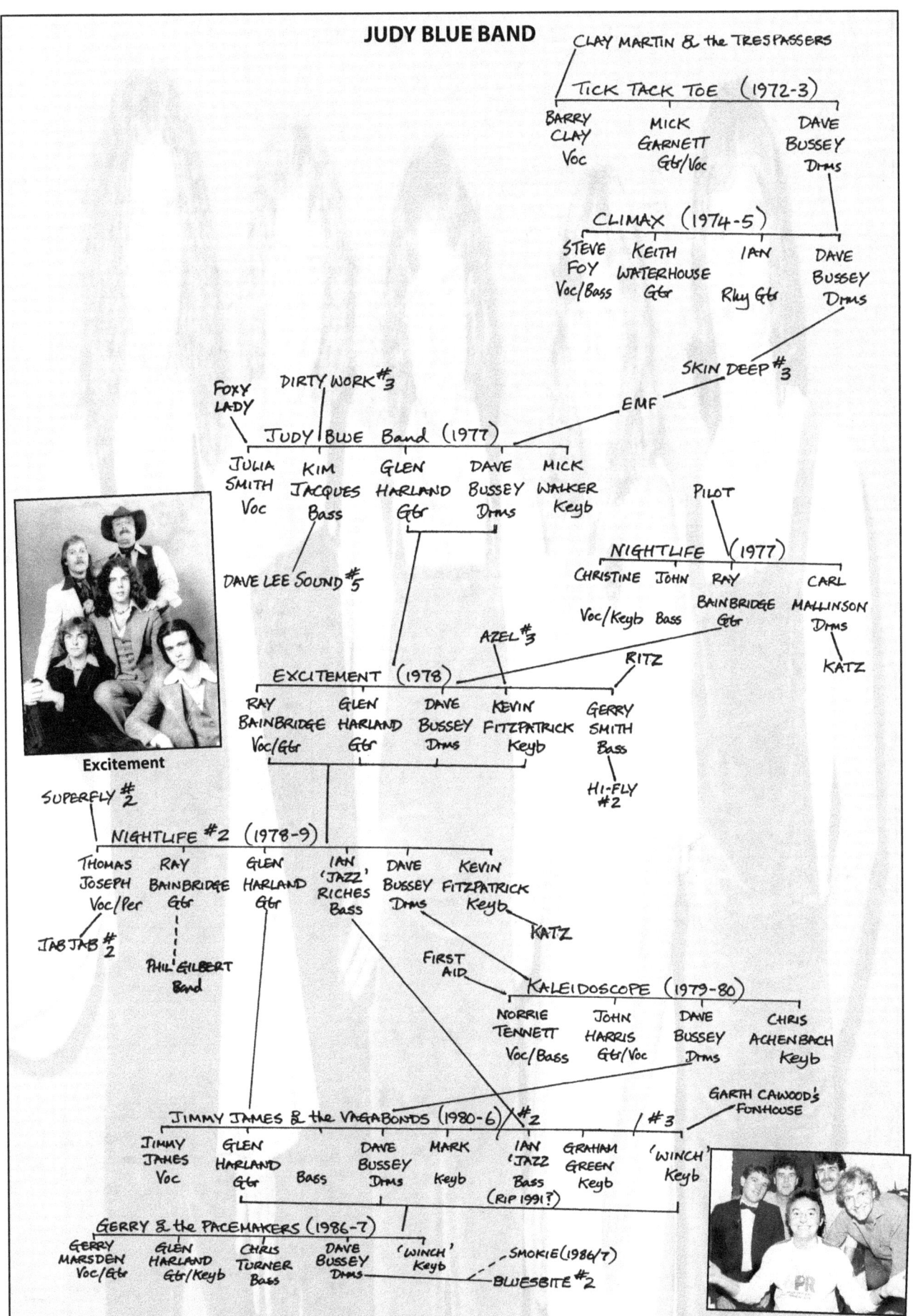

Excitement

127

THE SNEAKERS / ROY SUNDHOLM BAND

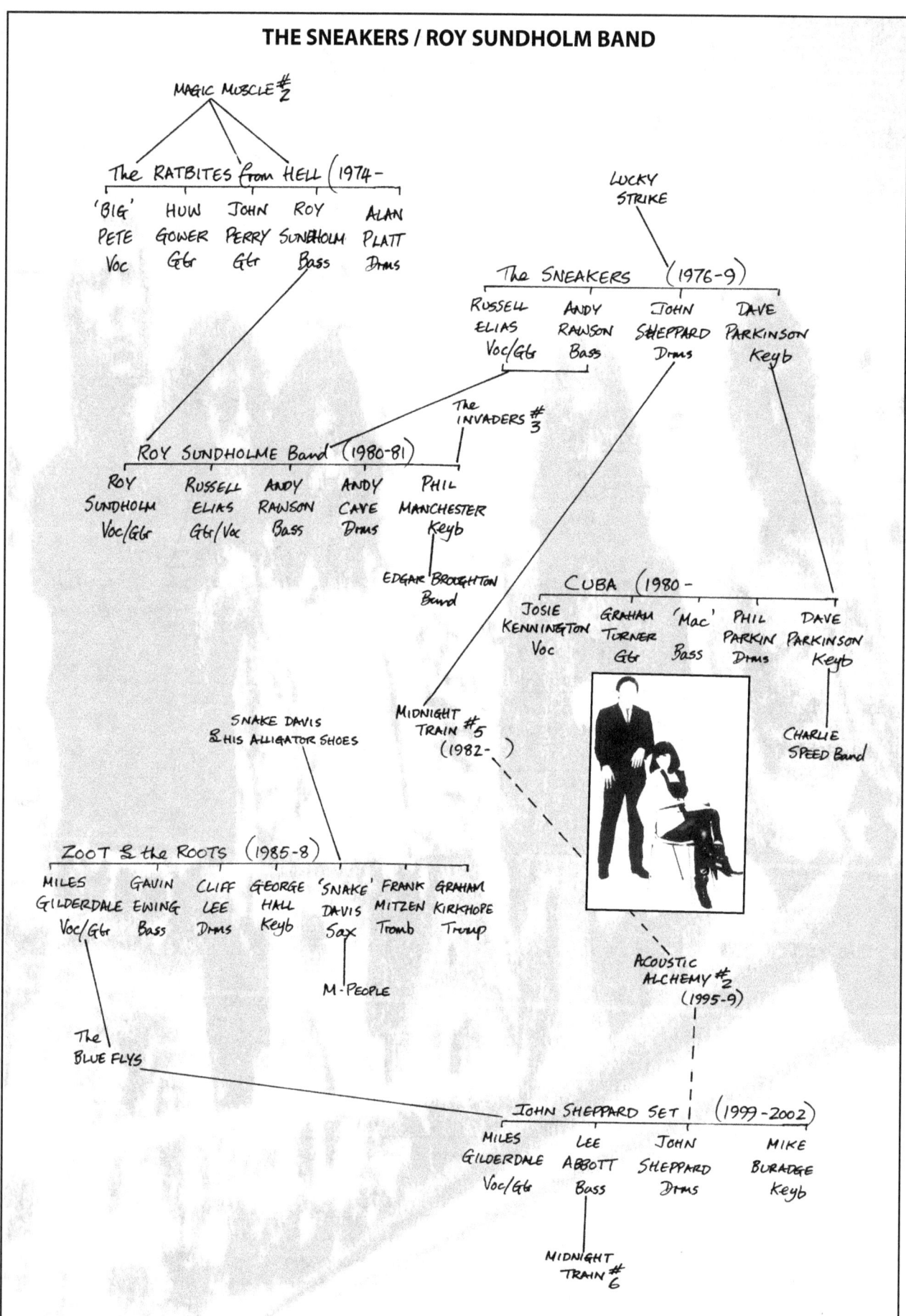

ROY SUNDHOLM

In 1979 local musician Roy Sundholm, a former member of the Spencer Davis Group, released his first solo album, *The Chinese Method*, on Ensign Records. It featured Brian Robertson of Thin Lizzy as a guest guitarist.

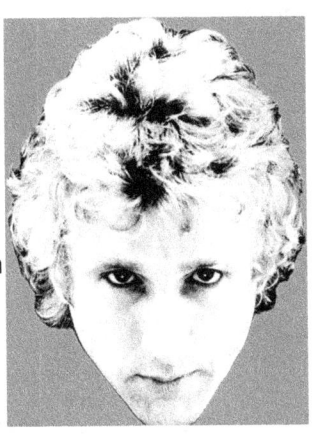

Roy made a second LP, *East To West*, in 1981 which featured Bradford musicians including Phil Manchester on keyboards.

OCEAN

In 1980, local cabaret / club band Ocean released the double A sided soft-rock ballad 7" single *Don't Want You To Love Me / I Must Be Dreaming* on their own Little Black Plastic Records label.

The single was recorded at JSG Studios in Bingley and was produced by Paul Smith, bassist in jazz-rock band Middle 8. The front cover graphic was by Peter Pryimuk.

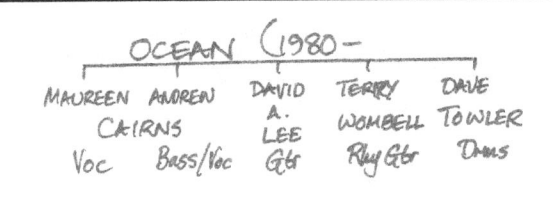

PHOENIX SECOND ALBUM

John Verity's Phoenix released the follow up to their 1976 self-titled debut in 1980 after moving to Charisma Records. *In Full View* was recorded at studios in Los Angeles and London.

On this album, John played guitar and bass and retained the services of Bob Henrit on drums with the addition of extra guitarist Ray Minhinnett.

Former Argent members Rod Argent and Russ Ballard both appeared on the album. Rod Argent played keyboards on the track *Into Your Blood* and Ballard sang backing vocals on two tracks and had written the opening track, *Just Another Day*. Former bassist Jim Rodford had left to join The Kinks in 1978 and was followed by Bob Henrit in 1984.

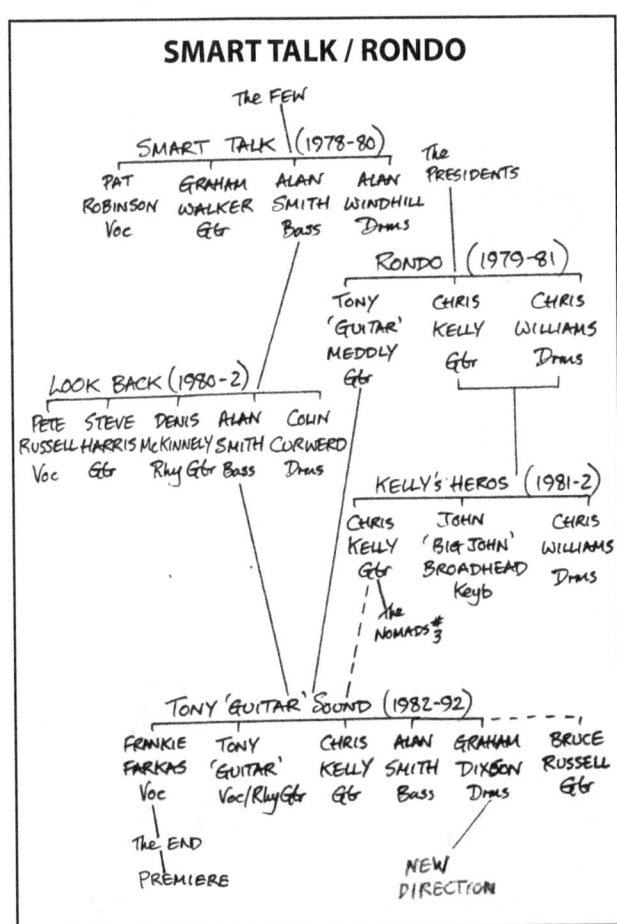

At the end of 1977, the bands **Fireswan** and **Skinny Cat** from Pudsey were on the local scene.

NEW WAVE OF BRITISH HEAVY METAL

By 1978, in a parallel reaction to the punk movement, hundreds of grassroots heavy metal bands had formed all over the UK. This explosion was called the 'New Wave Of British Heavy Metal' (NWOBHM) - a term coined by *Sounds* scribbler Geoff Barton.

Besides the Princeville Rock Club, other venues sprang up to cater for the new rock movement. In its first weeks, the Rock Club at the Victoria Hotel, Manningham, had Kukulkan and Dawnwatcher on the bill. There were also gigs at the Peacock Hotel in Yeadon, where major rock bands like Saxon and Girlschool played. (2)

Some of the more prominent bands on the NWOHM scene were;

BABY TUCKOO

Out of the ashes of the band QED who were on the scene during 1976-77, Baby Tuckoo formed in 1979 around key members guitarist Neil 'Sak' Saxton and bassist Paul 'Smiggy' Smith and became stalwarts of the local heavy metal scene. The first lineup splintered in 1980 when singer Steve Holton joined Cryka and drummer Pete Edmonds left to join Turbo.

With singer Rob Armitage and bassist Tony 'Suggy' Sugden on board, Baby Tucko went from strength to strength, initially with Andy 'Tiddy' Wells on keyboards before he left to join Verity.

They released the single *Mony Mony / Baby's Rockin' Tonight* on the heavy rock label Ultra Noise in 1984, now with Andy Barrott on keyboards and guitar.

Baby Tuckoo's first LP *First Born* (1984) was produced by local rock legend John Verity, on Ultra Noise Records. It featured former EMF/Oral Sax/Somebody's Brother saxophonist Tony Ziwick guesting on the track *Things*.

In 1986, they released the non-album single *Tears Of A Clown / Over You* on the Fun After All label.

Their second album was called *Force Majeure* and appeared on the Music For Nations label in 1986. The LP's first track, *Rock Rock*, was released as a single.

Vocalist Rob Armitage later joined German rock band Accept.

SHADOWFAX

Shaddowfax released the 1979 7' single *Really Into You / Spare Wheel Driver* on their own BFD Records label in 1979. Many years later a self released CD single version appeared with the extra track *Maybe I'm A Fool*.

CHAPTER 4 - PUNK / NEW WAVE / HEAVY METAL 1977 - 1980

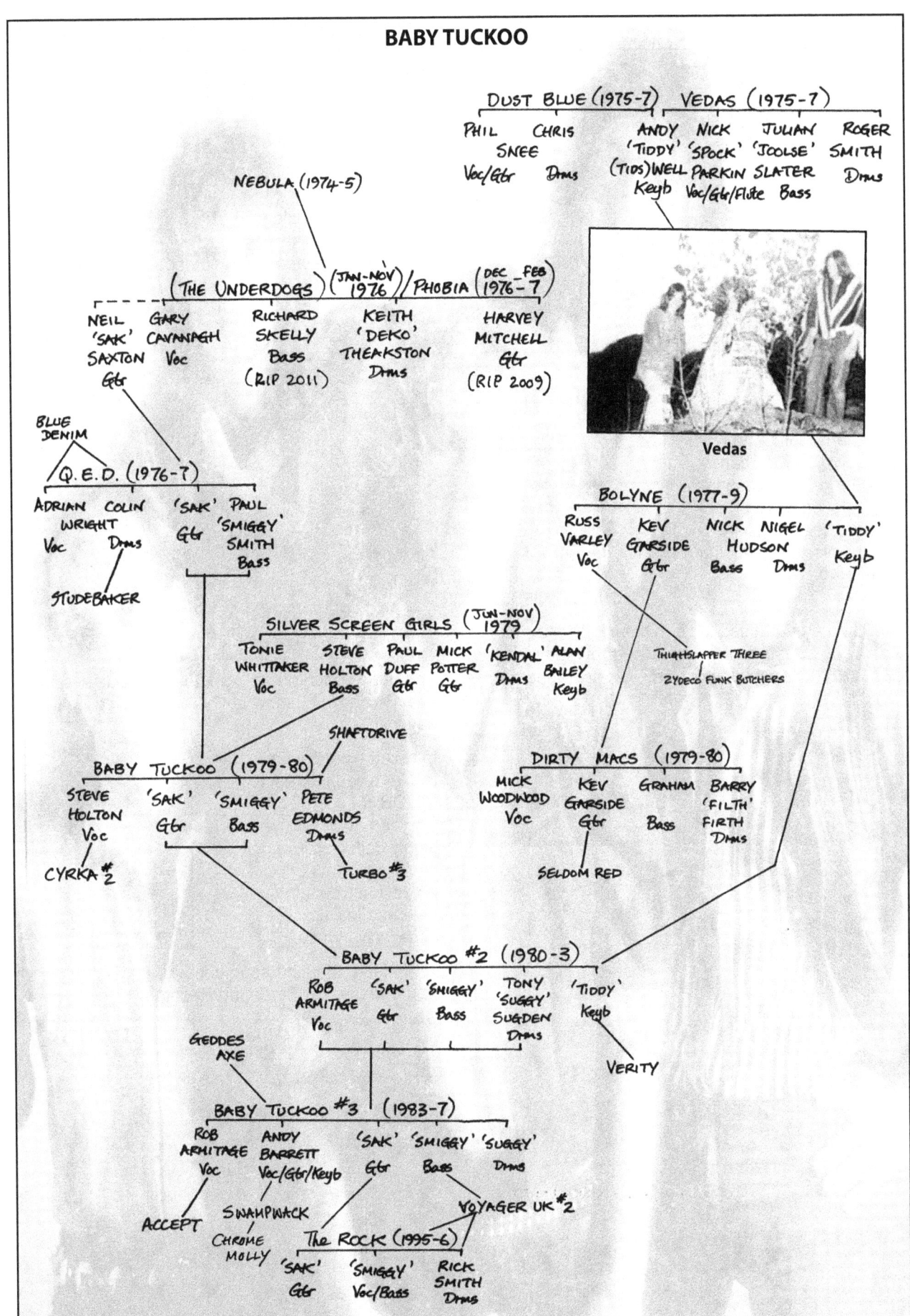

Vedas

DAWNWATCHER

This Keighley-based band formed in 1977 and went on to achieve a well-earned reputation and a large following as a heavy/prog rock band on the NWOBHM scene. They played regularly around West Yorkshire and the North East doing three or four gigs a week.

In 1980 they produced the self-financed seven-inch single *Spellbound / Hall Of Mirrors* on their own label. It received strong reviews and appeared in the Sounds Heavy Metal Chart, reaching number five. Subsequently the single was bootlegged and sold more copies than the originally pressed 1,000.

Their second single was the double A-side *Backlash / Salvador's Dream*, again on their own label, released in 1982.

The band continued to gig with a tour bus and their own PA and light show until they finally called it a day in 1983.

In recent years, with the renewed interest in NWOBHM scene, their singles have become highly collectable and there is still lots of interest surrounding the band in Europe, especially in Italy.

Years later, the nine-song compilation CD *Anthology* was released on Barbarian Records.

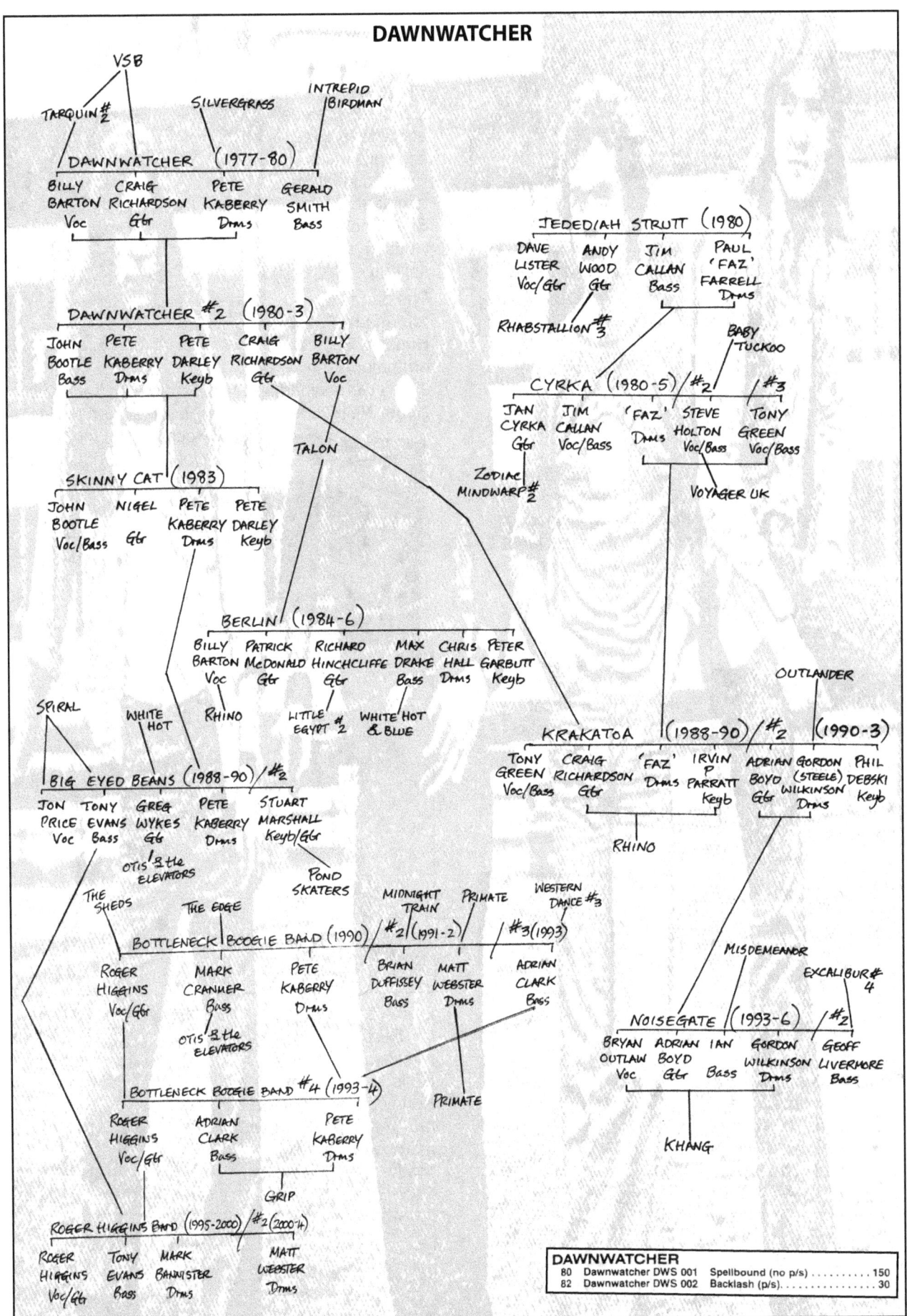

DEDRINGER

These Leeds/Bradford rockers got together in 1977 as the covers band Deadringer before writing their own material. After dropping the 'a' and becoming Dedringer they supported Michael Schenker on his 1979 British tour.

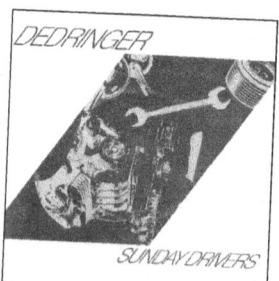

When initial interest from Virgin Records led to nothing, they signed to pop/new romantic label Dindisc in 1980. Their debut single was the 7-inch *Sunday Drivers / We Don't Mind*.

In 1981, Dindisc put out the first Dedringer album, *Direct Line*, produced by former Gong bassist / vocalist Mike Howlett.

The first single from the album was released a a double 7-inch pack in a gatefold sleeve.

Side one on disc one was *Maxine*, taken from the album, backed by *Innocent 'Til Proven Guilty*, recorded live at Nottingham's Rock City. The second disc features non-album tracks *Took A Long Time* and a re-recorded version of their debut single b-side *We Don't Mind*.

A third Dindisc single was the album's title track, *Direct Line*.

Due to poor sales and after a car accident which resulted in injuries to guitarists Al Scott and Neil Hudson, the band split up.

The band reformed in 1982. Hudson, Scott and drummer Kenny Jones were joined by Chris Graham on bass and singer Neil Garfitt. This new lineup signed to Neat Records and their single *Hot Lady / Hot Licks & Rock 'N' Roll* came out that year.

Al Scott left the band and was replaced by former Plexus and Atmosfear guitarist Mick 'Krem' Kremastoules.

By the time their next LP, *Second Arising*, was released in 1983, Neil Hudson and drummer Kenny Jones were the only remaining original members. Dedringer finally called it a day in 1985.

```
DEDRINGER
80   DinDisc DIN 10    Sunday Drivers/We Don't Mind (p/s) . . . . . . . . . . . . . . . . . 5
80   DinDisc DIN 11    Innocent 'Till Proven Guilty/Maxine//Took A Long Time/
                       We Don't Mind (double pack). . . . . . . . . . . . . . . . . . . . . 10
81   DinDisc DIN 12    Direct Line/She's Not Ready (p/s) . . . . . . . . . . . . . . . . . 5
82   Neat NEAT 18      Hot Lady/Hot Licks And Rock'N'Roll (p/s) . . . . . . . . . . . . 5
81   DinDisc DID 7     DIRECT LINE (LP) . . . . . . . . . . . . . . . . . . . . . . . . . . . . 15
83   Neat NEAT 1009    SECOND RISING (LP, with inner sleeve) . . . . . . . . . . . . 12
```

CHAPTER 4 - PUNK / NEW WAVE / HEAVY METAL   1977 - 1980

DEDRINGER

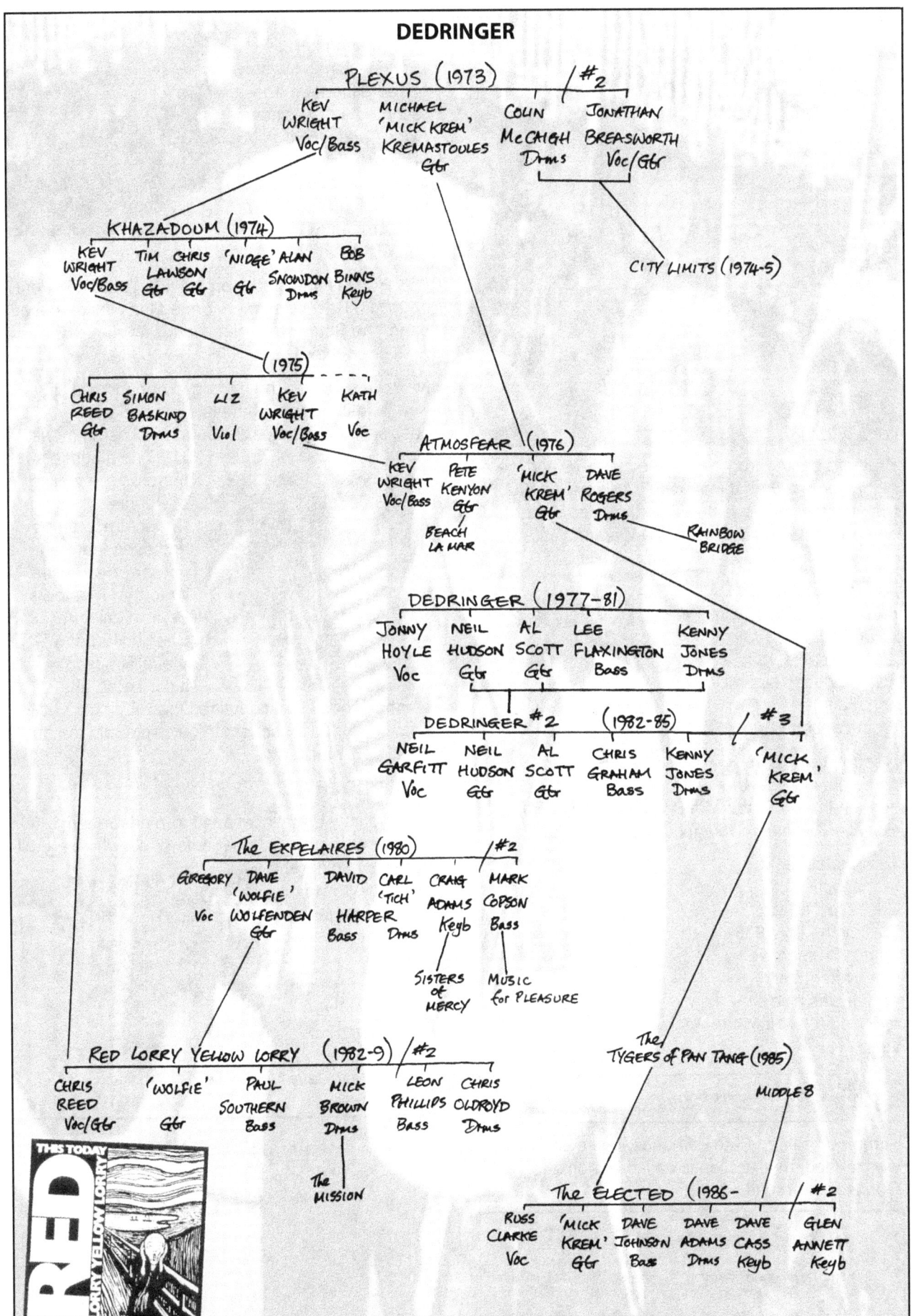

TURBO

Bradford band Turbo also formed in 1979 and were highly regarded on the NWOBHM scene. In 1980, their track *Running* featured on the Logo Records compilation album *New Electric Warriors*.

Cargo Records released the band's three-track EP *Stallion / Running / Take My Life* that same year. It was produced by Fall and Gang Of Four producer John Brierly.

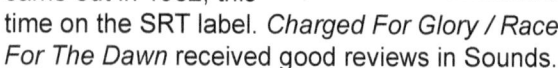

A second single in came out in 1982, this time on the SRT label. *Charged For Glory / Race For The Dawn* received good reviews in Sounds.

Turbo released a retrospective LP/ Cassette *The Last Warrior* in May 1988 on the German Noise label, after they'd split. It was also re-released the following year.

TURBO
80 Cargo CRS 004   STALLION (EP, p/s).........................100
82 Turbo CUS 1261 Charged For Glory/Race For The Dawn.........8

Turbo's drummer, Pete Edmonds, had a sister who formed an all-girl band called Handmade Goddesses around 1980.

HAND MADE GODDESSES (MAY 1980-				(FORMERLY: PHANTASY)
SANDIE EMMONDS Voc	CAROL FLANAGAN Gtr	MARIA TARPY Bass/Voc	TRUDI CROOK Drms	SHARON JOHNSON Keyb

After the band split in 1984, guitarist Pete Mayhew joined Burnley-based Silhouette and recorded two 7" singles, *I Can Take A Hint* (1984) and *Make The Most Of It* (1985) before relocating to Germany and forming AOR band TurboRed who released a LP in 1991.

Des Horsfall, the singer on the first Turbo EP, went on to join Raw Deal, then formed the Halifax-based band The Spurs who released the 7" single *The Soldier* on their Outback label in 1988.

Next, Des formed the roots-rocker band Kuschty Rye, and in honour of the late Small Faces' bassist Ronnie Lane released the CD album *The Good Gentleman's Tonic* in 2011. The album mirrored the feeling of Ronnie's Slim Chance recordings and even featured guest appearances by former members Benny Gallagher, Charlie Hart and Steve Simpson. It consisted of a

hardback book that contained the CD and a pocket which included a sachet of Yorkshire Gold tea and a metal bookmark.

AFTER HOURS

After Hours were a local band formed around 1980. They were a group of ex-Bradford folk who were all students at different universities who got together in the holidays to form a band.

They released a single, *All Over Town / Suspicious*, on the JSG label, produced by Dave Brimacombe.

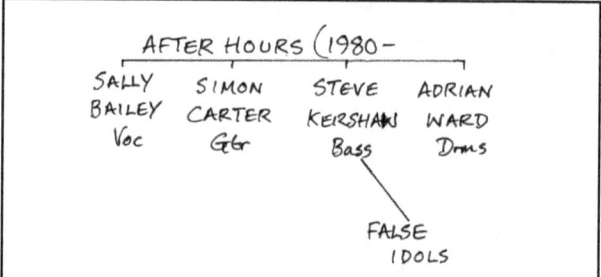

AFTER HOURS (1980-			
SALLY BAILEY Voc	SIMON CARTER Gtr	STEVE KERSHAW Bass	ADRIAN WARD Drms
		FALSE IDOLS	

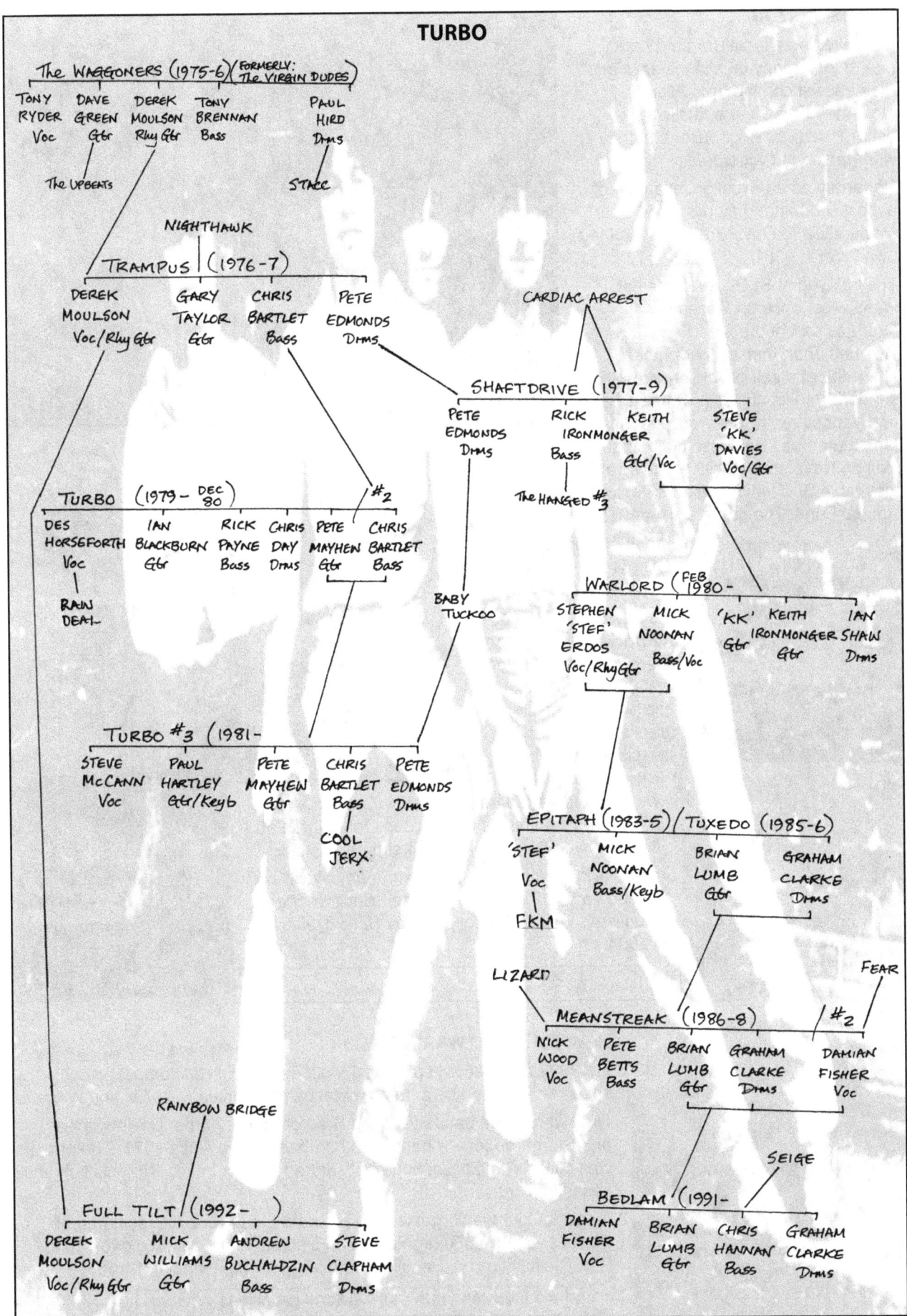

RHABSTALLION

Perceived as a local Bradford band, due to their many gigs in the area and their bassist coming from Allerton, most members were actually from either Halifax or Brighouse, and they were based in Calderdale.

Regarded as an excellent example of a local HM band, they produced one single, *Day To Day / Breadline*, on their own label in 1981.

They played at St George's Hall at least twice; once on December 11, 1980, as part of the *New Electric Warriors Tour*, then on November 26, 1982, at a self-promoted gig with support from local bands Vengeance and Vancouver, where over a thousand fans turned up. They also did a charity gig at Queen's Hall on November 4, 1983, with The Word and The Inevitable Split which raised £250 for the Jeff Naylor Appeal Fund. The group split in 1985.

In 1994, a posthumous CD of their material was released on Vinyl Tap. *Day To Day* contained 12 tracks. Ten of those were recorded between 1980 and 1984, including the single, compilation tracks, old recording sessions and two live tracks. There were also two newly recorded tracks from 1993 when all three of the band's guitarists, Thompson, Toddington and Wood, played together for the first time.

Rhabstallion reformed in 2018 with Andy Wood now on lead vocals. They released their *Back In The Saddle* album in 2021, followed by *Bat Shit Crazy* in 2004.

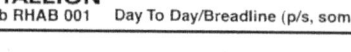

```
RHABSTALLION
81   Rhab RHAB 001   Day To Day/Breadline (p/s, some with badge) .. 30/20
```

NEW ELECTRIC WARRIORS

In 1980 Logo Records released a budget-priced HM compilation of sixteen bands up and coming metal bands entitled *New Electric Warriors*.

On it were three bands from the Bradford area: Turbo, Dawnwatcher and Stormtrooper – a band who had been going since 1977. Their track was called *Grind'n'Heat*. It also featured Halifax bands Rhabstallion and Jedediah Strut.

A special tour was organised to promote the LP and the local part of the tour was at St George's Hall on December 11, with a gig featuring Rhabstallion, Turbo, Bastille, Stormtrooper and Jedediah Strut.

```
80   Logo MOGO 4011   NEW ELECTRIC WARRIORS ....... 20
```

CHAPTER 4 - PUNK / NEW WAVE / HEAVY METAL 1977 - 1980

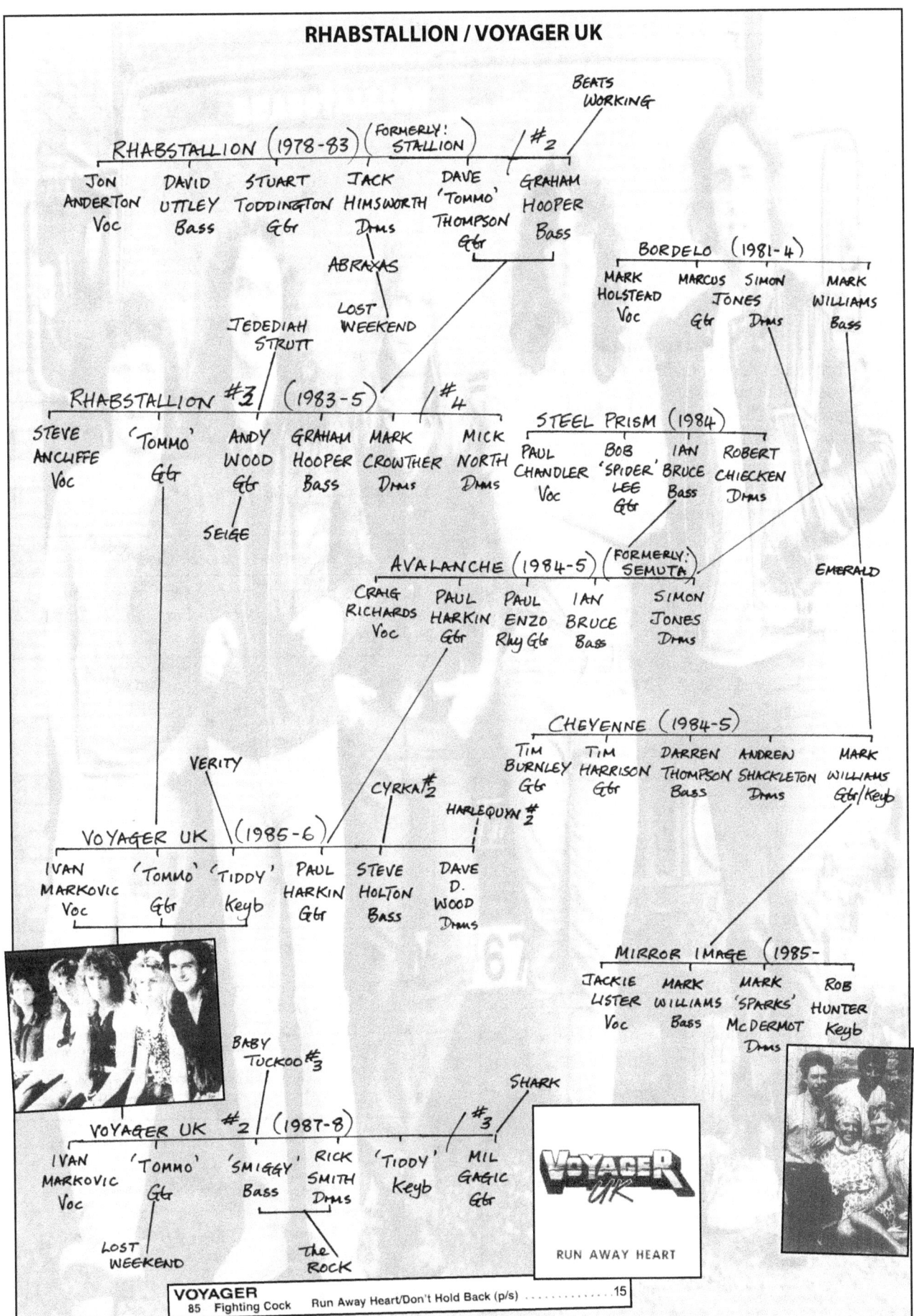

RHABSTALLION / VOYAGER UK

STORMER

Castleford band Method reached the final of TV's *New Faces* talent show in 1975. They signed to Jonathan King's UK Records and released six singles with little success.

The band then signed to Ringo Starr's Ring-O-Records. With the new label came a new name, Stormer. Original Kindness/Smokestack drummer Ron Kelly was brought in when initial sessions with the original drummer didn't go well.

Stormer recorded a full album's worth of material at Ringo's Starling Studios at the famous Tittenhurst Park, once owned by John Lennon.

They released the 7" single, *My Home Town / Shake It Baby* in February 1978 and posed with Ringo for publicity shots with a mock-up of the LP cover.

Unfortunately, Ringo's label was shut down by his manager as it was losing money and the album was never released.

STORMER
78 Ring O' 2017 113 My Home Town/Shake It Baby (some in promo p/s)...70/40

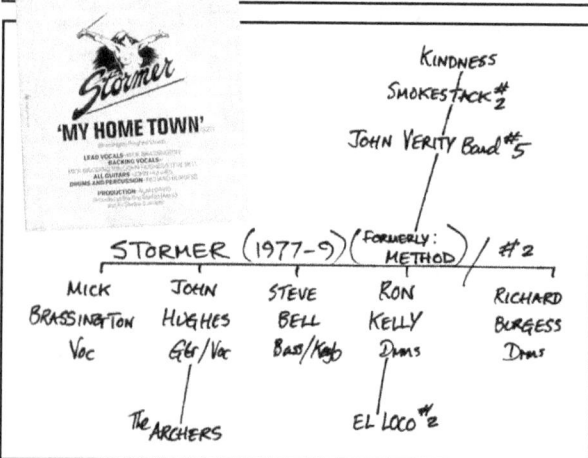

CHALLENGER

Keighley band Challenger were only active between 1980 and 1981 but manEged to release a highly collectable 7" single *So Sure Of Yourself / Out To Kill* on their CMC label.

CHALLENGER
81 CMC CM 0001 So Sure Of Yourself/Out To Kill 40

The band's rhythm section of Martin Keighley and Alastair Wiseman went on to form the trio Single File in 1982.

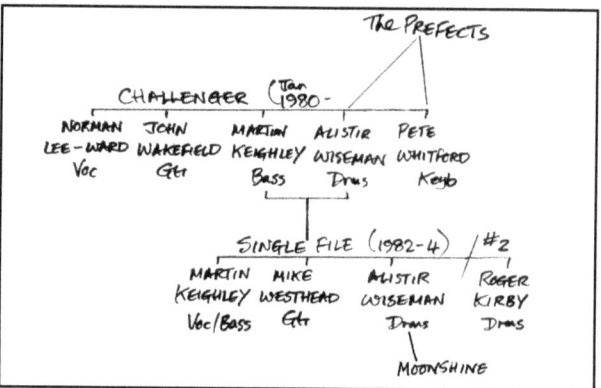

STORMTROOPER

A local metal band started around 1977 who featured former John Verity Band drummer Roland Dawson. Their track *Grind'n'Heat* featured on the 1980 NWOBHM compilation *New Electric Warriors* on Logo Records, which also featured tracks from Dawnwatcher, Rhabstallion and Turbo.

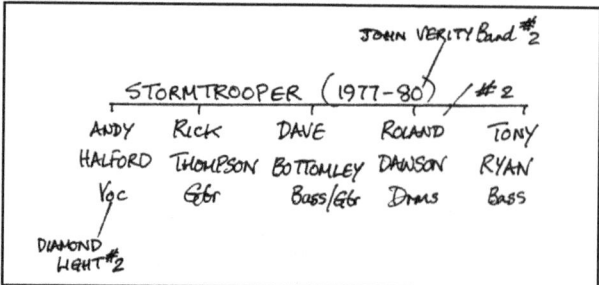

BLACK ONYX

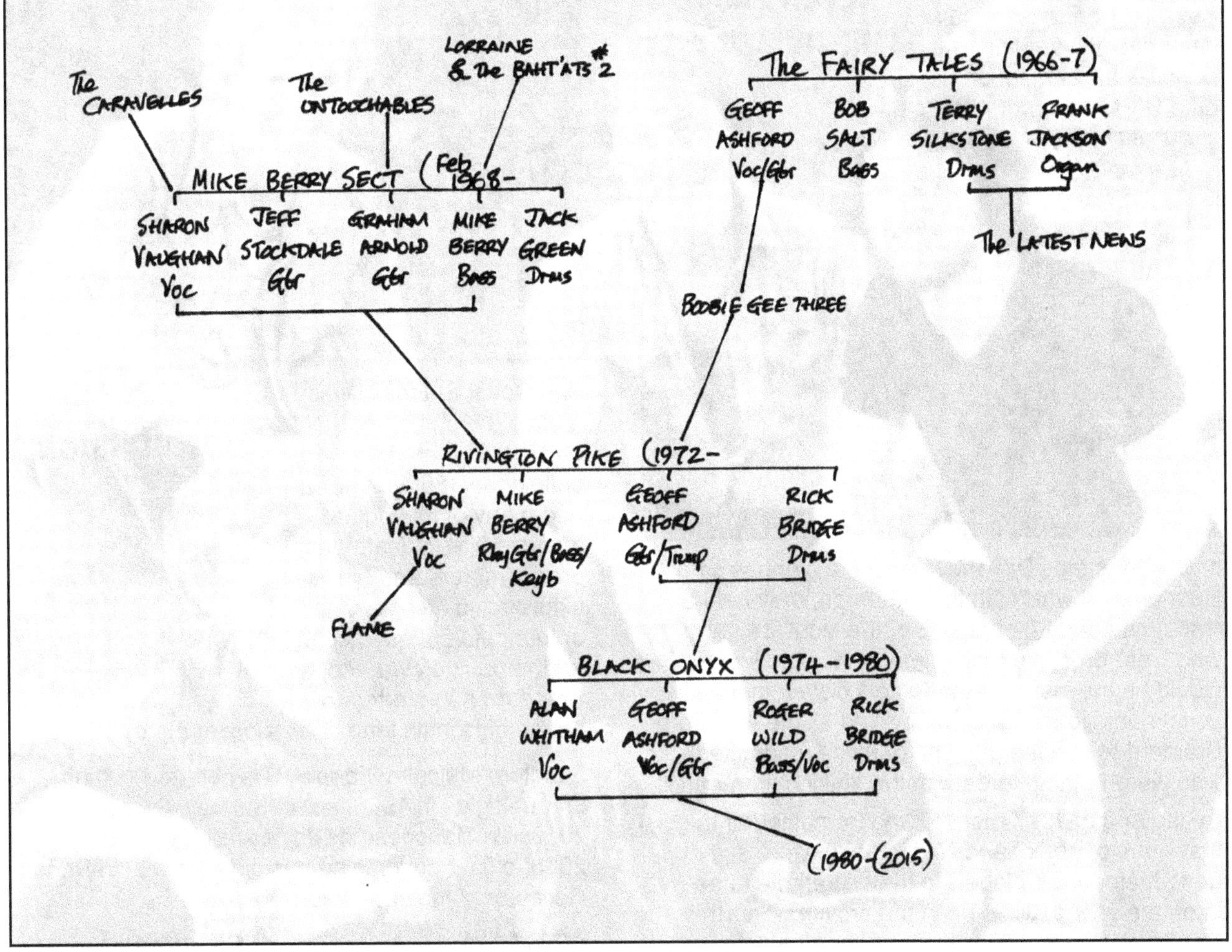

BLACK ONYX

Black Onyx were a comedy showband, formed from the remnants of Bradford pop band Rivington Pike. They appeared on the TV talent show *Opportunity Knocks* in 1974.

They became one of the North of England's best-loved club bands for many years.

In 1980, the band released their only 7" single, containing three tracks; *I Didn't Mean To Make You Cry / Greatest Performance Of My Life / If I Never Sing Another Song*. It was recorded at Mick Robson's Ric-Rac Studios in Leeds and released on the in-house label Luggage Records.

After guitarist Geoff Ashford left around 1980, the band became a trio and continued to perform until at least 2015.

In 2009, Black Onyx were the closing act on comedy actor Ricky Tomlinson's *Laugher Show*, where he appeared in the guise of Jim Royle, his character from TV's *The Royle Family* fame.

THE PUNK / NEW WAVE SCENE

In November 1977 the Sex Pistols released their infamous *Never Mind The Bollocks* LP and set off on a UK tour to promote

it. On Christmas Day they arrived at Ivanhoe's in Huddersfield where, in the afternoon, they held a Christmas party for the kids of the local firemen who were on strike at the time. That night's gig would be the last time the Pistols played in the UK. Local punk Johna Johnson walked all the way from Bradford to see the gig, one of the few admitted who were nothing to do with the striking firemen. (3)

By the end of 1977 most of what remained of the first wave of punk bands in the south were signed up to major record labels in their scramble to be in on the scene, while up in the provincial north Bradford's punk scene was only really getting started by 1978.

Only a few local bands, such as The Negatives, The Misfits (formed in 1977 with Justin Sullivan, Stuart Morrow and Phil Thompkins who developed into New Model Army) and Cameras In Cars, had begun by 1978, but they soon had a growing fan base on the local scene.

Pretty soon venues like the Royal Standard on Manningham Lane and the Vaults Bar were putting on gigs as well as local bands organising their own at nightspots like Scamps.

THE ROYAL STANDARD

The Royal Standard was a big old Victorian pub on Manningham Lane, built in the 1860s. It still had many of its original features like intricate and ornate mirrors and bar fixtures and fittings. One of the first venues to cater for the punk crowd, the Standard had started to put on gigs in its long back room in the mid-1970s.

THE ROYAL STANDARD
Presents
JOY DIVISION
plus
EMERGENCY
& DISCO
SUNDAY SEPTEMBER 10th
(Late Bar)
22, Manningham Lane, Bradford.

Landlord Malcolm 'Fairplay' Day started putting on punk gigs in 1978, as on Sunday, September 10, when Manchester's Joy Division played. (In 2005, a flyer advertising this gig was sold in Record Collector Magazine for £120!)

Other examples of the first generation of punk/new wave bands that played included; Adam & The Ants (12/1/79 and 22/7/79 on their Zerox Tour), The Ruts (22/7/79), Generation X, UK Subs, and a pre-Nazi version of Skrewdriver (21/1/79).

Malcolm was accused of uttering racist slurs and his reputation diminished when he even asked local bands for payment to play. He left in April 1980.

Under new ownership The Royal Standard continued to put on gigs throughout the eighties with various different promoters, including The 1 In 12 Club in 1985. It was a popular hangout for many bands and people on the local music scene until a mysterious fire gutted the building in 1991. The grade two listed building, with its stained glass windows and finely crafted fixtures and fittings, suffered massive structural damage in the blaze and was therefore allowed to be demolished and yet another of Bradford's landmark Victorian venues was lost.

The surviving fixtures were sold off to Andy Thornton of Elland who still make and sell reproductions of the old bar.

THE VAULTS BAR

An influential place on the 1970s scene, the Vaults Bar was based in the Alexandra Annex and was part of Bradford College. (4)

From 1978 to 1984 it was run by manager John Farquar who put on a wide range of gigs by local up and coming bands in its cavernous back room.

Other venues that tolerated the new punk/new wave explosion were the student haunts like the Queen's Hall and Bradford University.

HOKUM

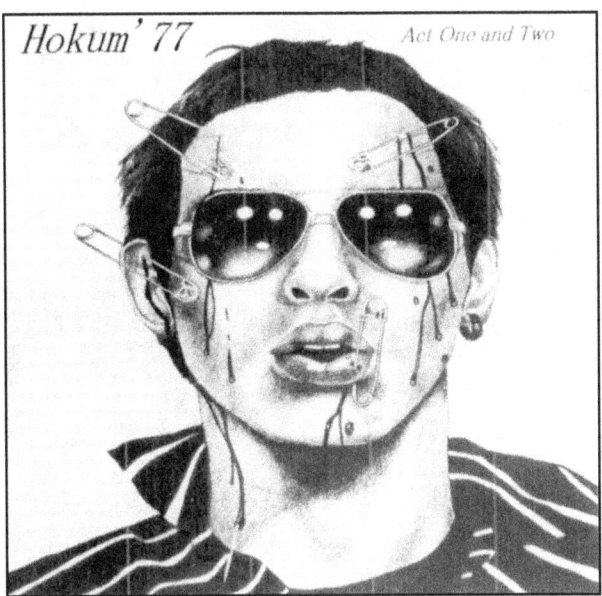

The punk musicial *Hokum' 77* was staged at Bradford University in June and November 1977. It was written by three students, Graham McAndrew, Glyn Adgie and Phil Wharton.

The poster for the event was designed by Mark Manning who went on to have chart success as his alter-ego Zodiac Mindwarp with his band The Love Reaction.

A cassette of the live performance and some studio tracks was released and it was transferred to CD in 2016.

Graham McAndrew went on to form The Pools Winners From Kent (1988-89) before forming the duo Clocks & Clouds (1989-91) with keyboard player Martin Griffin.

THE INVADERS

This Brighouse-based band formed in 1977 and were augmented by Bradford lad Phil Manchester on keyboards from 1979. Their early sound was said to be reminiscent of The Stranglers and pretty soon after they were offered a record deal with Polydor. They moved to London and released two singles, *Girls In Action / Secrets* and *Best Thing I Ever Did / Closer Still*. Both were produced by Sham 69 singer Jimmy Pursey.

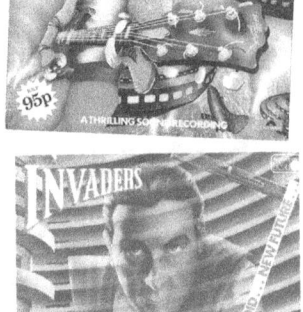

Girls In Action was Kid Jenson's record of the week. On August 9, 1979, the group played at the Marquee Club in London. Sounds described them as 'almost the most melodic of the post-punk bands'.

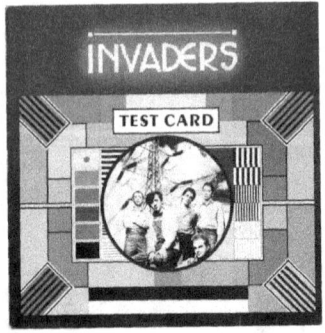

By the time they released their only LP, *Test Card*, in 1980 they were a six-piece, with David rogers on bass and Soo Lucas on backing vocals. The album and single covers were pastiches of 1950s sci-fi b-movies, designed by Alwyn Clayden who created sleeves for many bands including Visage, Sham 69, Slade and Vangelis.

The Invaders were one of four post-punk bands on the Polydor Records compilation LP *Made In Britain*.

Each band supplied four songs to the album, with Side A comprising two Bradford bands, The Invaders and Excel, while Side B featured tracks by Sheffield's Comsat Angels and Belfast's Protex.

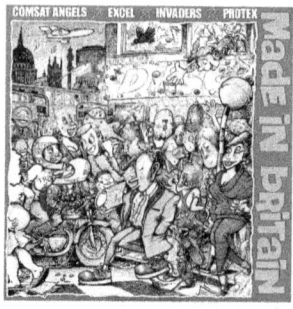

The Invaders' four tracks, *Magic Mirror (their third single)*, *Personality Profile*, *Backstreet Romeo* and *Rock Methodology*, were all tracks from their album. *Backstreet Romeo / Rock Methodology* was also the band's fourth and final single.

The band's vocalist/guitarist Slavo 'Sid' Sidelnyk was of Ukrainian descent and his brother Steve 'Little Sid' Sidnelyk played in local bands Vex and Idle Rich before moving to London in the early 1980s and becoming a renowned session drummer. He played at Live Aid with Paul Weller's The Style Council, Alison Moyet, Annie Lennox, Primal Scream. The Verve and many, many others as well as being Madonna's drummer on her albums between 2001-07.

SMASH HITS

In November 1978 a new music glossy magazine called *Smash Hits* hit the shelves. It was the brainchild of former *NME* editor Nick Logan. The first issue featured Blondie on the front cover. In contrast to the black and white newsprint style of the *NME*,

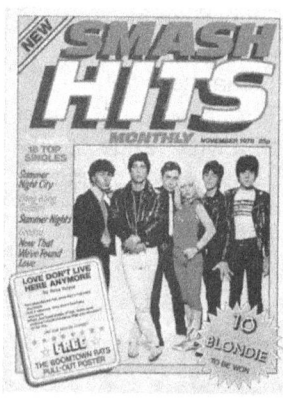

Melody Maker and *Sounds*, *Smash Hits* chronicled the 1980s generation of pop stars in full colour. Alongside glossy spreads and frothy interviews aimed more at the teen market were reproduced lyrics of current hits by the likes of The Boomtown Rats, Abba and The Police. It ceased publication in February 2000 when it had to admit it was no longer relevant to the *YouTube/Facebook* generation.

CHAPTER 4 - PUNK / NEW WAVE / HEAVY METAL   1977 - 1980

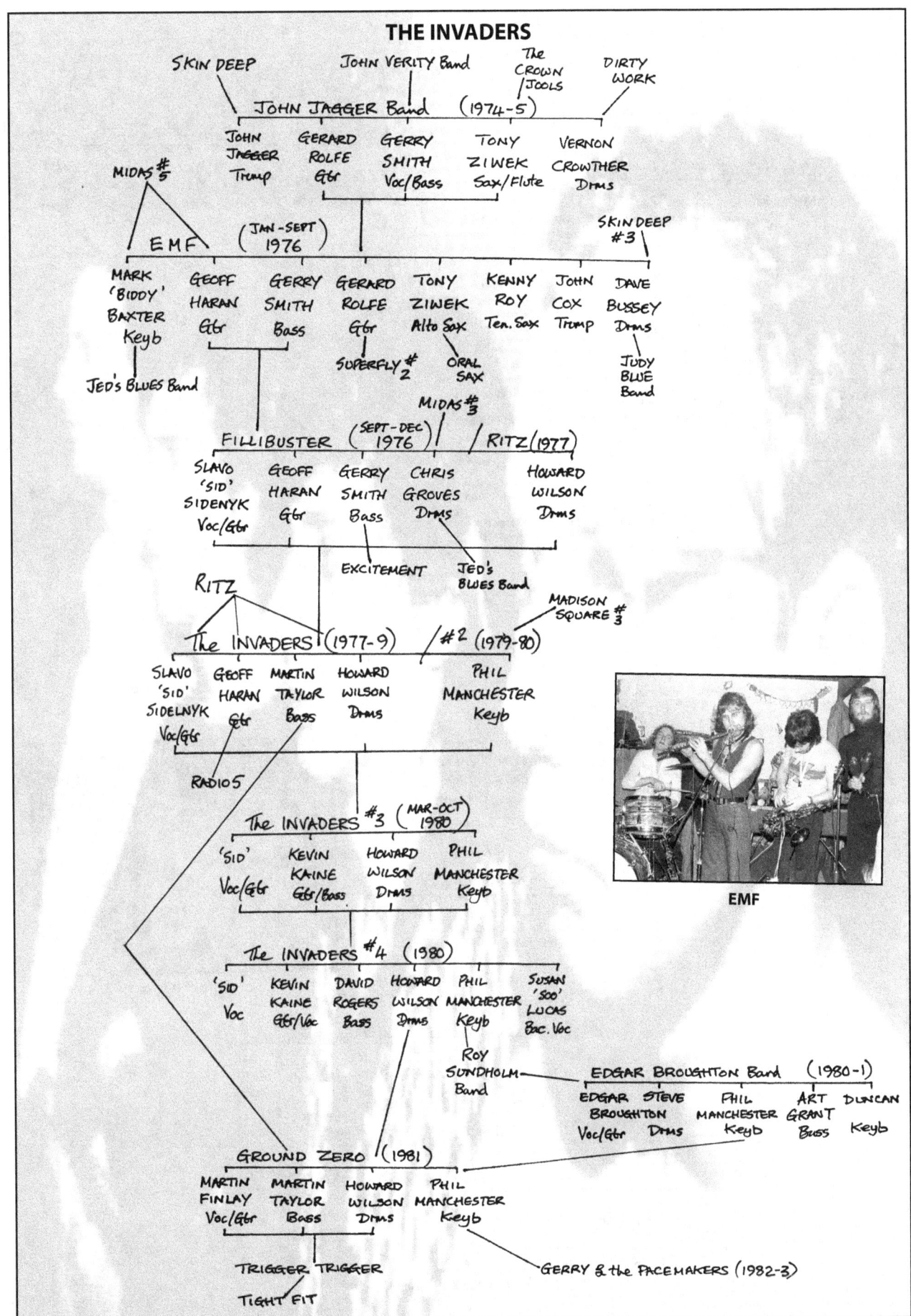

EMF

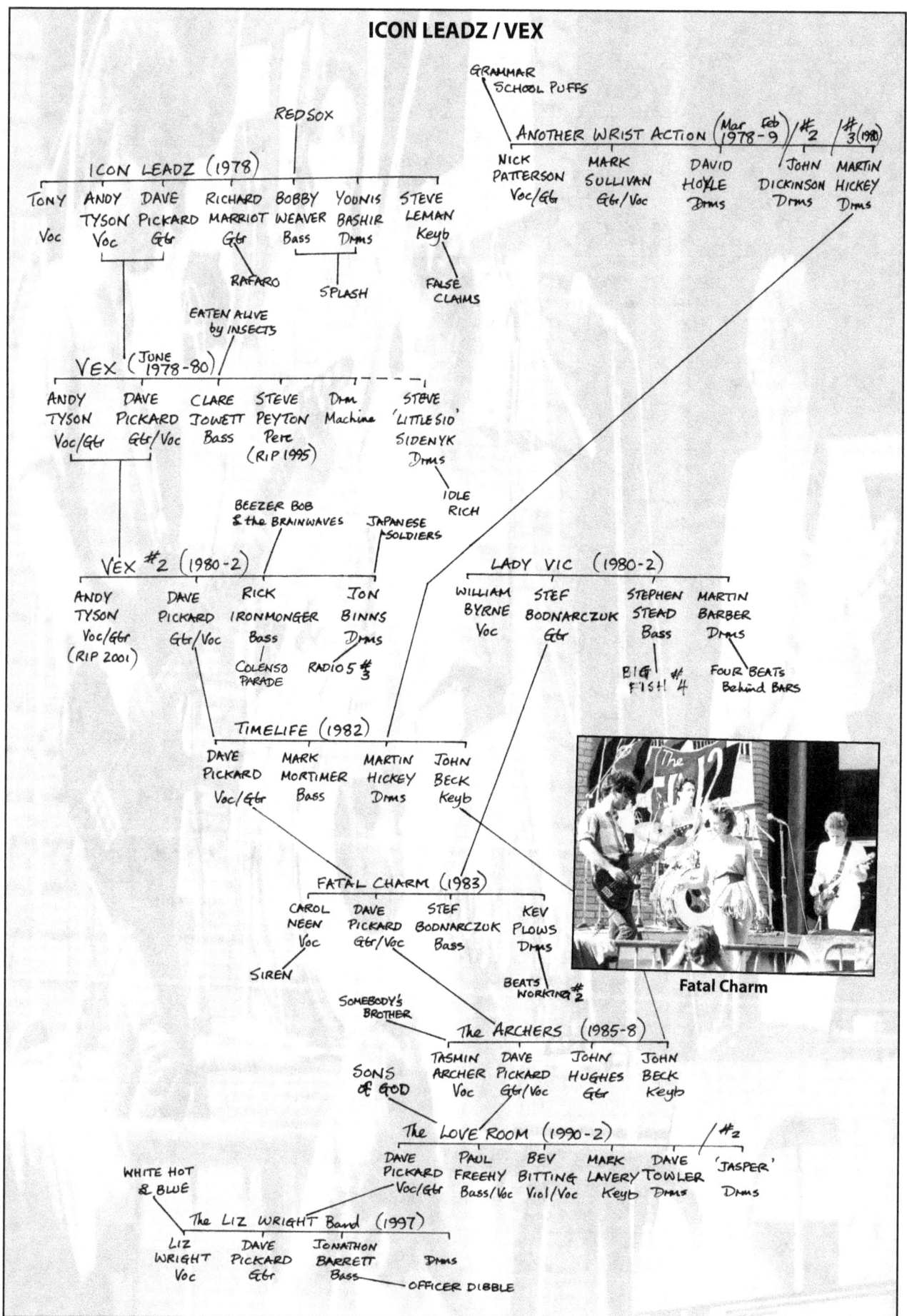
Fatal Charm

CHAPTER 4 - PUNK / NEW WAVE / HEAVY METAL   1977 - 1980

VEX

Formed in 1978, Vex evolved into a tight electro-pop oriented new wave outfit, with some strong material. The band recorded a three track cassette tape at Rochdale's famous Cargo Studios in 1980. The songs were *Stranger Station / (So This Is) Disco / Project Alien Emotion*.

As part of the Bradford Music & Art Workshop the band organised a gig at Bradford Playhouse (now the Priestley Centre) on Sunday November 9, 1980 with other local acts Cameras In Cars, Policeman With A Loaf Of Bread, ranters Nick Toczek, Little Brother and Sheffield band Vendino Pact (who included vocalist Martin Fry, later of ABC fame). A live cassette tape of the whole event later appeared on the local Tapir label called *Focus On Bradford*.

On December 11, 1981, Vex and local act Yeah, Yeah, Yeah played a presitious gig at Bradford University's Communal Building supporting the late DJ John Peel. (5) The band finally split around 1983, with members moving on to other bands.

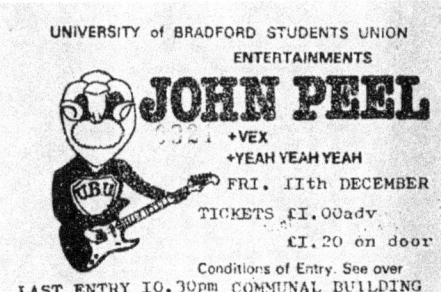

EXCEL

This Cleckheaton band formed in 1976 while still at school and were one of the first to embrace the punk/new wave scene in the Bradford area.

EXCEL			
79	ARSS XL1	If It Rains/Rolling Home/She's One Of The Boys/Rock Show (EP, p/s)	100
80	Polydor POSP 110	What Went Wrong?/Junita (p/s)	8

They released their debut seven-inch EP *If It Rains* on their own label, before being signed up by Polydor in 1979 and moving to London. All members were still teenagers when they released their first Polydor single *What Went Wrong / Junita* in February.

Slots on kids' TV shows followed, as well as tours in UK and a residency in Germany. Excel were also on the Polydor Records *Made In Britain* compilation.

A few CD compilations of the band's material appeared years later.

The band's singer Allan Walsh later played in Red Hot Stilettoes and The Bantus, while bassist Stephen Smith ended up in London-based act Miracle Mile in the mid-1980s.

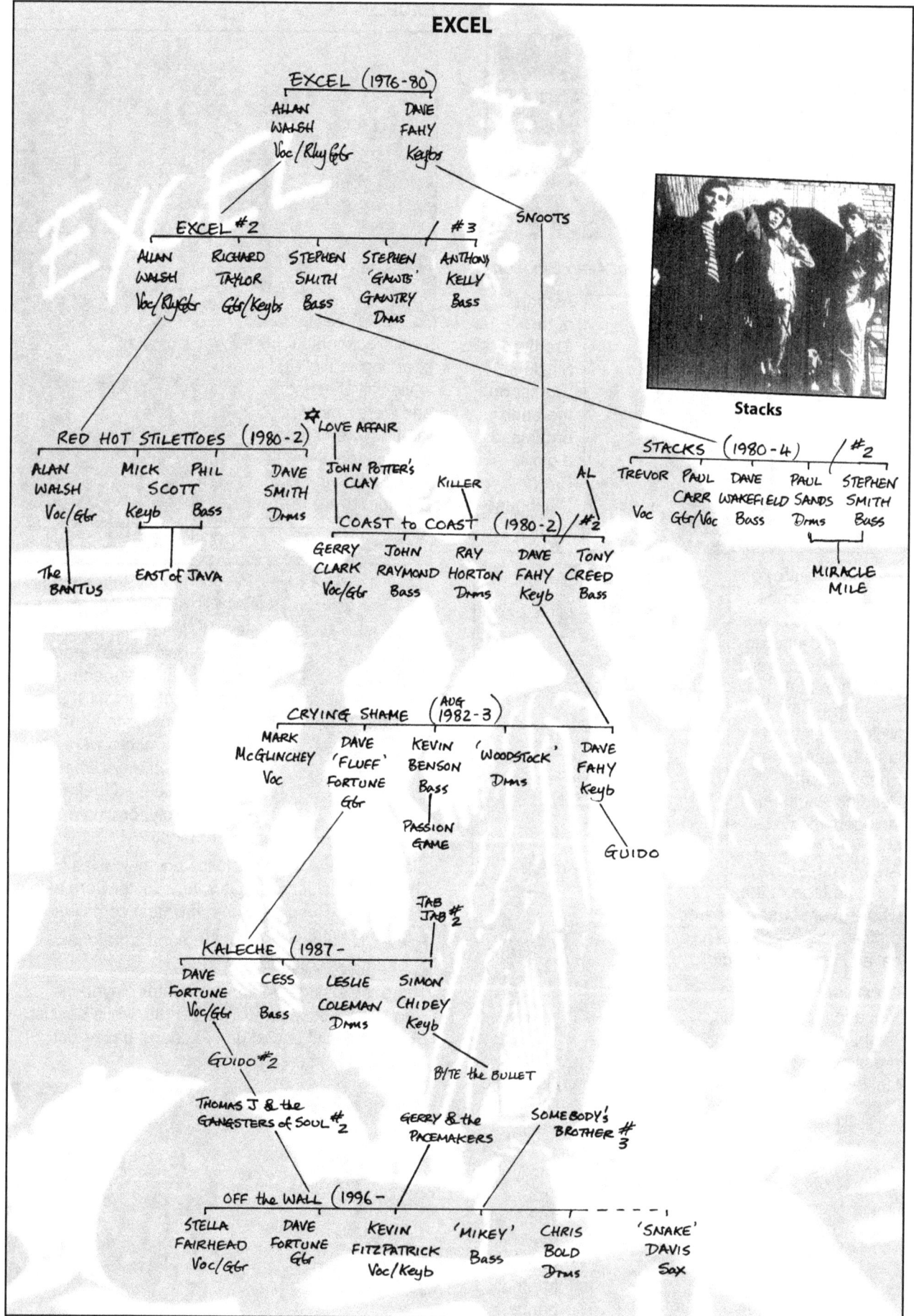

CHAPTER 4 - PUNK / NEW WAVE / HEAVY METAL 1977 - 1980

ROCK AGAINST RACISM FREE FESTIVAL

In September 1978 Bradford's first free Rock Against Racism Festival was held at the 'Halaq Stadium', a large area of waste ground off Woodhead Road which was often used as a football pitch on weekends by local youths.

A march paraded from Manningham to the site and went off without incident.

Over five hundred people turned up to watch many local bands, including The Scene, Icon Leadz, The Negatives, Shadowfax, Jab Jab and The Drive.

The only unfortunate incident on the day was a scuffle on stage caused by a sexist joke from an Icon Leadz roadie prior to their performance.

The Provost of Bradford, the Very Rev. Brandon Jackson, shows his views at the Multi Racial March on Saturday. Picture by Derek Chapman.

As a result a group of irate women stormed the stage to demand an apology and a fight ensued as one woman was thrown from the stage. The concert was brought to a sudden end as police removed the violent protesters, arresting eleven, of whom five were women.

'Some people thought the joke sexist and some lesbians in the audience took exception,' said Bradford University's Student Union President John Rimmer, who was a joint organiser of the festival.

Labour activist and Anti-Nazi League organiser the late Geoff Robinson (RIP 2006), who was also the older brother of The Negatives bassist Bob, said, *'It was just a minor incident in a sense that all the other events (films, sideshows, exhibitions and a children's circus all held in the University's Communal building) went off excellently without any problems at all.'* (6)

FASCIST ATTACKS ALTERNATIVE BOOKSHOP

In the 1970s the National Front (NF) and the British Movement (BM) fascist organisations and their ilk started to attack black immigrants, wreck Asian shops, trash Labour Party offices and try to burn down left-wing bookshops. The intention was to use the boot and the knuckle to win the battle of the streets and promote their brand of white supremacy all over the UK.

In Bradford, after a spate of racially motivated attacks on black individuals and property during 1977-79, the staff at the Fourth Idea Bookshop started to receive anonymous phone calls. One threatened, *'We'll burn you to the ground you Jewish bastard, Heil Hitler'.*

The shop also received ominous and threatening letters, including one from a far-right organisation in the USA. There followed constant harassment of the bookshop staff, culminating in members of the NF (Jack Smith, G Wright and F Harris) smashing the windows of Fourth Idea and four Asian shops in November 1978. They were all convicted over these incidents.

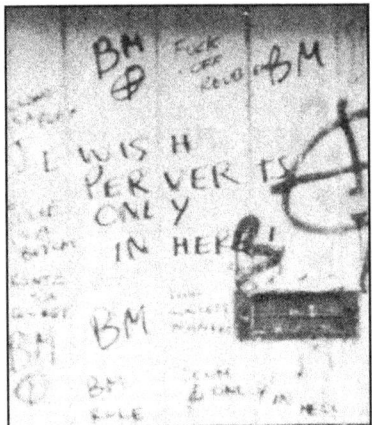

The previous September, fascist vandals had broken in, destroying books and shelves, tearing up magazines (i.e. *Gay News, Black Flag*, and *New Internationalist*) and stealing Anti-Nazi League and Rock Against Racism badges. (7)

Around the end of 1979, Gary Cavanagh joined the staff of the bookshop's collective as a volunteer member and hepled set up Bradford Claimants Union, which was based at Fourth Idea. At that time, the main collective members, after the untimely death of founding member Andy Swinson, were Jenny Gordon, Judith Watson, Di Morris, Roland Rance and Reuben Goldberg. (8)

THE NEGATIVES

Bradford's first and premier punk band formed in 1978 as a four-piece playing raw, loud and catchy self-penned tunes. They soon attracted a hardcore following of dedicated fans.

On November 30, 1978, they played a Rock Against Racism (RAR) benefit at Dudley Hill & Tong Socialist Club with other local groups The Drive and Icon Leadz.

They played at another RAR benefit with Leeds group The Mekons at Bradford's Queens Hall in October 1979.

In the same year, they released their only single, the classic double A-sided *Love Is Not Real / Stakeout* on Look Records, which was financed by a loan from local novelty shop owner Guy Watson. Initial copies of the single sold out on the first day and it was subsequently repressed.

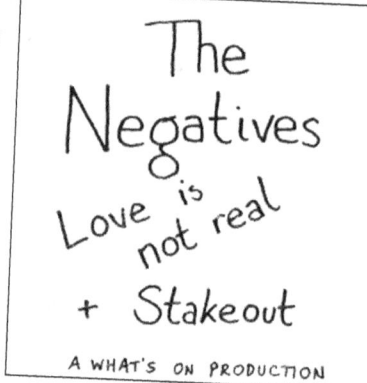

Years later, it became a very collectable record. The single was a favourite of John Peel, and it was discovered in his famous ultimate travelling DJ box after his death in 2005.

Singer Dave Wilcox suddenly quit the band in 1980, and the other three-quarters of the band became a reggae-influenced group called Mysterious Footsteps who went on to release a single, *Like They Do In The Movies / White Dread*, on their own Yeti label.

Dave Wilcox formed a new version of the band called The Negativz in 1982 which included none of the other original members but played the old set..

Punk rockers in witness appeal to 'tribal battle'

An appeal was made at Bradford City Court for witnesses of a scene which could have looked like a tribal battle. It was stated to involve punk rockers with multi-coloured hair and safety pins through their ears and noses.

A dozen youths and girls appeared before the magistrates accused of using threatening behaviour in Manningham Lane, Bradford, on July 9. The case was adjourned to November 7.

Mr. Stephen Couch, defending solicitor, asked for reporting restrictions to be lifted, and appealed for witnesses to come forward to assist the dfence

He said the inmident had involved punk rockers who might have given passers-by and eye-witnesses the impression of a scene reminiscent of a tribal battle, and one which they would remember.

Despite their ferocious appearance none of those involved felt they started or took part in any breach of the peace.

Before the court were: Gary Albison, 17, of Grantham Road, Bradford; Russell Hitchcock, 17, of Grantham Road, Bradford; Susan Inslip, 19, of Tufton Street, Silsden; Christopher Laughlin, 20, of Northolan Road, Keighley; Peter Stobbs, 19, of Avenue Road, Bradford; Hayden Watson, 20, of Worthdale House, Keighley; David Thomas Wilcox, 18, of Roundwood Glen, Bradford; Stuart Paul Williams, 19, of Springwood Terrace, Bradford; Mark Franch, 17, of Braithwaite Avenue, Keighley; and two 16-year-old boys, and a 15-year-old girl, all from Bradford.

Courtesy of the Telegraph & Argus

In 2001, a Swedish record collector bought a copy of The Negatives single on the internet for £350!

This renewed interest in the band led to a re-formation by three-quarters of the original group after Sussex-based Detour Records re-released the single and the other track from the same session, *(We're From) Bradford*, on a punk compilation.

The re-formed trio then recorded a song for Bradford City Football Club.

Original drummer Tino Palmer carried on with a new version of The Negatives, recording and playing gigs until he left in 2008.

LOOK RECORDS

This West Yorkshire record label started in the mid 1970s by Dave and Bob Whitely and Stephen Goddard. They were based at their studio September Sounds in Golcar, Huddersfield, where Bob did most of the engineering on the LPs and singles released.

The label's releases seem to be mainly local brass bands and choirs from the surrounding Kirklees area. But they also released a few punk / post-punk singles and albums by artists such as The Negatives, The Elements (pre-Skeletal Family), Welfare State, Moonchild and Roger Sutcliffe.

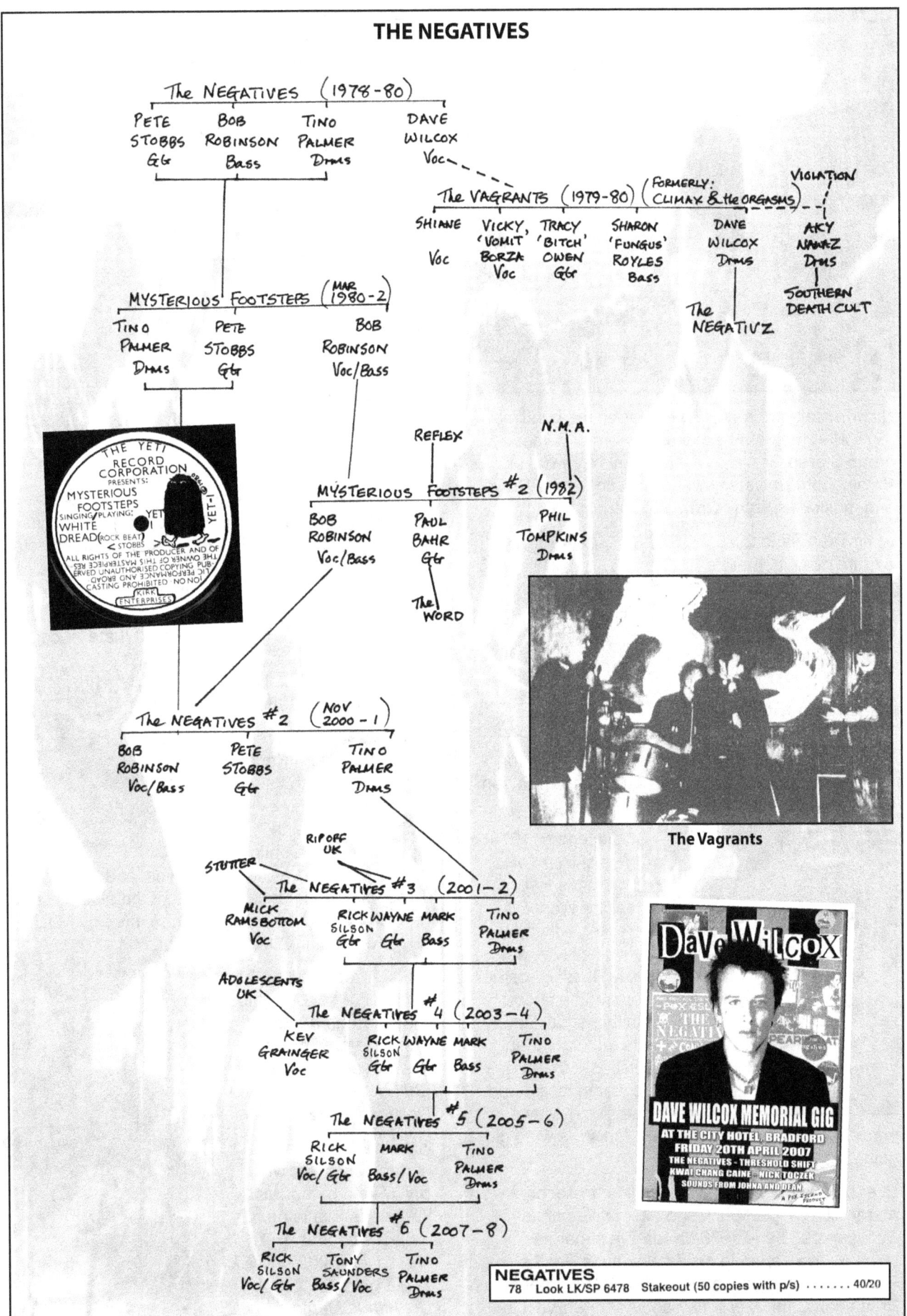

ULTERIOR MOTIVES

Nick Toczek and Kay Russell started the band in 1978 after the demise of their performance/poetry group Stereo Graffiti, formed when they were at Birmingham University with fellow poet John Rowe and musicians Frank Crow and Ron Bates.

At first, the band used a drum machine before acquiring a real drummer. They then released their only single, *Another Lover / Y'Gotta Shout,* on their own Motive Music label in 1979.

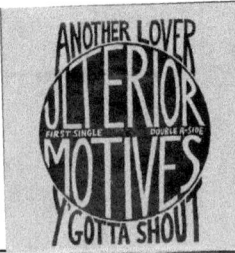

ULTERIOR MOTIVES			
79	Motive Music MMR 1	Another Lover (p/s)	30

Nick continued the group with various lineups for another three years after Kay had left to join Susan Fassbender and form Fassbender-Russell.

In December 1979 the first issue of Bradford's first fanzine *Wool City Rocker,* edited by Nick (initially with Kay Russell), came out for the price of thirty pence. During its run of thirteen issues (1979-81), it covered local band profiles, reviews, articles, cartoons and a monthly Yorkshire-wide gig guide.

Ever a busy man, Nick also had time to become a promoter of local punk and alternative bands. Between 1982 and 1986 he ran five separate clubs on five separate nights at venues like the Palm Cove and Manhattan Club in Bradford and Brannigan's, the Bier Keller and Adam & Eve's in Leeds. In the process, he brought many innovative punk and indie groups to the area, usually supported by one of the legion of local bands.

He moved on to run an alternative cabaret club with Wild Willi Beckett under the title *Stereo Graffiti.*

Nick later became a full-time freelance journalist and creative writer who produced numerous books/booklets of poetry, short stories and prose. He also wrote the political book *Hater, Baiters And Would-Be Dictators*, an overview of the development and activities of the right wing in Britain during the 20th century

He continued as a solo performer as well as collaborating with various bands on musical projects, including Nick Toczek's Britanarchists *More to Hate Than Meets The Eye* EP on Martyhate Records (recorded with The Burial and Spectre) in 1986.

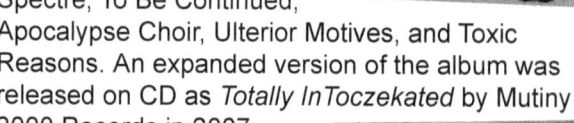

For his 1987 *InToczekated* album on Bluurg Records, Nick worked with various bands backing him, including The Burial, Spectre, To Be Continued, Apocalypse Choir, Ulterior Motives, and Toxic Reasons. An expanded version of the album was released on CD as *Totally InToczekated* by Mutiny 2000 Records in 2007.

He later recorded an EP and then a series of albums with German anarchist Thies Marsen including *The Bavariations Album (2012/19), Death & Other Destinations (2021).*

His other recording partenership was with *BNOTV* co-author Matt Webster's Signia Alpha project *Shooting The Messenger (2020), Walking The Tightrope (2021), The Columbus Memoirs (2022).*

CHAPTER 4 - PUNK / NEW WAVE / HEAVY METAL   1977 - 1980

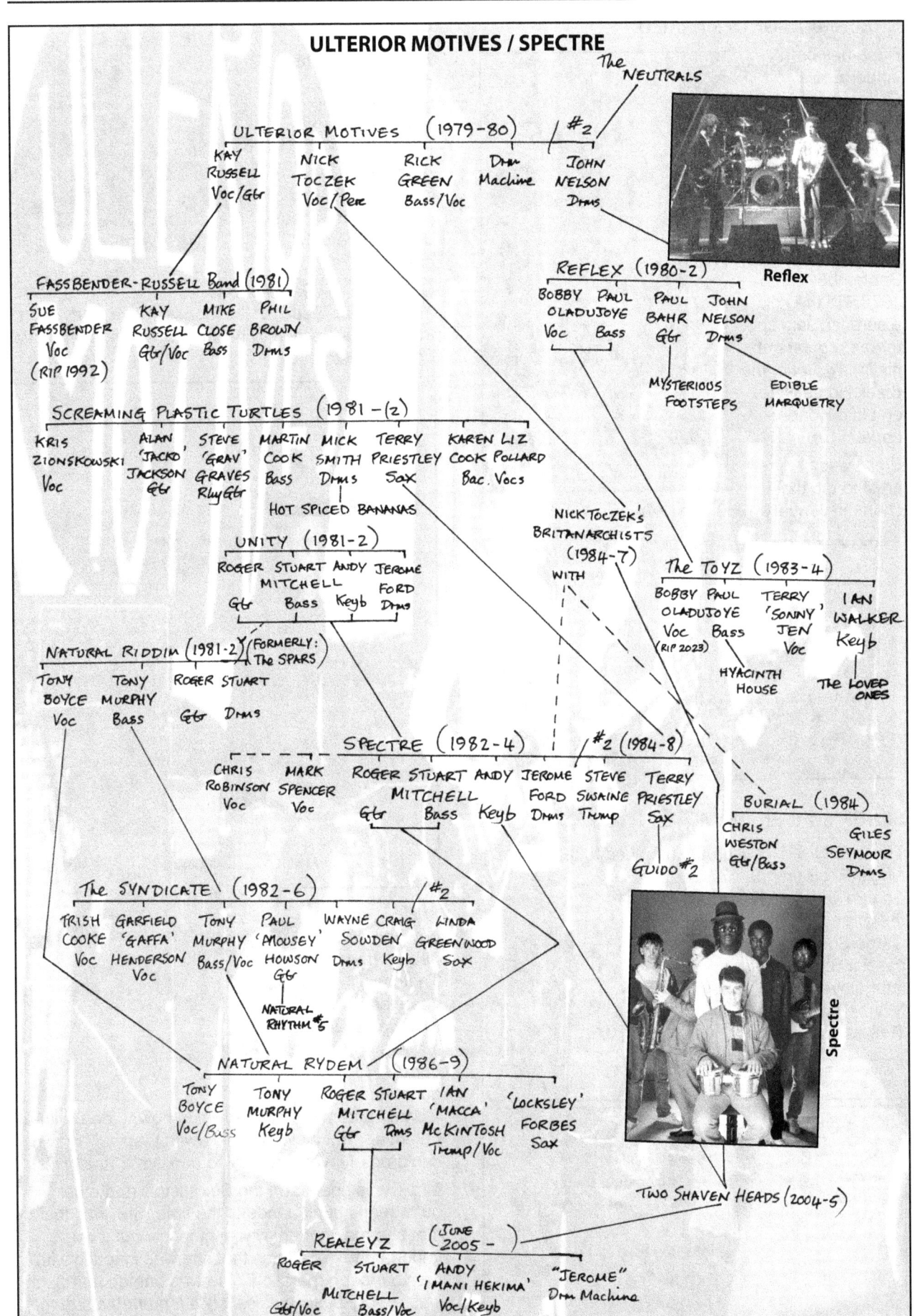

CHECKMATE GETS MARRIED

Bahamas born singer Emile (Sweatman) Ford, of the multiracial group The Checkmates, secretly married Bradford model and racing driver Valli Stack on September 6, 1978. He then did a surprise solo spot for the regulars at his in-laws' pub, the Black Horse Hotel, on Little Horton Lane.

Emile was the first artist to top the charts in January 1960 with *What Do You Want To Make Those Eyes At Me For* on PYE Records. He followed his number one record with four more top twenty singles during 1960, including a number three hit with *On A Slow Boat To China*.

SILVER SCREEN GIRLS

This short lived local group managed to release a 7" single *Photographs / Silver Screen Girls* in 1980 on the Siren label, recorded at Cargo Studios. The band's bassist Steve Holton later played in two local NWOBHM bands; Baby Tuckoo and Voyager UK.

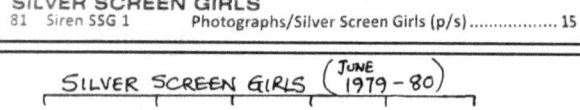

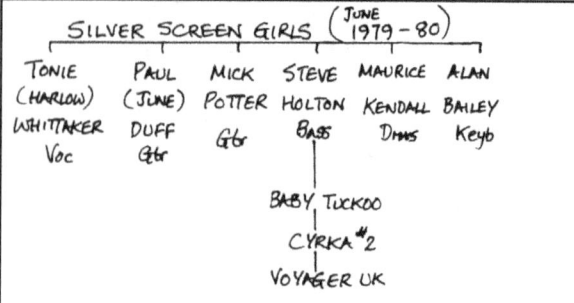

SID & MAGGIE

Elsewhere, culture-defining events were taking place. In February 1979, in a New York hotel room, the Sex Pistols bass guitarist Sid Vicious died of a heroin overdose.

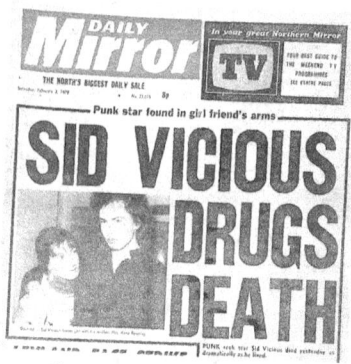

On May 3, 1979, Margaret Thatcher, as leader of the Conservative Party, won the general election to become Britain's first female prime minister.

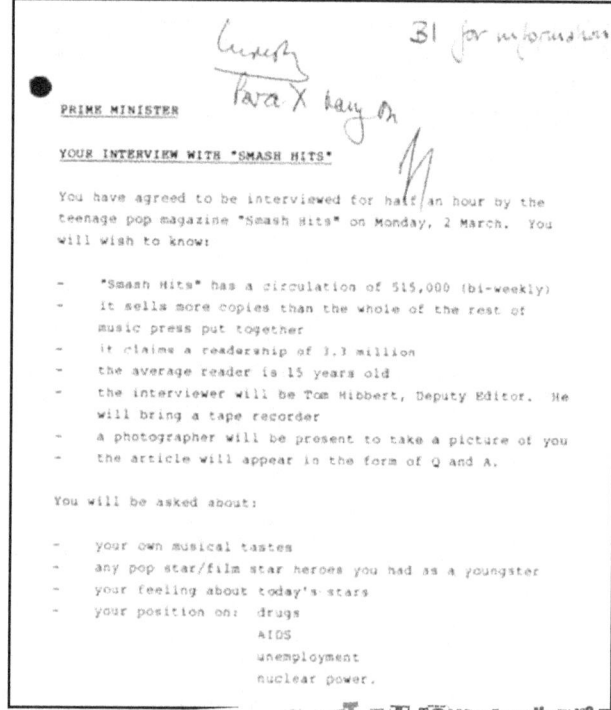

In 2017, governmental papers from Thatcher's years as PM were released into the public domain. One document was a briefing from her staff advising how to deal with a potentially troubling interview with that well-known cauldron of investigational journalism *Smash Hits!*

Mrs T was briefed on the Sex Pistols and other outrageous punk bands of the time. She was told that she may not enjoy the interview but it was important to get across that she was in touch with the younger generation. She was briefed that punk was a *'very basic musical style featuring a strange bunch of anti-establishment acts'*.

THE DONKEYS

The Donkeys initial trio of bassist Dave Owen and the Ferguson brothers Neil and Tony were formed in Normanton (near Wakefield) in 1978. After playing for the first four months with a pre-recorded drum track, they were augmented by Bradford lad Mark Wellham on drums.

Their first single, *What I Want / Four Letters*, was released on the Manchester label Rhesus Records in October 1979. It was re-released by Deram Records and reached number ninety in the charts.

On August 4, 1979, they supported Northern Irish band The Undertones at London's Marquee Club. They supported another Northern Irish band, Stiff Little Fingers, at a BBC *In Concert* session.

In May 1980, they released their second single, No *Way / You Jane*, on Backdoor - a low-key subsidiary of Phonogram Records. A third single, *Don't Go / Living Legends*, soon followed, again on Rhesus. Two Donkeys tracks, *No Way* and *You Jane* appeared on one side of a split 12-inch with Dalek I on Mercury Records.

As a trio after the departure of Dave Owen, their fourth single *Let's Float / Strike Talks* appeared on MCA Records in 1980. A final single, *Listen To Your Radio*, appeared on MCA in 1981 as The Donkees.

In 2000, the Japanese label 1977 Records reissued all five Donkeys/Donkees singles as well as the previously unreleased track *Shipwreck* on vinyl 7-inch for the first time, backed by *Listen To Your Radio (A Long Version)*.

The 1977 Records CD compilation *Monkey Business* came out in 2004. It included all single A and B sides plus extra tracks. Detour Records followed suit with a retrospective Donkeys compilation in the same year. *Television Anarchy* was a double CD and double vinyl set of their singles and more unreleased tracks recorded between 1978 and 1982..

Guitarist Neil Ferguson set up Woodland Studios in Castleford and engineer on many bands including Anti-System's 1984 LP *No Laughing Matter*, Excalibur's 1985 mini-LP *The Bitter End* and The Bobby Charltons' 7" single *Hole In The Sky / Bastard Town* in 1991.

Neil played guitar in a later version of the Leeds-based Anarcho band Chumbawamba.

The DONKEYS (1978-80)

DAVE OWEN	NEIL FERGUSON	TONY FERGUSON	MARK WELLHAM
Voc/Bass	Voc/Gtr	RhyGtr	Drms

The DONKEYS #2 / DONKEES (1980-82)

NEIL FERGUSON	TONY FERGUSON	MARK WELLHAM
Voc/Gtr	RhyGtr/Bass	Drms

DONKEYS
80	Rhesus GO APE 102	What I Want/Four Letters (yellow or orange label, p/s)	20
80	Rhesus GO APE 3	No Way/You Jane (p/s)	20
80	Rhesus GO APE 105	Don't Go/Living Legends (p/s)	20
80	Back Door DOOR 006	No Way/You Jane (reissue, p/s)	7
80	Deram DM-R 431	What I Want/Four Letters (reissue, p/s)	8
81	MCA MCA 682	Don't Go/Living Legends (reissue, p/s)	5
81	MCA MCA 721	Let's Float/Watched By Everyone (p/s)	7
81	MCA MCA 737	Listen To Your Radio/Watched By Everyone (as Donkees) (p/s)	7

LOCAL COMICS

From the late 1960s and early 1970s, besides American Marvel and DC comics and UK comics like *The Eagle, The Beano, Dandy, Victor* etc., that were available to young British teenagers, there was the growth of 'adult only' UK independent underground comics. Such as *Cosmic Comics* at 20p with off-shoot titles like *Nasty Tales, Zip, Sin City,* and *Half-Assed Funnies.*

More sensationalist and controversial mainstream titles appeared in the 1970s with the publication of titles like *Battle* (which notably included *Charley's War* by Pat Mills and Joe Colquhoun with its realistic interpretation of the reality of life in First World War trenches) and *Action* which was banned in 1976 after a front cover depicting teenagers attacking police in the futuristic story *Kids Rule OK* lead to a campaign by Mary Whitehouse and newspapers like The Sun and the Evening Standard.

Action editor Pat Mills launched the sci-fi comic anthology 2000AD in 1977 at the height of the punk rock explosion in the UK and is still going strong today after over 40 years of continous publication.

2000AD is the home of fascist future anti-hero cop Judge Dredd, created by fellow Battle and Action contributors John Wagner and Carlos Ezquerra and has spawned several spin-offs including the *Judge Dredd Megazine* in 1991 and the short lived adult themed *Crisis* (1988-1991) that gave publicity to global environmental and political issues.

Other adult themed comics created by 2000AD writers and artists include *Deadline* (1988-1995) which featured the *Tank Girl* strip, *Revolver* (1990-1991) and *Toxic!* (1991).

Regular early contributor to 2000AD, Northampton's Alan Moore was famous for his graphic novels *V For Vendetta* and *Watchmen* (both later made into films).

As the popularity of adult comics and graphic novels began to grow more and more independent and small press productions appeared.

By the early 1980s, there was Knockabout Comics with cartoon strips by artists like Hunt Emerson, Clifford Harper and Steve Bell. In 1987, Valykrie Comics of Bristol started printing the graphic novel *The Adventures of Luther Arkwright* by Bryan Talbot.

In Bradford, local artist Tony Grogan had helped start *Free News* around 1979/1980, based at Bradford College as a local magazine with local

CHAPTER 4 - PUNK / NEW WAVE / HEAVY METAL   1977 - 1980

and current social/political topics interspersed with his cartoons. A free comic *Horribul Fings* was a one off, before he produced the first issue of *New Reality Komic* in 1980 at 45p with the invitation to future contributors to *'...produce a wider range of ideas and artwork, so if you have a creative anarchistic urge get in touch.'*

In 1979, Anthony Webster and Howard Priestley of Boothtown, Halifax produced at least two issues of *Shok Therapy* at 35p as an *'amateur non-profit comic, whose aim is to help frustrated artists, writers, inkers and anyone intersted in surrealism, fantasy or art to get their work published.'*

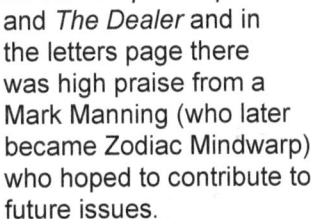

The comics two main strips were called *Space Opera* and *The Dealer* and in the letters page there was high praise from a Mark Manning (who later became Zodiac Mindwarp) who hoped to contribute to future issues.

In Leeds, the Women Against Facism & Racism produced the free *ARGGHHH* comic in 1979, while local artist PD produced at least three issues of *PD (Pages Decadent)* for 40p, which had cartoons from Jon Langford of the Three Johns/Mekons.

While over in Slaithwaite near Huddersfield, Kev Hopgood produced the excellently drawn *Crisis Comix* in 1980 at 15p, telling the story of *The Rise & Fall Of Johnny No-One*. Kev also contributed cartoon strips to Nick Tozcek's *Wool City Rocker* fanzine and had offered strips to the lads at *Shok Therapy*.

THE BAVARIA

The Bavaria Pub on Heaton Road in Manningham, had the occasional gig, as well as putting on local disco nights.

LOCAL SOUND SYSTEMS

As the migration of people from the West Indies to the UK in the 1950s, that 'Windrush' generation had brought their labour, skills and their music too – calypso, ska and reggae.

At parties held amongst the Caribbean community, music was initially on local home-made sound systems, playing imported vinyl with MC's who 'toasted' over the records.

In Bradford, one of the earliest sound systems was run by Ronald Mitchell, whose sons Roger, Stuart and Andy (Imani) would later form the ska band Spectre. (9)

The 1980 film Babylon, directed by Franko Rosso with music by Dennis Bovell, stared Brindsley Forde (of Asward) and the late comedian Mel Smith (of *Not The Nine O'Clock News* fame) and showed the culture of sound systems and the life struggle of the British West Indian community.

During the 1980s and '90s, the Palm Cove Club on Hollings Road had many nights of local and national sound system 'battles' with some of the best MCs and toasters around.

BRADFORD'S EXPERIMENTAL ELECTRONIC NOISE SCENE

This scene was hugely influenced by US composers John Cage, Walter Carlos, Suicide and William Burroughs (spoken monologues) as well as the German mid-1970s pioneering 'Krautrock' of Kraftwerk, Tangerine Dream, Can, Amon Duul, Faust, and Neu! who explored electronic sounds with synthesisers, mellotrons and early samplers.

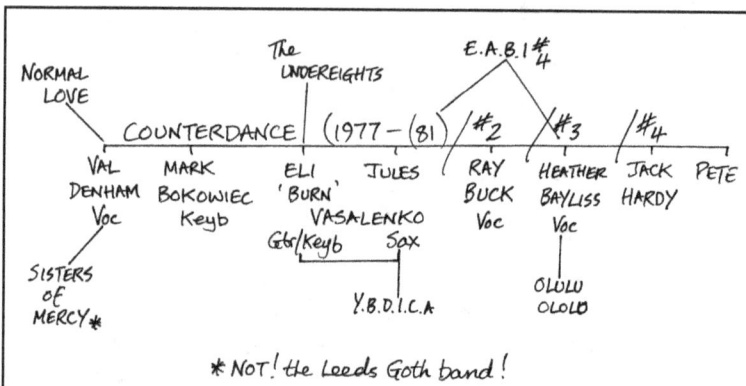

COUNTERDANCE

Formed in 1977 by a bunch of art college freaks, Counterdance led the way on the local electronic scene and were compared to Sheffield's Cabaret Voltaire. They continued to perform, with various line-up changes, until at least November 6, 1981, when they played a gig at Bradford's Queen's Hall.

Mark Bokowiec, one of the founding members, had by the late 1980s, become a composer of 'soundscapes' made from tape loops and experimental 'sound diffusion' noises. He later wrote influential research papers on interactive new technology and also recorded 'sonic art' pieces while working in the music department of Huddersfield University.

EATEN ALIVE BY INSECTS

Formed around the pivotal figure of Phill Harding in 1979, these 'noise merchants' were partly influenced by Sheffield's industrial bands, Throbbing Gristle and 'free jazz' artist Peter Brotzmann. They

produced two cassette releases; the first, *Insect Comix,* only had a run of 25, their second, the three-song *Dead Sparrows Can't Boogie / Do the Cedric / The Outskirts*, was on local tape label Tapir Products. (10)

At the Palm Cove Club on January 18, 1980, they staged an evening of experimental music, *Giraffes Over Bradford*, with another local group Mephisto Waltz and a one-off group Mesopotamears, which featured Phill Harding and others.

One of their best gigs turned out to be a private party in a barn at Nab Wood where over two hundred people attended, and they also played John Keenan's *Futurama 2*. They influenced two new bands formed in 1980; Manray's Haircut (taken from the title of an EABI song), and Industry Suits - a bunch of Halifax lads who were based in Bradford for gigs.

In Manchester, the remaining members of Joy Division resurfaced as New Order with the single Ceremony in 1981, after the suicide of singer Ian Curtis in May 1980 at the age of only 23.

At the same time, a group of electronic 'noise terrorists' made up of ex-members of Come and Whitehouse formed a new band also called New Order. The LP they put out has a strange title that has a connection to Bradford. It was called *Bradford Red Light District*, released on Come Org Records.

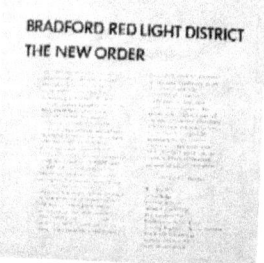

NEW ORDER			
81	Come Org. CARA12	BRADFORD RED LIGHT DISTRICT (LP)	110

THE SCENE

Local mod-influenced band The Scene formed in 1979, and wrote short catchy tunes that you could dance to. Their only single was the self-financed *Hey Girl / Reach The Top* on Hole-In-The-Wall Records, which is now very collectable, distributed by York's Red Rhino label.

CAMERAS IN CARS

Formed in 1978, this local band managed to put out a self-financed three-track EP on their own label, priced 99p.

They split in 1982 with some members forming a new band called Height who had a track on the double compilation album *Your Secret's Safe With Us*.

CHAPTER 4 - PUNK / NEW WAVE / HEAVY METAL 1977 - 1980

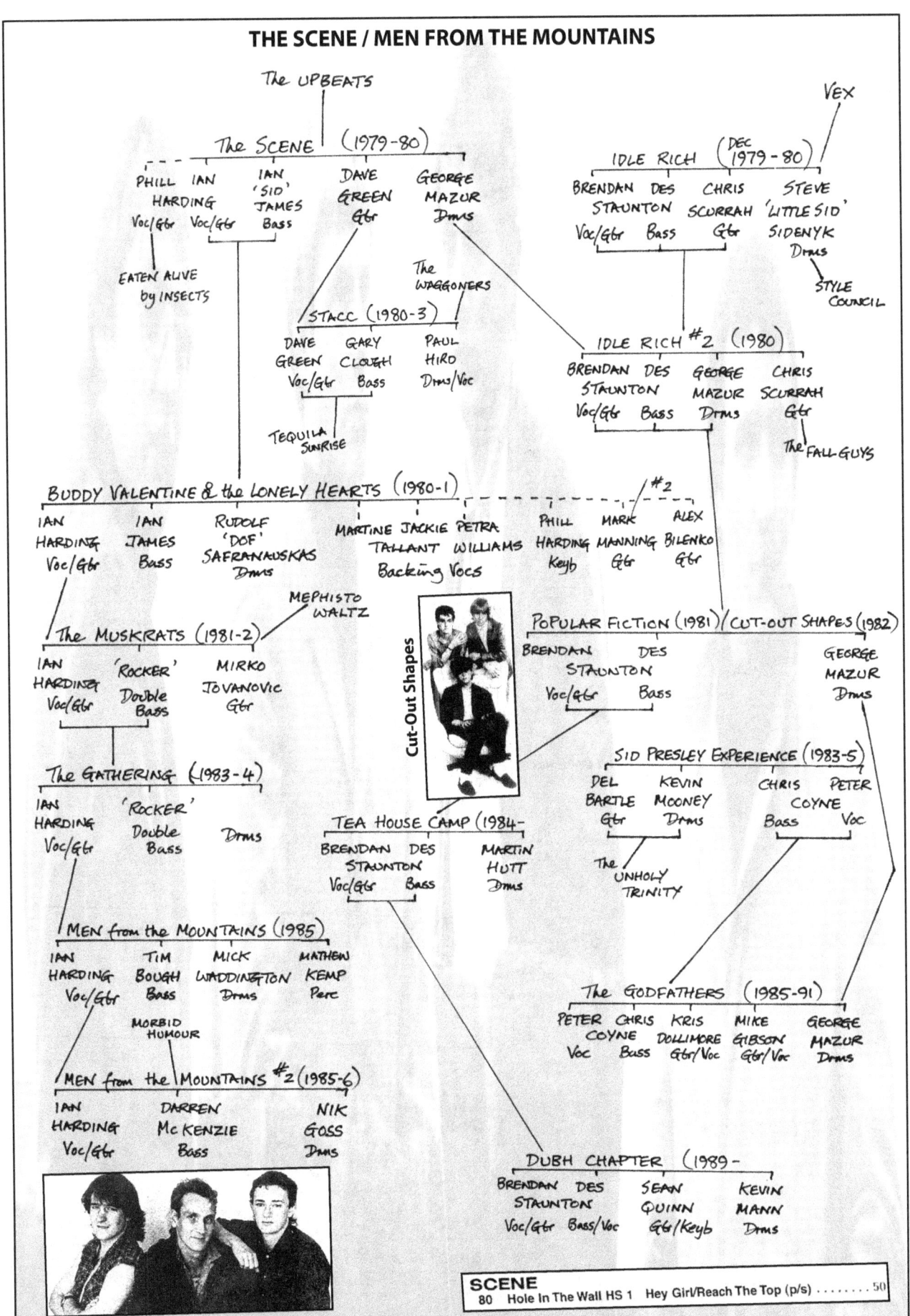

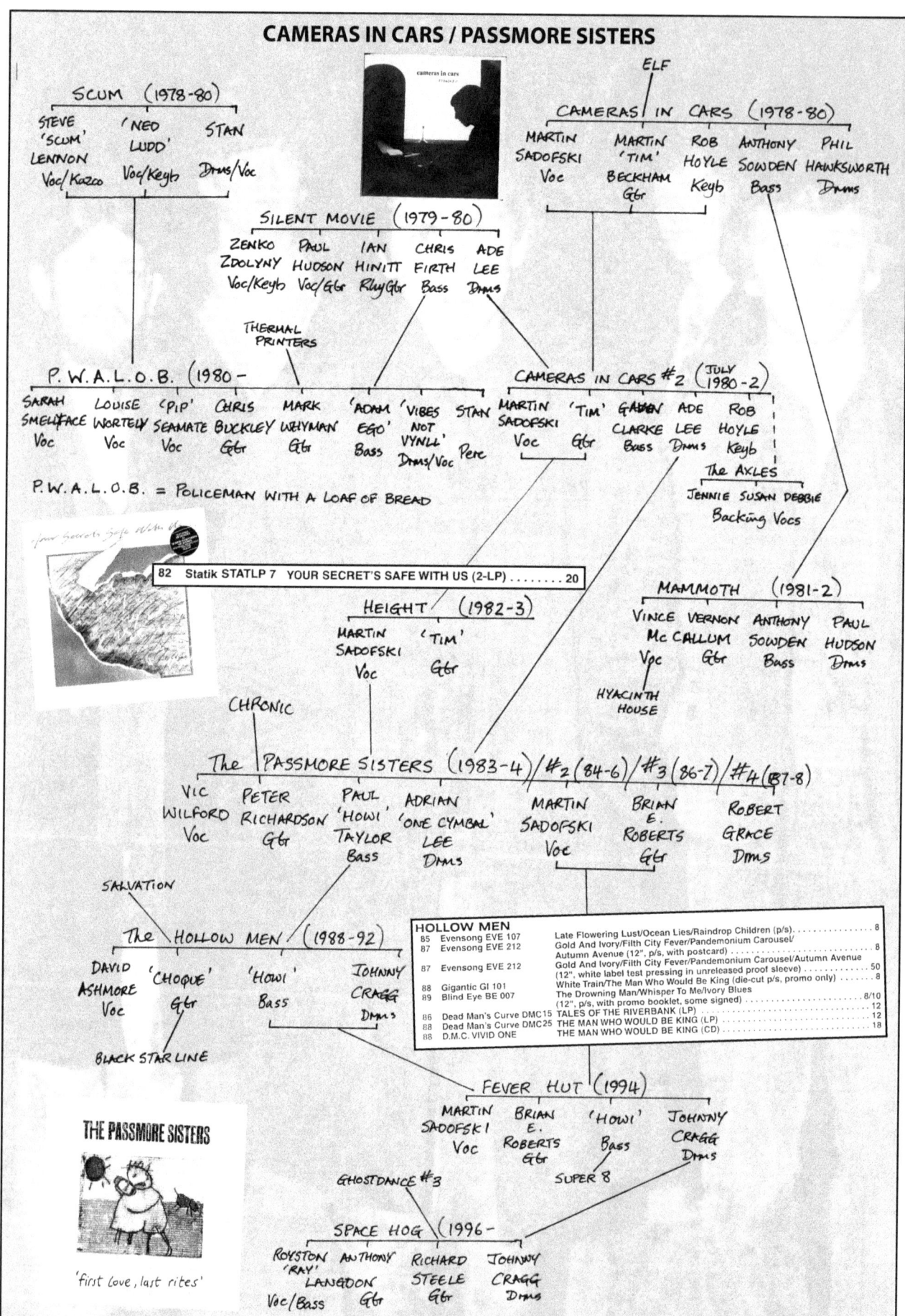

CHAPTER 4 - PUNK / NEW WAVE / HEAVY METAL 1977 - 1980

EATEN ALIVE BY INSECTS

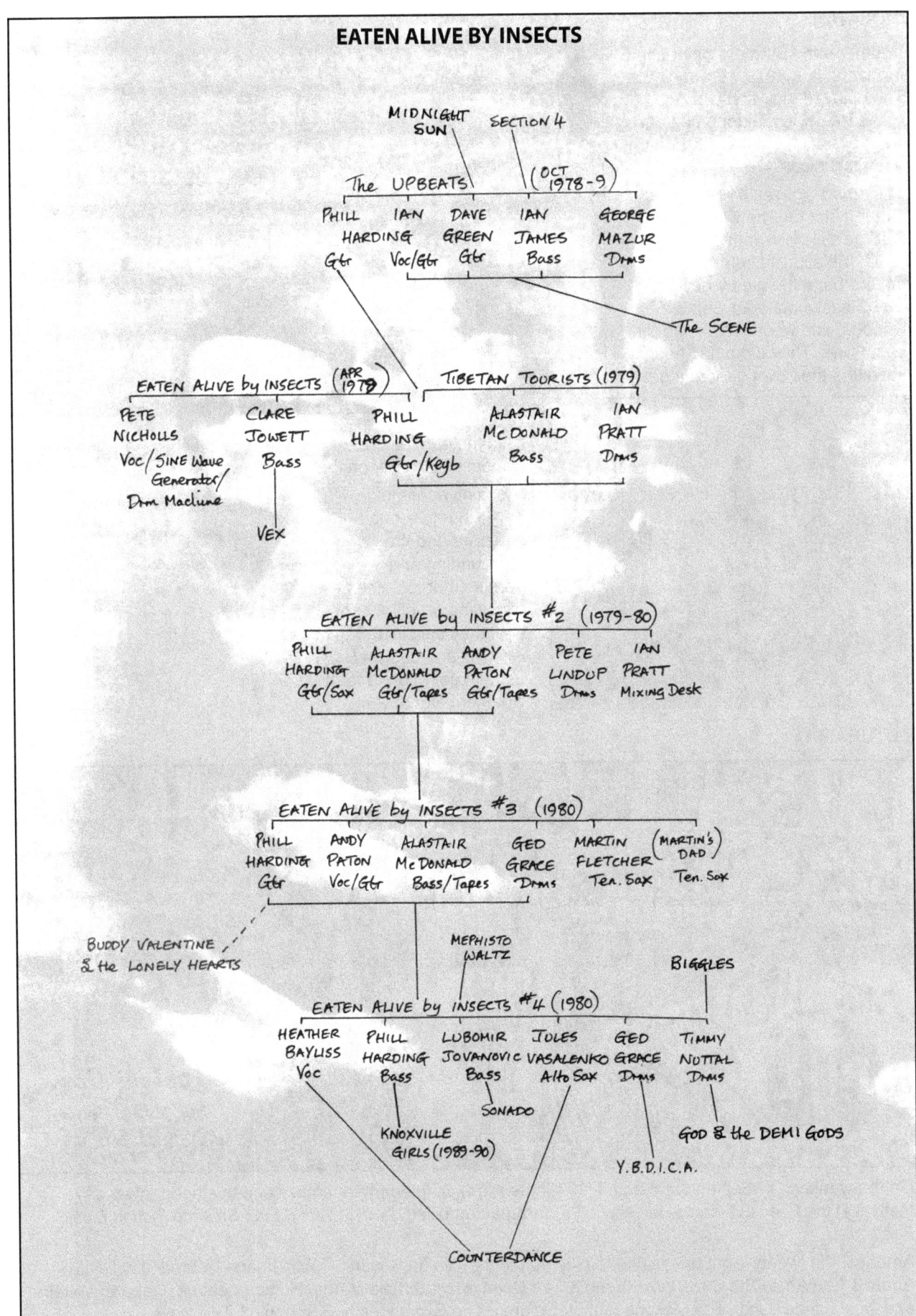

VIOLATION

Another early Bradford punk band formed in late 1979 were Violation. They played their first two gigs at the Palm Cove supporting The Negatives and Total Confusion on both occasions.

Their third gig was a prestigious support slot for The Clash at St George's Hall on January 19, 1980. Violation's Drummer Aki had got the band the gig by pestering The Clash's manager Bernie Rhodes, and wouldn't take no for an answer. They did a half-hour set using their own gear and got

paid the sum of £25. At the time The Clash were using local bands in each city on the tour to give them some exposure.

Violation continued to gig in and around Bradford and the surrounding area at venues that took the risk of putting on punk bands until they split in 1981, with Aki and bassist Barry Jepson going on to form Southern Death Cult.

FUTURAMA

On the weekend of September 8 and 9, 1979, the F(an) Club promoter John Keenan staged a two-day festival at the Leeds Queen's Hall entitled Futurama and billed as *'The World First Science Fiction Music Festival'*.

Amongst the twenty-eight bands due to play during the two days were; Public Image Limited, Joy Division, Adam & The Ants, The Cure, Wire, Echo & The Bunnymen, Simple Minds, Human League, Cabaret Voltaire and local Leeds bands The Mekons, Agony Column, The Expelaires and Sheeny & The Goys.

CHAPTER 4 - PUNK / NEW WAVE / HEAVY METAL 1977 - 1980

RED SOX / THE IGUANAS

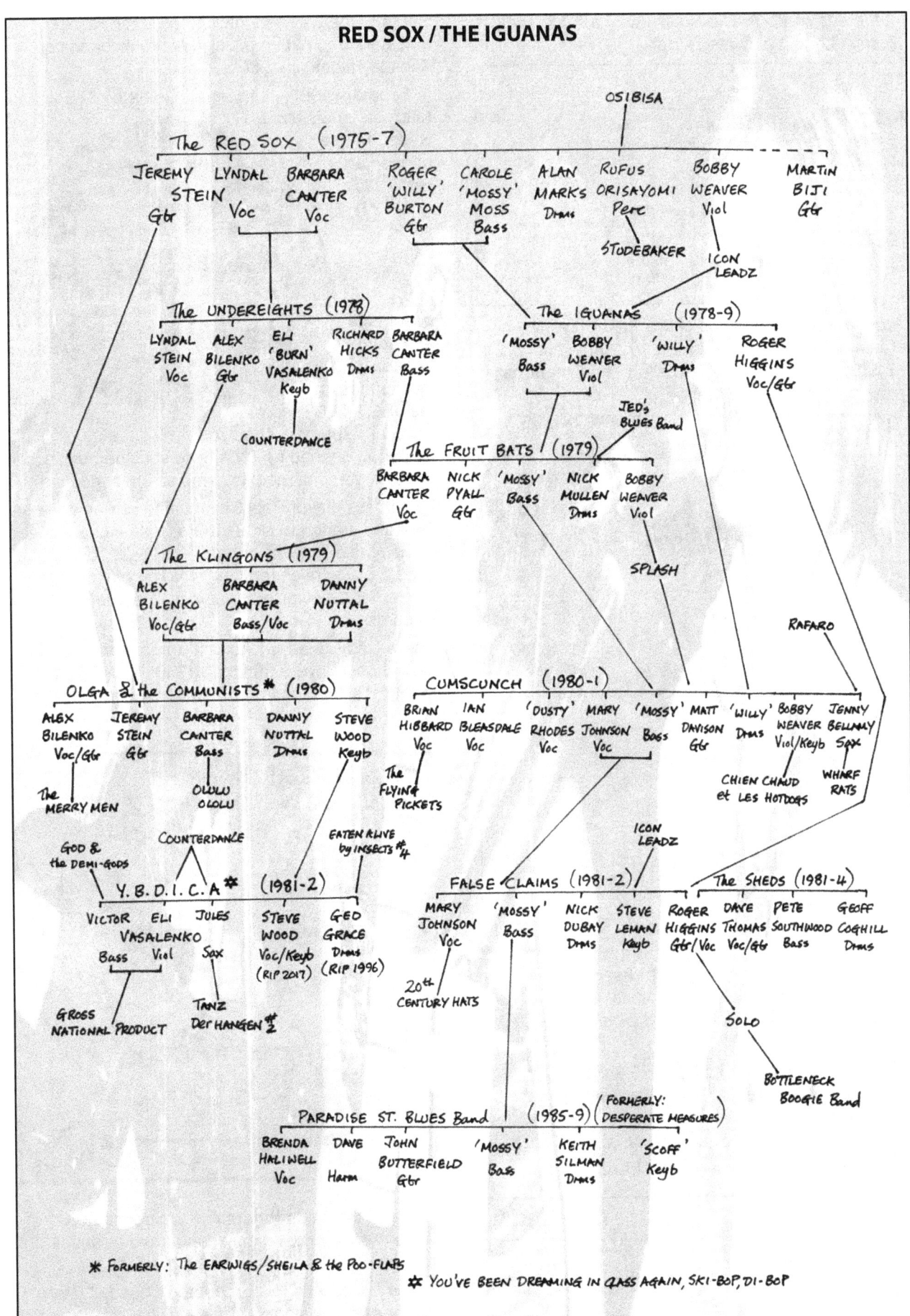

At the end of 1979, The Ruts played a *Rock Against Racism* benefit at Queen's Hall.

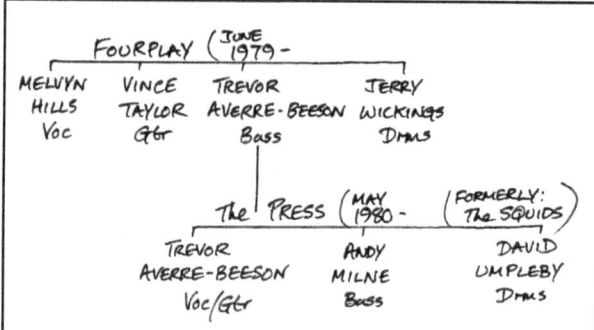

Around this time a bunch of Bradford University students formed a band called **Fourplay**, and a group of fourteen-year-olds called **The Fractions** played at Bingley Arts Centre.

The Fractions

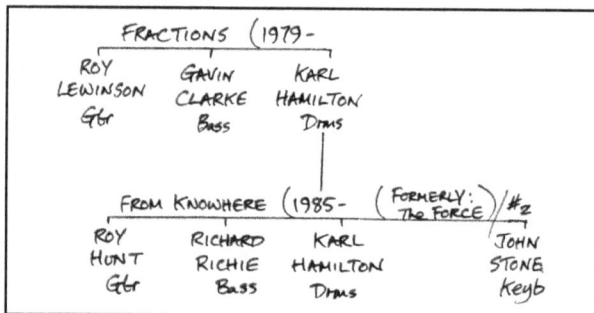

Skipton group Muggins Blight released a self-financed EP single on Look Records, *Mr Somebody / They Go Up, They Go Down / Malcolm Where's The Talcum?*

During the first six months of 1979 around ninety new independent record labels were set up in the UK, and a new music magazine called Record Collector was started by a certain Sean O'Mahoney.

In Halifax, there was the group **Airkraft**.

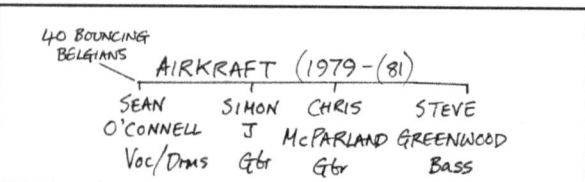

Splash One was a nightclub on Bolton Road that started to put on mainly electronic bands on Tuesday nights in 1980.

In February 1980, John Stuart Gothard of JSG Music, at 108B Main Street, Bingley, opened an eight-track recording studio called Fagend in the basement and started to release local bands on the JSG label. The musical instrument shop had been opened by John, who sold the business in 1988; it later changed its name to Spectresound.

Local bass player Paul Smith answered an ad in the *T&A* and started work at JSG as a service engineer in the studio. He was a member of Jazz rock group Middle 8 who released their instrumental debut single, *Misadventure / Countess Of Lyme,* on JSG Records.

Paul's Dad Edgar had been a trumpet and saxophone player during the 1940s and 50s in many local big bands like The Ken Henderson Big Band.

In March the **Cat's Pyjamas** shop opened on Morley Street, trading in second-hand clothing, LPs and handicrafts.

In July **Pearson's Records** shop closed; it later reopened as Bostocks.

RADIO 5

The four-piece indie band Radio 5 were formed in 1980 and had in their lineup two stalwarts of the city's 1970s music scene. Guitarist Geoff Haran and drummer Chris Groves, besides being members of many local combos were both in Midas (1971-72) and Fillibuster (1976).

Future incarnations of the band revolved around the other guitarist/vocalist 'Jock' Cotton (a cousin of The Cure's Robert Smith).

The band released their self-financed 7" single *Japanese Art / True Colours* in February 1980 on their Air Play label. It was recorded at Rochdale's Cargo Studios and co-produced by John Brierly.

After the B-side *True Colours* appeared as a track on Rockburgh Records compilation *Hicks From The Sticks* in late 1980, the label released it as a 7" single with the track *Animal Connections* on the B-side. The single was released in France on Polydor Records with different sleeve art.

John Peel discovered Radio 5 via the *Hicks From The Sticks* album and played True Colours half a dozen times on his show. On May 6, 1980, Radio 5 recorded four tracks, *True Colours / Animal Connections / Expressionless / Dancing With Germany*, for a John Peel session which was broadcast on May 13 and repeated in June and July.

Afterwards, Geoff left to form the band Seldom Red. Chris also left, and the rest of the band continued as a trio with new drummer John Wallis.

In 1983, the band morphed into The Word.

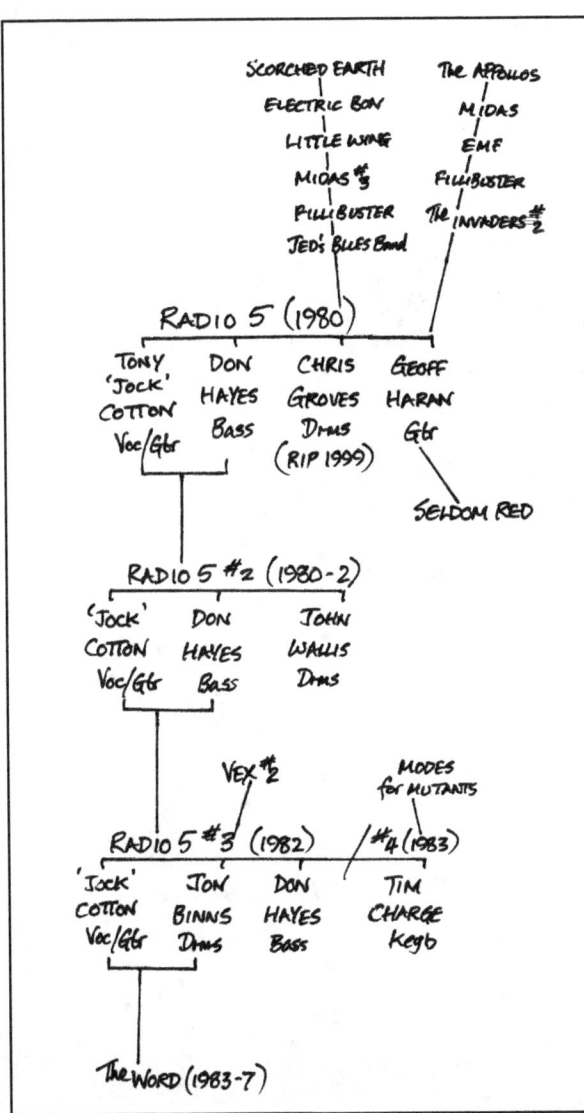

HICKS FROM THE STICKS

In 1980 music journalist Des Moines (Nigel Burnham) conceived and compiled an album of provincial northern bands entitled *Hicks From The Sticks* on Rockburgh Records. This sixteen-track compilation album included the song *True Colours* by Radio 5, the only Bradford band on the LP. It also featured two Leeds bands, The Expelaires and Music For Pleasure, as well as Halifax band Air Kraft. Rockburgh Records also released *True Colours* and the Expelaires track *Sympathy (Don't Be Taken In)* as singles.

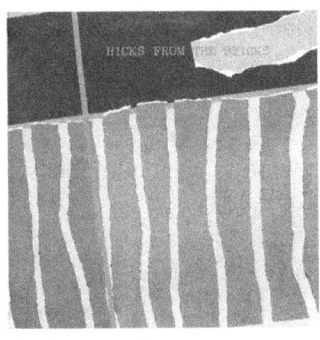

THE ELEMENTS

The band were formed in 1979 as Sulphate Attack, originally with singer Simeon Warburton who soon left to form Modes For Mutants. The band played their first gig at the Beeches Hotel, Keighley.

Now with vocalist Jayne Tretton on board, they gained a solid local following and had support slots on US band Bad Brains and British punk band UK Subs tours. They recorded a four-song promo cassette at JSG Studios, Bradford which included the tracks *Cannot Carry On*, *So Strange*, *Happiness Is Chemical* and *Fools Paradise*.

In 2006, the CD compilation *Beginnings 1980 To 1982* was released on Roach Daddy Records. It included early demos, studio tracks and tracks from their *Morton Institute Rehearsals* tape from June 1981.

In 1980, Jayne left The Elements and went on to sing for a number of bands including the dance-oriented Jayver and Rodeo Jones.

The band recruited new singer Trish, who had just left the pre-New Model Army Hustler Street Band. The re-christened NMA played their first gig supporting The Elements at Scamp's nightclub on October 23, 1980.

She was replaced by Rosemary Robb by the time the band went into Leeds' Ric Rac Studios to record a six-track demo.

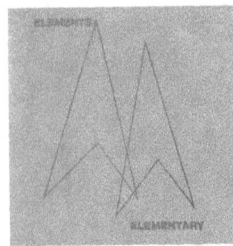

The band's only vinyl offering was the LP *Elementary* with an initial 500 pressing quickly selling out and having to be repressed. After Rose departed, Elements backing singer Ann-Marie Hurst took over lead vocal duties and the band emerged as the more well-known Skeletal Family.

The Elements reformed in 2019. Singer Jayne Tretton joined original members Stan Greenwood, Roger Nowell, Karl Heinz Taylor and Skeletal Family drummer Ozzy for a gig at Keighley's Exchange Bar on October 11, 2019. Gigs planned for 2020 and 2021 were cancelled due to Covid-19.

The band played in 2025 supporting Lene Lovoch (in whose band Stan Greenwood was playing) at The 1 In 12 Club on Saturday, October 11.

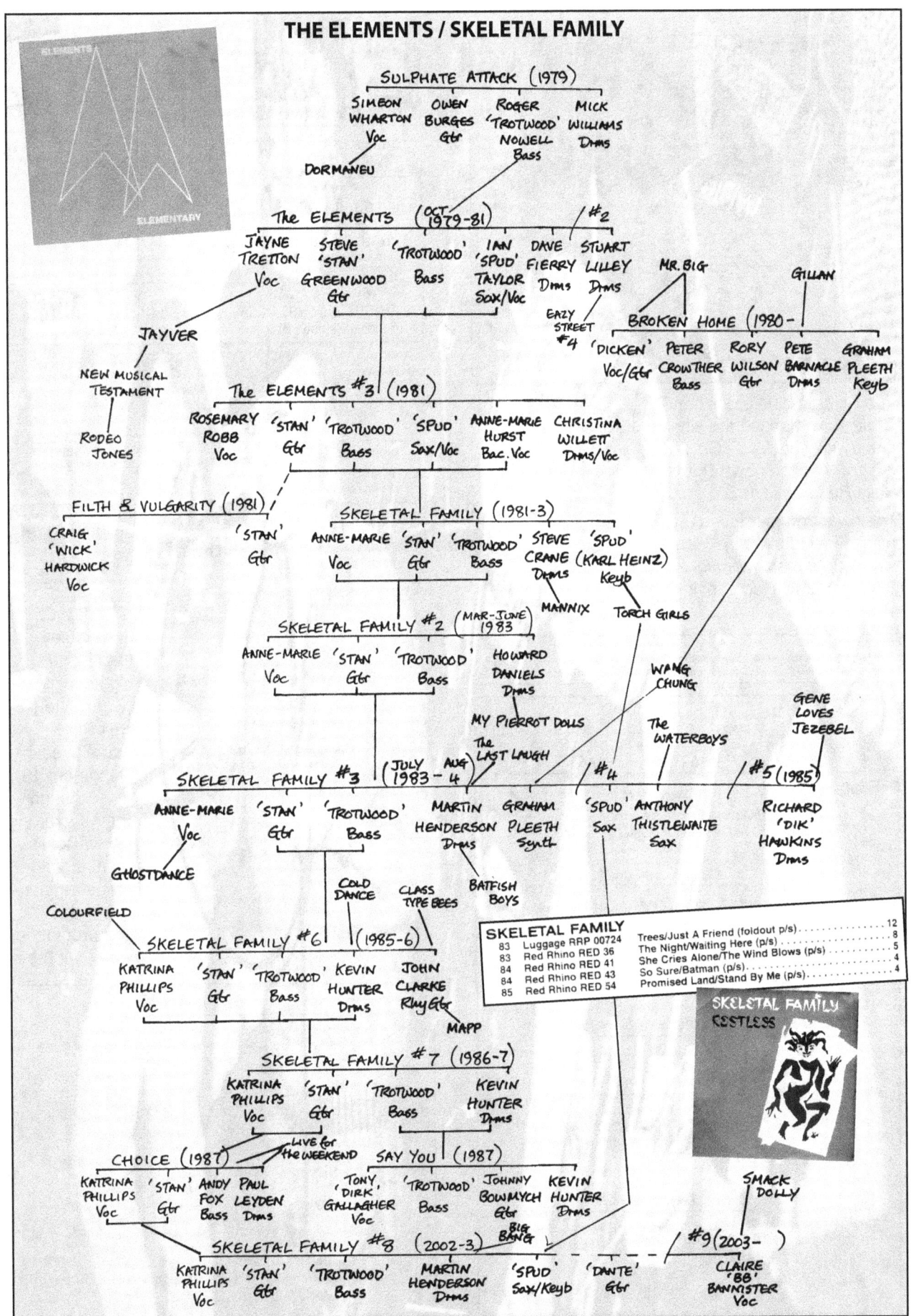

CHAINSAW

The Skipton blues rock band Chainsaw released the single *Lonely Without You / On The Highway* on their own Pot Belly Records in 1980.

They went on to release a further single, *Long Legged Woman / Midnight Blue*, on GMC Records, in 1984.

CHAINSAW			
80	Pot Belly EJSP 9462	Lonely Without You/On The Highway	35
84	GMC CS 001	Long Legged Woman/Midnight Blue	30

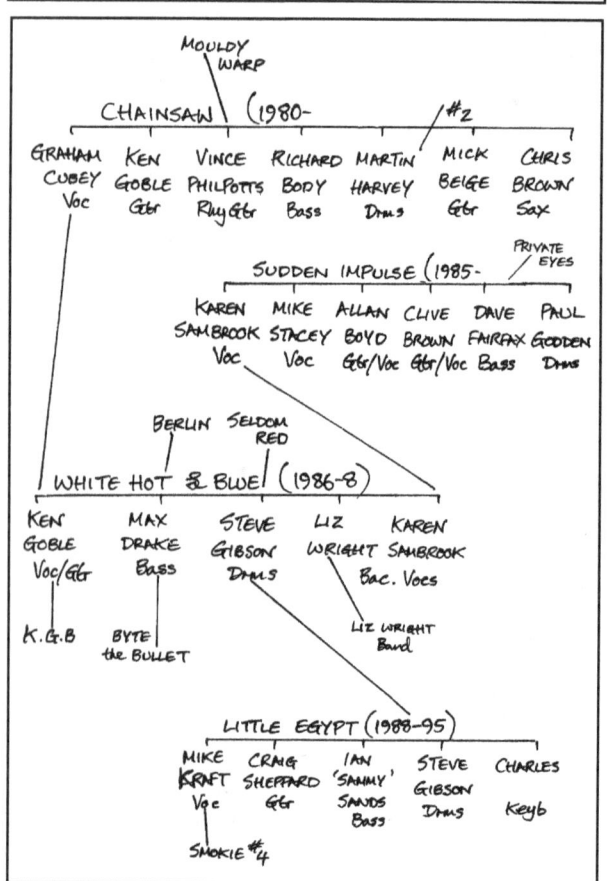

In Keighley, the **Nikkers** nightspot (where the Sex Pistols had played on December 19, 1977, during their secret *'Spots'* tour) continued to stage regular gig nights through to the early 1980s.

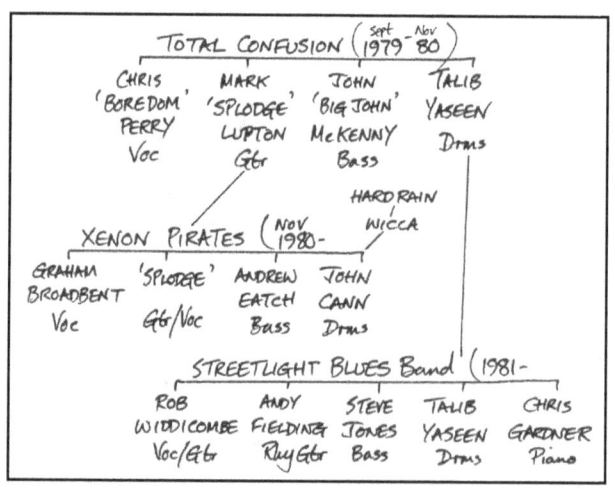

CHAPTER 5
POST PUNK ANARCHO PUNK Goth
1980 - 1983

During 1980 Britain slipped further under the grip of Thatcherite economic conservatism and general apathy, and suffered ever-rising mass unemployment, which in Bradford was 11,812 - seven percent of the population. Against this decaying social and political backdrop, the music scene that rose from the ashes of the first wave of punk was darker, more liberating and more experimental. The post-punk scene was spearheaded by a range of musically diverse bands like Joy Division, Killing Joke, The Fall, Gang of Four, Durutti Column, The Cure, and Wire.

Up until this time most rock bands had traditionally been male-dominated, but now women were making an impact - not just as singers, but as bassists, guitarists and even drummers. All female groups like The Slits and The Raincoats were joined by other mixed groups like The Passions and The Au Pairs.

These and other post-punk bands up and down the country were starting to feature on the new independent record labels, formed as a direct result of punk's DIY ethic. This in turn started the first national independent single and album charts in the trade paper *Record Business*.

BOB AND JOHN

1980 was the year the music world lost two of its most influential musicians and songwriters. On May 11, Bob Marley, the man who had almost single-handedly been responsible for introducing Jamaican reggae to an international audience, died from cancer, aged only 36.

On December 8, ex-Beatle John Lennon was shot dead by the fanatic Mark Chapman outside the Dakota Buildings, his New York home, after returning from a recording session. In some ways, his death marked an end to the era of free spirit and hope that began in the sixties and the beginning of the ruthless pursuit of money and materialistic goals that became the trademark of the eighties.

FUTURAMA 2

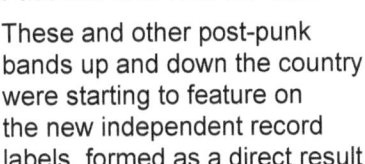

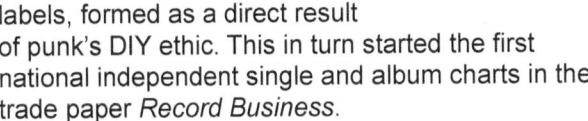

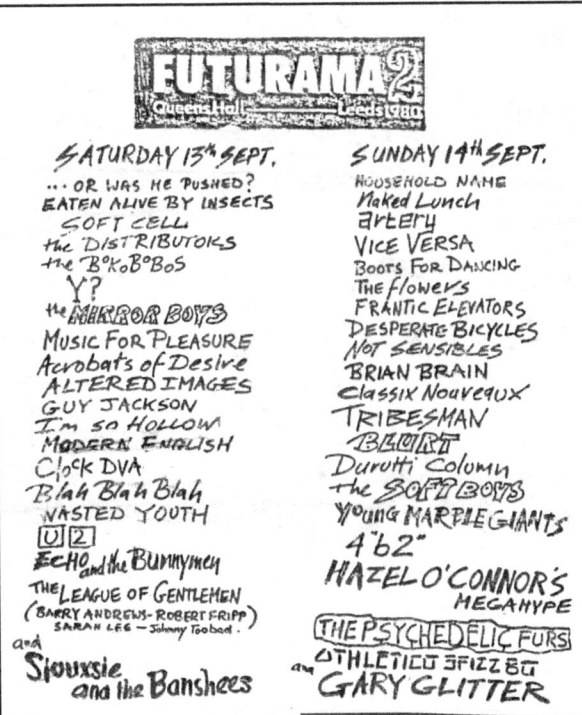

The Futurama event was organised for a second consecutive year by promoter John Keenan and took place over the weekend of September 13 & 14, 1980, at the Leeds Queen's Hall.

Gary Cavanagh remembers, *'I managed to get to the Saturday gig and as I got in I was fortunate to see the end of Eaten Alive By Insects set…the only Bradford band on the weekend's line-up. Of that day's bands, some who impressed me were – Durutti Column, and an early U2, before I had to run to the railway station to catch the last train back to Bradford.'*

ANARCHO PUNK HITS BRADFORD

Aki (the drummer in local act Violation) and his brother Rab organised a local gig for anarcho-punk bands Crass and Poison Girls at The Sweatbox (the ex-Italian Club), off Leeds Road, on October 13, 1980.

These two innovative and influential bands were formed in 1977 as a reaction to the 'no future' nihilism of the early punk movement. The latter were originally based in Brighton, forming the Vault Club and the fanzine *Spitting Blood* before linking up with the former in 1978.

Crass had been started by drummer Penny Rimbaud and vocalist Steve Ignorant at a communal house in Epping Forest and formed a loose collective of around nine members of the band. These anarchist 'noise terrorists' advocated pacifism, nuclear disarmament, animal rights, vegan/vegetarianism and the anti-commodification of society. Their banner at the gig stated, *'Oppose all power, fight war not wars, war can never be won.'*

They also founded their own record label, releasing singles and their first album *Stations Of The Crass* in 1980 and the *Penis Envy* LP in 1981. The band disavowed the profit motive on all their releases making them as cheap as possible with the famous *'Pay no more than…'* sticker on the cover.

Both bands also produced magazines; Crass's was *International Anthem* whilst the Poison Girls produced *Impossible Dream*. The publications expressed their anti-capitalist views using text and stunning photomontage graphics.

Crass as a band counted down to 'Year Zero' -1984 - the time they said they would, and in fact did, split up and cease to exist.

At the Sweatbox gig that night there were over four hundred punks crammed into the venue, many who had travelled from distance to be there. Poison Girls vocalist/guitarist Vi Subversa said, *'We prefer the atmosphere at this gig to some of the commercial clubs on this tour. It's more relaxed and not 'stiff'*

like clubs who are only paranoid about wall fittings and things getting damaged by shocking punks ..ha ha.' (2)

Both bands played many of their more famous numbers, a set enhanced by a multi-media backdrop of anti-war film images during the show. As the last encore numbers *Banned From The Roxy* and *Shaved Women* finished, the crowd were beginning to understand why the venue was called the 'Sweatbox'.

Crass's collaboration with and influence inspired a host of other anarcho-punk bands that followed, like Zounds, The Mob, Anti-Sect, Rudimentary Peni, Omega Tribe and Flux of Pink Indians.

The Brighton-based Poison Girls, led by singer/guitarist Vi Subversa (who was in her forties when the band started in 1977) returned to Bradford another four times over the next few years; at the Palm Cove Club on December 7 1981; at Queen's Hall in October 1983; a special Guy Fawkes gig for the 1 In 12 Club at Checkpoint on November 5, 1984; and at Benson's nightspot, supported by Chumbawamba, in 1985.

Sadly, their singer Vi passed away aged 81, in February 2016.

CHAPTER 5 - POST PUNK / ANARCHO PUNK / GOTH   1980 - 1983

FASSBENDER - RUSSELL BAND

The late Susan Fassbender (d.1991) was born Susan Whincup in Wibsey in 1959. She teamed up with ex-Ulterior Motives guitarist Kay Russell to release three singles on CBS.

Alan Brown, the manager of Kitchen's Music on North Parade, Bradford, had heard them practising on instruments in his shop. He was so impressed that he bought them guitars and keyboards and helped them get their first recording contract.

Courtesy of the Telegraph & Argus

POP stars Susan Fassbender (centre) and Kay Russell pay a surprise visit to Stewart Hannah, recovering from an operation in hospital.

Their first single, *Twilight Café / Get Around It*, reached 21 in the singles chart in January 1981 and led to two appearances on BBC's *Top Of the Pops*. The single had originally been released in November 1980 on Criminal Records before being taken up by CBS.

In April 1981, they released another single, *Stay / Ca Va*, this time as Fassbender-Russell. It was produced by Adam & The Ants drummer Chis 'Merrick' Hughes.

They appeared on TV show *Cheggers Plays Pop* to promote the single.

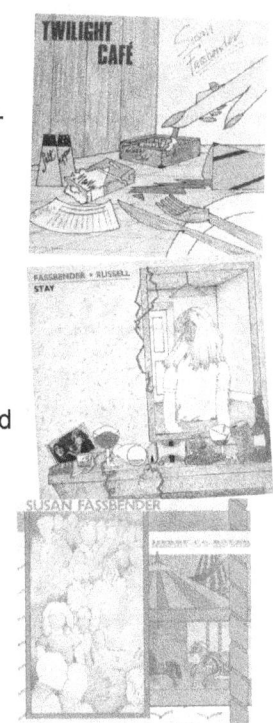

The band released a final single, *Merry-Go-Round / Reasons*, which was credited to Susan Fassbender Featuring The Fassbender/Russell Band. Their band was completed by bassist Mike Close and drummer Gary Walsh. *Merry Go Round* also failed to chart despite an appearance on Noel Edmond's Multi-Coloured Swap Shop in January 1982.

All three singles were co-written by Fassbender/Russell with sleeve artwork by Hilary Goodwright.

An album of unreleased Fassbender and Russell tracks entitled *Twilight Café (The Demo Collection 1981–1985)* was released in 2012 on Platform Records. Two further collections were released in 2016 using tapes of demos and other recordings preserved by Kay Russell. *Building A Dream (The Demo Collection Volume 2)* contained 17 tracks and their 10-track *Live In Concert (1981)* album was taken from a live tape.

Tragically, Susan (born Susan Kathryn Whincup) died in 1991, aged only 32. Kay Russell passed away in 2024, aged 72.

Pop stars call to see their No. 1 fan in hospital

SCHOOLBOY Stewart Hannah's day in hospital was brightened up by a visit from his two favourite pop stars (right).

For Stewart, 15, of 18 Church Lane, Brighouse, has been a fan of Bradford pop duo Fassbender Russell since they brought out their first single, Twylight Cafe, and he is the No. 1 member of their fan club.

So he was delighted when Susan Fassbender, Kay Russell and members of their band and management called to see him in Bradford Royal Infirmary, where he is recovering after a major lung operation.

Stewart, who goes to Rastrick Grammar School, used to cycle ten miles to hear the duo rehearsing in their Halifax studio. He is particularly fond of the group now that Merrick, of Adam and the Ants, his other favourite band, has produced their latest single, Stay.

And although cheered up by their visit, it also consoles him to know that he is missing O levels by being in hospital.

Susan Fassbender and Kay Russell met in Bradford at a Christmas party, and decided to perform together. They used to practise on instruments at Kitchen's music shop in Bradford, where they were heard by manager Alan Brown, who bought them keyboards and guitar and set up their first recording contract.

Twylight Cafe went to No. 21 in the UK singles charts.

Now, Stay is just climbing into the charts, and the duo, who have a band with drummer Phil Brown and bass player Mike Close, are touring from Bradford. Stewart hopes that he will be out of hospital in time for their gig on June 13 at Bradford University.

Meanwhile, Susan Fassbender, who used to be a nurse at Thornton View Hospital, Bradford, is trying to get him fit again.

PALM COVE

The Palm Cove, on Hollings Road, was a private ex-working men's club run by Robbie and Diane Lawrence. It became a popular venue for local bands and indie groups (like The Fall - 19/3/82), as well as mod and two-tone bands. Events were organised by Chris Groves (the drummer in Jed's Blues Band) on behalf of Robbie and Di.

The Palm Cove Club was also a popular venue for smaller punk gigs such as the Hustler Street Band (featuring Justin Sullivan and Stuart Morrow and soon to morph into New Model Army).

It was also the haunt of many other local punk bands including Chronic and Living Dead who produced and sold their local fanzine *Apathy* and released a Flexi Disc with a track by each band, for the princely sum of 40p.

Other bands who regularly turned out at the Palm Cove during the early 1980s included The Negativz, Complete Disorder, Requiem, Rip Snort, Friction Agitators, The Abhorred, Anti-System who played their own gigs or supported the likes of the Subhumanz, The Fall, and Urban Dogs.

Nick Toczek's *Gory Details* was the main promotor of punk during 1982/83. Among the many bands that featured were Chelsea, The Vibrators, The Exploited, GBH, Blitz/Violators, King Kurt, Poison Girls/Rubella Ballet, Bad Brains/Skeletal Family (5/5/83), The Meteors/The Gathering (24/3/83), Peter & The Test Tube Babies and many more.

Apart from the midweek punk nights, the Palm Cove was still predominantly a reggae club and there were lots of DJs and 'toasters' battling it out through reggae sound systems most weekends.

The Cove survived until 2001 when there were objections to its licence renewal *'on the grounds of noise and disturbance allegedly emanating from the premises and traffic congestion allegedly caused by patrons of the premises.'*

The Cove shut down after being the venue for many bands and DJs including, Griff's Magic Theatre (1986-96), Joe Strummer (1988) and hosts of reggae and garage nights. Griff's night closing shout of, *'If you want a drink, then get one now!'* may still echo through the empty building...

THE PALM COVE CLUB, HOLLINGS RD. BRADFORD

CHAPTER 5 - POST PUNK / ANARCHO PUNK / GOTH   1980 - 1983

CLUBS AND VENUES

Lots of other small or medium sized venues at this time were putting on occaisional gigs with punk and new wave bands in the city. Venues including Panache on Darley Street, The Royal Standard on Manningham Lane, The Vaults Bar on Great Horton Road, and The Manhattan Club (Bibi's) on Cornwall Terrace just by Bradford City's football ground were all helping to create a good local live music scene.

PANACHE

Panache, at 45 Darley Street, was briefly a bustling nightspot for punk and post-punk types in 1980 after opening as an American diner and bar in 1979. In addition to DJ nights, it also put on bands like The Negatives and New Model Army before its closure.

The venue was the original site of the famous Betty's Café which was started in 1919 by Swiss caterer Frederick Belmont. Years later, it moved to The Grove in Ilkley where it still provides its famous tea and cakes.

In January 1981, the lone parent organisation Gingerbread took over the building on a peppercorn rent of one red rose a year and was based there until closing in March 2008.

THE MANHATTAN CLUB – BIBI'S

The venue on Cornwall Terrace, situated just by the City football ground, was formerly Bradford City's Edwardian Club. It was bought and run by Gladstone 'Bibi' Minott. Bibi had arrived in Bradford from St Thomas in the West Indies in the early 1960s to work on the buses. His family was related to the West Indian 'toaster' Sugar Minott. The club was a popular venue for a period in the mid-eighties, although it became increasingly difficult to attract a decent size audience.

After a name change to the Capricorn Club, it became a popular venue on the acid house scene in the early 1990s and later moved to a new site at the corner of City Road and Preston Street.

Bibi's daughter Karin would later be a member of the group Unique 3 (1988-91) who had a minor chart hit, reaching number 41 in November 1990 with *Rhythm Takes Control*.

Sadly, Bibi died in 2007.

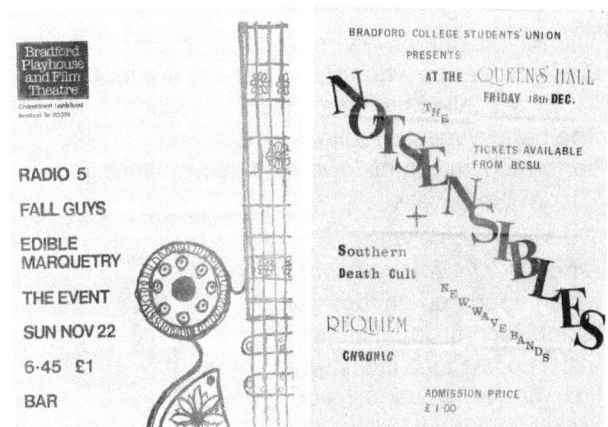

Two posters from local gigs at the Playhouse, off Leeds Road, and from Queen's Hall during 1981, show a snap-shot of the local band scene.

SWEATBOX II

In May, Rab (brother of Violation drummer Aky) was trying to start gigs at Gatsby's on a Thursday night. He had already lined up hardcore punk band Discharge and Kirk Brandon's Theatre of Hate to play but had to find somewhere else as the venue owners panicked at the idea of punks and their 'glue-sniffing' habits.

Soul legend **Marvin Gaye** played a string of his Motown hits at St George's Hall on Friday, June 25, to a small but appreciative audience of soul fans.

In Leeds, on Saturday, July 4, a free open-air festival was organised under the banner of the Anti-Nazi League/Rock Against Racism at Potternewton Park. Headlinering the *Northern Carnival Against Racism* were The Specials (who, within a week, would be topping the singles chart with *Ghost Town*) supported by Misty, The Au Pairs, and local bands The Mirror Boys, Another Colour, Reflex and poet Joolz Denby.

NEW MODEL ARMY

Formed as an initial three-piece in late 1980, NMA were to be one of the first Bradford bands in the 1980s to make an impact on the national independent music scene. They broke through the general bland music of the time with their hard-hitting political stance, original intelligent lyrics based around social injustice, and a powerful stage presence.

The band's name was derived from the English Civil War period when Parliamentary leader Oliver Cromwell called his troops the 'New Model Army'. The band's vocalist/guitarist Justin Sullivan also performed solo in his own right as his alter ego 'Slade The Leveller'.

Their first single was *Bittersweet / Betcha / Tension* which appeared on their own Quiet Records label in 1983. Initial copies also included a flexi disc of live versions of crowd favourites *Fashion* and

The Cause to discourage the sale of various NMA bootlegs which were appearing for sale. It reached number seventeen in the indie charts.

Their second single, *Great Expectations / Waiting*, was a number 27 Indie Chart hit in November 1983, released on Abstract Records.

Their main breakthrough came in 1984 with the release of their influential first LP, *Vengeance*, which reached number one in the indie charts.

Their final Abstract release, *The Price / 1984*, was their first indie number one single.

By this time the band had built up a large and dedicated following through their constant gigging and popularised the wearing of clogs amongst their audience.

In 1985, after being first messed around by Charisma Records, New Model Army signed a deal with EMI Records. Their resulting *No Rest For The Wicked* album received well-earned critical acclaim thus silencing any claims of the band having sold out to a major label.

By the end of 1985, bassist Stuart Morrow had left the band and for the next thirteen years, Justin and Rob Heaton became the central axis in the band's development.

In 1989 they released the LP *Thunder And Consolation* which was co-produced by legendary US Producer Tom Dowd and contained four Top 50 singles. The first was the *White Coats EP* (No 50), then *Stupid Questions* (No 31), *Vagabonds* (No 37) and *The Green And The Grey* (No 37).

In all they were to have twelve chart singles between 1985 and 1991 with their first EMI single *No Rest / Heroin* (NMA1) being their highest entry, reaching number twenty-eight.

In 1998, drummer and co-writer Rob Heaton retired from the band due to a brain tumour. After he recovered he built his own Righteous Sound attic recording studio before helping set up the Mutiny 2000 studio and record label at The Mill on Thornton Road. In 2003 he began into recording and promoting other local bands with other musicians in the *Fresh Milk* collective. Tragically Rob died suddenly aged only 43 in November 2004.

New Model Army continued with Justin as the only original member. They continued to play regularly to their army of dedicated fans all over the UK and Europe and released records on their Attack, Attack label, including the album *High* in 2007.

In 2020 they played an online show from their studio at The Mill, Bradford, to mark their 40th anniversary.

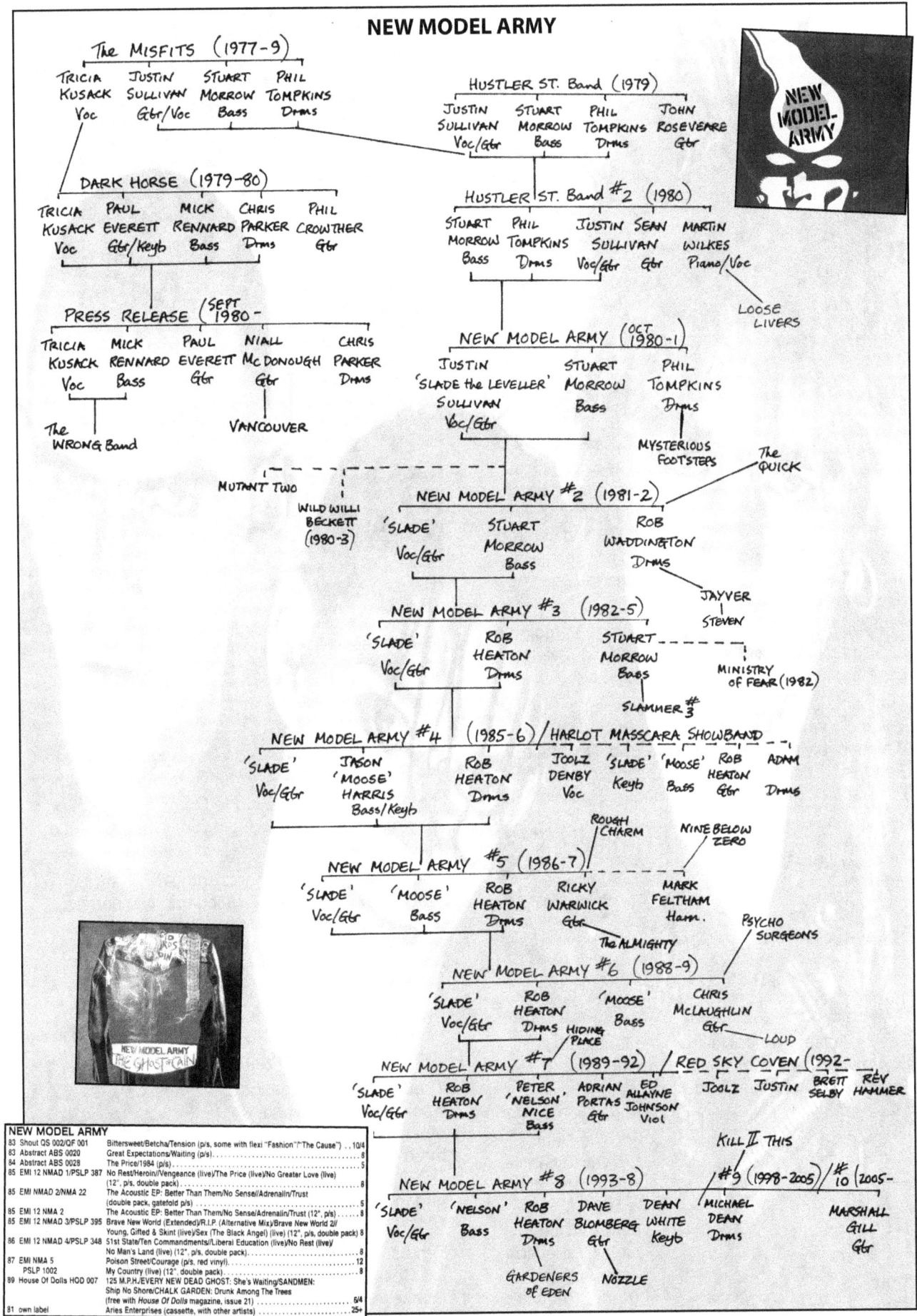

CHRONIC / LIVING DEAD

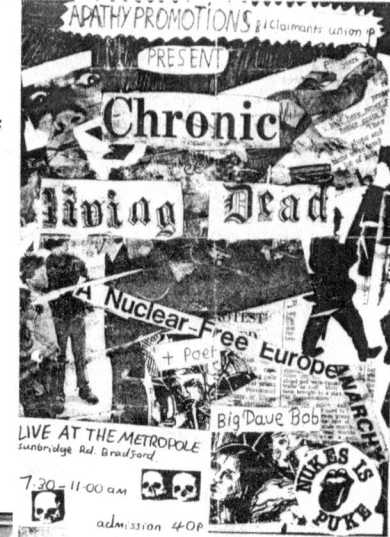

These two local Bradford bands were formed in 1979 and centred around the Clash-obsessed Ashton brothers. They set up their own DIY record label and fanzine known as Apathy Productions.

The *Apathy* fanzine was produced in 1981 (going on to at least three issues) and featured gig reviews, band profiles, jokes, photo montages, etc.

Their first tape release was the compilation *Apathy Volume 1* which featured nine local bands Chronic, Violation, Living Dead, Big Dave Bob, Distortion, Requiem, Friction Agitators, Abomination as well as Partizans (Birmingham) and Xpozez (Huddersfield).

They released two tracks from the tape as a split flexi-disc single, with *No Time* by Chronic and *Procession* by Living Dead.

Their second Apathy compilation tape was *Music For The Deaf Era* which came out on cassette in 1982. The bands included on this collection were Anthrax (Kent), Requiem, Friction Agitators, Chronic, Partizans (Birmingham), Living Dead, Stuff and Microsounds.

The last Apaphy release was the *Chronic* tape, a mixture of demos and live tracks.

Chronic and Living Dead were very active on the local gig scene with a large and

loyal following, until Chronic disintegrated. Andy Ashton joined Requiem in 1983.

In the mid-1980s, the Ashton clan relocated to Cornwall. As Chronic, they released their *Moondragon Dance* cassette album.

The three Ashton brothers, Andy, Paul and Tim formed a new band which had two names, Moondragon or Lordryk (the Cornish name for Moondragon). As psychedelic rock band Moondragon, they released the albums *Dream* (1991), *Live At The Kaos* (1994) and *Synaesthesia* (1996).

Their Lordryk incarnation was a Celtic/folk/world music band that released three CD albums *Lordryk* (1993), *Fushwacu* (1997) and the live *Combined Chaos* (1999).

Tim Ashton went on to form the Celtic folk band 3 Daft Monkeys.

CHAPTER 5 - POST PUNK / ANARCHO PUNK / GOTH 1980 - 1983

CHRONIC / LIVING DEAD / REQUIEM

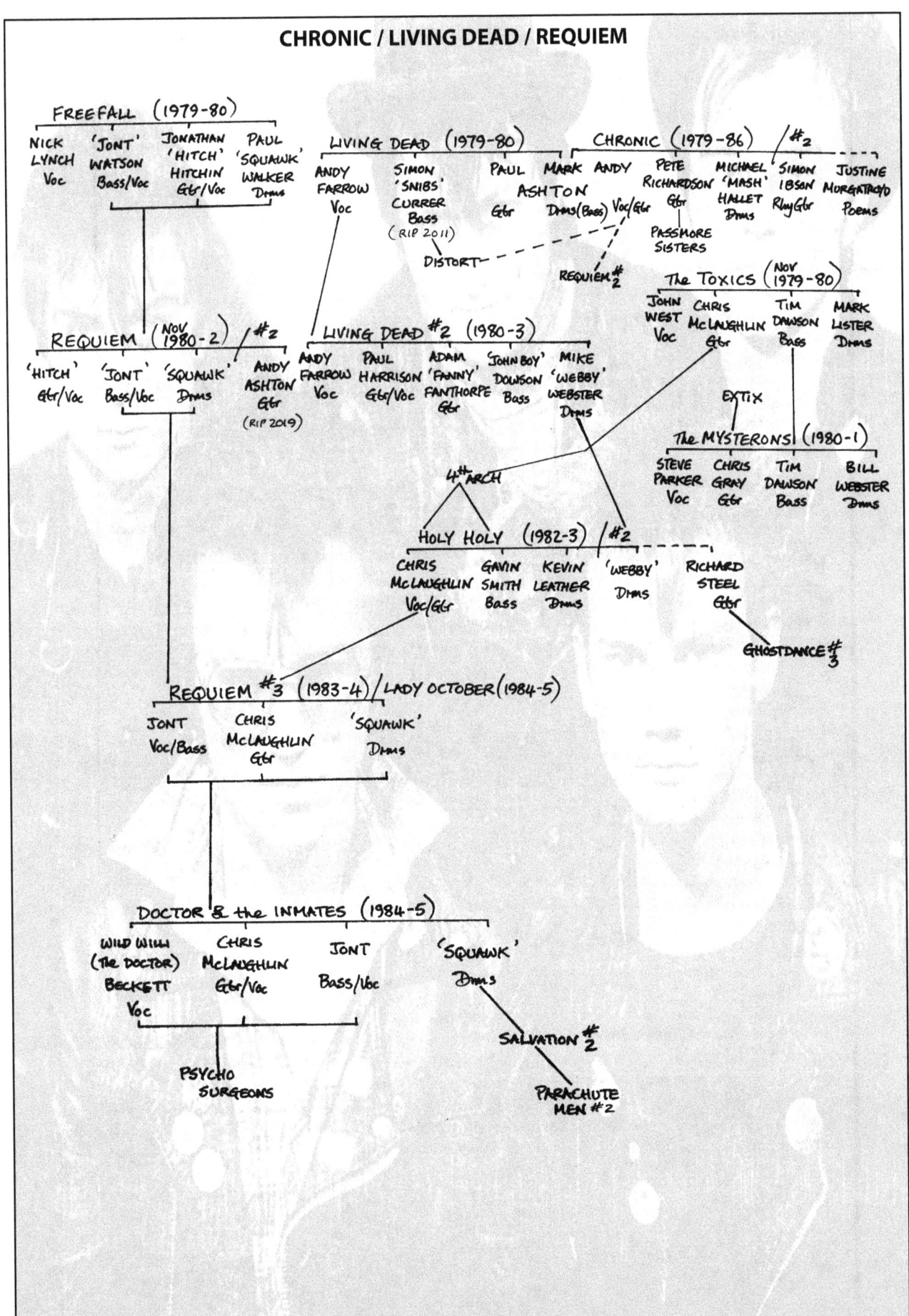

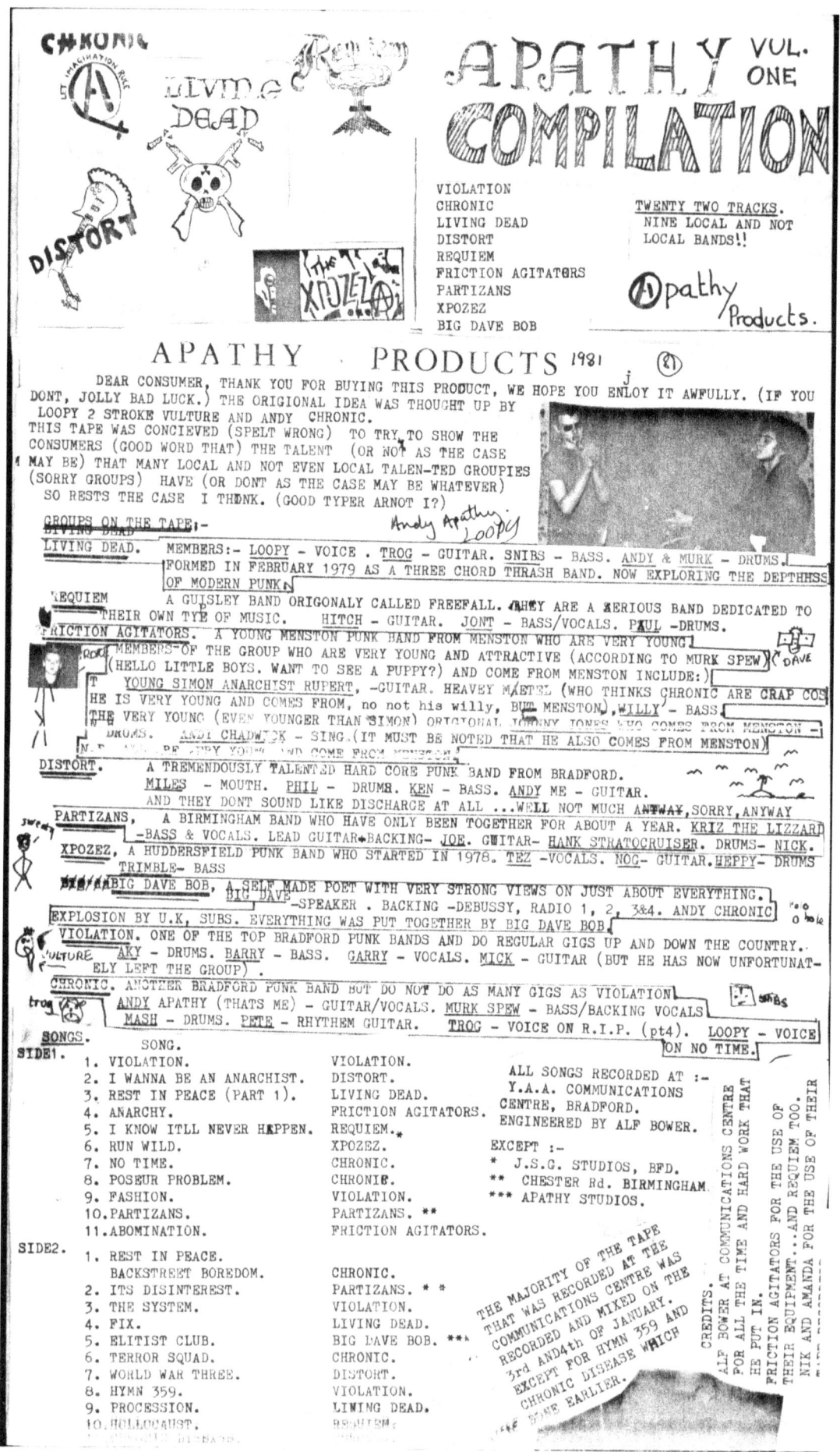

REQUIEM

This new wave group formed in 1980 with bassist Jont Watson, drummer Paul Walker and guitarist John Hitchin survivors of the earlier Freefall.

Requiem's post-punk style was reminiscent of early Cure. Their tracks *I Know It'll Never Happen* and *Holocaust* were recorded on 4-track tape at Yorkshire Arts, a small studio used for demos by a lot of early Bradford bands. Both tracks appeared on the *Apathy Volume 1* compilation tape in 1981.

Requiem played the usual venues of the day, like the Palm Cove, Queen's Hall and the 1 In 12 at various locations. They supported Sex Gang Children at The Manhattan Club in February 1983. Their track *Spartan Life* was released on *Enemies Of The State, The Worst Of The 1 In 12 Club Volume 3* vinyl compilation in 1984.

Hitch left and was replaced by Chronic's Andy Ashton on guitar by the time Requiem played the BCAU / 1 In 12 organised *Skive Off And Jive* festival in the amphitheatre at the back of Bradford University's Communal Building on Saturday, August 13, 1983.

Andy Ashton left and was replaced by guitarist Chris McLaughlin previously of The Toxics and Holy Holy.

This final lineup of Requiem morphed into Lady October (pictured bottom) before backing Wild Willi Beckett as Dr & The Inmates for a couple of gigs. Drummer Paul 'Squawk' Walker left to join Leeds goth band Salvation and was replaced by Barry 'Bambi' Gambles in what necame the original lineup of the Psycho Surgeons.

The Mutiny 2000 CD album *I Know It Will Never Happen* compiled Requiem studio tracks and a few live songs in 2003. It included tracks from early 1 In 12 compilations and their three-song demo, *Come On Down / Side Step Style / Myth*, recorded in 1983 at the new 24 track studio at Flexible Response.

THE CLAIMANTS UNION

In November the Raynor Report was published. It was a report commissioned by the Government looking to make cuts in staffing and services within the Department of Social Security (DHSS). Prime Minister Margaret Thatcher had asked Sir Derek Raynor, the head of Marks and Spencer, to also look into payments of benefits to the unemployed. The report came up with the startling statement that, *'1 in 12 claimants were defrauding the state, by claiming and working on the side'*. This was a ridiculous and arbitrary figure that both the CPSA (Union For Social Security Workers) and the Claimants Union thought was totally inaccurate and an attack on the unemployed.

The Claimants Union (CU) movement was a loose federation of local groups of unemployed who organised in their own area, supported claimants in the fight

for rights for those disadvantaged by being out of work. Nationally the CU attacked Government policies by advocating a scheme for a guaranteed minimum wage for all adult workers in an attempt to abolish the levels of poverty in society.

The local Bradford CU, which had started at the radical bookshop Fourth Idea in 1979, had in the meantime got its own room to work from at 9 Southbrook Terrace, near Bradford College. From this base, they provided mutual support for fellow claimants at DHSS interviews, as well as giving advice on aspects of the benefits system. They

also organised various fundraising activities such as jumble sales, etc., and produced their own magazine. *Free News* was a mixture of articles on current topics, cartoons, poems and a crossword.

Around this time, two other community organisations started in Bradford as part of the city's independent radical social provision.

Bradford Resource Centre (BRC) was a community-based project providing a range of facilities to support local activists in local and national campaigns, and Bradford Rape Crisis which was a service for support and counselling for victims of sexual assaults.

In February 1981 the Claimants Union decided to organise a benefit gig at Queen's Hall on Saturday the 7th featuring local Leeds and Bradford bands Pyramid, The Sheds, False Claims and You've Been Dreaming In Class Again, Ski Bop, Di Bop. After all expenses had been paid the CU netted around £60 which went towards paying off their phone bill.

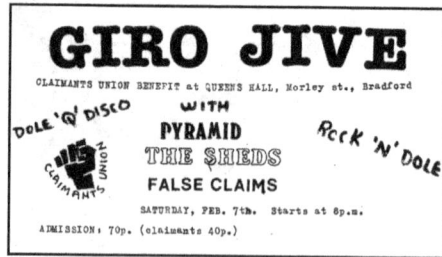

In early March members of the CU collected donations in buckets (which raised a fair few quid) at a rally outside City Hall as trade union leaders, including Len Murray and Arthur Scargill, spoke to the unemployed who were on The People's March For Jobs demo as it passed through the city on its way to London. (3)

Later that month anarcho-punk bands Crass and Poison Girls returned to Bradford to play a Socialist Workers' Party organised Rock Against Racism benefit at Queen's Hall.

A delegation from the CU visited Crass before the gig and got into a discussion with vocalist Steve Ignorant. The CU were asking the band to change their 'one price for all' door policy for the gig and reduce the price for UB40 holders so that the hordes of punk kids queuing outside around block could afford to get in. Steve couldn't handle the impassioned arguments of one female CU member and in a temper attempted to strike out at her! Although he quickly apologised for his actions the debate ended as a stalemate, leaving some unfortunate punk kids who couldn't afford the door price and didn't see the gig.

1981 RIOTS

In early April the first of many riots in mainland Britain that summer happened in Brixton, sparked by the racial harassment of the stop and search SUS laws and general police heavy handedness. Petrol bombs (Molotov Cocktails) were used by rioters for the first time on the streets of the UK.

These disturbances quickly spread to other urban

inner cities areas like Toxteth in Liverpool and Moss Side in Manchester. During the summer as another twenty seven towns and cities, including Leeds, Huddersfield and Halifax in West Yorkshire, all experienced rioting in reaction to the continued inner city decline, high unemployment and growing poverty.

Gary Cavanagh recollects, *'As I was involved with Fourth Idea bookshop as a volunteer at the time, I soon began to encourage some of the local punks (mainly the Apathy crowd) to hang out upstairs at the shop on Saturday afternoons, where they played their newly bought singles on an old stereo while having a cuppa.'*

'The collective staff had noticed that punks in the shop were a deterrent to Nazi skinheads and boot boys as a rival 'tribal' culture. Those brave 'Aryan Supermen' suddenly shied away from confronting a bunch of young leather-clad punks, where previously they had enjoyed baiting and intimidating the staff's female workers.'

THE BIRTH OF THE 1 IN 12 CLUB

'When asked by fellow workers to engage these local punk groups into doing a benefit for the shop, I said I would give it a go.

So, in March, I organised my first gig, which featured six bands and three poets at Bradford University Communal Building. They were;

Violation, Chronic, New Model Army, Joolz, Boys From The East, Little Brother, Living Dead, Big Dave Bob and Requiem.'

Chronic (above) and Living Dead's Andy Farrow

'It turned out to be a great night with a good turn-out of folks from the local Bradford punk scene. It was only marred by one stupid incident, when a certain bunch of idiots turned on a water hose at the side of the stage and drenched the last band Violation (it also turned to be their last gig) during the beginning of their third number. Due to all their gear being soaked and the chances of electrocution the gig had to be stopped. It was a bad end to a great night.

'Following the partial success of this gig and the previously organised benefits, some of the local CU members (Tony Grogan, Steve Leman, Lisa and

1 In 12 members on the door

The stage is set at The Metropole

Lusca Zychowicz and myself) got together at the Metropole Hotel one night to discuss the possibility of starting our own club in Bradford.' (4)

'The idea was to put on regular weekly gigs with admission as cheap as possible for the unemployed, and to focus on the virtually untapped source of up and coming local bands who were finding it hard to get anywhere to play in the city.'

'We soon agreed terms for hiring the upstairs room of the venue for a fiver a night with 'Polish Stan', the landlord of the Metropole Hotel on Sunbridge Road. The Club started on Wednesday April 29, 1981, and the first gig featured stalwart CU bands False Claims and The Sheds. The venue was named The 1 In 12 Club in response to the previous November's Raynor Report - now we all could be enemies of the state!

'Within a few weeks of starting the Club, it had attracted many new people to get involved at the gigs and extended the list of local bands and poets to groups from as far as Leeds and Manchester. It was originally publicised by word of mouth, then soon by the fly posting of A3 Day-Glo posters around town that advertised the next three gigs.' (5)

From the onset of The 1 In 12 Club gigs were run on a strict door cut of 75% to the bands and 25% to the Club for room hire, publicity, etc. Bands got no guarantees or guest lists, and how much they got paid was dependent on how many people turned up on the night.

Dancers at the 1 in 12 club

THE 1 in 12 Club for claimants at the Metropole, Bradford, looks like it is here to stay.

The club was started because young unemployed people in Bradford could not afford ordinary admission prices to clubs and concerts.

The Claimants Union was started in London to look after the interests of people claiming unemployment benefit or social security.

The Bradford branch decided to start a weekly club which provides cheap live music and also a much-needed venue for Bradford bands. They fixed on the Metropole pub in Sunbridge Road, Bradford.

Admission to the events is fixed at 40 pence for non-earners and claimants and 60 pence for everyone else. Each Week the 1 in 12 club has to pay out £5 for the room hire, £3 for posters and leaflets and £5 for disco and PA equipment, unless the band brings its own.

After these expenses are met, the proceeds are split, 75 per cent to the band and 25 per cent to the Claimants Union.

How much the band earns depends on the number of people who attend, and varies a lot. However, no-one gets in free, even volunteers helping run the gig — or the Telegraph & Argus reporter.

All the decisions about the club are made in a co-operative way, with an open meeting every Thursday at 7 p.m. before the gig and representatives of the Claimants Union on Tuesdays between 10 a.m. and 3 p.m. at 9 Southbrook Terrace, Bradford 308970.

Forthcoming attractions at the 1 in 12 Club are The Modern Scene and Boys from the East on Thursday, Vengeance and Mainline on September 17, The Clause and Reflex on September 24 and other bands. However, anyone interested in playing will be very welcome.

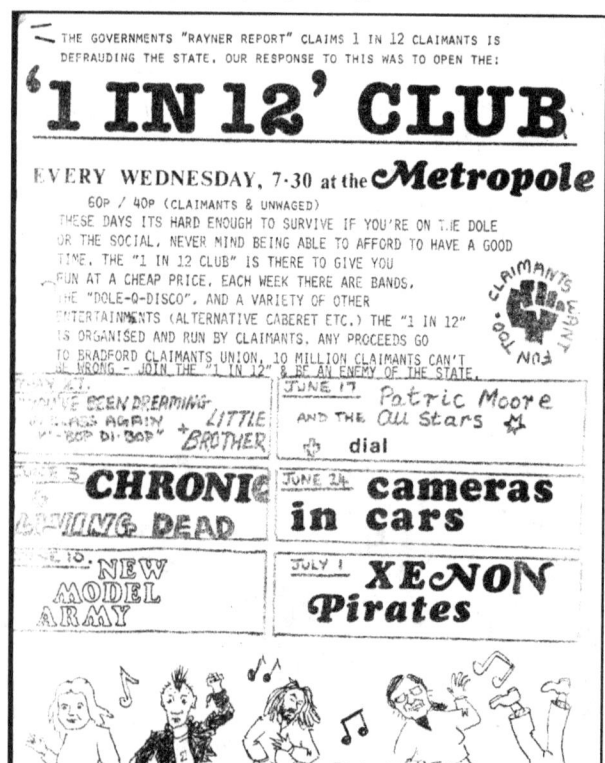

CHAPTER 5 - POST PUNK / ANARCHO PUNK / GOTH   1980 - 1983

The Club's principles were libertarian, with no bosses and no hierarchies, and a strong anti-racist/sexist policy encouraged cooperation and mutual aid amongst members of the audience and the bands alike. Everyone mucked in, volunteering to take turns on the door or to help fly posting and leaflet printing, and bands usually shared their backline gear.

Before long it had a hired twin turntable each week for the *Dole-Q Disco* which was ably run by DJ Mark 'Maz' Mazurke spinning some of the latest new wave hits prior to the gigs. The Club even got a positive bit of publicity courtesy of an article in the T&A's *Rock On* column by Celia Barlow, who gave the club lots of support between 1981 and 1983.

New Model Army was one of many local bands who supported The 1 In 12 Club through playing gigs, benefits and festivals in the Club's early years.

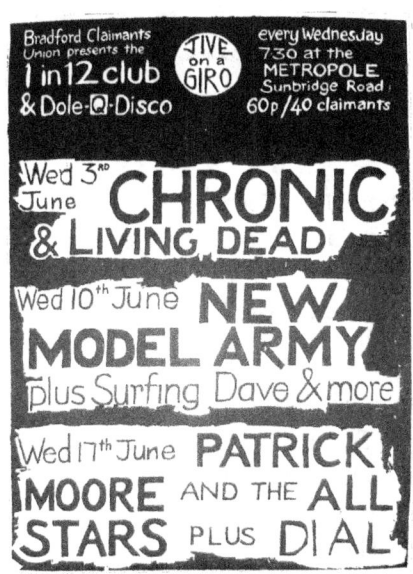

Many new local groups formed in and around Bradford in the early eighties, contributing to a thriving music scene full of energy and musical experimentation. The musical diversity of the bands included post-punk/new wave, mod influence and reggae dub styles, and produced the city's first multi-racial bands from an Asian background, including Boys From The East, The Vindaloos, The Abhorred, and Complete Disorder.

Since its inception in April 1981 at the Metropole Hotel on Grattan Road, Bradford's 1 In 12 Club had travelled the 'nomad trail' from venue to venue in the years 1981-87, until it opened its own members owned and run venue at 21-23 Albion Street in June 1988.

During that period it organised over 275 gigs, three free outdoor festivals at the amphitheatre behind the University's Communal Building and over a dozen benefit gigs. It also produced three vinyl compilation LPs featuring bands that had played the Club.

A few posters from gigs at The Metropole show some of the bands who played regularly during these early days. They were designed by various 1 In 12 Club members and screenprinted using hand-cut stencils at the Community Printshop on Thornton Road.

183

1 IN 12 CLUB GIGS AT THE METROPLE

APRIL 1981
29 - False Claims / The Sheds / Dole Q Disco

MAY 1981
6 - Reflex / University Of Sydney
13 - Requiem / Joolz
20 - Mammoth / Boys From The East / Dark Pheonix
27 - You've Been Dreaming In Class Again, Ski Bop, Di-Bop / Little Brother

JUNE 1981
3 - Chronic / Living Dead
10 - New Model Army / Surfin' Dave / Seething Wells / Joolz
17 - Patrick Moore & The All Stars / Dial
24 - Open To Offers / Mike Parkinson / Little Brother

JULY 1981
1 - Falls Guys
8 - Cameras In Cars / Seething Wells
15 - Backslider
22 - Bone Idle / Ajna Janet Cook
29 - Terrorist Guitars / Dinner Ladies / The Collapsable Deckchairs

AUGUST 1981
5 - Chainsaw / Nick Toczek
12 - Radio 5
18 - Living Dead / Requiem / Admass
27 - Dial / Stacc

SEPTEMBER 1981
3 - Surfi'n Dave & The Absent Legends / The Volunteers / Arts Course Of GB
10 - The Modern Scene / Boys From The East / The Vindaloos
17 - The Vengence
24 - The Cause / Mike Parkinson
30 - Rot In Flesh / Friction Alligators / The Insane

OCTOBER 1981
8 - Prophecy / Raider
15 - 96 Tears
22 - Southern Death Cult / Edible Marquetry
29 - Folk Nite

NOVEMBER 1981
5 - Shake Appeal / Mill City Blues Band / Seething Wells
12 - The Unconventional / Helter Skelter
19 - The Volunteers / Joolz / Surfin' Dave
26 - Fall Guys / The Vindaloos

DECEMBER 1981
3 - Sudden Red / Wild Willi Beckett
10 - Stacc / Industrial Aktion

JANUARY 1982
28 - New Model Army / Little Brother

FEBRUARY 1982
4 - Dry Ice
11 - Requiem / The Abhorred
18 - Yeah Yeah Yeah / Alf
25 - The Mysterons / Anthrax

MARCH 1982
4 - Apocolypse Choir / Nick Toczek
11 - Boys From The East / The Vindaloos
18 - Ichor / Wardance
25 - Mutant 2 / Joolz / Little Brother

APRIL 1982
1 - Ik / Friktion Agitators
8 - Chronic / Living Dead
15 - Wild Willi Beckett / Joolz / Weaving Sheels
22 - The Bitter End
29 - Surfin' Dave / The Three Johns / Little Brother

MAY 1982
6 - 4th Arch / Anthrax
13 - Victim / Complete Disorder / The Abhorred / Dachau
21 at Queen's Hall - 1K / Admit One / Wild Willi Beckett

JULY 1982
20 at Queen's Hall - Living Dead / Daka / Necromancy / Complete Disorder

BOP AGAINST THE BLUES
Bradford University Amphitheatre
July 24 - Harlem Spirit / Chronic / Seething Wells / Radio 5 / Little Brother / New Model Army / Joolz / Nick Toczek / Boys From The East / The Negatives / The Prowlers

1 IN 12 CLUB GIGS AT TICKLES

FEBRUARY 1983
25 - **The Textile Hall** - The Three Johns / Wild Willi Beckett / The Word / Monkey On A Rope

MARCH 1983
30 - The Negatives / The Convulsions

APRIL 1983
6 - Requiem / Holy Holy / Passmore Sisters
13 - Anti-System / The Convulsions / Social Spastix
20 - Monkey On A Rope / Mr Soft / The Gathering
27 - The Chumbawamba / 20th Century Hats / La Dulce Vita / Tebbits Law

MAY 1983
4 - Rip Snort / Wild Willi Beckett / Bash St Kids
11 - The Shakes / Little Brother / Monkey On A Rope
18 - The Beckoning / Figures From The Cold
25 - The Word / Age Of Chance / Ricky

JUNE 1983
1 - Silent Community / Vermin / Four Naughty Nuns / Raw / The Convulsions / Subvert / Warhead
8 - Colenso Parade / The Sunbeams / Dirk Spig
15 - Boys From The East / Beyond The Veil
22 - The Inevitable Split / Surfin' Dave
29 - Seven Antelopes / To The Jade Kitchen / Stupefaction

JULY 1983
6 - The Three Johns / Little Brother / Seething Wells
13 - Skeletal Family / The Bantus / Sweet Life
20 - Chumbawamba / Icon AD / Warhead / Passion Killers
27 - Passmore Sisters / A Touch Of Hysteria

AUGUST 1983
3 - Stallion / Ichor
10 - Camera Obscura / Citron Girls

SKIVE OFF & JIVE
Bradford University Amphitheatre
August 13 - The Three Johns / Spectre / The Toys / Skeletal Family / Fatal Charm / Requiem / Anti-System / Inevitable Split / Boys From The East / 20th Century Hats

17 - Snake Davies & His Alligator Shoes / Dirk Spig
24 - Walter Mitty's Little White Lies / The Toyz
31 - The Mighty Clifton Brothers

SEPTEMBER 1983
7 - Holy Holy / Living Dead / Legion
14 - The Ex / Alerta / The Three Johns
21 - Fatal Charm / If, But And Why
28 - Surfin' Dave & The B'Nee Teas / The Bitter End

OCTOBER 1983
5 - MRA / Household Name
12 - Chronic / Living Dead / Legion
19 - The Indiscriminate Hoax Fund / Dry Ice / The Bantu's
26 - The Word / Wild Willi Beckett / Rip Snort

NOVEMBER 1983
2 - The Negatives / The Convulsions / Neon Wolf
9 - Little Brother / Swells / Joolz / Wild Willi Beckett / Slade The Leveller / G McAndrew
10 - Eton Crop / Cowboys And Indians
16 - Blu Electric

1 IN 12 GIGS AT THE MARKET TAVERN

23 - Spectre / Those Frayed Edges
30 - Loose Livers / Dirk Spig / Little Germany

DECEMBER 1983
7 - Photomontage / Chinese Gangster Element
14 - Anti-System / The Instigators / Vermin
21 - Requiem / Seven Antelopes
28 - Passion Killers / Dan / Skum Dribblers / Odesa / Chumbawamba / Kulturo

THE WORD

Formed from the ashes of the band Radio 5, this group soon gathered a strong local following and became regular supporters/members of The 1 In 12 Club over the next few years.

They released their self-financed first single *Colour It / Recuring* on their own Menace Music label in 1983.

'Instead of sending a tape to the bigger record companies, who rarely seem to listen to them, we produced and recorded our own, to help promote the band, get bookings and to attract critical notice - especially on the radio if all goes well,' the band told the T&A's *Rock On* reporter.

The band also played at The 1 In 12 Club about ten times, including the 1984 *Not The International Garden Festival* outdoor gig.

In 1984 they released a four-track 12-inch EP entitled *The Next Big Thing*, again on their Menace label. The tracks were *Wide Awake / Shining Things / Immaculate / Different*.

Their 7-inch single *Schoolboy Saint / Word To The Girls* came out on Abstract Records in 1985. The A-side was recorded at Flexible Response while the B-side was done at Lion Studios.

On Friday, September 30, The Word appeared on Yorkshire TV's tea time local news programme *Calendar*, playing their single live.

One notable gig of theirs was in April 1983 when they headlined at St George's Hall with support from The Jazz Hipsters, Dry Ice, Toranaga, Let's Eat, Surfin' Dave and Wild Willi Beckett.

In 1987 The Word split up. Bassist Paul Bahr, later known as Nagbea, was in the band Hyacinth House in 1988. Jock Cotton and Jon Binns resurfaced in the 1990s with Poppy Factory who were signed to Chrysalis and released four chart singles. The lineup was completed by bass guitarist and keyboard player Mick Dale, later of Embrace.

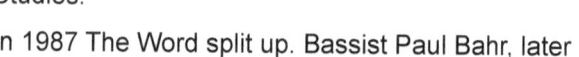

CHAPTER 5 - POST PUNK / ANARCHO PUNK / GOTH   1980 - 1983

RADIO 5 / THE WORD

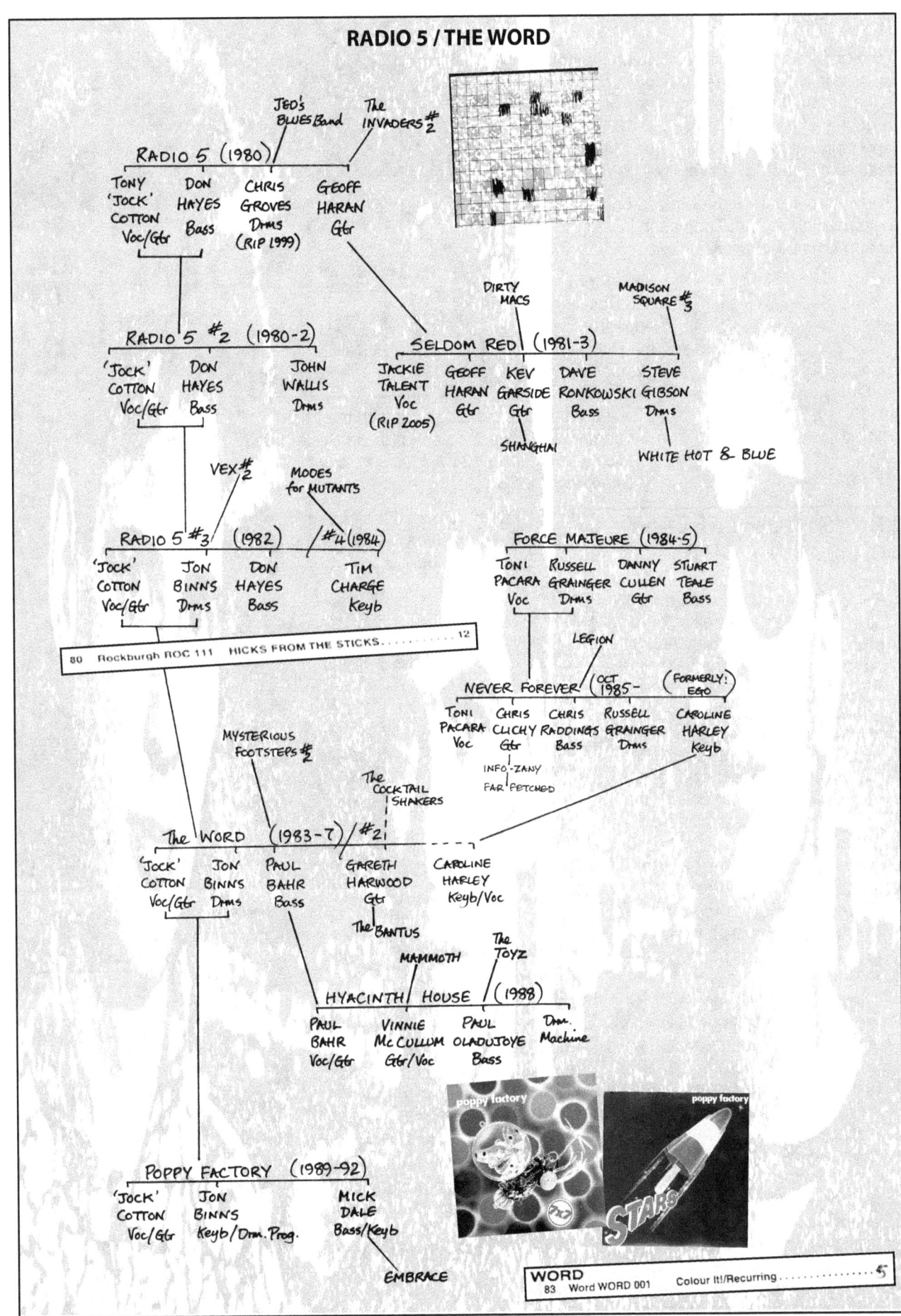

RADIO 5 (1980) — from JED's BLUES BAND / The INVADERS #2
- TONY 'JOCK' COTTON — Voc/Gtr
- DON HAYES — Bass
- CHRIS GROVES — Drms (RIP 1999)
- GEOFF HARAN — Gtr

RADIO 5 #2 (1980-2)
- 'JOCK' COTTON — Voc/Gtr
- DON HAYES — Bass
- JOHN WALLIS — Drms

SELDOM RED (1981-3) — DIRTY MACS / MADISON SQUARE #3
- JACKIE TALENT — Voc (RIP 2005)
- GEOFF HARAN — Gtr
- KEV GARSIDE — Gtr → SHANGHAI
- DAVE RONKOWSKI — Bass
- STEVE GIBSON — Drms → WHITE HOT & BLUE

RADIO 5 #3 (1982) — VEX #2 / MODES for MUTANTS #4 (1984)
- 'JOCK' COTTON — Voc/Gtr
- JON BINNS — Drms
- DON HAYES — Bass
- TIM CHARGE — Keyb

80 Rockburgh ROC 111 HICKS FROM THE STICKS 12

FORCE MAJEURE (1984-5)
- TONI PACARA — Voc
- RUSSELL GRAINGER — Drms
- DANNY CULLEN — Gtr
- STUART TEALE — Bass

LEGION

NEVER FOREVER (OCT 1985-) (FORMERLY: EGO)
- TONI PACARA — Voc
- CHRIS CLICHY — Gtr
- CHRIS RADDINGS — Bass
- RUSSELL GRAINGER — Drms
- CAROLINE HARLEY — Keyb
  - INFO-ZANY
  - FAR FETCHED

MYSTERIOUS FOOTSTEPS #2

The COCKTAIL SHAKERS

The WORD (1983-7) / #2 !
- 'JOCK' COTTON — Voc/Gtr
- JON BINNS — Drms
- PAUL BAHR — Bass
- GARETH HARWOOD — Gtr
- CAROLINE HARLEY — Keyb/Voc

The BANTUS / MAMMOTH / The TOYZ

HYACINTH HOUSE (1988)
- PAUL BAHR — Voc/Gtr
- VINNIE McCULLUM — Gtr/Voc
- PAUL OLADUJOYE — Bass
- Drm. Machine

POPPY FACTORY (1989-92)
- 'JOCK' COTTON — Voc/Gtr
- JON BINNS — Keyb/Drm. Prog.
- MICK DALE — Bass/Keyb
  - EMBRACE

WORD
83 Word WORD 001 Colour It!/Recurring 5

187

BOYS FROM THE EAST

One of the first multi-racial Eurasian bands to form in Bradford, they quickly became a fixture on the local scene. They played regularly at venues like the 1 In 12 Club, appearing at the Club's first free outdoor festival at Bradford University in 1982.

They were initially a three-piece until keyboard player Jim Thompson joined the lineup from Bill Presley's Coat.

Boys From The East appeared on the Club's *Worst Of The 1 In 12 Club Volume 2* cassette tape with the track *Subterranean Subterfuge* and also on *Systembeat 2: Worst Of The 1 In 12 Club Volume 5* with *Young & Beautiful* in 1985.

In 1984, they released their debut 7" single, *Eastern Eyes / Work Hard* on the Kirk Enterprises label.

On April 24, 1985, they did a Benefit at Queens Hall with The Three Johns and Little Brother for the Anti-Fascist 12. The gig was reviewed by the Seething Wells in the *NME*. (6)

On January 29, 1986, they played at the daytime *Red Wedge* gig at Queen's Hall with Joolz, Western Dance and 8 Day Fued.

Their second single, *Brilliant*, came out on 7 and 12-inch on Final Cut Records in 1987.

The band later shortened their name to The East before their final demise as the three members moved on to other musical projects. Drummer Mian Rahman, bassist Raj and Jim Thompson went on to Oktober, with Mian swapping his drumsticks for a guitar and a microphone. In 1991 Mian and Raj teamed up with three-quarters of the band Fundamental to form Detrimental.

BOYS FROM THE EAST
Bradford Queens Hall

BRADFORD has for sometime been establishing itself as the stud farm for some natty *pop* bands. Boys From The East are a Eurasian three piece with a very much un-sneezed at line in stroppy romanticism. They have tended in the past, as pop bands will, to exaggerate their sugar, spice and all things nice qualities at the expense of rats, snails and puppy dogs' tails.

  Brisk, brittle and aggressive. Lyrical twistings of the yawn yawn Heterolust outpourings of the current crop of chart non-entities were slyly poked past reverberating, clangy melodies. They ably caught the mood of a crowd gathered to raise cash for the defence of twelve assorted anti-fascists arrested opposing a recent slope-shouldered Master Race Appreciation Society rally.

  MEANWHILE back in the real world dot dot dot spoilt lower-middle class brats quote pre-war avant-garde manifesto's and play with chainsaws. Pah phooey!

Susan Williams

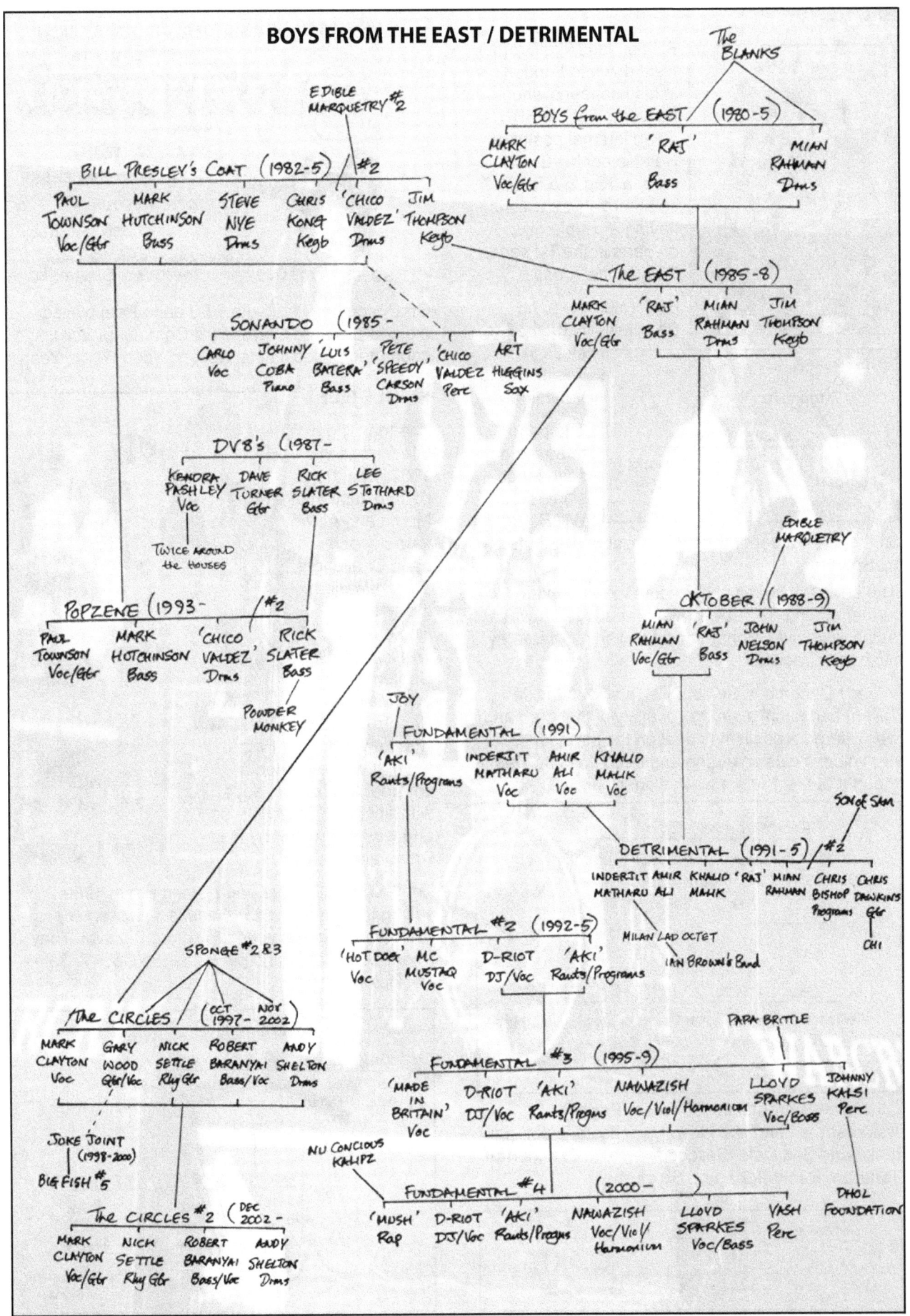

BAD NEWS 1

Bingley lad Mike Groth went down to London in his late teens where he worked at the BBC as an internal postman. He also got his Equity card, acting in a few commercials as well as having a couple of walk-on parts in the TV series *The Gentle Touch*.

He formed the band Bad News in 1981 after stints in Trickster and Valentino.

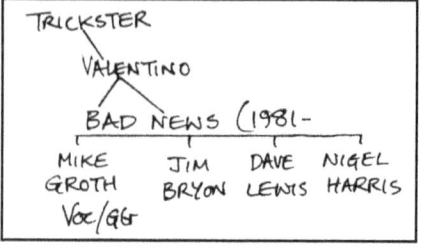

The band released a seven-inch single *Boys Will Be Boys* on the small independent V-Tone label distributed by Spartan.

The city's fragile racial harmony was put under further strain on Friday, November 20, 1981, when Asian taxi driver Mohammed Arif was murdered by suspected racists.

In early December, Seldom Red's singer Jackie Tallent had such *'a strong vocal style'* that the band was offered a publishing deal on the strength of her voice. It was so strong and deep that she was thought at first to be a black singer.

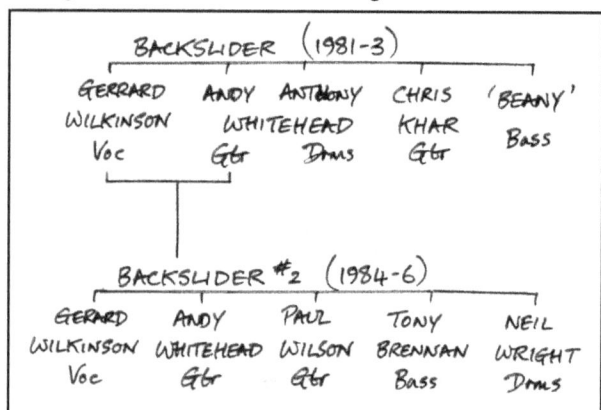

Other bands around in 1981 were **English Assassin**, a band likened to Manchester's soft-pop/rock band Sad Café, Baildon five-piece **Pre-Mental Tension**, **Backslider**, and **Strongbow**.

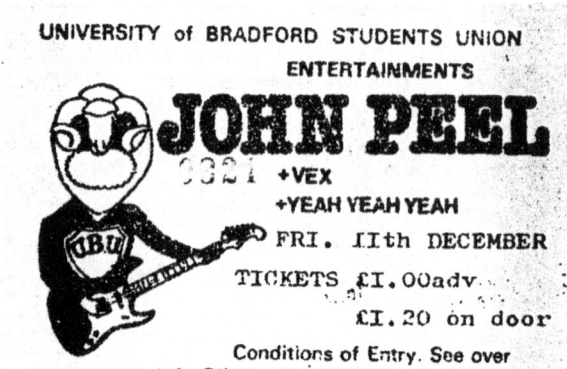

On December 11, Radio 1 DJ John Peel played a gig at Bradford University's Communal Building supported by local acts Vex and Yeah, Yeah, Yeah.

SINGLE FILE

The trio Single File formed in 1982, with the rhythm section of Martin and Alistir formerly of the band Challenger. They released their debut 7" single *Out In Traffic / Cracked Cup* on their own Mainline Records in 1986, with new drummer Roger Kirby. It was recorded at Off Beat Studios in Leeds with engineer Tony Bonner and was distributed by Red Rhino and the Cartel.

They were still active and playing live in 1989, selling their cassette LP *Biscuits & Broken Glass* at gigs during that year's Bradford Festival. They reformed in 2017, and played at the Cock & Bottle in Skipton on July 8.

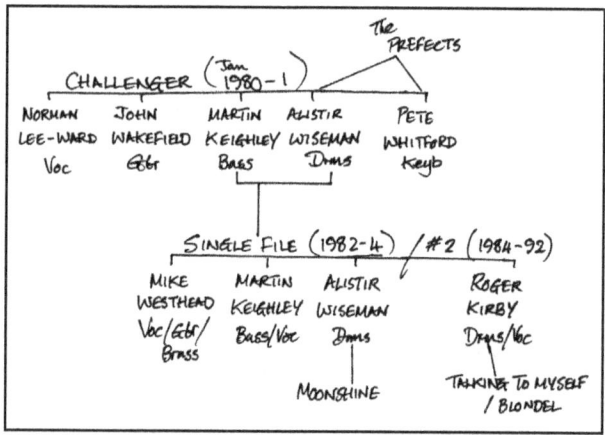

CHAPTER 5 - POST PUNK / ANARCHO PUNK / GOTH   1980 - 1983

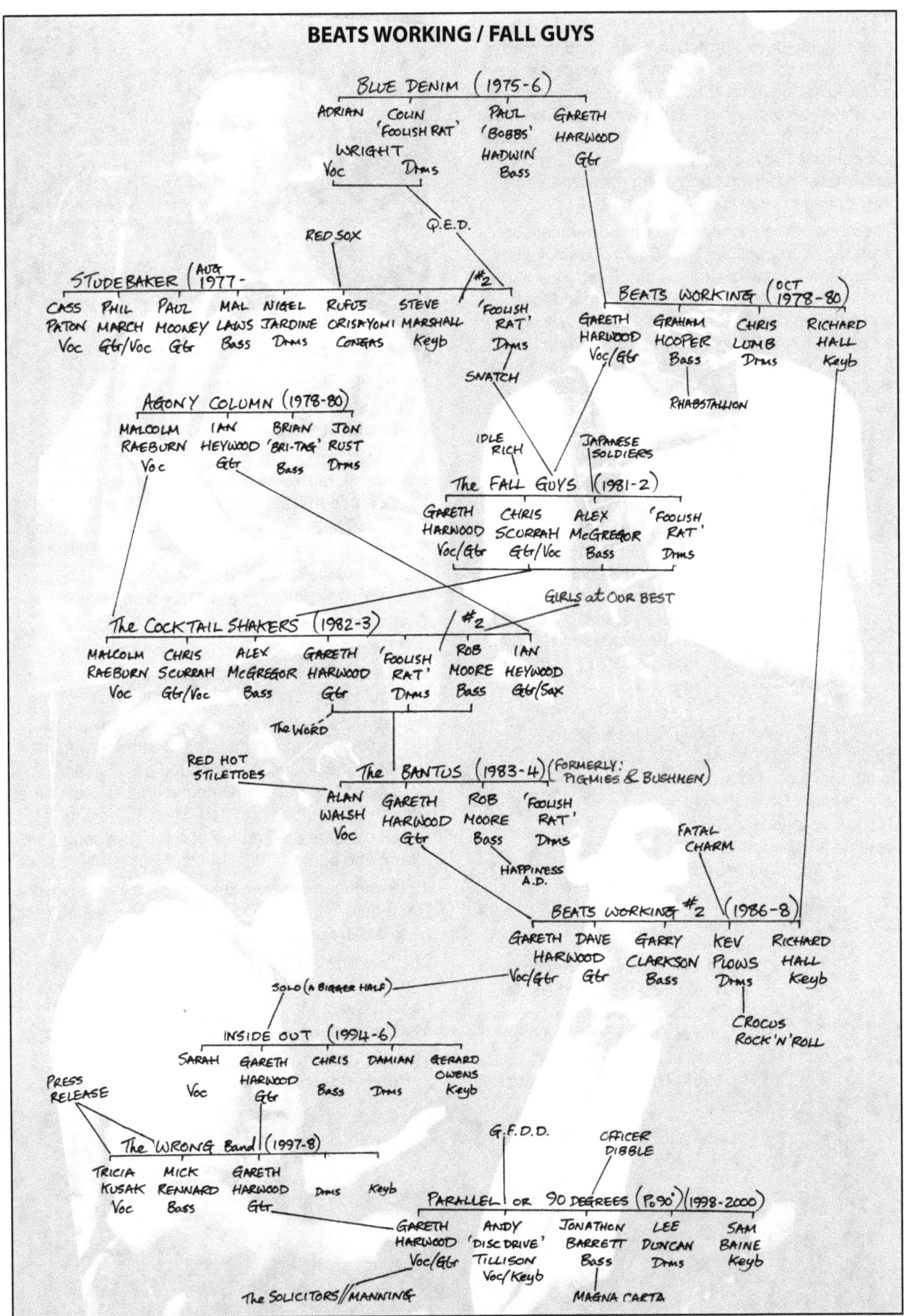

191

1919

This Shipley-based prototype Goth band formed in 1979 under the name Heaven 17. They released a flexi-disc single called *Something's Wrong* on Bubastis Records which was given away free with issue 12 of Nick Toczek's *Wool City Rocker* fanzine in February 1981. Shortly after, due to the more well-known Sheffield band using the same name, they changed from Heaven 17 to 1919.

The band made a limited 500 run of a white label pressing of *Repulsion / Tear Down These Walls*, a copy of which was sent to John Peel. Peel was impressed and arranged to meet the band for a drink in Shipley where he asked them to record a session for his show at the famous Maida Vale Studios. On the strength of that session, they were signed by the York-based label Red Rhino Records.

They released their first single, *Caged / After The Fall* (Red14), in July 1982. It was followed by an official release of their promo disc *Repulsion / Tear Down These Walls* (Red22). Both singles featured a cover with the band's logo, the only difference being the colour of the background. *Caged* was red while *Repulsion* was blue.

The only LP from their original incarnation, *Machine* (Red25), went to number seven in the Independent Chart in April 1983. A second Radio One session followed, this time for *The Kid Jensen Show*.

Having signed to London-based Abstract Records, they released their third single, *Cry Wolf*, which got to number fourteen in the indie singles chart in September 1983. Their last release was the 12-inch EP *Earthsong*, which reached number seventeen in August 1984.

After the group disbanded, Ian Tilliard, Mark Tighe and Steve Madden went on to form the band Another Cinema. They released two singles, *Hallucination Spires* and *Midnight Blue* on Red Rhino. Tilliard and Tighe went on to Zap Gun Virus in 1987.

Anagram Records released *The Complete Collection* 1919 CD compilation in 2001.

In 2005, original guitarist Mark Tighe decided to resurrect 1919 with a new line-up and recorded a new mini-album called *Dark Temple*.

By the mid-2010s, Tighe was writing with singer Rio Goldhammer and decided to put a new 1919 together. Karl Donner was added on bass and drummer Mick Reed re-joined in time to record their *Bloodline* CD album in 2016. Mark Tighe was forced to pull out after the first leg of a tour to support the album and sadly died in January 2017.

1919 continued to play to honour his memory with Reed now the only member with a connection to the band's early days.

The new lineup's 2019 album *Futricide* featured Tighe on the track *Stop The World* and *Cry Wolf*-era bassist Steve Madden on the track *Isolation*. Steve Madden passed away prior to the album's release.

The 2021 album *Citizens Of Nowhere* featured Reed and Goldhammer.

CHAPTER 5 - POST PUNK / ANARCHO PUNK / GOTH — 1980 - 1983

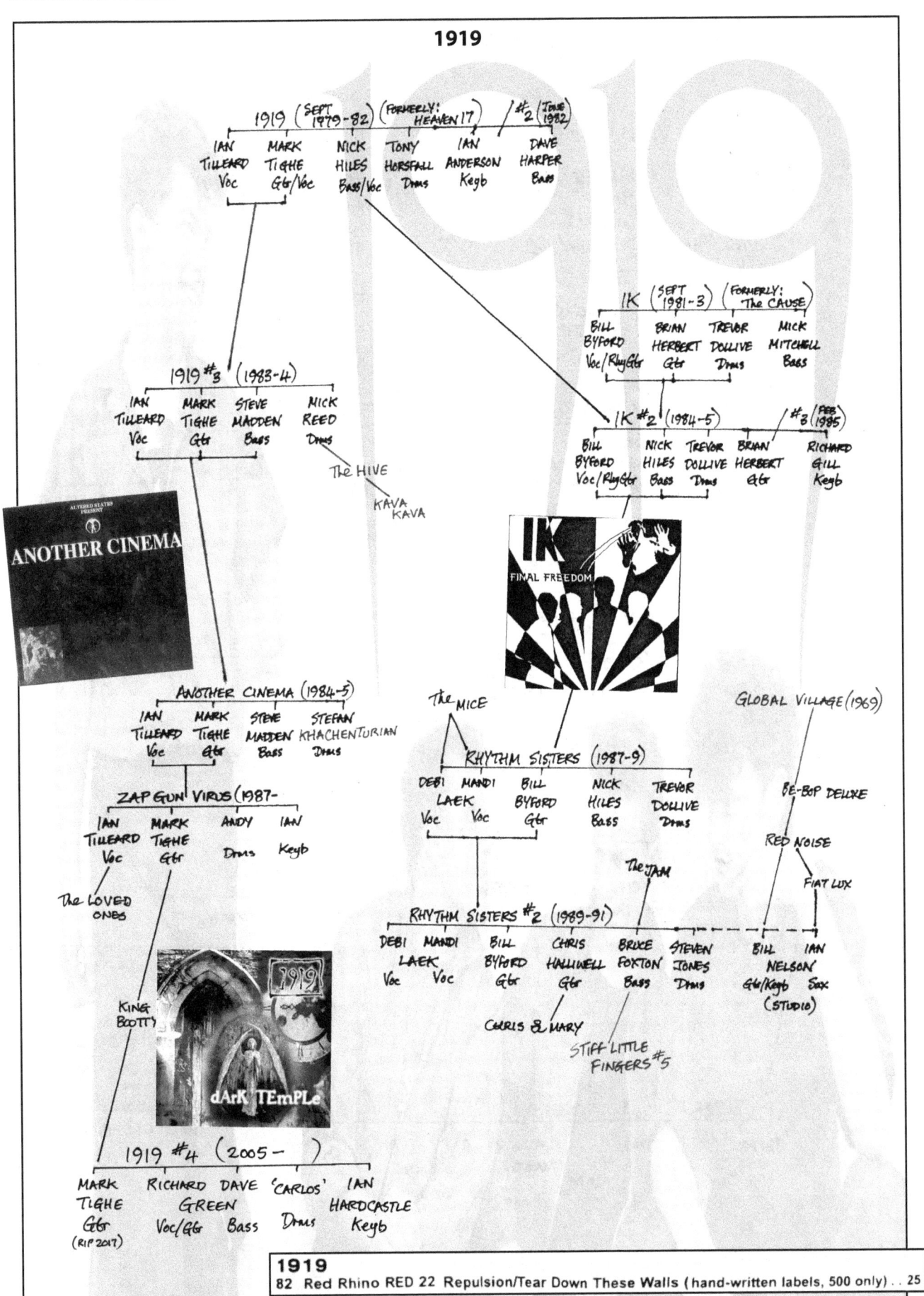

THE VINDALOOS

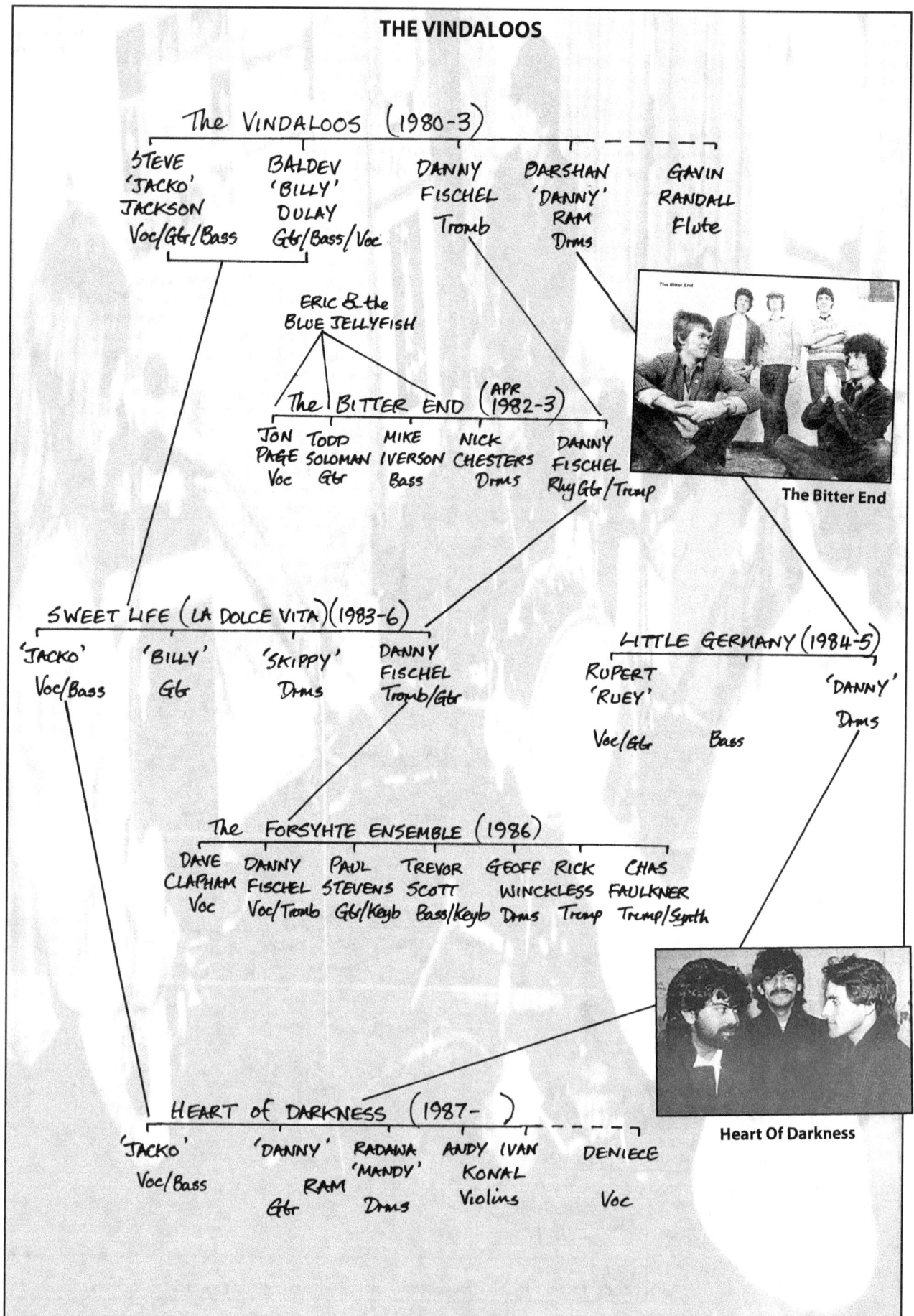

CHAPTER 5 - POST PUNK / ANARCHO PUNK / GOTH   1980 - 1983

GUIDO

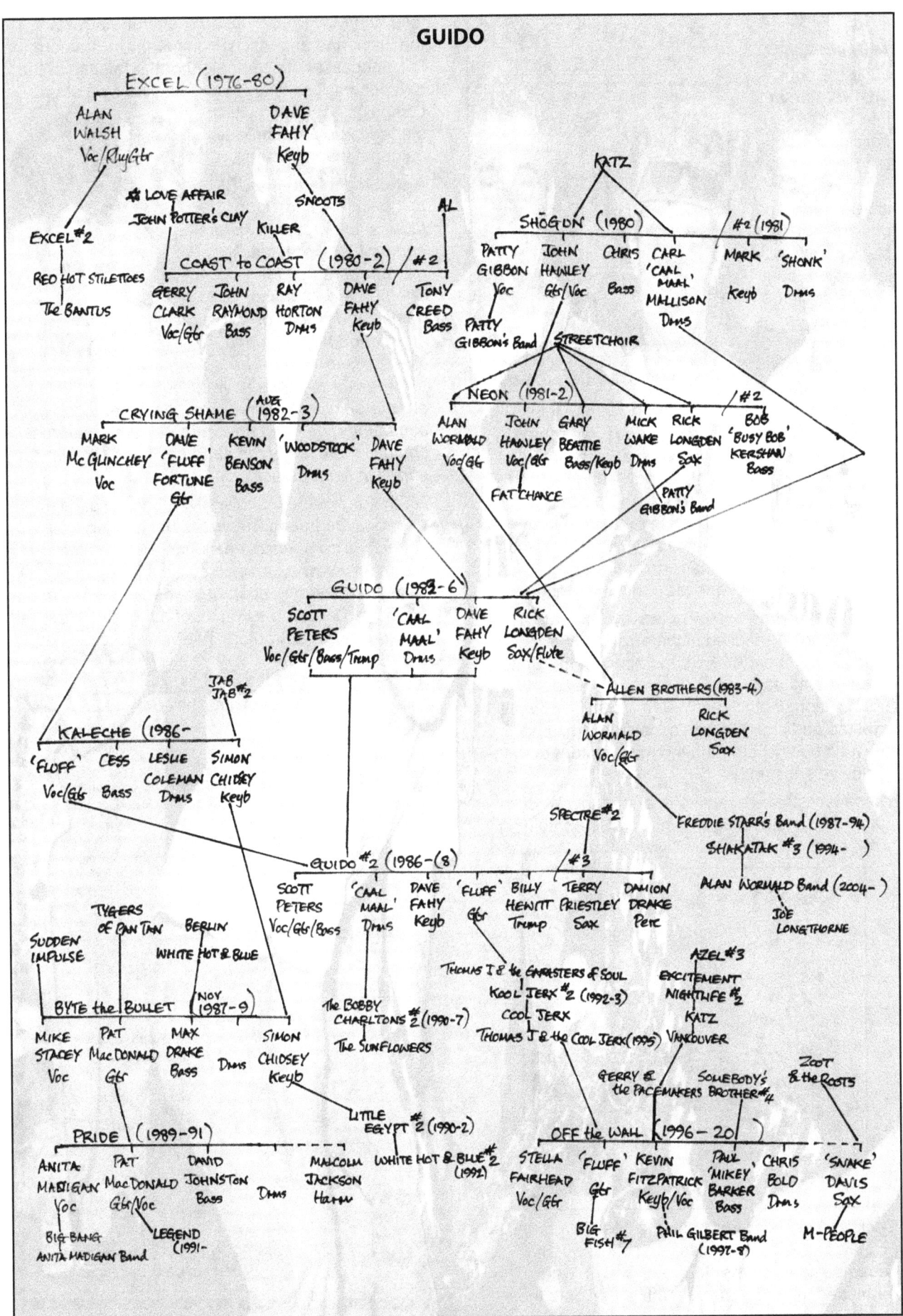

BRADFORD 12

After the April/June UK riots, the Government intensified its policies towards the black community by increasing police powers. The black community in Bradford had seen a spate of attacks by gangs of racists and were anticipating further incidents.

On the night of July 11, following the previous evening's riot in Chapeltown, Leeds, over three hundred mainly white youths rioted in Bradford's Westgate area, smashing windows and causing damage. In *T&A* reports it stated that some of the disturbances were attributable to fascists from out of town. Rumours circulated around the city and the atmosphere was full of tension at the prospect of further attacks by skinheads and NF members.

A series of dawn raids by police in Bradford on July 30 and 31 resulted in the arrest of twelve young Asian men. All were members of the United Black Youth League (UBYL) - an independent organisation of black and Asian youth. They were arrested and charged with conspiracy to cause grievous bodily harm and the manufacture of explosive substances. (7)

These arrests were related to a gardener at St Luke's Hospital finding two milk crates containing thirty-eight milk bottles filled with petrol (Molotov

Cocktails) in undergrowth on the hospital grounds on July 17. The young men, who subsequently became known as the Bradford Twelve, were remanded in police custody until a trial date the following May (1982). Directly after the arrests, the black and anti-fascist community in Bradford felt it necessary to campaign for the release of the defendants. The twelve were backed by a strong campaign of support which started locally and quickly gained national interest.

A statement from the UBYL at the time stated, *'Our fathers and mothers, sisters and brothers, are attacked and murdered on the streets. The police do nothing. Our homes and places of worship are burned to the ground. Nobody is arrested. The politicians and police have failed us. Our youth are our only protection… They have defended our community, we must now defend them. Their real crime in the eyes of the state has been their lawful efforts in fighting racism.'*

On the day of the trial over five hundred people were outside Leeds Crown Court chanting, *'self defence is no offence'* - a slogan that the black community saw as a basic political freedom. After an eight-week-long court case, on June 16, a multi-racial jury delivered a verdict of not guilty on all the charges and the Bradford Twelve were acquitted.

THE WEST INDIAN COMMUNITY IN BRADFORD

The small West Indian community in Bradford had settled in the city during the late 1950s to the early 1960s, putting down roots and integrating into the wider multi-racial community. In defence of their interests, they acquired strong links with the local anti-fascist/racist resistance during the turbulent 1970s and rallied to any suspected intimidation of their community.

This was evident on October 15, 1980, with the arrest of Gary Pemberton on charges of assaulting PC Colin McKenzie. Gary, a West Indian worker at Bradford Students' Union, was at Queen's Hall when he was confronted by PC McKenzie who said that somebody had called the police. Gary said he didn't know anything about this but went to check. The police officer had already entered the building. When confronted, Gary said he would not answer any questions before he talked to his employers. The police officer grabbed him and attempted to take him outside. A struggle ensued and six more police officers arrived, using excessive force. They transported Gary to the police station where he was charged, only to be released some hours later, late at night. A local campaign gathered pace to support Gary against this police intimidation. At his trial on November 25, 1980, he was acquitted. (8)

On August 15, 1981, a mysterious fire destroyed the top floor of Textile Hall, Westgate, where the Bradford West Indian community had been running regular Friday night events. These discos and two-tone nights had been running there since 1977. Later on, the organisers moved further down Westgate and took over the old Pentagon nightspot, renaming it Checkpoint. It was where local West Indian groups and artists like Tasmin Archer and the young ska band Spectre rehearsed.

Around this time, the National Film Institute made a film called Black Future, set in Bradford in 1984 and using local young people. It appeared on the BBC2 programme Open Door and was later shown at a 1 In 12 Club gig night in December 1981.

TRISH COOKE

Bradford born Trish, whose parents had emigrated from Dominica in the West Indies, grew up as one of ten children. She played in local ska band The Syndicate before getting a degree in performing arts and moving to London where she began working for television and contributing to BBC's children's programme *Playdays* which she presented for nine years. She also wrote material for the TV soap *Eastenders* and has won many awards for her children's books. She now again lives in her home town with her partner and their two children.

ROOTS RECORDS

This reggae/dub record outlet was based at the bottom of Lumb Lane and stocked all the latest 12" singles and LPs. It was run by local 'dread' Barry. Upstairs a small studio rehearsal space was run as Flexible Response by Phil 'Puss' Edwards which later moved to new premises in Chapel Street, Little Germany.

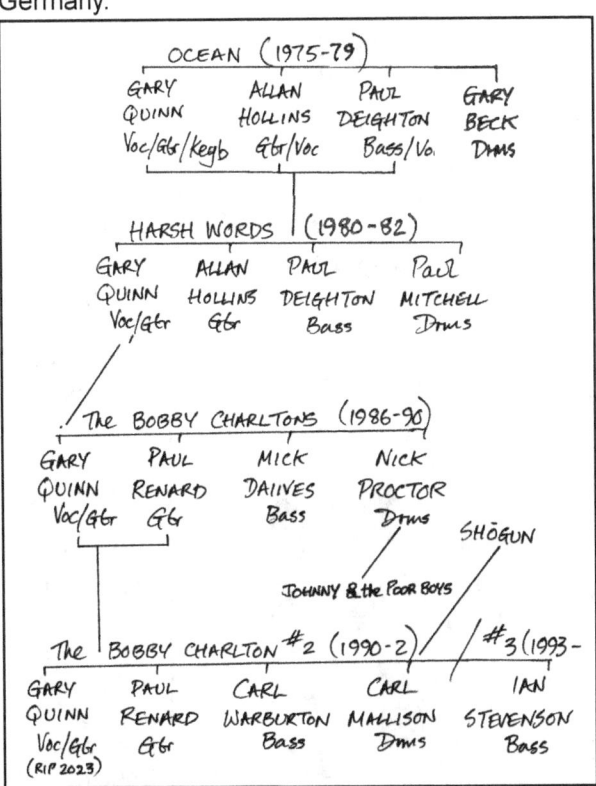

RAMON MARTINO

Bingley's JSG studio / record label's third release was a 7" four track EP, *No Problem /Maria Elena / Always/ Memories Of Andalusia / Marta,* by the quirky Spanish baritone Ramon Martino in 1981.

The EP featured a picture sleeve of Ramon on a horse next to a sign saying Spain one way and Ilkley the other. It had been printed and designed at Raiseprint in Keighley.

The EP was arranged and directed by Reg Hargreaves. Ramon had previously released the 7" single *Hotel Selomar* on the Benidorm label in Spain in 1978.

COMPLETE DISORDER

This multi-racial punk band formed in late 1981 and were regulars on the local scene for around a year, before disbanding. Its members relocating to other bands including Vermin and War Babies. Guitarist Dom Watts went on to form Anti-System.

SCREAMING PLASTIC TURTLES

Screaming Plastic Turtles were a Christian rock band, formed in Idle in 1981. They played around the local area during the early 1980s. Sax player Terry Priestley later became a member of popular local ska band Spectre.

WHEELCHAIR RHYTHM '81
A MUSIC FESTIVAL

FEATURING
NOSFERATU V   DAWNWATCHER
PATRICK MOORE & THE ALLSTARS
THE SHAKES   SURFACE TENSION
GOFF JACKSON & THE HUNS
WITH GUESTS
AGONY COLUMN
NON-STOP MUSIC FROM 2.00 — 9.00pm

SATURDAY JULY 25TH 1981
GATES OPEN 1.30 P.M.
VICTORIA PARK, KEIGHLEY
TICKETS AVAILABLE FROM: HERE
ALL PROCEEDS TO I.Y.D.P. LOCAL APPEALS — TICKETS: £3·00

On Saturday, July 25 1981, an open-air non-stop music festival was organised at Keighley's Victoria Park in aid of the International Year Of The Disabled, called *Wheelchair Rhythm '81*.

A host of local bands and artists took part in the event, aimed at showcasing musical talent from new wave to folk, all for £3 entrance fee.

The organisers expected a large crowd and hoped

Disabled festival

AGONY COLUMN, Shake Appeal, Surface Tension and **Dawnwatcher** are among the bands appearing at a benefit gig at Keighley Victoria Park on July 25 in aid of the International Year Of The Disabled.

The festival will run from 2pm to 9pm and other bands playing will include **New Model Army, The Shakes, Patrick Moore And The All-Stars, Nosferatu V, Geoff Jackson And The Huns, Liz Narey** and **Little Brother.**

Tickets are priced at £3 and are available from Music Exchange and Sundial Solarium of Keighley, Virgin in Leeds, HMV of Bradford, JSG of Bingley, Bradley's of Huddersfield and Halifax, Scene And Heard of Halifax and the White Lion Hotel in Huddersfield.

to make around £10,000 to go towards buying a caravan for the Keighley MENCAP Society. Apart from raising money, their primary object was to provide live music for the disabled and able-bodied alike.

CHAPTER 5 - POST PUNK / ANARCHO PUNK / GOTH   1980 - 1983

THE HANGED / EDIBLE MARQUETRY

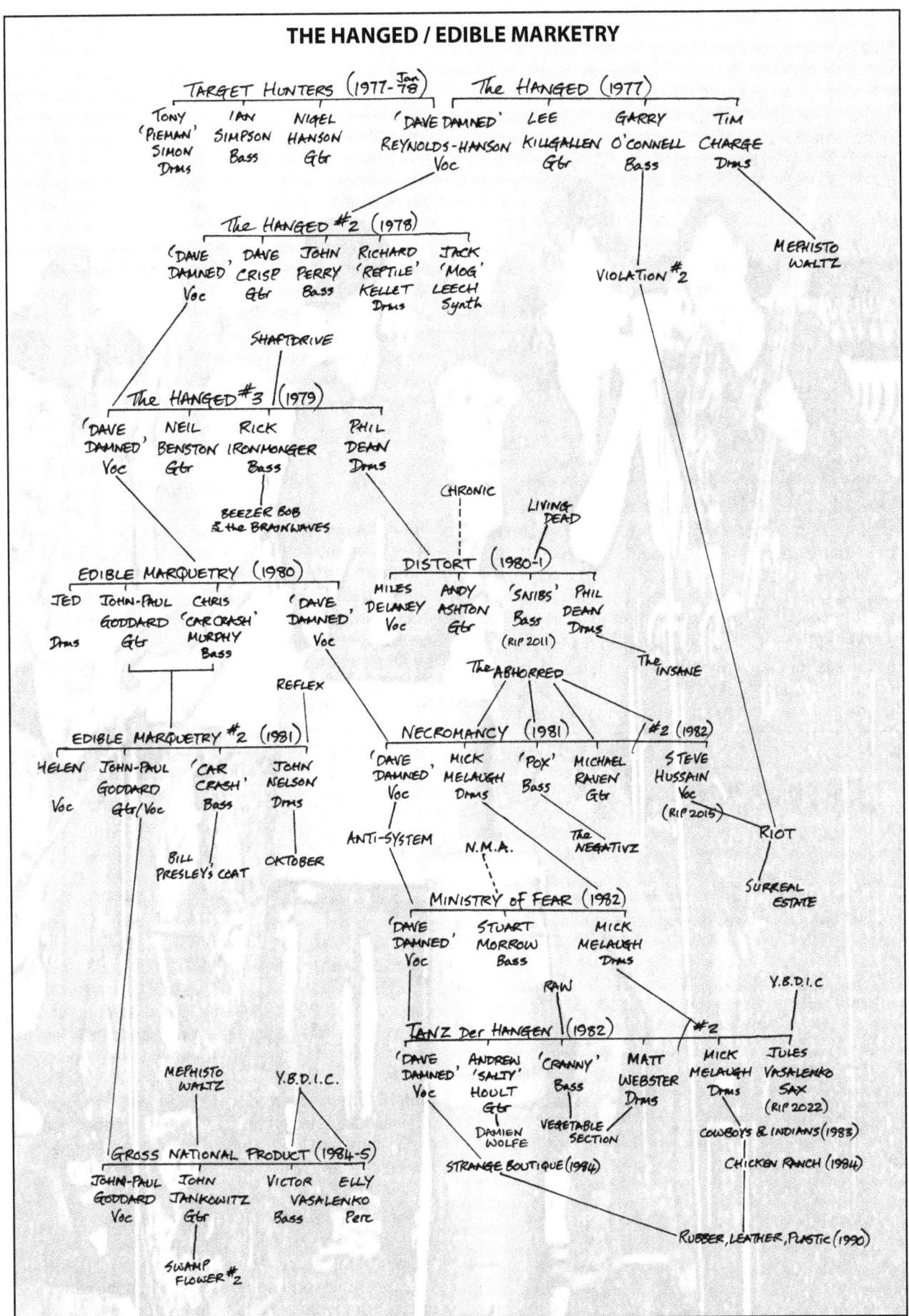

SOUTHERN DEATH CULT

This legendary Bradford band was formed by ex-Violation drummer Aky and bassist Barry Jepson, with local guitarist David 'Buzz' Burrows and vocalist Ian Astbury. Ian had settled in Bradford after being in the army for a while, then becoming a punk and a camp follower of Crass and Poison Girls.

Southern Death Cult played their debut gig to a packed room at The 1 In 12 Club on October 22, 1981.

After a few more local gigs in Bradford and Leeds, they started to gain a small following around the country. Heralded as *'the new form of positive punk'* they were labelled 'The Lost Tribe' - mainly due to Ian's interest in North American Native Indian culture and his on-stage war dancing (he had lived in Canada for five years and had visited Native Indian reservations). Their sound could be called the start of the Goth movement along with Bauhaus, Theatre Of Hate (with whom they toured), Sex Gang Children, etc.

On April 2, 1982, they headlined an anti-fascist gig with Requiem, Anthrax and The Abhorred at Eccleshill School, after which there was some trouble as skinheads tried to antagonise local punks on the way out of the venue.

They supported punk band Chelsea at the Marquee in London and received an encouraging review in *Sounds*. The music paper published a full-page article on the band in April 1982.

SDC recorded a demo at the Communications Centre (a 4-track studio charging £3.50 per hour in Chapel Street, Little Germany) which was run by Alf Bower and Moya. A session for the *John Peel Show* on Radio 1 followed on May 21.

More support for the band came from the NME's Paul Morley in October with another positive full-page article and a front cover shot of Ian. After signing to Situation 2 Records they released their first single *Fat Man / Moya* in December 1982 which shot straight to the number one spot in the Independent Chart.

This early success indicated a bright future but by early 1983 the band, who had been in existence for less than two years, started to disintegrate. They split up, with Ian Astbury taking two-thirds of the name to continue as Death Cult, then later, and more famously, The Cult.

An album, called simply *Southern Death Cult*, was released on the Beggar's Banquet label in 1983 after the band's demise. It included the demos, radio sessions (from Peel and a January 1983 Kid Jenson show), and some feedback enshrouded live tracks from a gig at Rafters in Manchester.

+ EDIBLE MARQUETRY   22nd OCT. 1981

Punters were slow to arrive although the bar downstairs was packed, but by the time the 1st band - **EDIBLE MARQUETRY** were on stage and ready to begin they were arriving in large no's eventually totalling 80 or more. Which goes as one of the best-attended nights to date. It's difficult to give an objective account of either band, as I'm no familiar with either's set (REASON: both bands 1st gigs) but I was impressed with both bands.

EDIBLE MARQUETRY played a sound set to a mildly interested audience but there was little response between songs. The rhythm section maintained a continuous (perhaps P.I.L. like) beat while jarring guitar and vocals were haphazardly thrown on top.

A satisfactory basis for **SOUTHERN DEATH CULT** - who, it has to be said, are a strikingly visual band but unfortunately they were hardly enhanced by their surroundings and the sound quality. Despite this the atmosphere was expectant, this being their debut gig. AKY's tribal drumming (?) and a grinding but often melodic bass line was interwoven with interesting one-string guitar efforts. However I couldn't help thinking that most of their power on the night came from the energetic vocals but perhaps this was because the drums weren't coming through as well as they should. They performed 5 or 6 songs competently and even inspired 4 or 5 people into dancin', myself amongst them. (THERE GOES MY STREET CREDIBILITY).

Again they did not receive the applause they deserved but the gig if nothing else will serve as a warm up for the band.

CONCLUSION: INSPIRING

A totally unbiased summary by JONT.

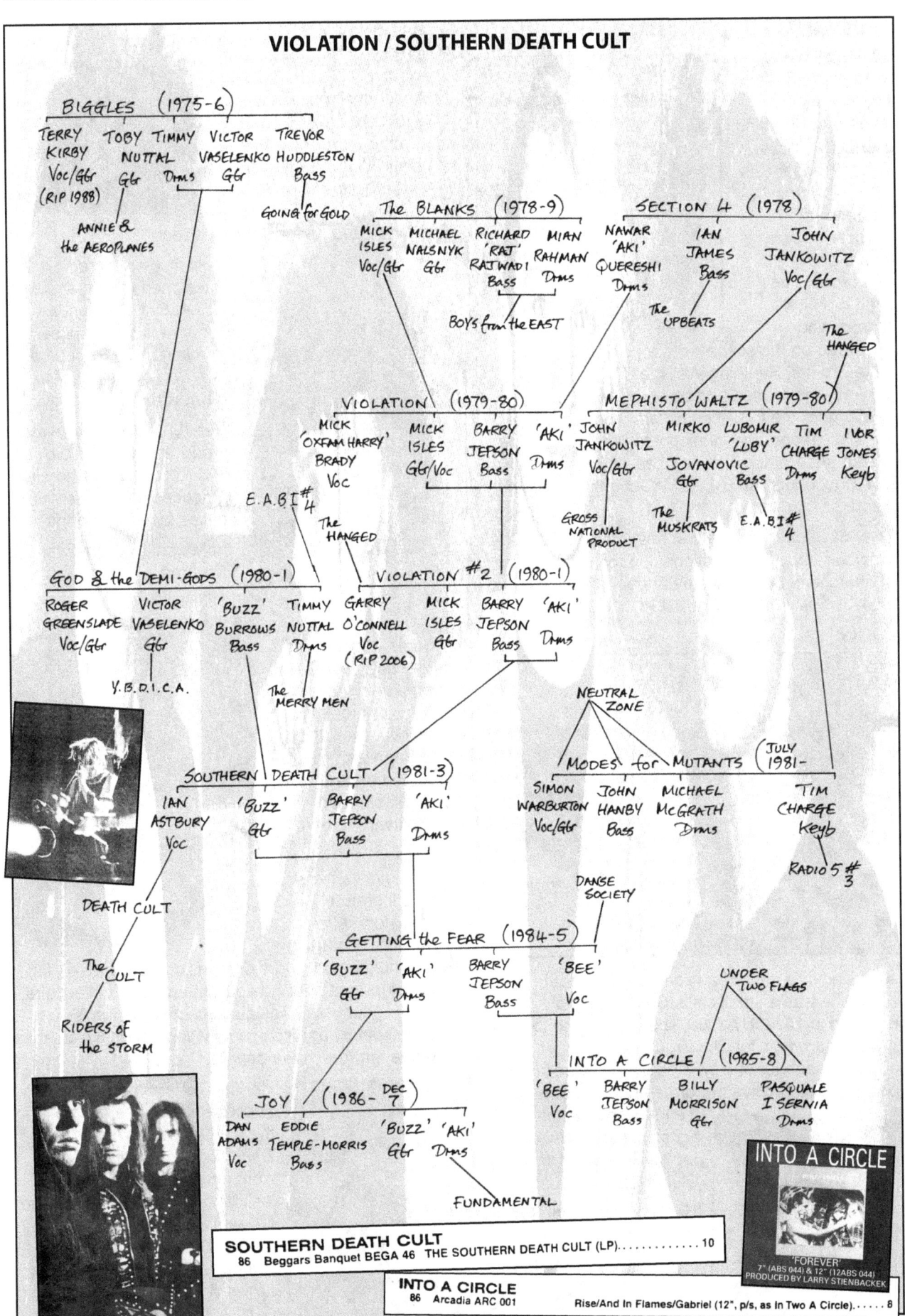

THE BRADFORD POETS / RANTERS

During the post-punk period (1980-83), Bradford became a breeding ground for a new style of modern poetry - sharp, aggressive, political, socially aware and humorous. The Bradford poets/ranters who

appeared on the scene were a collective of Joolz, Little Brother, Seething Wells and Wild Willi Beckett who formed and co-ordinated work in 1980 under the title Aries Enterprises. They took their inspiration from punk poets like John Cooper-Clarke and Patrick Fitzgerald as well as the 1960s Liverpool poets like Roger McGough and Adrian Henri.

They developed a style that both challenged previous literary conventions and the static values of Thatcher's Britain and by appearing at gigs and festivals rekindled an interest in modern poetry.

JOOLZ

Joolz Denby's family had settled in Harrogate when she was a small child. She moved to Bradford in 1974. By 1980, she had helped form *Aries Enterprises* for The Bradford Poets and was also the manager of New Model Army. She soon became a strong live performer of her poems on

the local and national gig circuit, performing regularly at The 1 In 12 Club in its early years.

Her recorded work was released by Abstract Records, with her own artwork illustrating the covers. One such release was the 12 inch EP *Denise*, produced by Jah Wobble IN 1983. A second Abstract single *The Kiss*, again produced by Jah Wobble with music by Justin Sullivan, Wobble and others. Her 1985 spoken word LP *Never Never Land* was also on Abstract.

Joolz also appeared on She signed to EMI and was backed by New Model Army for her next three singles, *Love Is (Sweet Romance), Mad, Bad And Dangerous To Know* and *Protection*.

Her 1987 album *Hex* was produced by Justin Sullivan and Rob Heaton who also produced the album with mixes by Glynn Johns.

In March 1983 she was featured on the cover of *Time Out* magazine.

Joolz was dubbed *'the queen of British spoken word'* as her work took her all over the UK and Europe with regular appearances at Glastonbury Festival's cabaret tent.

Her involvement with literature and story-telling included lecturing and holding seminars on performance and reader development. She has published many collections of her poetry and has also accepted commissions to write special poems such as *Northlands* which she wrote for Yorkshire Forward.

Her first novel *Stone Baby* was published in 2000 and won the Crime Writer's Association *Debut Dagger Award*. She went on to write more novels, including *Corazon* (2001), *Billie Morgan* (2004), *Borrowed Light* (2006), *A True Account of the Curious Mystery of Miss Lydia Larkin & The Widow Marvell* (2011) and *Wild Thing* (2012).

CHAPTER 5 - POST PUNK / ANARCHO PUNK / GOTH   1980 - 1983

LITTLE BROTHER

Bradford lad Dave Stockell originally worked on the buses for two years as a conductor before developing chronic varicose veins and having to leave. His experience on the buses may have helped his comedic poetry as his bitterly observed poems were poignant on the harshness of everyday life. Dave's strength as a poet/ranter was his humour and delivery which could be said to be akin to the great tradition of the Northern club comedian.

He gigged regularly up and down the country, from supporting The Clash and The Gang Of Four to appearing at the Hyde Park CND Rally in front of 250,000 people. On August 28, 1982, the *NME* gave him a two-page interview and article, and he later appeared on TV's *Oxford Roadshow*. Dave performed his brand of poetic humour and MC'd many local events.

The split 7-inch EP Seething Wells / Little Brother – *The Rising Sons Of Rising Verse* was released by Radical Wallpaper Records in 1982. It contained six poems by Little Brother.

His 1986 EP *No Relation* was released on Rouska Records. On this 7-inch he was backed by members of local blues rock band Somebody's Brother who were, you've guessed it, no relation to Dave! The same musicians backed him on his 1988 LP *Champion The Underdog*, also on Rouska.

Little Brother also appeared on numerous compliations over the years

For many years he presented his own *University Of The Open Mind* show on local radio station Bradford Community Broadcasting (BCB).

SEETHING WELLS

Having settled in Bradford in 1968, Swindon-born Steven 'Swells' Wells worked on the buses at the same time as Little Brother. In 1976 they had both been in a band called The Luddites but never did a gig.

He delivered his hard-hitting acerbic wit through his poems, reviews and articles for the public and music press alike. You will find many of his reviews scattered throughout this book. He did his first gig as the ferocious snarling ranter 'Seething Wells' in 1979. As a political animal, he advocated the party line of the Socialist Workers Party (SWP) and occasionally clashed with other left-wing groups such as The 1 In 12 Club over organisational and ideological policies even though he played there many times.

In 1981 he produced and edited *Molotov Comics*, a poetry zine which included reviews, cartoons and graphics, and featured poems by him and fellow Aries Enterprises poets.

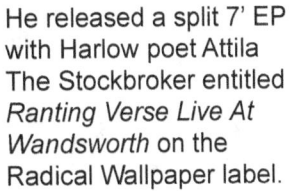

He released a split 7' EP with Harlow poet Attila The Stockbroker entitled *Ranting Verse Live At Wandsworth* on the Radical Wallpaper label.

In 1982 he put out a split EP with Little Brother. *The Rising Sons Of Ranting Verse* also became the title of a book he wrote with Atilla The Stockbroker, published by Unwin Press in 1985.

In the mid-1980s he became an *NME* reviewer, originally under the alias Susan Williams, which led to regular employment at the *NME* as a staff writer.

In the 1990s he appeared on TV as a cultural commentator of the punk era. He founded Attack! Books in the late 1990s when

> We can't remix the highlights of Rock Against Racism every time we mention the National Front. Instead you should refer to last spring's Ten Thousand Light Years Since Punk issues in which Steven Wells reflected on how he single-handedly took the fascist pigs to the cleaners in the toilets of the Bradford One In Twelve Club. – LB

based in London, publishing his first novel *Tits Out Teenage Terror Totty*.

Swells later settled in the USA where he tragically died at his home in Philadelphia on June 23, 2009.

WILD WILLI BECKETT

Wild Willi Beckett (Bennett) was born on October 26, 1947, in Middlesbrough, Teesside. He arrived in Bradford in the late 1970s to do a degree in Russian and French at Bradford University. While teaching French in Bradford schools, in 1980, he became part of the *Aries Enterprises Poet Group* with Joolz, Swells, Little Brother and others. He toure the UK with his own unique brand of poetry, usually dressed either as a nun on roller skates (wielding a blood-stained axe) or as his alter ego The Doctor.

From the mid to late-1980s Willi and Nick Toczek ran *Stereo Graffiti*, an alternative cabaeret which featured up-and-coming comedians like Steve Coogan, Joe Brand and Henry Normal. The pair also founded the Bradford Writers' Group in 1987.

As a long-time member of the late Screaming Lord Sutch's Monster Raving Loony Party, Willi entered two local elections as a candidate for MP. He stood for the Bradford North constituency in 1990 after his *Don't Be Silli Vote For Willi* campaign and received 210 votes. He stood again in 1992, increasing his vote count to 350.

Willi was also heavily involved with the Bradford Soup Run, going out in all types of weather to feed the city's homeless, as well as supporting other charity events. In 1986, his band the Psycho Surgeons (with Boys From The East, The Word, Spectre and The Best Way To Walk) did an open-air charity gig at the university's amphitheatre for a Unicef campaign to fight killer diseases in children in the Third World. Proceeds from his final Psycho Surgeons concert, *One Last One* in 2006, were donated to Water Aid.

NICK TOCZEK

After the demise of the band Ulterior Motives, Nick continued to perform as a poet on the local and national scenes. He has gone on to publish many pamphlets of his poetry as well as numerous children's books. Nick's poem *Responsibilities* was used in an award-winning TV advert for the Provincial Building Society, was voiced by *Boys From The Blackstuff* actor Bernard Hill.

In 1998 Nick's *Dragon* poems were set to music by composer Malcolm Singer were performed as The Dragons Cantata at London's Royal Albert Hall with a full symphony orchestra and an eight-hundred-strong combined schools choir. Their football cantata Perfect Pitch was premiered at the London Barbican in January 2004. A play script by Nick set around songs from the cantata called Dragons! The Musical was published in December 2005. A new version of the Dragons musical was premiered in Watford in March, 2025.

Coming full circle, Nick co-wrote a biography of fellow ranter Seething Wells in 2025.

DIRK SPIG

Mike Hughes was an ex-hospital porter who took to ranting poetry in the mid-'80s under his alias Dirk Spig. He also played keyboards for the band The Nerve Agents.

Spig was one of the comperes (with Wild WIlli Beckett and Seething

Wells) at the 1 In 12 *Not The International Garden Festival* outdoor all-dayer in 1984.

Mike went on to be a successful executive in a Leeds-based NHS Trust.

GINGER JOHN THE DOOMSDAY COMMANDO

L to r: Ginger John, two band members, Seething Wells, Nick Toczek, Gaynor Toczek

John Lunn was another Bradford based ranter who gigged regularly up and down the country. He did early eighties *The Intolerance Tour* with Swells and Toczek.

He was also DJ and right-hand-man at many Toczek promoted gigs in Leeds and Bradford.

Ginger John appeared at many benefit gigs also played The 1 In 12 Club at Tickles with Burial and The Nerve Agents on June 13, 1984.

As well as having poems published in many fanzines John also produced a number of poetry pamphlets like his hand drawn *Ranting On The Barricades* which sold for 40p.

In 2023, he announced his last ever tour.

All through the 1980s, a range of other poets/ranters continued to emerge and perform on the Bradford gig scene, such as Andy (Dave The Dog) Yeadon, Michael Parkinson, Andy Darlington, Graham McAndrew, the Asian ranter Hikmet Shah aka Dark Phoenix and the skinhead poet Rudi Cousins.

ROCK AGAINST RACISM 1982

Many local bands organised gigs around the *Rock Against Racism* banner, like the one at Eccleshill School in April 1982.

The gig was headlined by Southern Death Cult, riding high after their recent John Peel session and just prior to their Indie Chart number one hit *Fat Man / Moya*. Requiem, Anthrax and The Abhorred.

Apart from Requiem, every band had Bradford-Asian members. After the gig, a group of far-right skinheads harassed young punks leaving the venue.

THE WORST OF THE 1 IN 12 CLUB

At the beginning of 1982, the national unemployed figures for the UK reached the three million mark as the country shifted deeper into economic recession.

Yet the 1 In 12 Club was going from strength to strength. So much so that it caught up with the C60 tape revolution of the time by releasing two cassette compilation tapes, *The Worst Of The 1 In 12 Club Volumes 1 and 2*. These cassettes featured many bands/artists who performed at the Club during the first year or so.

Volume 1, which had been compiled and edited at Fairview Studios in Hull, quickly sold out mainly at gig nights. As did *Volume 2*, when it came out in early 1982. The master tapes were edited together by Martin 'Protag' Neish at Street Level Recordings at Ladbroke Grove, London. The studio was unique, as it was in the back of a converted transit van with a power line coming from a nearby squat - truly street level. Both tapes were copied in London at Fuck Off Tapes, who, in their distribution lists, gave them both this encouraging review; *'Some really good performances only strengthening the view that so much talent is localised and unexploited.'*

Along with the Apathy tape, these were vital early records of the Bradford scene at the beginning of the 1980s.

Volume 1 included a version of the original New Model Army live favourite *The Cause* alongside a live version of Southern Death Cult's first single, *Fat Man*. The other acts on the tape were False Claims, Cameras In Cars, Reflex, Requiem, Joolz, Ski-Bop Di Bop, Living Dead, Chronic, Modern Scene, Surfin' Dave, Helter Skelter, Dial, Fall Guys, Wild Willi Beckett, Volunteers, Shake Appeal, and Patrick Moore.

Volume 2 featured Boys From The East, The Abhorred, Terrorist Guitars, Little Brother, Radio 5, The Three Johns, Anthrax, Complete Disorder, Apocalipse Choir, Dry Ice, Wardance, Seething Wells, Edible Marquetry, Vindaloos, Nick Toczek, Ichor and Backslider.

For armchair rock devotees

FOR just £2, armchair rock fans in Bradford can find out what they've been missing for the last ten months.

The 1 in 12 Club has issued a cassette compilation of work from 19 bands and artists who have performed at that hallowed local venue since it opened last April.

The cassette entitled The Worst of the 1 in 12 Club, contains a varied mixture of material, both live and recorded, from such bands as Southern Death Cult, Shake Appeal, New Model Army, Helter Skelter, Reflex, False Claims, Living Dead and Cameras In Cars.

Some of these bands have since split up so the cassette is also a tangible piece of rock history.

Other artists featured include local poets Joolz and Wild Willie Beckett (plus backing band).

Reproduction quality is good, and at just £2, The Worst of the 1 in 12 Club is excellent value.

It can be obtained from HMV, Roots Records, Fourth Idea, Something Else and the club itself. But be warned, stocks are limited. Miss it to your cost.

City Sounds on tape

WORST OF THE 1 in 12 CLUB — Volume 2.

ALL the best of Bradford's music contributors have gone on tape to pay homage to the 1 in 12 Club.

From the soothing strains of Boys From The East the tape pounds into The Abhorred — remember these blistering punks before their demise recently?

Nearest band to match them for two-chord chaos comes from Kenny's Complete Disorder, whose track Violent Age would have a BBC bleep-man working overtime.

More tracks from 3 Johns, Apocalypse Choir, Vindaloos and the fine Tetley Bittermen poem from Seething Wells. Listen out too for the splendid finale from Backslider.

Well worth forking out a couples of notes.

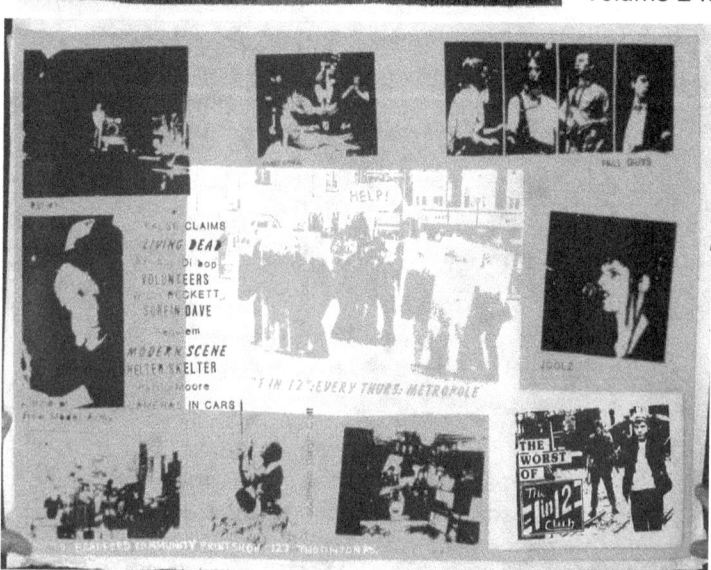

THE CATHEDRAL CENTRE

The former Cathedral School, which had been empty for some time, opened as a training centre in 1982 and offered YOP (Youth Opportunities Programme) courses in office skills, woodwork, screen printing and community projects. There was also a 'Radio Team', an audio production course that produced the *Bradford Cassette For The Blind*; a talking magazine for the blind and partially sighted. Trainees wrote news items, read poetry, and described and recorded visits to museums. They recorded and edited the material to fit on a C60 cassette, which was then distributed via post.

For the creatively inclined, the primitive recording facilities on cast-off BBC equipment offered the intoxicating promise of a recording studio. The 'Printing Team' taught trainees to screenprint posters for school fairs and charity auctions. This gave eager young musicians the chance to produce posters, T-shirts and leaflets to promote their own gigs and bands, aided and abetted by tutor Andy Drake.

The Cathedral Centre, and those two courses in particular, proved to be a magnet for young, unemployed punks, ska boys and rockers who saw the place as an opportunity to meet up to talk music all day and receive a weekly government payment of twenty five quid.

Virtually every punk band of the time, including The Convulsions, Raw, Anti System, Negativz, Morbid Humour, Isolation, and Vegetable Section had one or more members on the various courses. This led to several gigs in the half-built canteen area.

The first was on July 22, with Autumn Gold, a local Christian rock band, and The Desire Crew, who were a primitive Joy Division-influenced post-punk band which included the core of the future Vegetable Section and members of fledgling hardcore punk outfits Raw and The Convulsions.

Autumn Gold at the time rehearsed in Centre's studio and, when politely asked to move out due to its refurbishment, trashed and spray painted the room when they left, leaving the mainly young punk rocker trainees to clean up the mess! One - nil to the heathens.

The second gig was the infamous Christmas gig by Raw, Anti System and Isolation (with appearances by The Hassled and Social Spastix) on December 22, 1982. Cathedral Centre Director Anne Sheikh brought the night to a premature end by wading onto the stage and turning off the power halfway through Raw's chaotic set after songs like *Rock Against Rehearsal* and *Shit* and singer Liam Sheeran's raucous shouted song introductions, including, 'F**k the Queen with an Exocet Missile!'

It was almost a year before bands played again when Vegetable Section, The Convulsions and ska band Spectre packed out another part of the building on November 18, 1983. This proved to be the last gig there. The building was developed into a more regimented training area and most of the more free-thinking staff moved on. It now seems a very unlikely setting for such anarchic proceedings to have taken place.

ROGER HIGGINS

Another highlight in the early days of the Cathedral Centre was the music workshop that ran on Friday afternoons from 1982 to 1986 and gave young musicians the chance to pick up and play decent instruments.

The workshop was run by nationally renowned bottleneck blues guitarist Roger Higgins, at the time a member of local bands The Sheds and Doctor Socket, who later formed his own three-piece blues outfits The Bottleneck Boogie Band (1990-1994) and The Roger Higgins Band (1995-2005) and performed as a solo artist, later often backed by bass guitarist Tony Evans. Roger, originally from Manchester, stayed in Bradford after finishing his degree and became a resident of Great Horton. He played hundreds of gigs around the north of England and was a regular at many blues festivals up and down the country, including the Burnley Blues Festival and the Colne Blues Festival.

GEORGE BLAKE

An interesting revelation came to light around this time, concerning the father of local drummer Sean Randal (of 20th Century Hats). During the 1960s, Mike Randal (who later became a lecturer at Bradford University) and his wife Anne had been 'peaceniks' (active supporters of CND) and, along with another activist Pat Pootle, were responsible for helping in the dramatic escape of spy George Blake to Moscow via Berlin. The escape from Wormwood Scrubs Prison on the night of October 22, 1966, had been orchestrated by fellow ex-cellmate, Irishman Sean Bourke.

The Randals' part was to transport Blake, hidden inside a concealed compartment in a BMW camper van to East Berlin via a ferry from Dover.

George Blake had been imprisoned in 1961, sentenced to forty-two years (at the time the longest ever sentence under English law) when caught spying for the KGB (Soviet Russia's secret service) while working as a Foreign Office aide in Berlin. (9)

WOW IT'S NOW

During 1982 Jack 'Artmovement' Hardy's *Wow It's Now* promotions started to promote gigs at the Palm Cove Club. These included The Fall on March 19, The Passage on March 28, and later, Discharge/ Anti-Sect and Twisted Nerve. Lots of local bands also played as support or main acts on Jack's nights. In fact, on the none-too-rare occasions when the main band failed to turn up, the audience was treated to a replacement local act which was usually either pub rock oi punks Rip Snort or Kenny Thomas's hardcore punk outfit Complete Disorder, and sometimes both!

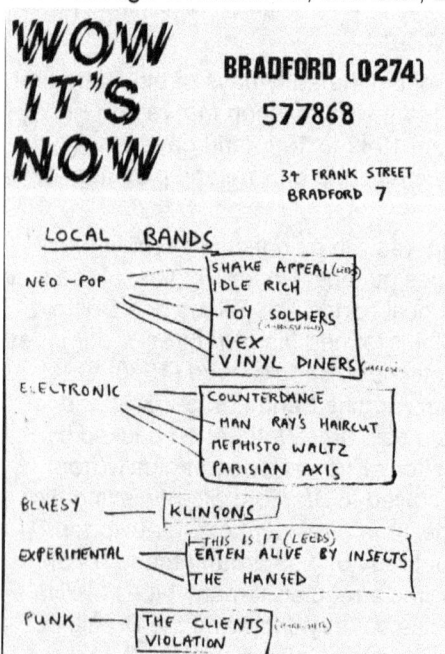

RIP SNORT (1981-3) / #2			
MARTIN ELLIS Voc/Gtr	RICHARD RHODES Bass	'MIRKO' Drms	PAUL PURCELL Bass

CANNIBAL FEAST

The local band Cannibal Feast only played around ten gigs, their first at the YMCA, Idle, and their second at Eccleshill School. Later, through Nick Toczek's gig nights at various venues, they supported such bands as The Vibrators and Sex Gang Children.

CANNIBAL FEAST (1982-3)			
BRENDAN 'MEL' MELON Voc	'BAZ' Gtr	GREG BURKE Bass	JIMMY 'RENT-A-RUCK' Drms

On April 2, 1982, the Falklands (Malvinas) War started. It ended on July 14, when the islands were retaken and the Argentinean soldiers surrendered.

SOMETHING ELSE

On April 23, BBC2 broadcast a Community Arts programme called *Something Else* which focused on music in Bradford, especially The 1 In 12 Club and local bands Southern Death Cult, Boys From The East and The Vindaloos. A minibus for some of the people involved went down to the filming of the programme at the BBC Wood Lane Studios. The programme when aired also featured Fun Boy Three as the studio band.

CHAPTER 5 - POST PUNK / ANARCHO PUNK / GOTH   1980 - 1983

THE BEGINNING OF FLEXIBLE RESPONSE

This multi-racial co-operative was headed by Phillip Edwards with support from Aky of Southern Death Cult. In 1982 they set up a recording studio with rehearsal rooms at Chapel Street in the Little Germany district with a grant from the council's Economic Development Department. Their aim as told to the *T&A* by Phillip was to *'...create channels to get material by local bands recorded and published. It is important that this service is available for black bands as there are many young bands but very few are black.'*

THE 1 IN 12 FIRST ANNIVERSARY

On April 29, 1982, the 1 In 12 had its first anniversary gig at the Metropole, featuring The Three Johns, Surfin' Dave and Little Brother.

Two weeks later, on May 13, the Club played host to the three-piece Belfast band Victim (then based in Manchester), whose lineup included drummer Mike Joyce, later of The Smiths. That gig unfortunately would

— Year of progress —

BRADFORD'S 1 in 12 Club celebrates a year of progress this week. The club was established at the Metropole, Sunbridge Road, by a small group of unemployed people keen to provide a cheap venue for live music.

As well as staging regular gigs during its first year of operation, the 1 in 12 has produced three fanzines and an excellent compilation cassette featuring local bands. It has also obtained its own 100 watt P.A., lights and a twin turntable disco unit.

It is run as a co-operative which is hoping to be able to obtain more equipment during the coming months for the benefit of the musicians who appear at the club.

"More people are getting involved in the running of the club and hopefully the idea of self-management will spread," said Tony Grogan, a member of the co-operative.

VICTIM (above), a three-piece Belfast band now based in Manchester, are currently planning gigs for next month and a new single to be released on their own Final Fling label. In the meantime they will be on show at Liverpool Pyramid Club May 11, Bradford One in Twelve Club 13, Coventry General Wolfe 15, Bolton Gaiety Club 18, Guildford Wooden Bridge 20, Manchester Portland Bars 27. Rudi will also be appearing at the Liverpool and Coventry gigs.

be the last 1 In 12 gig at the Metropole at that time because a certain bunch of drunken punks stole bottles of beer from the upstairs bar, forcing landlord Stan to stop allowing the Club to use the venue. The Club then began its search for another suitable venue for its base. venue for its base.

...goodbye

BRADFORD'S 1-in-12 Club is no more! Promoter Gary Cavanagh was forced to wind down the club this week, which operated from the Metropole Hotel, Sunbridge Road.

Full details are not yet known about the closure, but it is thought to be prompted by recent disturbances within the club.

A cartoon from the Claimants Union magazine Free News by Tony Grogan

FANZINES

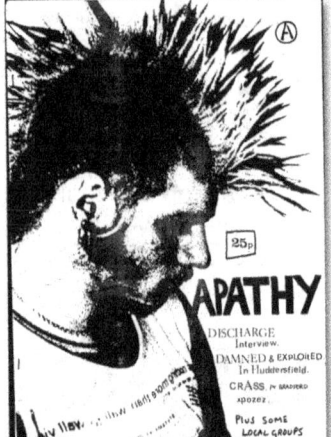

Since punk rock began, fanzines had become the intellectual consciousness of the DIY culture.

Bradford's first fanzine was **Wool City Rocker**, started in late 1979 by Nick Toczek, initially with Kay Russell.

It was mainly hand written with occasional typed pieces and covered profiles of local bands, gig reviews, new releases, interviews, cartoons, crosswords and classified ads. Bands featured in early issues included Violation, The Negatives, Shaftdrive, Shadowfax, Hustler Street Band, Dawnwatcher, Vex and Eaten Alive By Insects.

A lot of the writing in the monthly mag was done by Nick although many others submitted reviews, cartoons, photos and features. Early issues featured hand drawn covers and cartoons by Stan Engel and other contributors included Ken Turner, Keith E Rice, Brian Rushgrove, Kev Hopgood (cartoons) Mo Maklouf (covers), Mick Mitchell, John Tempest and others.

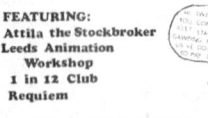

Issue 12 in February 1981 featured a free flexi disc by Shipley band Heaven Seventeen (soon to be known as 1919). Another flexi disc, this time featuring new bands from Hull, was given away with No 14, which proved to be the final issue.

CHAPTER 5 - POST PUNK / ANARCHO PUNK / GOTH   1980 - 1983

 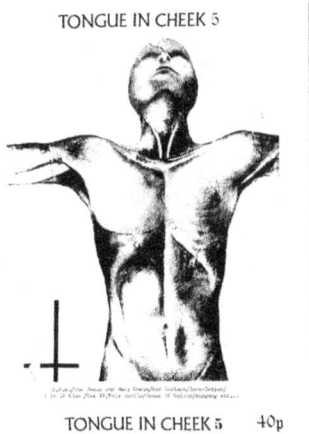 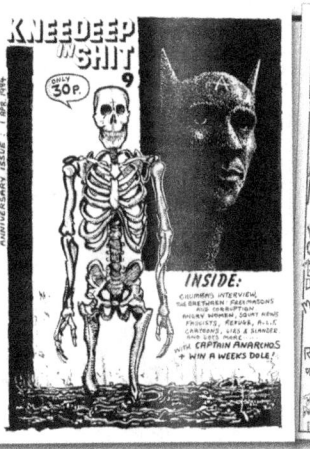 

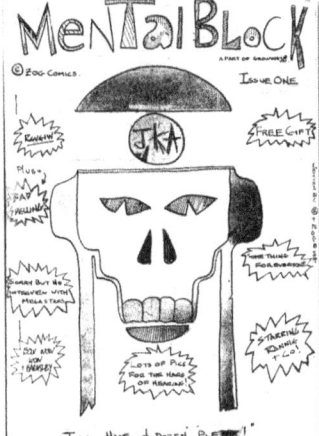

The early eighties saw a flurry of other DIY fanzines emerging, such as **Apathy**, by the Chronic / Living Dead punk crowd, and **Shiny Callipers** which was produced by Hitch of the band Requiem.

Molotov Comics was home of the city's ranters and poets and Aries Ents crowd, including Seething Wells, Wild Willi Beckett, Joolz, Gaius and Little Brother.

The 1 In 12 Club also soon had its own 'zine called **Knee Deep In Shit (KDIS)** featuring reviews, cartoons, poems and various articles and montages. **KDIS** as 'the voice of the 1 In 12' continued to be issued sporadically throughout the 1980s, sold mainly at gig nights, and gained a long list of contributors over the years. Other important 1980s local 'zines included **Subvert**, edited by Richard Jevons and Andy Plews from Keighley, Ruth Johnson's **Noise In The Valleys** from Burley-in-Wharfedale, future Sounds reviewer Ian Cheek's **Tongue In Cheek** from Ilkley and from Leeds **Roar**, **Rouska** and James Brown's **Attack On Bzag**.

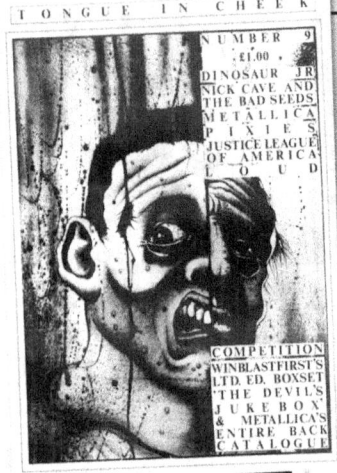   

Fanzines were cheaply printed from metal or even paper plates on traditional offset litho printing machines. They were hand written or typed on a typewriter and literally cut and pasted, usually using poisonous aerosol glue such as Spraymount or Photomount.

They used a lot of hand drawn images and meticulously resized and dot screened photos which involved extensive use of dark rooms, massive repro cameras, and more hazardous chemicals.
Produced before the days of cheap photocopying, and well before the era of desktop publishing and computer scanners and printers, these hand made music mags were real labours of love.

They all contributed highly individualised writing styles to the DIY format of fanzines, and would inspire future 'zines in the 1990s and more recent, slicker examples such as Bradford fanzine **'mono'** which featured pieces from original 'ziner **Wool City Rocker**'s Nick Toczek.

CHAPTER 5 - POST PUNK / ANARCHO PUNK / GOTH   1980 - 1983

GORY DETAILS

On Monday nights in early March 1982, promoter Nick Toczek began promoting punk gigs at The Funhouse in Keighley, naming the nights *Gory Details*. The gigs featured national bands with support from local bands and a door charge of around £1.50. The local support band policy was, as Nick said, *'to showcase rising local bands while they are still raw, exciting and energetic and before they quit the club circuit in favour of college and city hall gigs.'*

By early 1983, under his new promotional company title *Twisted Pleasures & Drastic Measures*, he was running five separate club nights. Two were in Leeds at Brannigan's. Monday nights went under the banner of 1984 and were post-punk and indie orientated whilst Wednesday's *Natural Disasters* featured bands from the punk scene. In Bradford *Fatal Shocks* at the Manhattan Club on Mondays and *Contrast* at Fagin's, John Street, also on Wednesdays, featured a lot of up-and-coming acts. Thursday's *Gory Details* at The Palm Cove featured more established punk acts like Chelsea, Conflict, Subhumans and UK Subs, often with local support bands.

Natural Disasters moved to the larger venue Leeds Bier Keller in late 1983 and continued to put on punk bands. Two memorable festive gigs were *The Negativz Xmas Party* on December 21, which featured Bradford's The Negativz, The Toy Dolls, Icon AD, Xpozez, The Instigators and Criminal Justice, and *The Underdogs New Years Bash* a week later with The Underdogs, Major Accident, The Fits, Uproar, The Convulsions and Civilised Society.

In 1984 he started *The Assassination Club* at Leeds Bier Keller, which was an alternative social political cabaret of bands and poets. He also organised all-day punk festivals at this time.

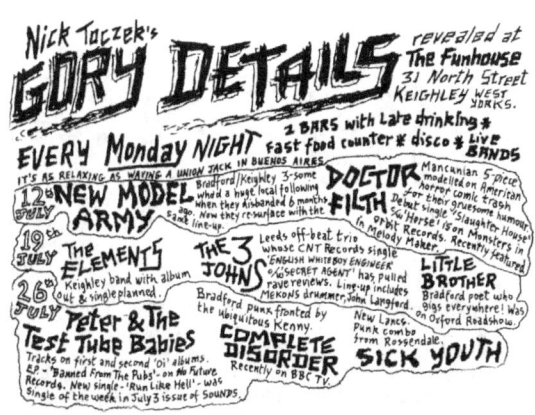

BRADFORD CENTRE AGAINST UNEMPLOYMENT BOP AGAINST THE BLUES

BOP AGAINST THE BLUES
Open Air Free Carnival

Bradford Centre Against Unemployment / 1 in 12 Collective

Saturday 24th July
2pm till 8pm. FREE

Bradford University Amphitheatre

Harlem Spirit - Line Up - Boys from the East -
New Model Army - The Prowlers - Chronic -
Bradford poets -
plus theatre groups, inflatables & jugglers.

While The 1 In 12 Club was suffering a forced hiatus due to the end of gigs at The Metropole, they were approached by a new organisation in the city.

Bradford's Centre Against Unemployment had been set up with the backing of the trade unions to help the city's large pool of unemployed people. The head of the centre's team, Matthew Kirkpatrick, approached The 1 In 12 Club to help coordinate and organise some free musical entertainment for the city's unemployed. Because of the Club's contacts in the music scene, they felt they were the ideal group to help coordinate this.

Two free gigs were organised at Queen's Hall. The first, on May 21, featured IK, Admit One and Wild Willi Beckett and the second, on July 20, featured Living Dead, Daka, Necromancy and Complete Disorder. The success of these two free gigs gave the BCAU the idea of organising a free outdoor festival.

With backing and help from The 1 In 12 Club, a festival package was organised for Saturday, July 24, 1982, at Bradford University's amphitheatre, at the back of the Communal Building. The festival was entitled *Bop Against The Blues* and though, despite the *T&A*'s claim that it was, it was not Bradford's first open-air rock festival (that was the 1978 *Rock Against Racism Festival* mentioned in Chapter 4) it was still a great success that summer.

The festival featured six local bands, four poets and a headlining reggae band from Manchester called Harlem Spirit. Fine weather on the day and local community stalls, plus bouncy castle activities for the kids provided by Playspace, meant that the people who attended the eight-hour musical carnival had a great time.

Where the action is!

A WEEK of action by the Bradford Centre Against Unemployment ends with a bang on Saturday with an open-air carnival.

The organisers say it is the first of its kind in Bradford and it has a bit of something for everyone.

There are numerous bands, local and from out of town, a feminist theatre group, poets and stalls. There will also be buskers, jugglers and inflatables for kids to jump around on.

The event will offer exposure for the first time to the newly reformed group Negatives, who were quite big around Bradford in the hey-day of Punk.

Among others appearing will be Joolz, Radio Five and Boys from the East — but unfortunately Southern Death Cult have had to pull out.

The stalls will be run by local community groups, and the afternoon's events kick off at 2 p.m. in the University Amphitheatre — admission absolutely free!

Festival fails to land Ian Dury's band

ALL'S set for the open air rock festival at Bradford University this Saturday despite disappointment over the failure to secure an appearance by Ian Dury and the Blockheads.

Although efforts to get a big name headlining act have failed, the musical bonanza goes ahead with a whole host of local bands covering all areas of rock music.

And the event, organised by the Bradford Centre Against Unemployment, is entirely free.

Heading the bill is a Manchester-based reggae band, Harlem Spirit, with Bradford band The Negatives providing strong support.

Backing up are Boys From The East, Radio Five, Chronic, New Model Army, and Seething Wells, all from Bradford.

BRADFORD'S FIRST OPEN AIR ROCK FESTIVAL

The bill is completed with appearances by Manchester jazz group Line-Up, and Leeds rhythm 'n' blues band The Prowlers.

In addition to music there will be jugglers and side stalls to gave Bradford's first ever open air festival a true carnival spirit.

The extravaganza starts at 1 p.m. at the Amphitheatre behind the communal building at the University. The festival is due to run through to 9 p.m., and all bands will be donating their services free.

Matthew Kirkpatrick, of the Bradford Centre Against Unemployment, said he had been hopeful of securing Ian Dury and The Blockheads to top the bill.

He said: "We could have got Ian Dury who was quite interested in playing the festival, but he wanted a much larger affair, with a bigger site where more people could come.

"We have done this whole thing on a very small budget, with no cash help from the council, and felt we could not really make it any bigger."

He said the only financial outlay for the festival had been the hiring of a PA system. The stage is being borrowed from the University.

Another concert organised by the BCAU takes place at the Queens Hall, Bradford, tonight.

Rock bands The Living Dead, Dachau, and Necromancy do the honours, and again it is free for the unemployed, but 50p for others.

CHAPTER 5 - POST PUNK / ANARCHO PUNK / GOTH 1980 - 1983

THE RETURN OF THE 1 IN 12 CLUB

While The 1 In 12 Club looked for a new venue it organised a free gig at the Textile Hall on February 23, featuring The Three Johns, The Word, Monkey On A Rope and Wild Willi Beckett. The gig was packed and all the artists put on a sterling show. It was also the first time that a 1 In 12 Club gig was reviewed in a national music paper - the *New Musical Express (NME)*.

COMPLETE HARMONY?

A group of Bradford punks gathered outside the registry office on Manor Row to celebrate the wedding of Complete Disorder vocalist Kenny Thomas to Debbie Padgett. Their wedding was featured in the *T&A*. The day was topped off by a gig at The Metropole.

WEDDINGS are supposed to be colourful affairs, but it'll take a lot to beat this one in Bradford on Saturday.

For Kenny Thomas, lead singer of Bradford "hard core" punk band "Complete Disorder" is getting hitched to fellow punk Debbie Padgett at Bradford Register Office.

Gold ear-studs and a striking Mohican hairstyle will make this a far from ordinary occasion and the reception carrys on the off-beat style of the day.

Friends and strangers are welcome to the evening 'do' when Kenny, of Parkfield Road, Manningham, will be celebrating by fronting his band at the Metropole on Sunbridge Road in the town centre.

And for the entry fee of 30p you could be a wedding guest too!

The fun starts at 8 p.m.

Rock On — By John Mahoney

The 3 Johns

1 in 12 back — and free!

PINKO PINUPS

THE THREE JOHNS
Bradford Textile Hall

HOW DO you describe a band as complex, worrying and disastrously original as The Three Johns? Ignore the obvious 'hack' interpretations that limit their appearance on the Leeds music scene as typical of the Northern tradition of 'stern-faced politicos' and 'boring art-grad Marxists'. This is the naive critic's niche, a safe retreat from confronting the fact that The Three Johns are one of the best bands in Leeds today.

They confuse and are often illogical, straining the imagination and overloading the speakers with a solid dangerous sound that has forced desperate comparisons that range from The Doors to The Mekons, PIL and early Skids. It's the bewildering diversity and strange articulation of their ideas (eg. 'Men Like Monkeys') that prevents the instant flat recognition that meets so much of the contrived pap fed up as 'unique shared experience' to passive, ripe young markets.

Quick-fire conversation between bass and lead guitars get cynical anarchists on their feet in heads-down dancing. Hyatt's elastic vocal chords stretch whining and sliding from quirky sarcasm to general hysteria. It's the formidable Langford on lead guitar who puts Beefheart belligerence into the vocals of 'English White Boy Engineer' and 'Fruitflies'.

So far The Three Johns have attracted attention from all strains of youth cultures but aren't interested in leading another: they encourage the audience to get involved. Positive ideas are put into action — they're currently running a weekly course 'It's Only Rock 'n Roll' for the unemployed.

It's easy to be objective about the usual unimaginative band fixed by its own limits of style and pretention. It's painstaking and aggravating trying to decide how to describe The Three Johns. Get a chance to see them or hear the newly released single 'Pink Headed Bug' and take on the challenge.

Julie Brandon

The Upstage Club, behind The Castle pub on Barry Street was another venue running at this time.

Other bands around at the end of 1982 included a five piece all female band called **Rhythm 21** and an electro pop duo called **Silent Congress.**

On March 25, 1983, there was a CND benefit at Bingley Arts Centre with Keighley punk band The Shakes, Spiral and Wild Willi Beckett.

215

THE KEIGHLEY SCENE

As a town in its own right, Keighley had been overshadowed by Bradford since the 1974 reorganisation, but it still continued to produce a fine crop of new local punk and new wave bands including The Quick, Speed, Teenage & The Wildlife (pictured below), The Elements, The Shakes, Cheap'N'Nasty, The Last Laugh (above), Total Confusion and others.

TEENAGE & THE WILDLIFE

Teenage & The Wildlife's *Get the Hell Out of Here / Colours* 7-inch single was released on the band's own label in 1978.

Singer Daz Robb and bassist Tronk went into the band Speed in 1980 and both weere in the original lineup of The Big Bang.

Teenage & The Wildlife made a comeback in 2021. They released an album of newly recorded material in 2024.

THE SHAKES

The Shakes received death threats after their final gig at Bingley Arts Centre on July 12, 1984, due to their controversial 1982 single *Funeral Rites / I Kill God*, which was released on their own label.

New Model Army covered their song *51st State Of America* (written by Shakes singer Ashley Cartwright) and their version was a chart hit, reaching number 35, and was played regularly on ITV's *Music Box* in 1986.

Former Shakes Ashley Cartwright, Jeff Rowland and Steve Wilson went on to form The Hunting Party in 1987.

Both Wilson and Rowland both joined Keighley legends The Big Bang, a band formed by Skeletal Family's Stan Greenwood.

Sadly, drummer John Mason passed away in 2006 and Ashley Cartwright passed away in 2016.

Steve Wilson and Jeff Rowland formed new version of The Shakes in time for a Keighley band reunion on December 29, 2021, at the Exchange Bar. The Elements, Teenage & The Wildlife and The Shakes were all due to play but The Elements had to pull out due to one of the band catching Covid-19.

CHAPTER 5 - POST PUNK / ANARCHO PUNK / GOTH — 1980 - 1983

THE QUICK / THE SHAKES

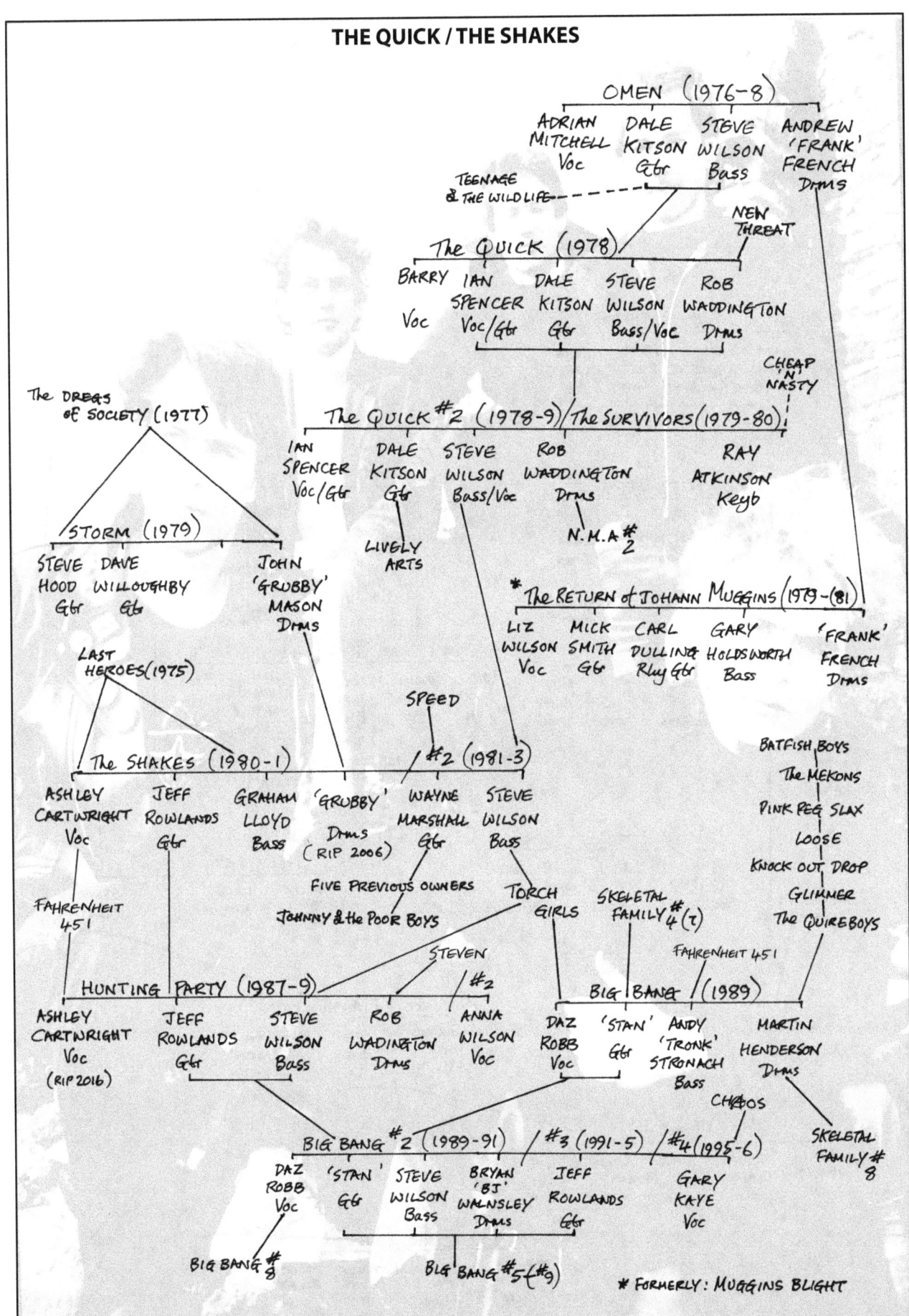

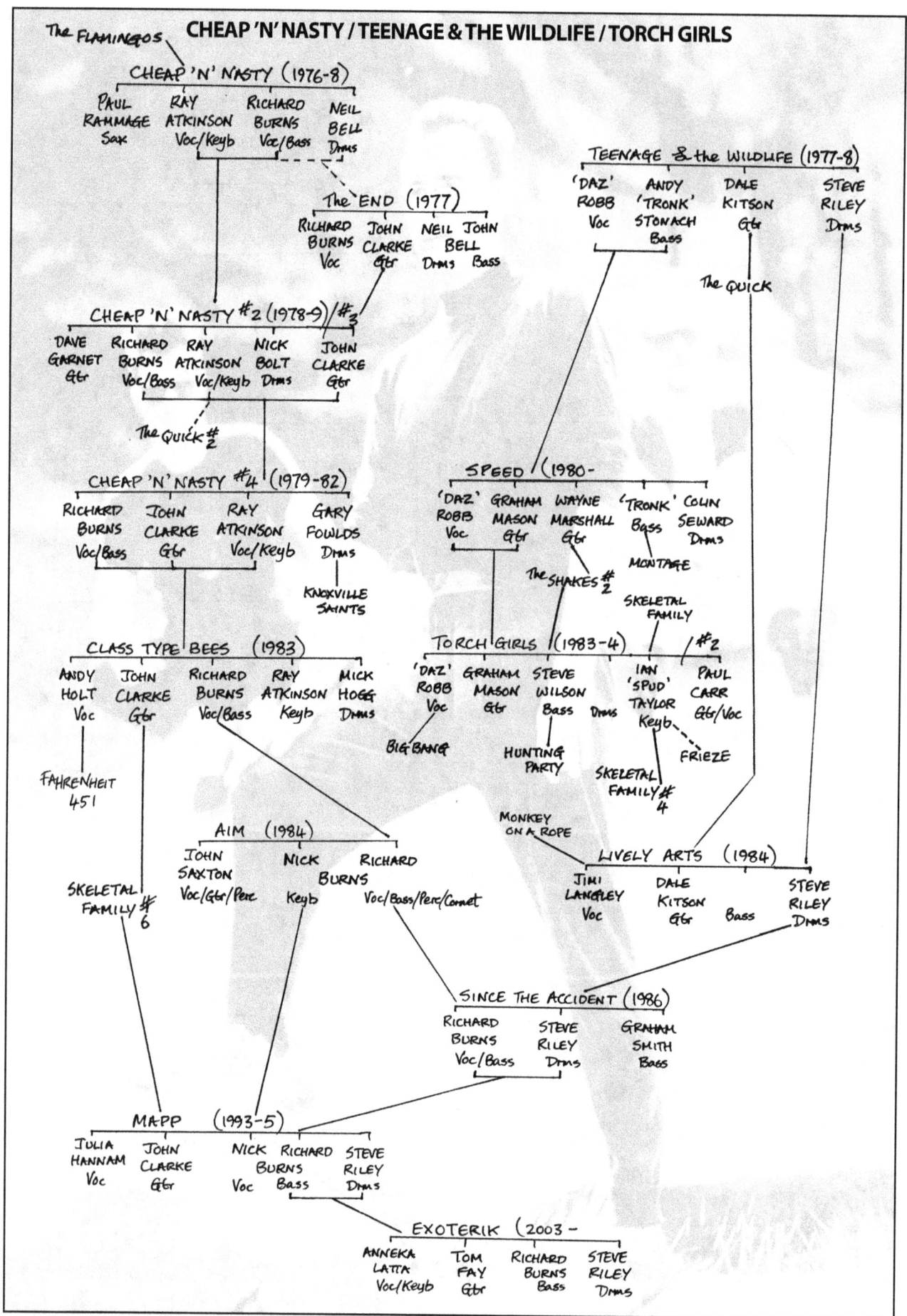

SKELETAL FAMILY

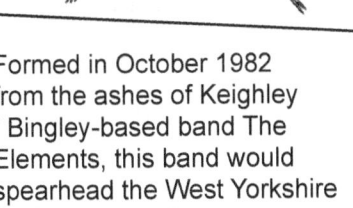

Formed in October 1982 from the ashes of Keighley / Bingley-based band The Elements, this band would spearhead the West Yorkshire Goth movement.

Their self-financed debut single *Trees / Just A Friend* was released on the Leeds-based Luggage record label in March 1983. The record was played regularly by John Peel and from this they gained Radio 1 sessions for Peel and later Kid Jensen and Janice Long.

Regular airplay on Peel's show led to a London debut at the Fulham Greyhound, a good review in *Sounds*, and support slots with Sex Gang Children and Play Dead.

They signed to York-based independent label Red Rhino in 1984 and in June released the single *The Night* which rose to number forty-one in the Indie charts.

Further single releases for Red Rhino, *She Cries Alone, Recollects, So Sure* and *Promised Land* all charted in the Indies at numbers 8, 7, 2 and 2 respectively. Their first LP *Burning Oil* went to the top of the Indie LP charts in September 1984, and their second LP *Futile Combat* (Red 57) got to number seven when released in May 1985.

When Anne-Marie left to form her own band Ghost Dance in 1985 she was replaced by ex-Colourfield vocalist Katrina Philips. This new look Skeletal Family released two singles after signing to major label Chrysalis Records, *Restless* and *Just A Minute*, both of which enjoyed moderate chart success.

Even though the band were a big draw on the British and European gig circuits they became disillusioned and broke up during the recording of demos for a new album.

With renewed interest in Goth acts from the 1990s onwards, Skeletal Family reformed on their 21st anniversary in June 2002 and went on to record new material and perform regularly in Britain and Europe.

Anne-Marie and Stan at 'Skive Off And Jive'

MUGGIN'S BLIGHT

Muggin's Blight's three-track 7-inch single *Mr Somebody / They Go Up! They Go Down! / Malcolm Where's The Talcum?* came out in 1979. It was another Look Records release.

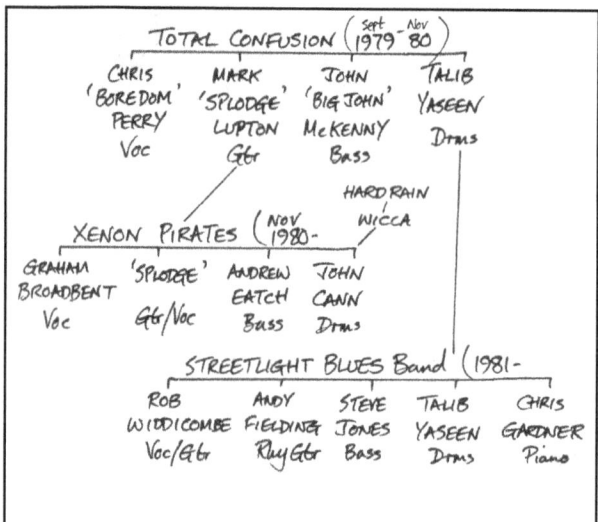

MONTAGE

This Keighley jazz rock band featured ex-Elements singer Jayne Tretton and guitarist Jon Harvison. Jon moved away from the rock circuit in the mid-1980s and built up a strong reputation on the folk scene as a skilful and powerful performer.

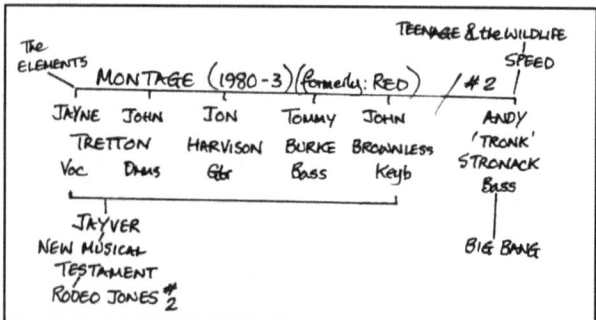

As well as the **Nikkers** nightspot, Keighley had a number of punk and new wave venues. The **Downtown Club** closed in November 1979; it had been a venue for many local bands. During 1980 the **Alternative Club** at Victoria Hotel (Keighley) ran fortnightly gigs, which were free to claimants with UB40, and was promoted by David McGlichey. The **Keighley Funhouse** became the main Keighley venue for numerous punk bands from around the country.

Other Keighley groups around at this time were Bovver & The Wombats, B-Team, Misty (a five-piece) and Edgar Ullmer.

BRADFORD INTERNATIONAL JAZZ FESTIVAL

Between March 18 and 20, 1983, a jazz festival was held at St George's Hall, organised by local enthusiasts Geoff Amos, Peter Martin and Eddie Fenn.

The weekend of concerts, films and fringe events was enjoyed by jazz fans from near and far, including snooker champion Steve Davis. The highlight of the weekend was the concert of Gil Evans (real name Ian Ernest 'Gilmore' Green) backed by a British ensemble. He inspired them to create a *'dynamic and stunning set of musical textures.'* Evans had been the arranger and conductor on three Miles Davis albums, the most notable being the 1960 LP *Sketches Of Spain*.

CHAPTER 5 - POST PUNK / ANARCHO PUNK / GOTH   1980 - 1983

THE 1 IN 12 CLUB AT TICKLES

After the Textile Hall free gig The 1 In 12 Club, was able to resume weekly gigs when it negotiated the use of the new venue Tickles, run by landlords Tim and Pete.

Tickles, on Westgate, had formerly been The Tavern In the Town and The 1 In 12 Club was unconsciously carrying on the previous tradition of running an independent club at the venue, like the rock club that was there in the 1970s.

On the Club's opening night of Wednesday, March 30, it played host to a revamped The Negativz supported by another local band The Convulsions from Thackley.

At the same time, the Club was enquiring into ways of eventually obtaining their own premises and was approaching the local council. It was decided that to help the case it should start an annual membership scheme making the 1 In 12 a members' club. At £1 (or 50p for unwaged) for the year people would get into the gigs cheaper with a member's card. Within a few months, the membership was soon approaching a thousand and the extra funds went towards buying a PA system.

During the nine months from March to November that the 1 In 12 was based at Tickles, it put on bands mainly from the Bradford and Leeds area. It soon started to gain a reputation as groups from all over West and North Yorkshire and Lancashire began to want to play there.

THE EX

Thanks to contacts of Leeds band The Three Johns, the Club played host to its first international groups on September 14, 1983, when Dutch bands The Ex and Alerta appeared as part of their *Red Dance Package* tour of the UK with Leeds band The Three Johns as support. The Ex and Alerta had just recorded two tracks each at KG Music studios in Bridlington, for the 12" *The Red Dance Package* EP released on Leeds-based CNT Records that would come out later that year.

The Ex thrilled the 1 In 12 crowd with their urban noise attack style and politically charged lyrics. They would continue a long association of playing at the Club with other Dutch bands over the next few years.

The Ex next played the 1 In 12 in 1985 when it was based at Queen's Hall, and again in 1987 at the Metropole Hotel, supported by Chumbawamba. Once the Club's Albion Street building was opened, they returned to play four times during 1988-91.

```
Knee Deep In Shit
No.10
30p

Strongly-principled anarchistic
zine with articles on the Miners;
  nuclear bunkers (& their
locations); 'What Is Anarchism?';
& - best of all - an exposé of
freemasonry in Bradford, & the
councillors & politicians
involved in it - & the corruption
that ensues. You've got to read
it - it's amazing. These masons
deserve to be wiped out. Get it
from the "1 in 12" club or from
c/o 127 Thornton Rd., Bradford 1.
```

During this time period the Club continued to periodically produce their fanzine *Knee Deep In Shit* (KDIS).

Left is a review from Leeds 'zine *Roar*.

Mickey Knowles left to play bass for Anti-System followed by Liam Sheeran a few months later. Mark Cranmer and drummer Mark 'Sharky' Mulhone continued Raw for a few months, sometimes as Raw Babies before playing again with Liam in The Nerve Agents and Liam and Mickey in Western Dance.

Tickles was also the venue for other gigs during this time, including a benefit on June 1, 1983, featuring Silent Community, Vermin, 4 Naughty Nuns, Raw, The Convulsions, Subvert and Warhead.

Tickles was also the venue for a Young Socialists Benefit featuring The Negativz, Anti-System, Morbid Humour, The Amazing Poxy Blowjobs (The Convulsions with Raw's Cranny standing in for guitarist Heystack), Spectre and Manray's Haircut on June 28. The venue put on live music under various different guises until 1986.

RAW

This youthful hardcore punk were known for creating their own slashed denim legwear that became known as 'Raw jeans' amongst the Bradford punk crowd. The sixteen-year-old punks were from Thorpe Edge and formed at the Springfield Youth Club. Singer Liam Sheeran, bassist Mark 'Cranny' Cranmer and guitarist Mickey Knowles were all on the YOP course at the Cathedral Centre. They played the usual punk venues at the time, 1 In 12, Tickles, Palm Cove and Queen's Hall.

Their songs *Shit* and *No Rehearsal* appeared on the We're From Bradford compilation tape.

ISOLATION / FIGURES FROM THE COLD

Isolation were a band formed by twins Andy and Wayne Yeadon (pictured with Convulsions Matt Webster) with old school friends while on a YOP course at the Cathedral Centre in 1982. The played the 1 In 12 and supported bands like The Negativz at Queen's Hall. They changed their name to Figures From The Cold before playing with The Convulsions and Raw at the Idle YMCA on April 18, 1983. The band split a few months later.

Singer Andy Yeadon also appeared as a ranting poet under the name Dave The Dog. He went on to play bass for goth band Damien Wolfe. Drummer Bambi became drummer for the Psycho Surgeons.

ANTI-SYSTEM

Bradford's premier anarcho-punk band formed in 1982 around the central figures of drummer Phil Dean and guitarist Dom Watts. After only playing one gig at Palm Cove on September 14, vocalist Dave Damned was replaced by local Odsal lad Nogsy who played his first gig with the band at the Cathedral Centre on December 22, a chaotic punk night with Raw, Isolation, The Hassled and Social Spastix.

After recording a demo at Tony Bonner's Leeds Lions Studios the band were picked up by Marcus Fetherby's Sheffield-based Pax label.

Their tracks *Breakout* and *Man's World* on the 1983 Pax compilation LP *Punk's Dead? Nah, Mate The Smell Is Just Summink In Yer Underpants* were recorded at Rochdale's Cargo Studios because Phil Dean wanted the same kind of drum sound that Discharge had got when they recorded there.

Their next release was *The Defence Of The Realm EP* (Pax 11) by which time bassist George Clarke had been replaced by Mickey Knowles (left) from Raw. A further two tracks, *Why Should It Happen?* and *Schoolboy*, appeared on the 1983 Pax compilation *Bollox To The Gonads, Here's The Testicles*.

Another line-up change came when vocalist Nogsy left the band soon after, to be replaced by Liam Sheeran, also late of Raw. Before long he too left, along with bass player Mickey Knowles and founder member guitarist Dom Watts, leaving only Phil Dean from the original band.

The new Anti-System released the split 7" EP *Strangelove* the Pax subsidiary label Reconciliation. Bradford's other anarcho-punk band Morbid Humour (featuring Nogsy on vocals) on the other side. It got to number twenty-six in the Independent Charts.

By 1984 the band's ferocious guitar and new twin vocal sound gave the group a large local following. They played regularly in and around Bradford, especially at The 1 In 12 Club where most of the band were members.

Their LP *No Laughing Matter* was released in March 1985, again on their own label, and reached 21 in the Indie Charts.

The 12" EP *A Look At Life* followed in 1986 reaching No 19 before the band split.

The band's demise was partly because two members, Mick and Mark, had received prison terms. This was after committing various nocturnal 'guerrilla actions' as the Angry Veggies which included smashing up butchers' shops, trashing over fifty top-range cars and finally breaking into Bradford's abattoir on Leeds Road and releasing all the cattle onto the city's early morning streets.

Former members Varik,

Mark Keane and Mickey Knowles reformed Anti-System in 2016. They recorded the 12" EP *At What Price Is Freedom?* and played gigs in the UK and EU. Nogsy joined the band on stage at a gig in Sheffield.

ANTI SYSTEM		
83	Reconcilliation RECON 3	Strangelove/Oh My God 25
83	Paragon/Pax PAX 11	DEFENCE OF THE REALM (EP) 20
85	Reconcilliation RECON 1	NO LAUGHING MATTER (LP) 30

From 2018, guitarist Varik, the only member from the 1980s, continued the band with different lineups.

Over the years, there have been various re-releases of the band's earlier material, including Vile Records 2024 vinyl compilation *In Defence Of Who's Realm?* which comprises the first EP, Pax compilation tracks and the *A Look At Life* EP.

MORBID HUMOUR

Anti-System released the first single Stranglove / So Long on their own Reconcilliation label in 1985 as a split 7" with the by then defunct Morbid Humour's Oh My God (Parts 1 & 2). Both bands were long-time friends and had interchangeable lineups.

The band Subvert was formed in 1983 by Teale brothers Mark 'Varik and Mick, bassist Mark Kean, and drummer Eddie Noonan. The band soon folded and Varik joined a new band with former

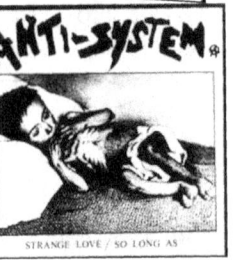

Anti-System singer Nogsy, Mark 'Mugsy' Muller, guitarist Phil Hobson, bassist Darren McKenzie and drummer Kev Grainger.

Morbid Humour played the same gigs as the rest of what became known as Bradford's UK82 bands. They only recorded a few tracks but these ended up on vinyl. *Oh My God (Parts 1 & 2)* and *Give Us This Day* were featured on the third Pax Records compilation LP *Daffodils To The Daffodils Here's The Daffodils* alongside tracks by the Mau Maus and others.

The Teale brothers, Mark Kean and Phil Hobson then all joined Phil Dean, the only remaining original member, in a new lineup of Anti-System. Simon 'Nogsy' Nolan went on to play guitar in various bands including indie-rockers Zed in 1989 with Requiem bassist Jont.

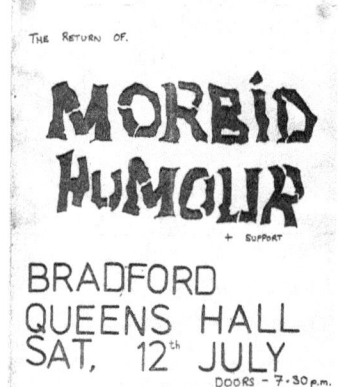

CHAPTER 5 - POST PUNK / ANARCHO PUNK / GOTH — 1980 - 1983

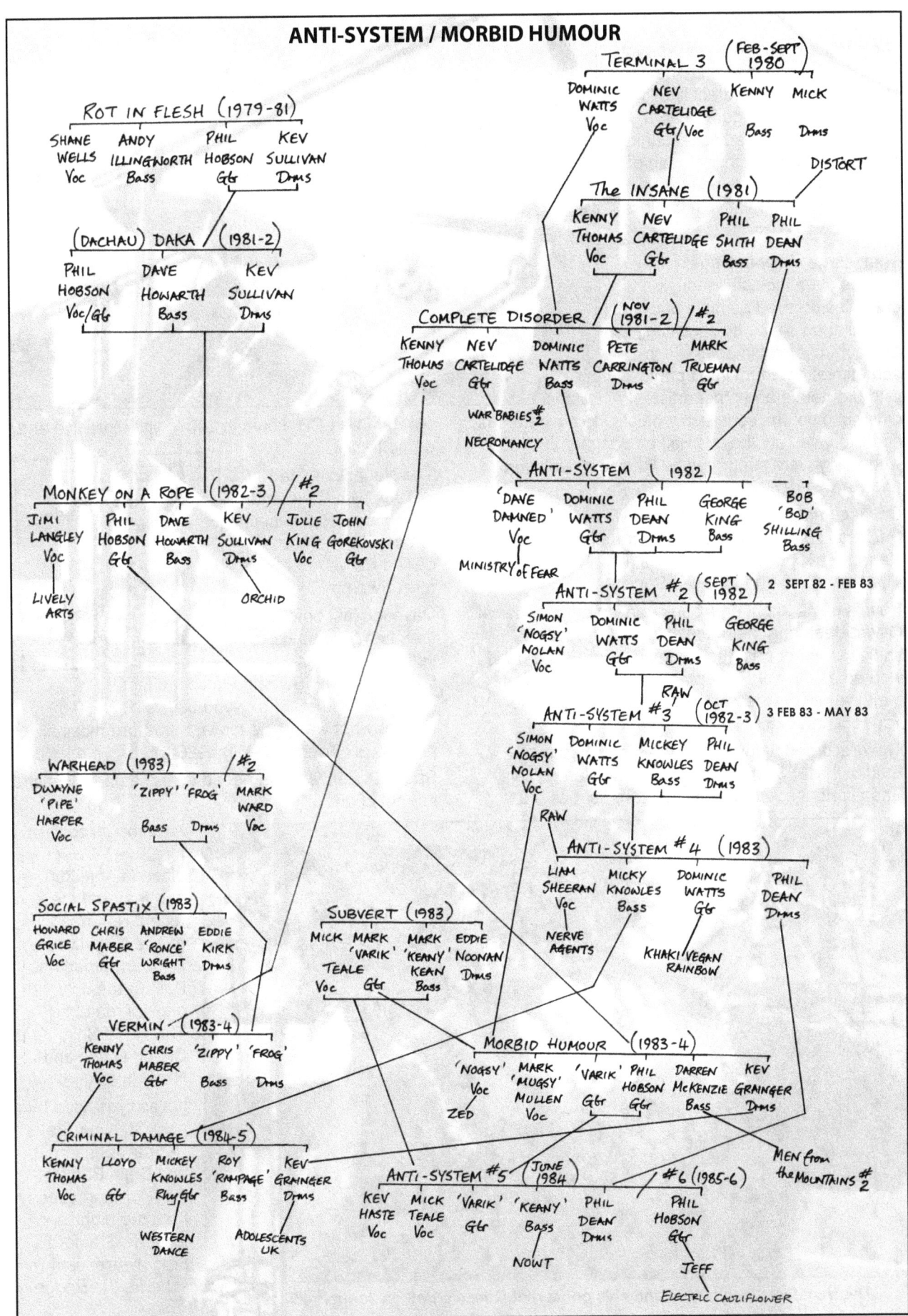

THE NEGATIVZ

Dave Wilcox formed a new version of his late seventies band The Negatives with a different line-up in 1982. The Negativz had a more tuneful and traditional punk style than the most recent crop of hardcore punk bands and quickly became very popular with the local punk crowd.

Their stage show at bigger venues often included shop dummies dressed as nuns and a slide show featuring shocking and controversial images which sometimes got them into trouble with promoters and other artists.

One such riotous occaision was at One such riotous occasion was at Queen's Hall on January 29, 1983, when they were supported by Requiem, Isolation and Raw.

On December 21, 1983, *The Negativz Xmas Party* took place at the Leeds Bier Keller with The Negativz supported by Toy Dolls, Icon AD, Xpozez, The Instigators and Civilised Society.

Dave's plans to put on a punk version of the musical Oliver!, featuring members of local punk bands sadly never got past the planning stages. The band worked a cover of *Reviewing The Situation* into their live set, a video of which found its way onto YouTube in 2025.

They recorded a seven-song demo at Cargo Studios in 1983, engineered by John Bierley. This wasn't released at the time but came out as the *Mental Case* CD album in 2007, with extra live and demo tracks.

The Negativz folded in 1984 with Dave and bass player Pox joining forces with members of The Nerve Agents to form Swamp Flower.

Dave left just before their first recording session but later teamed up with Swamp Flower guitarist, Negativz drummer Foxy and bassist Ross Terry to form what was to be his last Bradford musical project, Six Feet Under, in 1986-87.

Sadly, Dave was found dead in his flat in Newcastle in April 2006.

A memorial concert for Dave Wilcox took place in April 2007 and featured the recent re-formation of The Negatives (with drummer Tino Palmer the only original mamber), Threshold Shift, Kwai Chang Caine and Nick Toczek.

It was organised by punk stalwart Steve 'Johna' Johnson and Delia Bartlett-Perry, the proceeds from the night went towards Bradford's drug awareness scheme the *Bridge Project*.

The Negativz at a typically anarchic concert at Queen's Hall on January 29, 1983

CHAPTER 5 - POST PUNK / ANARCHO PUNK / GOTH — 1980 - 1983

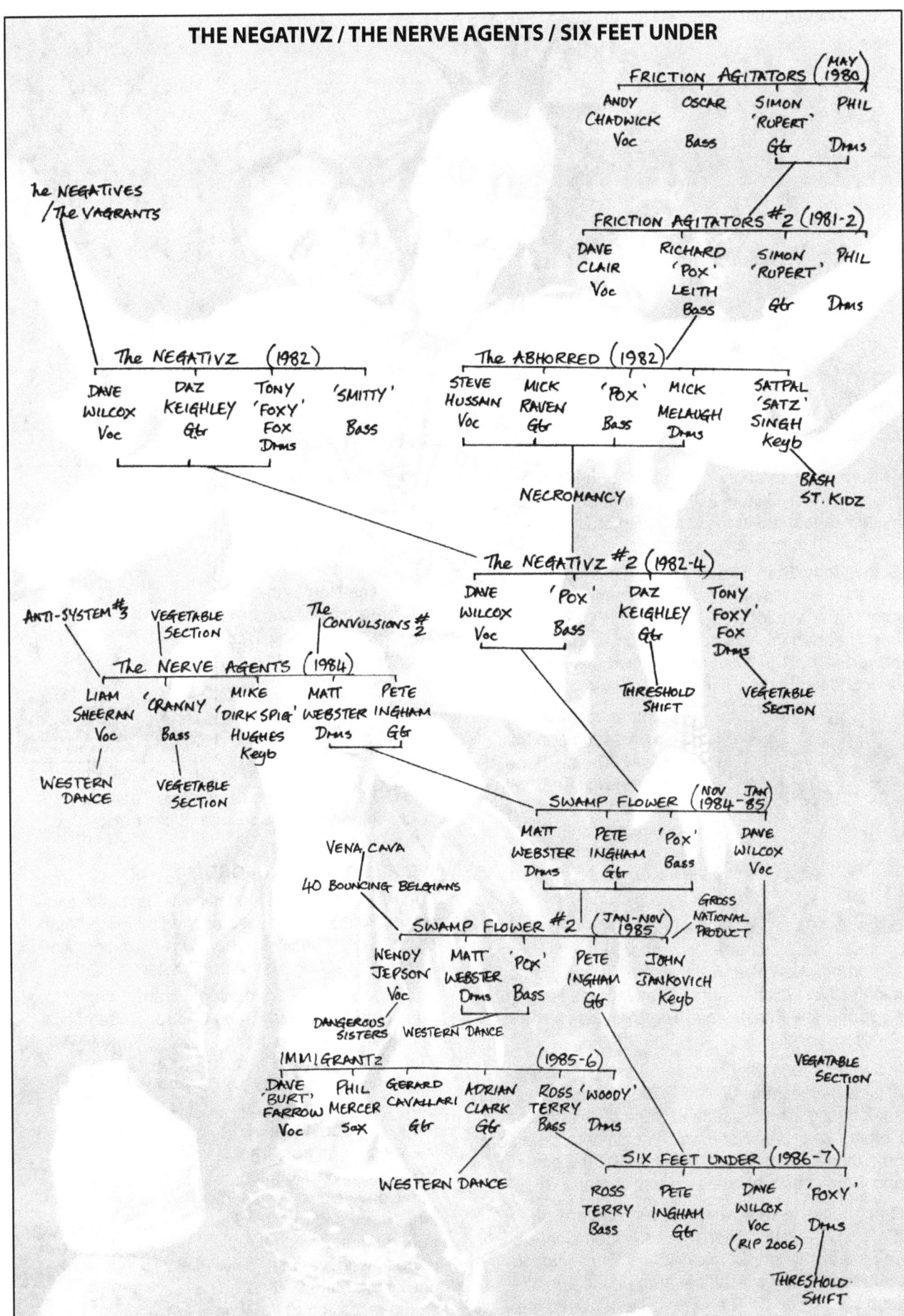

227

THE CONVULSIONS

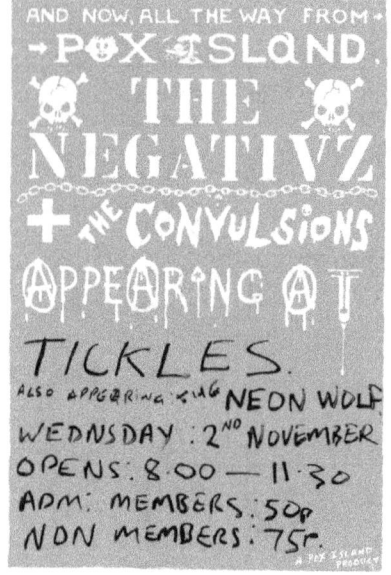

The Convulsions in customary chaotic style at Tickles November 1983

This youthful hardcore punk band formed while still at Hanson School in the summer of 1982 and initially rehearsed in the clubhouse of Thackley Football Club before being politely asked to leave.

Singer Tony 'Stan' Flaherty joined in January 1983 and the band played their first gig shortly after at Idle YMCA with local rockers Reefer. Thereafter the band hassled for gigs at all the punk venues and played at the 1 In 12 numerou times and could often be found supporting The Negativz.

In 1983 they recorded their seven-song *Electro Convulsive Therapy* tape at Lion Studios in Leeds with engineer len Liggins. They proceeded to push their tape at local gigs, along with the accompanying t-shirt.

They were on the bill at the Leeds Bier Kellar on December 18, 1983, for the Underdogs New Year Bash' at the Toczek promoted mini-festival which featured The Underdogs, Major Accident, The Fits, Uproar, The Convulsions and Civilised Society.

In January 1984 they recorded a second session at Lion Studios, this time with Tony Bonner engineering. The cassette EP lead off with the track *Coming Your Way Soon* which contained samples from the recently shown *Threads* BBC TV show about the effects of a nuclear strike on the UK.

Other tracks were newly recorded versions of *Electro Convulsive Therapy* and *Hatred Controls* (in tune this time!) with new songs *You're Nobody* and *Media Punx* which appeared on the 1 In 12 Club's *Enemies Of The State* LP and played the closing slot at the *Not The International Garden Festival*.

The band folded shortly after drummer Matt left to join The Nerve Agents. Kenny Armitage and Tony Palmer formed The Skidmarks. Bass player Kenny later joined punk band Threshold Shift with singer Mick Barrett and ex-Negativz Foxy and Daz (later replaced by Convulsions' Phil Hey).

The CD album *Electro Convulsive Therapy*, containing their two demos and live tracks, was released in 2001

WE'RE FROM BRADFORD

The refrain from The Negativz live favourite show closer *Bradford* was used as the title for the punk compilation tape *We're From Bradford*, compiled by Convulsions drummer Matt Webster.

The tape sold well from out of a carrier bag at local punk gigs and the favourite Saturday afternoon punk hang-outs like the West Riding Bar at Forster Square and The Spinx (now The Exchange) on Market Street. It featured live recordings from The Negativz, Raw, Requiem, The Convulsions, Isolation and others and also tracks from the first demo by Anti-System who were the only one of the bands with a studio recording at the time.

CHAPTER 5 - POST PUNK / ANARCHO PUNK / GOTH   1980 - 1983

THE CONVULSIONS / VEGETABLE SECTION / THRESHOLD SHIFT

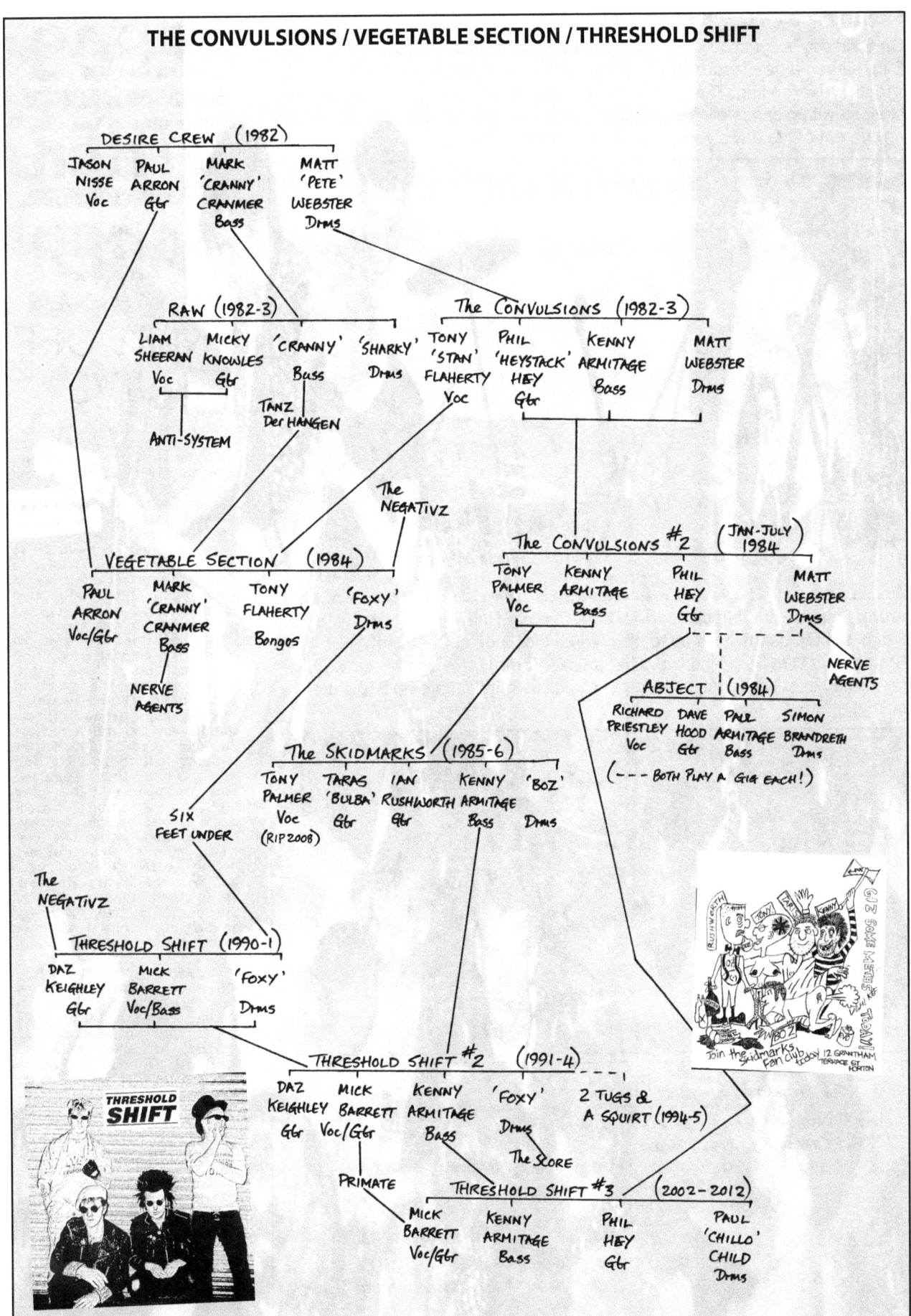

SKIVE OFF & JIVE FREE FESTIVAL

On Saturday, August 13, 1983, the collaboration of BCAU and The 1 In 12 Club staged a free festival at the university's natural amphitheatre for the second year running. That year's festival was called *Skive Off & Jive* and was blessed with glorious all-day sunshine which went a long way to enhance the enjoyment of the day's very large crowd of mixed revellers.

Around midday, the fun started with 20th Century Hats (above) who were the first of the ten bands lined up to play. Three local poets, Seething Wells, Little Brother and Dirk Spig, and two other artists, Surfin' Dave and Mister Soft, performed in between the day's groups, including Inevitable Split (pictured below).

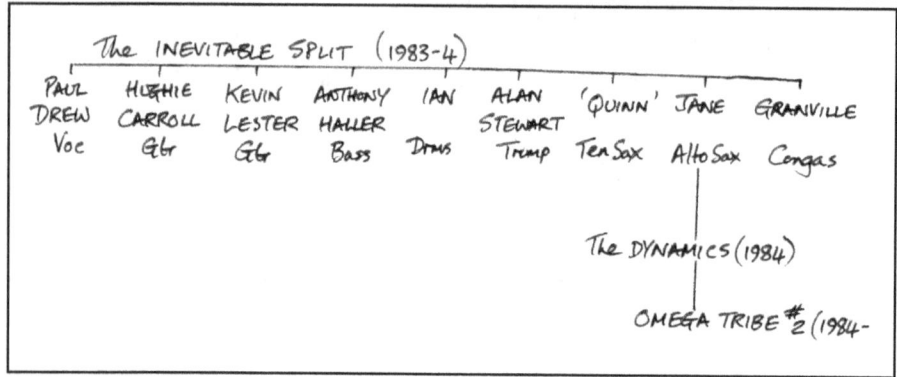

The INEVITABLE SPLIT (1983-4)

PAUL DREW	HUGHIE CARROLL	KEVIN LESTER	ANTHONY HALLER	IAN	ALAN STEWART	'QUINN'	JANE	GRANVILLE
Voc	Gtr	Gtr	Bass	Drms	Tromp	Ten Sax	Alto Sax	Congas

The DYNAMICS (1984)

OMEGA TRIBE #2 (1984-

LEEDS OTHER PAPER
REVIEW/PREVIEW
SKIVE OFF & JIVE

Sometimes strange characters turn up at the "1 IN 12" Club on a Wednesday night, like the two pictured here. these two stiff looking blokes arrived identically dressed in new gear and spent 4½ hours with only a half pint each, having, to judge from their looks, a thoroughly miserable time. It was punk night, with five local bands on. Everyone else thought it was great.

One of the two was so bored that he started writing in a notepad a one point.

Last on was the excellent punk band **Chumbawamba**, their strong visual anti-war theme was too much for the duo to bear, and after noticing that their photo had been taken, they departed and disappeared into the night in a smart hatchback saloon parked nearby. No-one knew who the two were, or what their interest in the "1 IN 12" Club was, but perhaps a cryptic clue as to their identity lay in the motif on their T-shirts, advertising now defunct Britol punks, "The Vice-Squad".

Meanwhile, the "1 IN 12" Club, along with B.C.A.U. are busy organising the second annual free open-air festival to be held on Saturday 13 August at the back of Bradford University. Bands playing include *The 3-Johns, Anti-System, Skeletal Family, Spectre, Boys From the East, Requiem, Inevitable Split, Fatal Charm, 20th Century Hats* and *The Toyz*, plus local poets and performance artists. Also there will be an abundance of stalls, food and drink, with inflatables and a puppet show for the kids.

Nowt else is happening of this nature in the area, so don't miss it! Starts at noon sharp.

Terry

CHAPTER 5 - POST PUNK / ANARCHO PUNK / GOTH — 1980 - 1983

PYRAMID / SURE MOVES / 20TH CENTURY HATS

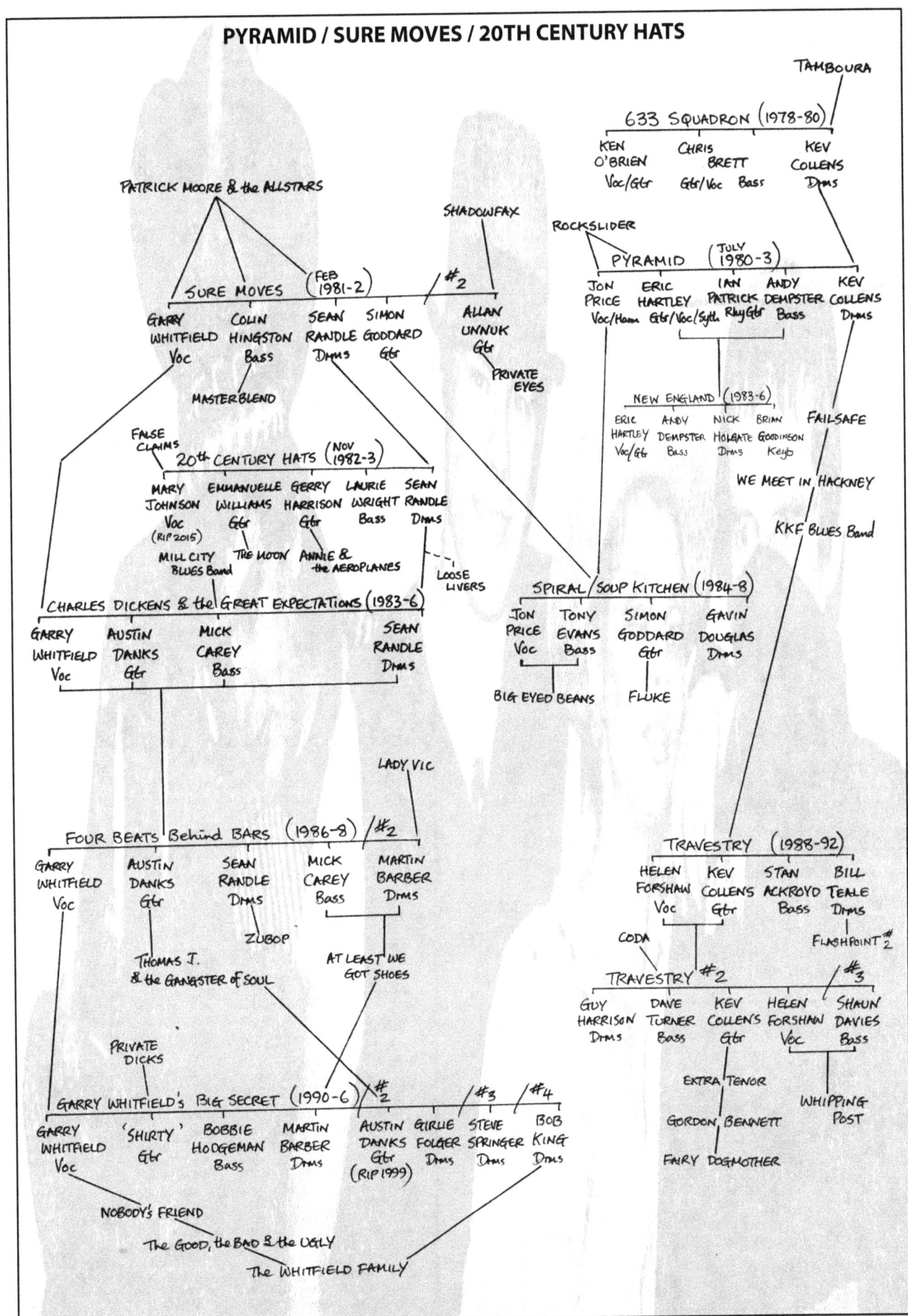

1980 - 1983 BRADFORD'S NOISE OF THE VALLEYS VOLUME 1

Anti-System

During the day lots of local punks and revellers pogoed and danced to local bands Anti-System, Requiem and Skeletal Family as they each gave excellent performances, as did the other more differently styled groups on the day, including a nine-piece group of Ilkley College students called The Inevitable Split who were managed by their trumpet player Alan Stewart.

Big mouth strikes again!

As the sun began to set the headlining group The Three Johns took to the stage, and in the darkening twilight they topped off the day by delivering a stunning performance that had everyone still present dancing with sheer enjoyment.

The festival was filmed by video production Acorn Video, who were based at the Cathedral Centre. One Thursday night in late October, The 1 In 12 held a *Video Night* at a pub off Manor Row where the unedited footage was shown to Club members.

Rock On By John Mahoney

Roaring open air success

HOW many groups can boast of playing their sound-check in front of 3,000 onlookers?

And Bradford University's Free Rock Festival got it all right by getting bands out on stage as swiftly as they could, while the audience sat in the sun and soaked it all up.

The Hawaiian-shirted Surfing Dave rattled out his Beach Boys renditions while punks and skins jived at the front, the quick-fire wit of Seething Wells, brought early afternoon ranting with more poems about Tetley Bittermen, and Little Brother, acting as compere, finally had his own excellent 15-minute set.

Only Mr. Soft, a painted blend of mime and rant, looked out of place on stage and appeared to bore everyone stiff.

The music satisfied all tastes, from gentle pop in the form of 20th Century Hats, Boys From The East and Requiem, to punk, alive and pogoing with Anti-System and The Toyz.

On came the Skeletal Family, late, for a shortened set, with Anne-Marie sporting a shock of flamingo hair. Still well up to scratch in the open air, the band played their debut Trees single and also the far superior Night disc.

As the sun began to set the Three Johns from Leeds had those fans back up on their feet for the final bop of the day.

From the faultless PA system to the ideal setting in the University grounds the event was an undisputed success.

The festival took shape following months of hard graft from the Bradford Centre Against Unemployment and the 1 in 12 Club. Both groups deserve a pat on the back for their efforts. They created a day to remember.

CHAPTER 5 - POST PUNK / ANARCHO PUNK / GOTH   1980 - 1983

The Toyz

Requiem

FRITZ THE CAT

Local photographer Fritz The Cat took the photos of *Skive Off And Jive* printed here, as well as hundreds of photos of local bands and gigs during the 1980s.

Lots of Fritz's photos were used as band publicity shots and many now adorn the pages of this book.

Based in a studio in the Bradford Cathedral Centre, Fritz and fellow 1 In 12 member Martin McGarragle also designed posters and record covers, including the first three vinyl 1 in 12 Club albums, and were known as Putsch Graphics.

In a later incarnation, Fritz became a top local rave DJ and was involved in the Stimulations Rave collective.

Sir — May I through your readers' column congratulate the Bradford Centre Against Umemployment and co--promoters the "1 in 12" club for the splendid festival they put together last Saturday.

It proved just what can be achieved with good organisation and "low profile" stewarding that despite the heat and the diverse make-up of the audience not one spot of bother was recorded in nine hours non-stop entertainment.

It must surely be the event of the year for Bradford's legion of unemployed, whose behaviour was exemplary.

In conclusion I might also add that Bradford Council showed true foresight when deciding to take in the funding of the city's, Centre Against Unemployment. The staff have their fingers firmly on the pulse of the TRUE needs of the city's jobless and deserve full support.

MR. C. BROWN,
7 Langton Avenue,
Bierley,
Bradford 4.

233

FUTURAMA 5

On the weekend of August 17 & 18, 1983 promoter John Keenan held another *Futurama* at Leeds Queen's Hall. The previous two years' *Futuramas* had been at New Bingley Hall in Stafford and Deeside Leisure Centre in Chester respectively.

Saturday's headliners were Death Cult Ian Astbury's post-Southern Death Cult band, supported on the day by Bradford's only representatives at the festival New Model Army and Joolz.

IF YOU BELIEVE WHAT YOU READ IN THE NME...

In late September The 1 In 12 Club got its first *NME* review for a Surfin' Dave gig at Tickles, courtesy of local scribe Seething Wells writing under his alias Susan Williams. Swells had first got a review in the *NME* earlier that year by reviewing an imaginary gig at a made-up venue in Bradford and hoodwinking the *NME* into printing it. (10)

By early November, he had written reviews for two

SURFIN' DAVE   28/9/83
Bradford 1 In 12 Club
SWEET GLEAMING on his naked skull, the salivating Surfin' Dave prods back his massive spectacles with a single thin finger as they once again start their slow slide down his slick and shiny proboscis. He struts, sneers and sings:
"There are grey skies above/The house my Baby lves in/And if that's not enough/She's taken to her bed with the 'flu".
Artists! Armed with one guitar, two ideas and three chords he sports a shirt of the sort which hasn't been seen since Jack Lord assumed full artistic control of *Hawaii Five-O*. Surfin' Dave has his audience's undivided hostility with his torrid tales of insubstantial physique and romantic disaster.
A genius? A plagiarist? Is he just taking the piss? One thing's for certain — if Buddy Holly had been born a Yorkshireman he would have sounded nothing like Surfin' Dave, Neato!
Susan Williams

City verdict: 'Give it some clog'

THE NEGATIVZ
ETON CROP
COWBOYS AND INDIANS
Bradford 1 In 12 Club

A SPECTACULARLY acne-encrusted man-child stalks the outer bar prising drunks with his teetering mohican and malevolent smiles. Inside unfolds a monochrome Babycham advertisement wherein the Dickensian spawn of McLaren's brainstorm still keep the faith — this is the hardcore, the rock-chinned residue of punk rock's devotees, some of them going back at least three years to that first fatal dose of Crass-mania.

The ghosts of a hundred sacred cows float like dope smoke above the crowd. Their blackened, hideously mutilated hides sporting the white painted Who's Who of those at whom it's still hip to spit in the inner city kindergarten.

D. Wilcox, Bradford's oldest surviving practitioner of late '70s sartorial inelegance and Negativz spokesthing, displays a torso of the sort desired and admired by myriad aspiring principal boys and East European gymnasts. As flat as an ironing board, as thin as an Oxfam poster, he smears several pints of glutinous plasma over flaccid nipples — whether in an attempt to remove them as focal points of sexual desire or in an exhibition of pathetically gratuitous self mutilation, it is hard to tell.

Ms. Lu Wong may be ex of the yapping boys but the cutesy-wutesy whimperings of plastic savagery linger on. Cowboys And Indians look nicer, sing sweeter and dance with more style than the Scummy Dogbreath Cult ever did — which is a bit like saying that *Blankety-Blank* piddles on *Celebrity Squares*. Anyway, their girlfriends clapped and smiled so that's all right.

Acting in a manner far more befitting ambassadors of Dutch culture than their rather thuggish football supporters, Eton Crop still contrived to give it some clog. Four staggeringly clean-cut types roped in Leeds '78 style anti-freeze with the whackiest drumming this side of our Cozy. Anarcho-syndicalist naivete is diced with unblinkered Whickerisms in 'Gay Boys On A Battlefield' wherein Erwin Blom wonders why Frankie Goes To Hollywood have never had a Top Ten hit in the People's Republic of China, where, officially, homosexuality is non-existent.

Der Crop view the world askew whilst the tribal sheep bleat the shrinkwrapped ideologies of the cultural pygmy, regurgitate a stolen image and sniff the results.
Susan Williams

more Club gigs for the *NME* - one featuring The Negativz and Dutch band Eton Crop under the title *Give It Some Clog*.

On November 16, the Club put on its last gig at Tickles. It then moved around the corner to the Market Tavern where landlords Peter and Tim had just taken over the running of the venue which was at the top end of the Arndale Centre on Duke Street.

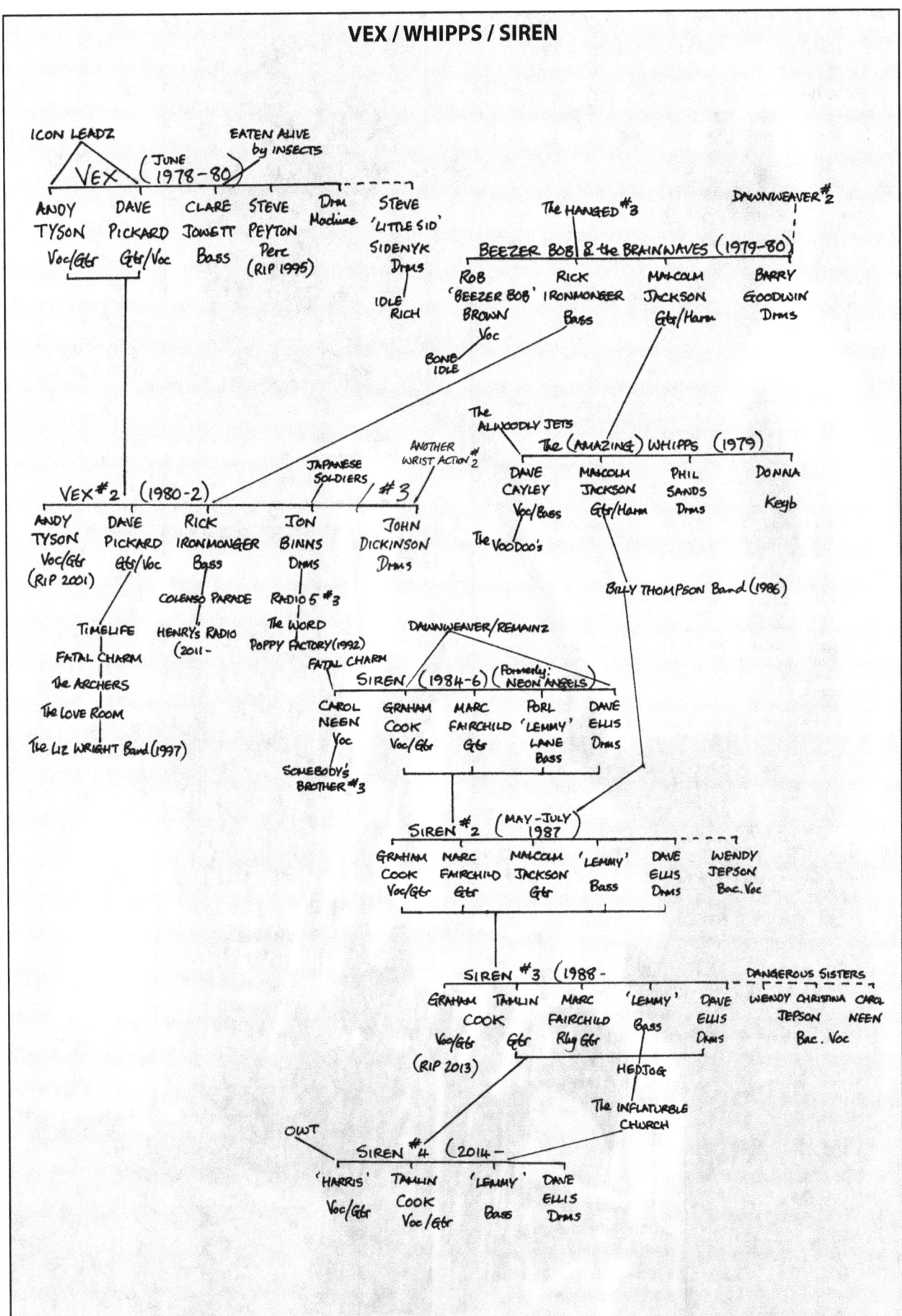

THE 1 IN 12 AT THE MARKET TAVERN 1983-85

The 1 In 12 Club moved venues from Ticlkes, on Westgate to the Market Tavern on Godwin Street, which was built into the Arndale Centre in November 1983. It remained based there for twenty-one months until July 1985 when it moved to the Queen's Hall.

The first night's gig was on November 23, by local ska band Spectre, supported by Those Frayed Edges (formerly Isolation/Figures From The Cold).

> **LOOSE LIVERS**
> **DIRK SPIG**   30/11/83
> **LITTLE GERMANY**
> *Bradford 1 In 12 Club*
>
> HARK HARK the Doom Dogs bark! Stay a while, sniff a little. Spring is in the air! The sweet jingle-jangle of polyester geetar! The dyslexick (sic) mono stumble of mail order drum kit! The Woolworths bass chokes and fumbles, thin fingers pound its shuddering, pale remains. The dank hiccough of Buddy Holly vocals spat through a pallid sock. I orgasm (metaphysically), thrust back to those HeyNoddyNoddy (spit spit) halcyon Pogo Stomps of the Golden Age when the 1st wave of Power Pop shook the International Cock Rock Conspiracy to its strained pubic roots with:
> *This is Poonk Rock! As it should be! As it always will be!*
> A malignant dwarf not a shambling corpse. Move me Baby, Move me! Little Germany were more than just good – they were *jolly* good, despite too many Lou 'Lung Machine' Reed references for my liking.
> Dirk Spig is the 4th most boring person in Bradford (307th in the world rating) and a HERO. Like all such men-of-action the hairline crack between masochism and guts is hard to discern, but despite having his wrist bent back to an impossible angle by an outraged seeker of gob-zip who then proceeded to scream his less than astute criticisms from very close range, Dirk was determined to 'Carry On Ranting!' which, of course, will make a great title for a film one day (Hattie Jacques as Attila).
> Colour me Pink! The kitchen sink lies smashed and crumbled as three black-clad chicks flirt with the patriarchy. The beards and kaftans of the jerking, spurting backing band were *disgusting*, counterpointed by the N.Y sleaze of the canny bopping lasses who comprise the Loose Livers front line. Sexual politics, a shuffle and a smile. (This is not an Oi band.) Groovy.
>   **Susan Williams**

The next week's gig featured Loose Livers, ranter Dirk Spig and Little Germany. It was the first review of Club gigs at The Market Tavern that appeared in the *NME* by 'Susan Williams' and another local reviewer Dave Jennings, as the 1 In 12 began a long residency there from 1983 to 1985.

During its stay at the Market Tavern it put on 110 gigs with an average attendance of between seventy to over a hundred, initially on Tuesdays and later, twice a week, on Tuesdays and Thursdays.

> * Goth, a kind of John The Baptist poor relation to the approaching mighty crust machine, takes The Look out for a dummy-run. Long hair, lots of black, smelling funny and signing on are the basic tenets. Strong in northern fortresses of doom like the Bradford 1-In-12 Club.

Some of the bands that played in the downstairs cellar room were among the cream of the national punk/new wave scene and the Club had sixteen reviews in the

NME over that period. The 1 In 12 Club also had a mention in music magazine *Select* during this period when it was referred to as *'a fortress of doom.'*

Bands that played regularly (some more than once) at the 1 In 12 during that market tavern period included local bands such as Requiem, The Convulsions, Anti-System, Morbid Humour, Passmore Sisters, **Surreal Estate** (above) and Skeletal Family, Leeds bands **The Three Johns** (below), Chumbawamba and Age Of Chance, Sheffield bands Pulp and One Thousand Violins, Manchester bands A Witness (below), Tools You Can Trust, Big Flame, Inca Babies and Marc Riley & The Creepers (AKA BBC Radio DJ 'Lard' formerly of The Fall), Leicester's Yeah, Yeah, Noh and Bomb Party, Blackpool's The Membranes, Barnsley's Party Day and from London Ruebella Ballet, Omega Tribe, Flowers In The Dustbin, The InStinks and Five Go Down To The Sea to name a few.

Pictures on this page courtesy of the Fritz The Cat

PEOPLE'S SQUAT FOR PEACE

The Convulsions with stand in vocalist Nogsy

Certain members of The 1 In 12 Club and others decided to revive Bradford's long-lost squat scene by squatting an old, disused garage off Ivanhoe Road in the Great Horton district.

During their short stay as *The People's Squat For Peace* they managed to put on a free New Year's Eve gig in 1983.

The local groups who featured on that chaotic night were The Word, Anti-System, The Convulsions, Pagan Hero, Screaming Jellyfish, Potential Victim, Nottingham's Scum Dribblurz and Batley's Civilised Society.

```
                CMS (1983-
       CHRISTOPHER    SIMON      MICHAEL
         JONES        WITHEY     WILKINSON
          Gtr         Rhy Gtr     Drms
```

CMS were a three-piece instrumental band made up of fourteen- and fifteen-year-old grammar school lads from Bingley, Keighley and Haworth.

SOCIAL SPASTIX

Social Spastix were a short-lived hardcore band that played from the end of 1982 to mid-83. They usually did short sets supporting bands like The Negativz and Anti System. They played with Anti-System and The Convulsions at Tickles on April 18, 1983.

Guitarist Chris Maber was another Cathedral Centre punk although he was dismissed from the YOP course for throwing a cigarette end into a plastic cup full of screen wash in the screen printing room and causing a fire. Quick-thinking tutor Andy Drake smothered the fire with a coat saving a batch of freshly printed Convulsions posters!

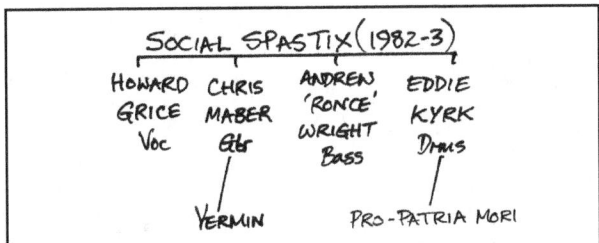

Around this time, as in other periods, there were a number of other bands around who we haven't gone into great detail about. Bands who had a record out, appeared on a compilation, played the 1 In 12 or other known venues we usually have some record about. Others, however, we have only heard mention of, maybe in the *T&A* or on a band family tree.

Reefer were a rock band who played a couple of gigs in 1983. Their bassist Gavin Wilkinson was a Thackley lad who went to Hanson School and sadly passed away in 2022.

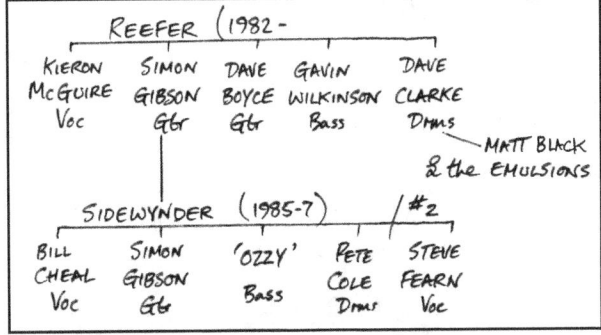

At the end of 1983 there was a band called **East Park**, a Bradford band based in Leicester.

Chapter 6
indie ALTERNATIVE ROCK
1984 - 1986

As 1984 dawned, George Orwell's prophetic predictions of mass compliance and police state oppression in his novel of a Big Brother-dominated society seemed to have become almost a reality in Thatcher's Britain. The country was in social and political turmoil, with massive inequalities of life chances, and industrial and urban disintegration, counterpoised with sections of society wallowing in rampant greed as the selfish 'yuppie' (young and upwardly mobile) culture was born.

The mid-1980s saw the alternative to the pop charts defined by the Independent Charts which featured a mixed bag of innovative musical styles including punk, post-punk, anarcho-punk, American-influenced hardcore-punk, gothic, experimental noise, jangly pop, jazz funk and dub reggae. Most bands were a hybrid crossover of some of these styles that had morphed into their own sub-genres.

THE 1 IN 12 CLUB AT THE MARKET TAVERN

The 'grim up north' urban resistance soundscape continued in Bradford, as The 1 In 12 Club settled into its new home at the Market Tavern on Godwin Street.

The Club thrived during its residence at the Tavern and developed an excellent scene in both the upstairs bar and the basement gig room at their regular Thursday night gigs from 1983 to 1985.

A succession of new up-and-coming local bands played, as well as the usual array of stalwarts. A handful of bands from outside the area begin to venture over, like Bolton's Mass Of Black, 13 Horses Legs, ex-Fall member Marc Riley & The Creepers and Blackpool's The Membranes. (1)

Growing word of mouth on the gig scene, and the club's reputation for not ripping off bands was attracting a regular audience. The odd review in the *NME* also helped to raise the Club's profile on an even broader national basis.

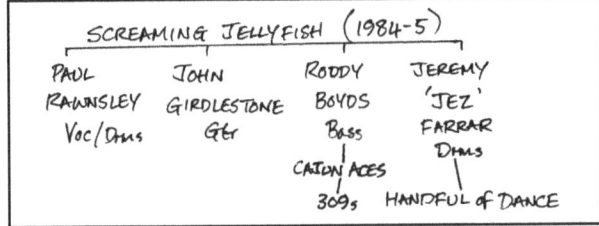

THE SCREAMING JELLYFISH
Bradford 1 In 12 Club

THE CHAP allowed the task of verbalising the group's angst and fury bears more than a passing resemblance to a rather cuddly Bull Mastiff. One does not blame him for this: we can't *all* live up to the slim, small-bottomed yet rugged stereotype perpetuated by the fat and greasy, huge-arsed slugs of the advertising media. One simply mentions it.

But, cry anguished readers, what of the *music*? This is after all *not* the *Dog Breeders' Express* but a journal dedicated to that segment of our throbbing cultural funny-farm known jokingly as Pop Music. And so Dear Reader, it is to the *music* that we now turn our attention.

Despite the name with its manifold nudge-nudge wink-wink "who's been knocking back the old psychedelic wibbeldy-wobbeldy pills then –?" connotations, The Screaming Jelly Fish are first and foremost a Punk Rock Band. This is established by their inability to play their instruments with any degree of technical skill, their tight trousers and their rather unnerving habit of grinning sheepishly at one another during the occasional accidental discord rather than pretending that the awful noise thus made is made on purpose in an attempt to emulate, say, Jimi Hendrix or some other recognised Master of the Electric Guitar whose reputation is based solely on their complete inability to play the instrument properly (unlike, say, Hank Marvin).

Doubtless they are politically aware to an extent betrayed by such masterfully ambiguous statements as: "This one's about people who say they like the army and they're going to join the Terriers when they're 18 but don't and it's a TRUE STORY!".

They are FUN. Which fact dooms them to obscurity until such time as the prevalant morbid obsession with the grim and mock serious can be said no longer to prevail.

The Enigmatic Susan Williams

Squat battle

Council bid to evict young protesters

By Sian James

YOUNG squatters who forced their way into an empty building are to be ousted by Bradford Council.

The authority, which bought the three-storey property in Claremont, Great Horton, in May for £105,000, is taking legal action.

The squatters, who call themselves The Free Space Collective, moved in a week ago last Sunday. Their numbers vary between eight and 15 and they are all unemployed.

All are aged between 16 years and 23 years, and claim they are homeless because the council and private landlords have failed them.

Worse

One of the group, Stan Archibald, 18, said: "Squatting has become a necessity. Council housing is impossible to get for single young people.

"Private landlords don't want to know and it has got worse since the change in housing benefits.

"We don't want to be dependent on anybody. We are willing to pay the council rent."

They have electricity and gas and say they have accounts with both in the name of Robert Crabtree.

The collective aims to live in the building, once a Ukrainian club, and use it as a meeting place for organisations in the city.

But Bradford Council has different ideas. It bought the building with a view to re-housing Bradford College Students' Union, based in the Alhambra Theatre complex.

As the students are staying where they are, the council is planning to lease or sell the Claremont building.

A spokesman for the authority's legal department said: "Unless they move out voluntarily we shall apply to the county court to get possession."

They were not willing to negotiate with the group as some of its members had squatted in another council property last year.

Posters outside the building said the squatters would only be moved by legal action. They have taken advice from the Bradford Law Centre.

From left: Robert Brooke, 20, Robert Crabtree, 20, Naway Osciffa, 23, Stan Archibald, 18 and Stan Reed, 17, squatting in the house.

Courtesy of the Telegraph & Argus

We the occupants of the PEOPLES SQUAT FOR LIFE - The Free Space collective have taken over the building at 13-15, Claremont. We are renovating and decorating the building and have legally turned the gas, electric and water over to our responsibility, which we pay for by fund raising activities and donations.

We intend to use the building to provide a Community Centre for unemployed people in Bradford, offering the following facilities:-

- A Vegan/Vegetarian Cafe and Meeting Place
- An Alternative Bookshop
- Cheap Rehearsal Space for local bands
- A regular venue for Theatre Groups, Dance Groups and Bands.

We will also initiate discussion groups on a variety of topics from Unemployment to feminism and Workshops on Creative Writing, Music, Politics, Theatre, The Arts, Photography and Graphic Design, to name but a few.

We would point out to the Council that other Metropolitan Authorities in London, Bristol and Cardiff have granted licenses and leases to projects of a similar nature to our own.

We urge the Council to acknowledge our sincerity and the value of this unpaid service to the Bradford Community and we ask them not to seek an unnecessary dispute with us.

The Free Space Collective.

Free Space communique sent to Bradford Council

PEOPLE'S SQUAT FOR LIFE

In early March, a bunch of 1 In 12 members autonomously decided to squat the ex-Ukrainian Social Club on Claremont, a one-way street off Great Horton Road just opposite the university. Although the building was only occupied for around two weeks before the squatters were evicted, they still managed to hold a free gig on Friday, March 2, with The Negativz, Vegetable Section and Dirk Spig in the large staged concert area at the back of the building.

CHAPTER 6 - INDIE ALTERNATIVE ROCK — 1984 - 1986

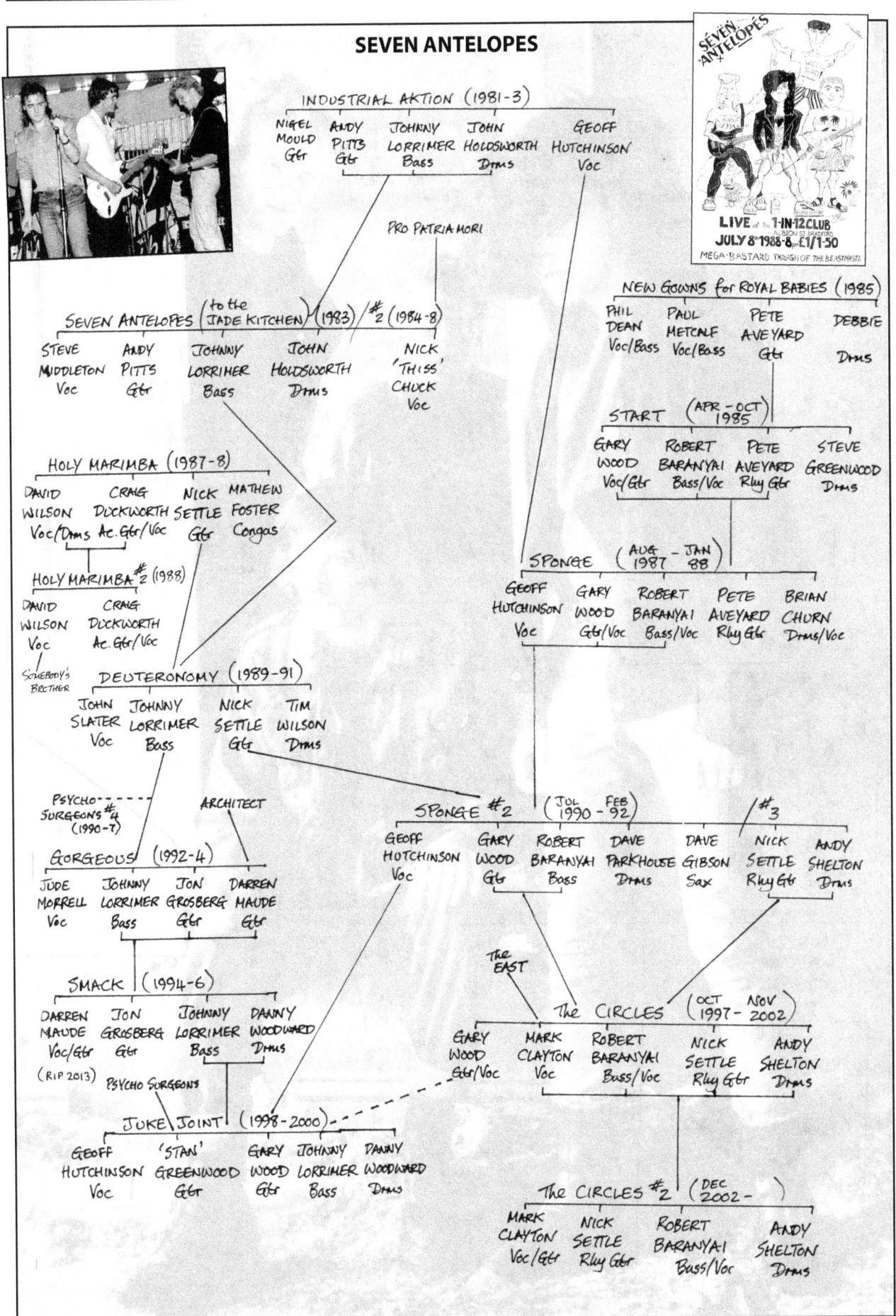

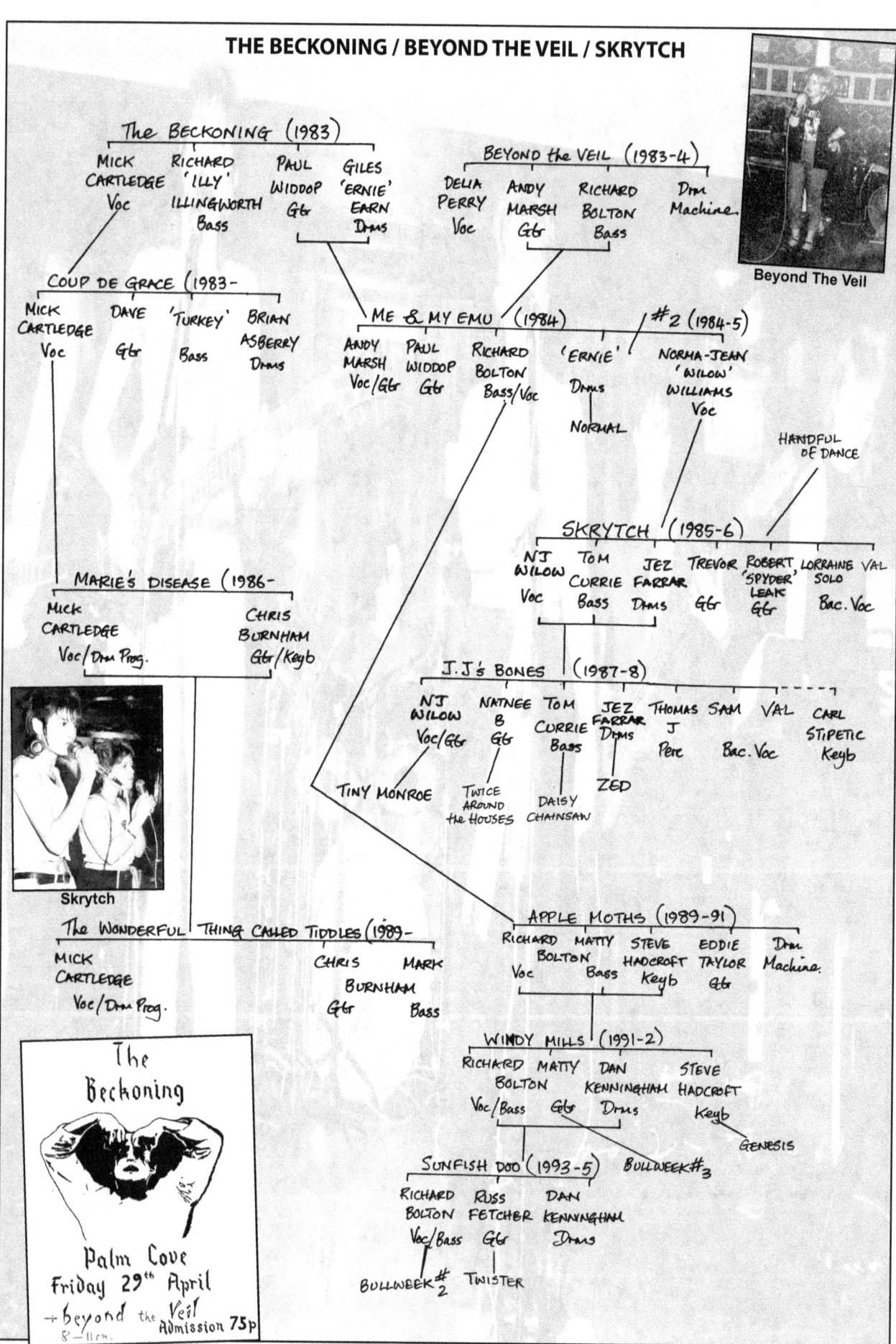

Other bank doors were super-glued and a Securicor van escaped being overturned because it was found to be too heavy before the protestors regrouped in the central city area. The protestors then repeatedly broke out to cause yet more confusion to the police and authorities. The day ended with a clear tactical victory for the anti-capitalist protestors.

Returning to Bradford exhausted but elated in the early hours of the following morning after a midnight drive up the motorway, the 1 In 12 Club demonstrators had only had one member arrested for obstruction who was later released without charge.

STOP THE CITY II

The second *Stop The City* demo was an early anti-capitalist, anti-globalisation protest aimed at shutting down and disturbing the workings of the money markets in the City of London's banking sector which took place on March 29, 1984. A transit van full of 1 In 12 activists travelled down to London to take part.

The day turned out to be more successful than the previous year's demo as over one and a half thousand people attended, causing mayhem for the police with impromptu theatre acts, carnival jugglers and mass breakouts of the heavily policed central area.

On one such breakout, hundreds of peaceful protestors chased down Aldgate, with red and black anarchist flags flying and smoke bombs drifting in the air, to smash forty plate glass windows, causing damage estimated at £10,000. Those banks attacked included Barclays, who funded and supported South Africa's apartheid regime at the time.

A SUITED City gent lectures a group of punks who were part of a demo in the City of London today.

Punks in City demo

PUNKS, anarchists, nuclear disarmers, vegetarians and anti-vivisectionists converged on the City today in a bid to halt the capital's business life.

Police were out in force as fluorescent pink hair styles mingled with the pin-stripes. Several people were arrested at the 'Stop The City' demo, chiefly against the arms trade.

Many of the demonstrators were searched by police who kept the groups moving on.

THE 1 IN 12 CLUB

Between 1981-87, The 1 In 12 Club emerged as the premiere organisation promoting regular weekly punk/new wave/alternative gigs in Bradford.

Originally starting at the Metropole on Grattan Road in April 1981, then moving around town to Tickles, Market Tavern, Queen's Hall, Royal Standard before ending back at the Metropole. The 1 In 12 Club in this period organised over 300 gigs including three outdoor free festivals and over a dozen benefit gigs for various causes. The Club gained a reputation for 'straight-dealing with a no hassle policy' that endeared it to the many local and national bands on the music scene, despite being seen as a threat to the existing local political elites because the club promoted libertarian ideas. (2)

1 IN 12 CLUB GIGS

After The 1 In 12 Club moved from the Market Tavern to the Queen's Hall, where it was based from October 1985 until August 1986, it relocated briefly to the Royal Standard on Mannigham Lane from September to November 1986.

It then returned to its original venue, the Metropole Hotel, for the rest of its 'nomad' existence, where it stayed throughout 1987 and up to the opening of its permanent home on Albion Street.

THE MARKET TAVERN

JANUARY 1984
4 - Ministry Of Fear / Vegetable Section
11 - The Mighty Clifton Brothers / The Pranksters
18 - IK / Wild Willi Beckett

FEBRUARY 1984
1 - Somebody's Brother / Screaming Jellyfish
8 - Those Frayed Edges / Pariah
15 - Party Dress / Al Beach / Graham McAndrew
22 - The Word / Boys From The East
29 - Little Germany / Outrage

MARCH 1984
7 - Near Legendary / Blind Eye / Absolute Beginners
14 - Marc Riley & The Creepers / Implied Consent
21 - The Three Johns / The Membranes
28 - Household Name / Indiscriminate Hoax Fund

APRIL 1984
4 - Chinese Gangster Element / Gross National Product
8 Third Anniversary - Party Day / The Three Johns / The She-Hee's / Dirk Spig / Pariah / Wild Willi Beckett / Requiem / Morbid Humour / Screaming Jellyfish
11 - The Crypt / Cynical Few
18 - Chronic / Legion
25 - Grrr / The Mighty Clifton Brothers

1 IN 12 CLUB GIGS AT THE MARKET TAVERN

MAY 1984
2 - 13 Horses Legs / Victor Matures
9 - Me And My Emu / Anarchist Kitchen
16 - The Lively Arts / Syberian Run
23 - Bak-Lash / Mass Of Black
30 - Requiem / The Cynical Few

JUNE 1984
6 - The She-Hees
8 Miners Benefit at Checkpoint - The Word / Morbid Humour / Spectre
11 Rape Crisis Benefit at Checkpoint - Toxic Shock / Indiscriminate Hoax Jun Fund / Passion Killers
13 - Burial / Nerve Agents / Ginger John
19 - Dik Dik Diamorphic / Single File
21 - Mau Maus / Morbid Humour / Silent Community
2? - Toxic Reasons / iconaclast
26 - Spectre

JULY 1984
3 - Matamba / Bok Bok
5 - Seven Antelopes
10 - The Chorus / Seething Wells
12 - The Membranes / The Men From The Mountains
17 - Five Go Down To The Sea / Little Brother
19 - Skeletal Family / Flowers In The Dustbin
24 - The Three Johns / Dr & The Inmates
26 - Sense / August Assembly

NOT THE INTERNATIONAL GARDEN FESTIVAL
Bradford University Amphitheatre
28 - The Convulsions / Matamba / Chronic / The Word / Morbid Humour / Little Brother / The She-Hees / Wild Willi Beckett / Chumbawamba / Dirk Spig / Little Germany

31 - The Instigators / The Convulsions / The Subvertives / Stagnant Era

AUGUST 1984
2 - A Witness
7 - Surfin' Dave
9 - The Prowlers
14 - Pagan Idols

16 - Screaming Jellyfish
21 - Indiscriminate Hoax Fund / When It's Hot
23 - Accident / Little Germany / Civilised Society
24 Hindles Dispute Benefit at Checkpoint
- Johnny Jumps The Bandwagon / The Nerve Agents
28 - Citron Girls / The Syndicate

SEPTEMBER 1984
4 - The Cassandra Complex / The Hallion Battalion / Son Of Sam
6 - The Word / 13 Horses Legs
11 - Big Flame / Passion Day
13 - The Edge / Freezone / Photomontage
18 - Chronic / The Mighty Strangers
20 - Chat Show / Paul Dunbar / Bogshead
25 - Tools You Can Trust / Passmore Sisters
27 - The Blood Brothers / Richard Rouska
29 - Matamba / Chronic / Boys From The East

OCTOBER 1984
2 - Violent Carsons / Steel Prism
4 - The Nerve Agents / Yeah Yeah Noh
9 - The Inca Babies / The First International
11 - The Vanishing Point / The Living Daylights
16 - Mass Of Black / Rejuvenation
18 - Omega Tribe / Chumbawamba / Grout
23 - Morbid Humour / Category A
25 - Spectre
30 - One Thousand Violins / AIM

NOVEMBER 1984
1 - Jazz Hipsters / God Dog
5 at Checkpoint - Poison Girls / The Three Johns
6 - Chicken Ranch / Dik Dik Diamorphic
8 - Burial / The Clues
13 - The In - Stinks / The Vibes
15 - The Bomb Party / The Heads
20 - Near Legendary Blind Eye / The Sinister Cleaners
22 - Citron Girls / Dig Vs Drill
27 - Rubella Ballet
29 - Leitmotiv / Richard Rouska / Dirk Spig

1 IN 12 CLUB GIGS AT THE MARKET TAVERN

DECEMBER 1984
1 at Checkpoint - The Three Johns / The Mekons / Big Flame
4 - Post Mottem / Pagan Idols
6 - The Linkmen / Domestic Enemies
11 - Persion Version / The Massacars
13 - My Perriot Dolls / Delicious Poison
15 at Checkpoint - The Word / Vegetable Section / Jazz Hipsters / Edwards Voice
18 - Doctor & The Inmates / Sam The Juggler
20 - The First International / Seven Antelopes

JANUARY 1985
1 - Chinese Gangster Element / The Shee-Hees
3 - Vegatable Section / Legion
8 - ICI / Nick Toczek / Mad Macca
10 - Toxic Shock - No! Puppies
15 - The Three Johns / A Witness
17 - Pulp / The Hubcapstealers
22 - Free State / The Chorus
24 - Flesh Puppets / Silent Community / Retaliate
30 - The Men From The Mountains / Tin God Trap

FEBRUARY 1984
6 - Five Go Down To The Sea / Bogshed
13 - Dorian Grey / The Vox
20 - Marc Riley & The Creepers / Kiss The Blade
27 - Tools You Can Trust / Flowers Of Evil

MARCH 1985
6 - Age of Chance / Silent Ambition
9 - Vegetable Section / Olulu Olulu / Swamp Flower
13 - Ik / Giant Treads Clean / Wild Willi Beckett
16 at Checkpoint - Mau Maus / Spectre / Dave Douglas
20 - Olulu Olulu / Tree House
27 - Party Day / Surreal Estate

APRIL 1985
3 - Bomb Party / Yeah Yeah Noh
10 - The Xpozez / The Instigators
17 - Vandels In Africa / Children Of A Lesser God

April 24 Anti-Fascist Defence Benefit at Queen's Hall - The Three Johns / Boys From The East / Little Brother

MAY 1985
1 - Implied Consent / Son Of Sam
8 - Anabas / The Rub
15 - I'll Show Harry / Dirk Spig / All Over The Carpet
29 - The Membranes / Butter Cookies
31 Fourth Anniversay at Checkpoint - When It's Hot

JUNE 1985
5 - Akimbo
13 Bradford City Fire Disaster Benefit at Queen's Hall - Icicle Works / The Word / Spectre / Doctor & The Inmates
19 - Rubella Ballet / Seven Antelopes
26 - Big Flame / Domestic Enemies

JULY 1985
3 - The 1 In 12 Cowboys / The Self Righteous Brothers / Wild Willi Beckett

AUGUST 1985
23 Anti-fascist Defence Benefit at Checkpoint - Doctor & The Inmates / Men From The Mountains

OCTOBER 1985
4 Benefit at Checkpoint - Eton Crop / The Best Way To Walk

THE 1 IN 12 CLUB AT QUEEN'S HALL

23 - The Inca Babies / The Wedding Present
30 - The Passmore Sisters / Ritzun, Ratzun, Rotzun

NOVEMBER 1985
6 - The Sinister Cleaners
13 - 3-Action / Pleasure Garden
20 - The Ex / First International
27 - Vee VV / Little Richards

DECEMBER 1985
11 - Anti-System / Category A
18 - Ausgang / Urban Desolation

1 IN 12 CLUB GIGS AT QUEEN'S HALL

JANUARY 1986
8 - Communal Drop / Hang The Dance
15 - Mr Morality / Pulp / Dig Vis Drill
22 - Party Day / Chinese Gangster Element
29 - Joici Causa / Hang The Dance

FEBRUARY 1986
6 - The Best Way To Walk / Another Cuba
13 - The Loudest Shout / Living With The Gun / Max Betamax
20 - The Napalm Stars / Nothing Before
27 - Red Lorry, Yellow Lorry / Lifting The Veil / Seven Antelopes

MARCH 1986
4 - APB / The Coloured Pencils
20 - Boys From The East / Seething Wells
27 - AC Temple / Maries Disease

APRIL 1986
2 - Joolz / Jean Gittens / Slade The Leveller / Hammer And Sickle / Wild Willi Beckett
3 - Spectre / Natural Riddim
5 - Desmond Down (Rock Opera) / Ritzun, Ratzun, Rotzun / Sweet Valentine Cowboys / Zip Gunn & The Bayou Bigshots
10 - The Wedding Present / Little Brother / Third Circle
17 - Psycho Surgeons / Swift Nick / Vicious Circle

MAY 1986
1 - First International / Pete The Poet / Autonomy
8 - The Second Coming / Mark Jackson & The Swinging Lovers
15 - Blythe Power / Das Tor Zu Der Wett
22 - Skeletal Family / Sinister Cleaners
29 - Midnight Choir / 3-Action

JUNE 1986
5 - The Walking Seeds / The Right Stuff
12 - Seven Antelopes / Civilised Society / Autonomy
19 - Age Of Chance / Dorothy's Cottage
26 - The Passmore Sisters / Giant Treads Clean

JULY 1986
3 - Cassandra Complex / Leon Nightmare
10 - Dig Vis Drill / Screaming Trees / Henry Normal
17 - Johnny Jumps The Bandwagon / The Wild Dogs
24 - Skidmarks / Wild Willi Beckett
31 - Another Cuba / Dust Devils

AUGUST 1986
1 PA Benefit at Checkpoint - The Word / The Best Way To Walk
7 - The Beat Of The Beast / The Jackals
21 - Conspiracy / Das Tor
28 - Chumbawamba / Peudo / Celtic Folk

THE 1 IN 12 CLUB AT THE ROYAL STANDARD

SEPTEMBER 1986
11 - Western Dance / Out Of The Blue
18 - Bleeding Hearts / Original Sin / Pete The Poet
25 - Happy Content / The Little Richards

OCTOBER 1986
2 - Happiness AD / Pete The Poet
9 - Mr Morality / Lay Of The Land
16 - Akimbo
23 - The Monkey Run / Sense Of Purpose
30 - Half-Crazed Mess / The Food Scientists

NOVEMBER 1986
6 - Civilised Society / Boilerhouse
13 - Sinister Cleaners / Big Red Gunn
20 - Out Of The Blue / Lifting The Veil

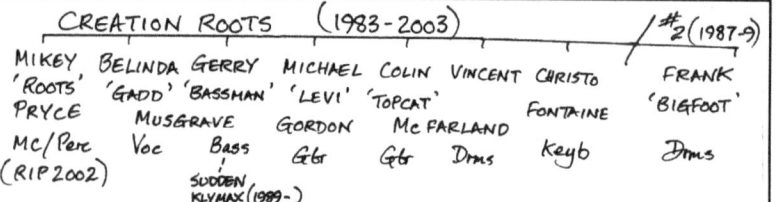

Estate raised artist at Scholemoor Cemetery. The band decided to call it a day soon after, although some members, like Bassman Gerry, continued with a solo career.

The MAPA Centre produced the *Rasta Struggle* magazine in the 1980s.

CREATION ROOTS

Creation Roots were Bradford's premier Rasta reggae band. Formed in 1983, they used the MAPA Centre in West Bowling as their base. During the band's twenty-year career, they gained respect all over the UK for their live shows and charity gigs which included supporting the cream of the UK and Jamaican reggae bands, including Aswad, Black Slate and Barrington Levy.

The band's first single *Selassie I Lives*, was released on the independent Quatro World Music label in 1989 and received a rave review in Black Echoes magazine. Their next release was the EP *Girls / Pye Pye Lovin'* which they put out on their own Graphics label in 1992. These tracks were very popular in their live set. The band's only LP, *Troddin'*, was produced by Mad Professor and released in 1999; again on their own Graphics label. The album highlighted the band's musicianship with a mixture of roots tunes and drum 'n' bass tracks.

When the band's MC Mikey Roots (Michael Pryce) tragically died aged only 33 in March 2002, hundreds of mourners attended the Egyptian-style ceremony for the Jamaican-born and Canterbury

THE ROOTSMAN

After settling in Bradford in 1983 John Bolloten immersed himself in the local reggae scene. He worked for over two years at Roots record shop on Lumb Lane where he became known as Rootsman. As a DJ he had been doing sound systems since 1985 then founded his extremely successful club nigh *Dub Me Crazy* in 1991.

Rootsman's debut 10-inch white label EP *Koyaanisqati* was released in May 1994 on the Soundclash label to critical acclaim in the music press and has gone on to become very collectable. After another highly rated EP, *Soundclash City Rockers*, he left to continue his career on his own Third Eye Music label.

Also around on the black music scene in the 1980s were B Bop Promotions, based at the Checkpoint nightclub, who organised jazz and fusion gigs for acts including local jazz funk band Osiris.

In 1984 ten young men aged between fourteen and twenty from Bradford, Keighley and Leeds formed the break-dance troupe Solar City Rockers.

In 1985 the prominent and hard gigging band Jab Jab released their second single *Keep On Smiling* on their own Rip Off label distributed by York's Red Rhino. The reggae band was from Huddersfield, Leeds and Bradford and had been around in various forms since 1972.

CHAPTER 6 - INDIE ALTERNATIVE ROCK — 1984 - 1986

THIRD ANNIVERSARY OF THE 1 IN 12 CLUB

On Sunday, April 8, The 1 In 12 Club celebrated its third anniversary with an all-day lock-in at The Market Tavern. Local bands Screaming Jellyfish, Morbid Humour, Requiem, and Pariah, plus poets Wild Willi Beckett and Dirk Spig, entertained a

The Three Johns at The Market Tavern

packed house between 1 pm and 7 pm. Due to the Sunday licensing laws landlords Tim and Pete were not legally allowed to serve alcohol but with everyone locked in they continued the afternoon's refreshments uninterrupted. Leeds bands The She-Hees and The Three Johns provided the evening's entertainment before Barnsley band Party Day finished off a brilliant day's celebration. (3)

During the next couple of months two more international bands played at the club. The first was a band called GRRR from Holland (friends of previous Club giggers The Ex) on April 25, and then in June Toxic

Reasons from San Francisco became the first US band to perform there.

As the demand to play at the 1 In 12 increased, and demo tapes from all over the country arrived each week, the Club began to put on gigs twice a week, on Tuesday and Thursday nights, from the beginning of June 1984, in an attempt to live up to the policy of trying to give every artist who applied a chance to perform at least once.

One of the limitations of the Market Tavern as a venue for The 1 In 12 Club was the amount of money that could be raised purely from their percentage of the door take (with seventy-five percent going to the bands), as the club

had no income from the bar takings. To expand, the Club needed control over a venue of its own, to be able to use all the skills of members in organising events and to be a focal point for people to develop ideas and initiatives that reflected all the members' needs and aspirations.

At a Sunday meeting in mid-1984, the Club decided to apply through the local Council's Policy Unit for a one-off capital (only) grant from the Department of the Environment to purchase a building. The Club believed that they had already established that there was a need for the existence of such a venue as no venue in Bradford catered for the particular section of the community (i.e. mainly the unemployed music fans) that the 1 In 12 encompassed.

After a lot of hard preparation work an application for a total of just under £64,000 to obtain a permanent building in which the Club could carry on and expand their activities was sent in before the September expiry date. Now all The 1 In 12 Club had to do was wait and hope. (3)

THE MINERS' STRIKE

By the time the 1 In 12 organised its first (official) miners' benefit in June the strike had already been going for four months.

The Miners' Union (NUM) had called a national strike in early March 1984, after rejecting the final offer of the National Coal Board (NCB) on its proposed programme of pit closures.

Between 1974 and 1984 the mining industry had been reduced from a workforce of 250,000 and 259 pits to 181,000 and 174 pits and any more pit closures would further decimate the mining communities. As the strike progressed the miners' mass pickets of the pit-heads also led to the picketing of the coking depots where massive stockpiles were held for the power stations.

On the 8th June a nation watched TV images of one depot picket and the resulting footage of police baton and mounted horse charges into groups of defenceless miners became known as the *Battle Of Orgreave*. As with virtually all the general media coverage during the strike, the commentary had a distorted bias against the miners. The strikers were portrayed as the 'enemy within' by Prime Minister Margaret Thatcher and the media followed the government's line. (5)

Many mining communities experienced a prolonged heavy police presence, 'big brother' type surveillance, intimidation and brutality.

From the start of the strike the miners' wives formed local support groups in order to organise food distribution, and started communal community kitchens in all mining areas, especially the solid Yorkshire coalfield. This helped to alleviate some

of the striking families' dire hardship as most of them received no support from the DHSS. These previously un-political women showed remarkable practical solidarity with their husbands and families, helping to keep the fight alive and determined not to be starved back to work. (6)

At the beginning of the strike in March The 1 In 12 Club, like the majority of trade unionists, left-wing activists, and thousands of ordinary people, quickly showed support to the beleaguered

miners. The club made every gig a kind of benefit for the miners, with collections of money and food, and most bands even waived payment. (7)

The club also organised a series of miners' benefits at the Checkpoint nightclub. The first featured The Word, Morbid Humour and Spectre, the second featured The Three Johns, The Mekons and Big Flame on the 1st December, and the third was on the

16th March 1985 and featured Sheffield's The Mau Mau's, Spectre (again), Rudy the Punk Poet and an informative talk about the strike from NUM official Dave Douglas of Hatfield Main Pit. Money raised from these benefits and collections was taken by club members to miners' social clubs where support groups were based. (8)

Despite international support, with food parcels donated to the miners from Italy, Poland, Russia and elsewhere, the continuity of the strike was threatened by the government's sequestering of the NUM's funds. The slow return to work of 'scab' miners who were encouraged to break the solidarity by crossing the picket lines and the forming of the Midlands breakaway 'free' (sic) unions went a long way to undermining the strike.

In the early months of 1985, as the strike solidarity waived and the miners needed support at certain pits, some 1 In 12 members joined picket lines but only when they were asked to by the pickets themselves.

In the end, despite national support from all sections of society, the strike ended after over a year of struggle. Thatcher's Tory government finally got their revenge for the humiliation of the miners' strikes of the 1970s and finally broke the strength of the unions in what was the last great union struggle in the UK.

CHAPTER 6 - INDIE ALTERNATIVE ROCK
1984 - 1986

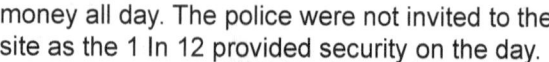

NOT THE INTERNATIONAL GARDEN FESTIVAL

For the third year running, The 1 In 12 Club and BCAU staged a free festival at the university's natural amphitheatre behind the Communal Building.

The 1984 event, which took place on Saturday, July 28, was entitled *Not The International Garden Festival*.

This particular year, due to the ongoing miners' struggle, the festival became an all-day benefit for the strikers. A TUC sponsored march and rally for the miners was held on the same day in Bradford city centre but the local council banned any street collections. After the rally, the miners and their families were invited to the festival, where collection buckets raised money all day. The police were not invited to the site as the 1 In 12 provided security on the day.

The afternoon's entertainment was provided by Bradford bands The Convulsions, Morbid Humour, Chronic, Little Germany and The Word, with Leeds bands Chumbawamba, The She-Hees and reggae group Matamba. Local ranters Wild Willi Beckett, Little Brother and Dirk Spig did support slots and compered the event.

Morbid Humour

Matamba

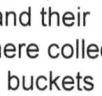

Wild Willi Beckett

Another great day was had by all with local band The Convulsions finishing off the day with a storming set of their punk rock tunes.

A couple of incidents slightly marred the festival atmosphere; once when a knife was drawn in the audience and later some teenage punks were hassled around the bouncy castle area, but this was untypical of all three of the 1 In 12 outdoor festivals, of which this was the last.

These events were a celebration of local music and were enjoyed by a diverse range of people who watched live music in the sunshine. They paved the way for the International *Festival Of Youth* which continued the open-air concert theme in Lister Park the following year.

RUNNING ORDER

- 12pm LITTLE GERMANY
- 1 CHUMBAWUMBA
- 2 SHE-HE'S
- 3 MORBID HUMOUR
- 4 THE WORD
- 5 CHRONIC
- 6 COPTIC ROOTS
- 7 CONVULSIONS

MUSIC STARTS 11 a.m.
OFF STAGE ENTS & STALLS

(this was decided by drawing names from a hat.)

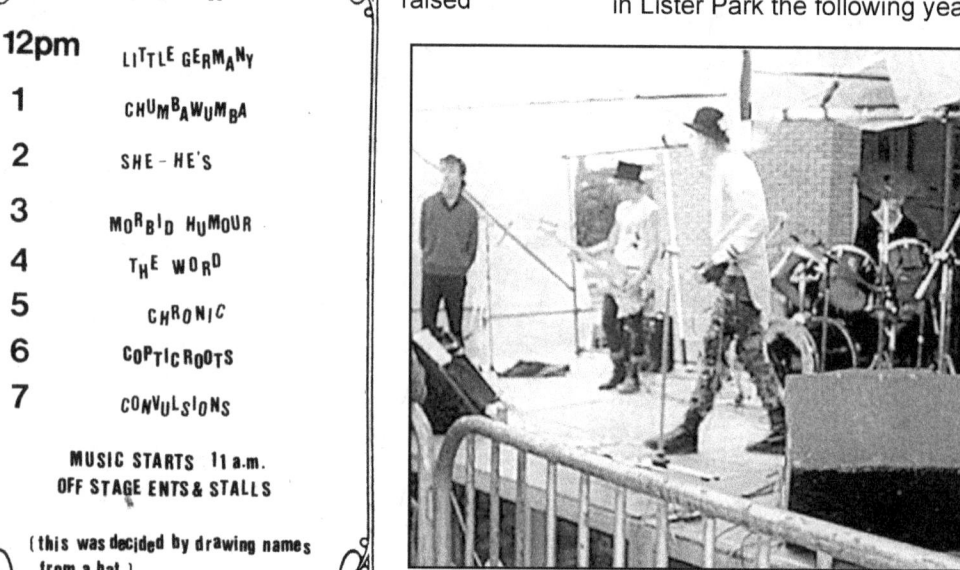

The Convulsions close the 1 In 12 Club's third outdoor festival

CHAPTER 6 - INDIE ALTERNATIVE ROCK   1984 - 1986

ENEMIES OF THE STATE

In July, the 1 In 12 Record Collective continued to document the musical diversity of bands that had played at the club by releasing their first vinyl LP, *Enemies Of The State – The Worst Of The 1 In 12 Club Volume 3*.

It contained fifteen bands/artists who contributed a track each and was mastered (cut onto metal for pressing) in London at George Peckham's famous Porky's Studios. Only a thousand copies were pressed and the album was nationally distributed by Backs Records of Norwich.

The record sleeves were done by a local Bradford firm to designs by 1 In 12 members Martin and Fritz. The back cover featured a Fritz the Cat picture of a derelict terrace street with numerous response from the T&A's new *Rock On* columnist Gill Gosling and a good review by Seething 'Susan Williams' Wells in the NME and another from Peace News.

John Peel had been a keen supporter of Bradford bands since the late 1960s due to his wife's family living in Shipley. A copy of the LP was sent to his home address so he could listen to it before his Monday night BBC radio programme. On the Monday night he played two tracks, *Eldridge* by the Leeds band The Mighty Clifton Brothers and *Boy's Choir* by The Word.

In the forthcoming nights and weeks he played several other tracks from the album. *The World's On Fire* by Halifax's Chinese Gangster Element impressed John Peel enough to give the band a Peel Session. Of the group he said '*...probably my favourite track, rather wonderful I think. Any record with talking in it like that is ok with me.*' (8)

DEAD GOOD DISC!

VARIOUS ARTISTS
Enemies Of The State *(1 in 12 Records)*

YEA, THOUGH I prance through the valley of the downturn I shall not aspire to catholic tastes. Fear not, woolly ones, I shall not lead you astray. Believe me when I say that this record is really rather good.

Dog's droppings first in the shape of Dirk Spig's appallingly un-original 'The Russians Are Coming' which reminds one of nothing so much as Atilla the Stockbroker in a sensory deprivation chamber – yes, *that* bad! Household Name's toytown white funk 'The Race Is On': Jesus – they make even New Order (spit spit) sound good. Play that plastic muzak white boy.

Great gleaming dollops of gold! Especially Chinese Gangster Element's 'The World On Fire' which is a 100% bona fide punk crassic. Garagegarage go the guitars Tinkletinkle go the voices. Epic! Mega! Quite nice! goes the hack. The Word are the best 'pop' band not only in Bradford but in all of Christendom. If Nick Heyward and Elvis Costello had been members of the original Gang Of Four then they would have given their back teeth, their right arms and their entire cnsp-packet collections to write a song that was worthy enough to sniff the pert bottom of 'Boy's Choir'.

Chronic, as their name suggests, were once an awesomely dire glue-head thrash machine. 'Who Cares' possesses a staggered inter-melodic rhapsody of chimes and non-buckshee bansheeist grunting that'll stick in your powdered, empty heads for hours. From the mouths of cak-merchants shall a mighty roaring grow.

The Three Johns! The Ex! Eton Crop! Surfing Dave and the B'nee Teas! K-Tel eat your heart out!

— Susan Woolyams

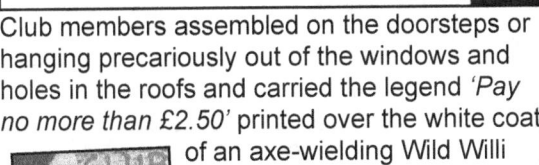

```
                    Enemies Of The State
                    (Worst Of The 1 in 12 Club Vol.3) £2.50

                    Vols.1 & 2 were on cassette format only.
                    Vol.3 however, is a vinyl platter. The
                    tracks vary in style from the typically
                    N. England dirge-riff masterpieces of
The Mighty Clifton Brothers (now The First International),
and Requiem,.....to the dream-machine neo-Gang Of Human
League Household Name. The 'rants' of Wild Willi Beckett &
Dirk Spig lack any poetic quality, unpretentiously forcing
home their political points point-blank. Others featured
include the ubiquitous 3 Johns(unfortunately not a very good
track), Surfin' Dave (5 stars for his contribution), Sweet
Life, Chinese Gangster Element, The Word, Chronic, Seven
Antelopes, & The Convulsions (all from Leeds/Bradford)......
plus a track each from Dutch bands Eton Crop & The Ex who
are windmill-buddies of the 3Js. An excellent record &
completely indispensible for anyone who claims to be
seriously into the local scene. Your copy is gettable from:
c/o 127 Thornton Rd., Bradford 1, or by ordering at your
local record shop(from Red Rhino/The Cartel).        Roar 12
```

Club members assembled on the doorsteps or hanging precariously out of the windows and holes in the roofs and carried the legend *'Pay no more than £2.50'* printed over the white coat of an axe-wielding Wild Willi Beckett.

The album received a positive

HEAVY METAL ROCK 2

Heavy Rock had always been a big part of the Bradford music scene and never went away, despite the influx of the punk/post-punk scene.

After the Princeville Rock Club stopped flying the flag for rockers in 1982, other local promoters carried on the tradition. One was Ronnie Corboz. HE began organising gigs on Friday nights, first from the George Hotel in Girlington, then at The Melborn on White Abbey Road, and gigs at The Wheatsheaf on Little Horton Lane from 1983 to 1985.

In 1984, Ronnie also staged shows on Friday nights at Thornton WMC where, in the first months, Siren, Tush and Chainsaw all played. In June, one memorable gig featured Northern Dancer (with Pauline Gillan, sister of ex-Deep Purple singer Ian, on vocals) and local support from Cheyenne.

This healthy local scene soon inspired a resurgence of spirit. The burgeoning NWOBHM scene led to the formation of a new generation of young Bradford-based bands.

EXCALIBUR

Formed initially in 1981 as a school band, Excalibur only really started playing live in early 1983. They mainly performed at youth clubs but also played the odd working men's club gig if it came their way.

The band released the three-track cassette demo tape, *Back Before Dawn*, in 1984.

In 1985, with a new drummer on board and finally having left school, the lads managed to get a deal with Conquest Records and released a six-track mini-LP called *The Bitter End*.

It received much

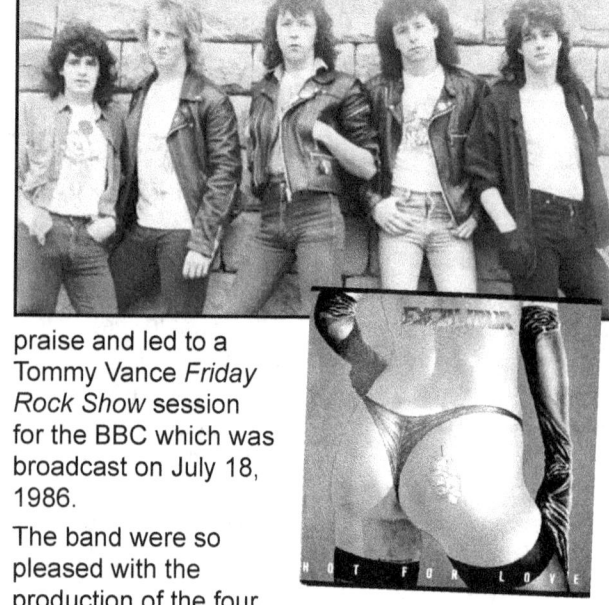

praise and led to a Tommy Vance *Friday Rock Show* session for the BBC which was broadcast on July 18, 1986.

The band were so pleased with the production of the four tracks recorded at the session by ex-Mott The Hoople drummer Dale Griffin that they organised a licensing deal with the BBC. The resulting 12" EP, entitled *Hot For Love*, came out later on the Clay Records label in 1988.

In 1989, after replacing original bassist Martin Hawthorn, Excalibur signed to Active Records.

They recorded their only full LP *One Strange Night* for the

label in 1990. The album sold very well and a series of headlining gigs as well as a support slot on Saxon's UK tour followed.

The single *Carloe Ann* was released from the LP.

The band were finally torn apart by defections in 1992 but remained on good enough terms to do a farewell tour. Their last show was at the Rio, Bradford, on June 13, 1992.

In 2021, an expanded version of *The Bitter End* appeared on No Remorse Records, adding four demo tracks.

CHAPTER 6 - INDIE ALTERNATIVE ROCK   1984 - 1986

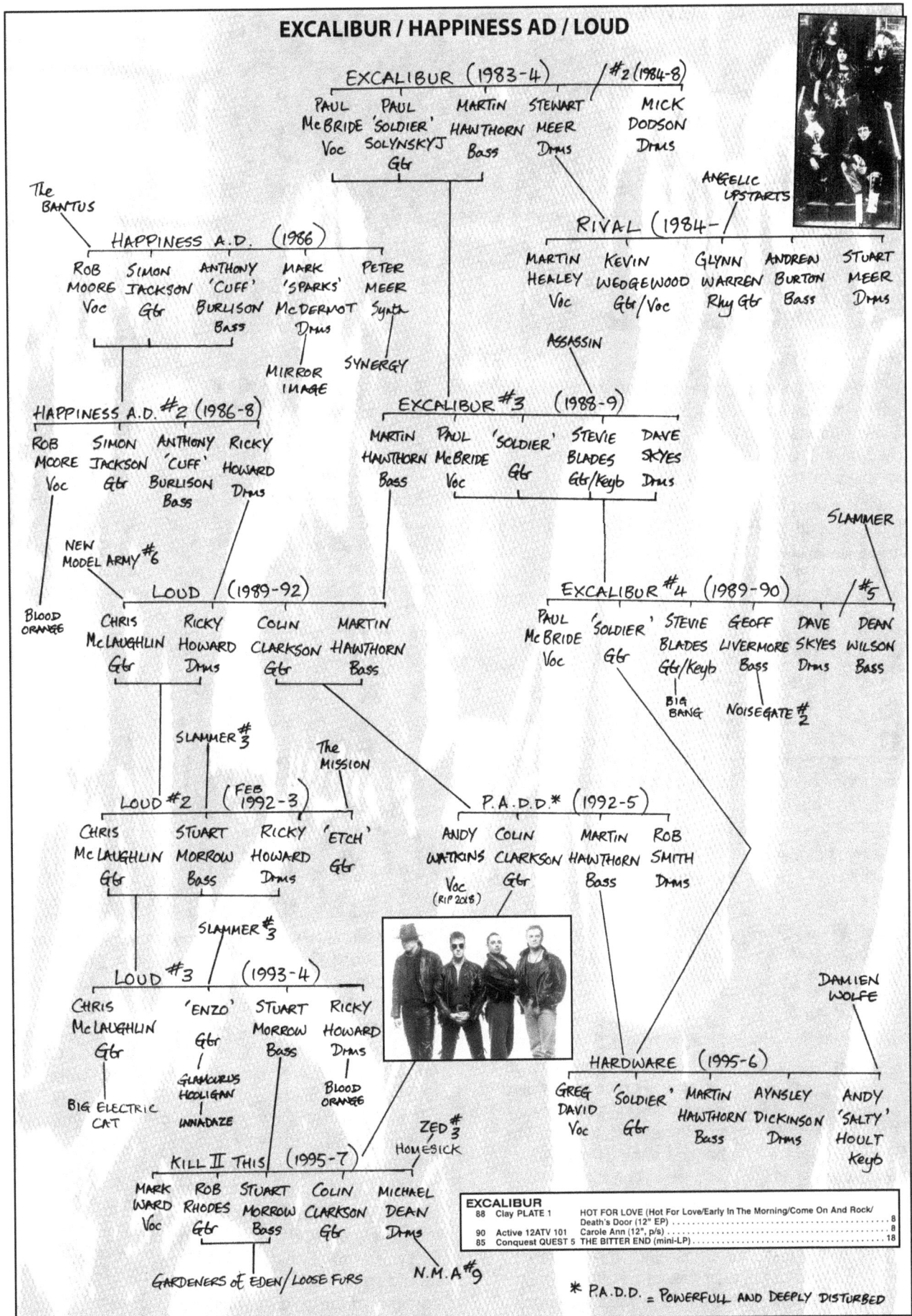

EXCALIBUR / HAPPINESS AD / LOUD

HARLEQUYN

When local band Bobo's vocalist Vic Wright left to join Salisbury based band Tokyo Blade guitarist, Tim Walker joined forces with members of Glass Opera to form the glam rock influenced band Harlequyn in 1984.

Over the next few years the band impressed local rock fans with their over the top stage show. In 1985 they came second to Boys From The East in a local *Battle Of The Bands* competition.

When manager Andy Farrow (ex-Living Dead vocalist) took an office in the Flexible Response building for his Starlight Music Agency in 1986 the band took over the running of the rehearsal facilities there and also ran a rudimentary 4-track studio, expanding it to the 8 track Crystal Cave in 1988.

Their first single *Burn / Experience Revolver* was the only release on Starlight Records and sold well at their gigs.

Andy Farrow's Far North Music (now Northern Music) released a four band, 7 inch compilation EP entitled *Thwak!* (FNR01) in 1988. It featured Harlequyn and other Far North handled bands Scarehunters, Boolean Matrix and The One Eyed Jacks. The bands on the EP played a showcase gig at the Marquee in London.

Harleqyn played a further three London gigs at Dingwalls.

After Flexible Response closed in 1989, guitarist Tim 'Titus' Walker and singer Paul Mother set up their own recording studio and rehearsal rooms, originally named Revolver, at Theatre Royal Workshops, just off Manningham Lane, parallel to the newly built road Hamm Strasse.

They recorded and released the LP *The Order Of The Golden Dawn* on their Voltage Records label in 1989. It received good reviews in *Kerrang!*, *Metal Forces*, and *Sounds*. The album tour included dates with Zodiac Mindwarp, Uriah Heep, Ghost Dance, Skeletal Family and Tygers Of Pan Tang.

In 1990 they re-formed as the group Architect under which guise they released the 12 inch EP *More Than Before* (VEP93) in 1991, and the LP *Poets & Thieves* (VCD127) in 1992 which got a good review in *Q Magazine* and the tour to promote the album included dates with Big Country, Dr & The Medics and Catherine Wheel.

In 1993 singer Paul Mother recorded *Bolanesque*, a CD EP of T-Rex cover versions, while Tim still runs Voltage Studios/Records which moved to St Stephens Mill, Ripley Street, Bradford, in 2004, and has over the years played host to many established artists and record labels, including Paradise Lost (Music For Nations), his own band Worm (Voltage), Loud (China), Slammer (WEA), My Dying Bride (Peaceville), The Downfall (Voltage) and members of Killing Joke, Terrorvision, Feeder, Skunk Anansie and others.

Harlequyn reunited in 2007 for a show at Bradford's Gasworks and began recording an album of new versions of their old material.

CHAPTER 6 - INDIE ALTERNATIVE ROCK 1984 - 1986

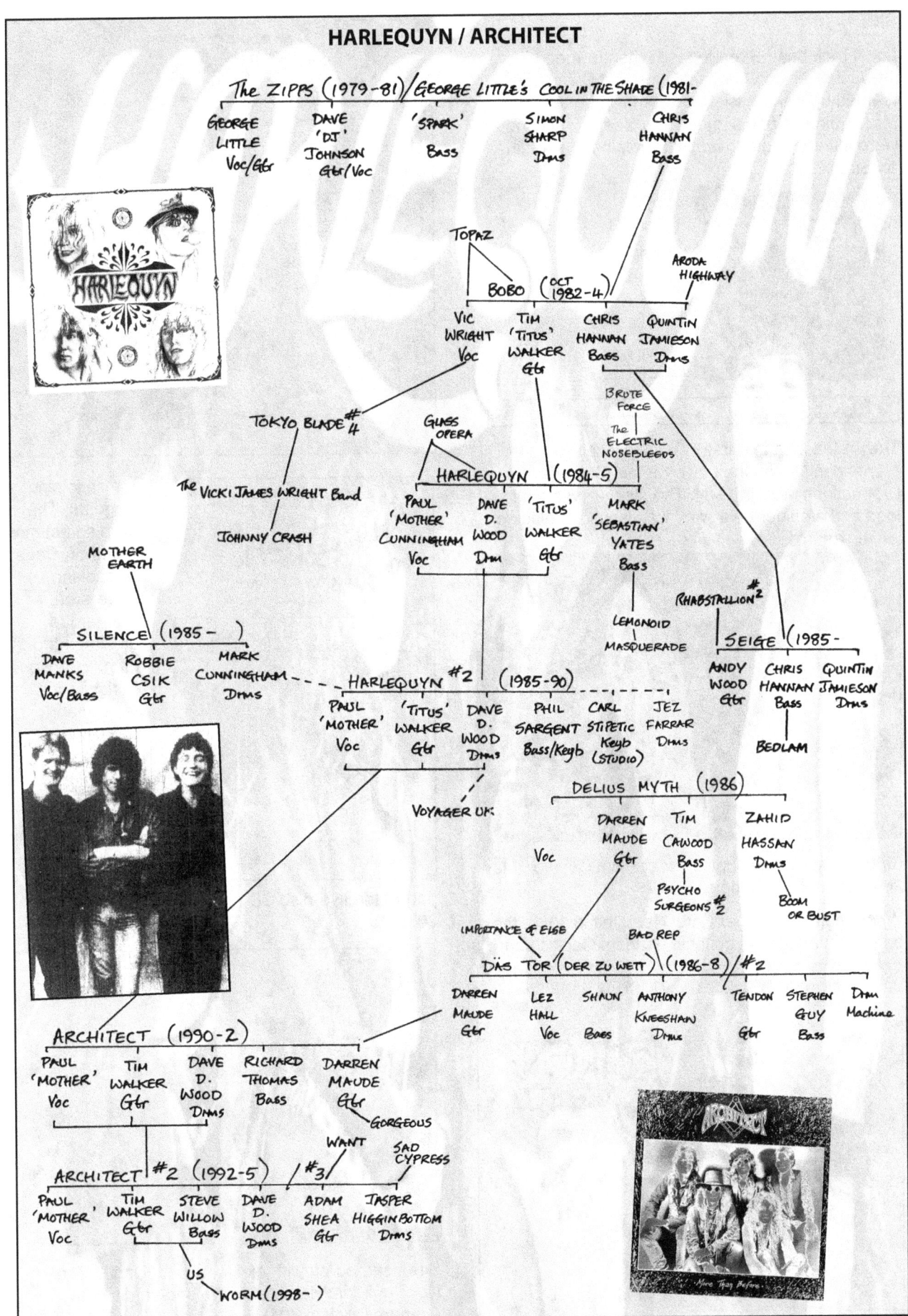

SIREN

Local rock band Siren formed when former Dawnweaver duo Graham Cook and Dave Ellis teamed up with bassist Porl 'Lemmy' Lane, guitarist Marc Fairchild and singer Carlo Neen. The band were initially named Neopn Angels before settling on Siren.

SIREN	
84 Distant Cousins DC4R Deceiving Lies/American Girl (white or black sleeve)	10

They released their first 7" single Deceiving Lies / American Girl on their own Distant Cousins Productions label in 1984. The sleeve, with their logo and a spider on a web, was issued in black or white variants.

Siren played a midnight show at Palm Cove on May 26 to promote the single.

When their lead singer Carol Neen left in 1986, the band continued with guitarist Graham Cook's son

Tamlin joining on guitar. They were sometimes joined on stage by backing singers the Dangerous Sisters, a trio of Wendy Jepson, Christina Jepson and Carol Neen.

The band released various cassette albums between 1984-97, which later became part of the five-disc CD retrospective compilation in 2010.

Siren carried on with ex-Handful Of Dance/Zed/ Nowt guitarist Harris after the sad demise of Graham Cook in 2013.

CHAPTER 6 - INDIE ALTERNATIVE ROCK — 1984 - 1986

DAWNWEAVER / SIREN

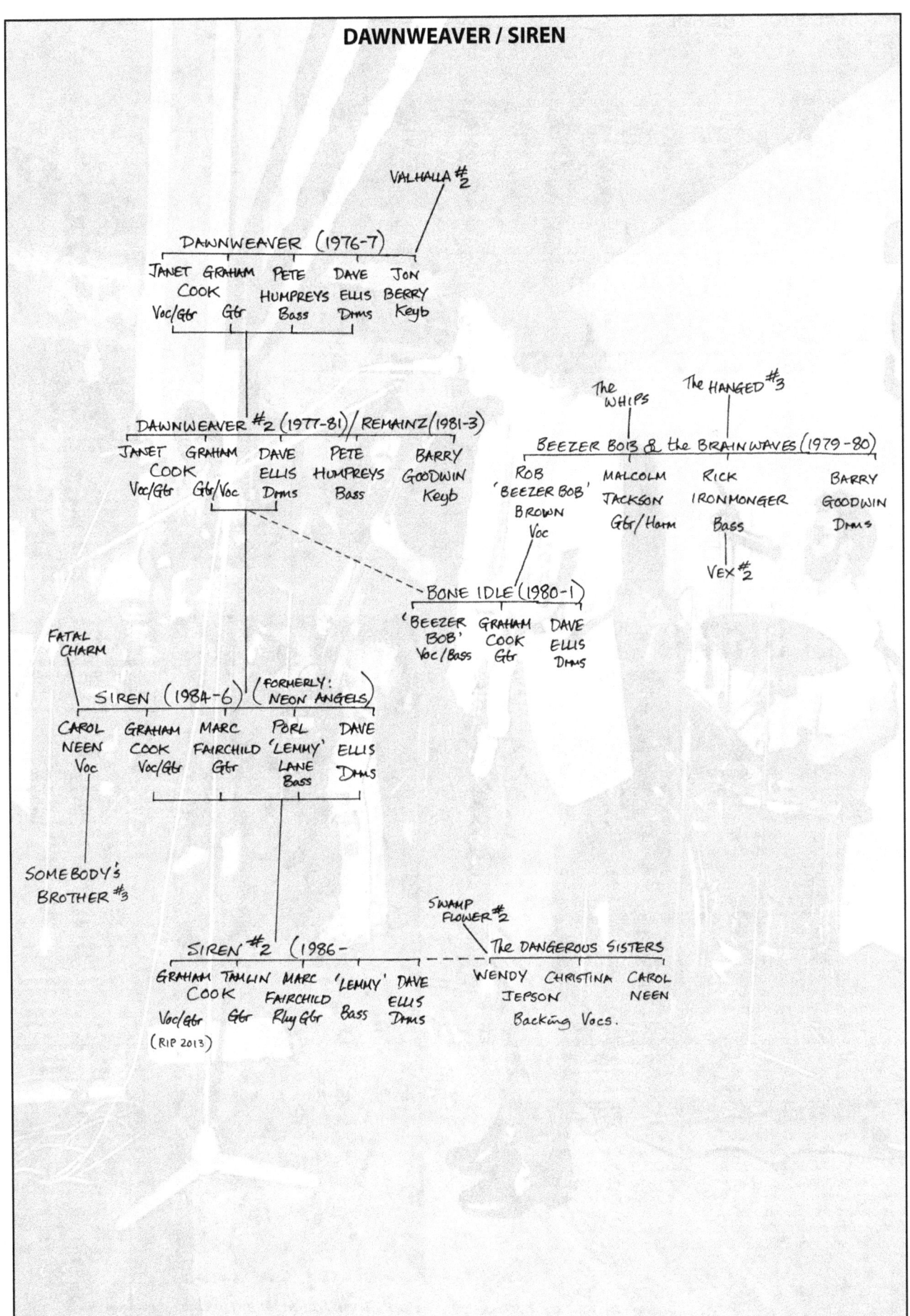

REVIEWS FROM THE NME

'Basstid!!!' Club members on watch for S. Williams, who scarpered when it was her round... *Pic Fritz the Cat*

IT'S GOOD, IT'S CHEAP, AND IT'S OURS!!

SUSAN WILLIAMS at the 1 in 12 in Bradford — "*whose* round??"

...(Days later) The rush is on — " "they've found Susan, — she's gettin' 'em in!!!"

Pic Fritz the Cat

In Bradford there's pubs choc-a-bloc with t'lads. Casual? Fila Lacoste and Pringle may have replaced the cloth caps and mufflers but the attitudes remain pretty constant. There are mate-markets disguised as discos where the main-stream kulture cattle are herded by gibbering Radio One clones called Chris or Steve. There are clubs that welcome you with open palms during the summer vac, but spit in your eye when the students come back. Late-night watering holes blast reggae 'n' soul. All life is there including the pimps, prostitutes and their clientele.

But if you are young, free and possessed of a modicum of taste, if you don't shop at Wally at C&A, if you're not rolling in oodles of ackers, if you're not possessed of that precious NUS card, if you have style but lack brass, it's The One in Twelve Club.

The name comes from HMG's estimate that one in 12 of all claimants are on the fiddle, unemployment being very close to the heart of this club, which sprang from the hearts and minds of activists in the Claimants Union in 1981. Gary: "Price of gigs these days – you're talking about £1.50 to £2.00 at *least*. It seems stupid that we can't afford the gigs at St. Georges Hall and the University. There was a hell of a lot of local bands breaking-up every week 'cos there was nowhere else to play."

You pays yer 50p and yer takes yer choice; The Membranes, The Three Johns, New Model Army, The Sisters of Mercy. Bands are paid on a 25%–75% door split. With a capacity of a few hundred, nobody plays here for the money. They play here because, as a venue, it is unique . . . and a lot of the time because there's nowhere else to play.

There's no grasping promoter to whine "I'm only doing this for the kids!" There are just the kids themselves. There's over a thousand of them in the co-operative (including me), several hundred of whom are active in running the club. This pool includes photographers, typists, sound and lighting engineers, journalists, humpers, printers and layout artists. Everybody that a self-respecting club can utilise but would never exploit.

The club has been shunted from pub to pub as landlords attempt (and fail) to move upmarket and attract the non-existent hordes of upwardly socially mobile.

Tammy: "The Hacienda? Where's that? Manchester? That's miles away! All this stuff about working class kids swanning round in taxis is total shit, they're making it up! This place is 50p to get in and *we* run it".

The 1 in 12 album is being pressed and the club is in receipt of a £63,000 council grant to buy its own premises. A fanzine of stunning verbosity – *Knee Deep In Shit* – is produced at irregular intervals.

Downstairs the DJ smashes the eardrums with splattered selection of noisy row from three generations of punk, pop and soul. Upstairs conversation ranges from squatting to striking to the price of hairdye. The atmosphere is refreshingly drug-free. Junkies and dealers are shown the door.

The 1 in 12 club is run upon lines so idealistic that many would have predicted a cot-death. The black/red logo, the miner's collection box and the 'Bradford Militia' T-shirts are not Clash-style graspings at elusive credibility but a reflection of the club's recognition of the inseperability of politics and music.

There are no poxy, pouting prats, no 90p a pint, no two page spreads in *The Fake*. Every Tuesday and Thursday night at the Market Tavern. A night out in Bradford means taking control of your culture.

BULLSHIT DETECTOR!

THE MEMBRANES
Bradford 1 in 12 Club

THOSE WHO deny the existence of a dynamic working-class culture should have bands like this rammed down their throats till they choke. Social Surrealism – the antidote to the cultural downturn and the cure for Factory style death-grip miserablism. Proof that the Johns Three are no-way alone in being able to assault stupidity through the medium of the daft. Fat Rob bangs bits of metal and plays the melodica. "Faster!" shout the kids. Rob sweats and plays faster.

Mick Green of The Pirates through Wilko through the Gang Of Four's Andy Gill through the Third John. A school of blues guitar that attempts the impossible and achieves the ridiculously sublime. There is no 'right way' to be an urban folkie. This is not to excuse the sloppy or the crass. To clown and to sustain requires a skill and a discipline which few possess. Five Go Down To The Sea, Shehe – they can do it. This is parody at the highest level and you never see a Membrane smile because a joke explained is a joke castrated and too much space has been wasted on the lame-brained 'piss-take' and isn't it simply hilarious that good ole ZTT can sell the same shit in 200 different wrappers?!? Chortle snort.

"Faster!" Fat Rob Membrane a-blur. Pic: Alastair Robt'n

When we make heroes of entrepreneurs we pat the back of the parasite that rides our backs, saps our spirit and poisons our culture. Rave on and scream the praises of the new shock-haired, unshaven thin/fat man and make Mr Tebbit smile. There are no pictures of Richard Branson on my wall. Crap is crap is crap is crap no matter how slick the video or witty the pimp's patter and The Membranes for 50p on a Thursday night in dirty stinky Bradford with my dirty stinky punk-rock friends in an atmosphere pungent with the heady scent of rabid anti-fascist/ anti-scab propaganda to my mind exposes the falsity of your much vaunted 'honest' moral stance, Paulie baby.

But then again I suppose that we just don't realise how pop-music is made in the '80s, do we (sic)? Up yer bum.

– Susan Williams

Stop! Stop! You're killing me!

RATTLE!
BRADFORD BONES HAVE SHAKE APPEAL

SKELETAL FAMILY
FLOWER IN THE DUSTBIN
Bradford 1 In 12 Club

THE SIMPLEST was I can think of to sum up Flowers In The Dustbin is to say that they're like a more sincere four-piece, guitar-playing Soft Cell. Their music is a curious mixture of anger and sentimentality, warmth and sheer downright perversity, all given life by an uninhibited singer named Gerard. Physically, Gerard resembles the Pistols' Helen Of Troy; like her, he is approximately 12 inches too short to be welcomed as a friend by most of his fellow humans. Offer him your pity, though, and he would quite rightly spit it back in your face, as songs like the extraordinarily personal 'Aim For The Sky' made clear to anyone in the 1 In 12 Club who cared to listen.

I didn't actually get to *see* much of Skeletal Family's performance; the peculiarly formal combination of dancing and unarmed combat which went on near the stage made that virtually impossible. But for all the tribal fever they generate, Skeletal Family hypnotise rather than brutalise; their music is hard and fast, and yet the best of it manages to be thoughtful and lyrical at the same time. They can write dry-eyed, dispassionate observations on human frailty, but the wildest Skeletal songs seem like exorcisms of trapped, lonely emotion.

Whether or not the band have all the creative abilities necessary to keep moving onwards and upwards will only really be seen when their imminent debut LP appears. But right now, Skeletal Family are providing some of the most exhilarating nights out to be had in West Yorks' .e.

– Dave Jennings

CHAPTER 6 - INDIE ALTERNATIVE ROCK   1984 - 1986

ACCIDENT
LITTLE GERMANY
Bradford 1 In 12 Club

FOUR WEEKS previously, I had seen Little Germany playing at the annual 1 In 12 Club festival, and had hated then with a fierce passion. On that occasion, their performance had seemed like one long arrogant sneer, directed partly at the audience, partly at themselves, but mainly at anyone whose political outlook happened to be less cruelly intolerant than their own. Tonight, though, they just seemed drab and dispirited, struggling as they were against malfunctioning equipment and unresponsive listeners. Little Germany *can* write tunes, and the sort of warped rockabilly they produce *is* a more original sound than most. I just think it's rather sad that they use these talents to put over a vision that is relentlessy joyless, loveless and hopeless.

Accident employed the *Clockwork Orange* visual style which has been the hallmark of any number of irresponsible idiots over the years, from Steve Harley to ADX. They sang anthems about "psychos" and schizophrenia, as though mental illness was something exciting and admirable and not the bleak personal tragedy it is for those who suffer from it. Generally, Accident were like a much less thoughtful and intelligent version of the early Angelic Upstarts. A few loyal supporters did the flailing limb ritual down by the stage, but rather more people elected to leave early and have the last drink of the night somewhere else.
– *Dave Jennings*

Hype payola scandal! Post-industrial Marxist hooligan groupie, the lovely Susan Williams is caught in the act!

THE SYNDICATE
Bradford 1 in 12 Club

CHRIST, THEY'RE so *cynical* young people these days, so *decadent*! That's why London is the fashion capital of the entire world 'cos British kids are so *daring*, so *blasé*! They don't give a toss about anything! It's all so amazingly *groovy*, so *decadent*!

It should come as no surprise to learn that most of the adults concerned with the processing, packing and marketing of pop are amoral, infantile, gutless scum. Yet these Peter Pans, the folk who know-what-the-kids-want will amaze you again and again with their shallowness and deep, depressing, self-fulfilling cynicism. Press agents, journalists, record company 'people'. Prime examples of the new 'me' generation. The Thatcher spawn. It really should come as no surprise – Ho Hum! Bring on the dancing dogs and steady with the blow job, Rodney.

Happily the culture of the young working class moves too steadily at its own pace for it ever to be totally accommodated by the biz.

Let's talk 'hip', 'cool', 'style' and we're talking the shit that sells everything from battleships to

Beatlewigs – it is sales talk – a scam, a con, an angle and the nature of the merchandise doesn't matter. The quality of the product is irrelevant. What must be sold to the mug-punter is the *concept* of RAPID TURNOVER (read 'fashion' 'style', 'cool', 'hip').

The Syndicate mash dub/ska 'n' rapping. A 13-year old sprog plays the organ. Bass guitar and lead guitar handled by oversize adolescent limbs and bum-fluff moustaches. Pork pie hat,'shades and *that* crouched stance borrowed from the back of the original Special AKA album that his big brother lets him borrow or mebbee even his Dad's Prince Buster scrapbook.

These children, liberated from the confines of Carlton Bolling Youth Club can *DANCE*. Not the strange, rusty jerking of the mascara-laden middle-class berk (London calling), but a delightful, fluid skank as in a) uncool
 b) unhip
 c) unfashionable.
Everything is bastardised. Fringed wedge and Fred Perries, toniks and trainers. It's nice to know that whilst so much is being spent on Frankly, darling, shoddy goods, the youth of Undercliffe at least can still sift the grit from the shit.   – *Susan Williams*

From the beginning of July 1984 to the end of that year, The 1 In 12 Club began to focus on a series of appearances from nationally renowned indie groups, including The Inca Babies, Tools You Can Trust, A-Witness, Big Flame, Yeah, Yeah, Noh, Bomb Party, Omega Tribe, Five Go Down To The Sea, Rubella Ballet, The Instinks and The Vibes, alongside the usual range of local and regional bands. (10)

Courtesy of Friz the Cat

Rubella Ballet on stage at the Market Tavern

1984 - 1986 — BRADFORD'S NOISE OF THE VALLEYS VOLUME 1

CHAT SHOW
PAUL DUNBAR
BOG SHED
Bradford 1 in 12 Club

"THIS SONG'S about the pure enjoyment of killing people." Thus spake Phil Hartley of Bog Shed, by way of introduction to a number entitled 'The Necktie Murders'. I can't claim to have been thrilled by Bog Shed's music — it was determinedly ugly and full of unexciting non-danceable mid-tempo rhythms — but their lyrics were fascinating. Their name is no cheap gimmick: they do indeed sing about bathrooms and water-closets and the terrible experiences they have had therein. Anally-fixated they aren't, however: they also have songs concerning panties, budgies, and chips with gravy on them. They are, in short, compulsively repulsive.

Paul Dunbar describes himself as a "white rapper". On the evidence of this performance, a "white rapper" is simply a ranter with a better sense of rhythm than most, an abnormally humourless worldview, and a crippling case of acute racial guilt. In fairness, though, it should be noted that he said his piece without the aid of the backing tapes I'm told he usually employs; the tapes might possibly have made Dunbar's witless words more palatable.

There really must be a band like Chat Show in *every* city by now. Tribal markings, dramatic poses, and music on loan from Spear Of Mercy and Alien Cult Gang. Vocals, on this occasion were shared between a would-be Nick Cave and a would-be Lydia Lunch. It was all meant to sound sinister and portentious, but it was just depressingly predictable.

— *Dave Jennings*

Pic. Fritz The Cat

OLD GREY MELVYN BRAGG!

CHUMBAWUMBA
Bradford 1 in 12 Club

THE CATALYST for a brazen televisual renaissance that would banish forever the spectre of Lord Reith to the dankest corners of the collective sub-conscious *or* a Moscow funded floodgate through which would strut the communist-lesbian spokespeople of the dispised counter-culture, corrupting our children with their foul language and vegetarian cooking?

The nation waited with bets placed and breath bated. What horrors did Channel 4 have in store?

It steamed in, on that first night, with a 'feminist theatre group' of appalling banality. The spectacle of sleek middle-class women sing the word "prick" ad nauseam in an attempt to shock the patriachy to its knees must have deprived Channel 4 of millions of viewers for months to come.

In general, left-wing agit-prop theatre stinks. It uses a medium which is totally alien to most of its desired audience. The plots are weak, two-dimensional cartoon parodies, the characters are the corniest of cardboard cut-outs.

Chumbawumba are, I suppose, a 'rock band'. They use 'rock' music which, whilst both competent and furious, is hardly likely to topple George or Frankie from the pedestal of popular devotion. Nowt to piss yer knickers over. (In his Lego bungalow, Toytown, Nik Kershaw blows a sigh of relief, mops a spot free brow with a lacy hankie and carries on reading.)

They are young, committed and idealistic anarchists. At times the fury borders on self-righteousness (what Tony Allen calls the Anarcho-Stalinist syndrome).

It is their use of theatre which sets the Chumbas apart. Most of the audience sits, expecting and receiving a show rather than the usual tirade. Props are used, not in the usual manner of rock groups, to divert from lyrical limpness, but to emphasise and illustrate.

Those groups which attempt to communicate a sense of outrage (any group not composed of Young Conservatives that *doesn't* feel outraged should jolly well be ashamed; if you aren't angry at 16 you're a zombie; if you're still in a pop-band at the age of 30, then it's about time you grew up and got a proper job – only kidding, kids!) would learn much from observing Chumbawumba's skilful change of texture and pace.

They leaflet the audience mid-song with literature which assaults the pop-culture of which they are both a part of and opposed to.

This is the most acute of the contradictions facing them. We live in a society where everything, including protest pop *and* agit-prop pop-journalism, is packaged and sold as a consumer product.

Those who attempt to exist outside of the established market-place, to create an 'alternative', tend to make a virtue out of lack of popular appeal – to see the ghetto as a universe.

What do you want, Chumby-baby? An audience of millions or of hundreds? To compromise or rot in celibate purity? Is there still a middle ground?

Between The Redskins and the Chumbas lies a massive difference in how to approach the marketing of agit-prop. There are no victories to draw inspiration from, only mistakes which must not be repeated.

— *Susan Williams*

WHAT'S UP DOC?

DOCTOR AND THE INMATES
Bradford 1 in 12 Club

MOST DEFINITELY not to be confused with Doctor And The Medics in anyway . . . And The Inmates are the latest manifestation of William Beckett's violent desire to become anything other than a pop star. This is the man who sacked New Model Army because they left the top off the toothpaste, who ditched The Word because the bassist split his infinitives. Quite simply, this is the nicest man in Bradford.

Beckett's motto is madness. The whys and wherefores of being tapped and the conclusions to be drawn therefrom. The music is suitably manic, less fluid or flexible than his previous compositions, more reliant on angry thrashes of Teflon-coated riffing than sweet melody or bass-line meanderings. This reflects a change that has occurred in his lyrics which, in tune with the times, have acquired a hardness and a sense of purpose.

Wild William staggers angrily in the wasterland between Screaming Lord Sutch and Ted 'Tie Me Kangaroo Down' Hughes (had the latter been an anarchist hooligan rather than a royalist toad). Such talents are few and far between. 1984 will be the year of the ex-Tex (with hindsight and much subtle re-writing at the Ministroy of Hype or was that all last year's thing?).

— *Savage Susan Williams*

BIG FLAME
PASSION DAY
Bradford 1 In 12 Club

THE SOUND of Passion Day was like a frozen rain of percussion driving into their listeners' faces. The band has three members – a drummer, a bassist, and a man who starts their set as an extra drummer and finishes it as a second bass player. The latter two also bark out vocals, while trying very hard to look like stereotypical angry proles. There was a mesmerising power about the sheer noise they made; but cold fury was the only discernible emotion in their work, and they didn't convey that particularly convincingly. Their words might possibly have been provocative if they hadn't been completely unintelligible.

Big Flame acted like a group frantically fighting off normality. As soon as a song started to get into a groove, it would be wrenched away into another rhythm or another key. It took me about ten minutes to adjust to the demands of Big Flame's convulsive songwriting, and then I began to enjoy the scrambled code messages they were delivering; I couldn't resist a band with song titles like 'Man Of Few Syllables' and 'All The Irish Must Go To Heaven'. Big Flame were Feverish, and long may they remain so.

— *Dave Jennings*

Those London-based bands needing to be put up after gigs at the Club were usually taken to the Perseverance Pub on Lumb Lane for a late drink. While enjoying a nightcap, they were often regaled by local 'toasters' like Mikey Dread and were amazed by the multiracial atmosphere of the place.

The *NME* printed a total of eight gig reviews at the Market Tavern during this period, enhancing the prestige of The 1 In 12 Club nationally even more.

CHAPTER 6 - INDIE ALTERNATIVE ROCK 1984 - 1986

THE HINDLE'S GEARS DISPUTE

During August 1984, a group of striking workers from Hindle's Gears Limited released the self-financed single *Part Of The Union / A Year And A Bit* on their Catch 22 Records.

The A-side was a reworking of the January 1973 Strawbs number two hit. The music on the single was provided by local band Boys From The East and was recorded at Lion Studios, Leeds. The single got at least three plays on John Peel's night-time radio show between August and September.

The twenty-two workers from Hindle's Gears Limited had originally started the dispute over a wage claim in April 1983. The dispute escalated as the management sacked the workers through a ballot form which simply read, *'Tick this box if you want your job, or tick that box if you don't. Failure to do either, your contract will be terminated.'* Acting under union instructions the men took no notice of the form and went on strike.

In June 1984 the strikers occupied their workplace for four days before being forced to leave after the firm obtained a court injunction. Like the miners, the strikers' wives formed a support group and joined the picket line. Many local trade unionists and other workers supported the strike as did The 1 In 12 Club who held a benefit on August 24, 1984, at Checkpoint with Johnny Jumps The Bandwagon and The Nerve Agents (Requiem didn't play).

Unfortunately, after a twenty-seven-month-long struggle, the strikers gave up in June 1985. At a tribunal in October 1985 to determine whether they were unfairly dismissed, Norman Tebbitt's law was used to determine that they had been dismissed fairly - a sad end for workers attempting to exercise their rights.

Sometime after the dispute former striker Stuart Firth went into local band management and during the next few years (1985-1995) managed The Best Way To Walk, Gypsy, Happiness AD, Hyacinth House, Bedlam, Seal Team 6, The Bobby Charltons and Detrimental.

CHECKPOINT & 1 in 12 BENEFIT FOR THE HINDLE DISPUTE. AT CHECKPOINT WESTGATE. ON 24th AUGUST. 8pm till 2a.

HIT-PICK PICKETS!!

Twenty-two workers at Hindles Gears factory in Bradford have been on strike for the past 16 months. The dispute, originally over a wage claim, was escalated by management last April when the strikers were given their cards.

With West Yorks pop-heroes Boys From The East, the pickets have taken the unusual if not unprecedented step (Ford strikers, Oct '78, and others) of putting their grievances down on record.

The B-side, 'A Year And A Bit, is a self-penned plaintive reggae lilt which describes the frustrations of industrial struggle – hardly a topic close to the heart of the Radio One jocks or indeed many 'music journalists'. The A-side is a proud reworking of The Strawbs' 'Part Of The Union'.

The Strawbs ditty was largely lifted from Woodie Guthrie's heavily *pro*-union 'Union Maid'. The Strawbs turned the sentiments of the original around, making the song a sarcastic assault on those who have the guts to stand up and fight when conditions and living standards are under attack (the bully boys). This was a point clearly missed by some of their more partisan critics. Whilst Labour politicians applauded the single as a "workers anthem", a back-bench Tory attacked it as ". . . a serenade to the troublemakers". All of which indicates a rather low level of artistic appreciation amongst those who-knows-best.

The Hindle Pickets have reclaimed the song and play it straight, every line reflecting solidarity and optimism.

'Part Of The Union'/'A Year And A Bit' plus badge and information pack is available for £2.00 from Stuart Firth, 21 Throxenby Way, Clayton, Bradford BD14 6EU West Yorks.

— *Susan Williams*

THE NERVE AGENTS

This band mixed the more melodic side of The Damned with a bit of '60s psychedelia mixed in. Liam Sheeran and Mark 'Vernon Damurgis' Cranmer from the hardcore band Raw teamed up with former Halifax band Prospect Zero guitarist Pete 'Pete Peculiar' Ingham (later known as Wulf Ingham) in 1984. Poet Mike 'Dirk Spig' Hughes on keyboards and Convulsions drummer Matt 'Matt Nazul' Webster completed the lineup. The Nerve Agents recorded the six-song *To And Fro* demo at Lion Studios and played at venues like 1 In 12 and Manningham Community Centre.

After a few months, bassist Mark Cranmer left to reform the Vegetable Section and singer Liam was busy with work commitments. The Negativz had split up in the summer of 1984 so singer Dave Wilcox and bassist Rik 'Pox' Leith (later known as Felix Leith) joined Pete and Matt to form Swamp Flower.

SWAMP FLOWER

After three months writing and rehearsing, a recording session was booked for January 1985. However, singer Dave Wilcox decided to leave so the band recruited singer Wendy Jepson (Pete's partner at the time) to record their 'cassingle' *Shackles On The Mind / Swamp Flower*.

After recruiting keyboard player John Jankovich the band played many gigs throughout 1985 at venues like Queen's Hall, and Manningham Community Centre (where Dave Wilcox often guested on a cover of Pretty Vacant), and were regulars at Bibi's. They supported The Boothill Foot Tappers at Bradford University on March 13 and a 1 In 12 benefit at Checkpoint with Men From The Mountains. A crossover gig with jazz band The Moon as Moonflower took place at Bibi's on October 18.

Seething 'Susan Williams' Wells reviewed a gig with Swamp Flower, Vegetable Section and Little Brother at Queen's Hall on May 30, 1985 in the *NME*.

Swamp Flower disintegrated at the end of 1985 leaving the trio of Pete, Pox and Matt to play under the pseudonym **Purple Wizard** for a one-off at Bibi's. The band were told to stop playing after about 15 minutes of instrumental jamming when four of the eight in the audience tried to leave! Owner Bibi forced the customers to stay for another drink as background music played until they managed to escape when he left the bar.

CHAPTER 6 - INDIE ALTERNATIVE ROCK   1984 - 1986

THE VEGETABLE SECTION

After one gig as The Desire Crew in 1982 guitarist Paul Arron, bassist Mark Cranmer and drummer Matt Webster decided to contunue as a trio with Paul Arron taking over vocal duties from Jason Nisse. After a couple of rehearsals, Mark decided to focus on his hardcore punk band Raw and Matt on his other band The Convulsions.

Mark and Paul Arron carried on the project later playing a couple of gigs and recording with a drum machine until Simon 'Nogsy' Nolan played drums for them. After another hiatus when Mark was in The Nerve Agents, the duo reformed, this time with former Negativz drummer Foxy and former Convulsions singer Stan playing percussion.

They played at venues including the Cathedral Centre, Benson's Bier Keller, Queen's Hall and Checkpoint.

Their *Fruit Cake Jake* track, recorded in their artistically self-decorated shared house on Seaton Street, Barkerend, appeared on The 1 In 12 Club's *Systembeat* compilation LP.

MANNINGHAM COMMUNITY CENTRE

Manningham Community Association, who had organised a week of festivities in May, finally took over the old Conservative Club in Lumb Lane. After refurbishment, it was opened as the Manningham Community Centre. The centre was open to all Manningham residents, especially the unemployed. It had meeting rooms and a café and later had a stage built as live bands began to play there.

It became a popular venue for local bands including The Nerve Agents (21/7/84, 1/9/84), Jah Pox & The Skankers For Damurgis (1/8/84), Morbid Humour, Raw Babies (18/8/84), Swamp Flower (29/6/85, 27/7/85, 9/8/85, 29/9/85, 7/12/85) Surreal Estate, Vegetable Section (18/4/85), The Moon (14/9/85) 4 Beats Behind Bars (9/11/85), Skrytch, Handful Of Dance (2/11/85)

By the mid-1980s it was unfortunately allowed to be run into the ground and became a haunt for serious heroin users; it later closed down altogether.

SWAMP FLOWER VEGETABLE SECTION
Bradford Checkpoint

THE DEEP-EYED willow-woman who sings for Swamp Flower has a voice like the mad axeman in your average Americak mass-murder movie. Every now and then it bursts forth screaming from behind the woodwork of strictly-for-the-earthworms Siouxsie-style imagery and lops a few heads off.

Grim, chinsucking, frowning, snarling, looking *heavy*, Vegetable Section are not a jolly band. Maybe they are a bit nervous. Maybe they are dying from painful diseases. Maybe they are just making the usual and all too common mistake (one perpetuated by our leading 'fashion' magazines) that looking constipated is in some way inherently stylish. Maybe they're just a bunch of posy bastards. All in all it becomes rather difficult really to enjoy their rather naughty cross-fertilisation of frenzied Afro-drumming and limping HM geetar when the whole band looks on the verge of breaking into hysterical tears. Gruntled I am not.

Susan Williams ■

WOMEN'S MUSIC WORKSHOP COLLECTIVE

Since the birth of the women's movement in the 1960s, Bradford, like most major cities and towns, began to develop a loose network of highly politicised women's groups.

Rosies Revenge

They became involved in various campaigns highlighting the injustices and inequalities faced by women. With the liberating DIY ethos of punk, more and more women started to take up instruments and form bands.

The Bradford Women's Music Workshop Collective was formed to encourage women and girls to learn and share music recording and technical, mixing and playing skills.

The BWMWC obtained funding to buy their own PA and instruments. Workshops took place at various venues between 1984 and 1988 including Manningham Community Centre, MAPA and Shipley New Start. Bands formed from these workshops included Olulu Ololu, Green Bags and Rosie's Revenge.

BELLE & THE DEVOTIONS

Bradford singer Kit Rolfe's debut 7" single *The Wizard / Play Another Song* was released on DJM in 1980.

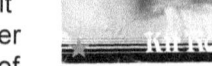

Female UK pop trio Belle & The Devotions was built around the Bradford singer Deirdre 'Kit' Rolfe (sister of guitarist and PA maestro Gerard Rolfe).

They released two 7"/12" singles *Where Did Love Go Wrong / When You're Alone* and *Got To Let You Know / Reach Out For Love* in 1983, again on the DJM label.

In 1984, with the addition of Laura James and Linda Sofeld on backing vocals, the group entered the UK heats of the *Eurovision Song Contest*. Their song, *Love Games*, was an easy winner and they went on to represent the UK in the main contest in Luxembourg where they finished seventh.

The single was also a UK chart hit reaching number eleven in April after a performance on *Top Of The Pops*.

Another single, *All The Way Up*, released in June 1984, failed to get into the charts and the group split up soon after.

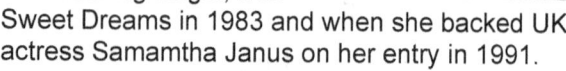

Kit Rolfe appeared at Eurovision two more times as a backing singer, with Sweet Dreams in 1983 and when she backed UK actress Samamtha Janus on her entry in 1991.

She also recorded the single *Fly Eddie Fly* with UK Olympic Skier Eddie 'The Eagle' Edwards.

In 1986 she released a cover of Abba's *SOS* and a dance track called *One More Hurt*.

Kit went on to run an equestrian and horse training centre in Sussex.

CHAPTER 6 - INDIE ALTERNATIVE ROCK 1984 - 1986

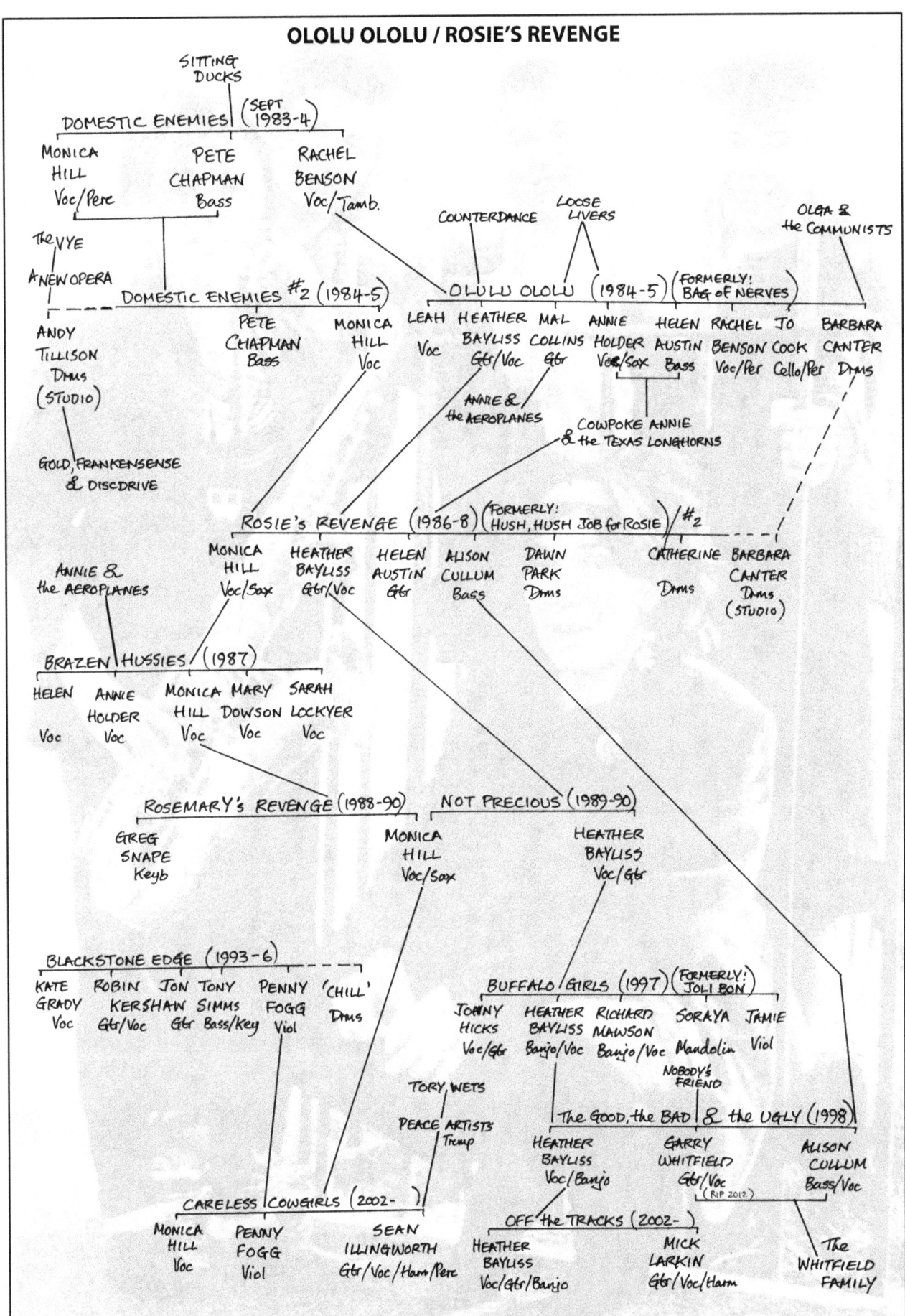

OLOLU OLOLU / ROSIE'S REVENGE

1984 - 1986 BRADFORD'S NOISE OF THE VALLEYS VOLUME 1

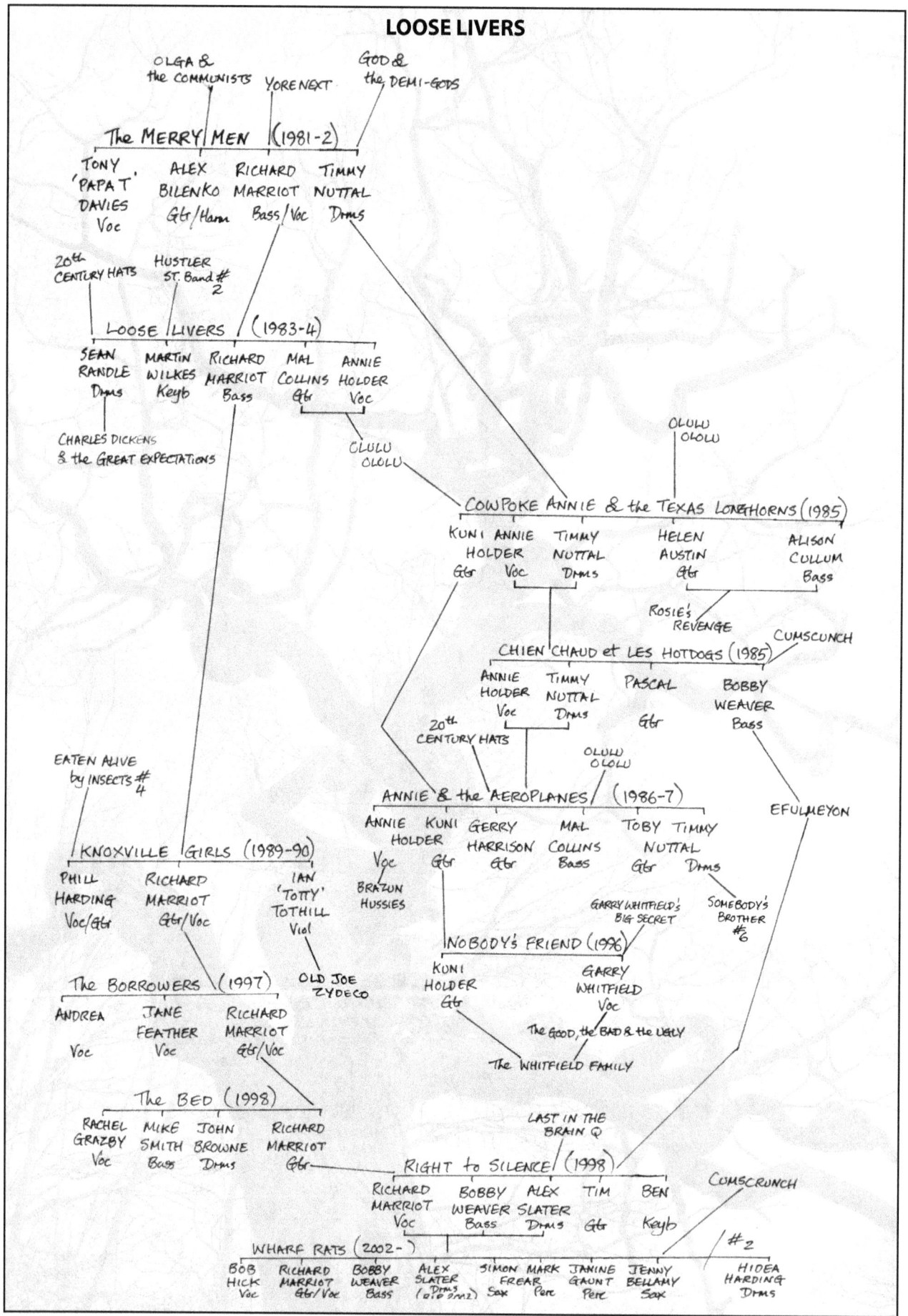

268

GRIFF'S MAGIC THEATRE

Local DJ Ian 'Griff' Griffiths began DJing above his parent's co-op shop in his Lincolnshire home town of Blyton in 1969, where he built his own sound and light systems and charged a shilling entrance fee.

After playing at various venues around the area and then venturing further afield, Griff moved to Bradford in 1979 and began spinning discs at The Brown Cow in Wyke.

In 1983, he brought his now legendary Griff's Magic Theatre to the city centre, playing rare sixties and seventies sounds accompanied by a psychedelic light show first at The Wheatsheaf, on Little Horton Lane, then at The Vaults Bar before moving to the Benson's Bier Keller, formerly The Fountains Hall, in 1985.

The elaborate '60s style light show with oil-filled slides and kaleidoscopic images that added so much to the atmosphere of Magic Theatre nights was the work of Max Jackman.

The Theatre was to later have long residencies at Palm Cove (1986-1996), Queen's Hall (1986-1993), The Beehive (1996-2006) and The Mill (2006 onwards) as well as stints at The Royal Standard, W's, Bradford University, the Spotted House, the Capricorn Club, the Windsor Baths and numerous one-off events and all dayers.

As well as running the regular Magic Theatre nights Griff has also provided musical support, lights and sound for a host of bands at countless venues, over the years as well as joining Zed and Wild Willi Beckett on the *Mad Dogs & Yorkshiremen European Tour* in 1990.

From 1994 onwards *Griff's Magic Theatre* has also been a weekly radio show on BCB.

Griff at Palm Cove with fellow DJ Linda Sprogis.

CHECKPOINT

During 1984 and 1985 The 1 In 12 Club organised a series of benefits and gigs at the West Indian Community's venue Checkpoint due to it having a larger sized hall than current Club venue, The Market Tavern.

Besides the miners and Hindles Benefits in 1984 already mentioned, there were benefits for the local Rape Crisis Centre on June 11, with Toxic Shock, Passion Killers and Indiscriminate Hoax Fund, then for Greenpeace on December 15, with The Word, Vegetable Section, Jazz Hipsters and Edward's Voice.

In March 1985 another benefit gig was held by the 1 In 12 at Checkpoint with Vegetable Section, Olulu Ololu and Swamp Flower. This time the benefit was to raise funds to support 1 In 12 members who were getting arrested for political actions.

Two other gigs at Checkpoint were Matamba, Chronic and Boys From The East on September 29, and a special 'Nice Try Guy' Bonfire Night party with Poison Girls (pictured above) and The Three Johns on Monday 5, November.

GETTING THE FEAR

Formed in 1984 from the ashes of Southern Death Cult, Aki, Buzz and Barry were joined by Paul 'Bee' Hampshire in the gothic ensemble Getting The Fear. Three early demo cassettes were released, but only at gigs, before they signed to RCA Records.

Their only vinyl release was the single *Last Salute / We Struggle* on 7' and 12' formats. After the band's demise, Barry and Bee formed Into A Circle while Aki and Buzz formed Joy. Both bands were short-lived. (14)

In 2021 Dais Records released a compilation album of unreleased tracks called *Death Is Bigger 1984-1985* on various coloured vinyl.

GETTING THE FEAR
84	RCA RCA 432	Last Salute/We Struggle (p/s)	5
84	RCA RCAT 432	Last Salute/We Struggle (12", p/s)	8

These other groups were on the circuit in 1984/85: **Lady Godiva, Tranquility, Jumping The Gun,** the duo **A-359s, Roulette,** and **Monterra Vice.**

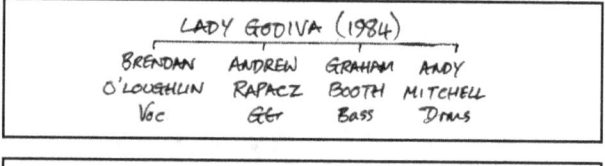

LADY GODIVA (1984)
BRENDAN O'LOUGHLIN	ANDREW RAPACZ	GRAHAM BOOTH	ANDY MITCHELL
Voc	Gtr	Bass	Drms

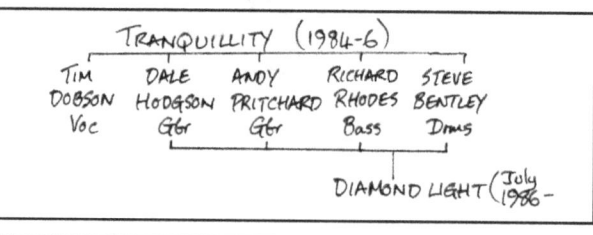

TRANQUILLITY (1984-6)
TIM DOBSON	DALE HODGSON	ANDY PRITCHARD	RICHARD RHODES	STEVE BENTLEY
Voc	Gtr	Gtr	Bass	Drms

DIAMOND LIGHT (July 1986-)

JUMPING the GUN (Jan 1984-)
ROY FONTAINE	DAVE FLERIN	KARL BENSON	DOM WELDON	SANDRA GRAHAM
Voc/Gtr	Gtr	Bass	Drms	Bac.Voc

TUXEDO

In 1986 the band Tuxedo released the Double-A-Sided single Take It Easy / Set Me Free on their Rushmore Records label before splitting up soon after.

VANISHING POINT

This melodic rock band formed in Dewsbury around early 1984 and included Bradford personel in its line-ups. In October 1984 played a gig at The 1 In 12 Club, supported by Leeds based band The Living Daylights. By 1990, the band had secured a deal with RCA Records and released the LP From Jump Street. The following year they released the 7" Better Than That from the LP in Holland.

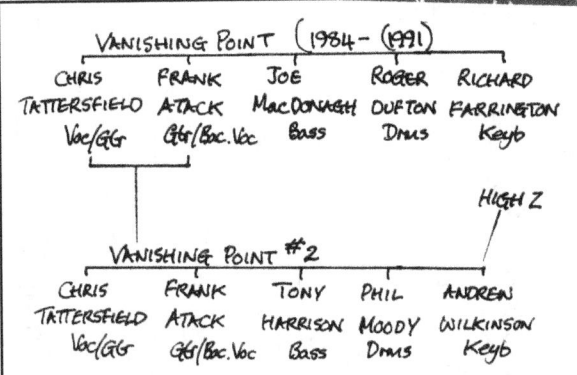

ANOTHER CINEMA

Formed in 1984 by three former members of Shipley based indie/goth band 1919. That same year, they released their debut 7" single Hallucination Spires I / I Had A Bad Dream Last Night on their own Altered States label. A second single on both 7" and 12" formats, Midnight Blue Oceans, followed in 1985, again on their own label.

Singer Ian Tilliard and guitarist Mark Tighe went on to form Zap Gun Virus in 1987. Ian later joined Ubik, then Bervas before helping to form The Loved Ones (1994 - 2010) then Henry's Radio in 2011.

Guitarist Mark Tighe reformed 1919 with drummer Mick Reed in the line-up. Sadly, both Mick and Mark passed away in 2017.

EL LOCO

This local combo were around from 1985-87. Their

formidable rhythm section included drummer Mick Wake who had been in bands since 1963. In

the 1970s he was in local rock acts like Howard & The Falcons (1970-73) and Smokestack (1975-77), Wishful Thinking (1977-78) and Streetchoir (1978-79). Bassist Mal Siswick had been in the original John Verity Band.

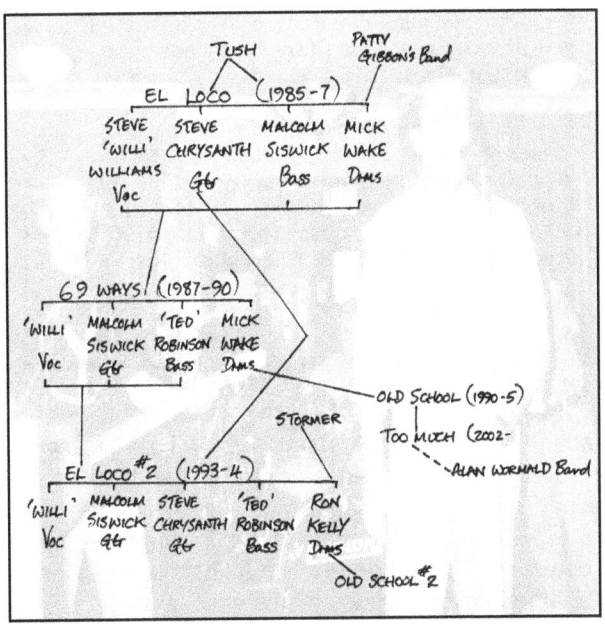

SHOCKING PINK

TOXIC SHOCK
Bradford 1 in 12 Club

A FURRY individual in a tea-cosy mumbles with *real* feeling "Yeeeah! Right on! Greeeeeeen-' am!'". Oh embarrassment! The platitudes dribble forth and congeal in the fur of the small Jack Russell that he has strapped to his chin.

To use a phrase that is the *teensy-weensiest* bit incongruous, Toxic Shock have got their audience firmly by the scrotal sac. Rarely, if ever, have I witnessed an act so totally in control of a performance situation (what we call a 'gig'). Having stunned the anarcho-pinklet horde into slack-jawed schtum, they follow through by swaggering amidst the piles of bodies, arms akimbo, bellowing in triumph.

The past 12 months have seen these brassy lasses blossom to a point where they can successfully pretend to be totally blasé about whether they are liked or not. Of course such apparent indifference is the hallmark of true professionals. To boldly grin whilst crapping oneself – a desirable ability I should think.

Lithesome, tight and spartan chunks of needle-sharp polemic plus that oh-so-important 'sense of humour'. A nasty habit of gobbing in your eye if you get too chummy, pal, but *nice* with it. Hackles were raised. Bums went unlicked. Toxic Shock often resort to the use of those theatrical techniques that, in the soft pink hands of lesser mortals, would merely be sniggerworthy.

The ability to communicate anger in an original and compelling manner is, alas, uncommon – hence the usually applicable directly inverse relationship between ideological soundness and listenability e.g The Flying Pickets: brilliantly, *amazingly* politically 'correct' but, Christ! What a *naff* band! If Trotsky himself molested that magnificent pop-thoroughbred 'Who's That Girl?' with such cack-handed disregard for aesthetic pleasantness, then I would seriously have to re-think my politics. (Only kidding, fellas!).

Toxic Shock are slithering from the snapping jaws of Pinko-cabaret into the harsh slimelight of popular attention. Nah . . . they're probably too good to ever be *that* popular. You could dig deeper into the rat's nest of escapist bilge that presently constitutes the vast bulk of our culture. Toxic Shock, will, for a small fee, come and dance on your grave, yeeah!

Susan Williams ∎

On January 1, 1985, The 1 In 12 Club continued its residency at The Market Tavern with a gig by Halifax's Chinese Gangster Element and Leeds's The She-Hees. On January 17, the then little-known Sheffield band Pulp played there for the first time before the Club ended its two nights per week and reverted to Wednesday nights only.

In early February a new record shop called *Rocks Off* was opened on Westgate by Alan Wrigley and Rick Zivanovic. During the shop's lifetime John Peel would be occasionally be seen rummaging through LPs on a Saturday when he was in town.

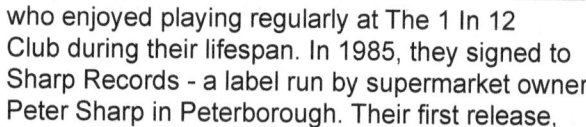

THE PASSMORE SISTERS

Formed in 1983, these Bradford/Leeds lads were a combo who enjoyed playing regularly at The 1 In 12 Club during their lifespan. In 1985, they signed to Sharp Records - a label run by supermarket owner Peter Sharp in Peterborough. Their first release, in September 1985, was the three-track 7-inch EP *Three Love Songs* which led to John Peel booking them for their first radio session.

Courtesy of Friz the Cat

By 1986 the band had recorded another session for Peel and one for Janice Long. They released two more singles; the four-song 12-inch *Violent Blue* and *Every Child In Heaven* which got to number sixteen in the Indie Charts in June 1986.

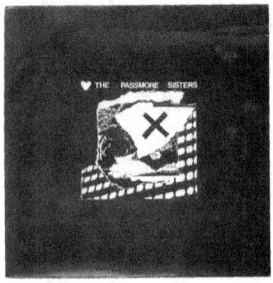

Another single, *A Safe Place To Hide*, followed in November 1987 and reached number twenty-three on the Indie Chart.

In February 1985, the band's vocalist Martin Sadofski turned his hand to a little 'extra' acting on TV when he appeared as a punk rocker in the Rovers Return on an episode of ITV's long-running soap *Coronation Street*.

By the time the band split up in 1988, they had released an LP for Sharp Records. *First Love, Last Rites* was a compilation of BBC session material.

THE BEST WAY TO WALK

The lads in The Best Way To Walk were originally from Black Rock, Dublin. They had moved over to Keighley College and met drummer Graham Wright. During 1986-87 the band released the three-track 12-inch single *Unbelievable* on Two Bad Records, recorded at Flexible Response, and gigged constantly in and around the area.

By 1988 they had relocated to London and later appeared as the house band in ITV's *The Paradise Club* – a drama about a music club in London starring former *Easterder* Leslie 'Dirty Den' Grantham.

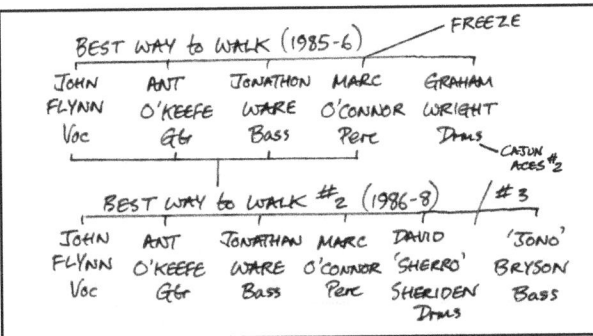

Another very tenuous Bradford connection was the TV *Auf Wiedersehen Pet* actor Jimmy Nail (real name James Bradford) who had a number three hit with *Love Don't Live Here Any More* in April 1985.

In January 1985 Police Sergeant John Speed was gunned down in Leeds city centre. The following police enquiry ended up questioning 41,000 people. As somebody had given the police the names of three 1 In 12 Club members they were all formally interviewed as part of the investigation in April. (12)

In May Bradford became the first UK city to elect an Asian Lord Mayor, Mohammed Ajeeb.

MARC RILEY AND THE CREEPERS
KISS THE BLADE
Bradford 1 In 12 Club

MARC RILEY and Paul Hanley share more than just their common status as Fall escapees. They also share a band, since Kiss The Blade consists of Hanley on drums, plus two members of The Creepers – guitarist and vocalist Paul Fletcher, and bassist Pete Keogh.

The sound of Kiss The Blade is very Mancunian, with lots of Peter Hook bass and kindred sombre tones. Hanley is an exceptionally skilful drummer – he demonstrated this during KTB's short set without dominating the proceedings – but the band was all too obviously in an early stage of development.

Marc Riley began his set with what is probably his finest song to date – 'Shadow Figure', a sour, sly narrative set to gentle piano melody. 'Fly The Nest', which followed, was similarly subdued – but then it was time for the boot to go in.

And go in it did – with Riley's words lashing out at ignorami of all kinds. But his loudest sneers are reserved for those who lurk behind the scenery of the music-biz.

'Location Bangladesh' – an inspired piece of black humour concerning the efforts of a party of pop aristocrats to make a video in the least glamorous location imaginable – is an example of Riley's caustic talent at its best.

At other times, though, he just seems petty and irritable. The great weakness in Riley's music is its lack of emotional range; he seems incapable of expressing affection or enthusiasm for anyone or anything. With his determination to face up to the ugliness of the world around him and to force his audience to do the same, Marc Riley could be a valuable treatment for those suffering from an overdose of sugary pop. But the antidote should be taken in small doses.

Too much of Riley's bitter medicine, and you can soon find yourself feeling numb, depressed and cynical.

Dave Jennings ■

GHOST DANCE

When Anne-Marie Hurst left Skeletal Family in 1985, she joined forces with ex-Sisters Of Mercy guitarist Gary Marx to form the 'super-Goth' band Ghost Dance.

Their first release was the 12-inch EP *River Of No Return* on Karbon Records in April 1986. It went straight to No 16 in the Indie charts.

Two more releases followed for the Karbon label in 1986.

Their cover version 7 and 12' *Heart Full Of Soul / Can The Can / Radar Love* single reached number four in the Indie charts in July. *The Grip Of Love / Where Spirits Fly* reached number nineteen in October and saw the introduction of former Requiem guitarist Richard Steel.

The 12-inch EP *A Word To The Wise* (including *When I Call / Fools Gold*) was another number four in August 1987.

In 1988, Karbon releases a compilation of all their singles and b-sides. The LP, *Gathering Dust*, reached number ten in February 1988.

The band then signed to Chrysalis Records and released the single *Down To The Wire / Blood Still Flows* in June 1989. The album *Stop The World* and the single *Celebrate* followed.

Ghost Dance parted company with Chrysalis during a tour with The Ramones. Their last gig in this first incarnation was in Amsterdam in December 1989.

A new version of Ghost Dance appeared in 2019 as Anne-Marie Hurst teamed up with three ex-members of Harlequyn, Tim Walker, Phil Noble and Dave Wood, and ex-Original Sin guitarist Stephen Derrig. Their 2023 album *The Silent Shout* went to No 1 in the iTunes 'Goth rock' chart.

In 2024, the lineup changed, with Anne-Marie and guitarist Tim Walker recruiting Sam Wilson, Billy Lockwood and Steve Brogden to play shows in the UK and Europe, including the *Rebellion Festival* in Blackpool.

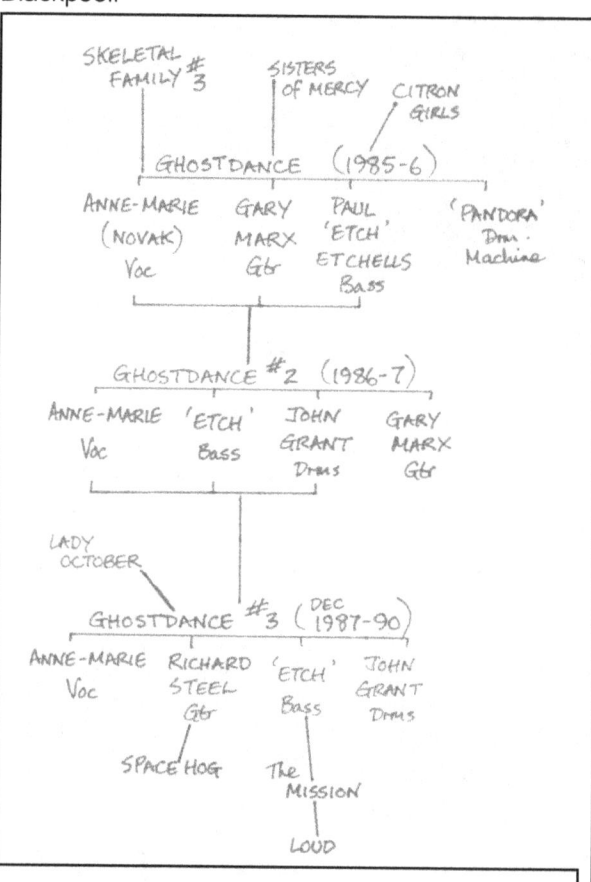

GHOST DANCE		
86	Karbon KAR 602T	River Of No Return/Yesterday Again/Both Ends Burning (12", p/s) 10
86	Karbon KAR 606	Heart Full Of Soul/Radar Love (promo only) 10
86	Karbon KAR 606T	Heart Full Of Soul/Radar Love (12", p/s) 8
86	Karbon KAR 604	The Grip Of Love/Where Spirits Fly (p/s) 8
86	Karbon KAR 604T	The Grip Of Love/Last Train/A Deeper Blue/ The Grip Of Love (Version) (12", p/s) 10
87	Karbon KAR 608T	A WORD TO THE WISE (12" EP) 8
86	Karbon KARXL 303	GATHERING DUST (LP) 12

ANTI-FASCIST 12

On Saturday, April 13, 1985, the fascist British National Party (BNP) hired an Eccleshill school hall for a public meeting, at which their leader John Tyndall was due to speak. They were confronted inside the meeting, which was disrupted, while outside an anti-nazi demonstration of over 200 people (1 In 12 members made up a third at least) jostled the police who were protecting the fascists. Twelve anti-fascist demonstrators were arrested on the day, including three members of The 1 In 12 Club, for obstruction, breach of the peace or assaulting a police officer.

A benefit gig was quickly organised for the defendants by a 'defence committee' and The 1 In 12 Club. On April 24, The Three Johns, Boys From The East and Little Brother played at Queen's Hall. Another benefit was staged on August 23, again at Queen's Hall, this time with Doctor & The Inmates and Men From The Mountains.

BOYS FROM THE EAST
Bradford Queens Hall

BRADFORD has for sometime been establishing itself as the stud farm for some natty *pop* bands. Boys From The East are a Eurasian three piece with a very much un-sneezed at line in stroppy romanticism. They have tended in the past, as pop bands will, to exaggerate their sugar, spice and all things nice qualities at the expense of rats, snails and puppy dogs' tails.

Brisk, brittle and aggressive. Lyrical twistings of the yawn yawn Heterolust outpourings of the current crop of chart non-entities were slyly poked past reverberating, clangy melodies. They ably caught the mood of a crowd gathered to raise cash for the defence of twelve assorted anti-fascists arrested opposing a recent slope-shouldered Master Race Appreciation Society rally.

MEANWHILE back in the real world dot dot dot spoilt lower-middle class brats quote pre-war avant-garde manifesto's and play with chainsaws. Pah phooey!

Susan Williams

The twelve went to court on September 9, when the police wasted the court's time as some officers did not attend to give evidence. Most charges were dismissed although a few anti-fascists were bound over, some for two years.

At the start of May, The 1 In 12 Club received notification that their bid to buy a building had been approved by the council, now all they had to do was to find suitable premises.

Around the same time as this news, a scurrilous front page article about the 1 In 12 appeared in the weekly paper the *Keighley News*. The article cobbled together bits of disconnected incidents in an attempt to make a sensationalist story aimed at blackening the Club's image.

CATCH 22

Bradford band Catch 22 released their only single, *Bantam Anthem / Who's Sorry Now*, on their own 22 Records label in 1985 in celebration of Bradford City winning the then Third Division Championship. It was recorded at Studio 21 in Denholme Gate, Bradford, and was produced by Barry R Pyatt. The band's guitarist Jeff Ryan, whose

father was City's commercial manager, encouraged the idea of the single as the band rehearsed at City's ground, Valley Parade.

City promotion goes on record

BRADFORD City's league success could lead to a record chart success. Bradford band Catch 22 (above) have made a record called Bantam Anthem — a celebration of City's promotion.

The group, a four piece heavy rock outfit, practise at Valley Parade.

Lead guitarist Jeff Ryan's father is City's commercial manager Mike Ryan and he provided Catch 22 with the idea for Bantam Anthem. Now 2,000 copies of the single have been released and are said to be selling well.

Courtesy of the Telegraph & Argus

	VENGEANCE #2		
	CATCH 22 (1984-6)		
DAVE MALT Voc	JEFF RYAN Gtr	KEVIN HILL Bass	ROY HANNAN Dms

THE BRADFORD CITY FIRE DISASTER

Over eleven thousand fans turned up at Valley Parade on Saturday, May 11, 1985, to see Bradford City's captain Peter Jackson presented with the Third Division Championship trophy before their end-of-season clash with Lincoln City.

What should have been a day of celebration turned to tragedy when, at approximately 3.44 pm, flames were visible in the seventy-seven-year-old wooden main stand. All the rubbish that had accumulated underneath the stand over the years had caught fire, possibly from a dropped match or cigarette according to later forensic evidence.

The fire quickly engulfed the whole stand within minutes as it travelled quicker than the three thousand fans in the stand at the time could escape. One fan, Stefan Krolak, observed, *'The smoke seemed to suddenly set on fire. People were falling onto each other and screaming. They did not have a chance. Tarpaulin fell on them and stuck to their clothes and then ignited. I saw one man lying on the ground burning from head to foot. There was hardly anything left of him.'*

One woman was seen running around the ground with no skin on her arms and face. She was hysterical and trying to find her three children. (13)

Countless acts of heroism by supporters, the police and firefighters took place as people frantically escaped onto the pitch. Members of City's infamous 'Ointment Crew' even used their leather jackets to extinguish flames on victims.

In the end, a total of fifty-six people lost their lives that day and a further two hundred and eighty-five people were injured. Many were treated by members of Bradford's Asian community in their homes near the club's ground.

The people of Bradford immediately rallied their community support and helped to start a disaster fund for the survivors and families of the victims. Hundreds of fundraising events were organised including a series of gigs in June at St George's Hall by Bradford guitarist John Verity.

CHAPTER 6 - INDIE ALTERNATIVE ROCK 1984 - 1986

THE CROWD

John Verity was also instrumental, with other Bradford musicians, in organising the charity fundraising single *You'll Never Walk Alone* – a cover of the 1960s hit by Gerry & The Pacemakers.

Gerry Marsden and other well-known names including Phil Lynott, Bruce Forsythe, Paul McCartney, Graham Gouldman, Lemmy of Motorhead, NMA's Rob Heaton and members of Smokie got together as The Crowd to record the single which got to number one for two weeks from June 15.

1 In 12 Club member Paddy Singh organised a disaster benefit at Queen's Hall on June 13, with Liverpool's The Icicle Works supported by local bands The Word, Spectre and Doctor & The Inmates. The gig raised £502.91 towards the disaster fund and a further £500 was raised by local group Happiness AD from the sales of their debut single.

One of the fire's victims, Matthew Wildman, organised a benefit at St George's Hall, which featured Lemonoid, Excalibur, Silence and Harlequyn. The money from this particular gig was for a much-needed hydro-therapy pool (costing around £40,000) to be installed for burns sufferers at St Luke's Hospital. Eventually, over £4m was raised. The majority of the money went to the survivors and the victims' families with some going to burns therapy research at specialist units.

In the aftermath of the disaster, a public enquiry was headed by Judge Oliver Popplewell. The resulting Popplewell Inquiry was published in July 1985 and led to new legislation governing safety at sports grounds and stadiums.

Valley Parade was eventually re-developed and re-opened on the 14th December 1986 when an England eleven were beaten 2-1 by a City side in a friendly match.

Two memorials were placed at each end of the main stand to remember those who perished and suffered on that fateful day. The ground is now a modern 25,000-seat stadium.

Bradford City announced that their famous claret and amber strip would henceforth include a black trim on their shirt collars and arms as a permanent mark of respect to those who died.

Another memorial, a sculpture donated by Bradford's twin city of Hamm, stands in Centenary Square in front of City Hall.

Our Sincere Thanks to: THE CROWD

Gerry Marsden, Tony Christie, Denny Laine, Tim Healy, Gary Holton, Ed Stewart, Tony Hicks, Kenny Lynch, Colin Blunstone, Chris Robinson, A. Curtis, Phil Lynott, Bernie Winters, Girls School, Black Lace, John Ottway, Rick Wakeman, Baron Knights, Tim Hinkley, Brendan Shine, John Verity, Rolf Harris, Rob Heaton, Patrick McDonald, Smokie, Bruce Forsythe, Johnny Logan, Colbert Hamilton, Dave Lee Travis, Rose Marie, Frank Allen, Jim Diamond, Graham Gouldman, Pete Spencer, Chris Norman, Gerard Kenny, The Nolans, Graham Dene, Suzy Grant, Peter Cook, The Foxes, Jess Conrad, Ki n Kelly, Motorhead, John Entwhistle, Jimmy Hennie, Joe Fagan, David Shilling, Karen Clark, Gary Hughes, Zac Starkey, Eddie Hardin, Paul McCartney, Kiki Dee, Keith Chegwin, The Chocolate Factory Studio, Ronnie French, Paul Hodsman, Walton & Green Advertising, Nigel Gilroy, Laura, CRS Printers, Trans Video Productions, Wot Productions Visuals, Ian Matthews, Bob Jones CTS Studios, Joe (Put the kettle on), CMCS Printers, Max Clifford, Harry Barter, British Telecom, Livingstone Studios, Derek Franks Keyboard Hire, Five Bells, ITN, Spartan Records, A.I. Records

Produced by Graham Gouldman/Ray Levy coordinated by David Thomas

All of the above people and companies gave their time and talent freely, to aid the Bradford City Disaster Fund.

We thank them.

Manufactured & Distributed by Spartan Records.

SYSTEMBEAT
WORST OF THE 1in12 CLUB. VOLUME. 4. PAY NO MORE THAN £2

In June 1985, the second vinyl LP release on 1 In 12 Club Records appeared. *Systembeat - The Worst Of The 1 In 12 Club Volume 4*, featured sixteen bands who had played at the Club during the previous year.

Seething Wells gave it an excellent review in the *NME*, as did Celia Barlow in the *Telegraph & Argus*. John Peel once again promoted a Bradford record release when he played tracks from the album on his nighttime Radio One show.

The track *Tremblin'* by The Men From The Mountains was described by Peel as 'dead catchy' and after he played it many times on his show the distribution company Backs convinced the Club to release it as a single.

A three-track 12-inch of the song was subsequently pressed and became the first single to be released on 1 In 12 Club Records.

FEATURING ON the sleeve a screaming policeman suspended on a cross composed of cruise missiles, this record contains 16 tracks from as many bands, all of whom have had the privilege of having played Bradford's fave anarchoholic slam dancing den.

Quite accurately reflected is the move by the majority of the nation's garage bands (or, in the case of Bradford, allotment shed bands) away from Krangkrang music towards the sort of pop one had hoped had rolled over and died when ABC went mental and Paul Morley got his gold American Express card. This is not necessarily something we approve of.

This record features beat combos with names like GodDog, Dik Dik Dimorphic and Dig Vis Drill. It features songs with titles like 'Fruitcake Jake', 'Mood Music For The British Empire' and 'How I Made A Million $ Leading Two And A Half Lives For The FBI'.

There are four tracks worth flaring one's nostrils about. 'Ideal Home' by Spectre (who must now rank as one of the UK's meanest, leanest and *least noticed* reggae acts), 'Cause' by A Witness, 'Debra' by Big Flame and 'My Mama's Dead' by The In-Stinks. These last three juicy little buggers are frenetic dance tunes for illiterate politicos – that is to say they are prime slices o' rock of a modern mode played with much aggression, little ear for melody and crudely stripped of lisping, poncing or ill-informed pontification.

Available from 31 Manor Row, Bradford 1 for £2.50 plus package and posting or *free* to anyone who sends in the remains of a destroyed copy of 'Meat Is Murder'.

What a bargain.

Steven Wells

A fair deal
'Systembeat' - The Worst of the 1 in 12 Club (Volume 4)

With the region's most (in)famous venue closed for the summer, **Systembeat** is a welcome exposition of the **Worst of the 1 in 12 Club**. There's sixteen bands featured on this fourth volume from Bradford's Market Tavern, and barely a soft-centre amongst them.

If L.P.s are a summer excursion then whilst most releases are content to stroll around the promenade, Systembeat is a hell-raising time at the fair. **Indiscriminate Hoax Fund's** Bulkhead' sets the pace for the day with an aggressive spin on the rota; they're joined by **Category "A"** and **Big Flame** giving it loads with 'Debra'.

Over to the waltzers where **Spectre's** 'Ideal Home' provides the most commercial sound on the album. In the next carriages are **The Sinister Cleaners**, **Dik Dik Dimorphic**, and an instrumental from **Son of Sam**. But the highlight is, without a doubt, the **Citron Girls**. With a title (and sound to match) like 'How I made a million $ by leading two and a half lives for the FBI' the big dipper is the only place for them.

On the dodgems 'I'm Hip, I'm Vain' from **Dig Vis Drill** is colliding with **The Blood Brothers**; and smashing into the rear are some unlikely 999-riffs in a melodic number from **The Effect**.

If the Fall were here they'd be on the big wheel. But they're not, so up there instead are **A-witness** and **The In-stinks** with 'My Mama's Dead'. (How come Bogshed missed out?)

And finally, wandering around mid-way between the coconut shy and hot dog stall (their feet rarely leaving the ground) are **GodDog**, **Vegetable Section** and **The Men from the Mountains**.

Entrance fee to the Worst of the 1 in 12 Club is only £2.50, so it's definitely recommended. It's available in all good record shops but for further information contact the 1 in 12 Record Collective, 31 Manor Row, Bradford 1.

D. Blake

At the end of June, The 1 In 12 Club ended its residency at The Market Tavern with a final gig featuring, among others, a scratch group called The 1 In 12 Cowboys

The Market Tavern was The 1 In 12 Club venue at the time the second and third vinyl *Worst Of...* compilations were released. Fritz The Cat, the Club's resident photographer, regularly snapped club events, including the various antics of Wild Willi Beckett (pictured above at the debut Dr & The Inmates Tavern gig) and promo pictures for the Enemies Of The State compilation, which were cannibalised and used on all three LP covers.

SING SING

**CHINESE GANGSTER ELEMENT
IAN
THE 1 IN 12 COWBOYS**
Bradford 1 in 12 Club
IMMODISHLY bedecked in the battered leathers of a Dylanesque rent-boy (which he most definitely is not), alternative Elvis impersonator Ian perches rigidly on a barstool and hammers with affection coy electric ballads in the style of the rotting white whale.

Goodbyes are mumbled and on trot the wholly uninfamous 1 In 12 Cowboys with much gusto, yeehawing and the like. They slap their chaps and proceed to crucify Boring Gary, a 1 in 12 Club central committee strong man, with 15 rosily barbed verses of 'Superstar', delivered smilingly so's the victim has to grit and bear it or stand accused of boorishness.

The personal and political divisions that lurk in the corridors of this institution like hordes of shamefully conceived brats are dragged forth screaming into the harsh daylight and incorporated into the art of the masses. Paris '68 or what? Probably 'or what'.

Chinese Gangster Element created the best moment on the great 1 in 12 Club LP. 'Disappointing' is a sad word and one which I squirm and wriggle to avoid *but* pop such as theirs should make a virtue of its potential gaudy starkness. Instead they were rather plain and not a trifle muddy. There were earthworms in the jelly and the blancmange stank of slug-pellets. I'm sure they can do better.
– *Susan Williams*

THE MILKY WAY CLUB

A new club opened on Friday nights at Benson's on Simes Street at the end of May. Called the Milky Way Club, it was organised by Wibsey lass Hayley Smiles. Within the first few months, King Kurt, Play Dead, Poison Girls and Skeletal Family played there. Benson's closed down in June 1986 after being mysteriously gutted by fire.

On May 29, The Membranes were supported by a new Leeds band called The Butter Cookies at The 1 In 12 Club. The Cookies were fronted by one James Brown, fanzine editor of *Attack On Bzag* fanzine. (14)

On Saturday, June 24, local musician Papa T and others organised a free outdoor festival called *International Festival Of Youth* at Lister Park in Manningham. Between 11.30 am and 10.30 pm over two thousand people tuned up to see an array of local talent such as The Word, Jab Jab, The Best Way To Walk, Spectre, Jed's Blues Band, Olulu Ololu, Doctor & The Inmates as well as The Membranes and Victor Brox's Blues Train.

Compere Wild Willi Beckett introduced the first and only performance by Stuart Morrow fronting his own band, fresh from leaving New Model Army.

Unfortunately, heavy rain spoiled the festivities and the gig was stopped before most bands got a chance to play due to fears of electrocution.

On July 13, it seemed that you couldn't avoid watching Bob Geldof's Ethiopian relief concert *Live Aid* which took place at Wembley Stadium.

Over two billion people were estimated to have watched via worldwide satellite links as the likes of Queen, Status Quo, The Who, U2, David Bowie and a host of others took the stage at the all-day event.

REBECCA STORM

Shipley-born singer Elizabeth Caroline Hewlett, known by her stage name Rebecca Storm, reached twenty-two in the singles charts with the single *The Show*. The song, on Towerbell Records, was the theme from the TV show *Connie*. In August 1986 she released a second single, *Widow's Tears*.

Doncaster lad John Parr got to number one in the US singles chart in September 1985 with *St Elmo's Fire* - the title track of the movie of the same name. It reached number six in the UK singles chart. John, had at one time been in a band called Ponder's End with Bradford lad Geoff Lyth, formerly of the John Verity Band.

There was a 1 In 12 organised gig at Checkpoint in early October, featuring Dutch band Eton Crop supported by The Best Way To Walk.

THE LIBERTY CLUB

In October 1985, a group of 1 In 12 members travelled to Lundwood Ex-Servicemen's Club in Barnsley to watch a play called *The Liberty Club*. Loosely based on The 1 In 12 Club, the play was written by 1 In 12 member Tony Grogan, who had won a prize in the South Yorkshire County Council Playrighting Competition earlier that year.

At the end of October, having left The Market Tavern, The 1 In 12 Club started gigs at a new venue, the Queen's Hall in Morley Street. On the first night, the Inca Babies supported by Leeds band Wedding Present kicked off the start of a new residency.

CHAPTER 6 - INDIE ALTERNATIVE ROCK 1984 - 1986

Systembeat 2 - The Worst Of The 1 In 12 Club Volume 5 was released in October 1985. This fifth *Worst Of...* compilation was the third to be issued on vinyl, as the first two volumes were on cassette.

It arrived hot on the heels of Volume 4 and again featured sixteen bands who had played at the Club in the past year.

Another NME review was forthcoming from Seething Wells, as was more airplay on John Peel's BBC radio show. Between 8 and 28 October, he played tracks by GRRR, One Thousand Violins (with whom he was very impressed), The Passmore Sisters and Inca Babies.

System Beat Two — The worst of the One In Twelve Club, Vol 5 — *Andrew Middleton*

The latest evidence of the fun and variety to be had at Bradford's Queens Hall on a Wednesday night. Sixteen bands, all for £2.50.

Young and beautiful is a nice, harmless track from **Boys From The East** complete with sweet violins. **The Shee Hees** say **Hello**, (yes the Lionel Ritchie song!) recorded live in a pool of laughing gas somewhere in Berlin. Mickey Mouse turns to opera and smuck.

Chimeras is soundtrack music to footage of alcoholic nausea. Spacey and haunting. God knows what it's really about, but that's the **The Chorus** for you.

The Jazz Hipsters appear reminiscent of the early Damned without Brian James. She don't care nor do I, by **Still Life**.

Quickly on to **The Passmore Sisters**, **Strong For Europe**, with a boppy bass line, swinging this into a succinct pop song with socio-soul roots. **Livin' In The Eighties** by yuk, I mean Ik. No, yuk will do.

Tragic Tale Of Daniel by Sheffield's **One Thousand Violins** could've been sung by Dusty Springfield, though this would appear to be a demo for Morrisey.

At last! **The Inca Babies**. The perfect, stereotypical 1 In 12 band. Round bass, thick guitar lines and splashy chords. What's more an idea of where rock 'n' roll should've been in '85. **Mass Of Black** do the **Rock 'N' Roll Hospital**. This is where the artform was in rural '78.

The clearest and most profound sentiments are expressed by **Domestic Extremes** in **Reproductive Ritual**. The contradictions of heterosexual male feminist sympathisers legion don't agree with me. Pass.

Grrr's, **Xenophobia** is a performance of a captivating, discordant nightmare. **Broken Bones** by the (not very) **Silent Community** wins the golden chainsaw award for '85.

Matamba are notably the only reggae band here. Excellent too, though haven't I and I heard this before!...a trifle unfair.

And finally **Doctor And The Inmates** give us some fast moving mental hysteria with grating, twangy guitar on **Never A Rebel**. Unlike System Beat One, a compilation for needle hoppers, but still worth the modest £2.50.

1984 - 1986   BRADFORD'S NOISE OF THE VALLEYS VOLUME 1

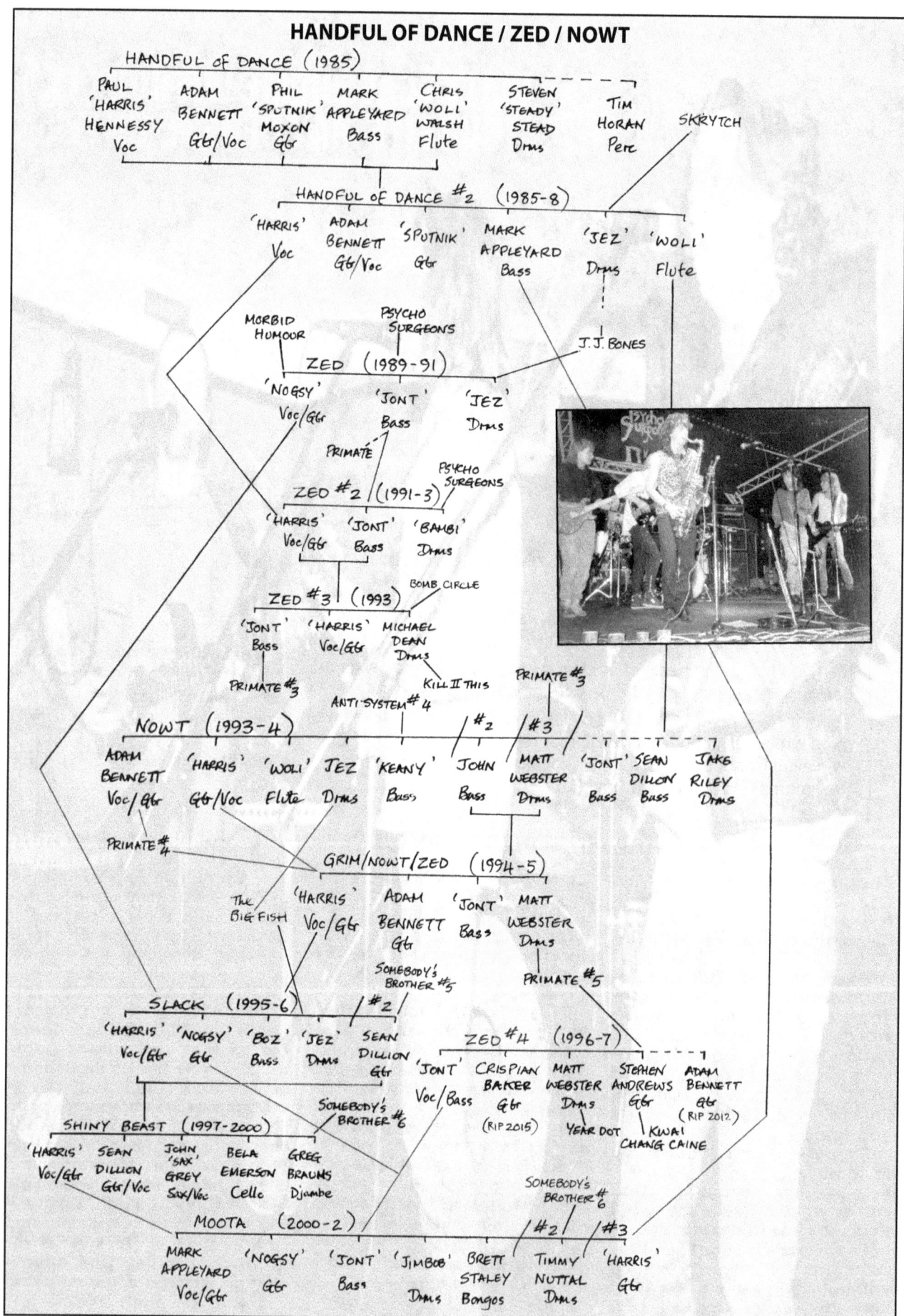

282

CHAPTER 6 - INDIE ALTERNATIVE ROCK 1984 - 1986

HANDFUL OF DANCE

A gig at the Manningham Community Centre on November 2 saw the live debut of Handful Of Dance.

Based around vocalist Harris, guitarist Adam Bennett and flautist Chris 'Woli' Walsh, Handful were a good time 60s and 70s-influenced band who became regulars on the local scene at clubs like Bibi's (below) and Queen's Hall.

Drummer Jez also stood in for Harlequyn and Leeds Goths Salvation amongst others before joining former Psycho Surgeon Jont to form rock band Zed in 1989.

Harris also joined Zed as guitarist in 1991 to record *The Articles Of Captain Mission* album on QTA Records, and the later released live Zed LP *Twelve Days In A Bunker*, originally broadcast live on Radio Praha during the band's tour of the Czech Republic in 1992.

Most original members of Handful Of Dance re-formed as Nowt in 1993 to play on the local scene until a version of the band relocated to Prague in the Czech Republic in 1994, where they played as both Nowt and Zed. That same line-up was later known as Grim.

Other Handful/Nowt/Zed crossover bands include Slack, Shiny Beast, The Horton Carpets and Moota – a band formed around original Handful bassist Mark Appleyard as singer/songwriter before he emigrated to Australia in 2004.

Vocalist Harris went on to perform with various acts, including Owt, Siren, Chiang and Signia Alpha.

THE KEIGHLEY SCENE

The music scene in Keighley was extremely vibrant during the mid-1980s, with local heroes The Skeletal Family leading the way.

New bands emerged,

RATTLESNAKE SHAKE (1985-				#2		TWILIGHT
MARTIN TARPY Voc	WARREN FYFFE Gtr	TONY McCOLGAN Bass	ROB KERSHAW Drms	TONY 'TRON' TRONELONE Keyb	DAMIEN 'HERMAN' SHORT Bass	GARY LAWSON Drms
MR. MEANA #2				HIDDEN WARFARE		

including Rattlesnake Shake (above), Suffering In Silence, American Housewives and heavy rock outfit Eazy Street.

One new band, Fahrenheit 451, were like a local supergroup made up of veterans of previous local bands. They played their first gig supporting Men From The Mountains in York.

Eazy Street

EAZY STREET (1984-6)				
JONATHAN KEIGHLEY Voc	PETER RUSH Gtr	ADRIAN MITCHELL Gtr	MICHAEL CASTLE Bass	PHIL LLOYD Drms
	The PARIS EFFECT	KICK	VIXEN	The ELEMENTS #2
EAZY STREET #2 (1986-7)			#3 (1988-	
JONATHAN KEIGHLEY Voc/Gtr	MARK RUSH Gtr	PETER GUEST Gtr	GORDON HARGREAVES Bass	JOHN (blank) Drms	PHIL LLOYD Bass	STUART LILLEY Drms

AMERICAN HOUSEWIVES / UNCLE ALBERT's ITCHY FEET (1985-90) / #2						
BOB MARSDEN Voc	MILES WRIGHT Sax	GRAHAM HARDCASTLE Gtr	SHAUN (blank) Bass	GRAHAM SMITH Drms	'SHAMUS' Harm	ANDY INGHAM Bass

ETHEL & the HEROES (1986-8)				
JONJO McCOLGAN Voc	DEREK MOUNTAIN Gtr/Voc	ANDY SALE Bass/Voc	PHIL STORTON Drms/Voc	DARRON MIDGLEY Keyb

283

BRADFORD'S BOUNCING BACK!

In 1986 Bradford Council announced a new campaign to bolster the city's image called *Bradford's Bouncing Back* (using a bear logo!) after the tragic previous year. The city hit the headlines straight away as local snooker player Joe Johnson beat Steve Davis to become world champion.

January 4 was a sad day for rock music nationally in Britain, as Thin Lizzy's Irish bassist/songwriter Phil Lynott died, aged 36.

In that month 1 In 12 Club Publications published its second book; *The Secret Society Of The Freemasons* - an exposé by A Cowan.

THE SATURDAY CLUB

From early January to July, a new club opened at Queens Hall called *The Saturday Club*, run by promoter Ali Briggs of Gigz '86 Promotions.

He gave many local bands a gig as well as putting on more established names like jazz guitarist Gary Boyle. In 1987 Ali started putting on gigs at Bibi's (Manhattan Club) in Manningham, including the very first gig by Spoilt Bratz who later changed their name to Terrorvision.

Ali went on to run the nightclub The Mill at his building at 262 Thornton Road from the late nineties, putting on all sorts of gigs and all-nighters. The venue also incorporated his Blueprint printing business Blue Noise studio, as well as being the home of various local acts including Griff's Magic Theatre, NMA, Paradise Lost, Mutiny 2000 Studios and Chumbawamba.

RED WEDGE TOUR

On January 29, the *Red Wedge Tour* came to Bradford's St George's Hall as part of a drive to raise awareness of the Labour Party to young voters. The concert featured The Style Council, Billy Bragg and The Communards.

As a forerunner to the evening's event, there was a local version of Red Wedge that afternoon in the Queen's Hall ballroom, featuring Joolz, Boys From The East, 8 Day Feud and Western Dance.

After the gig, a crowd of over a hundred were present as a panel of Billy Bragg, Paul Weller and Richard Corbridge of The Communards held an informal question and answer session prior to the evening's concert.

Most of the crowd asked the panel polite questions on unemployment, etc., until near the end one member of the crowd finally got to ask Billy Bragg why he had asked for £200 expenses to do a benefit for striking miners at The 1 In 12 Club during the recent miners' strike at a time he was promoting himself as 'have guitar will travel to play in your living room, if you feed and put me up'. He was clearly embarrassed by the question and mumbled a fudged answer along the lines of having to be careful of promoters. At that point, the panel's chairperson quickly terminated the session before any more awkward questions were fired at the political pop heroes.

IAN ASTBURY cultures some home truths with Pic below is by...HELEN MORLEY c 84.

Left to right: Wild Willy Beckett, Ian Astbury and Gary (of Bradford 1 in 12 club infamy.)

CHAPTER 6 - INDIE ALTERNATIVE ROCK 1984 - 1986

PSYCHIC WARDROBE / SUFFERING IN SILENCE

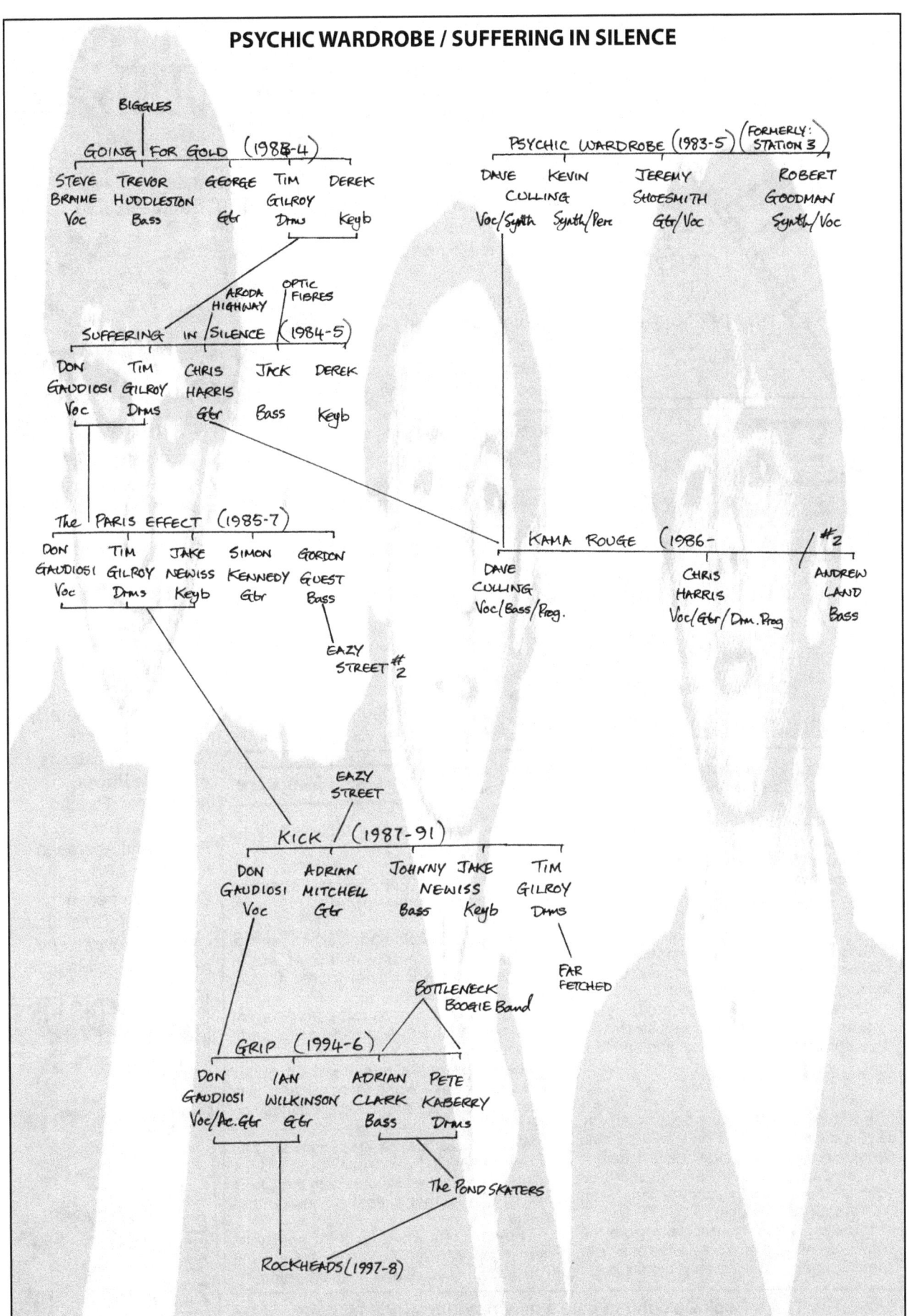

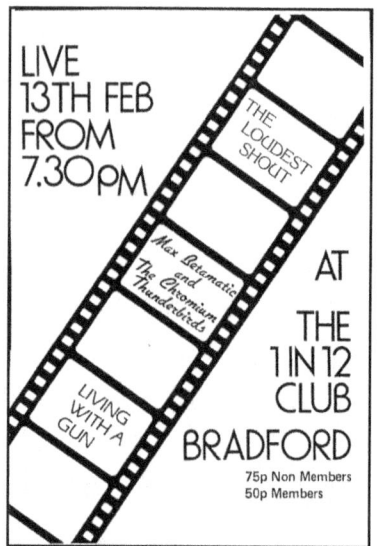

On February 27, 1986, Radio One DJ John Peel announced on that night's show, '…*talking about Wedding Present gigs, they're back in Yorkshire on April the 10th at the 1 In 12 Club, Bradford, which I'm now a member of, and the Pig (his nickname for his wife Sheila) too, although the Club probably don't know that yet.*' And yes, the Club didn't!

The following night fellow Leeds band Red Lorry Yellow Lorry played at the 1 In 12 and pulled in what turned out to be the biggest indoor audience in the Club's history. Hordes of Goths from god knows where were rammed into the Queen's Hall's Cellar Bar to see them, supported by local bands Seven Antelopes and Lifting The Veil.

Since The 1 In 12 Club had begun its residency at Queen's Hall it had staged a succession of well-attended gig nights featuring the likes of The Passmore Sisters, The Ex, Vee VV, Anti-System, and a Sheffield night with Pulp (again), Mr. Morality and Dig Vis Drill). Over the next few months the Club would host gigs by Blythe Power, AC Temple, Psycho Surgeons, Skeletal Family and Aberdeen funk boys APB.

During this period the *T&A's Rock On* column was taken over by new reporter Chris Maguire.

RED Lorry Yellow Lorry's relentless drive to success is gathering speed with the impending release of their second album.

by Chris Maguire

And the popular Leeds band are taking to the road to promote it.

They will be roaring into Bradford next Thursday when they play the 1 in 12 Club at the Queen's Hall Cellar Bar. In their convoy at the gig will be Bradford bands Lifting The Veil and Seven Antelopes.

Red Lorry Yellow Lorry's national tour begins tonight in Glasgow and takes them through to March 10 in Coventry.

On the way they will be stopping at, among others, Leeds Warehouse (March 3), Manchester, Birmingham and London.

Powerful

Paint Your Wagon, the second album, is released on March 7 on the Red Rhino label. Enclosed in a sleeve which opens into a poster, it promises to outsell their first LP, released in January last year, Talk About The Weather.

It drew great critical acclaim from the music press and radio as have many of their singles, most notably Monkeys on Juice, Hollow Eyes, and their last one, Spinning Round.

Since their formation in July 1982, they have consistently captured the attention of the public with their powerful, raunchy music.

Their unique sound has earned them a loyal following not only in the UK but in Europe and America. They toured abroad extensively last year.

And this year proves to be no different as a heavy touring schedule sees them travelling to Australia and Japan.

Their line-up is Chris Reed on guitar and vocals, Dave Wolfenden, guitar, Chris Oldroyd, drums, and Leon Phillips on bass guitar.

With one album and seven singles under their belt, Paint Your Wagon looks all set to be another winner with their fans and should attract a host of new enthusiasts.

They are renowned for their energetic live performances, so catch them next Thursday and you won't be disappointed.

The T&A's Rock On column gets a new reporter: Chris Maguire

THE FIFTH ANNIVERSARY OF THE 1 IN 12 CLUB

A four-day festival was organised to celebrate the respective fourth and fifth birthdays of Bradford Centre Against Unemployment (BCAU) and The 1 In 12 Club in April.

The first night launch at the Metropole on Sunbridge Road on April 2 was a poetry evening and benefit for Jean Gittins *Striking Stuff* book, another release by 1 In 12 Club Publications.

Jean gave readings from her book and was supported on the night by local poets Joolz, Wild Willi Beckett, Slade the Leveller (Justin from New Model Army) and Hammer & Sickle. All performed to a packed room for an admission of only one pound or seventy pence for members.

The remaining three events were all free and were held at the club's regular venue Queen's Hall. On Thursday local ska bands Spectre and Natural Riddim played, while on Friday a theatre group called Theatre Babel presented a spectacular surprise performance.

On Saturday an all-day extravaganza ran from twelve noon onwards with videos, a magic show, stalls and food, and live music from Zip Gun & The Bayou Bigshots, Ritzen Ratzun Rotzen and Sweet Valentine Cowboys. In the evening a conceptual 'rock opera' called *Desmond Down* was performed by a range of local musicians. The concept for the opera was written and developed by Jont of local group Requiem and narrated by Wild Willi Beckett.

During this birthday week, the 1 In 12 eventually found a suitable building for a permanent venue in an old four-storey warehouse at 21-23, Albion Street, off Sunbridge Road, which was funded with local government grant money.

Club members began the renovation work needed to convert it into an independent music venue..

1 IN 12 CLUB BUILDING COLLECTIVE

Over the past two and a half years members of the 1 in 12 Club have been desperate to find a building suitable for conversion to our own club. In such a building we intended to hold gigs, discos, meetings, and provide a space for the varied interests and activities of the Club's members.

We applied to Bradford Council for a grant to purchase and renovate a suitable building. Our application was duly approved.

We tried various buildings most of which were unsuitable. These buildings tended to be too small, too large, too expensive to purchase, or too badly in need of repair.

However, in March 1985, we stumbled across 21/23 Albion Street and, after lengthy investigations by club members, it was decided to buy this building. Really, we had no option left. The pressure on us to spend our grant money, after a long and exhausting search had become immense.

Trying to spend this money, however, turned out to be more difficult than we had anticipated.

The building had previously been in use as a clothing warehouse, and, it was necessary to obtain planning permission to change its use to that of a members social club.

Due to the incompetence / inefficiency of the powers that be at Bradford Council we encountered a severe delay in getting planning approval. This consequently set back the rest of the building program by many months. (We are not, of course, suggesting that these delays were deliberate !)

After getting planning permission we obtained the services of an architect (Rance, Booth and Smith). Since that time we have made considerable progress, and, in February 1986 four 1 in 12 Club members were appointed trustees for the Club and the building was purchased for the sum of £26,000.

So, after a lot of hard work, frustration, and red tape, we now own a building. That's right, all members of the Club share in the ownership of this building. It is now up to all of us to share in the responsibility and hard work that lies ahead of us.

If like us, you are sick of being treated like shit; and want to be more than a passive consumer / spectator / punter; if you want a space where you can create; a space where you can relax with friends and meet people in a hassle-free environment; a place where all members participate in the running of the club without elites or hierarchies; then, it goes without saying that, now, more than ever, **WE HAVE GOT TO GET OUR SHIT TOGETHER !!!**

The actual work on this building is going to be difficult. We are still short of money, and consequently are going to have to do a lot of work ourselves.

If you are a joiner, electrician, plumber, bricklayer, painter, decorator, roofer, etc., or even if you have no practical experience at all, then we need your help on the building. We need your energy and enthusiasm, the two things that have kept the club running for the past five years.

So don't moan if things don't seem to be working out - it's up to **ALL** of us to make it work.

In May, Leeds band and 1 In 12 stalwarts First International received a half-page feature article in the *NME*.

Two Keighley bands released debut singles, Single File with *Out In Traffic / Cracked Cup* on their Mainline label distributed by York's Red Rhino, and Suffer in Silence with their double A-sided *Remember This / Girls On The Dancefloor*.

In early June, the music paper *Sounds* printed its first review of a 1 In 12 gig when local fanzine scribe James Brown reviewed Liverpool band The Walking Seeds' gig on the 5th. James went on to write for Sounds for many years.

In July, DJs Linda Sprogis and Anna left Benson's and started a regular alternative disco on Saturday nights called the *Monster Club* at the Spotted House on Manningham Lane.

It soon became a popular haunt of the city's post-punk crowd and ran until late 1988.

Internationalists (left to right) Alan, Shawn and Terry.

FIRST AND FOREMOST

THE MATING of politics and pop has always been unappealing to me, but First International from Leeds manage it quite attractively. They join politics to power in songs that seem to merge the finer ideals of The Redskins with the guitar energy of bands like U2 and The Cult.

"We formed in May 1984," explains drummer Al, "and since then we've supported acts like The Three Johns, The Nightingales, The TVPs and Chumbawamba. We took our name from the first (and last) meeting of International Socialists, Anarchists, and Communists – subsequent internationals have not included anarchists. Most of our songs like 'Blood Money' and 'Strike' are fairly obvious in terms of their subject matter."

First International have spent a long time touring locally and have had tremendous support from Gary who helps organise Bradford's excellent 1 In 12 club. Their sound is rock-based, relying for the main part on thunderous drums and soaring guitars. Like all the best political songsmiths (Billy Bragg being the prime example) their songs work because they have excellent tunes.

"There's three of us in the band," continues Al. "Shawn the bassist comes up with most of the initial songs and then Terry (guitar and vocals) and I work on them. We recorded our initial demos in the basement of Chumbawamba's house with Boff their guitarist. I think it's important that young bands help each other. You'd be amazed how many bands who get a brief mention in the press wouldn't let you breathe on their drum riser let alone lend you a plectrum!"

Despite being one of the more interesting independent bands, First International still have trouble obtaining gigs in London. They appear on the excellent Skin and Bone tape, so hopefully things will soon change. In the meantime, promoters take note, they can be contacted at: 47 Headingley Avenue, Leeds 6.

Neil Taylor

CHAPTER 6 - INDIE ALTERNATIVE ROCK　　　　1984 - 1986

THE WALKING SEEDS/ THE RIGHT STUFF
Bradford 1 In 12 Club

THE RIGHT Stuff *a la* Wolfe they may be named but the 'right stuff' *a la* Chuck Yeager they have not. And no band aside of a slice of early Motown or a line of long since smoked-out Pistols is ever likely to.

Pretty, well dressed and clean cut; not smug enough to turn your stomachs but seemingly far more at home in the pages of *Elle* and *The Face* than playing their not so sunny Bunnymen songs in this militant anarchists' non-working cats club. If they used and abused the talent of their influences rather than just imitating them, The Right Stuff would probably produce some *good* stuff.

The Walking Seeds are sewn up by an attitude that bleeds self-destruction and despises success. Formerly Liverpool's Mel-O-Tones, they packed in when acclaim was too easily attained and now find themselves drawling out sit down, Hendrix-ridden rot shots, occasionally burning but on the whole still yearning. If we're talking speed, their revs per minute spin at 33.

A noisy, piss-stinken bag of hate, minus the pomposity and gloom of the last five years' gothic monsters. Sulking weeds, they mutter like bastards and crumble out their best song 'Mark Chapman', a loathsome ditty in praise of the pig who gunned down Lennon and proof that not everyone who bums the line of the Mersey loves and lives in the shadow of the city's supposed favourite son.

The Seeds' songs are lonely, private and independent and, until they brighten up, should remain that way.

JAMES BROWN

THE MOON

Modern Jazz band based around African guitarist Emannuel Williams, bassist Mark Cranmer and saxophonist Keith Jafrate. They gigged extensively around the Yorkshire area and were regulars at Bibi's, The Albert in Huddersfield and, as shown right (with Jab Jab's Thomas J guesting on percusssion) the Theatre Tavern.

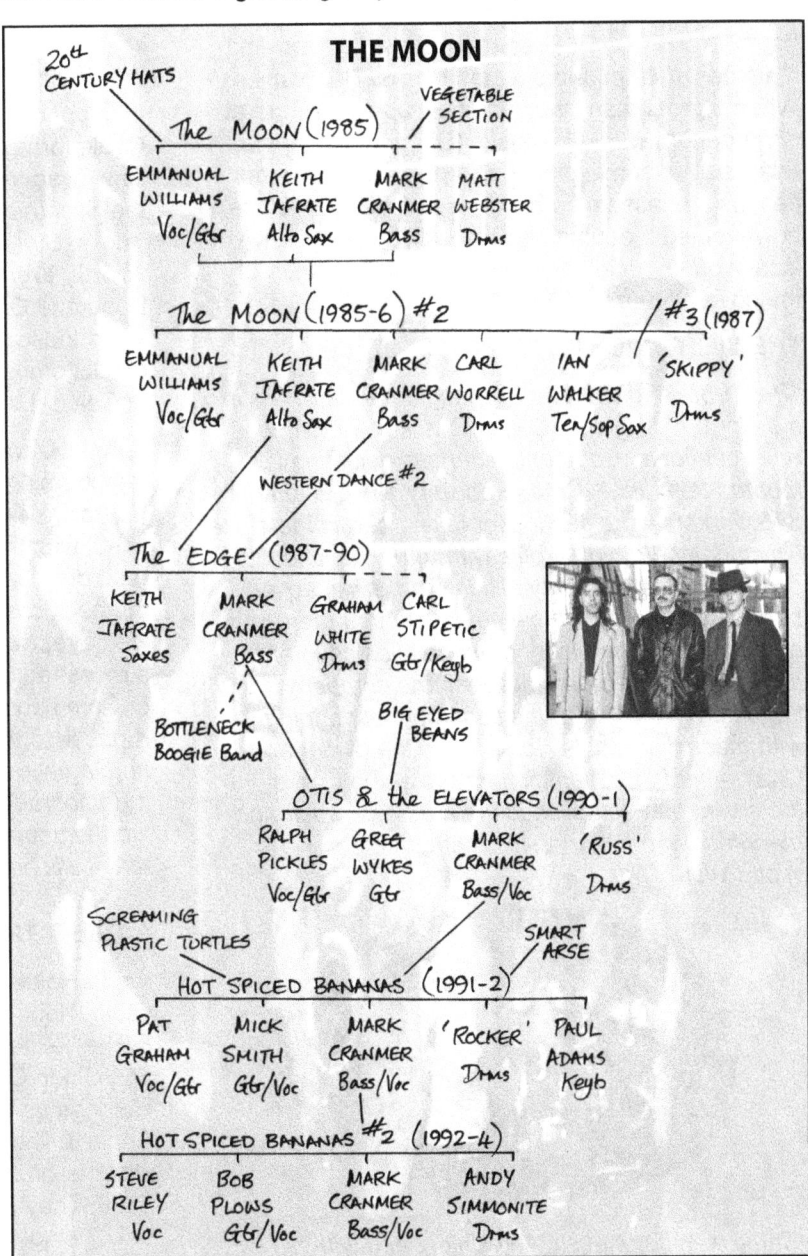

THE THEATRE TAVERN

Thomas J promoted local bands at a late-night Wednesday session at the Theatre Tavern on Manningham Lane. It ran from January 1986 until the pub was demolished to make way for the new Bradford link road Hamm Strasse in the summer of 1986.

MR LOVE

Shipley lass Elizabeth Caroline Hewlett, aka Rebecca Storm, put out the 7" single *Wrong Girl / Swansong* on Spirit Records in 1986.

In the same she year she also released the single *Mr Love / Mr King* on Columbia Records, which had music by Willy Russell and was recorded at Pink Studios, Liverpool. This was the title song of the film *Mr Love* starring Barry Jackson and Maurice Denham and directed by Roy Battersby. When a great many women show up at the funeral of gardener Donald Lovelace (Barry Jackson) his relatives are somewhat shocked – by all accounts he was a unassuming middle-aged man. Lovelace, however led a double life as a ladies' man, twelve local women recall their seduction at the hands of the covert lothario.

THE SILENTNIGHT STRIKE 1985-87

'The 1985-87 dispute at Silentnight had factories in the North of England (Barnoldswick & Sutton) was an exceptionally long and bitter strike, lasting 20 months from June 1985 - February 1987. A total of 346 workers were sacked for taking part in the strike which gained a high profile with remarkable levels of support and solidarity action. The Strike action began over the non-implementation of an agreed pay rise and compulsory redundancies counter to the existing agreement between the company and the union (FTAT), with the company responding with mass dismissals. Tom Clarke the owner and Chairman of the Silentnight group at the time of the strike, had established the mattress repair and manufacturing firm in Skipton after the second World War.

Clarke was notoriously Anti-Union, and with his senior managers were all Tory party members with close links to the party locally and nationally. The Strikers felt strongly that the denial of their pay rise and broken commitment over redundancies were motivated by greed of the company and especially the family that owned it.

Despite the failure of the recent Miners Strike (1984-85) the Labour movement and the far left gave continued support and donations to pickets / strikers outside the factories all through the dispute.

Two rallies were organised during the strike in support, the second was at Keighley in May 17,1986 with Dennis Skinner MP and others giving speeches.

The FTAT union called off the strike in November 1986, while 88 strikers continued unofficially until February 1987, when pickets and the dispute ended.'

JANET COOK

In support of the Silentnight strike, Janet Cook, former vocalist / guitarist with local band Dawnweaver / Remainz, produced and released the *Silentnight Strike EP* on 12" in 1986. The three tracks; *Strike Anthem / Blue Monday (In A Northern Town) / Working Week,* were recorded at Solid Bond and Offbeat Studios and mastered at the Townhouse in London on Cocomus Records of Colne, Lancashire.

Former Dawnweaver members and other musicians helped Janet with the recording, while on the back cover there was a reproduction of a message on House of Commons notepaper from the Labour leader Neil Kinnock to the strikers, *'The Silentnight strikers did nothing wrong- indeed they have done everything in a democratically right way. Their cause is just and worth support – so I back the boycott in the hope that it will help them to get a square deal.'*

ANNIE & THE AEROPLANES

Annie Holder had been in local bands Loose Livers, Olulu Olou, Cowpoke Annie & The Texas Longhorns and Chien Chaud Et Les Hotdogs before forming Annie & The Aeroplanes with her brother Kuni in 1986. They released their only 7"single *A Million Zillion Miles / Traveling Song* on the Pipedream Records label, recorded at the Home From Home Studios in 1988, and it is now very collectable.

```
ANNIE AND THE AEROPLANES
88   Pipedream PIPE 1    A Million Zillion Miles/Travelling Song..................15
```

CHAPTER 6 - INDIE ALTERNATIVE ROCK
1984 - 1986

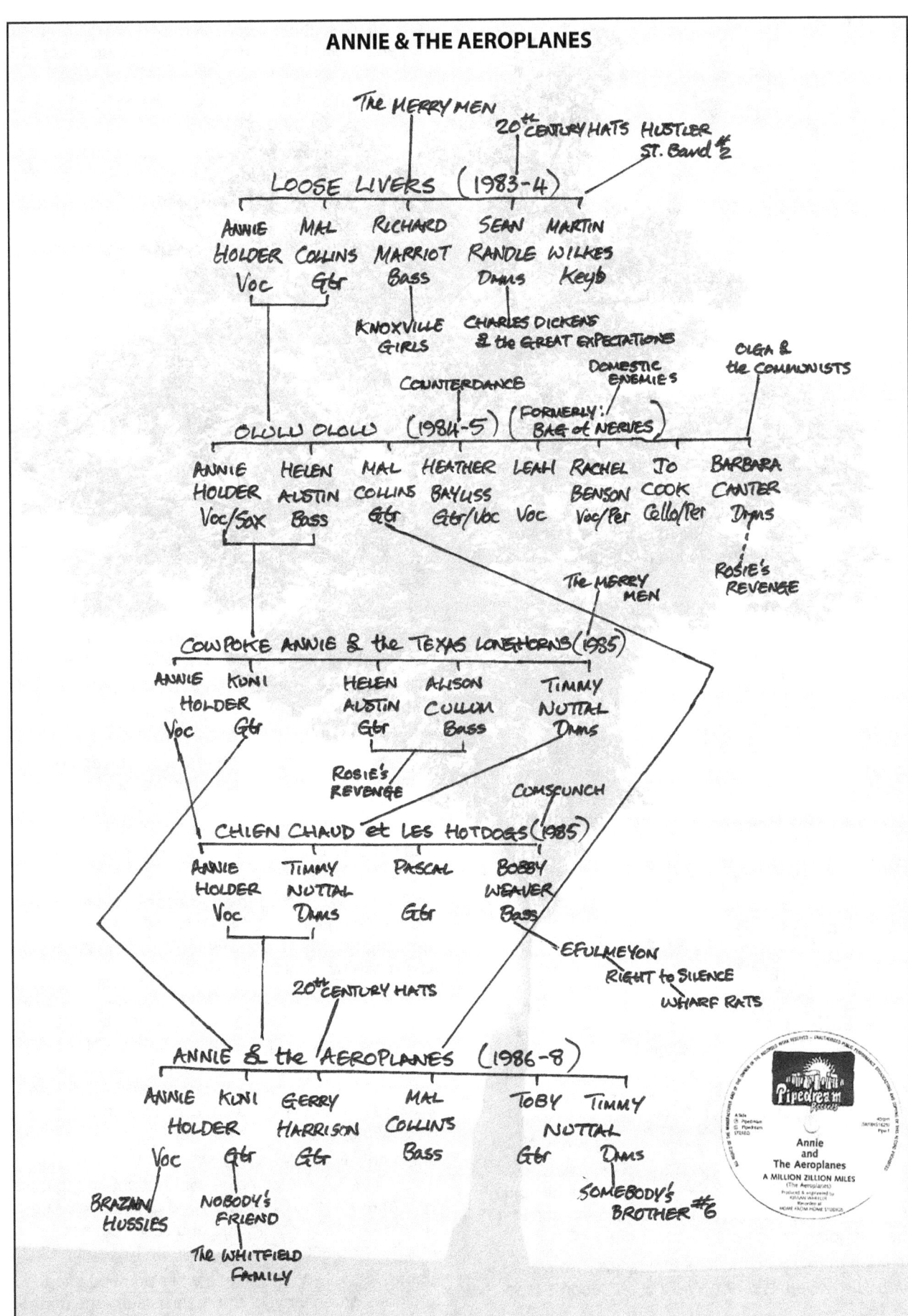

291

PSYCHO SURGEONS

Wild Willi Beckett had first put his poetry to music backed by an early line-up of New Model Army for live work which culminated in the recording of *Straw Hats* in 1981.

After working on the narration for the rock opera *Here's A Message From Desmond Down*, written by Requiem bassist Jont and performed at Benson's and later at Queen's Hall, Willi persuaded Requiem to perform a set based upon mental health issues personified by his alter ego 'The Doctor'. This became Doctor & The Inmates and a performance took place at The 1 In 12 Club (Market Tavern) in April 1985.

After a line-up adjustment as long-term drummer Bambi came on board, and a name change to avoid confusion with Doctor & The Medics, the Psycho Surgeons were born.

The band quickly built up a cult following, attracted by Willi's stage antics and theatrical costume changes as well as the band's tight, post-punk sound.

Their *Give A Man A Badge / Diagnosis* (FR001) single was the first release on Bradford's Flexible Response Records.

They supported New Model Army on their Brave New World tour in 1985, at which time EMI recorded a Surgeons live set for possible release as well as discussing a possible split single with NMA. Guitarist Chris McLaughlin left to become New Model Army's live second guitarist before going on to front the band Loud.

The band released their second single *The Book Of Job / Dirty Behaviour* on Willi's QTA Records label in 1987.

Jont left to form the band Zed and now with guitarist Tim and bassist Clive Hoey, the Surgeons recorded their *Madhouse* album, again on QTA in 1989.

The 12-inch single Panic On / Chasing The Dragon / R D Laing followed in 1990.

Zed, Wild Willi Beckett & Jont (poetry and bass) and Griff's Magic Theatre toured East Germany in 1990 as *The Mad Dogs And Yorkshiremen Tour*.

Willi took a new version of the band on tour to the Czech Republic in 1993, with Stan Greenwood on guitar, Rob Kershaw on drums and Johnny Lorrimer on bass, occasionally featuring Jont. When the brakes failed on the Surgeons' tour bus on a hill in Czech, driver Adi managed to steer the bus into a controlled crash and avert disaster. Willi slept through the whole event!

Newly inspired after a long break Willi remastered all the Surgeons' back catalogue at Mutiny 2000 Studios in 2003. The CD collections *Doctor & The Inmates*, *New Barbarians* and a re-master of the album *Madhouse* were the result.

Willi began recording the unfinished *Room 39* album, written about his time in a drying-out clinic, with a new lineup of the Surgeons in 2004.

After being diagnosed with terminal cancer, he organised a farewell concert for October 26, 2006, at the Bradford Rio - his 59th birthday. *One Last One* re-united past line-ups of the Psycho Surgeons with support from The Savages, The Fish Brothers and Griff's Magic Theatre.

The event was recorded and released for a double live album on Mutiny 2000 Records. A documentary featuring interviews and live footage from the night was made by local filmmaker Greg Brauns.

One final single, *Kingdom Come, Bring It On!*, was recorded as a tribute after Willi's untimely death in 2007, with Jont singing lead vocal. Excerpts of Will's voice from various sources including the demo version of the song were incorporated. The B-side is Willi's first-ever recording, the aforementioned *Straw Hats*, backed by New Model Army.

The single was released on Mutiny 2000 Records in November 2007 to coincide with a tribute gig put on by former Psycho Surgeons, and guests including Little Brother, Dave Savage and Nick Toczeck, which took place at The Beehive on November 3.

Controversially, Willi's ashes were pressed into the luminous green vinyl of the record itself - the first time that this has ever been done.

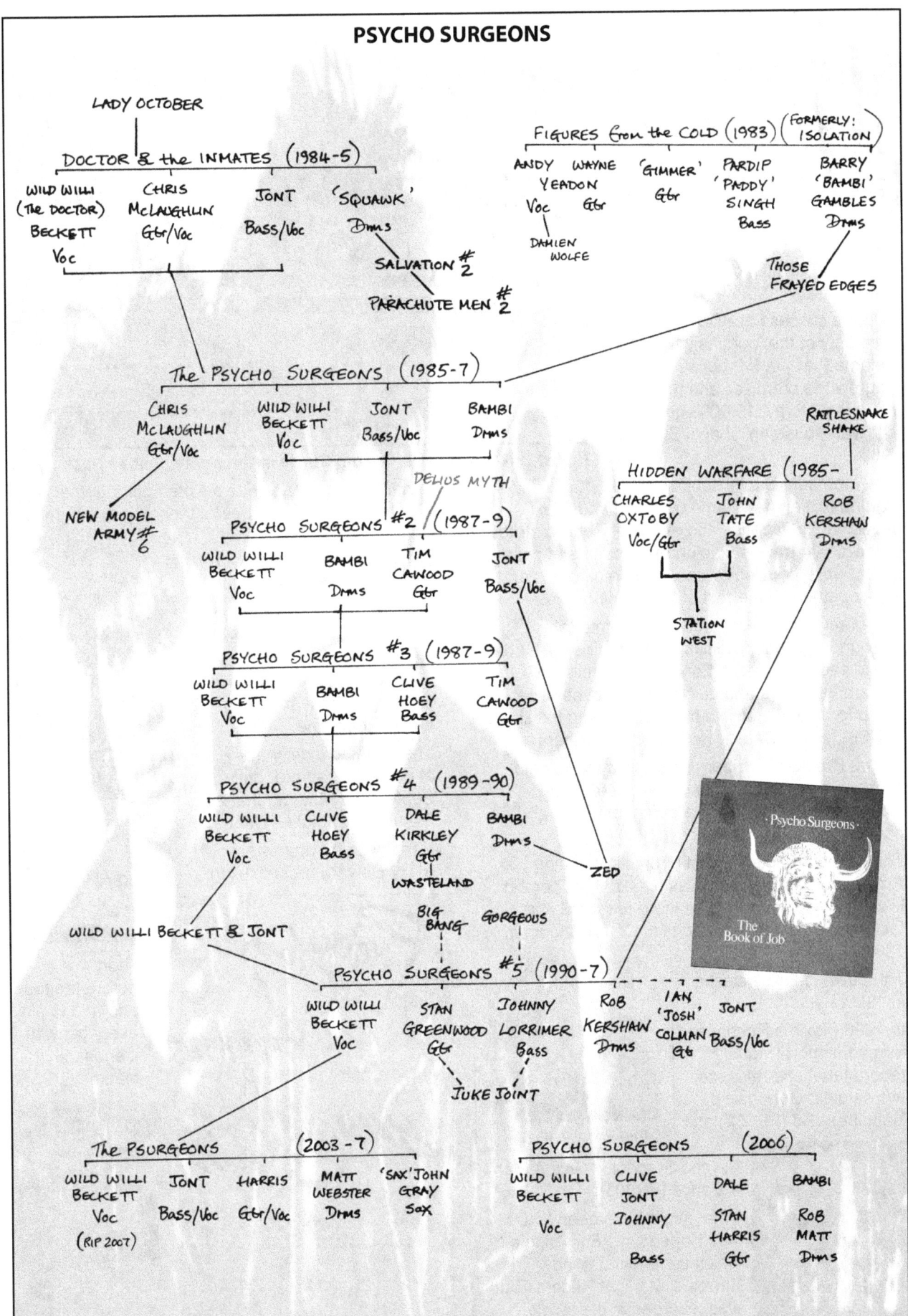

FLEXIBLE RESPONSE RECORDS

Brothers Phillip and Peter Edwards, along with the members of Southern Death Cult, had set up a small studio and rehearsal studio above Roots record shop in 1982.

With the success of SDC and the popularity of the facilities what had become Flexible Response quickly outgrew the premises and moved into a five-storey, 10,000-square-foot warehouse on Chapel Street in 1983.

Phillip Edwards observes Tom Currie in the newly built 24 track studio

New members Steve Robinson and Martina Robershaw came on board and 'Flexi' developed its facilities and eventually built a state-of-the-art 24-track studio on the ground and cellar floors, while housing offices, rehearsal rooms and a smaller studio in the rest of the building.

The practice rooms offered more comfortable surroundings than facilities in places like the Coda music shop on Church Bank and the cellar at Shearbridge Mills and quickly became the base camp for many Bradford bands, including the likes of NMA, Ghost Dance, Harlequyn and others.

Future Bradford number one songstress Tasmin Archer worked for a while in the office which included such luxuries as a coffee machine and a pool table.

The studio attracted a host of artists including American producer Don Was (of jazz funk combo Was Not Was) was enticed there to record a track for The Ward Brothers *Madness Of It All* album in 1986.

The building finally closed in 1989.

In 1986 Flexible Response formed a short-lived record label and released two singles; *Geburrah* by Happiness Ad (FR001) and the Psycho Surgeons' *Give A Man A Badge* (FR003).

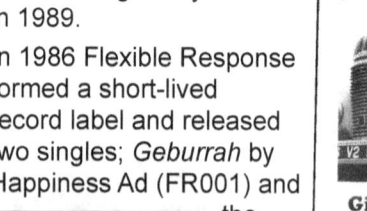

Give A Man A Badge

What might have been FR002 was Harlequyn's *Burn* single which came out on Andy Farrow's Starlight Records but was recorded at the studio.

Local manager Andy Farrow then put together a tour to showcase all three of these up-and-coming bands.

BRADFORD PACKAGE TOUR

The *Bradford Package Tour 86* saw the Psycho Surgeons, Harlequyn and Happiness AD set off on a tour which took in venues up and down the country, with the bands taking turns to headline.

The opening night was at Dollars, Bradford, on September 14, a gig that also featured Handful Of Dance.

Happiness Ad drummer Ricky Howard broke his leg shortly before the tour and had to play every gig with it encased in plaster.

CHAPTER 6 - INDIE ALTERNATIVE ROCK   1984 - 1986

HAPPINESS AD

In 1985 local group Happiness AD released their debut double A sided single *Love Can Be Cruel / Isolation* on the Leeds-based Off Beat label. The band's second seven inch, *Geburrah / Alone Again*, was released on the Flexible Response label.

They played many gigs on the local circuit and supported acts like New Model Army, Joolz, Fiction Factory and King Kurt. They played a shocase gig at Dingwalls, Camden Town, London on September 27, 1987.

Psycho Surgeon drummer Bambi took over the stickes when Ricky Howard teamed up with guitarist Chris McLaughlin to form Loud and record the albums *D-Generation* and *Psych 21* for China Records.

Ricky was reunited with vocalist Rob Moore to play in the bands Blood Orange, Moorzart, and Us in the nineties. In 2007 he formed Into The Clouds with Stuart Morrow and former Voyager UK singer Ivan Markovic a band which didn't get past rehearsals.

THE FROG AND TOAD

This new rock club opened on August 8, 1986, on the site of the old Zodiac Club on Little Horton Lane.

Owner Dennis Feather intended to promote HM/rock groups on a regular Thursday night basis, starting with Optic Nerve on the opening night.

For between £1 and £2, you could catch many local bands performing as well as more established rock acts like The Groundhogs who played on September 11.

It soon became a favourite venue for local heavy metal warriors who enjoyed headbanging at the club's excellent rock disco before and after the gigs. Unfortunately, the club stopped putting on gigs in July 1987.

The club moved to The Goldsborough, on Bolton Road, and was renamed Shades in the late 1980s.

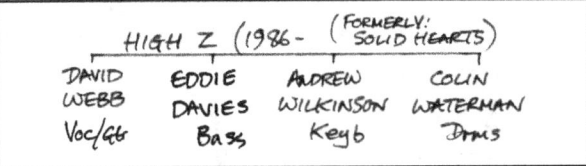

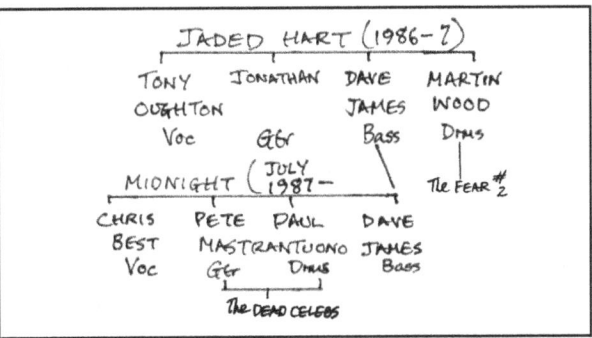

At the end of August, the last 1 In 12 Club gig at Queen's Hall featured Chumbawamba, before the Club again continued its search for a regular venue.

It moved to the Royal Standard on Manningham Lane. The first gig on September 11, featured local bands Western Dance and Out Of The Blue. The Club only lasted at the Royal Standard for a short period, eleven gigs in all, before moving on again.

WESTERN DANCE

After short-lived band The Nerve Agents split, frontman Liam Sheeran teamed up with guitarist Stephen Andrews. With the addition of fellow Agent Matt 'Matt Nazgul' Webster, Western Dance were formed.

Their high-energy power-pop indie-punk style quickly won them a large local following and the seven-song *Give Me The Moonlight* tape, their debut cassette release in April 1986, sold hundreds of copies at their gigs. This led to the release of two

live cassette albums and the seven-inch single *What Does It Take? / To And Fro / Give Me The Moonlight* (BREWD001) on Home Brewed Records label in March 1987.

The band played regularly at many Bradford venues, particularly Queen's Hall and every at 1 In 12 Club venue, and the band's continued flyposting campaigns brought a lot of local attention from local press and fanzines. Headline gigs in Manchester, Leeds and London lead to favourable national reviews and interest from several major labels.

IF you are a regular visitor to Bradford city centre you will be seldom in any doubt when local band Western Dance have a gig or a new record.

For posters like these, and matching stickers, tend to appear mysteriously on strategic walls and subways around the centre. Their style is instantly recognisable,

The man behind the eye-catching series of mini artworks is drummer Matt Nazgul. Matt, who's 21, hasn't had any formal art training, but his natural flair for the eye-catching and graphically striking could put many a professional to shame.

The 1987 cassette single *This Perfect Day* later appeared on the compilation album *Volnitza - The Worst Of The 1 In 12 Club Volume 6/7* in 1989 and received airplay on John Peel's show.

With a new set and a heavier sound, the band returned in the form of Primate from 1990 to 1995. Their track *Overwound* appeared on the 1 In 12 Club's *A Nightmare On Albion Street* album in 1990 and was played on Mark Radcliffe's Radio 1 show. This led to airplay on Mark Radcliffe and Marc 'Lard' Riley's *Hit The North* show on Radio 5 in 1993.

Singer Liam Sheeran and bassist Adrian Clark went on to form, Bullweek, from 1995 to 1999.

The pair reunited with drummer Matt Webster in 1999 and then guitarist Stephen Andrews in 2000 to become Kwai Chang Caine. They recorded two albums, both co-produced by Rob Heaton and released on Mutiny 2000 Records. *The Ones That Never Learn* (2002), and *Reel To Real Life*, which eventually saw the light of day in 2007. KCC also contributed tracks to the Mutiny 2000 compilation albums *White Abbey Road* in 2000 and *Soup Bowl Press* in 2002.

CD albums by Primate, *Mad Monkey*, and Western Dance, *Western Dance*, were released as part of Mutiny 2000's back catalogue in 2001.

Western Dance reformed for a 30th anniversary show at the Undergoround, Bradford, in November 2016, supported by Plastic Letters and released the compilation CD, *30*.

In 2020, the band reunited to record the 7-inch single *In The Distance / This Is Your...* as a comment on the Covid-19 lockdown.

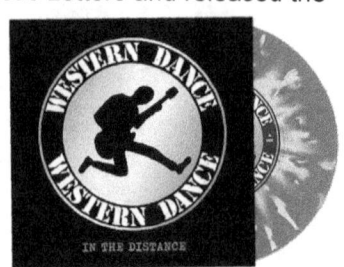

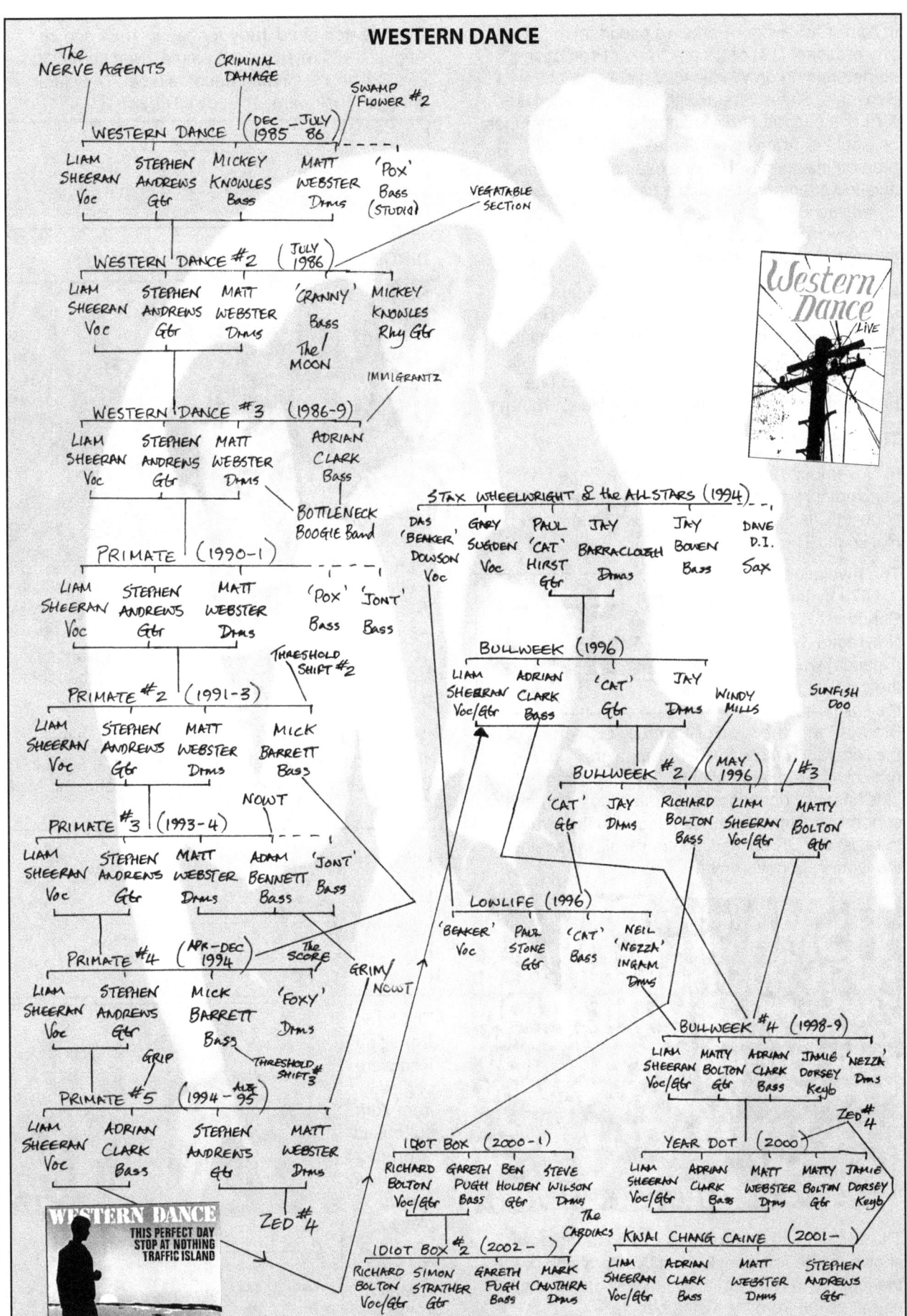

In April 1985, Honor Parker (a pseudonym for arty reasons) (15) of Honor Parker Promotions, started putting on Wednesday night gigs at Benson's, Simes Street, with Halifax's Langfield XY Love supported by Bradford's Seven Antelopes on April 24. Teaming up with a Halifax-based promotions agency, Honor explained, *'It's a long-awaited attempt to develop a type of promotional organisation to bring a spark of spectacular into the present music, to give them the confidence to express their talents and abilities.'* (16)

Langfield XY Love formed in mid-1983 and supported bands such as The Smiths and Section 25 as well as releasing a single on their own label, Moonboule Records, *Cinnamon Girl / Whistle & They'll Come*, which was produced by the late Factory Records in-house producer Martin Hannett.

THE TISMA PROJECT

In November 1986, it was the Tisma Project's first anniversary which they celebrated with a benefit show at Checkpoint featuring Hush-Hush Job For Rosie and The Moon.

The revolution in 1979 by the Sandanistas in Nicaragua (South America) was the catalyst for the linking of Bradford with the town of Tisma by supporters of the Nicaragua must Survive campaign. Thru the project vital aid (educational, health and recreation) plus financial donations were raised to help develop support and infrastructures needed in the struggle to resist the US backed Contra rebel war against the legitimate government.

The solidarity of Bradford folk in this struggle was shown by the few people from Bradford who made the journey to Nicaragua, with a welcoming warmth and affection from the Tisma people.

Cleckheaton band **Judy** formed in 1984 and in August 1985 released the single *Treatment Of Love / Follow* on the Cryptic Records label. They later changed their name to Judy's Dream.

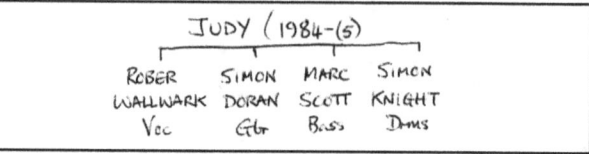

CIRCUS

Rock band Circus appeared on a metal compilation LP on the Ebony label in 1987. Their track *Down And Out* was on the *Rock Meets Metal Volume 1* album, one of a series of compilations featuring up-and-coming rock bands that the label put out between 1982 and 1987

Other bands around during the latter half of the 1980s included Tapestry Sky, a five-piece band from Cleckheaton which featured brothers John and Mick Gilman.

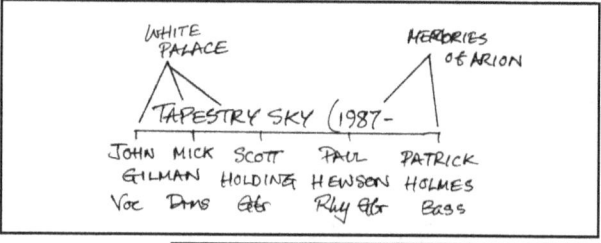

The band Condition Red were originally from York but based in Bradford. Their new line-up played London's Dingwalls in March 1988.

CHAPTER 6 - INDIE ALTERNATIVE ROCK   1984 - 1986

DAMIEN WOLFE

Courtesy of Friz the Cat

This Bradford goth band formed in 1986 and were named after their lead singer.

Guitarist Andrew 'Salty' Hoult went on to play keyboards for rock band Hardware. Bassist Andy Yeadon was formerly singer with Isolation/Figures From The Cold. His alter-ego was poet Dave The Dog.

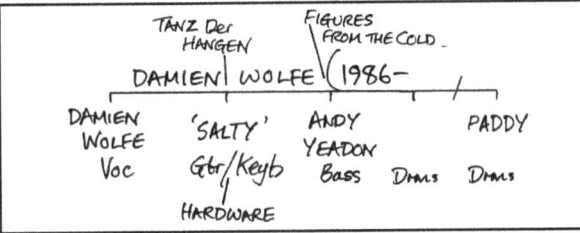

EAZY STREET

Keighley band Eazy Street released a single, *Quest For Glory*..

Skipton band Chainsaw's singles have also risen in value in the 2010 *Record Collectors Guide*.

Disguise were Bradford University students who were later renamed The Fortune Tellers.

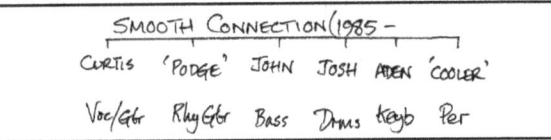

Another band around in 1985 were the duo **Face To Face** featuring Johnathan Breen and Steve Croft.

TALULA GOSH

This five piece 'jingly-jangly' indie-pop combo were based in Oxford, but included Bradford lass Elizabeth Price as one of their vocalists. Their debut 7" single *Beatnik Boy / My Best Friend* came out in 1986 on the Edinburgh label 53rd & 3rd and got to number 3 in the indie charts.

PRO-PATRIA MORI

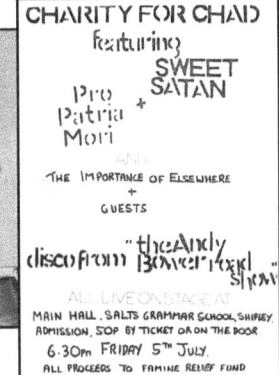

A short lived local punk band that played a charity gig at Salt's Grammar School with rock band Sweet Satan and The Importance Of Elsewhere in July 5, 1984 which had and entrance fee of 50p.

Pro-Patria Mori singer Nick Chuck went on to front local indie band Seven Antelopes and bassist Troy Bunn was later a member of Electric Cauliflower.

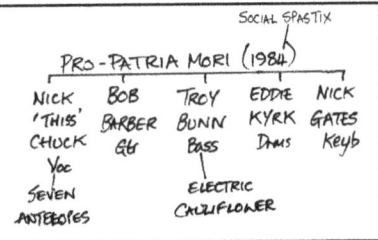

Following the DIY Punk fanzine ethic local lad Andrew Nixon produced the heavy rock fanzine *High Octane*, costing 60p, at the end of 1985.

The next home for The 1 In 12 Club was The Metropole on Sunbridge Road (coming full circle by moving back to their original home). The first gig featured two Sheffield bands, Midnight Choir and Screaming Trees, on December 4.

The second gig back at The Metropole, on December 11, 1986, was Aberdeen's The Shamen (who had previously been called Alone Again Or). The Shamen eventually went on to have many successes with their techno-rock fusion in the new dance scene, their most prominent hit was the September 1992 number one *Ebenezer Good*.

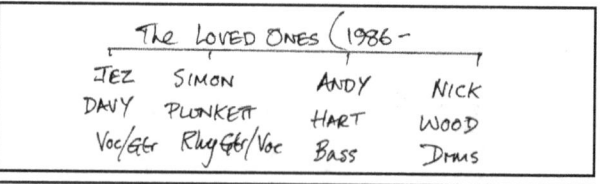

The Loved Ones (1986-			
JEZ DAVY Voc/Gtr	SIMON PLUNKETT Rhy Gtr/Voc	ANDY HART Bass	NICK WOOD Drms

SLOAN SQUARE EAST (1986-				(FORMERLY: SEMAI CRUISE)
PAUL DURKIN Voc	DARREN DUTSON-BROMLEY Gtr	TONY ISLES Bass	MAREK ZELINSKI Drms	TONY OTYKEL Keyb

Other bands around included **The Loved Ones**, **Sloan Square East,** and **Shady Dealz** (bellow).

ORIGINAL SIN (1986-				
JEZ COOK Voc	STEVE DERRIG Gtr	ROBERT BRICE Bass	LEE WELLS Drms	STEPHEN QUIN Keyb

SHADY DEALZ (Nov 1986-88)				#2 (1988-
GARY GELDEART Voc/Gtr	PETE SENIOR Gtr	RAY LONG Bass	BRIAN HODGSON Drms	BRIAN THOMPSON Voc

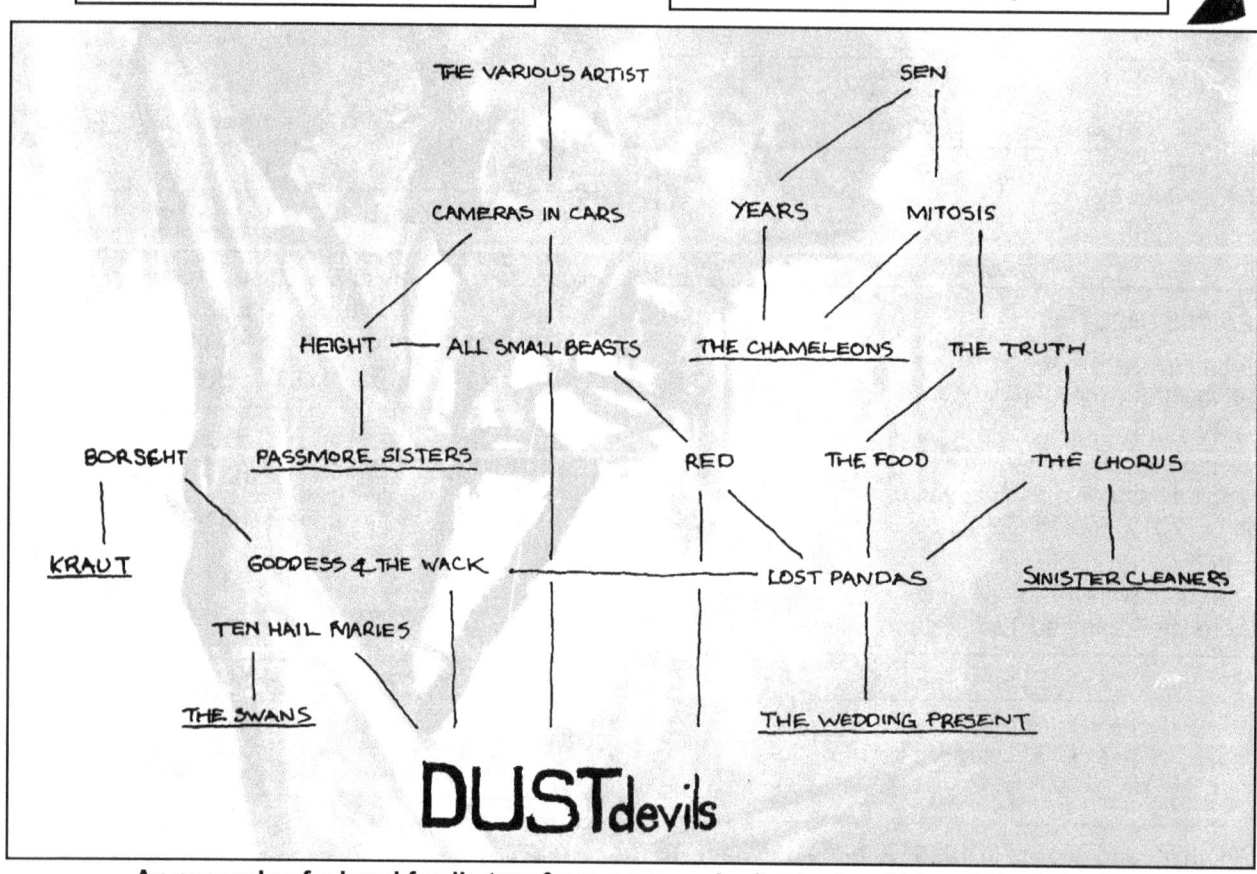

An example of a band family tree from a promo leaflet by Leeds band Dust Devils

Chapter 7
1987

Seen from a distance of four decades later, 1987 has become an important and pivotal year in the music history of the UK. That year a new disco/dance scene emerged with an energy reminiscent of the previous decade's punk/new wave explosion. It had begun slowly around late 1985 when American 'hip-hop' music developed new styles like 'house' from Chicago and 'techno' from Detroit. This started an underground scene of clubs and warehouse raves, where the designer drug of choice was MDMA (Ecstasy). The scene went overground when on January 2, 1987, Steve Silk Hurley's Jack Your Body single became the first UK house hit to go straight to the top of the UK charts.

Gradually, the UK scene introduced more dance music styles, like jungle, garage, drum 'n' bass, trip-hop, etc. A lot of record labels sprang up, seemingly overnight. Acid Jazz pioneered some of the hottest grooves on the scene through DJs Giles Peterson and Chris Bongs.

It was the year that the long-running BBC2 music programme *The Old Grey Whistle Test*, which first appeared in 1971, was finally pulled off the air, while on the local Bradford scene, there was a sudden emergence of a series of jazz funk combos.

FROM THE UNDERWORLD

This Shipley-based jazz-funk outfit was originally an 11-piece band which had met at Leeds Lions Studios. They later slimmed down to a seven-piece band as the previous members left to go to the Middle East. Their Harrogate guitarist, Guy Hatton, became an engineer/producer for bands including The Membranes and HDQ. He later performed as a jazz guitar soloist.

```
FROM the UNDERWORLD (1986 - (MAY/87))
DAVE    GUY      MARK      SIMON     MICHAEL   ANITA  SUSIE
GILL    HATTON   PRIESTLY  De SOUZA  STEAD            Bac. Voc
Voc     Gtr/Syn  Sax       Sax       Keyb
```

GUIDO

Funk band Guido has been around since 1982 and were going strong in 1987. Their name was derived from the 10th century Benedictine monk Guido D'Arezzo who had invented a way of teaching music through the use of fingers on a hand, and was the originator of the scale 'do, ray, me'.

The band had earned a support slot on The Commodores' 1985 UK tour. They released their only 7" single *I'm Alone* on Recoil Records in 1986. It was recorded at the Slaughterhouse Studios in Driffield and mixed and engineered by the band's vocalist and guitarist Scott Peters.

Guido reached the final of Circuit 22's *Battle Of The Bands* in 1988 after expanding to a seven-piece which included Bradford's Terry Priestley on sax.

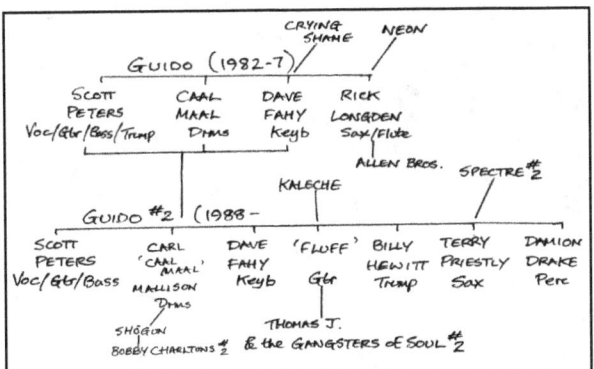

JAYVER

Based in Keighley, Jayver were a jazz funk band who had, at one time, ex-New Model Army Rob Waddington on the drum stool. It also featured ex-The Elements singer Jayne Tretton on vocals, who later sang backing vocals for 1990s Brit Pop bands like Placebo and Suede.

```
The
ELEMENTS
       JAYVER (1986 - (7)
  JAYNE    ANDREW    GRAHAM   GEORGE      JOHN        DAVID
  TRETTON  THROUPE   THUDD    FOTHERGILL  BROWNLESS   KRYSKO
  Voc      Gtr       Bass     Drms        Keyb        Keyb
```

JJ'S BONES

Formed from the bare bones of the band Skrytch, JJ's Bones quickly became popular on the local scene. After a successful performance at Dingwalls in London on November 1, 1987, they were asked back the following February to play at the prestigious venue's *Best Of '87* event.

They produced two cassette releases, *Hit On The Head* and *Hit On The Head Again*, which were sold locally.

When the band split in 1989 singer/songwriter Norma Jean 'NJ' Wilow and bassist Tom Currie relocated to London to pursue various musical projects.

Tom had a stint with indie chart darlings Daisy Chainsaw and Simon Napier Bell's boy band Zig Zag Park from Wales.

After various solo projects singer/songwriter NJ found Indie chart success when she formed the band Tiny Monroe in London in 1992.

The band released their debut single *VHF855V* on the Laurel record label in 1994. It was record of the week on Steve Lamacq's evening session on Radio 1 and led to sessions on Mark Radcliffe's show.

As part of the 'new wave of new wave' scene Tiny Monroe played many gigs with their peers including Elastica, Sleeper and Echobelly as well as emerging supergroups such as Suede and Radiohead.

They released the *Cream Bun* EP in 1994 and played at festivals including Glastonbury, Reading and Leeds and toured with The Pretenders and Curve.

Their album *Volcanoes* was released on Laurel Records in 1996, a year after it was recorded. The singles *She* and *Open Invitation* followed shortly before the band split.

After moving to La Palma, one of the Canary Islands, NJ, as 'Norma Wilow', recorded the solo albums *Indian Ocean* in 2004, *Goodbye Rock'n'Roll* in 2005 and *The Cyber Cafe* 2006.

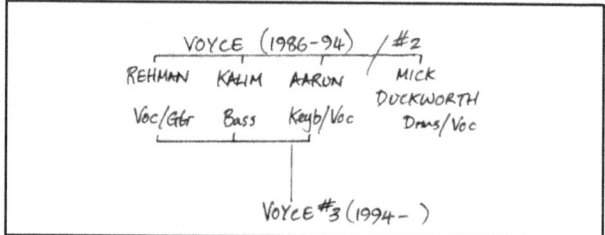

The predominantly Asian combo **Voyce** were another funky band on the scene.

MILAN LAD

The exceptional Bradford-born Asian jazz fusion guitarist Milan Lad started performing with his combo Slipstream around 1986. As well as playing solo, he occasionally worked with his own Milan Lad Octet. One gig the Octet played was at Leeds Irish Centre in October 1997. Milan is a highly skilled exponent of jazz, R&B and world music styles and has collected many accolades for his understated performances.

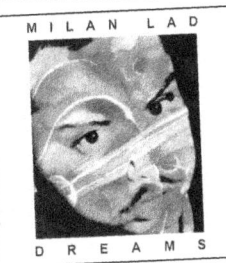

His debut CD, *Dreams*, released on the Small World record label, was launched at London's Jazz Cafe in 1995. It featured fellow UK jazz artists Jim Mullen on guitar and Andy Shepherd on sax.

He set up his own label/project entitled *Sangam* - the Hindi word meaning 'together' - with a host of like-minded musicians.

'It seems natural and almost inevitable therefore that 'Sangam' is a step forward, a reflection of his own personal development and philosophical outlook on life.'

'His music is an attempt to break down the barriers between people, using a blend of influences from R&B, jazz, acoustic, dance and ethnic Indian classical music. This is immediately evident through his choice of musicians and collaborators reflecting a wide diversity of ethnicity. He explores these genres whilst never denying his own Indian cultural heritage.' (1)

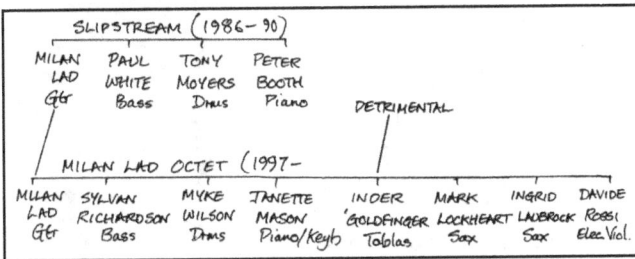

Now well-established back at its original venue The Metropole, The 1 In 12 Club played host to many local, national and European bands in the first six months of 1987.

Showcased groups included The Gargoyles, from Hull (twice) and 3-Action, featuring Swift Nick The Poet. Dutch hard-core band BGK played on March 5, supported by Scarborough two-piece Active Minds (who replaced Nottingham band Heresy on the bill).

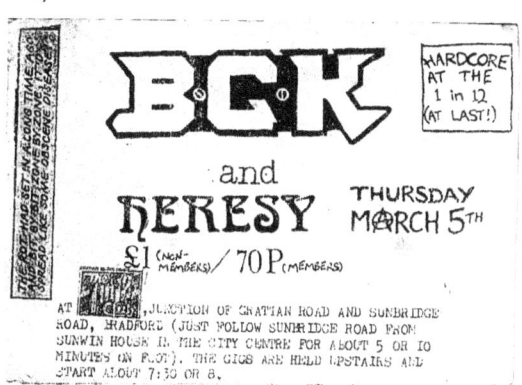

The following month, the Club celebrated its sixth anniversary with local Leeds regulars The Three Johns, supported by Scottish band Rote Kapelle.

In late April, a five-piece band from Blackburn supported local boys The Word at the Club. The band's name was Bradford. This tuneful power-pop band released a debut single *Skin Storm* on their own label. They put out two LPs; *Bradford* on Midnight Music in 1988, and *Shouting Quietly* on Sire Records in 1989.

In 1991, former Smiths lead singer and *Shouting Quietly* co-producer Morrissey recorded a cover version of *Skin Storm* as a b-side.

BRADFORD

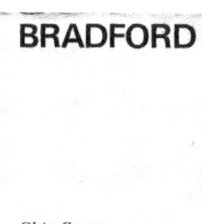

Skin Storm.

MALCOLM HANSON

Denholme-born guitarist Malcolm Hanson first came to prominence locally in rock bands Kaboss and Abyss.

He moved to London in 1974, and six months later to Hamburg in Germany where he wrote and performed the multi-media pop operetta *Prince Of Atlantis* with German baroness Angela Gisela Von Hamme.

After moving back to London he answered an ad in Melody Maker and joined Cheshire rock band Promenade in January 1975.

After a year with Promenade, he returned to London where he joined orchestral prog rock band The Enid as a keyboard player in 1978 (pictured right, with Dave Storey).

Malcolm released two 1980s solo albums as 'Malcolm Hansson', both recorded at Sketch Studios in Northampton; *The Naked Truth* in 1983 and *Traumadrome* in 1984.

After putting on several gigs to raise money for *Live Aid* in 1985 Malcolm, continued promoting bands in Northampton and set up the *Battle Of The Bands* under the banner of *Circuit 22 Promotions* at the Old Five Bells pub there in 1986.

The competition was a success and Malcolm decided to move it to Bradford and expand it to cover the north of England. Malcolm became the full-time promoter for Queen's Hall.

After leaving Queen's Hall in 1989, Malcolm took the *Battle Of The Bands* to the Royal Standard for heats with a final at St George's Hall which was won by Poisoned Electric Head.

The last *Battle Of The Bands* final was at the Communal Building in 1990 was won by Keighley rock outfit Premiere. After that, the competition was renamed the *Metal Mountain* and held at the Rio for the next two years.

Malcolm moved back to Northampton where he resumed promoting and used his German connections to set up the No-Ma music festival – a collaboration between Northampton and its twin town Marburg.

Returning to his Yorkshire roots, Malcolm took up residence in Skipton. He ran a full-time business called *Education Through Entertainment,* which involved working in schools on history projects, as well as organising school arts and musical events for the annual Keighley Festival.

He led local 'ghost walks' in the evenings in Skipton and Valletta in Malta. Malcolm went on to write several books on quirky local history and the supernatural.

In 2016, Malcolm was working with musician and producer Andy Wells (left) on a musical to be called *1612*, based on the Pendle Witches. Sadly, it was never finished although a couple of tracks appeared on *YouTube*.

After suffering a stroke in 2018, Malcolm returned to writing. From 2023, he published four volumes of his *Strange Yet True* books which are '...*bizarre, spooky, funny and always entertaining*'. They were sold in local book shops and distributed free to local hospitals and care homes.

CHAPTER 7 — 1987

BATTLE OF THE BANDS 1987

The annual *North Of England Battle Of The Bands* competition began at Queen's Hall in 1987. Run by *Malcolm Hanson's Circuit 22 Promotion*s, it offered a top prize of £1,000 and recording time for the winners. Many West Yorkshire bands entered and it quickly gained crowd support and became a very popular event in Bradford's musical calendar over the next few years.

The competition featured fifty-six bands over eighteen heats with three heats per week. The first heat on Thursday, April 23, featured Siren, Das Tor and Gypsy with Siren going through. It was judged by local music luminaries including *Rock On* columnist Chris Maguire, blues guitarist Roger Higgins and Far North Music.

The PA systems for the gigs were supplied by two local companies. King Voltz did the sound for all the gigs in the Cellar Bar whilst

Malcolm Hanson with PA maestro Gerard Rolfe

CONCERT PRODUCTION

Coast To Coast was run by guitarist Gerard Rolfe, formerly of local groups Superfly, Dignity and Sanction. He had set up the company, originally known as Yellow Cabs in the early eighties and provided PAs for hundreds of local gigs and festivals.

Gerard went on to do the sound for various touring bands nationally and internationally including the likes of Smokie and Martin Stephenson & The Dainties.

Coast To Coast was based for many years at the Bradford Rio and had several systems all running at the same time.

THE overwhelming success of the Battle Of The Bands has resulted in Malcolm Hanson permanently moving his southern-based CIRCUIT 22 Promotions company to Bradford.

For live music fans this could mean a blitz of top-flight acts descending on the city in the coming months.

The record crowds now attending the battles at the Queens Hall have proved fans will turn out to support such events.

Malcolm is personally knocked out with the support shown so far and he's also thrilled with the wealth of talent now treading the boards at the Queens Hall.

He said: "So many bands I have seen could, and should have had record deals years ago. Some of the sets have been riveting, and the overall standard of musicianship has shown itself to be sky high in this neck of the woods.

Circuit 22 was set up 18 months ago purely to promote live music on a pro-basis. Although most people think there is an army of people involved in the company, it is controlled solely by Malcolm but he offers a word of warning to would-be promoters.

"Promoting gigs is not just a matter of booking in bands and turning up on the night to collect the money. If it's to be done correctly one should look at a 60-hour week as easy meat. After that you can start paying yourself time and a quarter!

THE quarter-finals of the Battle of the Bands were finalised last week with Jester Turtle and Vital Force taking the last places —well, initially.

Vital Force's heavy rock, complete with dry ice and an army of fans, won them the day and duo Jester Turtle overcame all the odds to win through.

But Jester Turtle have had to pull out. They made the decision reluctantly, but possible deals in the film and publishing world have meant a trip to the capital tonight.

And that means a welcome place for Leitmotiv — the highest marked losers. In fact, the mark they achieved was one of the highest in the tournament.

The five quarter-finals — Siren, Act Natural and Slipstream battled it out last night — now read:

TONIGHT — Xero Slingsby and The Works/From The Underworld/Leitmotiv.

JULY 2 — Jayver/Cry/From Knowhere.

JULY 3 — Vital Force/Love It To Death/Somebody's Brother.

JULY 9 — Happiness Ad/Four Beats Behind Bars/No-Tick.

JULY 10 — Western Dance/High Z/Eazystreet.

Coast To Coast operated the rig for the bigger gigs in the Ballroom upstairs.

Over the next three months, bands battled it out to get to the final, with heats taking place in the Cellar Bar and gigs moving upstairs for the quarter-finals onwards.

The first semi final featured Somebody's Brother, Jayver and Leeds band Act Natural, on Friday, July 17.

The second semi took place Saturday, July 18, and featured Happiness Ad, three piece avante garde jazz band Xero Slingsby & The Works and South African pop duo Jester Turtle.

The following week the final featured the winners of each semi; Somebody's Brother and Xero Slingsby & The Works and the highest scored runner up Act Natural on Friday, July 24.

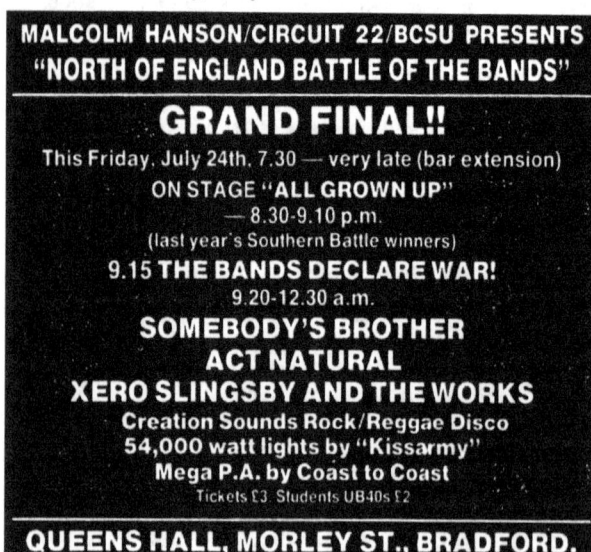

The eventual winners of *The Battle Of The Bands* were Xero Slingsby & The Works with Somebody's Brother finishing a close second.

Xero Slingsby & The Works were a Leeds-based combo fronted by the son of the owner of the Slingsby factory on Preston Street, which was opposite Bradford's legendary real ale pub The Fighting Cock.

The Battle was sponsored by a number of local companies including the Telegraph & Argus and Far North Music.

FAR NORTH MUSIC

Local manager Andy Farrow merged his AMF Music with promoter Gordon Roscoe to form the promotions and management company Far North.

From offices at Cheapside Chambers, they promoted bands from West Yorkshire and the north of England at venues in Leeds Duchess of York, Sheffield Take Two, Manchester International and London Dingwalls.

They managed an number of local bands including Slammer, Loud, Poppy Factory, Paradise Lost. After Gordon Rosco moved on to other things, Andy later moved his renamed Northern Music Co Ltd to offices in Saltaire.

It's the zero option

XERO Slingsby and The Works are the winners of the Northern Battle of the Bands.

The trio from Leeds beat off the challenge of Somebody's Brother and Act Natural at the Queen's Hall, Bradford, last night.

Their weird brand of avant-garde jazz, which includes Xero on bicycle pump, saxophone and other odds and ends, proved to be a winning combination on the night.

Somebody's Brother were Bradford's sole representatives and their infectious brand of blues/reggae/rock had most of the 700 plus crowd roaring support.

Alternative outfit, Act Natural, who hail from Leeds, gave a fine performance.

A total of £1,000 went to the winners, plus London dates including one at the top-rated 100 Club, and they also collected a host of other goodies provided by local shops. Somebody's Brother took £500 as runners-up and Act Natural £250.

CHAPTER 7 — 1987

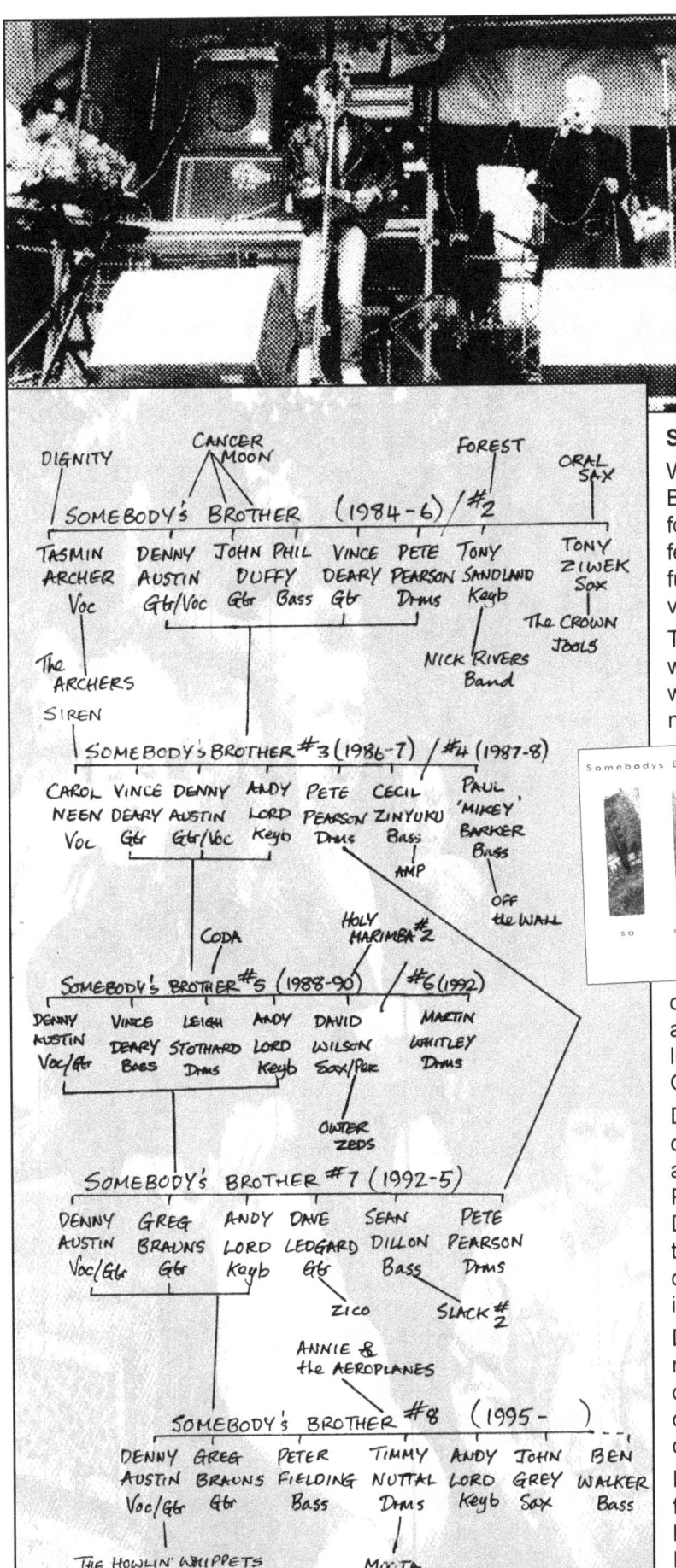

SOMEBODY'S BROTHER

When guitarist Denny Austin moved to Bradford from his native Sunderland he formed the band Somebody's Brother with fellow Maccams Jon and Phil Duffy and future number one artist Tasmin Archer on vocals.

The band became popular on the circuit with their blues and 70s-influenced sound with a mixture of covers and self-penned material.

In 1987 they released the three-track seven-inch *Soweto / It's Not For Long / So Damned True* on their own Tinza Records label and featuring Carol Neen on lead vocals.

The Brothers went through various line-up changes, with Denny as the main focus, and also sprouted various spin-off bands like country band Howlin' Whippets and Grateful Dead tribute Broken Bones.

Denny Austin also became a champion of local musicians and ran jam sessions at various Bradford venues including The Peel, The Melborn, MacRory's Bar and Delius throughout the 90s and 2000s. He teamed up with Rob Heaton and others to create local music endeavour *Fresh Milk* in 2002.

Denny's brother Ian Austin took over as manager of MacRory's Bar in 1988 and owner from 1991. He put on local bands on Wednesday and Sunday nights until it closed in 2004.

His annual *Ginger Fringe Festival*, featuring local bands, began in the MacRory's car park and later moved to Delius Lived Next Door.

During 1986/87 a second wave of glam metal bands emerged, including Bon Jovi, LA Guns, Poison and Guns'n'Roses.

These bands had a harder edged punk rock influence and some achieved strong commercial success, while the Bradford music scene again saw a resurgence of a new set of heavy metal/hard rock heroes.

ZODIAC MINDWARP AND THE LOVE REACTION

Mark Manning (aka Zodiac Mindwarp) was born in Armley in Leeds. By the mid to late 1970s, he had settled in Bradford and studied at Bradford Art College where he developed an early unhealthy interest in Nazi holocaust torture images.

By 1979 he had formed his first band with other local art school musicians before eventually relocating to London and bluffing his way onto the staff of the pop magazine *Flexi Pop* as a graphic designer. While working there he devised his mission to form the ultimate rock band.

Returning to Bradford he sought the assistance of his friend Buzz, the guitarist with the Southern Death Cult, and produced a demo in the basement of Roots Records.

Back in London, a chance meeting with Dave Balfe and Bill Drummond (both of KLF fame) led to them signing him to their Food record label. The rough demo became the first single by his cartoonish 'biker sex god' alter-ego Zodiac Mindwarp.

Wild Child, by Zodiac Mindwarp And The Love Reaction, got to number nine in the Indie Charts in late May 1986. The band soon became flavour of the month and appeared on the front cover of *Sounds* in July 1986 with the tag line, *'Hail Zodiac The Bikerdelic War Lord'!*

Their first EP on Food Records, *High Priest Of Love*, topped the Indie Charts in late 1986. In April 1987 their next single, *Prime Mover* (co-written with fellow Bradfordian Adrian Edmondson), was released on Mercury Records and reached eighteen..

That was followed in November 1987 by *Back Street Education* which reached 49 in the singles charts and a subsequent single *Planet Girl* reached No 63 in April 1988.

Their first LP *Tattooed Beat Messiah* was released on Vertigo Records and reached number twenty in February 1988. By this time guitarist Cobalt Stargazer had left the band to be replaced by Halifax guitarist Jan 'Flash Bastard' Cyrka. Jan had been a renowned guitarist on the local West Yorkshire gig scene with his own band Cyrka. (2)

After years of excessive booze, women and drugs on the trail of rock

superstardom, The Love Reaction ground to a halt around 1995. They next played live in 2001 and then occasionally until 2019.

Mark Manning became an established author with such rock autobiographies as *Bad Wisdom* (1996 with Bill Drummond), *Crucify Me Again*, *Get Your Cock Out* (2002) and *Fucked By Rock* (2001), *Collateral Damage* (2001), and *The Wild Highway* (2005 with Bill Drummond).

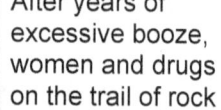

The band continued to release new material up to their last album, *We Are Volsung*, in 2010.

ZODIAC MINDWARP & THE LOVE REACTION

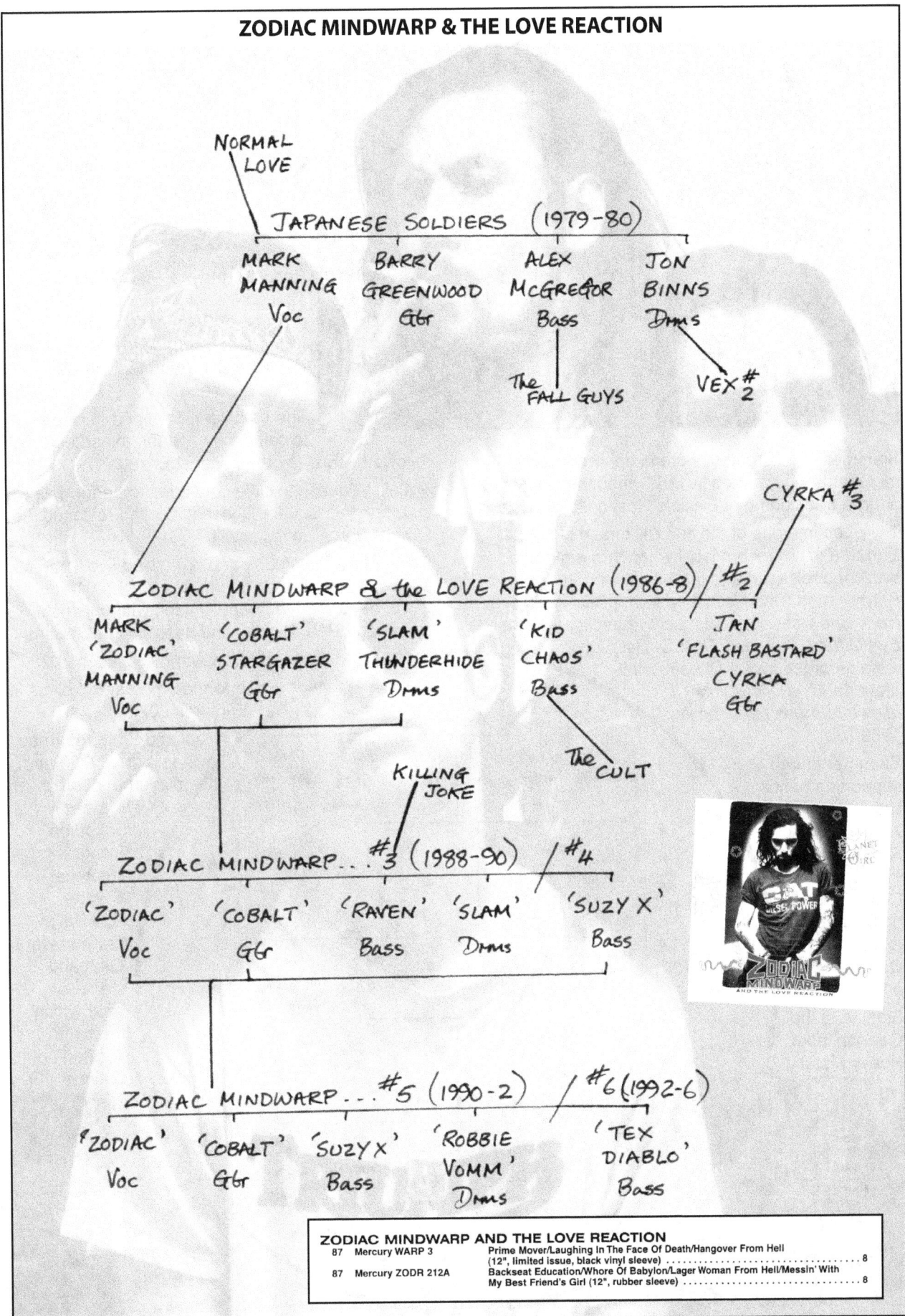

NORMAL LOVE →

JAPANESE SOLDIERS (1979-80)
- MARK MANNING — Voc
- BARRY GREENWOOD — Gtr
- ALEX McGREGOR — Bass → The FALL GUYS
- JON BINNS — Dms → VEX #2

CYRKA #3 →

ZODIAC MINDWARP & the LOVE REACTION (1986-8) / #2
- MARK 'ZODIAC' MANNING — Voc
- 'COBALT' STARGAZER — Gtr
- 'SLAM' THUNDERHIDE — Dms
- 'KID CHAOS' — Bass → The CULT
- JAN 'FLASH BASTARD' CYRKA — Gtr

KILLING JOKE →

ZODIAC MINDWARP... #3 (1988-90) / #4
- 'ZODIAC' — Voc
- 'COBALT' — Gtr
- 'RAVEN' — Bass
- 'SLAM' — Dms
- 'SUZY X' — Bass

ZODIAC MINDWARP... #5 (1990-2) / #6 (1992-6)
- 'ZODIAC' — Voc
- 'COBALT' — Gtr
- 'SUZY X' — Bass
- 'ROBBIE VOMM' — Dms
- 'TEX DIABLO' — Bass

ZODIAC MINDWARP AND THE LOVE REACTION

87	Mercury WARP 3	Prime Mover/Laughing In The Face Of Death/Hangover From Hell (12", limited issue, black vinyl sleeve)	8
87	Mercury ZODR 212A	Backseat Education/Whore Of Babylon/Lager Woman From Hell/Messin' With My Best Friend's Girl (12", rubber sleeve)	8

SLAMMER

Slammer were Bradford's premier thrash metal merchants who formed in 1987 when they recorded a three-track demo at Flexible Response Studios.

They became one of the first UK thrash bands to sign to a major record label when they signed to WEA and released a four-track 10-inch. It featured *Born For War* and *Hellbound* from BBC *Friday Rock Show* sessions and two live tracks, *If Thine Eye Offend Thee* and *Fight Or Fall*, which were recorded live at Queen's Hall. Their debut LP *The Work Of Idle Hands* was released in 1989.

Slammer toured supporting bands like Onslaught, Xentrix and Acid Reign and also supported Celtic Frost on their 1990 tour playing Queen's Hall on May 14.

Signing to the German label Heavy Metal Records, they released the four-song 12-inch *Insanity Addicts* in 1990. By the time of Slammer's second LP, *Nightmare Scenario* in 1991, former NMA bassist Stuart Morrow had joined the band.

The next year, the band decided to call it a day. Stuart joined Loud followed shortly by the guitarist Enzo.

Vocalist Paul Tunnicliffe continued to perform as a solo artist as Square Dog in 2006 and released the CD EP *Some Songs* in 2007. (3)

Paul set up *Beatitudes* and organised live acoustic sessions at various local venues from 2001. In 2018, he formed the band Chiang with guitarists Harris and Rob Rhodes and bassist Dom Sheard.

Guitarist Milo Zivanovic died in 2020.

Enzo formed the band Wolves In Winter in 2020.

Paul and Enzo reformed Slammer in 2023 and played the *Lords Of The Land 'Thrashathon'* in Glasgow on September 16, with Acid Reign, Lawnmower Deth and Xentrix, after which the band decided not to continue.

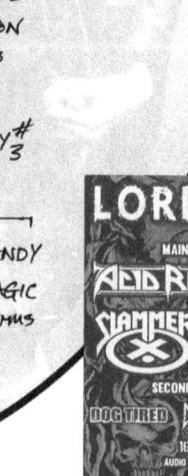

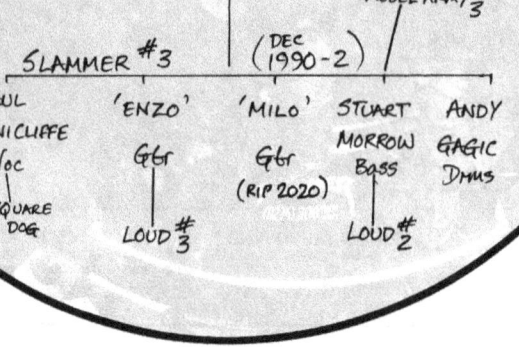

SPOILT BRATZ

Three Keighley lads formed the band Masquerade at Greenhead Grammar School and played their first gig in the sixth-form common room.

After leaving school the lads moved to Bradford and changed their name virtually every other week and still needed a vocalist. An advert was placed in Kerrang! magazine (No 148) stating 'Spoilt Bratz require vocalist. Alice-influenced'. Unfortunately, no-one came forward who was suitable.

Then with the chance meeting in 1986 of Mark Yates (who was DJing at the Wheatsheaf pub) and Bradford lad Tony Wright, they found the frontman they needed.

The band played their debut gig at a friend's party in Huddersfield and by 1988 they had made two demos; *Spoilt Bratz* and *Gasoline & Suicide*, before going into Slaughterhouse Studios in Driffield to cut a third demo called *Be My Guest*. This 1989 demo soon attracted the attention of *Kerrang!* writer Al Rhodes. He first tried to sign the band to his Major Records label but instead became their manager.

After a name change to Terrorvision (after the 1960s cult horror B-movie) and a few warm-up gigs the band played London's Marquee Club in 1990, gaining some interest from Chrysalis Records.

In 1991, with another demo *Pimp Action Sunshine* doing the rounds of record companies, they signed to EMI in October and were given their own imprint label Totally Vegas Recordings.

Their debut release in February 1992 was the EP *Thrive* which the band promoted on a support slot on a UK tour with Zodiac Mindwarp.

Their debut album *Formaldehyde* was released in December 1992, reaching number seventy five in the album charts.

They won the Best Band category in the *Kerrang! Readers Poll* for two consecutive years; 1995 and 1996. They released another three LPs; *How To Make Friends & Influence People* (1995), *Regular Suburban Survivors* (1996) and *Shaving Peaches* (1998), all reaching the UK album charts at numbers eighteen, eight and thirty-four respectively.

Terrorvision released over twenty singles, 16 reached the UK pop charts including three Top 10 hits, *Perseverance* (1996), *Bad Actress* (1996) and *Tequila* (1999) which reached numbers five, ten and two.

They left EMI in 1999 and in 2000 signed a new deal with Papillon Records, releasing the LP *Good To Go* in 2001.

The band called it a day after a farewell tour and a final concert at Pennington's Nightclub (the old Mecca Ballroom) on Manningham Lane on the 4th of October 2001.

Terrorvision first re-formed in 2005 to play two tours and went on to tour and record on a semi-permanent basis.

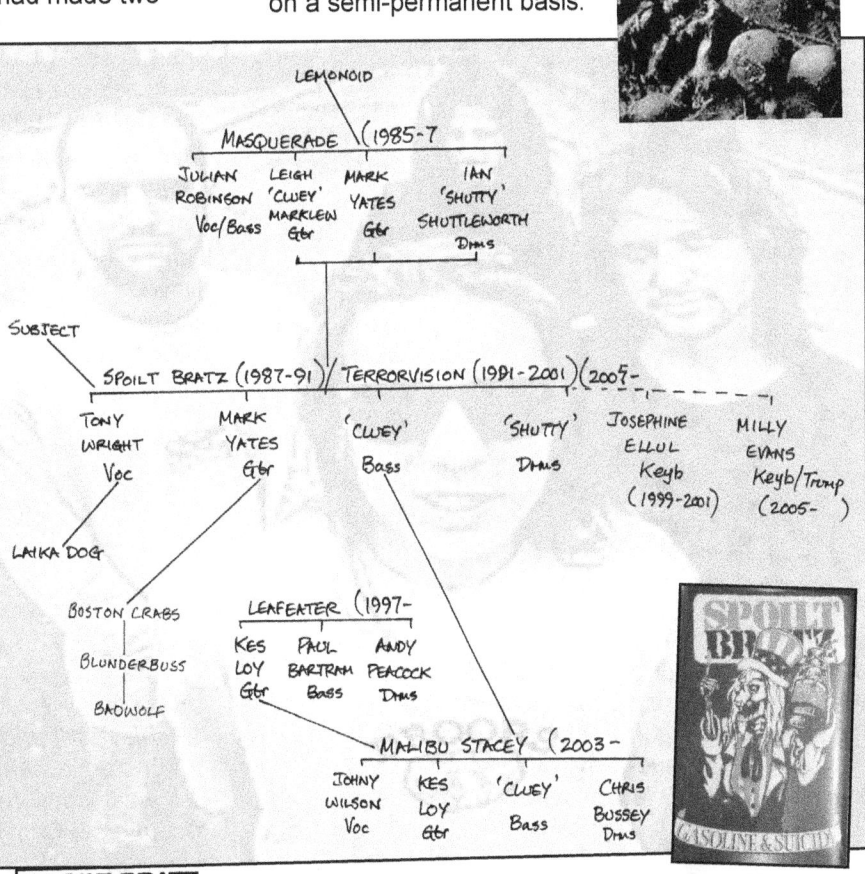

SPOILT BRATZ

88	Spoilt Bratz SB 1	SPOILT BRATZ: (Not So) Hot/You Talk Too Much/I Could Die/She's A Drag (cassette, private issue, 200 only) 50
88	Spoilt Bratz SB 2	GASOLINE & SUICIDE: Sex Doll, Love Cramp/Going Down Again/Stuck In A Rut/Crawling On Broken Glass (cassette, private issue, 200 only) ... 50
89	Spoilt Bratz BRAT 3	BE MY GUEST: Pain Reliever/Past Times/Ignorance (cassette, private issue) 50

A new local fanzine named *Uprising* appeared on the scene at this time, compiled by Mandy and Marie of Buttershaw. The fanzine cost 30p and ran to at least four issues.

In May 1987 local multi-racial band Boys From The East released their second single *Brilliant / Icarus* on their Livingstone Productions label.

At the beginning of July, a new West Yorkshire music magazine called *Live* appeared, based in Huddersfield and edited by Paul Dagg, Stuart Price, Debra Stretton and Tony Treacy.

Leeds-based fanzine *Northern Kickback* edited by Simon Jose and Simon Norfolk, ran from 1986 to early 1988 and covered the Yorkshire music scene with gig and record reviews, interviews and articles on local clubs and studios.

Northern Kickback 11 featured Ade Edmonson's Bad News of the front cover and included an interview with Bradford's Western Dance. The October 1987 issue came with the free vinyl 7 inch *Kickback* EP featuring tracks by Yorkshire bands Gun Law, 4 Majorcans, Sound And Fury and Reward.

During these early summer months, The 1 In 12 Club continued to flourish as volunteer members prepared their new building. Weekly gigs continued at the Metropole where a succession of bands played, including Final Warning, Leeds band Sinister Cleaners, two Welsh bands; Ahnrefn and Llwyer Llaethog, Leicester's Giant Treads Clean, Middlesbrough's Shrug and Scotland's Dog Faced Hermans.

JOHN PEEL COMES TO THE 1 IN 12 CLUB

On July 16, The 1 In 12 Club had another hard-core punk night featuring Larm (Holland), Heibel (Belgium), Filthy Christians (Sweden) and Nottingham's Heresy.

The gig attracted a very large crowd, crammed into the small upstairs gig room at the Metropole. Amongst those there was long-time supporter of the club Radio 1 DJ John Peel, visiting the club for the first time and hovering around the back of the crowded room. What he thought of the experience was recorded in his regular column for the Observer newspaper the following Sunday. (4)

On Saturday, July 18, there was an all-day *People's Festival* held at the Mapa Centre (Newby Square, West Bowling) from 12.30 until 7 pm featuring local bands Spectre, Natural Riddim, Somebody's Brother, Jumping The Gun, From Nowhere and Creation Roots.

During the summer of 1987, the new UK dance scene took off with the input of Ibiza's 'Balearic Beat Scene' which transferred to British clubs like Manchester's Hacienda. It became widely dubbed the 'Second Summer of Love'.

Meanwhile, the television programme *Antiques Roadshow* made its first Bradford appearance at the Richard Dunne Sports Centre.

During the month of August, The 1 In 12 Club played host to a range of bands such as Battle Of The Bands winners Xero Slingsby And The Works, Ilkley's Vast Hallucinations, Cleckheaton's Tapestry Sky, The Passmore Sisters and Scotland's We Three Kings, while in Keighley Skeletal Family's bassist Trotwood started to put on gigs at Vicki's Nightspot on East Parade.

```
VAST HALLUCINATIONS (1987-  (FORMERLY:
                               The EXPLODING
ERIC    DAVID    ANDREW    PETE  ELEPHANTS)
SPEAK   HANNEY   HIRST     TODD
Voc     Gtr      Bass      Drms
```

On Saturday, August 15, a free festival called *Keighley's Alternative Free Festival* (reprising the 1970s free festivals) was held at Cliffe Castle Park and was sponsored by the town's independent record shop Criminal Records.

It started at 6 pm and featured Nousommes, No Effect, Ice Child, Meanstreak, Tokyo, Sidewinder and a hybrid band made up of members of Excalibur and Baby Tuckoo.

Give me Hell any day

POP

Filthy Christians and Heresy in Bradford

JOHN PEEL

'AND a half a lager for me, please,' I whispered. 'Are you sure?' asked the barman, plainly worried. This was the Metropole, Sunbridge Road, Bradford, serious pints territory where members of the long-established 1 in 12 Club were gathered in an upper room to hear, amongst other bands, Nottingham's **Heresy**.

Fifteen years ago I won myself a sort of immortality through the inclusion in Pseud's Corner of my suggestion that the music of Pink Floyd was the sound of dying galaxies. Thoughts on Siouxsie and the Banshees were similarly honoured a decade later and last year I made the Corner for a third time by telling that a three-second-long track by the American band JFA was amongst my most treasured possessions. Since then the members of JFA have been exposed as time wasters by the Descendents whose song 'All' is one second long, and by Britain's very own Napalm Death with a track on their début LP, on Earache Records, which, it is claimed, is yet shorter.

Earache Records is run, from his Nottingham bedroom, by Digby Pearson, known as Dig. Dig was at the Metropole on Thursday to see Heresy, also on Earache, go about their business. Heresy have triggered such praise as 'mind numbing thrash barrage,' 'rapid chaos gone beserk' and 'a wanton obliterative trip' from American admirers, and their current LP, which they share with Concrete Sox, has sold, according to Dig, some 3,000 copies.

1 in 12 Club members showed all the signs of a culture in transition. T-shirts endorsed not only such ferocious bands as Big Black, Suicidal Tendencies and Stark Raving Mad but also rap ensembles Run-DMC. Baseball caps and baggy shorts were in evidence and haircuts ranged from decaying, spikey confections of the type admired by postcard manufacturers to state-of-the-art styles apparently wrought by chainsaw.

Heresy followed the Swedish band **Filthy Christians** on to the small stage. The Christians had played a set of staccato, rampaging songs with lyrics rendered in a language substantially beyond identification, but their work seemed seriously dream-like when set alongside the uproar created by Heresy.

Although some of Heresy's more extended works allow the four musicians to stray into what could be misread as demonstrations of squalid musicianship, they are at their best playing dislocated stuff at extreme speed. Mitch, Heresy's guitarist, studied his instrument with the air of a man bent upon craftsmanship, in marked contrast with bassist Kalv and John the singer, both of whom performed with abandon, the latter inspired in his presentation by some of the less inhibited film roles of Boris Karloff. In front of the band, celebrants hurled themselves about with a disconcerting lack of concern for personal safety, clambering on to the stage the better to launch themselves through the air and on to their peers.

Billy Joel enthusiasts who wrote to object to my remarks last Sunday would, I suspect, have imagined the Metropole to be some ante-chamber to hell. I preferred it considerably.

BRADFORD FESTIVAL 1987

A group of Bradford folk led and organised by local socialist activist Alan Brack, reprised the early 1970s Bradford arts festivals by holding a ten-day city centre festival between September 17 and 27, 1987.

Every day around fifty street acts performed between noon and 3 pm in five locations - outside the Arndale shopping centre, in front of Provincial House, and on Darley Street, Ivegate and Broadway. Acts included fire eaters, buskers, Morris dancers, clog dancers and illusionists.

At the Festival Pavilion outside Provincial House (now Centenary Square) there was free entertainment daily between 12 noon and 2.30 pm. The festival organisers hoped the colourful street entertainment would encourage people to buy tickets for the festival events at St George's Hall and Queen's Hall.

The Gospel

At the beginning of October, the local group Answering Machine released a four-track 12-inch EP called *The Last Rendezvous* on Playground Sounds which cost £2.50. The band's bassist Mark Blackburn had been in local bands since the late 1970s. At the time, his dad ran the historic Shoulder Of Mutton pub at the bottom of Kirkgate.

Matthew Wildman, the manager of Bradford rock band Aurora, played in a band called Sensai with ex-Lemonoid vocalist Richard Bell at this time.

On the night of October 16, the UK saw the worst storm since records began as embarrassed TV weatherman Michael Fish got it wrong. Massive damage was recorded when the hurricane storm hit the South of England.

On October 22, The 1 In 12 Club held another hardcore punk gig with the American band The Rhythm Pigs. The following week, October 29, The Prams played at what turned out to be the last Club gig at The Metropole Hotel as the 1 In 12 geared up to open its own long-awaited building in Albion Street.

VOLUNTEERS at the club, from left, Jeni Stork, Bogden Davies, Vad Taylor, Alison Goodyear, Kenzie and Angie Brown.

CLUB NEWS

The clubs building at 21-23 Albion st. is nearing completion thanks to 14 months of heavy toil by 1 IN 12 volunteers. Hopefully it should be open in October. The last remaining obstacles include a shortfall of about £4000 to furnish the place, and the granting of a "Registration Certificate" by local magistrates. However, providing certain conditions are met magistrates don't have the discretion to oppose this (unlike a "Public Licence"). It does mean though, that only members and guests signed in by them will be allowed in. New membership cards are now available, so get them soon. Cost is £2 unwaged and £5 waged for a year.

Even though 90% of the work has been done for free, the cost of buying the place, paying "professional" fees and buying materials has been horrendous. Around £90,000 has been spent - money from the D.o.E. and Bradford Council.

There will possibly be a booklet produced in the near future on just how this money was obtained without all the usual strings attatched, along with details on how all the numerous and heavily bureacratic authorities were dealt with, plus all the mistakes which were made along the way.

RHYTHM PIGS / VISIONS OF CHANGE
BRADFORD 1 IN 12 CLUB

LITTLE BRADFORD boys thrash with none of the intense savagery of US hardcore menagerie of whackomacho dimmies. Yorkshire knows nowt of the dumb rituals of the pit – they elbow each other in the face rather politely and dribble when the music speeds and stand still when the music slows. Upstairs the singer with a west coast US thrash band is apologising to George from Yugoslavia for pulling the Belgrade date. There is a worldwide scruff lumpenculture based around libertarian politics and tight-arsed rock. It is primitive, inelegant and political. For these three reasons it is largely ignored.

Visions of Change have what looks like a rat dressed in a liquidised tartan suitcase for a lead singer, the rest of the band have disgustedly long gurly haircuts. They used to be calling The Crap or The Shaton or something and they hail from Leamington Spa. Despite all this they sustained a constant bombardment of megagrade-rockfilth through a ropey PA.

The three Texan boys who are the Rhythm Pigs have little in common with the epsilon bottom shakers of the audience. They've been touring a month and they're still tanned. What they do have is communicated in short, sharp brutal thrashes, alternated with rock burlesque pieces probably lost on an audience keen on Tetleys fuelled catharsis rather than rock cabaret.

What makes the Rhythm Pigs special, their leaning towards acid wit rather than the Sid Lives retro-dirge, was mostly lost tonight. Their claim to be that part of the Global Punk Ghetto populated by Chumbawamba, Rabid Cat Records, the Buttholes and Culturecide was done no service. The album 'Choke On This' and the rest of their UK dates should put that right.

Steven Wells

BAD NEWS

This spoof heavy metal band made their TV debut in 1982 in series one of *The Comic Strip Presents...* episode four, *Bad News Tour*, was a fly-on-the-wall rockumentary following a chaotic heavy rock band. It starred Rick Mayall as Vim Fuego (vocals and lead guitar), Nigel Planer as Den Dennis (guitar), Peter Richardson as Spider Webb (drums) and local Bradford lad Adrian Edmondson as Vim Fuego (vocals and lead guitar). The actors all played their instruments. Ade also wrote the episode.

Adrian was a co-founder and co-writer of the series, created after the success of Peter Richardson's Comic Strip cabaret nights, built around comedy duos Richardson & Planer, Mayall & Edmondson, French & Saunders and compere Alexi Sayle.

Ade also appeared in the highly successful BBC TV series *The Young Ones* playing the punk Vyvyan alongside Rick Mayall and Nigel Planer. The comedy actors featured as backing vocalists on a re-recording of *Living Doll* with Cliff Richard made for *Comic Relief* which reached number one in March 1986.

Bad News reformed as a real band in 1986 to play the *Monsters Of Rock* festival at Castle Donnington on August 16.

The band released a self-titled LP on EMI in 1986, produced by Queen guitarist Brian May. The album included a cover single of Queen's *Bohemian Rhapsody* which reached number forty-four in the singles charts in September 1987. They followed this up with the non-album single *Cashing In On Christmas* on November 28, 1987.

They toured at universities and polytechnics and played Bradford St George's Hall in 1987 as well as that year's Reading Festival.

In 1988, the band's video release of their tour included footage from their appearance at the 1986 *Monsters Of Rock* at Castle Donnington when they played between the sets of Motorhead and Ozzy Osbourne.

A second *Comic Strip* TV show, *More Bad News*, was aired showing the band's performance from *Monsters Of Rock*.

They played a show at the Marquee in London on December 16, 1988, where they were joined on stage by legendary guitarists Jeff Beck and Brian May.

A second LP, *Bootleg*, was a mix of music and arguments between band members.

Ade sang with the Bonzo Dog Doo-Dah Band on their 2006 reformation tour and their 2007 album *Pour L'Amour Des Chiens*.

He also formed The Bad Shepherds in 2008, playing punk covers on mandolin, pipes and acoustic guitars.

```
BAD NEWS
87  EMI EM 24X    Bohemian Rhapsody/Life With Brian (scratch'n'sniff p/s) .................. 5
87  EMI EMP 24    Bohemian Rhapsody/Life With Brian (p/s, with sew-on patch) ............. 7
87  EMI 12EM 24   Bohemian Rhapsody/Pretty Woman/Life With Brian (12", standard p/s) ..... 8
87  EMI 12EM 24X  Bohemian Rhapsody/Pretty Woman/Life With Brian (12", scratch'n'sniff p/s) .. 10
87  EMI EM 36     Cashing In On Christmas/Bad News (p/s) ................................. 5
87  EMI EMG 36    Cashing In On Christmas/Bad News (Christmas card poster pack) .......... 7
87  EMI 12EM 36   Cashing In On Christmas (Let's Bank Mix)/Bad News/Cashing In On Christmas
                  (12", p/s) ............................................................. 8

BAD NEWS
87  EMI EMC 3535  BAD NEWS (LP, gatefold sleeve) ........................................ 12
88  EMI EMC 3542  BOOTLEG (LP, 1 track produced by Brian May) ........................... 12
```

1 IN 12 CLUB GIGS AT THE METROPOLE

DECEMBER 1986
4 - Midnight Choir / Screaming Heads / Peter Pax
11 - The Shamen
18 - This Burning Desire / Agit Rosa
27 - The Blood Brothers
29 - Matamba / Chronic / Boys From The East

JANUARY 1987
15 - This Perfect Kind / Peter Pax
22 - The Everly Sisters / The Pool
29 - Heart Of Darkness / Hope Street

FEBRUARY 1987
5 - Black Spot / Slughead 16
12 - Four Beats Behind Bars / Andy Faulkner
19 - The Gargoyles / The 3-Action
26 - Das Tor / Last In The Brain

MARCH 1987
5 - BGK / Active Minds
12 - Dog Faced Hermarns / Tree
19 - Seven Antelopes / 13th Friday
26 - Political Asylum / Dodgy Duo

APRIL 1987
2 - Bill Presley Coat / T-Dive
9 - The Three Johns / Rote Kapelle
16 - The Pick-Ups / Absolute
23 - Final Warning / Popeye / Little Brother
30 - The Word / Bradford

MAY 1987
7 - Another Cuba
14 - Anrefn / Llwybr Llaethog
21 - The Keep / Out To Lunch
28 - Western Dance / Shrug

JUNE 1987
4 - The Ex / Chumbawamba
11 - Upside Down / Pete Pax
18 - The Everly Sisters / Andrea
25 - The Gargoyles / Sinister Cleaners / Warriors Of Qoork

JULY 1987
2 - Dog Faced Hermans / The Gardiners
16 - Larm / Heibel / Heresy / Filthy Christians
23 - Rosie's Revenge / The Pool

AUGUST 1987
6 - Bloo & The Crazy 9 Mile Flares / 12 Guilty Men
13 - Passmore Sisters / Giant Treads Clean
20 - Xero Slingsby & The Works / Alex / Every Punks Mother
27 - Seven Antelopes / Slum Turkeys

SEPTEMBER 1987
3 - Tapestry Sky / The Vast Hallucinations
17 - Lethal Gospel / All Over The Carpet
24 - Generic / Kama Sutra

OCTOBER 1987
1 - August Avenue / Last In The Brain Q
8 - We Free Kings / The Motsons
15 - Who's In The Kitchen / Damage Done
22 - The Rhythm Pigs / Visions Of Change / Civilised Society
29 - The Prams / Altered States

During 1987, the 1 In 12 Club's publications collective produce the booklet *Doing Business: A Mischief Makers Handbook* by local ex-punk poet Dirk Spig. The handbook on how to research big companies and who owns them, using sources available in the local library. It explains in a DIY way, how to check copyright, libel laws and company records before going to print. It was aimed at people who wanted to uncover the shady world of business and power, but didn't know how to go about it.

LARM / HEIBEL / HERESY / THE FILTHY CHRISTIANS

1 in 12 Club, Bradford

THAT LACONIC old man with the ever tolerant, ever benign smile said he'd be there, and he was. Pope John Peel (deity of aural delinquents) came and went in a papal mist proving once again that his record spinning finger is still firmly on the pulse, and my, how that pulse was beating tonight.

This was a European megadeth - trash thrash anarcho/surfbastard/ beastiethrowback - night.

I'm sure that if I wanted to I could find the precise suitable adjective to describe the sorts of speeds the groups were playing at, but if I settle for fucking fast x N, you'll be able to imagine the shards of sound splintering into the collected bodies of the assembled Youth Culture (YC).

Filthy Christians (Sweden), fronted by a renegade baby viking wielding an axe - like voice gave a cathartic performance. With the sound of Sabbath ringing from behind him, his advice to the jerking urchins was "live the life you want to live." Nice one Ulvaeus, and goodnight... 6 points (pronounced 'sees pwant').

Continuing with the theme of blasphemy, **Heresy** (England's entry), tightened the pressure drip tourniquet fusing together white rasta rhythm with psychosis. Result; highly charged roof-reaching electricity and a sea of epileptic bodies working out the frustrations of the week. These boys were more co-ordinated than the Shadows (circa BC) substituting choreographed dancing with synchronised chaos. At a gig like this it's usually impossible to hear any of the song titles (if indeed there were any, songs or titles?), but these lads spared us the time for one traditional intro. He said, *"Make The Connection"* (a track on a Pleasure Disc compilation LP), followed by "T-shirts for sale"... Heresy, a different kind of commerce ('sept pwant').

Heibel looked extremely funny. I spied several dark clad yoofs popping in a crafty giggle at our Belgium buddies 'Beastie' togs. Miami meets Brooklyn in Belgium. The sound behind them was the same - they soundchecked with a chorus of *Stairway To Heaven*. Does anything ever change or does it just get louder and faster? - in fact, I'm almost certain that our peaked cap Belgium buddy was trying to give us a message in the music. No one heard him. On the slammometer these boys took the show. The highest leapers and the only band with two geetars which means they were the LOUDEST... 'dees pwant'!

Larm then had it all to do, and no time to do it in. Heibel overplayed a little. By now, the skateboarders (yes, they were on the dancefloor!) surf bastards, beastie metal men and anarcho syndicalist post-neon vegans were all pooped out. Well they had performed marvellously for almost two and a half hours, they deserved a rest. Larm would have got some points had the judges not suffered catatonic siezures by this time, we'll award them 'sees pwant' (with six more dates to play I'm sure they'll feature)... An International Knockout.

The post apocalyptic generation is alive and well and living in Bradford.

Paul B.

JOE JOHNSON

After beating Steve Davis to become Snooker World Champion in 1986, Joe Johnson released the 7" single *Bradford (Bouncing Back) / Tyke* on the London label Hit The Deck Records in 1987. Joe was backed by the local Hammond's Sauce Works (Brass Band). The single's concept and production was by Bradford's Far North Music.

CLUB RIO CAMPUS / RIO'S

After seven years of planning and eventually getting a late licence from the council, Steve Lawther opened a new club called *Rio Campus* on Woodhead Road in late November 1987.

The venue was converted from the old electrical and refrigeration engineers Southern & Redfern's building, Thorn House. The initial licence for this members-only club was for a trial six-month period as there had been many local concerns from Muslim worshippers at a nearby mosque over possible noise and late-night revelry.

In later years the club was taken over and renamed simply Rio's and then Bradford Rio and went on to become Bradford's premier venue for rock bands until it closed in 2007. The club then moved to a new venue in Leeds.

While this research has concentrated on venues that catered for the live music scene, we must also note the nightclubs that provided some social life for the rest of the population during the 1980s.

The three main city centre nightspots were Dollars & Dimes (at the old Mecca Ballroom), Blue Lace and Cloud Nine. The latter two catered for the top end of the city's affluent disco-goers. Cloud Nine refused entry to snooker star Alex 'Hurricane' Higgins because he was wearing trainers.

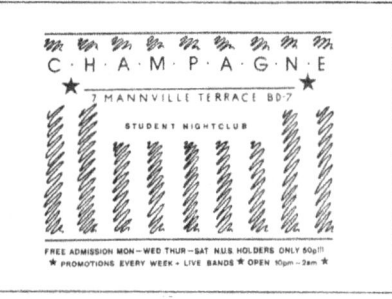

There were other clubs around the university and college area such as Unit 4+2, Champagnes and Tumblers all catering for the mainly student crowds.

Other groups around at this time included **Shoot The Dice**, **Toxic** and the rock band **606**.

At the end of 1987, the city's music scene was as healthy and diverse as ever with new bands forming all the time. The live scene was in a vibrant state, with numerous venues putting on local and national acts and gig-goers eager to go out and be entertained.

REFERENCES

The local Bradford evening newspaper, the *Telegraph & Argus*, provided a lot of the material for the research, particularly in the early chapters, the rest was gleaned from many other local sources, some of which are listed below, and the personal recollections of some of the people involved in the Bradford music scene during the relevant period.

PREFACE: 1963-66 FROM ROCK'N'ROLL TO THE BEAT BOOM

1. P 113 *Bradford's Rock 'N' Roll* - Derek Lister (1991) Bradford Libraries

2. P 95-96 *Bradford's Rock 'N' Roll* - Derek Lister (1991) Bradford Libraries

3. P 112-114 *Plebs: The Halifax Jazz Club 1961-68* - JS Wharton (2001) Sephton

4. *T&A* (1970)

5. The Esquire Club (1962-67) was started by local entrepreneur Terry Thornton after the success of his previous Jazz/R'n'B club Club 60 (1960-2) which had been run from the cellar of The Old Acorn pub in Shalesmoor. There was a range of well-known acts who appeared at the Esquire over the years, including The Kinks, The Small Faces, The Animals, The Who, US stars John Lee Hooker, Muddy Waters, and local boy Joe Cocker. At one point the club had an incredible 27,000 members!

When the five-year lease on the three storey old optical works, which had housed Sheffield's top venue, expired in 1967 Terry decided to move on and so the Esquire closed down. In 1980 the building was re-opened as The Leadmill, providing live music again after a gap of thirteen years. The Leadmill was closed in 2025.

Club 60 & The Esquire: Sheffield Sounds Of The Sixties - D Hale (2002) Ald Design & Print

6. *Kink* - Dave Davies, D (1996) Boxtree/Pan Books / *X-Ray* - Ray Davies (1994) Vikiing

7. After the Second World War Bradford continued its multi-ethnic heritage as new migrants and refugees from the Baltic and Eastern Europe settled here. One example was Ukrainian Ivan Prytulak who founded the famous Kolos Bakery on Great Horton Road in 1961, home to the nationally famous and delicious rye bread. (Kolos means 'ear of wheat' in Ukrainian).

8. Email from Tony Tretton.

9. P 107-108 *The Blues: From Robert Johnson To Robert Cray* - T Russell (2000) Carlton

10. *Halifax Courier* and *T&A*

CHAPTER 1: 1967-70 PSYCHEDELIA TO HEAVY ROCK

1. *T&A* (1970)

2. Ilkley Gazette (1967)

3. For a full list of bands/artists from the University Archives (1965-79)

   visit: www.bradford.ac.uk/library/special-collections/

4. In February 1972, Paul McCartney and his band Wings, visited Bradford University while on a day off from their UK tour, hoping to do an impromptu gig... alas they couldn't be accommodated at such short notice.

5. Kirkgate Market was eventually demolished on November 3, 1973, for the 'hideous' concrete Arndale centre.

6. *Telegraph & Argus (T&A)* 4/11/2006

7. The Paper Dolls were a trio of girls in blonde wigs and satin dresses from Northampton. Pauline Spider, Sue Copper and Suzi Tiger sang 'soulful middle of the road pop' vocals and released one album, *Paper Doll's House* in 1968, and five singles between 1968 and 1970. Their first single, *Something Here In My Heart*, got to number eleven in the charts.

8. Other 'art college freaks' like Al Beach and Mick Banks went on to form avant-garde theatre group John Bull's Puncture Repair Kit in 1970. Al also started the Northern Open Workshop in Halifax, as well as helping to run the Hebden Bridge festivals in the mid-1970s.

9. *Eyes On Stalks* – John Fox (2002) Methuen

10. President Records was set up in 1966 as an independent label and achieved its first chart successes with The Symbols and Eddie Grant's multi-racial group the Equals who reached number one with *Baby Come Back* in 1968. President is still in business and has become one of the longest established independent labels in the UK.

11. Skin Deep #2's vocalist Cindy-Ann Lee had previously worked with pianist Lenny Peters in London and had been managed by the infamous London gangsters the Kray Twins. This was before Lenny formed the pop duo Peters & Lee (taking Cindy-Ann's surname for the act) and had a 1973 number one with *Welcome Home*. Cindy-Ann was in the original cast of *Hair* on the West End stage in the late 1960s and also appears in the chorus on the LP of the show.

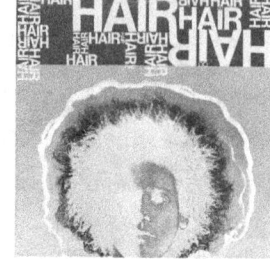

12. *T&A*, November 30, 1971

13. Global Village were recorded at the festival by Holyground Records, a label set up by Mike Levon and Dave Wood in Wakefield in 1966.

Hollyground was the first independent recording studio and record label in the UK, initially recording cabaret singers and mood music for Bingo halls. They put out their first album *Number Nine Bread St.* in 1967, followed by *A To Austr* in 1969. In early 1971 they recorded Bill Nelson's solo, private pressed LP, *Northern Dream*.

Due to problems in distribution of their LPs, and despite good reviews in the music press and support from John Peel, they went into hibernation in 1974. Holyground Records was revived in 1989 as interest in the collectability of their old releases led to re-releases and new material was recorded.

```
NUMBER NINE BREAD STREET
 67   Holy Ground HG 112/1109    NUMBER NINE BREAD STREET (LP, 250 copies only). . . . 400
```

14. Interestingly Leeds United asked the band to record a single for them, but being City fans they refused - Midnight Hearse website.

15. 1970 Bradford Festival Programme Booklet.

16. Email from Ken Waller.

17. *Halifax Courier* (1970)

CHAPTER 2: 1971-1976 PROG ROCK TO PUNK ROCK

1. Leeds Permanent Building Society advert featuring actor George Cole with Jimmy Iqbal (pictured right).

2. *Spenborough Guardian*, 15th January 1971

3. *T&A,*, November 2, 1971.

4. Chris Carter & Cosey Fanni Tutti were a performance art duo who joined the electronic performance art quartet Throbbing Gristle in 1975. The band, led by vocalist Genesis P. Orridge, started their own record Industrial Records label and released their first album *20 Jazz Funk Greats* in January 1980 which reached number five in the Independent LP Charts.

5. *T&A*, September 14, 1971.

6. *T&A*, October 17, 1971.

7. *T&A*, October 31, 1971.

8. Jeff Nuttall (1933-2004) was a Lancastrian by birth who played a key role in the underground press during the 1960s, writing for the *International Times* (IT) and also publishing his critique of the counter culture, *Bomb Culture* in 1968.

He was later a lecturer at Leeds Polytechnic and also performed as a poet, performance artist and jazz musician. In later life he became a prolific artist producing a series of expressionist landscapes as well as critical writings on popular culture.

His sons Danny and Timmy, both drummers, have played in various local Bradford based bands since the late 1970s, early 1980s.

9. Ticket stub kindly supplied by John Vinter.

10. *T&A*, August 28,1972.

REFERENCES 1963 - 1987

11. P 207, *Sound Effects: Youth, Leisure & The Politics Of Rock 'n' Roll* (revised version of *The Sociology Of Rock*) – Simon Frith (1983) Constable

12. P 130, *Alternative England & Wales* 1974 (1975)

13. During the 1970s, Bradford had a very strong Lesbian & Gay community who were very active on the UK scene. They had a PO Box at Fourth Idea Bookshop on Southgate and ran the local Gay Switchboard (Infomation Hotline).

14. *T&A*, June 8, 1974.

15. Roy 'Chubby' Brown, the 'blue' comedian whose real name is Royston Vasey - a name later used for the 'local' town in the radio and TV series *The League Of Gentlemen*.

16. *T&A*, April 24, 1976.

17. GYGAFO stood for 'Get Your Gear And F**K Off' – a regular response to bands from promoters! They were a Leeds based band who won the northern heat of the *Melody Maker's National Rock Contest* in September 1974.
They are infamous for releasing the highly collectable LP *Legend Of The Kingfisher* on Holyground Records in 1973.

18. *T&A*, March 13, 1976.

19. *T&A* 22.11.1997 *Pick of the Past* by Jim Appleby

CHAPTER 3: 1957-1987 LOCAL FOLK

1. P xii-xxvi, *The Penquin Book Of Folk Ballads Of The English Speaking World* - A Friedman (Ed) (1976) Penquin

2. *Pen & Pencil Drawings Of Bradford* - William Scruton (1985) Amethyst

3. On the wall at Guiseppe's Back Yard (Albion Court) is a Bradford City Heritage plaque which declares;

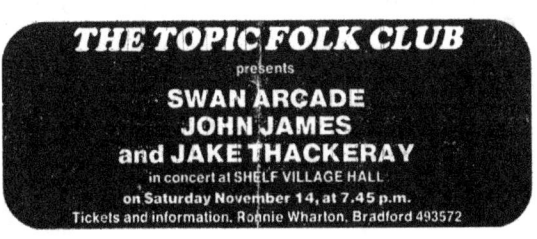

'It was in this building, founded by Tom Laycock in 1867 as Laycock's Temperance Hotel, that the Bradford Independent Labour Party was formed in 1891. This paved the way for the birth of the Independent Labour Party, in Bradford two years later. Laycock's became famous as 'The Bradford Parliament' – a public debating place.'

In 1887 the renowned Russian 'Anarchist Prince' Peter Kropotkin, author of the anarchist study 'Mutual Aid', spoke at a meeting there.

4. Alex Eaton's 30th Anniversary Notes and Topic Folk Club website.

5. *T&A*, September 14, 1971.

6. *T&A*, April 27, 1968.

7. *T&A*, October 1971.

8. *T&A*, August 31, 1971.

9. Bacca Pipes website.

10. German website review 2007.

11. Topic Folk Club website.

CHAPTER 4: 1977-80 PUNK ROCK / NEW WAVE / NWOBHM

1. In mid-1978, 'Green' Gartside left Leeds Art College for London and formed the archetype DIY band Scritti Politti (a bastardisation of the Italian phrase meaning 'political writing'). They produced their first single *Skank Bloc Bologna* as well as a photocopied booklet with a step by step guide on how to make and produce your own records.

2. The all girl group Girlschool were formed in 1978. After a series of line-up changes they were joined by lead guitarist Jackie Chambers, who was born in Bradford but grew up in Leeds, in 2000.

3. Steven 'Johna' Johnson later wrote two books about his experiences following the original Adam & The Ants, *Blood, Sweat, Leather & Tears Parts 1 & 2 (Old Dog Books, 2022)*.

4. The building was originally the Empire Theatre in 1899, where future

321

silent film stars such as Charlie Chaplin and Stan Laurel played in vaudeville shows. In 1918 it became the Empire Cinema. After fire damaged the building in 1952 it became the Alexandra Hotel (with the Vaults Bar at one end) - an annex of Bradford College. In 1984 it was demolished and is now a car park opposite the Love Apple café.

5. At that gig, Gary Cavanagh met the late great John Peel for the first time, and gave him a copy of the first volume of *Worst Of The 1 In 12 Club* compilation cassette tape. Peel was sent all subsequent volumes and he and Jello Biafra of the Dead Kennedys are probably the only people who have a full set of all the LPs.

6. *T&A*, 1978.

7. *The Leveller* #43 November 1980 / *Radical Bookseller* #4 Jan/Feb 1981.

8. 4th Idea's Collective member Reuben Goldberg (1952-1997) (pictured left) arrived in Bradford in 1972 to study sociology and literature at University. He soon joined the city's growing anti-fascist movement, eventually becoming chair of the city's Ad-Hoc Committee On Racism. In 1974-75 he became president of Bradford National Union Of Students.

After leaving 4th Idea, he started his own bookshop *The Starry Plough* (named after the flag used by James Connelly's Irish Citizens Army) on Edmund Street and in 1984 he became a Labour councillor for the Toller ward. He moved back to London in the late 1980s and sadly died in October 1997.

9. Ronald was interviewed for the BBC 4 programme, *The People's History Of Pop (1955-65)*, which was broadcast on 15.4.2016.

10. Bradford Music Collective was set up around 1980 and started making tapes of local bands under the title Tapir Product. The second tape was *The Focus On Bradford Tape*, recorded live at Bradford Playhouse (now the Priestley Centre) on the 9th October 1980. It featured Vex, Nick Toczek, PWALOB, Little Brother, Cameras In Cars and Sheffield band Vendino Pact (who included Martin Fry later of ABC).

CHAPTER 5: 1980-1983 POST PUNK / ANARCHO PUNK / GOTH

1. The Sweatbox was an ex-Italian club which had previously been the Sion Baptist Chapel, built in 1873. A Bradford City Heritage plaque adorns the building stating this. It is now a Sikh temple.

2. Quote from review of the gig in *Apathy* #2 fanzine by Stiff Shit.

3. After the rally members of the CU returned with the 'buckets of money' to their Southbrook Terrace base, only to realise that no-one had any keys to get in. One quick thinking member then shimmied up a drain pipe and through a toilet window at the back to let everyone in. As the members started to empty and count all the money three police officers appeared, having been alerted to a possible break-in. The CU members hastily explained the reasons for their unorthodox entry while trying to hide the piles of money on the floor. The police finally satisfied then left, much to the members' relief.

4. In late 1980 the Dole-Q Club had been started in Leeds by a collective of people who organised cheap (30p/40p) gigs at the Marquis Of Granby pub every fortnight. They also produced their own photocopied A4 *Chickenfeed* fanzine which had poems, cartoons, articles, reviews and photomontages. The prime movers were Kate and Anne, Wild Willi Beckett, and seventeen other contributors. The Dole-Q Club had close links with the drop-in/advice centre for young people called Off The Record, near Kirkgate Market in Leeds. Together they organised a free festival called 'Giro Jamboree' at Woodhouse Moor on 29th July 1981- the day of the royal wedding of Prince Charles and Diana Spencer.

5. All the 1 In 12 posters were hand printed by Club members at Bradford Community Printshop, based at 127, Thornton Road. The printshop had been set up in 1976 with Yorkshire Arts grants and was run by two full-time print workers, Jules and Ruth.

Its open door policy meant that anyone could turn up with an idea and be shown how to screenprint their own posters. Various community based groups from Bradford CND, Gay Switchboard, 1st Birstall Guides, St. Peters Church, to local music groups/bands used the premises over the years.

Unfortunately funding ran out in the late 1980s and its two paid workers were made redundant. The building was demolished for a college car-parking space.

REFERENCES 1963 - 1987

6. The Anti-Fascist 12 were arrested at Eccleshill School where they were protesting at a meeting of the National Front (NF). Six were arrested inside the hall and six outside.

7. The conspiracy laws were notorious for avoiding the safeguards that otherwise are afforded to defendants in other criminal cases, and if sentenced they carried a maximum of life imprisonment.

8. George Lindo was another Bradford West Indian man who fell foul of police harassment and was jailed. His campaign was later supported in song by dub poet Linton Kwesi Johnson. Sadly George died in 1998.

9. *The Springing Of George Blake* - Sean Bourke (1970) Cassel

10. Seething (Susan Williams) Wells' first NME gig review – fictitious bands at a non-existent venue! (pictured right)

CHAPTER 6: 1984-1986 INDIE / ALTERNATIVE ROCK

1. The Membranes became good comrades of The 1 In 12 Club and their singer/bassist John Robb also produced his own fanzine *The Roxx*. He later became a writer for the Melody Maker music paper and formed the band Goldblade.

Marc Riley later teamed up with BBC Radio 1 DJ Mark Radcliffe as the character and co-host 'Lard', initially on Radio 5s *Hit The North* how and then on various slots on Radio One.

2. Below is a scurrilous article by a *Keighley News* reporter trying to 'blacken' the reputation of the 1 in 12 Club.

GOING FOR A SNOG
A TALE OF CHEAP SEX ROCKERS

HELEN KELLER'S IRON LUNG
THE SEX OBJECTS
SHY TED

Bradford Mechanic's Arms

THE GROUP with the sickest name in the history of beat music are hard at work on the image. Local non-hero and lead singer Justin Alison (who you just *know* is a Grammar School boy) scratches a testicle, picks an inflamed nasal orifice, grunts and throws another shape. He mumbles darkly, an unlit Consulate dangling from decidedly virginal lips.

Their *piece de resistance* is a savagely mutilated version of The Cure's 'Killing An Arab' retitled 'Peeling A Camel', complete with animal scream and bog-eyed maniacal stare; I am torn between watching the entire set and going for a wee. Justin introduces the next song (their rendering of The Monkees' 'I'm A Believer' retitled 'Then I Chewed Her Leg') and I head for the Ladies.

I disengage rapidly, straight into The Sex Objects' accapella aural masturbatory fantasies. Sample song title – 'My Knob's Bigger Than Your Knob'. Instruments include plastic rulers and wastepaper bins. Imagine a suburban Test Department with a sense of their own absurdity and an obsession with male genitalia and you're half-way to realising why these boys'll never make the cover of your fave pop paper.

Shy Ted (geddit!!??!) is the latest 'poet' to infest this excuse for a city's cultural centre. Each piece of appallingly predictable Spartist verbiage is prefaced by a brief exchange of saliva with the literary dissidents stage front. The rising tide of pop sensuality?

I have seen the future of Rock and Roll and its palms are hairy.

Susan Williams

How public money is funding anarchy

EXCLUSIVE by Malcolm Evans

The Keighley News today reveals that a death threat to a top politician was printed on publicly funded equipment.

Bradford council has also pumped public money into organisations used by anarchists involved in violent and illegal activities.

Anarchists have wrecked a nuclear civil defence bunker at Keighley and shadowy groups are encouraging the destruction of other installations.

The Baildon home of West Yorkshire Tory Councillor Royston Moore two months ago suffered an arson attack. His car was wrecked and only prompt fire brigade action saved the house.

A death-threat letter followed but police inquiries have drawn a blank.

The stencilled letter referred to the closure of Thornton View Hospital by Bradford Health Authority, of which Councillor Moore is chairman.

It said: "R. has to go! The law of nature says he must die."

The Keighley News has traced the printing of the threat to Bradford Community Print Shop in Thornton Road, Bradford. The shop receives £4,500 a year from Bradford council and £6,500 from Yorkshire Arts.

When challenged by the KN, Print Shop partner Tony Grogan said: "This is all I need. It (the letter stencil) won't still be there. The people who use the shop aren't that stupid."

Grogan is a supporter of the anarchist group KDIS (Knee Deep In S**t), which uses the Print Shop as its contact address and produces inflammatory leaflets and magazines.

He is also a member of the Bradford 1 in 12 Club, which meets in pubs and clubs and which has received £4,700 from Bradford council.

The club will receive a council administered grant of £59,000 when it finds suitable permanent premises.

As well as promoting bona fide events for unemployed people the club, admits Grogan, "has a number of active members engaged in various activities and is the base for KDIS."

Two 1 in 12 members were arrested in February and are awaiting trial on charges of incitement to commit criminal damage.

Grogan is a member of the printers' union SOGAT, the assistant Bradford secretary of which is Bradford council's Labour chief whip Councillor Gerry Sutcliffe.

He says: "To the best of my knowledge the Print Shop were and still are a respectable organisation."

The KN has met a member of a militant peace-movement group calling itself Spies for Peace, which claims responsibility for the attck 18 months ago on the Royal Observer Corps nuclear-war monitoring bunker near Keighley Tarn.

There was an official hush-up over the incident. The bunker, secured by heavy padlocks, was broken into and set on fire. Papers were stolen.

The Spies for Peace member says: "So much relies on these bunkers they need destroying. It's like removing the bottom cans from a supermarket display."

He says Spies for Peace is a loose organisation of like-minded people.

3. The Three Johns were later asked to appear on the TV programme *The Tube*, produced in Newcastle. The band gave The 1 In 12 Club ten passes for people to attend as part of the band's entourage. The ten lucky winners were drawn from a lottery raffle held at the club on a gig night prior to the show and all ten people plus the rest of the band's entourage had a great time at the show.

4. At the time of the grant application other voluntary community groups were also applying for funding from the Council Policy Unit's community programme, which was funded by the Department for the Environment. In the end the policy unit's decision makers placed The 1 In 12 Club tenth in priority on their shortlist, with the top two community groups each asking for over £300,000. Incidentally, both these groups terminated within a year or so of opening.

Unemployed support you

I HAVE just finshed my second copy of the "Yorkshire Miner", which I obtained from the "One in 12" Club, in Bradford, (taken from a Rayner report statistic about one in 12 people defrauding the state).

This club supports the miners and last night a group called the Three Johns, from Leeds, played and over £100 was raised for the strike fund, no mean feat for such a small club.

The reports of the solidarity of all the families and communities and other members of the public in the Yorkshire area and elsewhere brought tears to my eyes.

I decided to write this letter, to express my solidarity as a "punk", unemployed for some four years to date.

I would like you to know that the unemployed of Bradford support your cause completely and I, for one, will continue to give money and food to your cause!

Victory to the miners!

I know about police harassment — you do tend to get harassed with blue hair, etc.

H. Caswell,
Manningham,
Bradford.

5. Over 6,000 pickets during the year-long strike were sufficiently injured to need hospital treatment, compared to 1,300 police officers. P 50 *Strike '84-'85*.

6. Each food parcel for the miners had to be under the value of £4 or the DHSS would count it as income.

7. Letter from 1 In 12 member Harvey Caswell in the NUM *Yorkshire Miner* newspaper.

8. The inscription on the plaque reads: *'Bradford 1 In 12 Club with many thanks for your help during the miners' strike 1984/85. Knottingly Miners' Wives Self Help Group.'*

9. Transcribed from John Peel BBC broadcasts by long-time listener and 1 In 12 Club member Ian 'Huddersfield' Browne.

10. Five Go Down To The Sea (1984-85, pictured right) were an Irish band from Cork who were, at the time, based in London. They played the 1 In 12 a couple of times, thrilling everyone with the quirky offbeat sound and the on/off stage antics of their vocalist, Donnelly. Later the singer and fellow Five guitarist Ricky formed the short-lived band Beethoven. Donnelly tragically drowned in the Thames in the late 1980s.

11. After Joy and Into A Circle split-up, Bee (Paul Hampshire) moved to Thailand and joined the Electro-rock group Futon with ex-Suede member Simon Gilbert. While Barry became a UK tour manager, Buzz retired to France and Aki created Nation Records and formed Fun-da-mental the political hip-hop group

12. John Speed's killer was identified as David Gricewith in 1988.

13. *The Guardian*, May 13, 1985.

14. James Brown started as a 17 year old fanzine writer, originally with co-editor Ben 'SIck Of War' (who ended up doing his own fanzine, *Raising Hell*), before becoming a freelance writer, then staff writer for the *NME*. By 1986 he had become a multi-media mogul as editor of the original lads mag *Loaded*. He later moved on to edit the magazine *GQ* in 1998, then his own men's mag, *Jack*.

In 2003 he sold his I Feel Good publishing company for £6.4m before becoming a cultural commentator as presenter of *I Predict A Riot* on the Bravo TV channel.

15. *Dismissal Of Strikers & Industrial Disputes 1985-87, Strike & Mass Sackings At Silentnight* - Dr. Stephen Mustchin, University Of Manchester (2014).

15. Alias of Kath Cannoville – co-founder of Nation Records

CHAPTER 7: 1987

1. Quoted from Raj Rajwadi on the Sangam website, sangam-music.co.uk.

2. When Jan Cyrka left the Love Reaction he went solo and produced two LPs for the Food For Thought label. His debut *Beyond The Common Ground* and the follow up album *Spirit* established him as a guitarist of note. He has since become big in Europe, especially France.

Nowadays he also makes a lucrative living from composing / recording music for TV ads for the likes of Irn Bru and Oil Of Olay, and TV theme-tunes for shows including *Wife Swap* and the *Jeremy Kyle Show*.

3. Slammer vocalist Paul's sister is the actress and comedien Jayne Tunnicliffe. Jayne, aka Mary Unfaithful in her T&A column, has become a comic poet on the comedy circuit, performing with Lily Savage, Peter Kaye, Johnny Vegas and others. She has recently been seen on the long-running tv soap *Coronation Street* as the character Yana Lumb, best friend of the character Cilla Battersby.

4. *The Observer* 19th July 1987

BIBLIOGRAPHY

Other invaluable reference material includes the following publications:

Record Collector's Rare Record Guide (2002-2006)

Alternative England & Wales 1974 (1975)

Encyclopedia Of British Beat Groups And Solo Artists Of The Sixties - C Cross (1980) Omnibus

Tapestry Of Delights - V Joynson - Online Website.

Indie Hits: 1980-89 – The Complete UK Independent Charts - B Lazell (1997) Cherry Red

Do You Want To Be In A Group?: Huddersfield Rock 'n' Roll Groups 1957-63 - R Mallinson (2004) Central Publishing

A Touch On The Times: Songs Of Social Change 1770-1914 - R Palmer (1974) Penguin Education

Then, Now & Rare, British Beat 1960-69 - T Rawlings (2002) Omnibus

Strike '84-'85, North Yorkshire Women Against Pit Closures (1985)

Rollbacktheyears website

And a special mention for Pete Frame's *Rock Family Trees (1979-93) Omnibus*. Pete's family trees have adorned a multitude of magazines, articles and record sleeves over the years and were a major source of inspiration for my own hand-drawn trees which adorn this book.

INDEX OF BANDS ON TREES

A

A1 41
Abacus 105
Abhorred 199, 227
Abject 229
Abraxas 139
Abyss 67, 107
Accept 131
Accent 14, 33, 71
Acid Gallery 21
Acoustic Alchemy 128
Adam's Apple 84
Adolescents UK 151, 225
Adora Highway 285
After Hours 136
Agents 99
Agony Column 191
Aim 218
Airkraft 164
Al 148, 195
Alan Wormald Band 84, 195, 271
Albion Country Band 111
Allan Holdsworth Band 43, 45
Allen Bros 195, 301
Allen Pound's Get Rich 14, 33, 57, 71, 77
All Fired Up 61
Alexis Korner's Blues Incorporated 39
Almighty 175
Alwoodly Jets 235
Ambition 59, 61
American Housewives 283
Amon Duul II 69
AMP 307
Andre Dudek 41
A New Opera 267
Angelic Upstarts 255
Anita Madigan Band/Big Bang 195
Annie & The Aeroplanes 201, 231, 267, 268, 291, 307
Another Cinema 193
Another Colour 119
Another Wrist Action 146, 235
Answering Machine 312
Anti-System 199, 225, 227, 229, 282
Apaches 84
Apollos 83
Apple 67
Apple Moths 242
Arab 100
Archers 140, 146, 307
Architect 241, 257
Argent 33, 77, 87
Argy Bargy 115
Aroda Highway 257, 285
Assassin 255
Atlanta 69
At Least We Got Shoes 231

Atmosfear 111, 135
Atomic Rooster 41
Auroborus (Thumb) 37, 43, 49, 69
Aurora 312
Autumn 19, 33
Avalanche (Semuta) 139
Avengers (Teen Beats) 9
Axis 59, 125
Axles 160
Azel 93, 127, 195

B

Baby Tuckoo 81, 87, 131, 133, 137, 139, 154
Back Door 99
Backslider 81, 111, 126, 190
Backstone Edge 267
Bad Company 13, 17
Bad Habits 93
Bad Rep 257
BAJ 71
Badwolf 311
Bantus (Pigmies & Bushmen) 148, 187, 255
Bartail – Godwit 107
Bash Street Kidz 225
Bastille 95
Batfish Boys 119, 163, 167, 217
Battered Ornaments 49
Beach La Mar 135
Beat Squad 13, 37, 43
Beats Working 139, 146, 191
Be-Bop Deluxe 193
Beckoning 242
Bed 268
Bedlam 137, 257
Beezer Bob & The Brainwaves 146, 199, 235, 259
Belvardos 9
Ben Crossland Quintet/Quartet 54
Berlin 133, 168, 195
Best Way To Walk 273
Beyond The Veil 242
Biffo The Storm 69
Big Bang 167, 217, 218, 293
Big Electric Cat 255
Big Eyed Beans 133, 231, 289
Big Fish 146, 189, 195
Biggles 161, 201, 285
Bill Presley's Coat 189, 199
Billy & The Four Masons 59, 61
Billy Ocean Band 41
Billy Thompson Trio 8
Billy Thompson Band 235
Bitter End 194
Black Cat Yard 123
Black Lace 87
Black Onyx 31, 141

Black Star Liner 180
Blackstone Edge 267
Blanks 189, 201
Block (Climax) 48, 77, 84
(Blue) Blood Group 14, 33
Blood Orange 255
Blues Bite 31, 59, 127
Blue Denim 131, 191
Blue Flys 128
Blue Murder 111
Blue Vein 73
Blunderbuss 311
Bobby Charltons 195, 197, 301
Bob Desant Trio 65
Bobo 257
Body Language 73
Bolyne 131
Bomb Circle 282
Bonafide 14, 33, 49, 71
Bone Idle 235, 259
Boom Or Bust 122, 257
Bordelo 139
Borderline 71
Borrowers 268
Boston Crabs 311
Box Of Tricks 41
Boys From The East 189, 201
Bradfords 9, 16
Branwell & The Bronte Beats (Phanthoms) 20
Brazen Hussies 267, 268
Breadline 13
Brenda & The Dominators 80
Brendan Croker & The 5 O'clock Shadows 117
British Lions 37, 39
Broken Home 167
Broomdusters (Jean & The Mistics) 49, 107
Brotherhood Of Man 99
Bruford 43, 45
Brute Force 257
Bryan Ferry Band 43
Buddy Valentine & The Lonely Hearts 159, 161
Buffalo Girls 267
Bullweek 242, 297
Burial 153
Bite The Bullet 148, 168, 195

C

Cajun Aces 239
Calderbeats 20
Calvary 35, 37, 69
Cameras In Cars 160
Camel 37
Cancer Moon 307

INDEX

Cannibal Feast 208
Caravanserai 113
Caravelles 9, 11, 141
Cardiacs 297
Cardiac Arrest 137
Careless Cowgirls 267
Carnal Horus 67
Castle 41
Casuals 31, 61, 73, 80, 100
Catch 22 83, 275
Catflap 81, 111, 122, 126
Ceremony 59
Chad Wayne & The Chessmen 20, 267, 268
Chainsaw 23, 168
Challenger 140, 190
Chaos 217
Charles Dickens & The Great Expectations 231, 268, 291
Charles 1st 52
Charlie 87
Charlie Speed Band 91, 117, 128
Charmers 85
Chatoyancy 49, 77
Cheap 'N' Nasty 217, 218
Cheats 20
Cheyenne 139
Chi 189
Chicken Ranch 199
Chicken Shack 39
Chien Chaud Et Les Hotdogs 268, 291
Chillas 5, 14, 33, 57
Choice 167
Chopyn 74
Chris & The Deltics 21, 49
Christie 21
Chris Farlowe's Thunderbirds 74
Chronic 160, 177, 1998
Chrome Molly 131
Chuck Layburn Band 13
Chumbawamba 115
Circles 189, 241
Citron Girls 274
City Limits 135
Clandestine Roots 69
Class Type Bees 167, 218
Clay Martin & The Trespassers (Great Pacifics) 14, 33, 59, 127
Climax 35
Clockwork Line 49
CMS 237
Coast To Coast 148, 195
Cocktail Shakers 187, 191
Coda 231, 307
Cold Dance 167
Colenso Parade 146, 235
Collection 5, 31, 45, 80, 84, 93
Colosseum 43
Colosseum II 43
Colourfield 167
Commitments 41
Company Road Show 88
Complete Disorder 225

Condition Red 298
Contrast 10
Convulsions 227, 229
Cornilious Webb 77
Counterdance 158, 161, 163, 227, 267, 291
Countdowns 31
Coup De Grace 242
Cowboys & Indians 199
Cowpoke Annie & The Texas Longhorns 291
Creation Roots 248
Cresters 9, 125
Criminal Damage 225, 297
Crocus Rock'n'Roll 191
Crown Jools 54, 124, 145, 307
Cruising 83, 97, 122
Crusaders (Dave Arran & The) 5, 31, 57, 80, 87, 99
Crying Shame 148, 195, 301
Crystalized Anthem 46
Cuba 128
Cumscrunch 89, 122, 163, 268, 291
Cunning Stunts 73
Cult 201, 309
Custer's Last Band 91
Cuttlers 110
Cyrka 131, 133, 139, 164, 309

D

Daisy Chainsaw 242
Dal Stevens & The Blue Jays 5, 8
Dal Stevens & The Four Dukes 5
Daka (Dachau) 225
Dakotas 5
Damien Wolfe 199, 255, 299
Dana Gillespie Band 41
Dangerous Sisters 227, 235, 259
Danse Society 201
Dantalian's Chariot 39
DPs 41
Dark Blues 39
Dark Horse 175
Das Tor Zu Wett 257
Dave Adams & The Belairs 107
Dave Berry Band 14, 33, 77
Dave Lee Sound 48, 77, 84, 85, 95, 127
Dave Sherwood & The Foresters 85
Dawnwatcher 95, 107, 133
Dawnweaver 93, 235, 259
Dealer 71
Dead Celebs 295
Death Cult 201
Dedringer 135
Deepbeats 9
Del-Fi 7
Delius Myth 257, 293
Delmonts 124
Depozer 89
Del Rio Four (Chapters) 9, 84
Delta Blues Band 60

Desire Crew 229
Detrimental 189
Deutronomy 241
Dial 83
Diamond 19, 73, 100
Diamond Head 93
Diamond Light 140
Dickie Valentine Band 21
Dignity 89
Dillinger (Fairground) 9, 59, 85, 125
Dingleberrys 48. 85
Dingos 5, 8, 9, 11
Dire Straits 117
Dirty Macs 131, 187
Dirty Work 81, 83, 91, 93, 97, 111, 122, 126, 127, 145
Disguise 299
Distort 177, 199, 225
Dhol Foundation 189
Dolce Vita 35
Doll By Doll 107
Don't Talk Wet 113
Domestic Enemies 267, 291
Donkeys 155
Don Partridge's Wild Fowl 125
Donovan's Open Road Band 49
Dormaneu 167
Doveston Brothers 40
Doctor & The Inmates 177, 298
Dregs Of Society 81, 126, 217
Dubh Chapter 159
Duchess 13
Dust Blue 131
DV8s 189
Dynamics 230

E

Earthquake Johnson 49, 57, 77, 107
East 189, 241
East Of Java 148
Eaten Alive By Insects 146, 158, 159, 161, 163, 167, 201, 235, 268
Eazy Street/ Bon Rue 167, 283, 285
Echo Four Two 115
Eclipse 107
Eddie & The Echoes 51
Edgar Broughton Band 93, 128, 145
Edge 289
Edible Marquetry 153, 189, 199
Edison's Phonograph 99
Efulmeyon 268, 291
Elastic Band 37
Elderberrys 8, 48
Elected 95, 135
Electric Bon 60
Electric Cauliflower 225, 299
Electric Love 310
Electric Nosebleeds
El Loco 84, 85, 140, 271
Elements 167, 283, 302
Elf 122, 160

INDEX

Ellis 37, 39
Ellison's Hogline 21, 49, 69, 99
Elizabethans 87
Embrace 187
Emerald 139
EMF 31, 35, 83, 89, 115, 127, 145
Empire 113
Emile Ford & The Checkmates 41
End 31
End (2) 93, 129, 218
Enid 31
English Rose 37
Epics 21
Epitaph 137
Eric & The Blue Jellyfish 194
Eric Burdon's New Animals 39
Ethel & The Heroes 283
Excalibur 133, 255, 310
Excel (XL) 148, 195
Excitement 93, 127, 145, 195
Exoterik 218
Expelaires 135
Extra Tenor 231
Extix 177

F

4th Arch 177
40 Bouncing Belgians 164, 227
Fact & Fiction 73
Factory 69
Fahrenheit 451/ Kurt's Company 217, 218
Failsafe 231
Fairy Dogmother 231
Fairy Tales 11, 141
Fallons 14, 18, 33, 35
Falconz Bluez (Lee Wayne & The Falcons) 10, 18
Falky's Forum 67
Fall Guys 95, 146, 163, 191, 309
False Claims 136, 231
False Idols 136
Family Dogg 77
Far Fetched 187, 285
Fargo 67, 107
Fassbender-Russell Band 153
Fatal Charm 146, 191, 235, 259
Fat Chance (Neat & Tidy) 61, 124, 195
Fear 137
Felix 19, 31, 73, 100
Fever Hut 160
Few 13, 129
Fiat Lux 193
Figures From The Cold (Isolation) 293, 299
Fillibuster 83, 145
Filth & Vulgarity 167
Financial Tymes 46
Firelace 60
First Aid 99, 127
Five Leighs 14, 33, 57
Five Previous Owners 217
FKM 137

Flamingos 218
Flashpoint 231
Flock 99
Fluke 231
Flying Pickets
FM 93
Focus 39
Fogg 84
Folkweave 112
Followera 18
Force Majeure 187
Forest 57, 83, 307
Forge Blues 71
Forgers 18
Forsythe Ensemble 194
Forum Trolls 19
Four Beats Behind Bars 89, 146, 231
Four Musketeers 5
Fourplay 164
Foxy Lady 83, 91, 97, 127
Fractions 164
Frankie Miller's Fullhouse 87
Freddie Starr's Band 124, 195
Freedom 71
Freefall 177
Free Expression 41, 61
Freeze 273
Fresh Garbage 57, 83
Friction Agitators 227
Friendship (Abacus) 71,
Frieze 218
From Knowhere (Force) 164
From The Underworld 301
Fruit Bats 122, 163
Full Tilt 81, 111, 126, 137
Fundamental 189, 201
Funeral 312

G

Gary Lane & The Rockets 77
Garry Lee Three 13, 17
Garry Whitfield's Big Secret 73, 89
Gathering 159
Gardeners Of Eden 175, 255
Garth Cawood & The Dingos 8
Garth Cawood & The Mike Stuart Sound 8
Garth Cawood's Funhouse 8, 35, 127
Gay Abandon 81
Geddes Axe 131
Gene Loves Jezebel 167
Genesis 242
Geno Washington & The Ram Jam Band 35
Gerry & The Pacemakers 31, 93, 195, 127, 143, 148
Get Rich 14
Getting The Fear 201
Ghandarva 60, 83
Ghost Dance 160, 163, 177, 274
Gillan 37, 167
Gingerbread 35

Ginn 46
Girls At Our Best 191
Glamorous Hooligan 255
Glass Opera 257
Gleneagles 84
Glen's Magical Roundabout 43, 99
Glimmer 217
Glitter Band 21
Global Village 193
God & The Demi-Gods 161, 163, 201, 268
Godfathers 159
Going For Gold 286
Golden Oldies 59
Gold, Frankensense & Discdrive 267
Gollies 77
Gong 43, 45
Good, The Bad & The Ugly 231, 267, 268
Gordon Bennett 231
Gorgeous 241, 257, 293
Gospel 312
GPO 95
Grace Notes 113, 117
Graham John Sound 67
Graham Lockwood Trio 8, 35
Graham Parker & The Rumour 119
Grammar School Puffs 146
Green Velvet 13
Grim 382, 297
Grip 17, 133, 285
Gross National Product 199, 201, 227
Grotesque Gnome 35
Ground Zero 93, 145
Guest 99
Guido 124, 148, 153, 195, 301
Gygafo 91
Gypsy 118

H

Hackensack 39
Hadrian's Wall 72
Handful Of Dance 239, 282
Hand Made Goddesses (Phantasy) 136
Hanged 137, 199, 201, 235, 259
Happiness Ad 191
Hard Rain 168
Hardware 255, 299
Harlequyn 139, 257
Harlot Masscara Showband 175
Harsh Words 197
Hawks (Rowdies) 97
Hawkwind 39
Heart Of Darkness 194
Heart & Soul 67
Hebric 108
Hebron Bros 33
Hedjog 235
Height 160
Helen & The Tomboys 9, 16
Henry's Radio 235
Hepworth's Good Impression 85
Herd 77

Hidden Warfare 283, 293
Hiding Place
Hi-Fly 20, 23, 48, 84, 127
Hightimers 89
High Z (Solid Hearts) 271, 295
Hive 193
Hobo 35
Hogsnort Rupert's Original Flagon Band 50
Hokupayshun Rode 107
Hollow Men 160
Holy Holy 177
Holy Marimba 241, 307
Homesick 255
Honeybus 74
Hooligans 87
Horsemen 117
Hot Pursuit 81, 111, 126
Hot Spiced Bananas 93, 153, 289
Hourglass 51
Howard & The Falcons 84
Howling Whippets 307
Huckleberry 99
Hunting Party 217, 218
Hurdy Gurdy 41
Hustler Street Band 175, 268, 291
Hyacinth House 153, 160, 187
Hype (David Bowie) 49

I

Ian J Bell & Eden Roc 35
Ian J Bell & The Memphis Sound 35
Ian Brown Band 189
Icebergs 35
Icon Leadz 89, 122, 146, 153, 235
IdiotBox 297
Idle Rich 146, 159, 191, 235
If 37
'Igginbottom 43, 45, 69, 99
Iguanas 163
IK (Cause) 193
Immigantz 227
Impact 84
Incredible Walker 38, 73
Indigo 71
Induction 67
Industrial Aktion 241
Inevitable Split 230
Inflatable Church 235
Info-Zany 187
Innadaze 255
Inner Mind / Tender Touch 54, 124
Insane 199, 225
Instant Eric 61, 83
Instruders 50
Into A Circle 201
Intrepid Birdman 133
Invaders 93, 128, 145, 165, 187
Inside Out 191
IOU 43
Iron Pig 61

Isengaard 60, 105
Isis 73
Isotope 117
Ivor Kenny Band 35

J

JB's Soul Nation 61
Jab Jab 89, 127, 148
Jackfield Farm (Noah's Ark) 17, 51
Jack Juma Band 83
Jaded Hart 295
Jam 193
Jan Dukes De Grey 106
Japanese Soldiers 146, 191, 235, 309
Jasper 93,
Jayver 81, 167, 175, 302
Jason's Flock 21, 69, 99
JCB Ceilidh Band 113
Jedediah Strut 133, 139
Jed's Blues Band 57, 81, 83, 91, 97, 122, 126, 145, 163, 165, 187
Jeff 225
Jefferson Love's Indigo 84
Jeff Green & The Bandits 11
Jellybread 33
Jimmy James & The Vagabonds 8, 127
Jinx 9, 11, 101, 125
JJ's Bones 242, 282
Joe Public 31, 59, 61, 80, 100, 124
John's Followers 22
John Shepard Set 69, 128
John Verity Band 21, 77, 84, 85, 87, 140, 145
Jon Jagger Band 35, 77, 83, 145
John Mayall's Bluesbreakers 39
John Potter's Clay 146, 195
Johnny & The Poor Boys 197, 217
Johnny Crash 257
Jon Strong Band 117
Jovial Crew 17, 110
Joy 189, 201
Jude Brown (Trust) 19, 20, 38
Judy (Judy's Dream) 299
Judy Blue Band 48, 127, 145
Juicy Lucy 39, 43
Juke Joint 189, 241, 293
Junior's Eyes 49, 69
Jumping The Gun 270
Just Before Dawn 41

K

Kaboss (Smokey Ring Hat Band) 67, 107
Kaleche 89, 148, 195, 301
Kaleidoscope 99, 127
Kama Rouge 219, 285
Katzz 31, 93, 124, 127, 195
Kava Kava
Keith Martin'S Trio 71
Kelly's Heroes 17, 129

Kevin Coyne Band 39
Keymen 13
KGB 61, 93, 165
Khaki Vegan Rainbow 225
Khang 133
Khazadoum 135
Kick 285
Kiki Dee Band 94
Kill II This 175, 255, 282
Killer 146
Killing Joke 309
Kindness 77, 84, 87, 140
King Bootty 193
King Crimson 41, 43, 45
Kingdonel Duo 61, 84
Kingpins 23
Kinks 39, 87
Kit Syke Will 115
KKF Blues Band 231
Klingons 163
Knock Out Drops 217
Knoxville Girls 161, 268, 291
Knoxville Saints 218
Kool Jerx 89, 195
Krakatoa 133
Kukulkan 91, 97
Kwai Chang Caine 297
Kweeny 19, 73

L

Lace 74
Lady Godiva 270
Ladykillers 23
Lady October 177, 274, 293
Lady Vic 146, 231
Laika Dog 311
Lainey Walker's Hot Stuff 8, 51
Last Heroes 217
Last In The Brain Q 268
Last Laugh 167
Late Night Transport 84
Latest News 11, 141
Lazy Days 69
Leafeater 311
Lee Chevin & The Ravers 9, 16
Left Hand Drive Band (Septimus Spider) 19, 38, 73
Legend 195
Legion 187
Lemathus 60, 91, 95, 97
Lemonoid 257, 311
Level 42 43, 45
Lifting The Veil 118
Lipsbury Pinfold (Blind Vison) 118
Little Egypt 87, 133, 168, 195
Little Germany 194
Little Nell 41
Little Wing 41, 60, 83
Little Women 49
Live For The Weekend 161, 167
Lively Arts 217, 225

INDEX

Living Dead 177, 199
Lizard 137
Liz Wright Band 146, 168, 235
Look Back 129
Loose 217
Loose Livers 175, 231, 267, 268, 291
Lorraine & The Baht'ats 11, 141
Lost Weekend 139
Love Affair 13, 37, 39
**Love Affair 148, 195
Love Cats 117
Loved Ones 153, 300
Loving Kind 74
Love Room 146, 235
Loud 175, 255, 274, 310
Lowlife 297
Lucky Strike 69,
Lykes Of Witch 43, 49

M

M People 195
Madison Square 31, 67, 80, 83, 93, 145, 187
Magic Dog (Iron Pig) 71
Magic Dog (2) 67
Magic Muscle 128
Magna Carta 91, 191
Maidenhead Farm 60, 71, 105
Malibu Stacey 311
Mammoth 160, 187
Manning 191
Mannix 167
Mapp 218
March Violets 119
Marie's Disease 242
Mark Almond 39
Mark Russell Four (Montanas) 17, 51
Martha's Graveyard 69
Masquerade 257, 311
Masterblend 122, 231
Math & Aftermath 49, 77
Matt Vinyl & The Emulsions
Maze 49, 77
Me & My Emu 242
Meanstreak 137
Medicine Head 39
Mekons 117, 119, 217
Mel Clarke Four (Unknown Four) 9
Mel Gibbs Sound 35
Memories Of Arion 298
Men From The Mountains 159, 225
Mephisto Waltz 159, 161199, 201
Merlin 97, 98
Merry Men 89, 163, 201, 268, 291
Mice 193
Mick & The Tornados 9, 11, 14
Mick Judge & The Jurymen 35, 45
Midas (Apollos) 60, 61, 83, 93, 111, 115, 122, 145
Midnight 295
Middle 31, 59, 95

Middle-8 135
Midnight Hearse 52
Midnight Train 21, 49, 69, 71, 99, 128, 133
Midnight Sun 81, 161
Midnite Blue 71
Mike Berry Sect 11, 141
Mike Cotton Sound 33
Mike Sagar & The Cresters 8
Mike Sagar Duo / Trio 85, 101, 1215
Milan Lad Octet 145, 189, 233, 303
Mill City Blues Band 231
Ministry Of Fear 175, 199, 225
Miracle Mile 148
Mirror Image 139
Misdemeanor 133
Misfits 175
Mission 135, 255, 274
Modbeats 115
Modes For Mutants 165, 187, 201
Monkey On A Rope 218, 225
Montage 218
Moon 231, 289
Moonchild 88
Moon De Lune 115
Moonkyte 49, 67, 107, 117
Moonshine 140
Moota 282, 307
Morbid Humour 159, 225, 282
Morocco 91, 97, 122
Morgan 37
Mort Draygon & The Diamonds 19
Mother Earth 195
Mott 37, 39
Mott The Hoople 37, 39
Mouldy Warp 23, 84, 107, 168
Mountain Ash 71, 113
Mountain Ash Band 113
Mr Big 167
Mr Meana 283
Museum 35, 37, 43, 45
Music For Pleasure
Muskrats 159, 201
Mutant Two (NMA) 175
Mutton Chops 48, 95
My Pierrot Dolls 167
Mysterious Footsteps 151, 153, 175, 187
Mysterons 177

N

1919 (Heaven 17) 193
National Health 43
Natural Riddim 153
Natural Rydem 153
Natural Rhythm 153
Neat Change 37
Nebula 131
Necromancy 199, 225, 227
Neon 84, 124, 195, 301
Negatives 151, 227
Negativz 151, 199, 227, 229
Nerve Agents 225, 227, 297

Neutrals 153
Neutral Zone 201
Never Forever (Ego) 189
New Direction 13, 17, 129
New England 231
New Gowns For Royal Babies 241
New Model Army 81, 151, 175, 199, 217, 293, 310
New Moon 115
Mew Musical Testament 167
New Orleans Jazz Band 71
New Threat 81, 217
Nick Rivers Band 307
Nighthawk 81, 137
Nightlife 57, 89, 93, 124, 127, 195
Nightshift 89
Nina Simone Band 99
Nine Below Zero 175
Niteshift 51
Nobody's Friend 267, 268, 291
Noisegate 133, 255
Nomads 7, 13, 17, 51
Normal 129
Normal Love 158, 309
Northern Lights 61, 71
Not Precious 267
Notting Hillbillies 117
Nowt 282, 297
Nozzle 175
Nu Conscious Kalipz 189
Nucleus 43, 45

O

1:1 312
Ocean 129, 197
Old Sckool 84, 85, 271
Off The Tracks 267
Off The Wall 89, 93, 148, 195, 307
Officer Dibble 146, 191
Oktober 189, 199
Old Joe Zydeco 268
Old Spice 17
Olga & The Communists (Sheila & The Poo Flaps) 163, 267, 268, 291
Olulu Ololu (Bag Of Nerves) 158, 163, 267, 268
Omega Tribe 230
Omen 81, 126, 217
Optic Fibres 285
Oral Sax 31, 59, 95, 145
Orange World Of Titan 91, 97
Orchid 225
Original Mirrors 74
Original Sin 300
Osibisa 163
Otherland 67
Otis & The Elevators 133, 289
Outlander 133
Outer Limits 13, 77
Outer Limits (Three G's + One) 21
Owl 69

INDEX

Owt 235
Owter Zeds 307
Ozo 49

P

PADD 255
Panache 95
Pandemonium 49
Papa Brittle 189
Paper Lace 125
Paradise Street Blues Band (Desperate Measures) 163
Parachute Men 177, 293
Parallel Or 90 (PO 90) 191
Paris Effect 283, 285
Parisian Axis 83
Passion 122
Passion Game 148
Passmore Sisters 160
Patrick Moore & The Allstars 60, 122, 231
Patty Gibbon's Band 48, 84, 85, 124, 195, 271
Paul Young 41
Peace Artists 267
Peach 67
Peppers 54
Peppercorn 13
Phantoms 20, 49
Phil Gilbert Band 127, 195
Phobia (Underdogs) 131
Phoenix 77, 87
Phoenix With Jean 49
Photomontage 312
Pilot 57, 127
Pink Fairies 49
Pink Peg Slax 119, 217
Planet 93
Plexus 135
Ploughshare 115
Pocket Orchestra 99, 124
Polytheen Tree 67
Ponders End 84
Pond Skaters 133, 285
Poppy Factory 187, 235
Popular Fiction / Cut Out Shapes 159
Popzene 189
Powder Monkey 189
Power Of Light 13, 67
Prefects 140
Premiere 129
Presidents 13, 129
Press (Squids) 164
Press Release 93, 175, 191
Pretty Things 119
Pride 195
Primate 133, 229, 282, 297
Private Dicks (White Lightning) 73, 89,
Private Eyes 97, 98, 168, 231
Progression 41
Pro Patria Mori 237, 241, 299
Proud Image 61, 67

Psurgeons 293
Psychedelic Feeling 91
Psychic Wardrobe (Station 3) 285
Psycho Surgeons 175, 177, 257, 282, 293
Punch 31, 99, 100
Policemen With A Loaf Of Bread 160
Pythagoras Squares 38
Pyramid 231

Q

Quare Fellows 19
QED 131, 191
Quiet Three 8, 9, 125
Quiet Farm 60, 105
Quick 81, 175, 217, 218
Quireboys 217
Quo Vardis 40

R

Radio 5 145, 146, 165, 187, 235
Rafaro 89, 122, 146, 163
Ragnarok 60, 91, 97, 105, 122
Ragman's Trumpet 111
Rainbow 43
Rainbow Bridge 81, 111, 126, 135, 137
Ratbites From Hell 128
Ratfinks 41, 67
Ratpack 41
Rattlers 8, 11, 125
Rattlesnake Shake 283, 293
Rats 49
Raw 199, 225, 229
Raw Deal 137
Ray Kennan & The Guvnors 9
Ray Kennan Trio 9
Realeyz 153
Really 117
Red Hot Stillettoes 191, 195
Red Lorry Yellow Lorry
Red Noise 193
Red Sox 146, 163, 191
Red Sky Coven 175
Reefer 237
Reflex 151, 153, 199
Remainz 235, 259
Replay 7, 13
Requiem 177
Return Of Johann Muggins (Muggins Blight) 217
Revelles 51
Rhabstallion 133, 139, 191, 257
Rhino 111, 126, 133
Rhythm Sisters 193
Richard Kent Style 77
Rickie Valance & The Northmen 7
Riders Of The Storm 201
Ridgerunner 310
Right To Silence 268, 291
Rio 87

Riot 199
Riot Squad 31
Rip Off UK 151
Rip Snort 208
Ritz 84, 127, 145
Rival 255
Rivington Pike 11, 141
Robin Hood & His Merry Men 14
Rock 131, 139
Rockabilly Rebs 123
Rockheads 17, 285
Rockslider 175, 231
Rodeo Jones 167
Roger Higgins Band 107, 133
Root & Jenny Jackson 21, 89
Rondo 13, 129
Rosie's Revenge 267, 268, 291
Rosemary's Revenge 267
Rot In Flesh 225
Rough Charm 175
Roxy Music 43
Royalists 14, 33, 84
Roy Blood Trio 59
Royce 39
Roy Sundholm Band 93, 128, 145
Rubber, Leather, Plastic 199
Russell, Linda & Bruce 13

S

633 Squadron 67, 231
69 Ways 84, 85, 271
789 Skiffle Group 5
Saagar 122
Sad Cypress 257
Sally Timms & The Drifting Cowgirls 117, 119
Salvation 160, 177, 293
Sanction 89
Sammy King & The Voltaires 9
Samson 93
Sanovanos 14
Satan & The Disciples 35, 84
Sawney-Beane 23, 107
Say You 167
Saxon (Son Of A Bitch) 77
Scene 81, 159, 161, 229
Scorched Earth 60, 83, 105
Score 297
Scum 160
Screaming Jellyfish 239
Screaming Plastic Turtles 153, 289
Sid Kane & The Skasville Dream 41, 67
Section 4 161, 201
Secrets 110
Secret Screams 97, 98
Seige 137, 257
Seldom Red 93, 131, 165, 178, 187
Senators 23
Sensible Shoestring Band 113
Seven Antelopes 241, 299
Seventh Dawn 19

INDEX

Sex Patels 115
Shadowfax 67, 97, 98, 231
Shadowfax (Hx)
Shady Dealz 300
Shaftdrive 81, 131, 137, 199
Shakatak 124, 195
Shakes 126, 217, 218
Shanghai 93, 187
Shark 139
Sheds 163
Sheeny & The Goys 117
Shiny Beast 282
Shirts 73
Shogun 84, 124, 195, 301
Shotgun Express 37
Sidewynder 237
Sid Presley Experience 159
Silas Warthelmet's Battering Ram 49, 107
Silence 257
Silent Movie 160
Silent Partners (Sidewalk) 122
Silvergrass 107, 133
Silver Screen Girls 131, 154
Since The Accident 218
Single File 140, 190
Siren (Neon Angels) 140, 259, 307
Sisters Of Mercy 274
Sisters Of Mercy* 158
Sitting Ducks 267
Six Feet Under 227, 229
Size 2 51
Size 5 17, 51
Skeletal Family 119, 167, 217, 218
Sketch 113, 117
Skidmarks 229
Skin Deep 8, 35, 127
Skinflint 57
Skinny Cat 133
Skip Bifferty 39
Skrytch 242, 282
Slack 282, 307
Slammer 175, 255, 310
Slipstream 303
Sloan Square East (Senai Cruise) 300
Smack 241
Smack Dolly 167
Smart Arse 61, 93, 289
Smart Talk 129
Smile 37
Smiley 102
Smokey / Smokie 5, 87, 127, 168
Smokestack 31, 61, 77, 80, 84, 87, 140
Smooth Connections 299
Snake Davis & The Alligator Shoes 128
Snatch 95, 191
Sneakers 69, 128
Sniffa 61
Snoots 148, 195
Social Spastix 225, 237, 299
So It Goes 126
Soft Machine 43, 45
Software 43, 45
Solid Gold 41, 59, 61, 67

Solomon Grundy 83
Solicitors 191
Somebody's Brother 31, 54, 83, 89, 146, 148, 195, 235, 241, 259, 268, 282, 291, 307
Sonando 189
Son Of Sam 189
Sons Of God 146
Soundsessions 312
Soul Revolution 73
Soul Survivors 37, 100
Soul Survivors (Hx) 19, 73
Soul System 49, 57
Sounds Around 35
Southern Death Cult 151, 201
Space Hog 160, 274
Spartans 17, 110
Spectre 153, 301
Spectres 43, 49, 295
Speed 217, 218
Spell 13, 35
Spiders From Mars 49
Spike 83
Spiral/Soup Kitchen 133, 231
Spiral Highway 69
Splash Alley 85, 125
Splash 85, 89, 122, 146, 163
Spoilt Bratz / Terrorvision 311
Spooky Tooth 39
Sponge 189, 241
Springfield Park 37
Spurs 73
Stacc 81, 137, 159
Stacks 148
Stage Fright 81, 126
Stairway 71
Stan-dins 59, 61
Start 241
Stax Wheelwright & The All Stars 297
Steel Prism 139
Steve Gadd Band 41
Steve Hackett 41
Steven 81, 175, 217
Stiff Little Fingers 193
Still Life 312
Stromin' Normans 81, 126
Strange Boutique 199
Street Choir 54, 61, 84, 99, 124, 195
Streetlight Blues Band 168
Strollers (Brian T &) 7
Stone The Crows 74
Strongbow 190
Storm 81, 126, 217
Stormer (Method) 77, 85, 140, 271
Stormtrooper 77, 140
Stormy Monday 71
Studebaker 95, 131, 163, 191
Stuvyxz 60, 83, 91
Stutter 151
Style Council 159
Subject 311
Subvert 225
Success 71

Sudden Impulse 98, 168, 195
Sudden Klymax 248
Suffering In Silence 285
Sulphate Attack 167
Sun 60
Sundown 59
Sunfish Doo 297
Sunflowers 195
Sunship 43, 45
Super 8 160
Superfly 89, 127
Sure Moves 97, 98, 122, 231
Surreal Estate 199
Survivors 217
Sutherland Bros & Quiver 49
Swakara 83, 97
Swan Arcade 81, 83, 111, 125, 126
Swamp Flower 199, 227, 259, 297
Swampwack 131
Sweeny Todd 84
Sweet 37
Sweet Life (La Dolce Vita) 194
Swift, Jonathan 74
Syndicate 153
Synergy 255

T

3 Beats 2 41, 67
309s 218
25 Rifles 119
20th Century Hats 163, 231, 268, 289, 291
2 Tugs & A Squirt 229
Taledos 9
Talon 107, 133
Talisman 110
Talisman (Hx) 40,
Tamboura 67, 291
Tanz Der Hangen 163, 199, 229, 299
Tapestry Sky 298
Target Hunters 199
Tarquin (Moondancer) 95
Tarquin 91, 97, 133
Tea House Camp 159
Teenage & The Wildlife 217, 218
Telecasters 11, 14
Tempest 43, 45
Tennesseans 9, 16
Tequila Sunrise 159
Terminal 3 225
Thermal Printers 160
Terry Sexton & The Telecasters 49
Thighslapper Three 131
Three Johns 93
Three Good Reasons 20, 84
Threefold 113
Threshold Shift 227, 229, 297
Thimbleriggers 22
Thin Lizzy 39
Thinking To Myself 190
Third Ear Band 37, 39
Thomas J & The Gangsters Of Soul 73,

INDEX

89, 148, 231, 301
Thomas J & The Cool Jerx 195
Those Frayed Edges 293
Thoughts 67, 93
Threads 115
Three Aviators 312
Three Johns 119
Thunderclap Newman 31
Tibet 107
Tibetan Tourists 161
Tick Tack Toe 33, 127
Tickle 49
Tie-Break 39
Tight Fit 145
Time & Motion Sound 13
Timelife 146, 235
Tiny Mo's Children 107
Tiny Monroe 242
Titan 91, 97
Toasted Growle 51
Tokyo Blade 257
Toledos 9, 125
Tony 'Guitar' Sound 129
Tony William's Lifetime 43, 45
Too Much 84, 124
Topaz 257
Torch Girls 167, 217, 218
Tornados 8
Tory Wets 267
Total Confusion 168
Tour 314
Toxics 177
Toyz 153, 187
Track 49, 77
Tranquillity 270
Trampus 81, 137
Travesty 231
Travelling Bilberries 7, 17
Tree 19, 38, 73, 100
Tribal Tech 43
Trigger Trigger 145
Tropicanos 35
T-Set 19, 20
Tumbling Dice 13
Tunnel 84
Turbo 81, 131, 137
Turning Point 99
Turnpike 107
Tush 77, 84, 85, 271
Tuxedo 137
Tuxedos 8, 11
Twice Around The Houses 189, 242
Twilight 283
Twister 242
Two Shaven Heads 153
Tygers Of Pan Tang 135, 195

U

Ulterior Motives 153
UK 43, 45
Unburst Bubble 74
Uncle Albert's Itchy Feet
Under Two Flags 201
Undereights 158, 163
Unholy Trinity 159
Unity 153
Untouchables 11
Upbeats 137, 159, 201
Upstarts 81
Uriah Heep 43
US 257

V

Vagrantz 151, 227
Valhalla 93, 259
Vancouver 93, 124, 175, 195
Vast Hallucinations 312
VBDICA 199, 201
Vedas 131
Vegetable Section 227, 229, 289, 297
Vena Cava 227
Vengeance 83, 275
Verity 87, 131, 140
Vermin 225, 237
Vex 146, 159, 161, 165, 187, 235, 259, 309
Vicki James Wright Band 257
Victorians 84
Vigilantes 10
Vindaloos 194
Vince Wayne & The Falcons 14, 18, 49
Vince Wayne Combo 18
Violation 151, 199, 201
VIPs 13
Virgin Dudes 81
VSB 95, 133
Voodoos 235
Voyager UK 87, 131, 133, 139, 154, 257
Voyce 302
Vye 267

W

Waco Bros 119
Waggoners (Virgin Dudes) 81, 137, 159
Walker Bros 41
Wallaby Finn 19, 73
Wang Chung 167
Want 257
War Babies 225
Ward Brothers 87
Warhead 225
Warlord 137
Warm Sounds 49
Wasteland 293
Waterboys 167
Wayward Sect 19
Welfare State 38, 115
Western Dance 133, 227, 289, 287
We Meet In Hackney 231
Wicca 168
Widowmaker 39
Wild Angels 41
Wild Life 93
Wishbone Ash 87
Wishful Thinking 31, 59, 61, 84, 124
Wharf Rats 163, 268, 291
Whips 235, 259
Whipping Post 231
Whiskey Mac 35
White Hot 133
White Hot & Blue 61, 133, 146, 168, 187, 195
White Palace 298
White Soul / Pockets 73
Whiticombe Fair 99
Whitfield Family 231, 267, 268, 291
Wild Oates 88
Wild Willi Beckett
Wilson's Expression 41
Windy Mills 242, 297
Witches Bane 113
Wonderful Thing Called Tiddles 242
World Of Sound 40
Word 151, 165, 187, 191, 235
Worm 257
Wrong Band 175, 191

X

Xenon Pirates 168

Y

Year Dot 297
Yes 87
Yore Next 89, 268
Yorkshire Miracle / Ploughshare 115
Young Generation / Wishful Thinking 59, 61
Young Tradition 111
You've Been Dreaming In Class Again... Ski-Bop, Di-Bop 158, 161, 163

Z

Zanties 52
Zany Woodruff Operation 35
Zap Gun Virus 193
Zed 225, 242, 255, 282, 293, 297
Zenith Band 89
Zico 307
Zipps (George Little's Cool In The Shade) 257
Zodiac Mindwarp & The Love Reaction 133, 309
Zombies 33
Zoot Money's Big Roll Band 39
Zoot & The Roots 128, 195
Zubop 231
Zydeco Funk Butchers 131
Zzebra 37

AFTERWORDS

When's this bloody book coming out?

While doing this project the most often passed comment was, *'When's this bloody book coming out?'* yet many people also said that this stuff should have been recorded before. I was asked on two separate occasions by two different musicians, neither of whom I had ever met before, *'Have you been sent by God?'* as I showed them my research on their careers. The only answer I could splurt out as my mind reeled was, *'Of course not, don't worry, the Devil has rock and roll.'*

Starting in 2001, I spoke to a few people and showed them the rough rock family trees I'd worked on. One of these was Matt Webster who immediately offered to do the layout and editing work when I was ready.

The book took so long because I had to start from scratch, tracing musicians, tracking them down like an amateur sleuth then piecing together the jigsaw of the interconnections of the local music scenes. Along the way, I met lots of different local musicians, most of whom I had never met before, and some have become new and honoured friends in the process.

Eventually, after many days and nights of research, and going out clutching sheets of paper to show people at various gigs, I finally had enough rough chapters ready, around 20,000 words, now it was time to bring Matt on board.

In early 2006 we started laying out the first pages and scanning in the hundreds of images used in the book, coming together one day a week for the next two years. It involved continually showing people, where possible, half finished trees to verify information, often needed additions and amendments as band members were suddenly remembered. Matt had a wealth of information about the Bradford scene in the 1980s which he added to what I had written. Pages changed week by week as more information was uncovered and rare pictures were acquired from various sources. Matt often likened it to kids collecting football cards and finding that elusive rare player.

By the end of 2008, we'd finally got a complete manuscript (barring a few tweaks!) and we were ready to start the greater challenge of raising the finance to get it published. But, if you're reading this, then we obviously managed it, cheers.

'It was a cold February morning, we'd been trying to perfect 'Smoke On The Water' for weeks, like most bands in Bradford at this time the only role models we had were Deep Purple and the like. Then at about 11 o'clock the guitarist (Harvey) burst into the room with a copy of the Ramones first album under his arm, this was February 1976 and as we listened to the album this was the moment that changed our lives. We trashed Smoke On The Water, we wrote a bunch of songs for ourselves including 'One More Vice' and, to those in the know, 'Down At Sweaty Harry's' yet within a year the band was no more and we all went our separate ways. Because nearly everyone who had been involved with a band in Bradford has a similar story to tell some have been more successful than others. Yet all are equally important to the legacy Bradford has given to the world of music. This book has been put together to preserve the unique part Bradford has played and stil plays in the UK's rock and roll history... don't let it die.'

Richard Skelly – Phobia

(RIP 2011)

I first met Gary, or Gary 1 In 12, or 'Supergaz' as Wild Willi used to call him, in 1982 when he was the guy you had to hassle to get gigs at The 1 In 12 Club, which I did on an almost weekly basis for my band, fabulous punk legends The Convulsions. He was also the person who put the Club compilation albums together, a thing I first tried with a local punk compilation tape in 1983.

When Gary approached me in 2001 I immediately volunteered to do the layout and design as this was my area and, having been involved with the local music for many years, it seemed like my ideal project.

I bumped into him at various times over the next few years with a slight variation on the main question, 'When's this bloody book going to start?' He usually made some feeble excuse, which I half believed, about having to do more research or having to see such and such a person or band before we could start and it wasn't until we finally did start that I realised the massive amount of work and research that Gary had done already. The later years came a bit easier as we both were active in the music scene at the time and had both kept hold of useful material and recordings, me - being very much younger than Gary - from about 1980 onwards.

Assembling the book was a bit like doing a massive jigsaw and we had to leave spaces for what was missing, hoping to find the name of the bassist from the fourth line-up of Midas or the cover of that single by Happiness Ad we knew existed. Often, just as we had a sequence of pages finished, a new bit of information or a great picture would be uncovered, involving a complete re-jig of what we had just done, only occasionally accompanied by an argument along the lines of, 'Can't we put that in the next chapter?' or 'Do we have to use that picture?.'

We did use virtually everything we could, bar the odd picture, and made an attempt to document every band we could find information about, without bias or personal taste influencing the content.

So, here it is, as complete as we could make it, for now...

A billboard on Broadway in Bradford which was a popular site for flyposters, circa 1986

Gary Cavanagh was born in Clayton, Bradford, and is a founder member of Bradford's 1 In 12 Club, a former university tutor in history and politics, and a local historian and archivist.

He has been a life-long Bradford City supporter and one time City Junior. If it hadn't been for that niggling knee injury....

Former vocalist with legendary local rock gods Phobia, he has been involved in the local music scene since the mid 1970s and was instrumental in the production of the 1 In 12 Club compilation LP series.

Matt Webster hails from Thackley, Bradford, and has been a drummer in numerous local bands since the early 1980s, including The Convulsions, The Nerve Agents, Swamp Flower, Western Dance, Primate, Nowt, Grim, Zed, The Horton Carpets and Kwai Chang Caine. Also known as Matt Nazgul and Pete, Matt is a graphic designer and recording engineer/producer, and co-founder of Mutiny 2000 Studios/Records.

He was an occasional music reviewer for the Bradford Star in the early 1990s during his time working in the Pre-Press Department at the Telegraph & Argus where he also used to sneak various bits onto the Rock On page when no-one was looking.

He was the editor of the non-existent Daily Mutiny and was also the original co-presenter of the Bradford Beat radio show on BCB, a programme which featured Bradford music and live local bands from 1995 to 1999.

Acknowledgements

Thanks to Ian Clayton for his forward.

We are grateful to the following for permission to reproduce certain articles: Telegraph & Argus (Peter Orme, David Barnett), Keighley News (David Knight), Spenborough Guardian, West Yorkshire Archive Service (Richard Brass), New Musical Express and Record Collector's Rare Record Guide.

This book would never have been possible without the help and assistance of the following people:

Barry Greenwood, Jont Watson, Andy Wells, Andy Farrow, Richard Skelly, Phil Manchester, Mary Johnson, Mark Clayton, Aki Nawaz, Justin Sullivan, Dave Wynne, Richard Bolton, Stan Greenwood, Derek Lister, Carole Moss, Dominic Watts, Jon Macdonald-Binns, Dave Pickard, Pete Chapman, Johnny Lorrimer, Grahame Kelly, Steve Isherwood, John Sheppard, Troy Bunn, Phil Hobson, Michael & Patrica Jackson, Alan & Josie Davies, Tony Grogan, Paul Tunnicliffe, Gill Parratt, Ade Clark, Liam Sheeran, Stephen Andrews, Kenny Armitage, Paul Armitage, Traci Teal, Paul Bahr, Nick Toczek, Pete Kaberry, Stuart Morrow, Polly Newsome, Jed Turner, Roger Mitchell, Terry Bainbridge, Heather Bayliss, Barry Moore, Gerard Rolfe, Charlie Inez, Phil Dean, Zoot Money, Bobby Weaver, Richard Marriot, Monica Hill, Penny Fogg, Stuart, Eve & Dawn Firth, Paul Hughes, Gareth Harwood, John Verity, Mal Siswick, Denny Austin, Martin Neish, Norman Hill, Kev Wright, Reuban Davison, Robert Baranyai, Nev Cartelidge, Mark Truman, Dave Reynolds-Hanson, Kenny Thomas, Tony Murphy, Tim Walker, Steve Jackson, Darshan Ram, Leigh Marklew, Garry Whitfield, Graham Darby, Steve Woods, Paul Solynskyj, Rachel Singleton, Nick Royles, Sharon Royles, 'Dob', John-Paul Goddard, Heather Hebron, Phill & Ian Harding, Mark Blackburn, John Hawley, Vicky Hawthorn, David Jennings, John 'Spud' Taylor, Kev Sullivan, Rod & Alan Owen, Philomena Hingston, Colin Hingston, Tim Gale, Belinda Noel, Gerry Musgrave, Dave Lowry, Dave Meir, Neil Roddis, Lynden Welch, Mick Dale, Mick Wake, Pete Bradley, Graham Lockwood, Kenny Rooke, Tony Wintony, John Radcliffe, Alan Wormald, Kev Garside, Kath Jarvis, Doug Lamb, Peter 'Skinny' Finan, Jeff Wilson, Richard Harding, Mike Sagar, Garth Cawood, 'Swinging' Sue Lee, Andy Greaves, Dave & Chris Stansfield, Angelina Minott, Ian Roper, Steven 'Johna' Johnson, Gary Wood, Dave & Julie Bussey, Mark Cunningham, Roger Higgins, Mick Williams, Brian Lumb, Derek Moulson, Susan Sharp & Mick Smith, Courtney Hay, Mark Cranmer, Tim Moon, Tommy & Mandy Hunt, Paul Smith, Bruce Lewis, Gordon Wilkinson, Jack Himsworth, Steve Whitehead, Dave Thompson, Mark Bokowiec, Pete Lancaster, Rick & Wendy Ironmonger, Griff, Dave Green, Alex Bilenko, Paul Taylor, Norma 'NJ' Wilow, Malcolm Hanson, David Wilson.

From Keighley: Tim Gilroy, Richard Burns, Bruce & Linda Russell, Ted Earle, 'Spike', Noel Coupland, Bernard Louth, David Boddy, Allan Smith, Mary Ashdown, Helen Forshaw, 'Trotwood' & 'Spud', Alan Rose, Martin Henderson, Ian Shackleton, Ian Sanderson, Chris Kelly, all the folk at The Red Pig - Shona Brunskill, Shaun & Louise Hardcastle, Danny, Kris & Lee, Chris, Lucy & Adam, and the landlord Bob. Rich Jevons, Terry Peaker, 'Wally' Waltons, Graham Richardson, Kev Collens, Sonia Atkins, Steve Wilson, Mick Thompson of Mmm Productions, Keith Tretton, Jonjo McCoglan.

We are also indebted to the following people for their permission to reproduce artefacts, photos, memorabilia from their personal archives: Matt Webster, Derek Lister, Alan & Josie Davis, Andy Wells, Heather Hebron, John Hawley, Phil Manchester, Pete Kaberry, Noel Coupland, Clive Royston, Brian Outlaw (snr), Bernard Louth, Marek 'Fritz The Cat' Skoczylas, Tony Grogan, Pete @ rollbacktheyears, Johna, Nick Toczek, Ian Roper, Alan Wormald, Neil Roddis, Kenny Armitage, Tommy & Mandy Hunt, Tim Moon, Delia Perry, Dave Lowry, Steve Whitehead, Dave Thompson, Rod Owen, Jed Turner, Steve Wilson, Mark Cranmer, Malcolm Hanson, Chris 'Woli' Walsh, Harris, Dave Bussey, Mike Sagar, Waterstones, Bradford.

Margery Webster (1927-2023) for the veggie bacon butties.

For help in researching rare discs: Mark Kershaw (Wall Of Sound), Tony (Metomorphosiz), Mike Levon (Holyground), David Wells (Wooden Hill), Dizzy (Detour Records).

All the staff at Bradford Gingerbread (2002-2007), for their support especially: Maria Pemberton, Helen Dover, Julie Lintern, Amy Milner for type input.

Special thanks to Bridget Izod for proof reading and helpful suggestions.

Also Susan Kasher for type input, Mike Quiggin at BRC, Chris Barker at CVS and finally all the staff at Bradford Reference Library for their help and assistance.

BRADFORD'S NOISE OF THE VALLEYS VOLUME ONE 1967 - 1987

AVAILABLE TO ORDER 4 CD SET

To get the 4 CD set that is a musical representation of the bands in this book, please order from:

bradfordnoise.com

or

mutiny2000.com

and visit our Facebook page
Bradford's Noise Of The Valleys - The Book
for updates and news of upcoming releases.

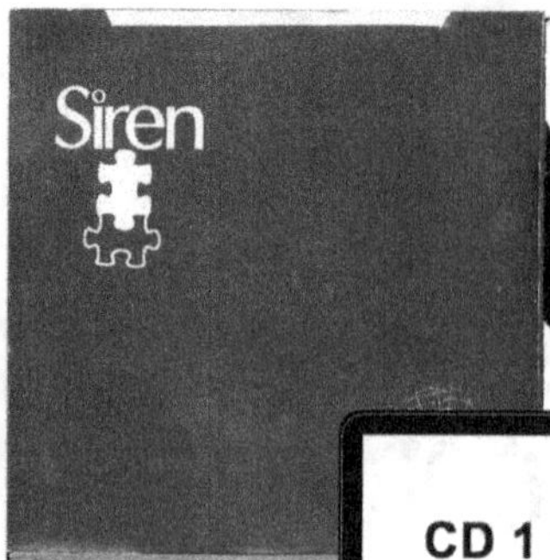

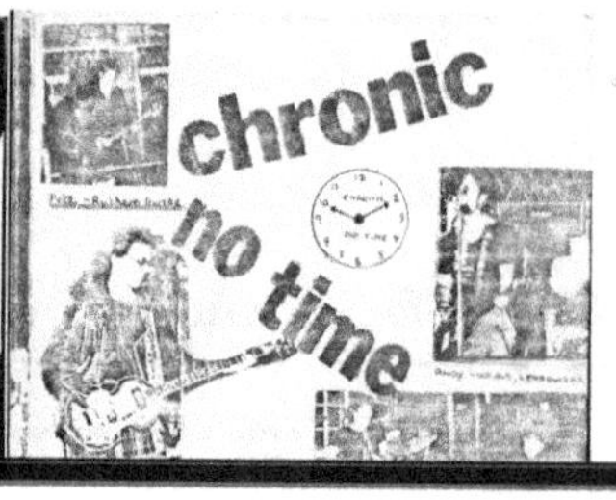

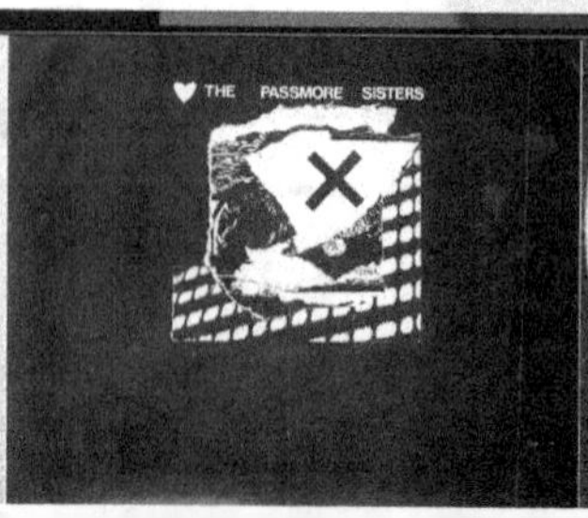

CD 1 1966-1976

1. **Allen Pound's Get Rich** - Searchin' In The Wilderness (Pound) © 1966 Toby Music
2. **The Accent** - Red Sky At Night (Davies/Beetham/Hebron/Birkett) © 1967 Getaway Songs
3. **The Outer Limits** - Great Train Robbery (Christie) © 1968 MCS Music Limited
4. **Love Affair** - Once Upon A Season (Michael Jackson) © 1968 Universal / Dick James Music Ltd
5. **Welfare State** - Silence Is Requested In The Ultimate Abyss (Coleman/Welfare State) © 1969
6. **'Igginbottom** - Golden Lakes (Holdsworth) © 1969 Universal / Dick James Music Ltd
7. **Junior's Eyes** - White Llight (Wayne) © 1969 Onward Music Ltd
8. **Free Expression** – Nightmares (Peaker) © 1970 Terry Peaker
9. **Barbara Moore** - Hot Heels (Moore) © 1971 De Wolfe Ltd
10. **Jan Dukes de Grey** - The Cheering Crowd (Noy) © 1970 Derek Alan Noy
11. **Jonathan Swift** - Clever Headed Spell (Swift/Hamilton) © 1971 Jelly Music Ltd
12. **Moonkyte** - Blues For Boadicea (Stansfield) © 1971 Endomorph Publishing
13. **Rick Hayward** - Weasel (Hayward) © 1971 Blue Horizon
14. **Martin Carter** - British Man O'War (Trad.Arr. Carter) © 1972 Copyright Control
15. **Mountain Ash Band** - The Outcast (King/Cripps) © 1975 Witches Bane Music
16. **John Verity Band** - Hitch-hiker (Verity) © 1973 Carling Music Corp
17. **Lazy Days** - Wait For Me (Wilson/Shepard) © 1973/2001 Holyground
18. **Dave Lee Sound** - Down The Line (Montgomery/Petty/Holly) © 1975 MPL Communications Ltd
19. **Smokie** - Back To Bradford (Norman/Spencer) © 1975 Universal Music Publishing
20. **Phoenix** - Easy (Verity) © 1976 Nereus Music
21. **Kukulkan** - Lady Heatwave (Kukulkan) © 1976 Copyright Control

CD2 1977-1982

1. **First Aid** - Shape Of Things To Come/Nostradamus/Epilogue (Excerpts from Nostradamus) (Wormald/Parsons) © 1977 Palace Music
2. **The Negatives** - Stake Out (Robinson/Palmer/Stubbs) © 1979/2000 Tandiz Music Ltd
3. **Ulterior Motives** - Another Lover (Russell/Toczek) © 1979 Motive Music
4. **Eaten Alive By Insects** - John Wayne's Jacket (Phill Harding/Paton) © 1979 Copyright Control
5. **The Scene** - Hey Girl (Ian Harding) © 1980 Hole In The Wall Records
6. **Mysterious Footsteps** - White Dread (Stobbs) © 1980 Copyright Control
7. **The Invaders** - Japanese Dreams (Invaders) © 1980 Copyright Control
8. **Rhabstallion** - Chain Reaction (Thompson) © 1980 EMI Music Publishing Ltd
9. **Dawnwatcher** – Spellbound (Dawnwatcher) © 1980 Copyright Control
10. **New Model Army** - The Cause (Sullivan) © 1981 Intersong Music Ltd
11. **Chronic** – No Time (Chronic) © 1981 1Noise12 Publishing
12. **Living Dead** – Procession (Living Dead) © 1981 1Noise12 Publishing
13. **Southern Death Cult** - Moya (Live) (Astbury/Burrows/Jepson/Nawaz) © 1981 Warner Chappell Music Ltd
14. **Dial** - In Love This Year (Dial) © 1981 1Noise12 Publishing
15. **Fall Guys** - New Start (Fall Guys) © 1981 1Noise12 Publishing
16. **The Vindaloos** – Problems (Vindaloos) © 1982 1 Noise12 Publishing
17. **Height** - Looking Through Glass (Sadofski) © 1982 Useful Music
18. **Radio 5** - We Burn So Well (Radio 5) © 1982 1Noise12 Publishing
19. **Timelife** - The Perfect Lives (Timelife) © 1982 Copyright Control
20. **Middle 8** - In The Dawn (Cass) © 1982 SBR

This compilation © 2009 Bradford Noise.
All tracks used courtesy of the original artists and copyright of the original recordings belongs to their individual owners.
All rights of the producer and the owner of the recorded works reserved.
Unauthorised copying, hiring, public performance and broadcasting of this record prohibited.

CD 3 1982-1984

1. *Skeletal Family* - Trees (Greenwood/Hirst/Nowell) © 1982 Kassner Associated Publishers
2. *Holy Holy* - The Judge (Holy Holy) © 1982 Copyright Control
3. *1919* - Storm (Tighe/Tilleard/Reed/Madden) © 1983 Big Life Music Ltd
4. *Requiem* - Spartan Life (Requiem) © 1983 1Noise12 Publishing
5. *Stacc* - Children Of The Night (Stacc) © 1983 Copyright Control
6. *Anti-System* - Service/1000 Rifles (Nolan/Watts) © 1983 Centa Music
7. *The Negativz* - Mental Case (Pete Stobbs) © 1984 Pox Island/Mutiny 2000
8. *The Convulsions* - Media Punx (Webster/Armitage) © 1983 Mutiny 2000
9. *Seven Antelopes* - Eat People (Seven Antelopes) © 1983 1Noise12 Publishing
10. *Malcolm Hansson* - The Naked Truth (Hanson) © 1983 Copyright Control
11. *Spectre* - Ideal Home (Spectre) © 1984 1Noise12 Publishing
12. *Men From The Mountains* - Trembling (Harding/Bough/Waddington) © 1984 1Noise12 Publishing
13. *The Word* – Immaculate (The Word) © 1984 Menace Music
14. *Morbid Humour* - Oh My God (Parts 1&2) (Morbid Humour) © 1984 Copyright Control
15. *The Nerve Agents* - To And Fro (Sheeran) © 1984 Home Brewed Music
16. *Vegetable Section* - Fruitcake Jake (Arron/Canmer) © 1985 1Noise12 Publishing
17. *Swamp Flower* - Swamp Flower (Ingham/Leith/Webster) © 1985 Home Brewed Music
18. *Joolz* - Audience Participation (Denby) © 1982 1Noise12 Publishing
19. *Seething Wells* - Tetley Bittermen (Stephen Wells) © 1982 1Noise12 Publishing
20. *Wild Willi Beckett* - Privilege (Beckett) © 1982 1Noise12 Publishing
21. *Little Brother* - Land Of The Rising? (Stockell/Austin) © 1982 Sixty Three

CD 4 1985-1987

1. *Brendan Croker & The 5 O'Clock Shadows* - Hard Times (Skip James) © 1985 Wynwood Music Co Inc
2. *Domestic Enemies* - Tiny Minds (Domestic Enemies) © 1985 1Noise12 Publishing
3. *Boys From The East* - Young & Beautiful (Boys from the East) © 1985 1Noise12 Publishing
4. *Passmore Sisters* - Strong For Europe (Taylor/Sadofski/Lee/Richardson) © 1985 1Noise12 Publishing
5. *Still Life* - She Don't Care (John/Burns/Walker) © 1985 1Noise12 Publishing
6. *Doctor & The Inmates* - Never A Rebel (Beckett) © 1985 QTA/Mutiny 2000
7. *The Skidmarks* - Dirty Old Man (Skidmarks) © 1986 Copyright Control
8. *Britanarchists (Nick Toczek & Spectre)* - Sheer Funk (Toczek) © 1986 Nick Toczek
9. *The Best Way To Walk* - Unbelievable (Ware/Flynn/Bryson/O'Conner) © 1986 Sony Music Ltd
10. *Happiness Ad* - Geburrah (Rob Moore) © 1986 Copyright Control/Flexible Response
11. *Psycho Surgeons* - Give A Man A Badge (Beckett) © 1986 QTA/Mutiny 2000
12. *Western Dance* - This Perfect Day (Andrews) © 1987 Home Brewed Music
13. *Verity* - Are You Ready For This? (Verity) © 1983 Verity Music
14. *Siren* - American Girl (Cook) © 1984 Distant Cousins
15. *Bobo* - Tall Talk & Rocking Horse Tales (Bobo) © 1985 Copyright Control
16. *Excalibur* - I'm Telling You (Solynskyj/McBride) © 1985 Solynskyj McBride
17. *Voyager UK* - Don't Hold Back (A Wells) © 1985 Copyright Control
18. *Tuxedo* - Set Me Free (Clarke/Erdos/Lumb/Noonan) © 1986 Copyright Control
19. *Baby Tuckoo* - I'm Your Man (Armitage/Barrott/Saxton/Smith/Sugden) © 1986 Derek Savage Music Ltd
20. *Harlequyn* – Caroseul (Mother/Walker) © 1987 Copyright Control
21. *Somebody's Brother* – Soweto (Austin/Lord/Neen) © 1987 Tinza
22. *The Crowd* - You'll Never Walk Alone (Rogers/Hammerstein) © 1985 EMI Music Publishing Limited

This compilation © 2009 Bradford Noise.

All tracks used courtesy of the original artists and copyright of the original recordings belongs to their individual owners.
All rights of the producer and the owner of the recorded works reserved.
Unauthorised copying, hiring, public performance and broadcasting of this record prohibited.

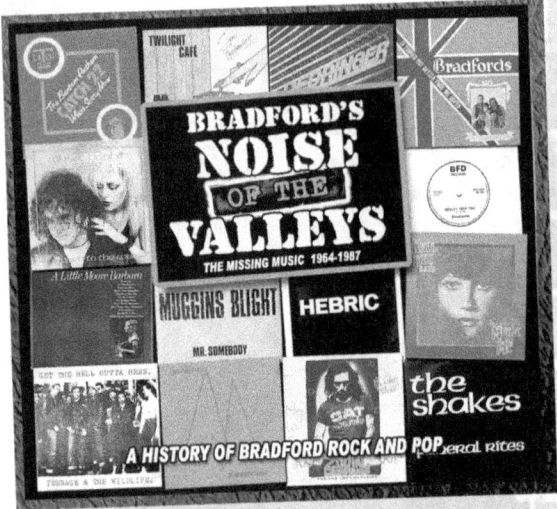
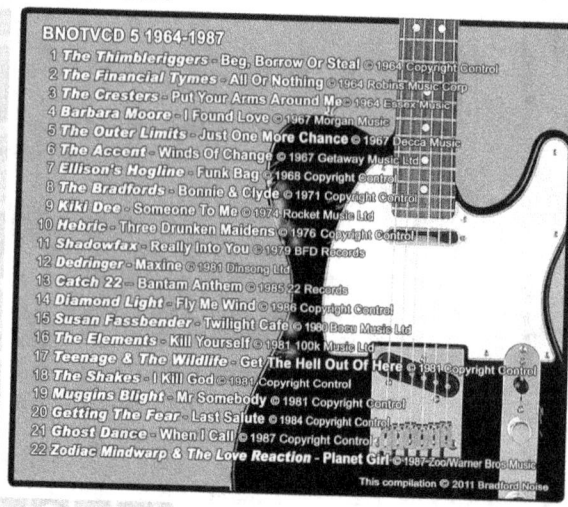

Also available are the two *Missing Music* CDs which capture some of the tracks we didn't have access to when *Bradford's Noise of The Valleys* was originally published in 2009.

These CDs form the bridge between *Volume One* and the forthcoming *Bradford's Noise Of The Valleys Volume 2* which continues the story of the Bradford music scene from 1988 to 1998.

Both of these CDs are available to order from **bradfordnoise.com**

A further 6 CDs will be available to accompany Volume 2, featuring more fabulous tracks from a diverse selection of bands and artists from the slightly unrecognised and unloved city that is Bradford.

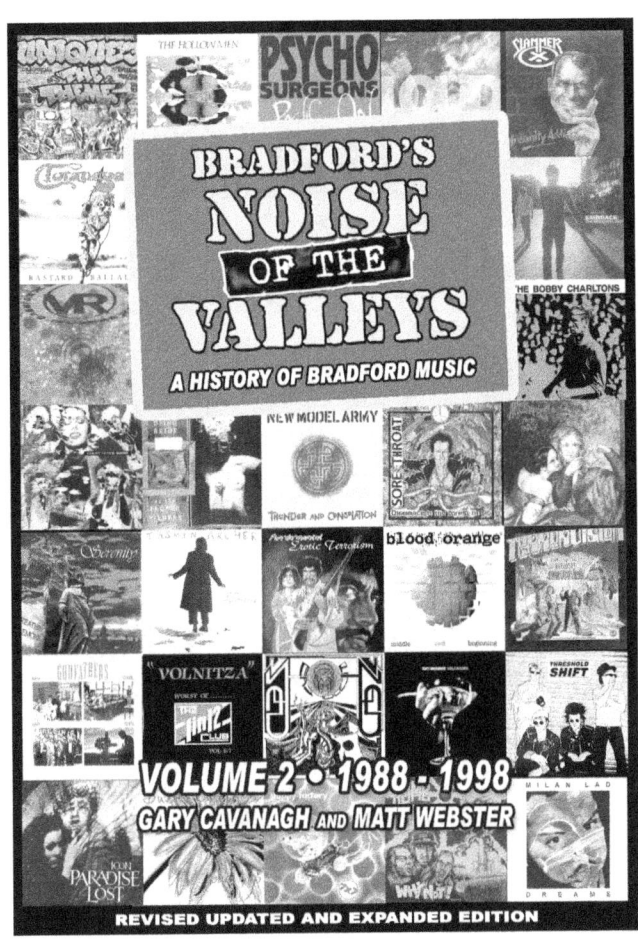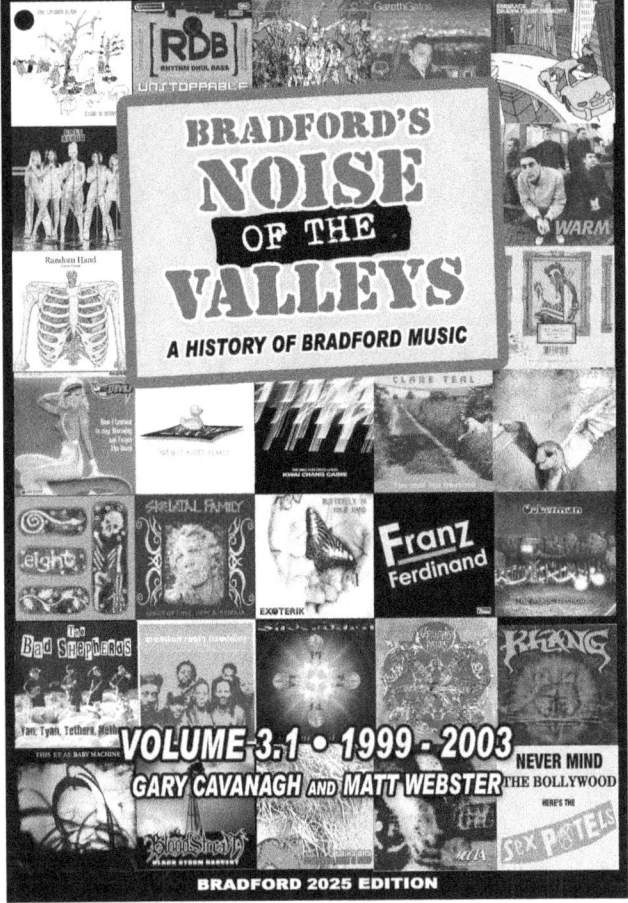

www.ingramcontent.com/pod-product-compliance
Lightning Source LLC
Chambersburg PA
CBHW081100070526
44583CB00018B/2504